The Fourteenth Dalai Lama's Stages of the Path

Publisher's Acknowledgment

The publisher gratefully acknowledges the generous help of the Hershey Family Foundation in sponsoring the production of this book.

The Fourteenth Dalai Lama's
Stages of the Path

VOL. 2: AN ANNOTATED COMMENTARY ON
THE FIFTH DALAI LAMA'S
ORAL TRANSMISSION OF MAÑJUŚRĪ

HIS HOLINESS THE DALAI LAMA

COMPILED AND EDITED BY HIS EMINENCE
Dagyab Kyabgön Rinpoché

Translated by Sophie McGrath

Wisdom Publications
132 Perry Street
New York, NY 10014 USA
wisdomexperience.org

Tibetan edition: *Rgyal ba'i dgongs gsal* ("Clarifying the Intent of the Conquerors"),
vol. 2: *'Jam dpal zhal lung zhal skong* ("Supplement to the Oral Teachings of Mañjuśrī"),
copyright © 2016 by The Dalai Lama Trust & Tibethaus Deutschland e. V.

Library of Congress Cataloging-in-Publication Data for volume 1
Names: Bstan-'dzin-rgya-mtsho, Dalai Lama XIV, 1935– author. |
Dagyab, Loden Sherab, editor. | Kilty, Gavin, translator.
Title: The Fourteenth Dalai Lama's stages of the path. Volume 1: Guidance for
the modern practitioner / His Holiness the Dalai Lama; compiled and edited
by his eminence Dagyab Kyabgön Rinpoché; translated by Gavin Kilty.
Description: First. | Somerville: Wisdom Publications, 2022. |
Includes bibliographical references and index.
Identifiers: LCCN 2021054566 (print) | LCCN 2021054567 (ebook) |
ISBN 9781614297932 (hardcover) | ISBN 9781614298175 (ebook)
Subjects: LCSH: Buddhism—Doctrines. | Mādhyamika (Buddhism) |
Spiritual life—Buddhism. | Happiness—Religious aspects—Buddhism.
Classification: LCC BQ7935.B774 F683 2022 (print) | LCC BQ7935.B774 (ebook) |
DDC 294.3/42—dc23/eng/20220223
LC record available at https://lccn.loc.gov/2021054566
LC ebook record available at https://lccn.loc.gov/2021054567

ISBN 978-1-61429-794-9   ebook ISBN 978-1-61429-818-2

27 26 25 24 23
5 4 3 2 1

Cover and interior design by Gopa & Ted 2. Typesetting by Tony Lulek.

Printed in Canada.

Contents

Preface by His Holiness the Fourteenth Dalai Lama   ix

Translator's Preface   xvii

Compiler's Introduction   xix

Foreword and Acknowledgments by Tibet House Germany   xxvii

Technical Note   xxxiii

THE VIRTUOUS BEGINNING: THE STARTING CONTENT   1

    The Expression of Homage   1

    The Pledge to Compose the Text   15

SHOWING THE GREATNESS OF THE TEACHING'S AUTHOR
IN ORDER TO INDICATE ITS PURE ORIGIN   19

    The Sacred Biography of the Great Fifth Dalai Lama   63

SHOWING THE GREATNESS OF THE TEACHINGS IN ORDER
TO ENGENDER RESPECT FOR THE INSTRUCTIONS   77

    The Meaning of "Stages of the Path to Enlightenment"   81

THE VIRTUOUS MIDDLE: THE EXPLANATION
OF THE MEANING OF THE TEXT   85

    How to Listen to and Explain the Teachings
    Possessing the Two Greatnesses   87

THE STAGES OF GUIDING DISCIPLES WITH THE
ACTUAL INSTRUCTIONS   111
    The Preliminary Mind of Refuge   113
    A Brief Instruction on How to Sustain the Meditation   171

AN EXHORTATION TO TAKE FULL ADVANTAGE
OF A LIFE OF LEISURE AND OPPORTUNITY   201

HOW TO TAKE FULL ADVANTAGE OF A LIFE
OF LEISURE AND OPPORTUNITY   213
    Training the Mind in the Stages of the Path Shared
      with Persons of Small Scope   217

CONTEMPLATING THE SUFFERINGS OF THE
LOWER REALMS   257
    Contemplating the Suffering of Bad Rebirths   259

THE METHOD FOR ACHIEVING HAPPINESS IN
FUTURE LIVES   279
    Taking Refuge   285

CULTIVATING CONVICTION IN KARMIC CAUSALITY:
THE ROOT OF ALL HAPPINESS AND GOOD   319

TRAINING THE MIND IN THE STAGES OF THE
PATH SHARED WITH PERSONS OF MEDIUM SCOPE   353
    Contemplating True Sufferings:
      The Drawbacks of Cyclic Existence   362

CONTEMPLATING ORIGINS: THE STAGES OF
ENTERING INTO CYCLIC EXISTENCE   393

CONTEMPLATING THE SUFFERING OF CYCLIC EXISTENCE
FROM THE VIEWPOINT OF THE TWELVE LINKS OF
DEPENDENT ORIGINATION   423

DETERMINING THE NATURE OF THE PATH LEADING
TO LIBERATION   435

TRAINING THE MIND IN THE STAGES OF THE PATH
FOR PERSONS OF GREAT SCOPE   451
   The Way to Develop Bodhicitta   466

HOW TO ADOPT BODHICITTA THROUGH ITS RITUAL   515

HOW TO TRAIN IN THE CONDUCT HAVING
GIVEN RISE TO BODHICITTA   535
   How to Train in the Six Perfections
    That Ripen One's Continuum   545

TRAINING IN THE PERFECTION OF GENEROSITY   547

TRAINING IN THE PERFECTION OF ETHICAL DISCIPLINE   561

TRAINING IN THE PERFECTION OF PATIENCE   571

TRAINING IN THE PERFECTION OF JOYOUS EFFORT   591

TRAINING IN THE PERFECTION OF CONCENTRATION   605

THE PERFECTION OF WISDOM:
TRAINING IN SPECIAL INSIGHT   639

TRAINING IN THE FOUR WAYS TO GATHER DISCIPLES
THAT RIPEN OTHERS' CONTINUA   691

THE VIRTUOUS END: THE CONCLUDING CONTENT   693
    The Fifth Dalai Lama's Colophon   700
    Compiler's Colophon   702

Appendix: Essence of Thought: A Summary of
    The Fourteenth Dalai Lama's Stages of the Path, Volume 2   715

Glossary   729

Notes   733

Bibliography   741

Index   751

A Short Biography of His Holiness the Fourteenth Dalai Lama   793

A Short Biography of His Eminence Dagyab Kyabgön Rinpoché   795

Preface by
His Holiness the Fourteenth Dalai Lama

THE FIRST VOLUME OF this work is a fairly detailed explanation of general points related to Buddhist concepts. It includes an introduction for today's Buddhists on the important and fundamental points of the philosophical tenets of Śākyamuni Buddha, explanations on the reality of base existence presented by Buddhism and modern science, and ways to integrate the essence of Buddhism into daily life.

The second volume, composed by way of analysis of modern-day realities, consists of supplementary annotations to the wonderful work *Oral Transmission of Mañjuśrī*—an exegesis on the *lamrim*, or stages of the path treatise, by the Great Fifth Dalai Lama, which is included in the classification known as the eight great works on the stages of the path.

I would like to talk a little about the reasons for this approach. In this twenty-first century the ongoing economic betterment of conditions for the peoples of this world has meant the overcoming of various immediate difficulties. By means of our human intellectual capabilities, alliances have been forged, great strides have been made in education, and, with the huge efforts expended by scientific research, great advances have been made in measurable understandings of the workings of the quantifiable external world. However, up to now, similar quantifiable understandings of the workings of the inner world of mind and experience have not been possible. Nevertheless, the ongoing search for ways to do so, fueled by an increasing interest in these areas, is an excellent sign.

However, at the same time there are the unprecedented phenomena of climate change, epidemics, environmental problems, health issues, and so on. Moreover, new troubles, such as terrorism, are continuing to beset the world. The reality is that these problems are man made. Many governments, communities, and individuals, driven by the energy of anger, desire, and wrong concepts, focus on their immediate needs without any thought for the long-term damage that might arise. Additionally, beset by intense sectarianism, they focus shortsightedly on the benefits to the individual or their own groups, not thinking of the effect their actions will have on the global community. There is no other way of resolving and improving these situations than to transform human thinking and conduct.

For such a transformation to take place, we can engage in the trainings of the views and conducts existing in religious traditions. In particular, we should work to benefit others by wholesome secular acts not necessarily linked with religious traditions, such as love, mindfulness, consideration, contentment, and patience, which are the basic attitudes for a conduct of accepting and discarding. These wholesome ways of behavior are found within all religious traditions, but they do not depend upon a particular religion for their existence, nor do they arise from those religions. In general, they arise by virtue of their being the very foundations of society. [viii] For example, abandoning the ten unvirtuous acts was adopted into Buddhist practice because these ten actions—such as killing and lying—did not bring about peace, harmony, and happiness within society. They were not newly decreed by the Buddha as being harmful. Therefore, abandoning these can be categorized as wholesome acts not specifically linked with any religious tradition. There are many such activities, and it is helpful to recognize them as such.

Whether we follow a religious tradition or not, I see it as incumbent upon us all to recognize the common goal of short- and long-term happiness and to see that this is our common responsibility as individuals and communities. Many people have no liking for religious traditions and tend to shun a particular training as if it were a contagious disease simply because it comes from a religious tradition. These people, when working for their own happiness, should try to recognize these fundamental trainings as practical methods for bringing about peace and happiness and apply them to their minds. If these trainings are allowed to disappear, ultimately it will be a loss to humanity. It is worth experimenting to see if this is true or not.

Human beings of all kinds, without differentiation, whether they have faith in religion or not, are young or old, traditional or progressive, whether they believe in change or not, are all united in wanting to live happy lives in a well-ordered and decent society. And, keeping in mind that working for the benefit of all beings is essential for this endeavor, we should consider it our responsibility to help as best we can all those who show an interest. Therefore, because we hold that the teachings of the Buddha are reality-based and verifiable by experience, a general introduction to Buddhism in eight chapters has been included in this two-volume work.

VOLUME 1

For many years, wherever I am in the world, I have worked hard to promote three beneficial commitments to be of benefit. The first of these commitments is to attempt to develop the intrinsic and fundamental qualities of goodness that exist in human beings. The second commitment is to increase harmony among world religions. The third is the commitment to the welfare of Tibet. These three are the focus of the first volume and are the context of the presentation of the general and specific points of Buddhism together with various historical narratives. In this general explanation are chapters on Buddhist philosophy on the reality of base existence, the relation between Buddhism and modern science, and how certain Buddhist trainings can be put into practice in tune with the necessities of daily life.

xii   THE FOURTEENTH DALAI LAMA'S STAGES OF THE PATH

I will explain briefly the fundamental issues on which the contents of these eight chapters are based. [ix] The conditions that give rise to our man-made troubles are due to the failure to value the wholesome qualities such as love and kindness, which are innate in human beings, and to not recognize them as being fundamental for the welfare of humanity. Not valuing these qualities, we make no effort to develop their potential.

These qualities are like seeds. If seeds of flowers are provided with the right external conditions of soil, fertilizer, warmth, water, and so on, and are nurtured and cared for, the full glory of the flowers' beauty, with their wonderful aromas, can blossom. If not, those seeds remain as potential only, unable to produce their results. Similarly, in order to manifest the potential of the love and kindness innate in each of us, we must nurture the right inner conditions of our attitudes, such as being compassionate, content, disciplined, and conscientious. Our happiness depends solely on others being happy, and therefore, if we alleviate the suffering of others, our own happiness will naturally and inevitably arise. When we understand this, these attitudes of love and kindness will develop unhindered, and the innate potential within human beings can emerge.

We must recognize that among the numerous troubles that have occurred in the world over the past thousand years or so, some have involved groups that follow religious traditions. These followers have shown little interest in taming their minds through reliance upon their religion, and they hold their religious views to be supreme and misuse their religion so that it becomes a cause for increasing anger and desire. This is such a tragic situation and it continues today.

The result of such abuse of religious teachings has been a widespread opinion that no religion can be effective in real-world situations. Followers of the major religious traditions that teach practices for taming the unruly mind have a responsibility to counter this unfortunate situation and to bring about the short- and long-term welfare of individuals and communities. A single religious tradition lacks the methods for fulfilling all the hopes and wishes of all living beings because such hopes are as numerous as the varied dispositions of living beings. I believe that followers of diverse religious traditions should willingly act to shed any resentment, apprehension, expectation, and competitiveness between them, fueled by attachment or dislike. Setting aside their history of hostility and distrust, they should work to foster harmonious relations by cultivating respect and a genuine appreciation of other religions.

Furthermore, it is important that we Tibetans who have faith in Buddhism understand that all the philosophical positions of the Tibetan Buddhist traditions and their subsects are ultimately of one intent. If we had some familiarity with the historical accounts of where and how these traditions developed, it would without a doubt act as nourishment for the respect and pure perception of each of them. [x] Therefore, it is worth having some interest in studying their histories.

The philosophical view of Buddhism is dependent origination, and its conduct is one of nonharming. Relying upon Buddhism can exert a beneficial influence on the way we spend our lives. In Buddhism we recognize that all actions operate solely within the process of cause and effect. On that basis, we devote ourselves to the antidotes to karma and mental affliction, which are phenomena to be abandoned, and we strive for the resultant phenomena, which are factors to be adopted and which bring happiness now and in the long term. To begin we need an introduction to the essence of Buddhism by way of a presentation on the four truths.

In this book it is possible that there is some repetition over the two volumes, but this is because of the particular emphasis of the way of explaining the subject matter.

It is not necessary to become a Buddhist in order to put the fundamental philosophy of Buddhism and its stages of training into practice. All can comprehend these worthy qualities and use them to enjoy a good life blessed with short- and long-term happiness for oneself and others; this is something we all have to do. This does not mean that you should have faith in Buddhism or that you must definitely practice it. We should respect the individual's right to have or not have faith in a religion. It goes without saying that it is acceptable to practice religion and also acceptable not to. However, given that we desire happiness and have no desire for suffering, if a religious tradition's practices for taming the mind and abandoning hurting others are sincerely brought into daily life, they will definitely be beneficial in bringing happiness to oneself and others. I consider it important to try to show that.

Concerning an actual practice of Buddhism, at the very heart of the Dharma of the Buddha is a presentation of karma, or cause and effect. The proposition that "if this is done, that arises" is held to be a fundamental truth. By adhering to the reality of all phenomena existing in a state of mutual dependence, Buddhism must be practiced in harmony with the principle of seeking truth from facts. Buddhism is not a tradition that adheres solely to scripture; it is one in which reason is paramount. Any doctrine that contradicts evidence or sound reasoning, or that contradicts that which is validated by direct experience, should not be accepted and should be discarded. New ways of explaining phenomena that emerge from the investigative skills of modern research and do not accord with traditional explanations found in Buddhist texts of the past should be willingly accepted.

Even the words of Śākyamuni Buddha himself should be practiced having first examined them as one would examine the purity of gold through burning, cutting, and polishing. [xi] This the Buddha himself advised us to do. His instructions are not to be held as objects of veneration, nor followed simply because they are the words of our teacher. This independence of thought decreed by the mighty Buddha is the central pillar and peerless feature of this tradition. Those religions that determine what is and what is not allowed on the basis of the controlling decrees of a creator or of a founding saint, do not accord, in this aspect, with this fundamental tenet of Buddhism. Therefore, when we actually apply ourselves to religious practice, except in those areas of working to benefit others, we cannot simultaneously engage in different traditions, like having a foot in each camp, because of these fundamental differences in the path. Nor would it be of any benefit.

These days, in the conspicuous race of the human intellect to investigate fields of knowledge, competitiveness has increased accordingly. Because of this, many open-minded people, including those who propound modern scientific views, are convinced that Buddhist philosophy and its related trainings stand up to scrutiny. Non-Buddhists are recognizing that Buddhism can provide practices for developing happiness and eradicating suffering, practices that are therefore effective in bringing peace and well-being to society. Such voices are becoming more pronounced. For those who seek out new fields of knowledge and who have taken on the responsibility of promoting the welfare of our human society, Buddhism has become a new area of interest. This clearly illustrates the unique prestige of this tradition. It continues to receive much praise from all quarters that not only is it not a poison, but it can be substantiated by verifiable evidence and experience that it is medicine. This inspires limitless and joyous confidence.

VOLUME 2

Volume 2 is a translation of *Oral Transmission of Mañjuśrī: Instructions on the Stages of the Path,* a Buddhist presentation comprising, for a person who seeks liberation, the essential ways to practice in a single meditation session. It is an example of the stages of the path genre, one of the many condensed and extensive stages of the path works composed by the great masters of the past. It was composed by the Great Fifth Dalai Lama, whose work was an unparalleled kindness for both the modern religious and secular systems of Tibet and for its people. He was genuinely a great being endowed with learning and accomplishment. This text takes as its foundation the unrivaled work *Extensive Exposition on the Stages of the Path*, composed by the all-knowing Tsongkhapa Losang Drakpa (1357–1419), [xii] and excellently summarizes the main points of practice.

I have taken *Oral Transmission of Mañjuśrī*, which was held in great esteem by many masters of the past, as a basis for the teachings in volume 2 and I have provided, with great respect and service, a somewhat expanded explanation in the form of a supplement.

The explanation in these volumes does not just follow the traditional modes of the past. It is in accordance with these changing times and follows the great ocean waves of beliefs and dispositions of the beings of this world, however they live. It is aimed at those who have a liking for religion in general, or specifically for Buddhism, and at those who are monks and nuns, lay men and women, Tibetan and non-Tibetan, who out of faith have entered into this doctrine. It is also for those who have hostility toward religion, or have no particular feeling toward it, and for those who hold various political views. It is a work compiling the wisdom of different valuable philosophies and the great ways of the bodhisattvas.

This work is a small gift for the discerning people of this vast world and is offered with the pure motivation that it will reveal the excellent path of immediate and permanent happiness by opening new eyes of wisdom in all those of unbiased minds.

The Buddhist monk and propounder, the Fourteenth Dalai Lama, Tenzin Gyatso, Thekchen Chöling, Dharamsala, India, the sixth day of the tenth month of fire monkey year of the seventeenth cycle, corresponding to December 5, 2016.

Translator's Preface

The Fourteenth Dalai Lama's Stages of the Path, vol 2, is a translation from the Tibetan text originally titled *A Clarification of the Intent of the Conqueror That Fulfills the Wishes of All Beings: An Interwoven Commentary on the Guide to the Stages of the Path to Enlightenment called "Oral Transmission of Mañjuśrī."*

The bold font throughout the translation is the root text: *Oral Transmission of Mañjuśrī* by the Fifth Dalai Lama, Ngawang Losang Gyatso (1617–1682). The commentary by His Holiness the Fourteenth Dalai Lama, as compiled by His Eminence Dagyab Kyabgön Rinpoché, is rendered in regular font.

Oral Transmission of Mañjuśrī is an example of the traditional stages of the path (*lam rim*) literature of Tibetan Buddhism, specifically belonging to the Gelug tradition. As such, it follows the original framework of Atiśa Dīpaṃkara Śrījñāna's (982–1054) *Lamp for the Path to Enlightenment*. It guides the practitioner through the motivations of the "three beings" of lesser, intermediate, and greater spiritual capacity to the end goal of full enlightenment.

In his root text the Great Fifth essentially follows the outlines of Tsongkhapa's *Great Treatise on the Stages of the Path to Enlightenment*, condensing the information and supplementing it with meditation instructions. His Holiness has further clarified this structure by directly including the outlines from the *Great Treatise on the Stages of the Path* and pointing out where they differ.

Each translator has their own preferred terms, and thus some terminology differs from that of volume 1. Variants are noted in the glossary.

The bibliographic information for Tibetan texts that are the sources of numerous quotes throughout the book were not extant in the original, as is common for Tibetan works. I have nonetheless included a bibliography with general referent information and have listed English translations where found.

I would like to thank Tibet House Germany for offering the opportunity to translate this precious text; Dagyab Rinpoché for kindly making himself available to meticulously answer my questions; Franziska Oertle for her hard work in checking my translation against the Tibetan; Rebecca Hufen for frequently conferring with me on the translation and helping to resolve doubts; Thupten Jinpa for kindly addressing some qualms; Andreas Ansmann for facilitating all points of communication for the entire journey of the translation and publication; and Alex Gardner for his excellent editing skills.

Compiler's Introduction

[XIII] I WOULD LIKE TO SET OUT the thinking and background to the wonderful opportunity I have had in compiling the two volumes of *The Fourteenth Dalai Lama's Stages of the Path* from the teachings of the great and all-knowing Fourteenth Dalai Lama.

On October 7, 1991, while His Holiness the Dalai Lama was giving teachings in Hamburg, Germany, I experienced the great fortune of being deemed worthy to be in his presence during the lunch that was offered to him in his residence at the Rabten Jangchup Chöling Dharma Center. In keeping the thought that we should receive his forever meaningful instructions wherever possible, I expressed a doubt concerning the manner in which texts primarily of the stages of the path genre were being commentated on, wondering whether some were not in tune with the dispositions of the changing times in this world, and I requested his advice on this matter.

It was His Holiness's opinion also that it was certainly the case that some of the more traditional ways of commenting were not appropriate, and that it was important for such commentaries to not fundamentally be in contradiction with progressive modern education and reasoning, and to be in harmony with practical reality

Therefore, with a view of not wanting Buddhism to be regarded as anachronistic, and still be relevant today, I requested that he might compose a work on the stages of the path that would suit the mental dispositions of numerous students. [xiv] This great treasure of compassion agreed that such a work was necessary and was of the opinion that it would be excellent if such a stages of the path compilation were based upon the four truths. However, because of the pressure of his busy schedule and increasing workload, it would have been difficult for him to give time to composing a text with his own hand, and so he said, "I will teach it and you, Rinpoché, will write it down. That would be good."

He had blessed me with a joyous festival of priceless words, and I experienced a feeling of faith, devotion, and happiness beyond description. However, because of his increasing activity in working for the welfare of the world, bringing harmony among the world's religions, and striving for the welfare of Tibet, the project did not immediately begin, and I did not have the confidence to ask him again and so left it as it was.

However, on June 5, 2006, after four days of teachings His Holiness had given in Brussels, Belgium, as he was preparing to leave, I was suddenly asked to see him in his room. His Holiness said that it would be worthwhile to compose a supplement to *Oral Transmission of Mañjuśrī* by the Great Fifth, and because I had received many teachings from His Holiness and was very familiar with his way of thinking, it was appropriate that I should compile the draft of this supplement. There would also be a general explanation consisting of an introduction to Buddhism and so on, as a preliminary, and therefore I should organize the production of "The Fourteenth Dalai Lama's Stages of the Path."

This was a kindness beyond measure and an unparalleled caring for me with an optimism that regarded a clod of earth as gold. [xv] There was no time to think about whether I could accomplish this task, or to ask his thoughts on how to proceed to carry it out. No sooner had I taken his command to the crown of my head I just uttered the one word, "Yes," and was lost for anything else to say.

Gradually, after this surprising turn of events became a little clearer, I thought about it and realized that it was connected to what His Holiness had said previously at lunch in Hamburg. Although I had no confidence in myself having the knowledge or capability to carry out such a service, I thought that by the power of the blessings of compassion from the lama, such an accomplishment might be possible. This lifted up my mind and gave me encouragement.

At the same time, from the Gaden Phodrang Private Office I requested and received CDs and other materials on His Holiness's introductory discourses on Buddhism, as well as his stages of the path teachings primarily on *Oral Transmission of Mañjuśrī*. These I used as a basis. Over time I collected the many published books of his teachings and compiled the various notes I had taken. From Tibetan language newspapers, journals, and the internet, I collected even the smallest teachings that had been published, as well as the various talks that were regularly given. In this way I set about the preparations for the compilation.

On December 18, 2006, at Varanasi, India, while His Holiness was giving a teaching, I had my first opportunity to ask for his opinion and advice on the notes I had made for this composition and on its content being in accord with modern thinking.

[xvi] From August 16 to 20, 2008, at Nantes in France, while His Holiness was giving teachings there, I was able show him a basic compilation of the draft I had completed thus far, and I received some profound advice. After that, as suggested by His Holiness, I went to Switzerland to meet with the academic scholar and geshé Thupten Jinpa, the interpreter for His Holiness. In informal and very helpful conversations on diverse topics, he suggested various improvements and put forward many ideas. On that basis I revised the draft.

Generally, the outlines to explanations of the stages of the path are straightforward. However, here, while it was perfectly acceptable to use the outlines established by the *Extensive Exposition on the Stages of the Path*, these were not copied verbatim but at times were abridged, and so the numbering only roughly corresponds.

General explanations of Buddhism have no outlines. Using the suggestions of Geshé Thupten Jinpa and others, I looked into laying out chapters and setting up a new structure, in particular making sure that there would not be much repetition of material and that everything would fit into its appropriate classification. Doing so meant that I was providing the opportunity for criticism from all quarters for my woeful lack of knowledge and ability. However, I have proceeded with whatever my mind was capable of understanding. Nevertheless, I remain doubtful that it conforms to the intentions of His Holiness, and while that is so, I cannot do other than to ask for tolerance of my errors.

[xvii] His Holiness's discourses are delivered in a phrasing that is easy to understand and their meanings are clear. They are timely, of profound potential, contain great counsel, are in tune with the developments of time and place, and are completely in accord with the beliefs, inclinations, attitudes, faculties, latent dispositions, and so on of listeners from different cultures. It is evident to everyone that they are enthusiastically regarded as unparalleled objects of praise and reverence.

When putting these discourses into writing so that the splendor and brilliance of His Holiness's profound words are clearly manifest, I maintained as best I could the prime importance of bringing out those elements that clarify his thought with no degeneration of the written language, and in the first volume especially, by supplementing with relevant material.

Discourses of His Holiness such as these are of great importance, and when writing the draft, I did not shy away from the amount of writing. However, whenever it was shown to His Holiness for his perusal, so as not to tire him from reading too much, those sections that definitely required his attention were written in blue ink. After his scrutiny, any advice he gave was recorded or noted down and revision made accordingly.

For the three days that ran between July 31 and August 9, 2010, at the Gaden Phodrang in Dharamsala, I specially convened with Professor Samdhong Rinpoché, Geshé Thupten Jinpa, and the interpreter Geshé Dramdul. [xviii] Together with His Holiness we discussed the draft text, and I revised the draft based on the advice and suggestions given at that time.

On December 22, 2012, I went to see Samdhong Rinpoché at Ashram, his private residence in Dharamsala. There for seventeen full days, uninterrupted by any of his other duties or functions and with a great sense of responsibility, he gave his full attention to all the notes that had so far been roughly compiled into the two volumes of the stages of the path and preliminary general explanation. In return I received peerless advice and suggestions from him. I improved the draft where necessary and over time sent sections to Rinpoché for review.

In 2015, over three days from May 19 to 21, in the Gaden Phodrang at Dharamsala, I met with Samdhong Rinpoché as well as with Sera Mé Monastery Lharampa Geshé Yangteng Rinpoché, who is the Private Office undersecretary. At that time His Holiness provided us with the pleasing reassurance of looking over the whole of stages of the path section. Taking the advice that we received from him on those parts still in need of improvement and of supplementing, I consulted with Samdhong Rinpoché and amended accordingly. With this, a draft of the second volume of *The Fourteenth Dalai Lama's Stages of the Path*, on the stages of the path, was complete.

Toward the end of December 2015, while His Holiness was teaching in South India, I consulted Samdhong Rinpoché on the first volume dealing with the general teachings and made revisions in accordance with his advice. On April 2, 2016, I came to Dharamsala to present the draft to His Holiness for his perusal.

This precious work, *The Fourteenth Dalai Lama's Stages of the Path*, reviewed and assessed by Samdhong Rinpoché and Yangteng Rinpoché, is a collection of teachings that bring out the very essence of the thoughts of His Holiness. It is an excellent teaching created from his actual words, from words that have his assent, and from words that he has blessed.[1] It is a contribution to a new-moon, authentic literary tradition that reveals a path to benefit all beings of this world equally without discrimination, and now the opportunity to present it to the people of this world, as a gift to ease their pain, has arrived.

His Holiness the Dalai Lama especially gave me this precious opportunity to gather the excellent merit of performing this act of devotion by preparing a draft of the two volumes of *The Fourteenth Dalai Lama's Stages of the Path*. It brings joy to my heart, and with gladness, faith, and devotion I prostrate before him and remember his kindness that knows no end.

As a key to open the vast door to His Holiness's profound collection of teachings, I compiled from these two volumes a summary, *Essence of Thought*, which contains the most succinct statements. The two sections of the summary are included as an appendix in each of the two volumes.

ACKNOWLEDGMENTS

To Professor Samdhong Rinpoché, who from beginning to end scrutinized the various drafts and constantly gave me peerless, abundant advice and guidance, I express gratitude that is beyond measure.

To the academic scholar and interpreter for His Holiness, Geshé Thupten Jinpa; to the director of Tibet House Delhi and interpreter for His Holiness, Geshé Dorjé Dramdul; [xx] and to Gaden Phodrang Private Office undersecretary, Sera Mé Lharampa Geshé Yangteng Rinpoché: for their peerless assistance by way of many gifts of ideas, guidance and discussion given over a long period, I rejoice from the depth of my heart.

To the Gaden Phodrang Private Office also, who provided much needed assistance for this undertaking and who granted us joint

copyright to publish in Tibetan, English, German, and Chinese languages these two volumes of His Holiness's book *The Fourteenth Dalai
Lama's Stages of the Path*, thereby fulfilling the aspirations of the Tibetan
Cultural and Educational Institute, known as Tibet House Germany,
which is sustained by the compassion of its honorary patron, His Holiness the Dalai Lama, I offer sincere thanks and gratitude.

Respectfully,

Dagyab Loden Sherab

Compiler

March 15, 2016

For an account by Rinpoché of His Holiness the Dalai Lama's many
achievements, please visit https://wisdomexperience.org
/wp-content/uploads/2023/01/Achievements-of-HHDL.pdf
or see volume 1.

Foreword and Acknowledgments by Tibet House Germany (Tibethaus Deutschland)

IT IS REPORTED OF GREAT INVENTORS that they suddenly had a brilliant inspiration, as if from nowhere, during a banal activity such as brushing their teeth. The fact that these inventions were preceded by many years of thought, one-pointed motivation, and intensive work is often glossed over. The idea for writing *The Fourteenth Dalai Lama's Stages of the Path* arose in a similar situation:

> More than a decade ago, during a short audience in Brussels, H. H. the Dalai Lama tasked me by the by—he was preparing to leave and was tying his shoelaces—to compile a contemporary lamrim on his behalf, based on his own teachings. It was to be his own commentary on the lamrim by the V. Dalai Lama. In addition, I was to compile a detailed introduction to Buddhism.

With these words, our revered spiritual director H. E. Dagyab Rinpoché described with a chuckle the moment of the "initial spark" for the creation of the two-volume work, the Tibetan title of which is *Gyalwé Gongsel* (*Rgyal ba'i dgongs gsal*).

As a result, Rinpoché, who had just retired after thirty-eight years at the University of Bonn, worked intensively on these books for more than ten years. What an impressive achievement! In this connection he traveled three times to Dharamsala to review and correct the text in detail with His Holiness. Professor Samdhong Rinpoché, Geshé

Thupten Jinpa, and Yangteng Rinpoché were also present at these meetings. The Tibetan edition was then jointly published by the Dalai Lama Trust and Tibet House Germany in December 2016 and presented to the public in the presence of His Holiness, Dagyab Rinpoché, and Mr. Phuntsok Tsering Düchung at a book lounge in India.

In this work, His Holiness has pointed out a number of new paths that Tibetan Buddhists in particular are encouraged to follow. For instance, the *geshé lharampa* title, introduced by the Fourth Panchen Lama, Losang Chökyi Gyaltsen (1570–1662), was only given to monks until just a few years ago. The Fourteenth Dalai Lama has initiated that this title be conferred to nuns as well. The first female geshé in the academic history of Tibetan Buddhism is the German nun Kelsang Wangmo, who earned her title in 2011. In addition, His Holiness has now directed that in the future this academic title be awarded to all graduates of Buddhist philosophy studies—regardless of ordination, gender, or race.

According to Dagyab Rinpoché, we can regard this work, comparable to the constitution of a country, as something we can always rely on. It is forward looking and of great importance for not only Buddhists but also for people without a spiritual background as well as for researchers.

The work has been translated into English, German, and Chinese under the direction of our Tibet House publishing house. And hopefully this is just the beginning...

Why does Tibet House Germany hold the copyright together with the Gaden Phodrang Foundation of the Dalai Lama? To answer this, we must briefly explain some of the history and orientation of our organization: Tibet House has been under the patronage of H. H. the Dalai Lama since 2005. It is a cultural and educational institute in the middle of the open multiethnic and multireligious cosmopolitan city of Frankfurt. It arose from a Buddhist predecessor organization that had already been working with Dagyab Rinpoché for over twenty years.

Our institute has had the honor of inviting His Holiness to Frankfurt a total of four times in recent years, enabling him to present to the public his heartfelt concerns (which are also ours): intercultural and interreligious dialogue, study, and the cultivation of Tibetan culture, and the cultivation of the global, nonreligious ethics he has developed. Particularly important and touching for us were his encounters with sometimes up to two thousand pupils as well as dialogue encounters on interreligious and secular topics.

Tibet House Germany builds bridges in both directions to create a connection between Tibetan culture and all those interested in it, and to create the necessary basis for this—for instance, by deepening communication with other Tibetan institutions in and outside Tibet, likewise with Western, Tibetan, and Chinese artists and scholars. The purpose is to support people in attaining happiness by providing differentiated information, study, and practice and to impart crucial core values.

According to the Dalai Lama's succinct formulation, these core values are the following:

1. The view is dependent origination.
2. The conduct is to do no harm.

Tibet, Tibetans, and Tibetan culture are the origin and source of the contents and concerns of Tibet House. The supporting pillars of Tibet House are Tibetans and Germans/Westerners alike. Undiluted study of Buddhist texts, application of the teachings in everyday life, appreciation of all traditions, and the overcoming of stereotyped thinking are all a matter of course for us. We also promote the connection between Buddhist knowledge and science. A good example of this is our Cultural Foundation's Phuntsok Tsering Scholarship project, which enables young Tibetans to study at the University of Hamburg under the guidance of Professor Dorji Wangchuk. Another concern is the overdue equality of Tibetan women scholars and practitioners, for many years a goal of the Dagyab Benefit Society (Dagyab Hilfsverein) and of our foundation. Just one more focal point should be mentioned: providing specific support for children and young people, who are, after all, our future.

Our School for Tibetan Children, or Sherab Ling ("Garden of Knowledge"), follows the secular SEE Learning method for teachers, which was initiated by the Dalai Lama (we have been a cooperation partner of Emory University/USA since 2016). We also host numerous visits by school classes and student groups, which are a great pleasure for us.

In this way we endeavor to put into practice as many of the important themes and thought-provoking ideas of this great two-volume work as possible.

Our special thanks go to the Gaden Phodrang Foundation of the Dalai Lama, which has financed a large part of the English translation from its endowment funds. The translation into English would not have been possible without this support. We would also like to thank them for entrusting us with the planning and coordination of the English, German, and Chinese translations. We would like to take this opportunity to express our gratitude to Mr. Kungo Tseten Chhökyapa and Mr. Tenzin Sewo for their outstanding cooperation.

Also, we wish to offer our thanks to Geshé Thupten Jinpa, who gave his precious advice at different stages of this publication.

With their outstanding linguistic and philosophical skills, Gavin Kilty and Sophie McGrath have produced translations that are both accurate and inspiring, making this extremely important work accessible to English readers. We wish to express our highest appreciation and deepest gratitude to them. We would also like to give our heartfelt thanks to Rebecca Hufen and Jürgen Manshardt, the German translators of the second volume, who contributed to the quality of the English translation by way of analyzing and comparing difficult parts of their translation with the English edition, and to Franziska Oertle, who compared the English and German translations of the second volume word for word with the Tibetan original.

We would very much like to thank Chandra Chiara Ehm for her inspiring translation of the summary, *Essence of Thought*, which can be found in the appendix of the two volumes.

The cooperation with the publication team of Wisdom Publications was always very pleasant and characterized by a high level of professionalism. We are very happy to know that this work is in good hands with this excellent publishing house. We would especially like to thank Laura Cunningham and Daniel Aitken for their excellent project management. In addition, Alex Gardner, as editor, and Ben Gleason, as production editor, have made a great contribution through their careful and meticulous work. Our sincere thanks!

At Tibet House we would like to express our special thanks to Phuntsok Tsering. He accompanied this project as codirector with great commitment before his all-too-early death. A big thank you goes to Claudia Heilmann for her support from the Tibet House Cultural Foundation, as well as to Judith Fries, who was able to collect a large number of donations for these translations with extraordinary dedication. Our heartfelt thanks also go to Matthias Atrott for his generous and professional legal advice. We would also like to thank from the bottom of our hearts all the people who, through their small and large donations, helped to make this translation possible.

Our wish is that many people will personally benefit from this work and contribute thereby to a better world.

Elke Hessel, Director, Tibet House Germany
Andreas Ansmann, Manager, Tibet House Publishing

Technical Note

THE SHORT TIBETAN TITLE of the two-volume work, of which the second volume is translated here, is *Rgyal ba'i dgongs gsal*, which might be translated as "clarifying the intent of the conquerors." Bracketed numbers embedded in the text refer to page numbers in the 2016 Tibetan edition published by the Dalai Lama Trust and Tibet House Germany in India (ISBN 978-93-83091-52-2).

The conventions for phonetic transcription of Tibetan words are those developed by the Institute of Tibetan Classics and Wisdom Publications. These reflect approximately the pronunciation of words by a modern Central Tibetan; Tibetan speakers from Ladakh, Kham, or Amdo, not to mention Mongolians, might pronounce the words quite differently. Sanskrit diacritics are used throughout except for Sanskrit terms that have been naturalized into English, such as samsara, nirvana, sutra, stupa, and mandala.

Except in some cases of titles frequently mentioned, works mentioned in the translation have typically had the author's name added by the translator for ease of reference by contemporary readers. It should be noted, therefore, that these names, although appearing without brackets, are not always present in the original Tibetan.

Pronunciation of Tibetan Phonetics
ph and *th* are aspirated *p* and *t*, as in *pet* and *tip*.
ö is similar to the *eu* in the French *seul*.
ü is similar to the *ü* in the German *füllen*.

ai is similar to the *e* in *bet*.

é is similar to the *e* in *prey*.

Pronunciation of Sanskrit

Palatal *ś* and retroflex *ṣ* are similar to the English unvoiced *sh*.

c is an unaspirated *ch* similar to the *ch* in *chill*.

The vowel *ṛ* is similar to the American *r* in *pretty*.

ñ is somewhat similar to the nasalized *ny* in *canyon*.

ṃ is similar to the *ng* in *sing* or *anger*.

The Virtuous Beginning:
The Starting Content

IN ORDER TO EXPLAIN the stages of the path (*lam rim*) to enlightenment called *Oral Transmission of Mañjuśrī*, this text is separated into three outlines:

1. The virtuous beginning: the starting content
2. The virtuous middle: the explanation of the meaning of the text
3. The virtuous end: the concluding content

The first outline, the virtuous beginning, has two parts:

1. The expression of homage
2. The pledge to compose the text

THE EXPRESSION OF HOMAGE

The expression of homage contains a supplication to the Lord of Teachings, the Teacher Bhagavān, and likewise to Nāgārjuna and Asaṅga, to Jowo Jé Atiśa Dīpaṃkara Śrījñāna (982–c.1055), the sole divinity, to the gentle protector Lama Tsongkhapa (1357–1419), and to Khöntön Paljor Lhundrup (1561–1637), from whom the great Fifth Dalai Lama received the teachings of the experiential guide on the stages of the path.

Thus, the first expression of homage to the Teacher Bhagavān is as follows:

> Born from the nurse[2] of the moon (the ocean), the two
> collections, the union of method and wisdom,
> the supreme fruit of a hundred tastes of omniscience of all
> aspects
> is ripened on the tips of the far-reaching branches of the
> marks and signs,[3] favorable to see.
> Supreme among beings, friend of the sun,[4] wish-granting tree,
> bestow good fortune!

This verse expresses the qualities of the guardian of the teachings, the lord of sages, the Teacher, supreme among beings and friend of the sun, by depicting him in the form of the wish-granting tree. [2] What qualities does he have? "Supreme among beings" is in reference to his enlightened deeds. The Buddha is the ultimate refuge because he possesses the *dharmakāya* and *rūpakāya*—the dharmakāya for one's own welfare, and the rūpakāya for the welfare of others. These are the culmination of the qualities of a buddha's body, speech, and mind, which accomplish the welfare of sentient beings through spontaneous and effortless enlightened deeds. Thus, "supreme among beings" can refer to the supreme enlightened deeds that are suitable for the dispositions and inclinations of all sentient beings. The enlightened deeds have arisen from actualizing the qualities of the dharmakāya—the mind omniscient of all aspects—and thus in this analogy the dharmakāya is manifest on the tips of the far-reaching branches of the Buddha's marks and signs of the body, favorable to see, possessed by the one who is represented as a wish-fulfilling tree ripe with fruits of a hundred tastes.

Alternatively, one might wonder if his possession of the ultimate rūpakāya for others' benefit that is favorable to see—that is, the rūpakāya adorned with marks and signs, whose nature is inseparable from the pristine wisdom dharmakāya—and his possession of both bodies of immeasurable qualities—namely the dharmakāya for one's own benefit and the rūpakāya for others' benefit—is a manner of possession that is changeless, permanent, and self-arisen, or whether they arose in dependence on causes and conditions.

The answer is that they are entirely arisen in dependence upon causes and conditions. Moreover, they are arisen in dependence upon the force of meditation on the path. Thus, the analogy used here is the far-reaching branches and ripened fruits of a hundred tastes belonging to a wish-granting tree that fulfills hopes. It is arisen from the nurse, or ocean,[5] that is the union of method and wisdom. The Buddha's nature is that of the two ultimate bodies: the rūpakāya for others' benefit, favorable to see, a body adorned with marks and signs, not of flesh and bone, not a coarse aggregation, but in the nature of pristine wisdom— in brief, of inseparable nature with the enlightened mind—and the dharmakāya for one's own benefit, which is a single pristine wisdom realizing modes and varieties,[6] and which is the mind directly realizing all phenomena in a single instant like a gooseberry placed in the palm of one's hand. Both arise from the force of complete habituation with the limitless two accumulations that are continuously familiarized with in order to easily achieve omniscience for an extended time over eons and eons. This is the marvelously complete cause that is *bodhicitta* and the method-conduct of generosity and so forth that is conjoined with it, and the pristine wisdom realizing emptiness, [3] both not separated but united as wisdom conjoined with method, and method conjoined with wisdom.

Moreover, for the sake of sentient beings who are the intended beneficiaries of the enlightened deeds, the actualization of those bodies, of which there are various divisions of two, three, and four, is to act for the welfare of sentient beings unceasingly by way of the twenty-seven enlightened deeds[7] and so forth, until the end of space, under the influence of great compassion. As explained by Nāgārjuna in his *Precious Garland of the Middle Way*, there is nothing within Buddhism that is not included among the accomplishing agents for high status or definite goodness. Moreover, since accomplishing high status depends upon the dharma of nonviolence, it requires faith in the dependent origination of cause and effect. Accomplishing definite goodness requires an understanding of the suchness that is the dependent origination of imputed existence acting as a direct antidote to the apprehension of true existence. Thus, Nāgārjuna states, "In brief, faith and wisdom." Through making praises with great faith in the guide, the Śākya lion, who became the supreme among beings through being skillful in excellently instructing on the two principles of Dharma—faith that accomplishes high status, and wisdom that accomplishes definite goodness—we supplicate him to bestow good fortune. [4]

In accordance with this, the gentle protector, king of Dharma, Lama Tsongkhapa authored the following homage in his *Great Treatise on the Stages of the Path*:

> To the one whose body was formed by ten million perfect
>   virtues,
> whose speech fulfills the hopes of limitless beings,
> whose mind sees all objects of knowledge as they are,
> I bow my head to the chief of the Śākyas

The message of the first line, that buddhahood is entirely arisen through a perfect collection of causes, pertaining to the dependent origination of cause and effect, is an incredibly significant point. To gain a thorough understanding of this one must know the presentation of the four truths. Perfectly ascertaining the presentation of the four truths requires understanding the presentation of the two truths, in which they are distinguished as being one nature but different isolates.

As for the second line of this verse, "whose speech fulfills the hopes of limitless beings," the hopes of beings for their temporary happiness and for their ultimate happiness both arise only in dependence upon compatible causes. This principle of dependent origination in which accomplishing temporary and ultimate happiness requires eliminating the discordant conditions and accomplishing the concordant conditions for either temporary or lasting aims was taught by the Buddha through his enlightened deed of speech. The Buddha possesses a body that is the miracle of emanation, speech that is the miracle of teaching, and a mind that is the miracle of total forbearance. That his speech, the miracle of teaching, is principal among his three miracles is taught in the *Treasury of Knowledge*, and also in the treatises on the perfection of wisdom sutras. In particular, the protector Nāgārjuna praises the Buddha for teaching subtle dependent arising:

> I prostrate to the Lord of Sages,
> who taught dependent origination
> by which he abandoned
> birth and disintegration.

And likewise, the majority of the protector Nāgārjuna's praises of the Lord of Sages are offerings of praise by reason of his teaching dependent origination. Likewise, Jé Rinpoché Tsongkhapa states:

> Out of all your deeds,
> your deed of speech is supreme. [5]

Thus, even more than the aforementioned dependent origination of cause and effect, the teaching of subtle dependent origination, i.e., the suchness of dependent origination, is principal among his enlightened deeds of speech.

Alternatively, with respect to the line "whose speech fulfills the hopes of limitless beings," instead of applying the meaning only to a limitless *number* of sentient beings, if it is taken to mean "whose speech fulfills the aims of diverse beings of limitless dispositions and inclinations, accordingly," then one can understand the existence of different styles of scriptural teachings, which, from a first, literal, reading deceptively appear to be taught to persons of different continua. Yet, in the stages of the path treatises they are arranged as a path for the three types of beings and their practice is consolidated for a single sitting session. This is because, with respect to the different vehicles proclaimed by the Teacher, (1) one must practice what was taught for when one's mental capacity is inferior, (2) it is suitable to practice what was taught for when one's mental capacity has slightly developed, and (3) one is capable of practicing what was taught for when one's mental capacity has become supreme. Thus one can see that these different stages that were taught on account of the vastness of attitudes and aspirations, the depth of wisdom, and so forth, are actually to be practiced by a single person in a single sitting session. Therefore, I think that the feature of the emergence of the Mahāyāna and Hīnayāna and four tenet systems can be posited from the perspective of vastness in attitude, or aspiration, and depth of wisdom.

What is the necessity and reason for the Buddha to teach differently from the perspective of wisdom? It is due to the different presentations of the view related to objects. [6] For example, although the views of coarse selflessness of persons and coarse selflessness of phenomena are not the final view, through the superimpositions of the innate apprehension of true existence that apprehends phenomena in our continua as truly existent, external forms, sounds, and so forth appear as outwardly existent objects regardless of whatever name is imputed. On top of that they appear to exist from the side of the object as the referent of the conception that apprehends them.

Whether that mode of apprehension is innate or not, since there are such appearances to our awareness, the agents that cause them to cease also need not be totally contrary to those. Even though something permanent, unitary, and independent does not appear to an innate awareness, things spontaneously appear as permanent, unitary, or autonomous, and therefore due to a single person having many levels of subtlety of self-grasping, one needs to know how to bring the means of subduing those into one's practice.

In any case, as noted above, the fact that all profound and vast Dharma taught by the Buddha is categorized as either an accomplishing agent for high status or definite goodness is as it is said in Nāgārjuna's *Precious Garland of the Middle Way*: "In brief, faith and wisdom."

The accomplishing agent for high status is faith in the process of cause and effect arisen from an understanding of dependent origination. The accomplishing agent for definite goodness is the understanding of the suchness of dependent origination—that is, dependent imputation—and the application of it as the direct antidote to the apprehension of true existence.

With respect to the third line, "whose mind sees all objects of knowledge as they are," the root of the Buddha's capability to proclaim all Dharma teachings, beginning with the dependent origination of cause and effect and the dependent origination of dependent imputation, arises from his being endowed with a mind that is omniscient of all aspects—of all modes and varieties of phenomena without exception. It states in the verse of homage of Maitreya's *Ornament for Clear Realization*:

> Through its perfect possession the subduers taught these
> varieties having all aspects . . .[8]

By reason of possessing these qualities, the Great Fifth's homage praises the Bhagavān's body from the viewpoint of excellent causes, his speech from the viewpoint of excellent results—or enlightened deeds—and his mind from the viewpoint of excellent nature, or excellent attributes of its nature. [7]

The verse of homage to Nāgārjuna and Asaṅga is as follows:

I praise those known as the two great trailblazers,
the renowned ones who transcended the domain of existence,
skilled in lifting up the vast and profound Dharma on the
back of the turtle of explanation, debate, and composition
when it sank into the inferior ocean of the world.

Due to being similar to great trailblazers who force their way down
a path with large wheels, thereby making it easier for other small-
wheeled vehicles to move with ease, Nāgārjuna and Asaṅga are known
as "the trailblazers who opened the way." Since these two great beings
excellently unraveled the exact intention of the victor, allowing num-
berless individuals, regardless of their country, to study them, they are
similar to great trailblazers. They are openers of a path that restored
the way of the sage's words after they had declined, and they developed what had not declined.

With respect to this, there are many categories of Buddhadharma in
general, and Mahāyāna Dharma in particular, and from that perspective it is incredibly vast. Likewise, from the perspective of profundity,
because the meaning of emptiness is a very difficult point, Mahāyāna
doctrine easily declines due to lack of understanding and misinterpre-
tation. It is for this reason the kind Teacher came to the land of āryas,
and was followed by the "seven successors to the teachings,"[9] great
beings who upheld the Dharma. However, after a while, when the
degeneration of the Mahāyāna teachings became so great, Nāgārjuna
and Asaṅga appeared in succession, in accordance with the scriptural
prophecies of the Teacher. They opened a path in which they created a
revival of the kind Teacher's Dharma in general, and specifically of the
vast and profound Dharma, both of which were temporarily defiled
by the stains of lack of realization and wrong understanding, and had
incurred degeneration. In doing so they opened the way for the vast
proliferation of the Buddha's system of teachings. [8] For this reason
Nāgārjuna is called the opener of the trailblazer way of the Madhya-

maka School, and Ārya Asaṅga is called the opener of the trailblazer way of the Yogācāra School.

The ancient story depicted here of the turtle—one of the ten avatars of Viṣṇu—who lifted up the earth when it disappeared into the depths of the ocean, comes to us from the oral history of pre-Buddhist India.

Praise is expressed via this metaphor to the two trailblazers, the stainless renowned ones who transcended the domain of existence, who, through their noble deeds of explanation, debate, and composition—portrayed as the turtle—were skilled in lifting the vast and profound Dharma system of the Mahāyāna—broad like the earth—that disappeared into the inferior ocean of the Hīnayāna sutras that were taught generally by the Buddha Bhagavān to common disciples.

In brief, the two supreme beings, protector Nāgārjuna and Ārya Asaṅga, are offered heartfelt praise for thoroughly illuminating the Bhagavān Teacher's general Dharma, and in particular his vast and profound Mahāyāna Dharma throughout the world at the right time.

Following that, the expression of homage to the glorious, incomparable Jowo Jé Atiśa, is as follows:

> **In the cool land surrounded by snow mountains,**
> **Atiśa dispelled the darkness of wrong views**
> **with the bright sun of Mahāyāna Dharma,**
> **simultaneously permeating Tibet with the light of the**
> **Subduer's teachings.**

This highly extolled supreme being was born into a royal line in current day Bangladesh, formerly ruled by India. Eventually he ordained in the Buddhist tradition and was called Dīpaṃkara Śrījñāna. He rose to the top among scholars of his own and all other schools of thought, and practiced to the level of his knowledge, and thus was a scholar-practitioner with a thoroughly tamed mind. This supreme being went to Tibet and spread the teachings with great kindness. [9]

Regarding this, the Buddhist Dharma was first spread in the cool land encircled by snow mountains during the time of the Tibetan king Thori Nyantsan, and in particular during the time of the Tibetan king Songtsen Gampo (617–650). During the time of the Dharma king Tri Songdetsen (742–796), the three known as the Abbot, Ācārya, and Dharma King gathered together and established a tradition of the Buddha's teachings that included Mahāyāna, Hīnayāna, and Tantrayāna, which gradually became as bright as the sun. However, following that, from the time of the Tibetan king Lang Darma onward, when the dire situation unfolded of the great degeneration of the Victor's teachings, Atiśa, the greatly kind, once again cleared away all darkness of lack of realization and wrong understanding with the powerful radiance of pure scripture and logic of the sun of the Buddha's teachings in general and in particular the Mahāyāna Dharma, and simultaneously pervaded the entirety of Tibet with the light of the nonerroneous teachings of the Subduer. He is thus praised.

In particular, the Incomparable Jowo Jé Atiśa arrived in Tibet and, having determined the dispositions, inclinations, and situation of the country of the Tibetan people, authored *Lamp for the Path to Enlightenment*, a treatise to concisely guide them on the stages of the path of the three beings, the intention of the Victor. Thus, Atiśa is also praised from the point of view of *Lamp for the Path* being the original model of all well-known teachings known as "stages of the path to enlightenment."

The verse of general praise for the upholders of the Kadam tradition, beginning with Dromtön Gyalwé Jungné (1004–64), the chief disciple of the incomparable Jowo Jé, is as follows:

How wondrous this Kadam tradition that pervades all
   directions,
whose excellent teachings are the supreme wish-fulfilling
   jewel, [10]

> that, placed at the pinnacle of the victory banner of listening,
> contemplation, and meditation,
> fulfills ultimate aspirations.

This special extolling of greatness that captivates the heart means the following: by placing the excellent teachings of Atiśa, the supreme wish-fulfilling jewel that accomplishes all hopes of myriad beings, at the pinnacle of the victory banner, beautified with the symbols of triumph over the army of ignorance that was accomplished by means of the actions of the three spheres of explanation and accomplishment, the Jowo Kadam tradition, pervading all directions, which fulfills all temporary and ultimate aspirations of oneself and others without exception, is indeed marvelous.

All topics of the triple basket of the Buddha's word are contained within Atiśa's scriptural tradition of *Lamp for the Path to Enlightenment* and other invaluable teachings such as his *Bodhisattva's Garland of Jewels* and so forth. Moreover, the entirety of the triple basket can be unlocked via the key of *Lamp for the Path*. Thus, the marvelous approach known as the "sevenfold divinity and teachings of the Kadam tradition" was comprised of (1) the internally and externally pure Dharma of the three types of beings in which the style of practice takes the Victor's teachings as practical instructions without forsaking a single word, and (2) reliance on the four deities of (a) the Teacher Bhagavān, because he is the deity who is the lord of teachings; (b) the most exalted Avalokiteśvara, because he is the deity of compassion; (c) Venerable Tārā, because she is the deity of enlightened deeds; and (d) Acala, because he eliminates obstacles. On top of this, a system renowned as the "New Kadam," emphasizing the path of unsurpassed secret mantra in which the meditation deities Guhyasamāja, Cakrasaṃvara, and Vajrabhairava are practiced inseparably, arose from the system of practice of the gentle protector, the Great Lama Tsongkhapa, and thus a verse of homage for Jé Rinpoché in this context follows:

Through merely raising the vast hundred-spoked vajra of your
finely analytical intelligence, [11]
you destroy the mountains of faulty explanations of countless
treatises by the stained and confused,
while simultaneously defeating all subtle-bodied arrogant
asuras, malicious antagonists, nascent in the womb.
May the omniscient Tsongkhapa, the unprecedented
Devendra, learned, righteous, and good, reign!

The meaning of this praise and homage is as follows: one can infer
from the system that is the supreme legacy of the gentle protector
Tsongkhapa's many excellent works—that eliminated all faults of
nonrealization and wrong understanding of the Victor's teachings
and that were taught through the experiences of his realizations of
the stages of the path that arose within him—that this protector possesses an incredibly vast and strongly analytical intelligence. His collected writings—spanning eighteen volumes—might not seem to be
many when compared to the collected works of the omniscient Butön
(1290–1364) and so forth. Yet they possess vast analytical perspectives
on myriad textual systems, and through the power of his excellently
written contributions—eloquent works of quality that tackle difficult
topics through his perfected understanding of such myriad textual
systems—he destroyed the forces of faulty explanation; that is, erroneous commentaries of textual systems by those confused by wrong
understanding or possessing the stains of a lack of realization of the
crucial points of the Subduer's intentions behind his teachings of sutra
and mantra, and he simultaneously stripped all malicious antagonists
of the power of their arrogance. May the omniscient Jé Tsongkhapa,
the unprecedented marvelous great being, learned, righteous, and
good, who upholds the teachings, portrayed here as Devendra, be
victorious!

Next follows a praise incorporating the name of Khöntön Paljor
Lhundrup from the region of Phabong, from whom the Great Fifth
Dalai Lama received the practice guide of the stages of the path:

> When the sun of the Victor set at the western mountain
> obscured by karma and affliction,
> you, lord of tutors, rose from the eastern mountain of my
>   inferior intellect, [12]
> Khöntön, friend of the jasmine flower, are the ornament on my
>   crown.
>
> Through the glory (*pal*) of your virtue in the beginning,
>   middle, and end,
> you endlessly bestow the wealth (*jor*) of holy Dharma,
> and through your mastery from Mañjuśrī entering your throat,
> you are the spiritual friend who is the source of the
>   spontaneously accomplished (*lhundrup*) four bodies.

Not only did the Great Fifth receive cycles of teachings on the stages
of the path from this venerable lama, but it was Khöntön Paljor Lhundrup who initially introduced him also to the teachings of the gentle
protector, the great Tsongkhapa of the New Kadam, and the crucial
points of secret mantra from the early translation period, and for this
reason he is venerated as one of his principal root gurus.

How are the qualities of this master lauded in these verses? By
stating "I honor, Khöntön, lord of all tutors, at the crown of my head,
O you the friend of the *kunda* flower, that is, the full moon, who arose
from the surface of the eastern mountain of inferior intellect and dispelled the darkness when the sun of the Victor's teachings subsided at
the western mountain, obscured by karma and affliction." Moreover,
through the glory of this spiritual friend Khöntön Paljor Lhundrup's

enlightened deeds, virtuous in the beginning, middle, and end, he endlessly bestows the wealth of the holy Dharma, and due to mastery that is akin to a state of Mañjuśrī himself entering into his throat, the Great Fifth respectfully bows to this great spiritual friend, his tutor who easily confers buddhahood that is by nature the four bodies.

> The cool moonrays of your white deeds
> cause the ocean of eloquent speech to swell
> from which comes the wish-fulfilling jewel of well-being in
>   current and future lives,
> you bestow to eliminate destitution in samsara and nirvana.
>
> In particular, the great streams of instructions of Nesur [and
>   the three Kadam brothers]
> Potowa, Chenga, [and Phuchung]
> that flow from the ever-cool Anavatapta Lake of the master
>   and disciple—
> Dīpaṃkara, the defender of five hundred, and his
>   spiritual son—
>
> have poured into the ocean of my mind.
> Thinking of the great debt of their kindness
> I will never be able to repay them [13]
> until I reach the far shore of enlightenment.
>
> Reflecting on this, I close my palms together at my heart.

Through the force of the deeds of speech of vast dissemination of the Dharma systems of sutra and tantra of this spiritual friend expanding the ocean of teachings that contend with the hundred thousand rays of the full white moon, the glory of benefit and happiness in this and future lives, similar to a wish-fulfilling jewel, is bestowed, and thus he has become the lord of benefactors[10] who dispels all suffering without exception in samsara and nirvana.

In particular, thinking of the kindness of their directing into the ocean of my mind the cool river of the tradition of instructions of the glorious, incomparable Jowo Jé Dīpaṃkara, supreme ornament on the crowns of the five hundred, and his chief disciple Dromtön Gyalwé Jungné, and likewise that excellently transmitted by the three Kadam brothers—Geshé Potowa Rinchen Sal (1027–1105), Chen-ngawa Tsultrim Bar (1038–1103), and Phuchungwa Shönu Gyaltsen (1031–1106)—goosebumps arise when the Great Fifth contemplates that he cannot repay their kindness until he reaches the essence of enlightenment. Thus he spontaneously presses his palms together at his heart.

THE PLEDGE TO COMPOSE THE TEXT

Next, the pledge to compose the text:

> **The nature of bodhisattva conduct is vast like the sky,**
> **and the intended meaning of reality is subtle like atoms.**
> **Thus, when someone like me takes on the burden of**
> ** expressing it,**
> **it is like measuring the ocean with a mango seed.**

As illustrated by the topic to be explained by this treatise, which is principally bodhicitta, and that takes as preliminaries to that the paths of the small and middle scope beings, the conduct of bodhisattvas is vast like the sky, and the intended meaning of final reality is incredibly difficult to realize, like subtle atoms, [14] and thus the Great Fifth compares his taking on the burden of composing a vast and profound treatise to an attempt to measure the breadth of the ocean with a mango seed. However, he states the following:

Yet, it is not that I call this treatise a guide
from merely having glanced at a text or having received an oral
    transmission.
The essence of the nectar of the speech of supreme lineage
    holders,
integrated into my own authentic experience, swirls within
    the jewel capsule of this treatise.

The Great Fifth indicates this is a vast and profound treatise that is incredibly prodigious. He does not label this text a guide based on his having merely glanced at written teachings or received a quick reading transmission. Rather, he listened well to the nondegenerated speech imbibed with the fragrance of blessings of transmission from one qualified sublime guru to the next, and that which he listened to he did not leave at the level of mere words of advice, but he incorporated mentally, giving rise to authentic experiences within his mindstream. Thus, the essence of this nectar swirls here in this invaluable capsule, this stages of the path scripture called *Oral Transmission of Mañjuśrī*. Together with showing the greatness of this treatise, he has thus made the pledge to complete the text.

I will now take the opportunity to weave some slight commentary into this masterpiece. He furthermore states: **This [treatise] is a summary of the entirety of the Sugata's teachings. In order to practically apply this guide on the stages of the three types of beings that leads persons of good fortune to buddhahood . . .**

The Great Fifth has not utilized detailed outlines in his text, but rather comments in the style of a summary of Tsongkhapa's *Great Treatise on the Stages of the Path*. Moreover, topics related to special insight were written using Tsongkhapa's *Middle-Length Stages of the Path* as a basis. Thus, this commentary will be an explanation on the basis of the main outlines from the *Great Treatise on the Stages of the Path* with some minor omissions and additions. [15]

As such, the guide to the stages of the path to enlightenment has four parts:

    I. Showing the greatness of the teaching's author in order to indicate its pure origin

   II. Showing the greatness of the teaching in order to engender respect for the instructions

 III. How to listen to and explain the teachings possessing the two greatnesses

 IV. The stages of guiding disciples with the actual instructions

Showing the Greatness of the Teaching's Author in Order to Indicate Its Pure Origin

THE GREATNESS of the author [has three parts]:

A. How he took rebirth in an excellent lineage
B. How he acquired good qualities on that basis
C. How Atiśa furthered the teachings having acquired good qualities

There is no need to comment in detail on the further subdivisions of these outlines as they can be learned from religious histories, Tsongkhapa's *Great Treatise on the Stages of the Path*, and so forth. Instead, a simple summary of the transmission of vast and profound instructions from the Teacher, king of subduers, to Jowo Atiśa, his spiritual sons, and so forth, will be made as nourishment for faith.

Just as the Dharma to be practiced should be one of pure origin, like a river meeting back to snow, **practitioners** of the Dharma of the stages of the path to enlightenment **should likewise hear from a spiritual friend** this advice that has been sequentially transmitted by supreme gurus of the **unbroken** vast conduct, profound view, and blessed practice **lineages** originating from the lord of teachings, the Bhagavān Teacher, and whose qualities of the greatness of their three secrets—that is, their body, speech, and mind—are as they extensively appear in the life stories and so forth of the lamrim lineage gurus. **The reason for this** is as the gentle protector Lama Tsongkhapa the great says:

The path of profound view and vast conduct
excellently transmitted from the two great trailblazers . . .

And,

Showing the greatness of the teaching's author in order to
indicate its pure origin . . .
And,

Having pith instructions transmitted uninterruptedly from
holy beings, starting with the fully enlightened one . . . [16]

These words are powerful if analyzed. Furthermore, with respect
to that, which is to say, showing how the origins of this Dharma are
pure, the succession of the lineage starting with our teacher, the
son of Śuddhodana, through to the great king of Dharma, Tsongkhapa, is in the unmistaken order as found in the *Requesting Prayer
to the Lamrim Lineage*. Moreover, from among the 84000 heaps of
Dharma taught by the kind Teacher, the most excellent, prime, and
supreme perfection of wisdom sutras are the extensive, middle-length,
and condensed *mothers* (*yum*) sometimes occasionally mispronounced
in Tibetan as the "extensive, middle-length, and condensed *hundred-
thousands* (*'bum*)." Thus, among those, the *Extensive Mother*; that is,
the *Mother in One Hundred Thousand Verses* contains twelve volumes,
the *Middle-Length Mother in Twenty-Thousand Verses* contains three volumes, and the *Condensed Mother in Eight-Thousand Verses* has one volume. To categorize them more precisely, the extensive, middle-length,
and condensed *mothers* are divided into the extensive of the extensive,
the middle-length of the extensive, and the condensed of the extensive; the middle-length is also further divided into the extensive of the
middle-length, the middle-length of the middle-length, and the condensed of the middle-length; and the condensed, too, is divided into

the extensive of the condensed, the middle-length of the condensed, and the condensed of the condensed. Moreover, the many perfection of wisdom treatises renowned as the "seventeen mothers and sons" are primary among the 84000 heaps of Dharma. They contain the *explicitly taught stages of emptiness* and the *stages of clear realization that are the concealed meaning*. From among those two, the explicitly taught stages of emptiness were clarified by the protector Nāgārjuna. Within the *mothers*, in the context of the stages of the profound path of the vast elucidation of the stages of emptiness, the way the stages of realization are born, and so forth, through the practice of clear realizations of the path are the stages concealed in the manner of being the subjects that are the bases of emptiness.

The protector Maitreya focused clearly on these hidden stages in his *Ornament for Clear Realization*, and Ārya Asaṅga excellently propagated the stages of clear realization that are the hidden meaning through the framework of the *seventy topics*. Together with these stages of the vast path, the two stages of the vast and profound arose. [17]

The perfection of wisdom sutras taught by the Buddha are Mahā-yāna treatises. The disciples for whom they were intended were a great gathering of not only human bodhisattvas but also nonhuman bodhi-sattva deities. Although there are a lot of conflicting explanations as to whether Mahāyāna scriptures belong in the canonized triple basket, Ācārya Bhāvaviveka taught in his *Blaze of Reason* how Maitreya, Mañ-juśrī, and so forth, compiled the teachings. As such, when the Buddha Bhagavān famously turned the wheel of Dharma, that which was taught to the general audience was Hīnayāna Dharma, of which there were naturally more teachings. Thus, for the disciples with an auspicious accumulation of karma and prayers, who were principally bodhisattva humans and deities of pure karma and high intelligence, the wheel of Mahāyāna Dharma was taught at Vulture's Peak and so forth.

As we can see for ourselves, although there is no space for hun-dreds of people to fit together on Vulture's Peak, it appears differently to those with pure karma. Present among the disciples to whom the Bhagavān directly taught the perfection of wisdom *mothers*, the stages of the profound path were transmitted to Mañjuśrī, and the stages of the vast path were transmitted to protector Maitreya, and the lineal transmissions occurred thus.

Although Maitreya and Mañjuśrī are buddhas in reality, when the kind Teacher taught the Dharma they were among the "eight great bodhisattvas"; that is, princely bodhisattvas in the retinue of the Teacher who listened to the Dharma and who were exceptional among the many in the assemblies. [18] Venerable Mañjuśrī is said to be the embodiment of the wisdom of all the buddhas. Accordingly, the quality of wisdom visibly appears as a heart disciple with face, hands, and so forth, and presents in a variety of forms such as someone in the Buddha's retinue, a principal deity, and so forth according to the inclinations and dispositions of disciples.

Out of the two sets of instructions transmitted successively from Maitreya and Mañjuśrī to both Nāgārjuna and Asaṅga, who independently commented on the intention behind the Buddha's teachings without relying on other humans to explain them, [Vasubandhu's] brother Asaṅga took on the stages of the vast path as his direct responsibility. Nāgārjuna made a profound impact on his immediate emphasis that was the stages of the profound path while addressing the stages of the vast path incidentally. This can be seen in his *Precious Garland of the Middle Way*, for instance, where the entire stages of both the vast and the profound paths are taught. Accordingly, Pandita Atiśa from the ārya land received both lineages of the vast and the profound. The stages of the vast path were transmitted via Guru Serlingpa, and the stages of the profound path were transmitted via Guru Vidyākokila. In Atiśa both the vast and the profound instructions merged into a single river that was then condensed into a single graded path, and in Tibet he authored the *Lamp for the Path to Enlightenment*, which became the foundation for all stages of the path of the teachings.

When Jowo Jé came to Tibet, the king Lha Lama Jangchup Ö (eleventh century) supplicated him to give a Dharma teaching that would be of benefit to all of Tibet. Jowo Jé, highly pleased with the manner of the request, starts his *Lamp for the Path* with the line "as requested by the noble student Jangchup Ö." Reflecting upon this, the way this bodhisattva Dharma king of Tibet took into consideration the welfare of the general populace of Tibet is an incredibly significant point. [19]

Generally speaking, the one known as Jowo Jé was a famous guru from India that they were able to invite to Tibet. Specifically, they did not make the request "please give me profound instructions of quick enlightenment of secret mantra that no one else possesses," but instead requested a teaching that would benefit all Tibetans. Not only that, they also requested that he reform the incorrect, wanton behavior connected to secret mantra that was the result of the tragedy of the damage wrought upon the Victor's teachings by Lang Darma, the forty-first king of Tibet. These were Atiśa's incredible accomplishments. Among the countless students that Jowo Jé had, Dromtön Gyalwé Jungné, a unique student and holy being who was a celibate holder of lay vows, was bequeathed whatever existed of the vast and profound instructions in their entirety. As illustrated by this, Atiśa exerted himself in a noble model life of restoration of the stainless teachings of the Victor.

The Dharma king Dromtön became the holder of the teachings of the Jowo Kadam tradition and founded Reting Monastery. He established the tradition of teachings of the sole divinity, Jowo Jé Dīpaṃkara, and transmitted the teachings of the stages of the path of the three beings by way of Jowo Jé's *Lamp for the Path to Enlightenment* to the Kadam scholar-practitioners such as Potowa and so forth. With respect to this successive transmission, the gentle protector Tsongkhapa the Great heard the Kadam scriptural lineage from the great Dragor abbot Chökyab Sangpo (thirteenth century), and both the Kadam stages of the path and Kadam pith instruction/oral instruction lineage from the mahāsiddha of Lhodrak Namkha Gyaltsen (1326–1401). The three lineages were then merged into a single river.

From then on, the learned and accomplished disciples who spread Jé Lama's teachings of scripture and realization in all directions were as numerous as the stars in the sky and the grains of dust on the earth. Thus, as they spread, **the lineages, too, became just as numerous. However, these days only the lineage lamas of one's own monastery are listed, and there are innumerable cases of teaching to others and so forth without a source for the transmissions that occurred in between.** [20]

Accordingly, the gentle protector Tsongkhapa the Great had distinguished disciples including those in groups such as the "eight pure retinue," and individuals who are mentioned in the life stories of Jé Lama. From among those, relevant to this context, there were disciples who excellently transmitted the stainless system of teachings of Tsongkhapa's stages of the path to enlightenment treatises uninterruptedly by way of upholding, preserving, and spreading them. Among those to whom we owe gratitude for those teachings being disseminated in all central and distant lands even at present are those of the most esteemed incarnation lineage of the Dalai Lamas who are among the lineage lamas of the *Great Treatise on the Stages of the Path.* A summary of the activities of the Dalai Lamas spanning from Jé Gendun Drup to the Great Fifth Dalai Lama now follows.

THE SACRED BIOGRAPHY OF GYALWANG GENDUN DRUP PALSANGPO

The First Dalai Lama, the omniscient Gendun Drup (1391–1474), was a direct heart disciple among the "four great sons whose deeds equaled space," and one of the renowned "three spiritual heirs."[11] In addition to "the seven heart sons who were genuinely predicted," and in accordance with the dream prophecy of Tokden Jampal Gyatso (1356–1428),

Jé Gendun Drup was twenty-five when he went to Ön Tashi Dokha and was accepted by the gentle protector Tsongkhapa the Great and became his heart disciple. For this reason he is included within the "eight heart sons who were prophesied."[12] [21]

I will give a small glimpse of the many independent sacred life accounts of Jé Gendun Drup Palsangpo's upholding, preserving, and spreading of the Victor's teachings through explanation and accomplishment.

How He Was Endowed with the Nine Sublime Traits

Jé Gendun Drup received both the extensive and abridged lamrim treatises authored by the gentle protector Tsongkhapa from Jé Lama himself and practiced them. He also heard them from the two heart sons and the glorious Sherab Sengé (1383–1445).

He received the stages of the path that had been transmitted from Sharawa (eleventh century) to Tumtön Lodrö Drakpa (1106–66), and also from Kamawa Sherab Ö (1057–1131) to Lumpawa Yeshé Jangchup (twelfth century), from his abbot in Narthang. He received the stages of the path that had been transmitted from Sharawa to Chekawa Yeshé Dorjé (fourteenth century), then to Sechil Buwa (fourteenth century), and then to Lha Chenpo (fourteenth century) and so forth, and particularly cycles of the whispered lineage (snyan brgyud) of mind training, from Lhasur Khangwa Sönam Lhundrup (fourteenth century). Having integrated them into his practice, exceptional realizations of bodhicitta were born. From Hortön (fourteenth century) he also received the mind training of the Jé tradition arranged as stages of the path.

The statement by the great lama, Jé Gendun Drup, that "this mind training is excellently explained and understood by us," is the genuine admission of his practice experience.

Moreover, he received the stages of the path that had been transmitted from Chen-ngawa to Chayulwa Shönu Ö (1075–1138), and likewise the cycles of teachings from Chayulwa, from Gyaltengpa Chen-nga Rinchen Phel (fourteenth century). In summary, our great lama Jé Gendun Drup possessed all the instructions of Jowo Jé.[13]

Jé Gendun Drup listened to the great Tsongkhapa thoroughly analyze difficult points with respect to Dharmakīrti's *Ascertainment of Valid Cognition*, and authored notes on this. He also listened to many teachings on treatises such as Nāgārjuna's *Fundamental Wisdom of the Middle Way*, Candrakīrti's *Entering the Middle Way*, Tsongkhapa's *Differentiating the Definitive and Interpretable*, and Tsongkhapa's *Commentary on Nāgārjuna's Fundamental Verses*. [22] Jé Rinpoché Tsongkhapa, having become incredibly pleased, also gave him a piece of his lower robe to create the auspiciousness for him to propagate exceptional teachings on the precepts and trainings within the Vinaya.

Prior to meeting Tsongkhapa, Gendun Drup listened to the explanations of the word meanings and difficult points of Dharmakīrti's *Commentary on Dignāga's "Compendium of Valid Cognition"* from the spiritual son of Jé Rinpoché, the great bodhisattva Kunsangwa (fourteenth century), expert in Madhyamaka, valid cognition, and secret tantra. He thus established a foundation in logical reasoning through the power of the fact. He later excellently studied Madhyamaka and valid cognition also from Sherab Sengé and Gyaltsab Darma Rinchen (1364–1432), and comprehended the intention of the great trailblazer.[14]

In general, he had a mere six lamas from whom he heard the Dharma. He said that among those the most kind in that lifetime were both the great abbot of Narthang, Drupa Sherab (1357–1423), erudite in the five sciences, and Jé Sherab Sengé, and that Tsongkhapa was the most kind throughout all lifetimes.[15]

Through the convergence of the nine sublime traits of (1) studying, (2) contemplation, (3) meditation on the vast, nonsectarian Tibetan Buddhist Dharma teachings and scriptures illustrated by those Old and New Kadam teachings from these masters, (4) explanation, (5) debate, (6) composition, (7) being learned, (8) being righteous, and (9) being good, he became supreme among those who upheld, preserved, and spread the teachings of the Victor.

Examples from the Sacred Life of a Pure Practitioner

In particular, Gendun Drup's equalization of the eight worldly concerns was equal to that of Dromtönpa. He was concerned only for the welfare of the teachings and sentient beings, and never cared for wealth, respect, fame, and so forth. He preferred to have only a few compatible students. Unlike other masters, he did not rebuke his students for having attended the religious colleges of others. He also did not monitor whether monks from elsewhere belonged to his own religious college. He never spoke with partiality toward any tradition or group. Although his equals or lessers tried to disparage him, he was not prone to anger. [23] He suppressed even mild respect from his followers. Even when relaxing his three doors of body, speech, and mind he incurred no faults of downfalls. He never complained. He was tolerant. He was not disturbed by the mistakes and mishaps of his disciples.

When he moved for the sake of others he did so without hustle and bustle, and he possessed not the haughtiness of the learned and righteous. He did not pretend to be calm and restrained. He had neither jealousy nor competitiveness. He did not praise himself or chastise others. Any food or clothing sufficed; he possessed no superficiality with respect to clothing or behavior. He did not seek to buy students or benefactors. He was not partial to any particular monk or sponsor, and he did not flatter them. In these qualities he exceeded the conduct of later lamas who claimed to be masters. He always passed his time with holy activities alone, and extensively explained the meaning of the triple basket and stages of the path of the three beings.[16]

Naturally Evident Signs of Prior Habituation

The exceptional signs that his studies were not focused outwardly and that he had internalized the meaning of what he studied were all visible to everyone.

Still, the successive proof that he had acquired confidence in the view and the warmth of meditation and gained mastery over the dynamism of his conduct from long ago was incredibly vast from the time of his youth. From the moment Jé Gendun Drup was born in 1391 to a nomadic family in the district of Sad in the Tsang region, his whole life was filled with accounts of infinite pure appearances beyond thought or conception. Among those, if one were to give a mere starting example: On the night he was born, his family camp was attacked by bandits. When they were stealing possessions and leading people away, his mother, Jomo Namkha Kyi, hid her small son among the rocks and fled. The next day a grandmother went to look for him and saw a raven next to the small boy with many predatory animals circling him. [24] When she fearfully ran to his side, she saw that the crow, large and dark, was protecting him, preventing the other animals from getting close. Astonished, she said, "If it were a god, the bandits probably would not have taken the camp, and yet, if it were a harmful spirit, it probably would not have protected the small boy," and she took the boy and left.[17]

For some time before they could set up a tent again, they lived off the help of acquaintances in towns and countryside. From the mere age of five when he was herding goats for the town and so forth, he carved the *mani* mantra onto many stones saying, "These are for purifying the obscurations of my parents." When reminded that his parents were still alive, he spoke of how there were many dead and undead parents of his. It is well known that many stones on which he carved the six-syllable, three-syllable, *hūṃ*, and *hrīḥ* mantras, along with many carved offering substances, still exist even today.

At age seven his father, Gönpo Dorjé, passed away. Having become very poor, they lived off the assistance of an uncle, Geshé Chöshé, in and around Narthang.[18] When Gendun Drup went to beg for food from the assembly of monastics in Narthang, the abbot of Narthang, Drupa Sherab, erudite in the five sciences, told him that it is a grave misdeed for the laity to partake in the donations of the monastic community. He suggested the boy should become a lay vow holder until he could acquire monastic robes, and thus bestowed him the lay vows. He was entrusted to Tsandrapala of Gyatön (fourteenth century) for reading tutelage, from whom he effortlessly learned different forms of the Tibetan script, as well as the Indic Lantsa and Wartu scripts, and likewise the Mongolian script. After becoming a monk, he trained many young students in reading and writing. Later on, when engaging in study himself, he wrote out by hand the majority of his religious scriptures. The majority of the *mani* stones, and names of gurus, buddhas and bodhisattvas on both interior and exterior walls around Tashi Lhunpo Monastery, and in particular the Lantsa script found within the temple, and essentially the majority of writings, would be handwritten by him.[19] [25]

In 1405, at the age of fifteen, he received his novice vows from the abbot of Narthang and so forth, and was given the name Gendun Drupa Palsangpo. Although he desired to engage in study and especially greatly desired to meet Jé Lama Tsongkhapa, the great abbot told him that he must greatly benefit others in this place for the time being. In particular, he told him he should definitely receive the Lachen lineage of full ordination vows within the Jowo's tradition of teachings.[20]

In 1410, when he was twenty years old, he received full ordination from this abbot. He also [spiritually] ripened him into the entrance of Vajrayāna and from whom he accepted the great burden of traveling to Ü, and thus Jé Gendun Drup considered the Narthang abbot one of his greatly kind lamas. Having already begun his study and contemplation of the great treatises, he traveled to Ü.[21] For twelve years he listened to vast teachings on sutra and tantra through correctly relying on many spiritual teachers such as Jé Tsongkhapa and his chief disciples. While continuously maintaining his samaya, or spiritual pledges, and practice, in the fire-horse year he traveled to Tsang and engaged in teaching and study in many areas.

Receiving the Title "Omniscient"

In the female iron-pig year (1431), at the age of forty-two, he had a passionate wish to meet Bodong Panchen Choklé Namgyal (1395–1475), so he went to Pema Chöding. He met the Panchen and listened to extensive Dharma teachings. The Panchen was delighted by the answers given to his many questions. He stated, "From now on you shall be known as 'the omniscient Gendun Drup," bestowing on him this honorary title.[22] [26]

Founding the Monastic Seat of Tashi Lhunpo and His Extensive Deeds of Erecting Sacred Representations, Making Offerings, and So Forth

Jé Gendun Drup followed in the footsteps of the three Kadam brothers, and, like Geshé Chen-ngawa only erected bases for the teachings and the three sacred supports of statues, stupas, and scriptures; like Geshé Phuchungwa, he focused on making offerings to the Three Jewels; and like Geshé Potowa, he left a great legacy through his efforts in helping Dharma teachers and students and the monastic community.[23]

Furthermore, like Chen-ngawa, in order to erect bases for the teachings and spiritual supports, he extensively toured all over exhorting virtue and collecting donations. Thus, in 1447, at the age of fifty-seven, on an auspicious day during the waxing moon of the sixth month of the female fire-hare year, Jé Gendun Drup, along with the patron Dargye-pa Pön Sönam Palsang, he went to the place where he would establish his monastery, performed the ground-consecration rituals and so forth, and laid the foundations for the main temple, lama residence, and living quarters. He thus founded the "Great Monastery of Glorious Tashi Lhunpo, the Sanctuary Victorious over All Directions." In the beginning there were around one hundred and ten monks, and over time that number got as high as sixteen hundred.

He newly constructed around fifteen temples.[24] He brought a large twenty-five-cubit Maitreya statue made of gold and copper,[25] along with statues of Bhaiṣajyaguru and Amoghasiddhi. He created a hanging tapestry of the Buddha measuring eighteen arm spans[26] in height and twelve arm spans in width, and also hanging tapestries of Tārā and Avalokiteśvara both measuring eight arm spans in height and six arm spans in width. There were furthermore numerous other large hanging tapestries and painted reliefs. Along with hand-written Kangyur texts and so forth, he vastly contributed to the creation of religious objects. [27]

For the sake of diligently worshipping the Three Jewels like Geshé Phuchungwa, he made extensive offerings during prayer ceremonies twice each year, at the prayer ceremony for the Period of Miracles, and also at the Trophu Ganden Temple. When consecrating the great Maitreya statue that had been erected in Tashi Lhunpo he made extensive offerings for seven days, and likewise at the age of eighty-four, in the wood-horse year, during the Period of Miracles at Tashi Lhunpo, he made extensive offerings for twelve days,[27] using at least three hundred loads[28] of barley to make food tormas decorated with beautiful ornaments such as the seven auspicious emblems created from colored butter

Using three thousand loads of butter to make butter lamps, in the Kongbu Gyatso Temple he offered large butter lamps in a square pattern measuring an arm span on each side, and in the outer courtyard at the Kelsang Temple they were set up with two sides measuring three arm spans and the other two sides measuring two arm spans each, and aside from that many butter lamps arranged in arm span lengths.

These, along with many offerings of a hundred sets of lamps filled entirely with white butter were offered, and it is said the light from the lamps was so bright the night stars could not be seen.

Likewise, he made offerings beyond words and thoughts, such as two rows of seven offering bowls that used two water buckets,[29] many sets of one-hundred offering bowls, a seven-heap mandala measuring one cubit, and made many offerings of fine cloth robes within his own and other monasteries.[30] [28]

How the Title "Panchen" Remained for a Long Time

In terms of his deeds of teaching and learning, like Geshé Potowa, at age thirty-five he taught and studied in Sangphu Monastery and so forth in central Tibet, for around twelve years.[31] Later he settled the meaning of many great treatises through teaching and study, such as the *four greatly difficult topics*, the *six collections of Madhyamaka reasoning*, the later treatises of Maitreya, Śāntideva's *Compendium of Trainings* and *Way of the Bodhisattva*, *Life Stories* and *Collection of Verses*, in many places within Tsang such as Narthang, the isolated place of Jangchen, Tanak Rakhu, and so forth.

In dependence upon the lamrim pith instructions from Jowo Jé and the pith instructions of the Mahāyāna mind training texts, Jé Gendun Drup did not distinguish the great treatises as Dharma to be explained and the pith instructions as Dharma to be practiced. Instead, he pointed out the pith instructions through the great treatises themselves. In particular, for twenty-eight years after establishing Tashi Lhunpo he was the master of the Buddha's teachings, directing construction, erecting spiritual supports, making offerings to such supports, serving the monastic community, and benefiting the lay householders as well, while never ceasing to teach and learn.[32]

His deeds were boundless, among which he founded institutes for scripture and reasoning, established general Vinaya rituals, and in particular the rituals of the three base monastic activities and so forth in the great assembly. Based on this, the four important subsidiary teachers such as the two Chöjé Topjor Rinpoches, the four monastic colleges, and many smaller schools were established, for which most of the great beings from the upper and lower parts of Tibet, too, authored praises out of faith.

Within that monastic seat, he instituted detailed explanation and learning of many principal treatises such as the three of the perfections, valid cognition, and Madhyamaka, and the two of Abhidharma and Vinaya, and established an authentic school of debate for the one thousand to twelve hundred monks present.

Furthermore, he engaged in uninterrupted teachings by giving transmissions of Kadam texts, the sacred biographies and collected works of Jé Rinpoché and his spiritual sons, along with guides on mind training and so forth, given either as public or private teachings as appropriate. [29] He furthermore bestowed many pith instructions, tantric empowerments, transmissions, and guides, and so forth, to close disciples.[33] He thus became renowned as "Panchen Gendun Drup," and from then onward whoever was the holder of the seat of Tashi Lhunpo became known by the title "Panchen.[34]"

Jé Gendun Drup mastered the ten sciences and became an expert and highly confident in explanation, debate, and composition. When he taught, his face was radiantly clear. His voice was rich and pleasing to hear, and could be heard from afar. His speech was well-paced and potent. He used analogies to drive home the point so that it touched the hearts of the students. Through his mere elocution when reading the text, the meaning could be understood.

When debating he would not fiercely shout or be intimidating but would immediately detect the faults in either semantics or meaning and strip the opponent of his haughty confidence. This is because, even when debating at length with others he would not mix assertions but rather each appeared as individual mounds largely discernable, as was apparent from the time he studied logic in Sangphu.

When composing, not only did his phrasing and use of adjectives captivate the minds of literary experts but his word commentaries for major Indian treatises and his commentaries on difficult points were also coherent and clear and conveyed much depth in meaning with few words. Their unique character is that they can be easily understood even by those of lesser intelligence.[35]

Later, when a conflict occurred between individual monasteries within Tashi Lhunpo, he also gave counsel at the assembly, in which he stated, "I have set a nine-month boundary for my retreat at Jangchen. If I am to maintain that period now, even I can have a superficial experience of the path since I have contemplated the stream of teachings and engaged in such teaching and learning, but now the final period of my teaching and learning has been robbed by attachment and anger." [30]

In summary, for close to fifty years, from age thirty-five to eighty-four, he gave up desire for gain, honor, and fame, and with the Buddha's teachings and sentient beings in mind he taught the great authoritative treatises on sutra and tantra and gave pith instructions. It is commonly known that through the power of his compassion, he did not allow a single thing to interrupt his daily Dharma teachings for that period.

The glorious Jé Gendun Drup's flourishing of spiritual deeds, in which he spent his lifetime only doing what was beneficial for the teachings and sentient beings, did not come about without causes or conditions. As well as the bodhicitta aspiration and definite intentional rebirths throughout his previous lifetimes such as when he was the emanation of Ārya Avalokiteśvara Dromtön Gyalwé Jungné, and so forth, and even from the perspective of this life alone, through it being obvious that he had powerful imprints from habituation in previous lifetimes, at the end of his extensive deeds of the three spheres of explanation and accomplishment his final words were, "Teachers and students, remember me and significantly contribute to the Buddha's teachings through Tashi Lhunpo!" In saying that he gave the keys to the masters, and in 1474 at the age of eighty-four the coarse display of his rūpakāya withdrew into the dharmadhātu.[36]

The representatives and successors of this protector are his sublime deeds of speech committed to writing that continue to nourish us through his kindness, that are his *Instruction Manual on the Seven-Point Mahāyāna Mind Training*, and his five eloquent volumes on the difficult topics from sutra and mantra pertaining to Madhyamaka, valid cognition, Vinaya, and so forth, which aspirants toward liberation can still utilize for study, contemplate, and meditation even today. [31]

THE SACRED BIOGRAPHY OF THE SECOND INCARNATION OF THE DALAI LAMA AND THE FIFTH THRONE HOLDER OF TASHI LHUNPO,[37] THE OMNISCIENT JÉ GENDUN GYATSO PALSANGPO

Clear Indications of His Intentional Rebirth and Recollection of Previous Lives

In the wood-sheep year (1475), Gendun Gyatso was born in Yölkar Dorjéden, Tanak district, in the region of Tsang, to his father Chöjé Rinpoché Kunga Gyaltsen and his mother Machik Kunga. At age three, upon being scolded by his mother, he stated, "This young boy is not staying. I am going to Tashi Lhunpo. The house is nicer there and I can even eat candy." He sang songs from the time of his previous life, and thus it was said these are the initial words in recollection of his previous life.

At the age of five, in the earth-pig year (1480), when he was staying with his father in a mountain camp, the summer thunder resounded, and he lifted his head from his father's lap to look. When his father asked him, "What happened?" he replied, "It was like the sound of father Tsongkhapa Losang Drakpa teaching the Dharma." His father enquired what he was like, and the boy confidently replied with the verses from Maitreya's *Ornament for the Mahāyāna Sūtras*, "Well, 'A spiritual master restrained, at peace, totally pacified ...'" and so forth. Then he turned to a small image of Jé Tsongkhapa and said, "This is father Losang Drakpa. Furthermore, with respect to a dark stone perfect for carving he said, "This is father Losang Drakpa" and carried it to where he danced. [32] As a seat he made a small throne and placed father Losang Drakpa on it, and if rain fell on it, he would cry.

Since he sang many songs of recollection of events in his past life on those occasions, it was widely acknowledged that "the omniscient one has been born in the upper valley of Tanak."

In the water-hare year (1483), at eight years old, he went with his father to Tashi Lhunpo. Immediately upon entering the assembly hall he climbed onto the throne and said, "When I taught the Dharma, I had a seat like this," and sat with his right leg outstretched and left leg tucked in. All of the many disciples from his past life that he recognized without any introduction, such as Chöjé Paljor and the elder Gendun Drayang, and so forth, developed great conviction.

From his father Chöjé Rinpoché he received empowerments, authorizations, transmissions, and pith instructions. Without having to put effort into memorizing the rituals using the liturgy, he naturally learned them through being present during his father's daily practice.

Recognition by Tashi Lhunpo Monastery as the Reincarnation of Jé Gendun Drup, and Exhibiting the Natural Signs of a Holy Being

In the wood-dragon year (1485), at the age of ten, after the masters such as Lungrik Gyatso (fifteenth century) the second throneholder of Tashi Lhunpo and so forth held discussions, this lord was recognized as the reincarnation of the omniscient Jé Gendun Drup and invited to Tashi Lhunpo.

In the fire-horse year (1487), at the age of twelve, he received the upāsaka vows and was given the name Gendun Gyatso Palsangpo. [33] At the winter session of teachings of that same year, he took novice ordination from Kunga Delek (fifteenth century), the close disciple and attendant of Jé Gendun Drup. He went on to study Dharmakīrti's *Commentary on Dignāga's "Compendium of Valid Cognition,"* and received teachings on sutra and mantra from Panchen Yeshé Tsemo (born 1433), the third throneholder of Tashi Lhunpo. At that time, it appeared that through becoming polluted, his memorization and so forth declined, thus he was scolded heavily by Panchen Yeshé Tsemo during his memorization examination on the topics of the perfections and valid cognition. Despite this it is said that he showed not the slightest disrespect in turn.

To improve his memorization, he received an oral transmission of the Indian sādhana cycles of White Mañjuśrī from Panchen Yeshé Tsemo and performed an approach retreat on the Venerable One. At dawn on the seventh day, he had a direct vision of the Venerable One's face and was blessed, activating the imprints from his previous lifetimes. He directly saw many of his past lives. It was said that from merely reading any scripture he was able to understand it in its entirety.

In the iron-dog year (1491), at age sixteen, he performed an approach retreat for White Mañjuśrī and Sarasvatī, which allowed him to famously memorize a hundred pages in the time it takes to drink a cup of tea, and for poetry to naturally flow forth from his heart. He was later glorified as the "Laughing Sarasvatī Gendun Gyatso."

At age twenty, from the wood-tiger year (1494) onward, he lived in Tashi Lhunpo and completed his studies of the great treatises under the tutelage of Panchen Lungrik Gyatso, Panchen Yeshé Tsemo, and so forth, and received countless empowerments, oral transmissions, and pith instructions from Panchen Yeshé Tsemo.

Continuing His Activities in Ü

While residing in Tashi Lhunpo, over time many people came to meet Jé Gendun Gyatso. Due to people crowding in to receive his Dharma teachings, those who came to meet and receive teachings from Panchen Yeshé Tsemo became few, [34] and through the magical trickery of Nenying Gyalpo it unfortunately seemed like Panchen Yeshé Tsemo was treated as an attendant. He thus became displeased with Jé Gendun Gyatso, and during the collective prayers it was announced that due to the detriment to the pursuance of offerings for the congregation, no monk should go to receive teachings and so forth from Jé Gendun Gyatso. Jé Gendun Gyatso was made to enter into retreat and so forth, and thus he no longer wished to reside in Tashi Lhunpo.

This lined up well with the invitations from the abbot of Drepung Loseling Monastery, Jamyang Lekpa Chöjor (1429–1503), and the great Ganden throneholder Mönlam Pelwa (1414–91). He thus went to the glorious Drepung Monastery in Ü and received the explanatory guides on Nāgārjuna's *Fundamental Verses* and Candrakīrti's *Entering the Middle Way*, as well as teachings on the great treatises relating to the perfections and valid cognition, as well as on sutra and mantra.

At the age of twenty-one, in the wood-hare year (1494), since the attendant Kunga Delek had traveled to Ü in the manner of a wandering ascetic, he was invited to Drepung where Jé Gendun Gyatso took full ordination from him.

In the ninth month of that year, in autumn, Jé Gendun Gyatso went turn by turn to Reting, Odé Gungyal, Samyé, and Chongyé. There, a heart disciple of Jé Gendun Drup called Panchen Choklha Öser (born 1429) said to him, "You are actually Dromtönpa. Although I am not Ngok Lekpé Sherab (tenth century), I am the holder of his seat (Sangphu Monastery). Through my supplication I request you to teach a volume of scripture of the Kadampas." Having accepted the request, he first read through the secret biography of Jé Tsongkhapa once to the masters and students of Riwo Dechen. He then gave appropriate teachings on sutra and mantra of the Kadam volumes of scripture as they desired. [35] This was Jé Gendun Gyatso's first turning of the wheel of Dharma. Scholars such as Panchen Choklha Öser and so forth showed supreme reverence and faith in him, stating what incredible intellect he had at such a young age. Thereafter he extensively fostered the teachings and sentient beings in many places.

He was invited by the great abbot of Jenyé Monastery, where he gave numerous teachings on Kadam scriptures, such as Tsongkhapa's *Lamp for the Five Stages*, and so forth to a large gathering in Tsethang, by which they were all delighted. It was also said that the offerings made, and the respect shown, was unprecedented by the people of Tsethang to any other lama. From then on, he would turn vast wheels of Dharma yearly in Tsethang, which all commonly agreed greatly benefited the teachings in general and in particular the teachings of Jé Tsongkhapa.

When he was twenty-four, in the earth-horse year (1498), Dönyö Dorjé (1462–1512), the [head of] the Rinpung family, which ruled Tsang, having formed an alliance with the Karma Kagyüs, aggressively rivaled the Geluks, and a large force of the Tsang Rinpungpa troops marched on Lhasa. Taklungpa, Ölkhawa, and the Seventh Karmapa, Chödrak Gyatso (1454–1506) acting as arbiters, arranged a settlement whereby the Nelpa Sakyong Ngawang Lhunpo (fifteenth century) and his family received an allotment and were sent into exile in Kyormo Lung, and Rinpung Sakyong Dönyö Dorjé took possession of the entirety of Nedong and so forth. Although no damage was done to the monastic estates of Sera and Drepung, from that year onward until twenty years later up to the earth-tiger year (1518), the monks of Sera and Drepung were not permitted to attend the Great Prayer Festival in Lhasa.

In 1499, at the age of twenty-five, Jé Gendun Gyatso received many Dharma teachings such as on the complete ancillary practices and astrology of the Kālacakra root tantras and commentaries, and so forth, from Khedrup Norsang Gyatso (1423–1513) in Densathil. [36]

He then went to Ngangkyal in Nyal, where he presided over an assembly at a great religious gathering that included all six districts of Nyal. To a huge gathering of one thousand monastics and many lay people he gave public lamrim teachings, and he gave full ordination to over a hundred monks. As illustrated, he traveled many times up and down Ü-Tsang, extensively turning the wheel of Dharma in many places.

Founding Chökhor Gyal Monastery and Ascending to the Throne of Tashi Lhunpo

In the earth-snake year (1509), at the age of thirty-five, he went to visit Chökhor Gyal and the divine lake of Palden Lhamo Latso, and founded Chökhor Gyal, the "Paradise Resounding with Eloquent Explanations, the Monastery Spontaneously Arisen through Good Fortune."

In the water-monkey year (1512), at the age of thirty-eight, a messenger from Tashi Lhunpo Monastery was sent by Panchen Yeshé Tsemo with a letter reading, "In the presence of the one who is the intentional incarnation of my lama, the omniscient Gendun Drupa Palsangpo, I, Yeshé Tsemo, an inferior disciple, humbly request . . ." and so forth, making a fervent appeal together with praises, for Jé Gendun Gyatso to return to Tashi Lhunpo by all means necessary.

Jé Gendun Gyatso's reaction was the following:

> While denying all my requests for an audience in the past, this present demeanor of respectful humility I interpret as the auspiciousness of my unerring correct reliance on the spiritual teacher. Although initially I never desired to be conferred a monastery in recognition, if it be the seat of Tashi Lhunpo then of course I would accept. Despite being previ-

ously inclined, due to the past aforementioned events I lost my desire to do so, and I have already founded Gyal Monastery. As such, I will never be the throneholder of Tashi Lhunpo. However, despite my previous devotion to the Panchen in the manner Dromtön was devoted to Lama Setsun, it got to the point where I had not the opportunity to see even his face. Therefore, if by my meeting him it would appease the minds of the masters and disciples then it would also fulfill my aspiration. [37] It would also close the door for those many beings lacking complete context of the situation to accumulate negativities toward myself and the masters and disciples. With this in mind I prepare to depart.

He then went to Lhasa and was invited to Sera Monastery. He was welcomed by the assembly, and from atop the throne of Jamchen Chöjé (1354–1435) he taught the Dharma to establish a spiritual connection. Lamas such as the learned Dönyö Palden (1445–1524), Jetsun Chökyi Gyaltsen, Chenpo Döndrup, Chenpo Yönten Shenyen, Rabjampa Tsultrim Öser, and so forth, showed incredible respect toward him.

He was then invited to Drepung. The lamas and entire congregation listened to his Dharma teachings. A religious hat was placed on his head. Unfathomable faith and respect was shown. In summary, it was said that such respect had not been shown to a lama since the time of Jetsun Tsongkhapa.

Then, as requested by a large monastic assembly comprised of the abbot, masters, and those with the scholastic degree of *karabjampa*, he became the fifth throneholder of Tashi Lhunpo.[38] He tended to the monastic seat for six years, passing his time by teaching the great treatises on sutra and mantra. In particular, it is famously said that never before in Tibet had there been so many students of the treatises on valid cognition in one place. Since an untold number of aspirants principally comprising the lamas, masters, and karabjampas from the majority of the Tsang monasteries were present, he excellently took care of them in terms of both spiritual and worldly matters.

He then went to Chökhor Gyal. He visited the majority of places in Dakpo and Kongpo and gave public teachings to boundless monastics and laity. [38] In summary, within the Kongpo area, all those who upheld the Geluk teachings, along with those belonging to the Sakya tradition, Karma Kagyü, Tshalpa Kagyü, and so forth, had faith in him, and he effected great benefit to beings without partiality.

The Empowering of Lhamo Latso, the Renowned Oracle Lake of Palden Lhamo

At the end of summer in the previous sheep year, Jé Gendun Gyatso had visions of an extraordinary lake in this place. After investigating it further, locals with knowledge of the area spoke of an extremely fierce lake where if you even spoke loudly by the shore, hail would strike. Having heard this, he sent people to search for it and they found the source. More than ten masters then set off to empower the lake.

Having reached the shores, the lamas visualized and invoked Palden Lhamo upon the glistening white lake. Upon doing so a snowstorm appeared in the east, descending upon it, and the lake immediately changed color. Sometimes a five-colored rainbow appeared, and sometimes a five-tiered palace together with a pagoda-like roof vividly came into view. The lake then split into two sky-like colors, from which two hills—one in the shape of a square and the other an oval—rose up as if touching the sky. It was an incredibly frightening spectacle. They were most likely to be understood as magical displays of the two attending deities of Palden Lhamo. At times the entire lake appeared to boil in the sky and turn to the color of milk. In brief, the water did not appear in its natural state, and the incredible appearances were commonly perceived by all who were present. From that time onward until now, within the five hundred or so times at most that prophetic visions were seen, there

were myriad identical visions of the palace of Palden Lhamo, her imple-
ments, her donkey mount of varied color and size, her black tempest
movement, the wish-granting tree, and other things. [39]

There were endless people who, never having witnessed it, could not
conceive of it upon hearing stories, and those who upon witnessing it
were totally overwhelmed through faith. Following that he accepted
an invitation from Tashi Lhunpo and gave extensive Dharma teachings
on sutra and mantra.

Installment as the Ninth Throneholder
of Drepung Monastery

Jé Gendun Gyatso then inquired of Palden Lhamo whether it would be
better to reside in both Tashi Lhunpo and Chökhor Gyal monasteries,
or both Gyal and Drepung. The divination came that it would be better
to stay at Gyal and Drepung. His response to this was the following:

> Although it was my sincere wish to be able to stay in Tashi
> Lhunpo, as my aspiration was to increase my previous
> imprints and activities of teaching and learning more than
> before, past and present fortunes did not align, and thus I
> could not stay.

At the age of forty-two, in the fire-mouse year (1516), he was invited
by the people of upper Nyang and Palkhor Dechen. It was as if the
crowds of monastics and laity filled the land, and thus he arrived to a
gathering larger than anything he had experienced up until that time.

After discussions about the appointment of a deputy to the seat of
Tashi Lhunpo, Lhatsun Losang Tenpa was selected. At that time, he
received a pressing decree from the Lhariwa of Shelnga and likewise
a letter of invitation from the office of Drepung regarding ascension of
the throne of Drepung.

He went to Lhari, and in the presence of the great master Khetsun Yönten Gyatso Tenpé Nyima Gyaltsen Palsangpo received many teachings such as the guru yoga and Vairocana Abhisambodhi empowerments, and so forth. Although he provided many reasons from many standpoints as to why he could not hold the seat of Drepung, the pressing response came that he must do so at all costs, to which he tentatively agreed to do as he was able. [40] This reply of clarification was also sent to the office of Drepung from Lhari.

At the age of forty-three in the fire-ox year (1517), with the order of Thönyön Gyalwa, the request from the office of Drepung, and royal decree of the great ruler Ngawang Tashi Drakpa of Nedong (1480–1564), he went to Ü where he became the ninth holder of the seat of Drepung Monastery, and in Chökhor Gyal Monastery he established the wheel of Dharma for many hundreds of monks. From then onward, each year he would spend winter and spring in Drepung, and summer and autumn in Gyal extensively propagating the Victor's teachings.

Becoming Lord of the Assembly Which Could Once Again Hold Prayers in Lhasa

At the age of forty-four, in the earth-tiger year (1518), regarding the holding of prayers that was originally established by Jé Tsongkhapa as the Great Prayer Festival and held continuously for ninety-one years, yet continued intermittently for the previous twenty years only by Sangphu Monastery, the Karmapa, and so forth due to the increase in power of the Rinpungpa rulers of Kyishö, Jé Gendun Gyatso petitioned the Phakdru Desi to allow Sera and Drepung to attend, which he approved. Due to the Tsangpa's declining power at the time, Sera and Drepung were able to attend the Great Lhasa Prayer Festival, and Jé Gendun Gyatso sat at the head of the assembly. From the time of his teachings in Chongyé and Tsethang onward and up until that year, he bestowed the vows of full ordination over three thousand times.

The Lama Estate Ganden Phodrang

At this time Ngawang Tashi Drakpa from Nedong offered the Nedong estate within Drepung famously known as the "Blue Stone House" to Jé Gendun Gyatso as a residence. [41] It was further renovated during the time of the Third Dalai Lama and called the "Ganden Phodrang." This residence of all future Dalai Lamas became known as the "Drepung Ganden Phodrang," and later from the time of the Great Fifth Dalai Lama onward became the name of the government of the great country of Tibet.

As clearly documented, in 2011, the Fourteenth Dalai Lama handed over all political power related to Tibet to the democratically elected Kalön Tripa, thus returning the Ganden Phodrang to its original purpose as a lama estate.

Installment as the Eleventh Throneholder of Sera Monastery, and Passing Away

At the age of fifty-one, in the wood-bird year (1525), as requested by the ruler Nedong Desi Ngawang Tashi Drakpa, and so forth, he became the eleventh holder of the seat of Sera Thekchen Ling.

At the age of sixty-seven, having offered the great torma for the first day of the water-tiger year (1542), he spoke of how his youth had gone and how there was no longer a need to remain for long. After attending the Great Prayer Festival, on the evening of the fifteenth day, the luster of his body waned slightly, and the vibrancy of his voice also slightly diminished. On the eighth day of the third autumn month his physical manifestation withdrew. Through his legacy—the commentaries on the great treatises and so forth in the form of three volumes of his works on sutra and tantra—the deeds of his enlightened speech did not decline, and the kindness connected to their widespread existence even today continues to nurture us. [42]

THE SACRED BIOGRAPHY OF THE VICTORIOUS THIRD DALAI LAMA, THE OMNISCIENT SÖNAM GYATSO[39]

His Rebirth as the Unmistaken Reincarnation of the Previous Victor, Jé Gendun Gyatso, and His Installment on the Throne

Jé Gendun Gyatso was born in the water-hare year (1543), to Depa Namgyal Drakpa and Peldzom Butri near Lhasa, at Khangsar Gong, Tölung Datsakha.

In the wood-snake year (1545), when he was three years old, he went to the great monastery of Kyormo Lung, and the people of that area became incredibly faithful on account of his behavior and so forth. Due to some people rumoring that "he seems like an incarnation of the omniscient Gendun Gyatso," Pönsa Dungyü Rinpoché Sönam Drakpa Gyaltsen (1478–1554) invited him to his estate. Since at that time the boy spoke endlessly of visions, recollections of his past life, and so forth, he was thus placed in a position of faith and devotion of the people. At that time the boy heard Panchen Sönam Drakpa teaching the *Son Dharma* collections of Jowo Atiśa and his spiritual son Dromtönpa, and proclaimed, "He is talking about my biography!" Thus, those who were present were certain he was an emanation of Dromtönpa.

His father then decided that his son should be tested to determine whether he was an extraordinary being, and so brought him to the elder Dawa of Kyormo Lung who received clear prophecies from Tārā. Having created the first boundary and performed a thorough analysis, he prophesied that he was the reincarnation of the omniscient one (that is, the Second Dalai Lama). [43] Many other confident yogis received direct prophecies that were in agreement.

In that way, from the mere age of three, he recalled and stated the entire life and deeds of Jé Gendun Gyatso, and thus became renowned as his tulku.

In the fire-horse year (1546), at the age of four, the great attendant Sungrabpa and the governing council of Drepung held discussions and recognized him as the reincarnation of the victorious Gendun Gyatso. He was then invited to Drepung and installed on the throne in his lama estate. He took upasāka vows from Panchen Sönam Drakpa and was given the name Sönam Gyatso Palsangpo Tenpé Nyima Chok Thamché Lé Nampar Gyalwa.

In the earth-bird year (1549), at the age of seven, he took novice ordination from Panchen Sönam Drakpa and received many teachings on sutra and mantra.

Ascending the Thrones of Sera and Drepung

In the water-mouse year (1552), at the age of ten, in accordance with supplications by Drepung Monastery, he ascended as the twelfth throneholder of this great monastery.

In the fire-dragon year (1556), when he was fourteen years old, due to discord between the Nedongpa and Chongyé Nangso, great civil strife erupted in Yarlung. He mediated between both parties and brought peace, which was greatly approved by all.

Phakdé Lotsāwa Ngakrampa invited Gendun Tashi from Chökhor Gyal to Drepung. He received many stages of empowerments, oral transmissions, and guides. [44] He also cleared up uncertainties with respect to the Vajra-Bell-Holder tradition with regard to practices of the four activities; dance, mandala proportions, and chants; and all major and minor rituals of torma making and so forth, and wrote an authoritative manual for a serviceability-approach retreat for one's superior deity.

In the earth horse year (1558), at age sixteen, he ascended as the fifteenth throneholder of Sera Thekchen Ling Monastery, bestowing vast teachings on the Kadam texts and so forth.

The regent then invited him to the great palace of Nedong, affording him all the honors suitable for a great lama.

In the iron-monkey year (1560), at age eighteen, he received countless Nyingma secret mantra empowerments, oral transmissions, pith instructions, rituals, and practices from Rinpoché Kunsang Tsepa.

Taking Full Ordination, Being Invited to Mongolia, and Held in High Esteem

In the wood-mouse year (1564), at age twenty-two, he took full ordination from the former Ganden Tripa Khedrup Gelek Palsangpo and so forth.

In the wood-pig year (1575), at the age of thirty-three, after concluding the new year and prayer festivities and while residing at Drepung, the chief of the Rinpung led an army of nearly ten thousand Tsarong people and set up an encampment at Tölung Gelpo Nakha. They destroyed Gelpo, Jang, Mönga, and so forth. They intended to eventually reach Kyishö and enter battle; however the tantric adept Aku Kunsang Tsepa, who was in Jé Sönam Gyatso's service, performed a tantric ritual, causing lightning and so forth to strike down on their camp. This led the Rinpungpa to think that while they could defeat men, they could not defeat gods, and so they turned back. [45]

Dzogé Aseng Lama explained the sacred life story of Jé Sönam Gyatso to the Mongolian Khalkha, or Chahar, Altan Khan, on account of which he grew faithful and sent messengers at different times to invite him to Mongolia. Jé Sönam Gyatso promised to come.

In the fire-bull year (1577), at the age of thirty-five, extensive offerings were arranged in the Lhasa Trülnang Temple. He bestowed ordination vows to Pabongkhapa Khöntön Paljor Lhundrup (1561–1637), imparted upon him many profound teachings, and installed him as a central pillar of the general and specific teachings.

Again, messengers arrived stating that the Mongolian king Altan

Khan would receive him at Tsokha. Accordingly, (in 1577,) on the twenty-sixth day of the eleventh lunar month, he rode from Drepung and went via Ganden Monastery at Mount Drok Riwoché, and then to Reting Monastery, the "Hermitage of Victors." Many great and powerful people such as the former Ganden Tripa, along with Bökharwa Rinpoché, Tsangpa Panchen Rigpa Sengé, Ensapa Sangyé Yeshé (1525–91), many abbots and students from the greater and smaller monastic seats, representatives from Tsegongkar, and Sakyong Tashi Rabten along with attendants, who had accompanied him thus far to Reting, bid him farewell.

When Jé Sönam Gyatso mounted his horse, Sakyong Tashi Rabten took hold of the stirrup and expressed two lines of verse:

> May your lotus feet remain firm, O guru, glory of the teachings.
> May great beings who uphold the teachings cover the earth!

However, welling up with tears, he could not continue the verse. Thus, the supreme victor, Jé Sönam Gyatso, spontaneously completed it:

> May patrons of the teachings increase in wealth and power!
> May there be auspiciousness for the teachings to remain long!

This verse of auspiciousness spread far and wide, and continues to be included within prayers even today.

Thereafter they set up camp as they progressed. Jé Sönam Gyatso gave public teachings to lay and ordained along the way, and gave full and regular ordination to nearly a thousand people. They crossed the Machu River and continued on to where the king's initial reception of around eight-hundred Mongolian riders had arrived. [46] When they eventually set up camp on the Arik Karpo plains, they were offered one thousand horses and some tens of thousands of livestock. At Hanggé the second reception including royalty and so forth met them with about three thousand riders. They went on to be met by yet another third reception and so forth, where they continued to be shown great respect and receive extensive gifts.

On the fifteenth day of the fifth month, with all the esteem appropriate for a great person, he was escorted by many thousands of Mongolian and Chinese riders. An enormous amount of offerings were made at the initial celebration for the meeting of preceptor and patron, supreme victor Jé Sönam Gyatso and Mongolian king Altan Khan.

The preceptor and patron then proceeded as a pair, like sun and moon, into the center of a public gathering of a hundred thousand people. A speech was made to all present by Hong Taiji, the translated contents of which were as follows:

> Although a preceptor-patron relationship was formed earlier with the Sakyas allowing the Dharma to spread, the practice of Buddhism ceased with the Zemur king. We relished in sinful actions and ate only flesh and blood, as if in a lake of darkness and blood. Through the kindness of preceptor and patron, the sun and moon, the path of holy Dharma was revealed, and the lake of blood transformed into milk. Due to our gratitude for this great kindness, all who live here— Chinese, Tibetan, Mongols, and so forth—must abide by the rules of the ten virtues. From this day forth there are new laws to be followed, particularly in the Chakar area of Mongolia. Although in prior times it was the custom to sacrifice wife, servants, horses, livestock, and so forth when a Mongol died, his livestock and appropriate items will now be offered to the monastic sangha and lamas, and dedication prayers will be made in return.
>
> If a person murders another and so forth as in the past, they are to be judicially executed and their wealth seized.

The former ritual known as *ongkö* in which images of the deceased were created and sacrificial offerings of livestock were made to them on the full, new, and eighth-day moon, along with the custom of yearly sacrificial offerings are to stop entirely. [47]

These images are to be burned and replaced with statues of Mahākāla, the Six-Armed Protector. Only the three pure substances are to be offered to it; blood and flesh offerings are prohibited. In the case someone does perform them, the equivalent of ten times the value of the sacrificed animals shall be seized. If an *ongkö* image has not been burned, the household shall be dispersed. In brief, as the people in the Tibetan lands of Ü and Tsang live virtuously, so shall we in this land.

All Mongolians were made to live in harmony with the Dharma in accordance with the many laws proclaimed.

The Supreme Victor and His Eminence Mutually Conferring Titles upon One Another

The ground of the meeting place of the Mongol king Altan and the Victor Sönam Gyatso was blessed for the building of a temple. The combination of temple and palace built by many skilled Chinese and Tibetan workers was called Thekchen Chökhor Ling. The consecration ceremony was performed, a community of monastics was established, and a celebration of enormous proportions was held. Jé Sönam Gyatso was presented with a seal made from one-hundred ounces of gold, inscribed with the words "Victory Seal of Vajradhara Dalai Lama" in Mongolian. From that time on the incarnation line of the Victors were customarily known as the Dalai Lamas, meaning "Ocean Lama," i.e., a lama possessing an ocean of qualities.

Jé Sönam Gyatso likewise respectfully conferred the title "Dharma King, Great Brahmā of the Gods" on Altan Khan.

Just as the "seven chosen ones" were ordained in the earlier time of the Tibetan king Tri Songdetsen, for the purpose of trialing it, one hundred people, headed by three princes, were set forth into monastic training. [48]

A great number of travelers were dispatched by the preceptor and patron, including Aseng Lama and so on, to offer silver mandalas and so forth to the Jowo Śākyamuni and Akṣobhya statues in Lhasa, and to make offerings to the monastics in the monasteries, principal of which were Sera, Drepung, and Ganden. Gifts were offered to all— high and low—including to those from Tsé, Gongkar, Gyari, Gaden and so forth.

He was then invited by the Ordos prince, Windu. He newly founded a temple there called Phuntsok Shenphen Monastery. He was given countless offerings of gold and silver, horse armor, cloth and silk, live-stock, camels, jewels, and so forth.

A great Mongolian ruler called Genju Dutang, who controlled thir-teen provinces, also invited him. He arrived with the greeting of music and displays of weaponry. Among the individual tribes along the way the leaders offered endless spectacles of equestrian sports and vari-eties of food. Having traversed seven out of the ten half-kilometers needed to reach the castle, they encountered around 130,000 troops dispatched by the king to receive them. They continued on to the pal-ace, where the Avalokiteśvara practice was translated into the Chinese, Uighur and Mongolian languages for the public. Around one hundred people took ordination. In previous times the Helta Mongolians had done extensive damage to the regions within the Great Wall of China. After the Dalai Lama bestowed religious advice to the Mongolians, he became a peerless protector of the Chinese.

At the age of thirty-seven, in the earth-hare year (1579), disputes arose between the Ordos and Orö Mongolians. The Dalai Lama counseled them and restored peace. An urgent letter was given to him beseeching him to return on behalf of all lay and ordained within Ü-Tsang.

He intended to build a great monastery within Lithang. In accordance with his request to dispatch artisans from Kyishö, around four Nepalese arrived such as Pūneshing and so forth. [49]

Altan Khan then requested that he return to Mongolia. Since he planned to establish a monastery at Lithang, he promised if it were completed and nothing pressing arose that would force him to return to Ü-Tsang, he would come to Mongolia. The preceptor and patron conferred and decided that ambassadors should be appointed. The leader Kholo Chechin Batur and entourage were placed at Tsokha, and the Tibetan representative Tongkhor Yönten Gyatso (1557–87) was temporarily stationed in Mongolia.

In the eighth month of that year, messengers sent by the Chinese emperor arrived with a very respectful invitation. Preceding the conferring of the title protector of all the empire "Jog Ching Śrī," seal of authority, garments of authority, edict, and so forth, he was met by three leaders of China along with a variety of grand musical performances. He was offered many luxuries of a palace, including the full Luhang golden outfit, along with gold, silver, cloth and silk, and so forth.

The letter stated that he had excellently fulfilled the wishes of his Mongolian subjects belonging to the forty great tribes, and of the leaders Genju Dutang and so forth. He was also invited to the great palace, and so forth. The treasurer was given the work and seal of Gushrī.

Founding Thupten Jamchen Ling Monastery in Lithang

At the age of thirty-eight, in the iron-dragon year (1580), the king of Jang Satham assembled the corvée laborers and artisans for the construction of the great monastery of Lithang. The temple and monastic residences were built without delay, together with a main statue called Thupchen Khamsum Silnön, "Mighty Subduer of the Three Realms," measuring sixty-four hand spans in height. An extensive consecration ceremony was performed. The monastery was named Thupten Jamchen Chok Thamché Lé Nampar Gyalwa. [50] In the eleventh month he set out to Markham by horse.

At the age of thirty-nine, in the iron-snake year (1581), on the road to Chamdo, he saw a statue of Vairocana made by the artisans of the Chinese queen; that is, the wife of king Songtsen Gampo. It transformed into Vairocana in actuality, and from the crown five-colored light rays radiated, and at the heart he clearly saw Mahākāla in a peaceful aspect. Through miraculous powers he performed one thousand circumambulations.

He was received by around two hundred riders consisting of high lamas and so forth headed by Jedrung Rinpoché Lhawang Chökyi Gyaltsen (1537–1603), and together with a procession of nearly four thousand monastic sangha he proceeded to Chamdo Jampaling.

Following that he went to Chökhor Ling on the invitation of Chöjé Lungrikpa, masters, and students. Having directly perceived that Altan Khan had passed away, he caused him to enter into the Cakrasaṃvara mandala and took care of him.

Founding Jé Kumbum Monastery in Amdo

At the age of forty-one, in the water-sheep year (1583), as per Shingkyong Nangso's invitation, he went to Jé Kumbum, the birthplace of the victor Tsongkhapa. He remained in retreat for a few days in a small room surrounded by deities that was newly constructed according to his request. That room is the origin for what is known nowadays as the "Upper Chamber." Jé Sönam Gyatso then principally requested the upholder of the Vinaya, Chöjé Gomchen Rinchen Tsöndrü Gyaltsen, and sponsors principally from the five tribes in Amdo to establish a monastery in this central hub of Tsongkha, speaking of its benefit now and in future. [51] They all wholeheartedly accepted the request with joy and devotion. The victor Sönam Gyatso gifted the monastery a thangka of himself, a thangka of Palden Lhamo, and a thangka of a dharmapāla. With his supportive kindness he performed the ground purification and blessed the site.

Within the Zina Lugya clan there is a family line, nowadays known as the Sharayugur, who he bound as spirit mediums of the deity Sung-gyal Draklha, a guardian of the Buddha's teachings made to spontaneously possess them. Since the protector deity pledged to remain with the family for thirteen generations, Jé Sönam Gyatso also supplied the value of a statue of the dharmapāla to be made using his own nose blood.

Thereafter the housing was constructed. In the first month the prayer sessions for the days of miracles were also held and the chiefs of Tsongön and the five clans took turns as sponsors. In accordance with an instruction from Gyalwang Rinpoché Sönam Gyatso, the reconciliation stupa was turned into an enlightenment stupa and excellently built together with deity images and their supports, and was then consecrated. Monastic colleges were newly established there, and the teachings were formally entrusted to the dharma protector deities.

He went to Chakyung Drak and bestowed full ordination and taught Dharma extensively. Eventually he arrived at Dantik Mountain. He furthermore confirmed Dantik as a holy place. On the face of the mountain many naturally arisen images of buddhas, bodhisattvas, eight auspicious signs, and so forth occurred. He then went to Dzomo Khar where Jamchen Chöjé resided. He mediated a dispute that arose between the Chinese and Hor Mongolians in Tsongkha, restoring the peace for all. He continued on to Tshokha via Tsongkha.

At the age of forty-three, in the wood-bird year (1585), Altan Khan's son, Turing Khan, sent messengers bearing an invitation. Jé Sönam Gyatso rode out to the banks of the Machu River. [52] Eventually he reached Blue Castle, where countless Tibetan nomads were encamped. From Chakar he went to see Namo Tai Hong Thaiji and was presented with tens of thousands of material offerings.

At the age of forty-six, at the end of the first month of the earth-mouse year (1588), he became slightly ill. The emperor of China sent a royal envoy [in a palanquin] carried on the backs of eight people, inviting him to the palace. He accepted to come to the palace. At the beginning of the third month, he became severely ill, and on the dawn of the twenty-sixth he passed away.

His body was cremated in Mongolia. His attendants Chamdzö Gushrī Palden Gyatso, Gyalé Kudunpa Chösang Trinlé, and so forth, took his remains and constructed a thirteen-cubit silver stupa. It was brought to Lhasa where it remained in Drepung.

THE SACRED BIOGRAPHY OF THE FOURTH INCARNATION OF THE GYALWANG, THE OMNISCIENT YÖNTEN GYATSO

The fourth of the Gyalwang line, the omniscient Yönten Gyatso, was born in the Blue Castle in Mongolia, on the first day of the first month of the earth-ox year (1589). His father was Sechen Chökhur, of the royal line of Genghis Khan and son to Altan Khan, and his mother was Bākhenjul. In the very same month, he called his father by his name and furthermore spoke a lot to the amazement of all. One day he told his mother to bring a volume of the Kangyur from the shrine room. [53] He looked at it and said, "This is my biography." He opened it at the life story of Amoghapāśa within the Lotus Sutra, and all stated they were certain he was an emanation of Avalokiteśvara. One day he had visions of many dharmapālas coming to him and he spoke of what they looked like, and he imitated them a lot.

After a year passed, when his father's shrine room was consecrated, the young tulku pointed to a statue of the previous victor Jé Sönam

Gyatso and said, "This is me." He also identified the rosary that had been given to his father by the previous Dalai Lama. Afterward Gushrī came to meet him, bringing a rosary and other items that belonged to the previous Dalai Lama. He mixed these up with around eleven fake items and let the boy see. The child identified all of them individually, thus inspiring great faith and becoming a source of conviction.

The head cook Tsultrim Gyatso and Nangso Kajupa then heard of these events and came to meet and investigate the boy. He placed his hand on the head of the former attendants such as the head cook and identified them each by name. They were left speechless and faithful.

At the age of three, in the iron-hare year (1591), he went to meet the king of Thumé. Although he was young, lacking fear or apprehension, with a smile he asked the king and his entourage if they were well. The king shed tears and experienced goosebumps from the longing of recollecting the previous Dalai Lama. The boy identified by name the artists who worked on the great deity statue of Lithang then present in the service of the king.

The great treasurer to whom the Chinese emperor gave the title Gushrī, whose real name was Palden Gyatso and who was known to all as "Treasurer Senge," had just completed the death anniversary prayers for Jé Sönam Gyatso in Ü. Based on talk that Jé Sönam Gyatso's supreme emanation had appeared in Mongolia, he consulted the prophesies of gods and lamas as part of the search. [54] In conformity with [the positive results] he set off for Mongolia, and identified Gyalwa Sönam Gyatso's reincarnation, who had reached three years of age.

The great Tibetan scholar and recently retired[40] Ganden Tripa, Gyalkhang Tsepa Paljor Gyatso (1526–99), conferred many times about immediate and long-term matters with Chamdzö Gushrī, who would leave on invitation to Mongolia, and in particular stated the following:

> I am old and thus cannot come as a representative to Mongolia, but as I am presently senior among Geluk lamas in

Ü-Tsang, it is suitable that I offer a name via the precious
attendant: the omniscient Yönten Gyatso.

Yönten Gyatso became renowned as such to all high and low. Although
great efforts were made to cordially bring the tulku to Tibet, his parents loved him dearly and delayed his leaving. He remained in Mongolia until he was fourteen.

Arriving in Ü-Tsang and Installation on the Ganden Phodrang Throne

In the water-hare year (1603), at the age of fourteen, Jé Yönten Gyatso
arrived in Ü having passed through Jé Kumbum. He first went to the
Reting Monastery, the hermitage of the victors, in the north. There he
went on invitation of the former Ganden Tri Rinpoché Sangyé Rinchen
(1540–1612). Following that he went to the source of the Dakpo Kagyü
tradition, a great seat of the glorious Phakmo Drupa, Taklung Monastery, where he was received by the Chamdzö and high government
officials and a procession of the monastic community. [55] At that time
he met with the majority of invitees including Sakyong Gandenpa
Miwang Yülgyal Norbu and his disciples, along with Önyer Kundun
Rinpoché Chösang Trinlé and so forth.

Afterward, upon arriving in the area of Phenpo, the incumbent Ganden Sertri Gendun Gyaltsen (1532–1607) went to receive him. He then
went on to the great seat of Ganden Nampar Gyalwé Ling. He closely
examined the temples, and in particular upon viewing the precious
golden reliquary he had a vision of Jé Rinpoché Tsongkhapa.

As he approached the heart of the snow land of Tibet, the great
Lhasa Trülnang Tsuklakhang, he was welcomed by a line of lay and
monastic riders numbering more than ten thousand, inviting him to
his estate, Ganden Khangsar. On the fifteenth day the monastic sangha
from countless monasteries in the vicinity such as Sera, Drepung, Gan-

den, and Kyormo Lung, formed a long procession. Together with an inconceivable amount of religious paraphernalia such as parasols, victory banners, hanging silk bands, music, flowers, and so forth, he was received by members of the lama estates, monastic sectors and house groups. He ascended the lion throne of the Ganden Phodrang within glorious Drepung, the sanctuary that conquers all directions. To the great assembly that had gathered to welcome and receive him, an enormous celebratory feast was held with portions of brown sugar, butter, meat and tsampa, wheat and pulses, along with continuous food. He was furthermore invited to the upper chamber, seven monasteries, masters' abodes, monastic sectors, house groups, and so forth and treated with supreme respect.

On an auspicious day in the great Lhasa Trülnang Tsuklakhang he took novice vows in the presence of the Jowo Śākyamuni statue with the former Ganden Tripa Sangyé Rinchen presiding as abbot and the current Ganden Tripa Gendun Gyaltsen as preceptor. [56]

Great lamas and great people gathered like monsoon clouds to welcome him to Tibet. In particular, the omniscient Shamar Garwang Chökyi Wangchuk (1584–1630) from Garchen sent a congratulatory letter. While the abbot and all disciples from Tashi Lhunpo in upper Tsang were on their way to meet him, the master Panchen Rinpoché Losang Chökyi Gyaltsen (1570–1662) had a vision of amazing signs such as an illusory white boy and so forth, which are clear in his own biography.

In accordance with Ganden Tri Rinpoché Gendun Gyaltsen's plan, having conferred with Shabdrung Rinpoché and the Chamdzö, it was proposed to Panchen Rinpoché Losang Chökyi Gyaltsen that he become the tutor, which he accepted. The master and student temporarily resided at Drepung Monastery, and many sets of teachings were given to him over the course of a few years.

At the age of sixteen, in the wood-dragon year (1604), he presided as head of the great prayer festival in Lhasa. Gongkar Shabdrung,

Gyeré Lhawa, and so forth, invited him to their estates and showed him great respect. Following that he went to Ölkha Dzingchi and the seat of the previous Dalai Lamas, the immutable and spontaneously accomplished temple of Chökhor Gyal.

Panchen Rinpoché also arrived for the sake of tutoring, and for many days offered teachings mostly in the form of oral transmissions. Via Maldro he was received with great respect from the monastics of Rinchen Ling. He gave Dharma teachings to the assembly. Via Dzingchi, Ölkha Tsé, Chökhor Gyal, and Kyishö, he arrived at Sera Thekchen Ling. He then went on to Drepung, and in the fire-horse year he rode out to Yarlung. He was invited to Chongyé Taktsé by Ngawang Sönam Drakpa and his brother. He visited greater and smaller monasteries from different sects, such as Riwo Dechen, Chenyepa, Phakdepa, Palri Drupdé, Tashi Dechen, Chö Lamrimpa, Dé Terwa, and so forth, and eventually returned to Drepung. [57]

Having accepted appeals by patrons in the Tsang area, Shartsé Lopön Dradül arrived bearing invitations from Tashi Lhunpo. On the day he arrived at Tashi Lhunpo, the lord of the teachings, Panchen Rinpoché Losang Chökyi Gyaltsen was at the forefront. He saw the masters and senior ones ride out for reception and he dismounted from his horse. Jé Yönten Gyatso entered the great institute of Tashi Lhunpo alongside a procession of nearly a thousand monastics. He received empowerments from Panchen Rinpoché and listened to teachings on the Dharma. The Tsang king Karma Phuntsok Namgyal (1587–1620) offered requisite fodder and fuel. He went to Gangchen Chöphel, Trophu, Lhunpotsé and so forth. When riding back to Lhasa he visited Gyaltsé Pelkhor Chödé, Nenying, and so forth.

At the age of twenty-three, in the iron-pig year (1611), he went to Drepung and received the Vajra Garland (*vajrāvali*) empowerment. Due to the Tsangpa Önshang becoming displeased that year, a large Tsangpa army arrived in Yargyab. Since the situation became such that the Yargyab leaders and ministers were forced to remain within their own territories, the Dalai Lama became known as "Thutop Gyatso," meaning "Powerful Ocean." During these years a great number of travelers from north and south arrived with an endless flow of offerings.

The Tsang king, Phuntsok Namgyal, went to Lhasa, where he requested the Dalai Lama to confer the one hundred long-life empowerments and eight-limbed vows. If the Dalai Lama would have conferred them, it likely would have been beneficial for both preceptor and patron. However, he was dissuaded by Rabjampa Sönam Drakpa, who said, "He should not be conferred such as he is an enemy of the Teachings!" [58]

Many great lamas from Amdo, China, and Mongolia such as Tongkhor Shabdrung, Śāntideva's tulku, Baso Tulku, Demo Tulku, Sherpang Tulku, and so forth came to greet him. He cut the crown hair of Baso Tulku and Śāntideva's tulku. He gave the Thirteen-Deity Yamāntaka empowerment and the oral transmission of fragments of the collected works of Jé Gendun Gyatso. When Demo Tulku first saw him, he said, "I assumed the omniscient one was ordained, but he appears as a layman in white clothing," to which those in the vicinity replied, "You did not see properly, he most certainly has the symbols of a monastic!" One time he said that he saw him in the aspect of a wrathful deity. One day when Jé Yönten Gyatso was standing in the window of the palace, Demo Tulku arrived immediately by himself and saw an image of Dromtönpa on a three-tiered throne, just as he is depicted in art nowadays, along with a figure of a smiling Jowo Jé Atiśa, one cubit in height, seated amid light rays. When Demo Tulku was left temporarily dumbfounded, Jé Yönten Gyatso told the tulku to sit down, which interrupted his psychic vision that he then relayed to Jé Yönten Gyatso, but he did not believe him, and said he was not seeing properly.

Taking Full Ordination and Receiving the
Golden Seal from Ming Wanli Emperor

At the age of twenty-six, on a virtuous day in the twelfth month of the wood-tiger year (1614), Jé Yönten Gyatso took full ordination at Palden Drepung Monastery in the middle of the requisite number of monks, from Panchen Losang Chögyen presiding as abbot, and Sönam Gelek Palsang (1594–1615), the tulku of Panchen Sönam Drakpa (1478–1554), acting as assistant preceptor. [59] He then received a variety of teachings on sutra and mantra from many lamas, including Tri Rinpoché Sangyé Rinchen, Tri Rinpoché Gendun Gyaltsen, Chönyer Drakpa, Pönlop Panchen Rinpoché, Zimkhang Gongma Tulku Sönam Gelek Palsang, Drungpa Khetsunpa from Ölkha, Jé Norbuwa, and so forth.

Following Jé Sangyé Rinchen's death, when his remains were offered into the fire, most of his upper body did not burn. At first this appeared to be a bad sign, and the corpse was brought to Jé Yönten Gyatso for inspection. To the shock of many present, Jé Yönten Gyatso took the upper body part with his hands and placed it on his head for a long time while making prayers.

Jé Yönten Gyatso performed countless recitations at the base of a statue containing a reliquary in which the entirety of the remains of Jetsun Rachen Lotsāwa (1016–1128)—the great trailblazer of the Black Opponent, Six-Faced One, and Bhairava tantras in Tibet, the sole eye of the world—[were interred], and that also contained clay figures moistened through Tsongkhapa's miraculous powers with the saliva produced from each recitation of a thousand Yamarāja mantras.

Among the qualities that holy beings are generally endowed with from the perspective of disciples, such as expertise, discipline, and righteousness and so forth, his entire life was principally dedicated to the stages of practice.

At the age of twenty-eight, in the third month of the fire-dragon year (1616), the Ming Wanli emperor sent a delegation of many Chinese such as Lama Sönam Lodrö and so forth. They offered him the author-itative title of a buddha, "Universal Lord Vajradhara," along with an authoritative hat, clothing, and seal. They invited the supreme victor to the Chinese residence within Drepung, where they offered gifts and provided much astonishing entertainment. [60] Upon their request that he visit China, he accepted it for the sake of auspiciousness.

During this time the Tsang king took control of the entire area of Kyishö, and gradually the majority of Ü-Tsang was taken over. While Jé Yönten Gyatso was still in good health, Chief Kholo Ché's two sons forcefully approached many times from Mongolia with their army, intending to battle with the Tsang king, but when they arrived near to Tibet the Dalai Lama sent a messenger, and the turmoil was pacified.

The Dalai Lama then displayed the aspect of becoming ill, and at the age of twenty-eight, on the fifteenth day of the twelfth month of the fire-dragon year, he departed to the realm of Tuṣita. For forty-nine days the sangha of the Upper and Lower tantric colleges and individual monasteries accomplished extensive memorial prayers. After Panchen Rinpoché offered his body into the fire, the skull, along with the three—heart, tongue, and eyes—and relic pills appeared. The Kalkha chief, Chökhur, took the skull, and the Thumé Taiji the heart and so forth, as objects of veneration, back to their respective homelands.

With the Kalkha Chökhur acting as patron, and Chamdzö Sönam Chöphel (1595–1658) otherwise known as Sönam Rabten or Gyalo Chödzé bearing responsibility, a silver memorial stupa was con-structed that was installed in Drepung Monastery.

THE SACRED BIOGRAPHY OF THE GREAT FIFTH DALAI LAMA

There were no longer any rivals in the way of building upon the incred-ible accomplishments of the previous supreme victors. The one who authored a large ocean of eloquent treatises related to sutra and tantra such as this text *Oral Transmission of Mañjuśrī,* who was incredibly kind to those of the snow land, was the Great Fifth Dalai Lama, Ngawang Losang Gyatso Jikmé Gocha Thupten Langtsö Dé, renowned as an emanation of the enlightened deeds of the Tibetan Dharma king, Tri Songdetsen. [61] Among the victor's supreme works that eliminated the stains of lack of understanding, misconceptions, and doubt toward the teachings, the *Oral Transmission of Mañjuśrī* is a treatise that unravels the intention behind Atiśa's *Lamp for the Path* and is a summary of *Tsongkhapa's Great Treatise on the Stages of the Path.* It has many profound qualities such as being clearly written, in that it is pithy yet solves all difficult points, and is entirely connected to the great Indian treatises. Thus, it fulfills the meaning behind Dromtönpa's statement of "Infinite in their deeds of explaining the final teachings."

There are two treatises that are supreme among the Great Fifth's works: (1) *Sacred Words of the Vidyādharas: A Dzogchen Manual,* belonging to the Nyingma tantras, and (2) *Oral Transmission of Mañjuśrī: A Manual on the Stages of the Path to Enlightenment.*

From the biography of Kachen Yongdzin Yeshé Gyaltsen (1713–93) authored by the Eighth Dalai Lama Gyalwa Jampal Gyatso (1758–1804):

> *Oral Transmission of Mañjuśrī* was taught every year during the time of Lama Jampa Rinpoché leading to the guide transmission of it becoming widespread. However, that gradually declined to the point where even the reading transmission was at risk of becoming broken. Kachen Yeshé Gyaltsen thought only of restoring the teachings that had declined. With respect to his request that those who were interested in this be given the explanatory transmission along with pith instructions of this guide to the path, the master's own words were as follows:

Oral Transmission of Mañjuśrī was composed as a
legacy for the Great Fifth's followers in the form
of a pithy instruction manual commenting on the
intention of the Buddha's teachings. [62] I, myself,
underwent great hardship to listen to these pith
instructions seven times in the presence of my precious guru, the gentle protector. Thereafter I went
into the mountains to practice them as much as
I could. I had wished to disseminate this path to
others since before, but there was no one who was
interested.

With great joy Kachen Yeshé Gyaltsen accepted his teacher
Kushab's recent instruction to restore this teaching.

He then went to Meru Dratsang. From the eighth day
onward, he bestowed oral instructions of the whispered lineage through a summarized guide of *Oral Transmission of
Mañjuśrī*—the stages of the path to enlightenment that is the
thoroughfare traversed by all victors and their spiritual heirs
of the three times—for one month, to an audience of more
than three thousand fortunate ones seeking liberation.

At that time, the level of understanding of those virtuous
ones who were renowned for their eyes of knowledge being
wide open with respect to authoritative treatises, and who
were confident in their own understanding and explanation
of this text, could not even compete with a small fraction of
this master's explanation. Thus, they said, "Ah, it is certainly
true that this holy being has come to spread the teachings of
the omniscient Great Fifth himself."

Based on the request that the summary he bestowed be
written down, together with a summary of the guiding
focal objects of meditation of the guide *Oral Transmission*

of Mañjuśrī, together with connecting passages, he extensively authored on the ritual for generating bodhicitta in
accordance with how it appears in Śāntideva's *Way of the
Bodhisattva.*

Thus, in this section wherein the greatness of the author is expressed,
a summary of the deeds of the Great Fifth Dalai Lama are presented.

The Great Fifth Dalai Lama, Ngawang Losang Gyatso, was born
on the twenty-third day of the ninth Tibetan month of the fire-snake
year (1617) of the tenth sexagenary cycle, in Chingwar Taktsé Castle at
Chongyé. The ruler Dudül Rabten of the Zahor people was his father,
and the noblewoman Kunga Lhadze was his mother. [63]

Panchen Losang Chökyi Gyaltsen and the Ganden Trichen Könchok Chöphel (1573–1646) both performed dough-ball divination in
the presence of the Jowo Jampal Dorjé statue at Reting, and in the
presence of the Jowo Śākyamuni in Lhasa. The divination came out
in accordance with the prophecies of the Dharma protectors, and the
boy was recognized as the reincarnation of the Fourth Dalai Lama
Yönten Gyatso. However, due to the power of the Tsangpa king at the
time, he could not be invited to his residence in Drepung, and so he
remained where he was for some years. Through the skillful request
from His Eminence Panchen Losang Chökyi Gyaltsen and Hong Taiji's
delegates, namely Chöjé Jinpa Dargyé and so forth, permission was
granted by the Tsangpa king.

In dependence upon this, at the age of six, Chamdzö Sönam Chöphel
was able to invite him to the seat of the Dalai Lamas, the Ganden Phodrang in Drepung Monastery. He was then installed on the throne of
the previous Dalai Lama.

At the age of nine, in the wood-bull year (1625), he took novice
ordination from Panchen Rinpoché presiding as abbot and Trichen
Könchok Chöphel as assistant preceptor. During the ceremony he
was given the name Ngawang Losang Gyatso Jikmé Gocha Thupten

Langtsö Dé, and received many streams of Dharma, such as empowerments, guides, and pith instructions one after another.

At the age of eleven, in the presence of the thirty-fifth holder of the Ganden throne, Ling Mepa Jamyang Könchok Chöphel, he began his studies of the five great authoritative treatises. Gradually he received teachings within the Sakya tradition from the sovereign lord Wangchuk Rabten (1558–1576) and the lord who pervades all Buddhist lineages, the protector of the wheel, Sönam Chokden Tenpé Gyaltsen. [64]

At the age of seventeen he received teachings on the Early and New translation periods of secret mantra in the presence of Khöntön Paljor Lhundrup.

From age twenty-two onward he received vast nonsectarian teachings illustrated by the Early Translation period secret mantra empowerments and guides from Zurchen Chöying Rangdröl (1604–69), Khyabdak Kangyurwa, Umdze Sönam Chokdrup, Rikzin Terdak Lingpa (1646–1714), Menlungpa Lochok Dorjé (1595–1671), and so forth. These are clear in the four-volume record of teachings he received [called] *Ganga River*. Additionally, he studied grammar and poetic composition with Möndröl Pandita Tsewang Döndrup (sixteenth century) Jamyang Wangyal Dorjé (sixteenth–seventeenth century) and his spiritual sons. With Lumpo Döndrup Wangyal he studied elemental astrology, Svarodaya astrology, and so forth, thus becoming a total expert on the ten traditional sciences.

At the age of twenty-two, in the earth-tiger year (1638), he received his initial bhikṣu vows (within the Lachen Gongpa Rabsel lineage) in the Lhasa Tsuklakhang in front of the Jowo Śākyamuni in the middle of a sangha fulfilling the requisite number, with Panchen Rinpoché Losang Chökyi Gyaltsen presiding as abbot and interviewer of private questions, Ganden Trichen Jamyang Könchok Chöphel as assistant preceptor, Jepa Jampa Mönlam as the recorder of the time, together with another nine monks who fulfilled the quorum. Starting five years after taking full ordination, he would go on to bestow novice and full ordination vows to many thousands of recipients until the end of his life. [65]

At the age of twenty-three he pursued studies in the Four Medical Tantras.

In 1642, at the age of twenty-six, the Great Fifth was invited to Shigatsé by Gushrī Khan, and together with a remarkably vast number of offerings he was handed total political authority over Tibet. As such, the Ganden Phodrang government was founded, and Chamdzö Sönam Chöphel was appointed as the first regent.

In the wood-bird year of 1645, at the age of twenty-nine, in addition to renovating and expanding the original eastern wall of the remains of the old Potala palace, the "White Palace" was newly constructed. After the palace was built, he shifted his residence from the Phodrang at Drepung to the Potala, where he carried out important duties related to both religion and politics.

In 1649, at the age of thirty-three, he founded the medical college Drophen Ling.[41] From age thirty-four, for the next twelve years he once again put great effort into extensive study of sutras, tantras, and the traditional sciences.

In the iron-tiger and iron-hare years (1650–51) of the eleventh sexagenary cycle, the Shunzhi emperor of the government of the Manchu Qing dynasty, sent many letters inviting the Dalai Lama to the Chinese capital of Beijing. Accordingly, in the water-dragon year (1652), at the age of thirty-six, he arrived gradually via Janglam and Tsongön, with an inconceivable number of persons greeting him along the way. He bestowed teachings at the larger monasteries in the districts of China and Mongolia and gave advice pertinent to what should be adopted and discarded in relation to monastic discipline.

There being no custom of a Chinese emperor going to receiving someone directly, the emperor used deer hunting as a pretext to encounter the Dalai Lama at the Nenyön grove. [66] There they encountered each other, and the emperor descended from his throne, and they exchanged greetings while standing together. Following that they sat together on their individual thrones, drank tea, and ate together. For many days afterward there were endless performances and offerings made, and the Great Fifth resided for some days in the Taikha Palace that the emperor had purposefully built for him.

After the emperor had returned to Beijing and the Great Fifth Dalai Lama also arrived there, he resided in what was well known as the "Yellow Temple," which the emperor had specially built for him. Before the new year dawned, the emperor sent two internal ministers, Kapala Ama and Askhen Ama to offer all of the apparel suitable of an imperial preceptor, including parasol, victory banner, silk banner, ribbon, incense burner, awning, conch and horn, and so forth. Not only that, but during the new year festivities of the water-snake year, the great emperor, princesses, internal and external great ministers and so forth all put on a grand celebration for him that lasted many days. When he was about to depart from Beijing, emperor Shunzhi himself also went to the Nenyön grove where he had arranged an enormous banquet.

While the Supreme Victor was at the Taikha Palace, in the presence of Li pu Shang, Shu'u Luo und Lang Qiu, and so forth, who were sent by the emperor, he was presented with a golden seal made out of fifty gold coins, and on its face the following words were written in Chinese, Tibetan, and Mongolian scripts parallel with each other:

> The ocean lama, unchangeable vajra holder, from the great abode of the gods in the west, where all beings under the sky are united under a single teaching that is the words of the Buddha abiding in virtue and bliss.

Along with fifteen gold bars the size of religious texts, four finger widths high and a hand span in width, with grand praises inscribed on their faces, at the end of which was written the following [67]:

I offer you the title of "The Perfected, Peaceful One of the West, the Omniscient Vajra Holder Dalai Lama, the Lord of the Buddhist Teachings among the Vast Enlightened Ones."

The supreme victor, the Dalai Lama, also offered the emperor the glorifying title "God of the Sky, Emperor Mañjuśrī, the Great Lord," written in Machu, Mongolian, and Tibetan.

At the age of thirty-eight he went to meet Panchen Rinpoché Losang Chökyi Gyaltsen at Tashi Lhunpo. In the earth-dog year (1658) Gushrī Khan's son, Tenzin Dorjé Dayan Khan (died 1668), was given the title of king. In that year, the Dalai Lama gave an audience to messengers sent with greetings by India's Bengal king, Śrī Hasujas Madāshasi.

After the regent Sönam Chöphel passed away in 1658, His Holiness the Dalai Lama maintained political authority for three years. Following that, the regents who were successively appointed were Jaisang Depa Drongmepa Trinlé Gyatso (the grandfather of Desi Sangyé Gyatso); Chöpön Losang Thutop; the storekeeper of Namgyal Monastery, Losang Jinpa, and Desi Sangyé Gyatso (1653–1705).

In the earth-pig year (1649), at the age of forty-three, he dispatched to Tsongön his representative Sönam Wangyal, who bound the feuding Mongolian chiefs to powerful religious oaths, making them vow to respect the orders of the Great Fifth Dalai Lama. This not only resolved the conflict of the Mongolians and helped to solidify the power of the Ganden Phodrang government, but also would prove instrumental in ending border disputes between China and Mongolia. [68]

At the age of fifty-one in the fire-sheep year (1667), war broke out between China and Mongolia at the southern border of Tsongön and the Manchu emperor urgently requested the Great Fifth to rectify the situation with the Mongolian chiefs and soldiers. Accordingly, specially sent representatives counseled the Mongolian chiefs, and thus a period of peace ensued between the Chinese and Mongolians.

In the iron-pig year (1671), Gushrī Khan's younger son, Könchok

Dalai Khan, was enthroned to the rank of his father along with the title of Tenzin Dalai Khan.

From the fire-bird year (1657) an interfering spirit born from distorted prayers had been harming the teachings and sentient beings in general and in particular in Dol Chumik Karmo. Due to this, the Great Fifth Dalai Lama performed pacifying activities such as building a new house for the spirit to settle in and so forth. In the early parts of the wood-tiger (1674) and wood-hare (1675) years the Great Fifth performed two interrogations, and it is clear in records that at the end of those a group of seven practitioners performed a fire ritual in which the spirit Dogyal was burned. These events can be understood in further detail from historical records. Indeed a few texts containing rebuttals and presentations of other positions appeared; however when analyzed from an unbiased perspective, they lack reasoning that leads to certainty of their arguments and answers, and fall back on hearsay and slander based on attachment and hatred. The fact that it is nothing other than opportunistic sectarian criticism is already clear as evidenced by historical records.

Dartsedo, on the eastern border between China and Tibet, was a major hub and a better place than others to find all sorts of goods and wares. However, it was missing authentic places of worship for effortlessly bestowing all resultant happiness of this life and future lives. A new tantric monastery, Drophen Ling, famously known as Ngachö Gön, was built as an agent to lead all beings there to high status and definite goodness. Additionally, the Dalai Lama also provided provisions for around 50 monks [in the form of food, wood, hay, and so forth] and assigned them merchants and nomadic settlements [from which they received part of their income]. [69]

In the fire-snake year (1677) he offered back the full ordination vows of the Lachen vow lineage he previously received. On the twenty-fifth of the tenth month of that year—the day of the Ganden Ngamchö festivities—at the peak of the Potala Palace, it is clear in the records[42] that the Great Fifth again correctly took the bhikṣu vows of full ordination in the lineage of Panchen Śākyaśrībhadra, in the center of a group of five, namely Khenchen Rinchen Sönam Chokdrup Tenpé Gyaltsen Palsangpo presiding as both abbot and preceptor, Tsangri Dzinpé Wangpo as interviewer of private questions, Neten Jamyang Drakpa as the recorder of the time, and both Chöpön Ngawang Sherab and Ratna Mañjuśrī to fulfill the requisite number.

To give a summary of the Great Fifth Dalai Lama's autobiography on the topic of his taking the vows of full ordination from the Lachen vow lineage first and then later again from the Panchen vow lineage:[43] When the lineage of pratimokṣa vows established in Tibet by Khenchen Bodhisattva Śāntarakṣita (eighth century) during the early dissemination period of Buddhism was annihilated by Lang Darma, the three monks known as Mar Śākyamuni, Yo Gejung, and Tsang Rabsel took mule loads of Vinaya texts and fled to Amdo via Ngari Janglam, and then settled in Dantik Yangdzong. An intelligent boy belonging to a Bön family but inclined toward Buddhism due to awakening of past-life imprints requested ordination from them. In addition to the three aforementioned upholders of the Vinaya, two Chinese monks named Hashang and Kebak filled the requisite number, and the young man received the full ordination name of Gongpa Rabsel (953–1035). Thereafter, the lineage that proliferated from the ten persons from Ü-Tsang who took full ordination from Lachen Gongpa Rabsel became well known as the "Lachen vow lineage." [70]

During the later dissemination period, initially the upholders of the Vinaya from the early period such as the great lotsāwa Rinchen Sangpo (958–1055) and so forth relied upon the Lachen vow lineage, but Trophu Lotsāwa Jampa Pal (1173–1236) endured enormous hardship and invited Sönam Panchen Śākyaśrībhadra (1127–1225) of Kashmir to Tibet, where he spread the Mūlasarvāstivādin lineage of ordination vows. He illuminated the Vinaya teachings like the sun and moon in the land of snow. It appears that Sakya Pandita Kunga Gyaltsen

(1182–1251), Drogön Chögyal Phakpa (1235–80), Lama Dampa Sönam Gyaltsen (1312–75), the omniscient Butön, Gyalsé Thokmé Sangpo (1295–1369, Ngorchen Kunga Sangpo (1382–1456), and so on, took vows in this lineage.

Although the Great Fifth had great success in reviving the embers of the Lachen vow lineage of the later dissemination period of the teachings in Tibet, old speculation still lingered about whether the two Chinese who fulfilled the requisite number when Lachen Rabsel took full ordination were emanations. In order to dispel these doubts, with the intention to increase conviction in a pure lineage of vows, the Great Fifth Dalai Lama once again took the Panchen lineage of vows. It states in his *Autobiography*:

> Jé Tsongkhapa also took the Panchen lineage of vows from Chakmik Khenchen Tsultrim Rinchen. Even though I had reached the old age of fifty-one, I endeavored with the wish to benefit myself and many others, and with Khenchen Rinchen Sönam Chokdrup Tenpé Gyaltsen Palsangpo presiding as both abbot and preceptor . . . I once again took the full ordination vows of a bhikṣu.[44]

In the earth-sheep year (1679) of the eleventh sexagenary cycle, Drongmepa Sangyé Gyatso was appointed as the regent. Thereafter not only was he consulted on the most important government matters, he principally dedicated himself only to religious activities such as explanation, debate, composition, and practice. [71] He upheld the religious traditions and tenet systems of Tibet, including that of the Bön, through nonsectarianism.

In addition to the Muslims, Nepalese, and so forth in Lhasa being allowed to practice whichever religion they wanted, the Muslims from Kashmir were permanently provided land within the city of Lhasa on which to build their mosque, along with places for festivities and an area to bury their dead. Such great and small deeds significantly garnered the appreciation of all people, high status or low, Buddhist or non-Buddhist.[45] In order to expand the printing of rare texts he newly built a printing house within Drepung Ganden Phodrang and a printing house behind the back entrance of the Potala Palace. He was greatly kind in his counseling of monasteries on their codes of conduct and advising on their studies of Buddhism. Whether it be in religion or politics, his forward-thinking actions were definitely effective.

In the water-dog year (1682) of the eleventh sexagenary cycle, having reached the age of sixty-six, as he was approaching his passage to peace, the Great Fifth urgently advised Desi Sangyé Gyatso on the need to keep his passing a secret for some years, together with the reasoning for that decision. As such, his passing was kept secret for thirteen years. His direct disciples Bhikṣu Jamyang Drakpa (seventeenth century) from Pabongkha Hermitage and Trerabpa from Namgyal Monastery had similar faces to the Dalai Lama and were thus made to serve as his double.[46] Since at that time the government of the Ganden Phodrang had not been in existence for more than forty years, there was doubt as to whether all religious and political matters could be carried out successfully, and thus the death was kept a tight secret. In the iron-horse year (1690) of the twelfth sexagenary cycle— eight years since the Dalai Lama passed into the sphere of peace—the construction of the red Potala Palace commenced, [72] and two years following that the actual production of a golden tomb—the sole ornament of the world—a resting place for the body of the Great Fifth Dalai Lama began.

In brief, with respect to religion, at a young age the Great Fifth Dalai Lama went to the Ganden Phodrang in Drepung, at which time he engaged in studies of vast treatises within the Geluk tradition, principal among which were the excellent works of Jé Rinpoché Tsongkhapa. From an early time, he had great interest in the teachings of the Nyingma tradition of secret mantra, with Khöntön Paljor Lhundrup first connecting him to the teachings, and in dependence upon which he received cycles of teachings from Zurchen Chöying Rangdröl and Terdak Lingpa. Together with cycles of old and new tantras principally from the Sakya cycles of teachings from Khöntön Paljor Lhundrup and cycles of teaching from the Geluk tradition from Panchen Losang Chökyi Gyaltsen and Trichen Könchok Chöphel, he received extensive stages of empowerments, oral transmissions, and pith instructions, and completed his studies of many scriptures.

Thus, as indicated by his understanding of all textual systems across the Tibetan Buddhist traditions, his knowledge was vast—whether it be in religion, politics, or traditional sciences. He was incomparable in his religious and political goodwill toward all, monastic and lay, and among the succession of Dalai Lamas he is among the most well-known inside and outside the grand nation surrounded by snow mountains and those whose impact was greatest.

Although I speak of him as if ordinary, he possessed all requisites needed in a leader—incredible shrewdness, strong fortitude, and so on. After we incurred the loss of Tibet's independence, one can understand from the above that the transformation of our government in exile into a democracy is a progressive succession of the Ganden Phodrang instituted by the Great Fifth Dalai Lama. [73]

The Fifth Dalai Lama's vast written contributions, including on the traditional sciences, span twenty-one volumes: four volumes of his records of teachings received, six volumes of sacred biographies, related to sutric treatises, such as *The Ornament of the Intention of the Intelligent* on the topic of the perfection of wisdom, *The Ship Sailing the Mahāyāna Ocean* related to Madhyamaka, and the *Trailblazing Jewel of Abhidharma*, as well as manuals on the new tantras such as his *Sakya Lamdré Instructions*, along with many liturgical arrangements and so forth, constituting a plethora of work on a variety of topics.

Within the four volumes of private teachings there exist vast cycles of teachings on the Nyingma principally concerning the eight sādhana teachings. Likewise, there are two volumes of teachings relating to the secret visions of the Great Fifth, thus comprising his public, private, and secret teachings.

This mere summary of the general outer activities of the supreme victor that are clear proof of his being a lord of nonsectarian teachings concludes the expression of greatness of the author for the sake of demonstrating an authentic source of the teachings.

Showing the Greatness of the Teachings in Order to Engender Respect for the Instructions

---

    A. The greatness of realizing that all teachings are free of contradiction

    B. The greatness of all scriptures appearing as instructions

    C. The greatness of easily finding the conqueror's intent

    D. The greatness of exceedingly negative behavior stopping by itself

These four outlines, which are present in Tsongkhapa's *Great Treatise on the Stages of the Path*, are explained by the Great Fifth in the following third outline on how to listen to the teachings. Thus, I will explain them in that section, and lightly discuss the general and specific greatnesses of the teachings here [74].

To generate respect for the instructions is to endeavor to acquire a discriminating conviction about the author and the intention of the scriptures based on reasoning; this is the intelligent approach. It is fundamental to understand that it is incorrect to enter into the Buddha Bhagavān's teachings merely through following in the footsteps of tradition, or because others have told you to, while not knowing what is required or what should be abandoned.

Teachings on the formation of the external universe can be found within Buddhist treatises: however not all of those accord with modern scientific conclusions. Those which do not accord with logic and are refuted through direct observations must be discarded. These, though, are merely of secondary importance; the inner reality of our mind along with the methods to train it are that which are primarily explained.

These explanations are, from among the many religious teachings in the world, the philosophies relating to the stages of practice of developing the mind as found in such depth and profundity within Buddhists texts. In particular, they teach the varying levels of subtlety of the mind. Not only do they teach meditations on wisdom, but also how to unify it with the door to the generation of the boundless supreme method of altruism, thus limitlessly increasing the exceptional mind of bodhicitta that cherishes others more than oneself. These practices that withstand the analysis of the intelligent are what are primarily explained.

Instructions on important mind training techniques derived from these teachings were passed down from Maitreya and Mañjuśrī, and Nāgārjuna and Asaṅga. [75] This entire lineage of the complete vast and profound instructions was then transmitted to Atiśa. This was subsequently transmitted to Potowa, Sharawa, and so forth, who transmitted it in the form of the renowned "six treatises of the Kadampas": the two treatises for inspiring faith—*Garland of Thirty-Four Birth Stories* and the *Compendium of Sayings*; the two treatises on conduct—*Compendium of Bodhisattva Trainings* and *Way of the Bodhisattva*; and the two treatises on concentration—*The Bodhisattva Grounds* and *The Ornament for the Mahāyāna Sūtras*. Those who upheld these collections of teachings were known as "Kadampas of Authoritative Treatises."

The Bodhisattva Grounds and the *Ornament for the Mahāyāna Sūtras* extensively expound on the Mahāyāna grounds and paths, and therefore are clearly not treatises related to meditative stabilization (*samādhi*) alone. The *Compendium of Bodhisattva Trainings* and *The Way of the Bodhisattva* both teach the conduct of bodhisattvas, and within that, the bodhisattva conduct of entering into practice, the conduct of actual practice, and the conduct of accomplishment, renowned as the "three conducts." Since these are complete in those texts, perhaps

SHOWING THE GREATNESS OF THE TEACHINGS 79

they are the so-called "treatises on great conduct." Since they engaged extensively in studying and explaining these texts, it was for this reason they became known as the "Kadampas of Authoritative Treatises."

The upholders of the tradition of practice guides relating primarily to the stages of the path and doctrine, as transmitted from Dromtönpa to Gönpawa and so forth, were known as the "Kadampas of the Stages of the Path." Rather than extensive and elaborative commentaries, it is a lineage of Kadam pith instructions transmitted from Jowo Atiśa and Dromtönpa to Chen-ngawa Tsultrim Bar and so forth, and summarizes Atiśa's *Dependent Origination, Two Truths,* and *Lamp for the Path*. These three uninterrupted Kadam lineages are presented clearly in *Opening the Door to the Supreme Path: A Supplication Prayer* [*to the Lamrim Lineage Gurus*].

The great lord Tsongkhapa possessed the entirety of these three Kadam lineages. [76] He composed the perfection of wisdom commentary *Golden Rosary,* and five treatises on Madhyamaka: *Great Chapter on Special Insight; Abridged Chapter on Special Insight; Ocean of Reasoning: A Thorough Exposition of Mūlamadhyamakakārikā; Elucidation of the Intention: A Thorough Exposition of Madhyamakāvatāra;* and *Essence of Eloquence: Differentiating the Provisional and Definitive Meanings.* Jé Tsongkhapa thus applied his profound explanations of the Madhyamaka view practically, in the manner of the instructions of the "Kadam Lineage of the Stages of the Path." The perfection treatises act as the support for his *Great Treatise on the Stages of the Path,* and the fact that Gyaltsab Darma Rinchen references lamrim in his *Ornament of the Essence* clearly shows that there is a relationship between the genres.

Furthermore, not adhering to the structure of a major treatise and giving instructions solely by way of extensive or abridged stages of the path is the tradition of the "Kadampas of the Stages of the Path."

The omniscient Tsongkhapa states in *The Great Treatise on the Stages of the Path*:

Those who know how to bring all these explanations into their practice seem to hardly exist. Therefore, I will create a separate summary of what to sustain in meditation.

This teaching of a separate summary that he mentions here is Jé Tsongkhapa's *Middle-Length Stages of the Path* itself, otherwise famously known as *Condensed Exposition on the Stages of the Path*. Following the intention behind that statement, many followers authored extensive and concise commentaries, such as the "eight great lamrim manuals" and so forth.[47] Such concise and extensive treatises are authored in the style of the lamrim instructions of the "Kadam Lineage of Pith Instructions."

Many Tibetan experts of different traditions authored stages of the path treatises, a few of which have minor differences in the arrangement of the text compared to the style of the present treatise, but nonetheless have the same intended meaning. Such texts include the omniscient Longchenpa's *Resting in the Nature of the Mind*, which is certainly a treatise on the stages of the path, the first volume of *Words of My Perfect Teacher*, an instruction on the Dzogchen preliminary practices by Patrul Rinpoché (1808–87); and likewise many other texts belonging to the Early Translation tradition teach lamrim. The Dharma Lord Sakya Pandita's text *Clarifying the Sage's Intent* is a combination of stages of the path and mind training, and the instruction manuals on the three perceptions within path-and-result literature are entirely lamrim. [77] Likewise, in his *Jewel Ornament of Liberation*, the incomparable physician from Dakpo, Gampopa, teaches the four thought transformations, which turn the mind toward Dharma in a slightly divergent order; however, the overall style of the texts are in accordance, as exemplified by the multitudes of teachings on the subject of lamrim.

Stages of the path literature condense the essence of all scriptures and are like introductions for clearly seeing the nature of our own body, speech, mind, in addition to their qualities and faults. Lamrim is furthermore an easy practice of profound advice correctly teaching what to adopt and discard and, therefore, when interested persons practice this system, the manner in which the text progresses and its outlines need not be followed in the exact order; rather, take them as examples and connect them back to the experience of your own contextualized environment, habits, capabilities, what you need to give up at present, and so forth. Take these medicinal lamrim texts as you see fit for your individual needs—adding and subtracting the extensive or condensed sections as necessary, and above all holding them as a means to benefit your being.

The source texts for that, renowned as the "stages of the path of the three persons," of course link back to the perfection of wisdom treatises contained in the Kangyur. Further illustrations are those texts that the Arhat Dharmatrāta composed in order to abridge the Buddha's teachings such as his *Collection of Verses* and its commentary, and the *Sūtra Requested by Sāgaramati* and so forth. As for treatise source texts in the Tengyur, there are the glorious protector Nāgārjuna's *Precious Garland*, *Letter to a Friend*, *Commentary on Bodhicitta*, and so forth, and Ārya Asaṅga's treatises related to the grounds (*bhūmi*). In particular, there are those texts related to training bodhicitta: Śāntideva's *Compendium of Trainings* and *Way of the Bodhisattva*. [78]

THE MEANING OF "STAGES OF THE PATH TO ENLIGHTENMENT"

The meaning of the word "enlightenment," or *jangchup* (*byang chub*) in Tibetan, is the purification of all faults through applying their antidotes. One thus becomes purified (*jang*), and achieves the complete perfection (*chub*) of all qualities in the mind for the sake of attaining our ultimate goal—complete, unsurpassable enlightenment. The methods for achieving this—that is, the development of one's mind—are the stages of the path of the three persons taught as a series of instructions for a single person to achieve awakening in a single sitting, and thus are called "stages of the path to enlightenment."

The word "person," or *puruṣa* in Sanskrit, in the phrase "three persons" refers to a capable being. As for ourselves, too, we will develop the courage to purify all stains of dualistic appearances and the negative behavior left by them and thus become capable in applying antidotes to the afflictions. And not only to our own afflictions, but those of all sentient beings. When one generates such enthusiasm and capability to train in the path, one is termed a puruṣa. How this applies to the presentation of persons of small, middle, and great scope is clear in the section below, "How to Take Full Advantage of a Life of Leisure and Opportunity."

Well then, what is the way to tame our mind based on the stages of the path of the three persons? When introducing our object of refuge in the context of the stages of the path in common with persons of small and middle scope, we are introduced to (1) the object to be achieved, the Dharma jewel that is nirvana; (2) the one who unerringly teaches how to achieve that, the Buddha; and (3) his followers, the Sangha. Accomplishing this ultimate goal exactly as intended depends on the immediately pressing need to restrain the discordant conditions—negative behavior arising from the afflictions.

Persons of Small Scope

One needs to see that there is fault in engaging in the afflicted behavior of the ten nonvirtues and that such behavior makes us vile. [79] If one does not have an informed conviction on the basis of karmic cause and effect of the actual practice of abandoning the ten nonvirtues through understanding the benefits of applying antidotes and restraining from such behavior, one cannot understand the need for practicing virtue and turning away from misdeeds.

Starting with refuge based on informed faith, one trains one's conviction in karmic causality, which is included in the precepts of refuge, and practices adopting and discarding certain behaviors. This is the essence of the stages of the path of persons of small scope. Regarding that, if one gets mixed up with the eight worldly concerns for this life, then one cannot develop a quality practice. However much one tries one will always be at risk of linking one's practice with deception and so forth. Thus, pure refuge comes from contemplating that this life is without essence and without remaining long we must go to the next life, and so too is the happiness and suffering of future lives and, especially, the suffering of the lower realms.

Therefore, the first stage involves restraining bad behavior by utilizing as secondary practices the contemplation of both (1) the difficulty of finding precious leisure and opportunity, and (2) death and impermanence.

In summary, aiming for a higher rebirth through abstaining from negative behavior that arises due to the afflictions constitutes the stages of the path in common with persons of small scope. Thus, when one begins refraining from negative behavior arising from afflictions, one has taken the first step toward liberation.

Persons of Middle Scope

Then, one holds as one's aim the abandonment of those afflictions that give rise to negative behavior through applying antidotes and the manifestation of nirvana—a separation in which afflictions are exhausted into the dharmadhātu. Taking these as one's goal, through the three trainings of *wisdom* that directly purifies afflictions, *concentration* that generates it, and the *ethics* that are the basis of that, one directly applies the antidotes to afflictions. These paths of purification are the stages of the path in common with persons of middle scope. [80] Therefore, the actual practice of the stages of the path is posited from the persons of middle scope onward.

Persons of Great Scope

Then, contemplating how one is tormented by the general and spe-cific sufferings of samsara, one experiences a powerful generation of renunciation seeking liberation. Based on that, one shifts focus to how other beings suffer in the same way, and through habituating oneself with this fact one generates the mind seeking the welfare of others. Furthermore, through understanding that it is possible for oneself to achieve liberation, one sees that all sentient beings are likewise able, if they each put in the effort. Thus, one gives rise to the attitude seeking enlightenment for the sake of all sentient beings. The stages of the path of persons of greater scope are the trainings in the general and specific bodhisattva conduct related to this mind.

The Boundaries for the Three Types of Beings

Taking a good look at oneself, until we have disengaged from the emphasis on this life—that is, so long as we still have strong clinging to food, clothing, and pleasant conversation, or to riches, possessions, and so forth—then we still have not reached the starting point of the person of small scope. Until one has disengaged from the emphasis on future lives, retaining strong clinging to the delights of cyclic existence, one has not reached the starting boundary of the person of middle scope. Lastly, until one has given rise to the uncontrived mind seeking enlightenment for the sake of others based on an attitude of cherishing others more than oneself, one has not reached the beginning boundary of the person of great scope.

The Virtuous Middle: The Explanation
of the Meaning of the Text

**The virtuous middle is the explanation of the meaning of the text.
With respect to the practice and so forth of the** stages of the path to
enlightenment applied to the **direct instructions,** there are a variety
of **instructions contained within the individual lineages I have put
great effort into listening to and contemplating,** such as explanatory
instructions, direct instructions (*dmar khrid*), experiential instructions
(*myong khrid*), and practice instructions (*nyams khrid*). [81] *Explanatory
instructions* are a tradition of instructions in which one primarily draws
conclusions based on scripture and logic. The great lord Lama Tsongkhapa authored his *Great Treatise on the Stages of the Path* primarily in
the style of explanatory instructions, in which there is a strong focus
on refuting others' views and asserting one's own position. This is
opposed to his *Middle-Length* treatise on the stages of the path in which
he emphasizes the sustaining of meditation observations and aspects,
thus not presenting instructions in which conclusions are drawn, just
as he said:

> Those who know how to bring all these explanations into
> their practice seem to hardly exist. Therefore, I will create a
> separate summary of what to sustain in meditation.

Direct instructions are like the instructions of a doctor, wherein they
cut open a corpse, laying bare the entrails such as the five vital organs
and six hollow organs, pointing things out in great detail. In the same

vein, the way one should meditate while practicing, and the way discursive thoughts appear to mind during meditation, and so forth, are pointed out by the guru through their own experience. Furthermore, while the disciple meditates in this manner, the guru sequentially bestows focal objects of meditation.

Experiential instructions teach the individual ways to sustain focal objects of authoritative texts through the experience of the guru. Until the disciple has given rise to experience during a round of focusing on an object, they are made to strive in sustaining certain observations and mental aspects; they are then instructed on a new round of contemplation in accordance with the stages of excellently generating experience. Whether it takes months, or even years, the instructions are given as the disciple meditates.

Practice instructions are not those in which a guru teaches from whatever experience they may have while the disciple accrues a general understanding of the words. It is a tradition of instruction in which one accumulates as much experience as possible while sustaining the instructed focal object.

In this regard, the Sakyas have the "four explanations"—a practice from the path-and-result tradition. At the conclusion of the daily teachings, the essence of the explanation is repeated once with a strong emphasis on the way to sustain the meditative focal objects. [82] Then, the meaning of that explanation is repeated in an even more concise manner, thus rendering three explanations. Then the following day, at the beginning of the teachings, another concise summary of those is given again, and so four explanations are given in total.

In their tradition, each day, after the teaching session has ended, the student returns to their dwelling and first performs either extensive or brief preparatory practices, or the seven-limb practice, in order to accumulate merit and purify obscurations. Then, they diligently bring to mind the daily instructions, engaging in analytical meditation on the reasonings related to each. At the end of the analysis, they sustain the instructed focal object in placement meditation. It is excellent if they can also do that in the early hours of the next morning. With the dedication of merit during the concluding part, the end is "ornamented," and thus the sessions and their breaks are mutually beneficial.

HOW TO LISTEN TO AND EXPLAIN THE TEACHINGS POSSESSING THE TWO GREATNESSES

How to listen to and explain the teachings possessing the two greatnesses has three parts:

- A. How to listen to the teachings
- B. How to explain the teachings
- C. How [a session] should be concluded in relation to both hearing and explaining the teachings

How to listen to the teachings [has three parts:]

1. Contemplating the benefits of listening to the teachings
2. Developing reverence for the teaching and the instructor
3. How to actually listen to the teachings

How to actually listen to the teachings has two parts:

a. Abandoning the three faults of a vessel
b. Reliance on the six discernments

Reliance on the six discernments has six parts:

1) Discernment of oneself as a patient
2) Discernment of the instructor as a doctor

3) Discernment of the instructions as medicine[48]
4) Discernment of serious practice as a cure
5) Discernment of the tathāgatas as excellent beings
6) Discernment that the teachings [should] remain for a long time

How to explain the teachings [has four parts:]

1. Contemplating the benefits of explaining the teachings [83]
2. Generating reverence for the teacher and the teachings
3. The requisite attitude and preparations for explaining the teachings
4. Differentiating between those to whom one should and should not explain the teaching

Regarding this, the teachings of the gentle protector Tsongkhapa's *Great Treatise on the Stages of the Path* were passed down **from** his direct disciple, **venerable Sherab Sengé**, to the omniscient Gendun Drup, then to Gendun Gyatso, Sönam Gyatso, and so forth, **up to the root guru** of the Great Fifth Dalai Lama. They were successively passed on from there, and I received the instruction lineage of this text, *Oral Transmission of Mañjuśrī*, from my abbot and tutor, Ling Rinpoché Dorjé Chang (1903–83).

Thus, without a break in the transmission of the extant instruction lineages of *The Oral Transmission of Mañjuśrī*, in conjunction with Panchen Losang Yeshe's (1663–1737) *Swift Path*, and likewise Panchen Losang Chökyi Gyaltsen's *Easy Path*, the following explanations and so forth were given:

A clean and appealing place . . .

One should **thoroughly clean one's dwelling that accords with the place and time**—whatever place is easy for you to practice in.

In keeping with that taught in the perfection of wisdom sutras, one should generate reverence for the Teacher and the teachings. The Teacher was free of all faults and was endowed with all qualities primarily due to his practice of the Dharma of the great mother—the perfection of wisdom. In the context of the perfection of wisdom treatises authored by the Bhagavan on the topic of the mother, just as the Teacher honored his own seat by arranging it himself and so forth, one should arrange a high seat such as a lion throne for one's Dharma teacher, ornamenting it with garlands of flowers and arranging offerings.

Arranging a seat with such respect is to demonstrate the greatness of the teachings, not to show the high status of the lama. [84] Erecting higher and lower thrones according to the status of the lama, and so on, are merely societal habits.

One should generate the respectful discrimination that the teacher of the Dharma is like a buddha. Through this one accumulates great waves of merit, as explained in the section below on the way to rely on the spiritual teacher. The guru first makes prostrations to the throne; however, they are not prostrations to an empty throne—in the space above the throne are the lineage gurus of the Dharma to be visualized. Three prostrations are made as one visualizes receiving their blessings. When sitting on the throne, one should recite from sutra:

> Like a star, hallucination, candle,
> magical illusion, dewdrop, bubble,
> dream, lightning or a cloud—
> view all compounded phenomena to be like this.

Having recited that, one should snap one's fingers and remember that all phenomena lack essence due to their impermanence. This is to combat the danger of generating pride when one sits on a throne. With regard to the guru who teaches the Dharma, **it says in the *Kṣiti-garbha Sūtra***:

> **Listen to the teaching with single-pointed faith and**
>   **veneration.**
> **Do not ridicule and deprecate [the teacher].**
> **To venerate the expounder of Dharma,**
> **is to recognize that they are akin to the Buddha.**

Just as **it is said that one should prevent inauspiciousness and disrespect from the outset,** one must listen to the teachings with great respect. Thus, contemplation of the benefits of listening to the Dharma first is for the sake of joy arising in the listener. It is important one first understands the benefits of listening to the Dharma. As it says in the *Garland of Birth Stories*:

> Listening is the lamp that dispels the darkness of ignorance;
> the highest jewel that thieves cannot steal;
> a weapon that destroys the enemy of delusion;
> the best of companions that instructs in methods;
> the stable friend in times of distress; [85]
> the surest medicine against sorrow;
> the strongest army to combat swathes of misdeeds;
> the highest treasure of glory and renown;
> the highest gift when meeting with virtuous beings;
> that which pleases congregations of wise ones.

If one contemplates the meaning of this, it is that listening to the Dharma and applying the meaning of it to oneself is beneficial in all contexts, and furthermore that there is benefit insofar as there are not feelings of hardship while listening to the teachings, and so forth. In order for listening to such beneficial Dharma to become like medicine for taming one's mind, from the outset one must listen with faith, respect, and joy, generating reverence for the Dharma and the teacher.

Whatever understanding the listener retains of the Dharma explanation, and however much confusion is cleared away through that, that is how much benefit the Dharma teacher receives. Furthermore, however much others' discernment is broadened, to that extent one's own discernment will increase; this we can bear witness to.

If one has the opportunity to listen to or teach the Dharma, **one should first recite the mantra subjugating demons that prevents them coming within one hundred leagues, as said in the *Sūtra Requested by Sāgaramati*. However, since it is possible one is not successful in reciting the mantra** correctly, **the *Heart Sūtra* must be recited three times as a substitute. Next, one should perform, in sequence, supplications to the entirety of the stages of the path lineage gurus from the Buddha to one's root guru, up to and including the mandala offering.**

It is not sufficient that beginners be taught practice manuals in the manner of a teacher giving finger-pointing explanations; that is, textual exegesis in which certain parts are emphasized and other parts left aside—**simple and easy Dharma** of vague explanations. Those listening to the Dharma should take it to heart as they are being introduced to their own minds, investigating if their mental attitudes during a twenty-four-hour period accord with the intention of the scriptures as taught by the guru. [86] Otherwise, if there is a huge disconnect between our mind and the Dharma, it is not helpful for taming our minds. Therefore, **it is vital to use one's intellect unstained by one's own fabrications to analyze the greater and finer points of the beginning, middle and end practices** mentioned above.

With correct altruistic intention and preparations in the context of listening to and explaining the Dharma, **for the sake of attaining the state of perfect, complete buddhahood for all sentient beings** equal to the limits of space, protector Nāgārjuna and Ārya Asaṅga, in dependence on the kindness of the two regents and through their own ability, without relying on other instructors, excellently opened the chariot way for all heaps of profound and vast excellent Dharma taught by the Teacher, the one gone to bliss. Atiśa Śrī Dīpaṃkara's excellent teachings are the single merging of these rivers of Dharma into the way of the Mahāyāna. Coming to an understanding of these teachings through hearing, contemplating, and meditation is the source of all happiness and good that comes from clearing away all the webs of existence and peace. As it says in the *Collection of Indicative Verses*:

> Through hearing one comes to understand all Dharma;
> through hearing one overcomes misdeeds;
> through hearing one abandons the improper;
> through hearing one attains nirvana.

Therefore, first settle your understanding of them through hearing. Without hearing the teachings, one cannot contemplate their meaning, and then there can be no meditation based on that contemplation. Therefore, it is extremely important to first listen.

Take an example of something in this life, like a well-paying occupation that is considered good and respectable work. If one has such a job it is generally considered to make life happier. In order to acquire the level of knowledge and skills necessary for such a position, one must first train with an expert and understand explanations contained in textbooks on the topic. [87] As one accumulates practical experience, one gains familiarity and certainty. Thus, one must become a skilled person in this way, and it is unfeasible that there could be an expert who has no training or experience. Likewise, if one must put effort into accumulating such a collection of causes in order to gain knowledge that gives happiness in just this life, what need to mention the collection of causes that must be accumulated to bring about a perpetually virtuous state in this life and the next, and for oneself and others.

Even if one has perfect external conditions, if one's mind is constrained by continuous jealously, rivalry, hopes, and fears, then both temporary and long-term happiness completely disappear. Therefore, one must understand that a happy life depends upon one's mind. Since we can bring about that happiness through Dharma instructions and practices, one must understand those first. If not, one will not know how to practice. Through correct understanding and continual, gradual, and thorough analysis, one finds trusting conviction. Through this decisiveness, one's mind is moved; through repeated familiarization with something, one's whole mind becomes the nature of that.

Take, for example, meditation on compassion. In the beginning one gains an understanding of compassion through hearing; then, through repeated contemplation on the benefits of compassion and the reasons for meditating on it, an awareness seeking it from the depths of one's heart gradually arises. Through further striving and meditation, the awareness seeking compassion and the compassion it seeks no longer remain separate; the original mind which gained an understanding of compassion transforms into compassion itself. One must develop the practice that shifts every single perspective to that of the object of meditation that thinks, "How terrible it is that all sentient beings are tormented by suffering." [88] Thus, one needs conviction in this from the depths of one's heart, gained through intense familiarization—it is not possible if one has shaky conviction.

Therefore, one must repeatedly engage in analysis and study from the outset. Thus, in dependence upon the wisdom arisen from hearing, one sequentially develops the wisdom arisen from contemplation and the wisdom arisen from meditation. Through hearing one generally comes to understand Dharma; in particular, through hearing the basket of discipline and practicing its subject—the training in ethical conduct—one stops misdeeds. Through listening to the basket of sutras one gains ascertainment of the training in meditative stabilization. Then, mental distractions are pacified, and awareness abides steadfast on the given focal object. Through that one is able to give up what is meaningless.

Through comprehensively hearing the subject matter of the basket of manifest knowledge, which is the wisdom realizing selflessness, then the wisdoms of contemplation and meditation arise in one's continuum. Acquainting oneself with those, one progressively perfects familiarization until one attains nirvana. Therefore, the way of hearing is as said **in the sutras:**

Listen well, thoroughly, and remember!

Abandon the three faults of a vessel: (1) being upside down, (2) dirty, and (3) having a leaky bottom.[49] The first, an upside-down vessel, refers to the time of listening to the teachings, when one is physically present but one is either falling asleep or one's mind wanders outside. If this is the case, then since our ears and mind are not focused, nothing is retained by our awareness. Just like an upside-down vessel, no matter how much water and so forth is poured, it will not enter. Instead, one should concentrate like a deer listening to beautiful sounds, with all parts of our mind undistracted. Watch the guru with your eyes and focus well on the Dharma they teach, up to the tone of their voice. In order to retain the meaning of what is taught we must concentrate single-pointedly. [89]

The second, the fault of a leaky vessel, refers to a vessel that, although not turned upside down, has a leaking base. No matter how much water and so forth is poured in, it cannot be filled, and just runs out the bottom. Likewise, although one might listen to the teachings of the guru, if one does not retain them, after the teachings finish nothing comes to mind having forgotten them. Thus, we become like a leaky pot. Therefore, when listening to the teachings, make a promise not to forget them and remind yourself as you listen. According to the occasion, record the teachings, take notes, and so forth, any active means to continually retain the meaning of the teachings. However, if one relies too heavily on taking notes and so forth, when one does not have them, then one cannot remember anything, just like the saying "knowledge left in the books."

Khunu Lama Rinpoché Tenzin Gyaltsen's (1894–1977) level of effort and exertion was so outstanding that he attained ultimate perfect recall. He was able to immediately reproduce all subtleties of teachings he had heard thirty or forty years prior without relying on any notes. Likewise, when I was receiving teachings on the fifth part of the *Kalāpa Grammar* from Yongdzin Ling Rinpoché, he informed me that because he had not seen the text since he last heard it thirty or forty years prior, he would have to scan over it quickly. He then went to take the text for the next day's teachings and read over it once briefly. The next day, when I was reading along and receiving the teaching, he was able to give a presentation of the meaning with no impediment and great certainty. We need to become like this. [90]

With respect to the third fault of a dirty vessel, if the vessel is unclean then whatever amazing food or drink you put in it will no longer be suitable to consume. In this way, if one's motivation is unclean when listening to the Dharma, or if one is preoccupied by something incompatible, it is unhelpful. It is wrong to ascertain the meaning of the words of Dharma solely for the sake of explaining them to others, or, especially in the case of tantric teachings, gaining fame and esteem through the acts of pacification, increase, magnetizing, and wrath[50] for the sake of the fleeting aims of this life of oneself and others. Likewise, being motivated by jealously, competition, triumphing over others, and so forth, is a huge mistake. Therefore, for the sake of all sentient beings—our mothers in past lives—listen to the words and remember the meaning of Dharma for the sake of attaining the state of complete, highest enlightenment. In the beginning, middle, and end we must be embraced by the essence of the pragmatic altruistic motivation; therefore the Bhagavān said, "Listen well, thoroughly, and remember!"

Following that, reliance on the six discernments was taught: thinking of (1) oneself as a patient, (2) the Dharma instructor as a doctor, (3) the teachings as medicine, (4) earnest practice as the way to cure disease, (5) the tathāgatas as holy beings, and (6) wishing that the teachings remain for a long time.

Discernment of Oneself as a Patient

All beings without exception want happiness and do not want suffering. The purpose of Dharma is to correctly show how to adopt virtue and discard nonvirtue, the causes of happiness and suffering. If we ourselves are able to seriously endeavor in multiple approaches to meditate on, for example, virtues such as compassion and faith through citing scripture, stating logical reasonings, and using concentration, only then will we be able to generate attitudes like compassion. [91] Such attitudes do not arise through minor conditions, unlike anger, pride, jealously, and so forth that do not require effort to bring about and need only the slightest of conditions, like a wood fire that bursts into flames upon adding some petrol.

Thus, that which leads to unhappiness, misfortune, birth, aging, sickness, and death—a variety of dependent sufferings—are the afflictions. They cause us to engage in actions that ruin ourselves and others, whereby we accumulate negative karma. Since this is the case, we must understand that afflictions, as exemplified by the three poisons, are ultimately the real enemy within us. Although they should be crushed as soon as they arise, our current situation is that we are heavily weighed down by afflictions, and due to this strong oppression we are at a point where, unable to rise up, we can barely catch a breath. Thus, because we are gripped by this chronic disease of afflictions, it is said we should maintain the discernment of ourselves as a patient.

Discernment of the Instructions as Medicine

The Buddhadharma is the supreme method that acts as an antidote to clear away the chronic disease of afflictions, and thus is like medicine.

Discernment of the Dharma Instructor as a Doctor

Someone who correctly gives instructions on the methods to clear away afflictions is like an adept doctor.

Discernment of Earnest Practice as the Way to Cure Disease

We need to actually take the medicine and rely on medical treatment in order to improve. We do not recover from sickness through making offerings and prostrations to the medicine. In this way, merely understanding the Dharma does not destroy one's afflictions; one must emphasize practical experience and maintain the discernment of earnest practice as the way to cure the disease of afflictions.

Discernment of the Tathāgatas as Holy Beings

Through the power of that attitude, the faith that sees the tathāgatas as the ultimate teachers and their qualities as kind, holy beings naturally generates from the depths of one's heart, and respectful discernment toward them arises. [92]

Wishing That the Teachings Remain for a Long Time

The teachings and instructions from such a teacher have, up until our lifetimes, been passed down in an undegenerated continuum as an instruction lineage, like stones passed from hand to hand. Through remembering the gurus' kindness, one naturally generates the discernment of thinking how wonderful it would be if these Dharma teachings remained for a long time.

In brief, bring to mind all the general and specific motivations, behaviors, and so forth related to listening to the Dharma and endeavor to listen. Regarding the holy Dharma to be heard, the

gently protecting lama and Dharma king, the great Tsongkhapa says
in his *Songs of Experience*:

> These stages of the path to enlightenment
> are the excellent transmissions from Nāgārjuna and Asaṅga—
> crown ornaments of the wise ones of this world,
> your banners of fame flutter resplendent among migrators.
>
> These transmissions are the king of powerful, precious oral
>   instructions,
> fulfilling the wishes of living beings.
> They are an ocean of glorious and excellent explanations,
> a confluence of the rivers of a thousand fine treatises.

The stages on the path to enlightenment, the great treasure of excellent
explanations which incorporate all important points of a thousand
fine treatises that extract the essence of the Bhagavān's teachings, are
superior by way of the four greatnesses and three special attributes.
Therefore, it is said:

> Through them one realizes all the Buddha's teachings are
>   noncontradictory,
> all teachings appear as personal instructions,
> one easily finds the intention of the conqueror,
> and one is protected from the abyss of terrible conduct.

This verse not only indicates the four greatnesses, but the attributes
of (1) the subject matter being perfectly complete, (2) being related to
the methods for taming the mind, and (3) a profound import related
to the guru's personal instructions. Thus *Songs of Experience* states
next:

If the great experts from India and Tibet,
those fortunate ones, relied upon the supreme instructions
of the stages of the path of the three beings, [93]
what intelligent person would not be captivated by these
    teachings?

All important points of the path traversed by all sugatas and the 84000 heaps of Dharma excellently expounded by the son of Śuddhodana, the Buddha, the incomparable guide, were first taught by the Teacher, and then the two charioteers independently commented on the intention of those teachings, which were in turn brought to definitive conclusion by the panditas—those foremost scholars of India—through excellent analysis and explanation. The mahāsiddhas put these into practice and gave rise to realizations, and thus the teachings became bases of conviction. All of these teachings that were unerringly transmitted from one to the other were condensed by the glorious Atiśa Dīpaṃkara, the Sole Deity, into the practice instructions of the stages of the path of the three persons, the *Lamp for the Path*, and so forth, which were propagated widely. Those that followed this system—the holders of the undegenerated conduct of scholasticism, ethics, and goodness, renowned as the Jowo Kadampas—pervaded this snowy land like the sky covers the earth. Thereafter, for the sake of once again eliminating the stains of misconceptions and a lack of realizations due to this degenerate age, Mañjughoṣa, the Dharma king Tsongkhapa, akin to a second great charioteer and wise in the dance of human existence, composed the renowned extensive and abridged treatises on the stages of the path. These unprecedented, excellently expounded great treatises do not engage in limited objects to be adopted and discarded on account of being biased toward particular higher and lower vehicle teachings of scripture and realization. Rather, they are in keeping with the meaning of the spiritual guide Dromtönpa when he said:

The one who knows how to practice the teachings as a four-sided path is my guru.[51]

The aforementioned treatises on the stages of the path that take *Lamp for the Path* as their foundation bring together all essential points of the Buddha's teachings into the stages of the path of the three beings. [94] Therefore, they are methods by which one can realize all teachings as noncontradictory.

Furthermore, from among the individual dispositions and inclinations of trainees, the Buddha taught to those of lesser aptitude, or beginners, that even slightly engaging in killing, stealing, sexual misconduct, lies, divisive speech, harsh speech, gossip, and so forth is by nature harmful, and lacks any benefit for others. The buddha never permitted those seven acts of body and speech—killing and so forth— in a context where it brought no benefit to others, and he prohibited turning the mind toward those. However, once the discernment of a person has considerably increased and one has an altruistic special intention that is stable and vast, then in extraordinary circumstances of time and place wherein there is an exceptional, great purpose to benefit others, performing those seven acts of body and speech was permitted.

For those beings who are unable to meditate on mind generation, which engenders positive mindsets for the sake of all sentient beings, it was emphatically stated that since one must achieve freedom from cyclic existence, the mind seeking liberation is extremely important and therefore one must generate the mind wishing for liberation. In other authoritative treatises, it was taught as a mistake to seek liberation from samsara for oneself alone, and therefore inappropriate to generate a mindset thinking, "If only I could attain liberation." It is more important to achieve the aims of others, and thus there exists instructions on having to remain in cyclic existence for that sake.

At first glance these may seem contradictory, but the Bhagavān gave different teachings regarding practices that accord with the stages of progression of the mind of a single being at earlier and later times. Therefore, they must be practiced in successive order. Only with some exceptions can we separate some aspects into principles of the path, and others into branches. [95] From this we can clearly understand that everything must be practiced, just as it is stated in the *Great Treatise on the Stages of the Path*. Thus, it is said that the greatness of being able to realize all teachings as noncontradictory comes in dependence on this treatise.

A person who has not generated the wish for liberation from the suffering of the three lower realms due to sincere fear—a mindset akin to the disgust a prisoner has toward their prison—which is taught in the context of the person of small scope, is not able to generate the uncontrived attitude of wishing for definite emergence from samsara taught in the context of the middle scope being which is seeing the nature of samsara as a blazing expanse due to having no desirous craving for the marvels of the higher states of gods and humans.

If the doctrine that it is proper to give up attachment to one's body, and that the body is something to be discarded, is taught to someone who is a beginner and a vessel for the path of persons of small scope, they will find themselves completely ungrounded. Instead of that, if it is explained to them that our present human body of leisure and fortune is extremely fundamental for achieving the aims of oneself and others, and is a precious opportunity full of potential that should not be wasted, it is much easier for them to take. Based on that, they develop the discernment of their human body having leisure and opportunities as a wish-fulfilling jewel. Aspiring to attain such a body even in their next life, they practice the ethics of abandoning the ten nonvirtues and so forth, developing the level of their mind in stages.

At a certain point, they are taught that even this human body that arose through the power of afflictions is unclean, has no essence, is to be discarded, and is not suitable to be attached to, and that one must achieve liberation in which the continuum of rebirth of these appropriated aggregates is severed. Everything must be practiced in accordance with the stages of development of the individual person; nothing is to be discarded, and there is no contradiction. [96]

Likewise, **without the slightest experience of disgust for samsara, how is it possible to generate fully qualified, uncontrived great compassion observing other sentient beings? Without great compassion, a bodhisattva who trains in the conduct of the six perfections and the attitude of generating the mind aimed at enlightenment is equivalent to a sky flower,** an example of something that does not exist. **Furthermore, the explicit teachings on the methods for liberation from lower realms and those on giving up one's own aims and taking responsibility for others are seemingly contradictory on a literal level and lead to doubt. However,** even though the explicit wording seems contradictory at first, **with respect to the meaning, in the manner of cause and effect, or of principals and branches of the path, all teachings must act as a support for the other as conditions for a single person to attain enlightenment.**

From the very outset, starting with training the mind with respect to leisure and opportunities, there is no contradiction with practicing the three trainings for the sake of attaining a good future rebirth and bringing an end to rebirth. On the contrary, they are completely related in that they are necessary to practice. Through those prerequisites, the focus of meditating on one's own suffering is shifted to that of others through meditating on compassion, and thus one trains in a cause-and-effect process in dependence on this teaching. Furthermore, everything taught in the lamrim literature is said to be a fundamental prerequisite, or branch, in the context of the secret mantra vehicle.

In summary, overcoming attachment to the experiences of this life, overcoming attachment to the experiences of the next life, and practicing the jewel of bodhicitta that discards the focus on one's own aims and holds others dearer than oneself, are all indispensable foundations even in the practice of secret mantra. Therefore, the first of the four greatnesses—**the greatness of realizing all teachings to be noncontradictory**—is possessed by this treatise. [97] Therefore, the lamrim literature possesses the greatness of expressive words. It is taught that the four greatnesses of their subject matter must be present in one's own continuum, and one must train in them by all means. Therefore, the various presentations of the path taught for the sake of the trainees of the three vehicles—the three lineage beings—are the prerequisite branches for entering into the Mahāyāna. In order to take care of the other lineage beings, knowledge of the śrāvaka path, the pratyekabuddha path, and the Mahāyāna path should all be generated, understood, and brought to completion, as taught in the perfection of wisdom sutras. As venerable Maitreya also said in the homage verse of the *Abhisamayālaṃkāra*:

> Those who benefit migrators and achieve the aims of this
> world only through the knower of paths . . .

This exemplifies that the Buddha's teachings that take into account the huge responsibility of bodhisattvas and tantric practitioners wherein they teach that they are not permitted to listen to nor contemplate śrāvaka treatises, nor that it is suitable for them to stay in the dwelling of a practitioner of śrāvaka Dharma for seven days, must also be meditated on as secondary, in order that one takes care of others and increases one's own realizations.

When practicing such points, it is as said in *Applying the Advice of the Three Jewels***:**

> **Although having listened extensively, one is bereft of**
> **Dharma.**
> **This is the fault of the teachings not appearing as instructions.**

This is a case of not understanding the vital point of proving the teachings of realization through the cause: an understanding of the scriptural teachings. Thus, the great yogi Jangchup Rinchen states:

> Someone who has reached certainty about a pithy little volume cannot be said to know all the topics of instructions; this is said about someone who understands all of the Buddha's teachings as instructions.

The method for achieving even the slightest happiness and so on of higher rebirths and definite goodness is contained either explicitly or implicitly the Buddha's stainless speech. However, since those are vast and profound, they were clarified further in śāstras commentaries, which unravel the intention for those beings who find them difficult to understand. [98] There are no unofficial pith instructions of practices left unexplained in the Buddha's discourses or the scholars' treatises. Ascertaining that all points extensively explained in those are condensed and complete in this stages of the path treatise in a comprehensive manner through the preparatory, actual, and conclusion stages is the greatness of all teachings appearing as instructions.

Some think that the great authoritative treatises function merely to eliminate the superimpositions of logic and refute certain Buddhist and non-Buddhist views and tenets, and thus that the essential meaning does not need to be practiced. Therefore, they think that studying is unnecessary, and that pith instructions that are the object of practice exist elsewhere. Saying that one has a consolidated Dharma practice even though one has not studied the authoritative treatises is a misunderstanding. Generally speaking, "personal instructions" refers to methods that cause one to easily realize the intended meaning of the Buddha's teachings on the vast and profound paths that accomplish liberation and omniscience. Therefore, if it is something that helps one understand the meaning of the spoken word of the Buddha, the Kangyur, numbering around one hundred volumes as translated into Tibetan, or to understand the approximately two-hundred-twenty-volume commentarial canon, the Tengyur of the scholars from the Land of the Āryas that unravels their intention, then it is a pith instruction.

Other than that, if one finds that however much one studies a so-called pith instruction that it leads to greater disconnect from the Kangyur or Tengyur, it is clearly either the fault of not thoroughly understanding the actual pith instruction, or a sign that one had no firm conviction in the treatise or instruction considered to be a pith instruction. Thus, "explanatory Dharma" and "practical Dharma" are not different things; the 84000 heaps of Dharma taught by the Buddha are all various methods for taming our own stubborn mind. [99]

Since this is the case, a treatise will enable us to see all teachings as instructions if it is able to holistically consolidate the teachings of the Kangyur and Tengyur as methods for taming our mind. In particular, since there are different phases of the minds of Dharma practitioners—juvenile, mature, and old—if one understands the different ways to practice, considering the different stages of development of the mind in accordance with those phases, then one realizes all of the Buddha's teachings as noncontradictory and all teachings without exception appear as instructions; thus, one must understand that all hearing, contemplation, and practice can come about through a single great treatise.

If all scriptures completely appear as instructions, and the aforementioned words of the Buddha and their expository treatises can be delineated through hearing and contemplation, then one might wonder why there are separate volumes given the names *Lamp for the Path*, *Stages of the Teachings*, or *Stages of the Path*. As the power of disciples' discriminating intellect declines due to the times, their meaning becomes more difficult to realize, and there is an inability

to clear up uncertainty regarding the numerous aspects of any given phrase. Therefore, in dependence on the pith instructions of an uninterrupted succession of holy beings, starting from the perfectly complete Buddha, they have been included within the lamrim treatises, and so forth.

Thus, do not think the extensive phrases and meaning contained within the 84000 heaps of Dharma, and so forth, do not fit into lamrim, and therefore that there must be omissions or additions, because it is not necessary that all of the words be completely included since all of the meaning is contained. For example, due to the huge aggregation of medicinal plants in camphor-25, a small dosage of it, which contains all varieties of medicines, will alleviate heat illnesses—one does not need to eat the entire mass of medicinal plants. For that reason these teachings possess the greatness of easily finding the intention of the victor in dependence on the guru's pith instructions. [100]

Thus, it is completely impossible that there could be an antidote to the two obscurations—the objects of abandonment in the context of one person progressing as an ordinary being toward buddhahood—that has not been taught in the Buddha's teachings and their commentaries. Furthermore, as the meaning of all teachings is subsumed in this treatise, through practicing this system all doors leading to faults are closed. From the *Sūtra Gathering All Threads*:

> Mañjuśrī, the karmic obscurations from discarding the holy Dharma are subtle. Mañjuśrī, perceiving some teachings of the Sugata as good and some as bad is to discard the Dharma.

Such faults of abandoning the Dharma are eliminated, and thus these teachings possess the greatness of exceedingly negative behavior stopping by itself.

Regarding the practice of the stages of guiding disciples through this actual instruction that possesses the four greatnesses, there are three stages: preliminary, actual, and conclusion.

First, with regard to the preliminaries, the earlier stages of the paths of the three beings act as preliminaries for the later ones. Therefore, taking the greater scope being's training in bodhicitta itself as the main basis, the small scope and middle scope beings are included within the preliminaries; however, since the methods of mind training and so forth share similarities, it is of course not unsuitable, as is said in the *Seven-Point Mind Training*:

> First train in the preliminaries.

In the section titled "training in the general conduct" it lists: (1) the general way to train in the Mahāyāna, and (2) the particular way to train in the Vajra Vehicle. Thus, in the context of mantra, the topics regarding conduct are also preliminaries. Regarding whether something is a preliminary or actual practice, generally the paths in common with persons of small and middle scope are preliminaries, and training in bodhicitta is the actual practice. Or, by way of the aforementioned division of the sections of general conduct, topics concerning tantra would be the actual practice, and the conduct of the stages of the path of the three types of beings would be preliminaries. [101]

Thus, whether something is a preliminary or an actual practice is relative; hence one needs to differentiate preliminaries and actual practices once the instructed focal object has been identified, otherwise it is just like designating a "close" mountain in dependence on a far mountain, and a "far" mountain in dependence on a close mountain. Many wander on a mistaken path having not identified the context; it is important that one relies on the existing lineage gurus for the practices instructions from holy lineage gurus of the past. Thus, from the topics of the difficulty finding leisure and

opportunity up to special insight, all must be practiced as the actual
paths in that system.

Concluding Verses

In the ears of those who are honest and have abandoned
the faults of an impure vessel, the melodious Dharma
heard from the mouth of the tutor
is received through eons of merit.

Specifically, the Dharma having four greatnesses,
the quintessence of the minds of all Indian and Tibetan
    masters,
the impartial medicine helping superior and inferior
    migrators,
and the rival of ambrosia, that path is difficult to find.

When those with the good fortune to practice such a supreme
    path
through hearing, contemplating, and meditating
find some small gain, they prolong its continuance,
their minds stirred by strong revulsion and disillusionment.

On the face of a high mountain away from hustle and bustle,
surrounded by green forest and flowers,
in a small stone hut that fits oneself
together with a friend who is one's second shadow,

Aside from the sounds of a gently flowing river
and the noises of calm wild animals,
idle chatter that generates the three poisons,
the thorn in the side of concentration, is absent.

With a broom, retreat clothing, and alms,

one is not tainted by the poison of livelihoods and improper
offerings.

one's body, speech, and mind can thus be moved toward the
virtuous and pure,

reaching the summit of eternal happiness. [102]

The Stages of Guiding Disciples with the Actual Instructions

WHEN EXPLAINING THE STAGES of guiding disciples with the actual instructions, first it is appropriate to briefly discuss foundational topics related to the instructions. Regarding this, Nāgārjuna, in his *Precious Garland of the Middle Way*, teaches sixteen Dharmas that are methods for first achieving higher rebirths. These are thirteen actions to be abandoned and three to be adopted: abandoning the ten nonvirtues, abstaining from alcohol, abandoning wrong livelihoods, abandoning violence, respectful generosity, making appropriate offerings, and love. Following that, he taught the stages for achieving definite goodness (*nges legs*), and within that context of achieving definite goodness he guides disciples through teaching emptiness.

Furthermore, in the protector Nāgārjuna's *Commentary on Bodhicitta*, he quotes the *Guhyasamāja Root Tantra* thus:

> Due to the sameness of phenomena in being selfless,
> one's mind is primordially unproduced,
> devoid of all entities,
> exempt from the skandhas, elements, sense-spheres,
> the apprehender and apprehended,
> in the nature of emptiness.

When commenting on this, Nāgārjuna first taught the view of selflessness—emptiness, or ultimate bodhicitta—and followed that with conventional bodhicitta. Finding ascertainment of the view of emptiness through contemplation, after gaining a correct understanding from hearing, if one excellently develops an experience arisen from meditation, one sees it is possible to generate a mind that damages grasping at true existence—the cause of suffering. One then realizes that suffering can be exhausted, and if one realizes that there are powerful antidotes for the causes of suffering, one sees that there is an end to the results that suffering produces, and then there will be no doubt that compassion longing for migrators will arise. Thus were the stages taught.

The *Commentary on Bodhicitta* is a treatise that comments on that root verse of the *Guhyasamāja Root Tantra*, which was taught to intended trainees of extremely sharp faculty. [103] Therefore, once those particular trainees ascertain the view, the way they are guided in training in the practices of the paths of methods assisted by wisdom is different. If we analyze the two aforementioned teachings of Nāgārjuna, it seems that the way beings are guided in the *Precious Garland of the Middle Way* is intended for a general audience, and the style in his *Commentary on Bodhicitta* is for specific individuals.

Here, "instructions" in the phrase "actual instructions" refers to instructions for achieving definite goodness—the states of liberation and omniscience—which are the primary, ultimate instructions of the Buddha Bhagavān. In order to understand this, one must first be able to conceive that it is possible to attain the state of liberation and omniscience through the assistance of wisdom; through that, one must generate the mind striving for liberation.

The fourth outline, the stages of guiding disciples with the actual instructions, contains two outlines:

A. **The preliminary of relying on the spiritual teacher—the root of the path**
B. The stages of training the mind having relied on a guru

[With respect to this first outline, there are furthermore] preliminaries for relying on the spiritual teacher, which are refuge and so forth.

This is divided into:

- The preliminary mind of refuge
- The actual practice of the path of relying on the spiritual teacher

THE PRELIMINARY MIND OF REFUGE

A scholar once said that the beginning of all Dharma is solely the manner of reliance on a spiritual teacher, and therefore there is no other preliminary Dharma to that. He presented many apparent sources for this position. However, if that were the case, then one would have to assert that a trainee for the stages of the path to enlightenment could train in the topics related to relying on a spiritual teacher [104] without having gone for refuge in the Three Jewels. This is not correct. Since that trainee has not gone for refuge, they do not fit the definition of being a Buddhist, and so could not be training in the stages of the path. Jowo Atiśa and Śāntipa differentiated Buddhists and non-Buddhists based on refuge, and it is said in the *Outlines of the Stages of the Path to Enlightenment* that "refuge is the entry door to the teachings."

Some say there is no contradiction with respect to mere refuge, but it is unreasonable with regard to mind generation, because the topics of the person of small scope come after that of relying on the spiritual teacher. I do not think such an explanation is logical, since the topics of the person of small scope contain actual practices of the person of small scope and also practices in common with them; out of those, the topic to be practiced in this context is not the seeking a mere higher future rebirth, but rather the practices in common with the person of small scope that form the basis of the paths of the persons of middle and great scope. Therefore, it was said:

> In order for beings with beginning karma
> to enter into the holy Dharma,
> the perfect Buddha taught the methods
> like an order of steps.

From the *Great Treatise on the Stages of the Path*:

> If the practices for the persons of small and medium scopes are preliminaries for the person of great scope, then they may as well be considered stages for the path of the person of great scope. Otherwise, why use the expression, "stages of the path shared with persons of small and medium scope"?

Therefore, the explanation in this context is directed at trainees of great scope, with persons of small scope taught as preliminaries. For this reason, not only is there no fault that it be qualified by mind generation, but it is excellent! The modes of Dharma of different contexts are taught in whichever way is appropriate.

If explained from the perspective of the Pāli Dharma lineage originating in India, the practices for relying on the resident teacher, abbot, and preceptor are rudimentary. [105] When we practice the Buddhadharma lineage of Nālandā that spread in the snowy land of Tibet, which includes the Mahāyāna, Hīnayāna, and Tantra Vehicle, we map out the path from the beginning, and follow those coordinates on the map up until the practice of highest yoga tantra. This is the reason why relying on a spiritual teacher is taught before beginning the stages of the path of persons of small scope. If one were to independently practice the path of persons of small scope, whether one would need to rely on a spiritual teacher as described in the stages of the path is doubtful.

When persons of small or medium scope are now mentioned in regard to the stages of the path, what should be understood are the stages of the path in common with persons of small and medium scope, as we are not discussing the paths that are unique to small and medium scope persons. However, it is the case that among practitioners of the path of small and medium scope there do exist practitioners who solely follow that of the small and medium scope, and therefore, in order to bring about maximum benefit to persons of high, average, and lesser intellect, training in the mindset of seeking higher rebirths is taught first. If it is taught how to achieve higher rebirths having generated that mind, those of lesser intellect have received exactly the Dharma topics that benefit them, and thus, according to the four thought transformations, one contemplates the difficulty of finding leisure and fortune, death and impermanence, karmic cause and effect, and the drawbacks of samsara; having done those, relying on the spiritual teacher, refuge, and so forth, are attributes that follow later.

In general, it is assumed that Tibetans either follow Buddhism or the Bon religion from a young age based on their birth region and the traditions of their parents. Before they receive Dharma teachings from a lama, they learn from their parents about the hells, [106] how it is wrong to kill insects, how they must recite the *oṃ maṇi padme hūṃ* mantra, and so forth—general presentations on virtue and negative actions, and karma and effect. This style of teaching Dharma is cultural. Alternatively, when giving a complete explanation of the vast and profound stages of Buddhism, as in Śāntideva's *Way of the Bodhisattva* and Āryadeva's *Four Hundred Verses*, many opposing views are debated, and thus the style of teaching revolves around refuting others, presenting one's own view, and disposing of further objections.

When the stages of the path literature is presented to them, the primary focus is on stages of easier practices.

Many stages of the path manuals start out with a section on relying on the spiritual teacher. It is explained that in order to have a real practice of relying on the spiritual teacher, one must rely by way of the two thoughts and actions—faith in the guru and respect that remembers their kindness. To increase faith and respect, the unique connection between the guru and buddhas is taught; it is impossible for the disciple to develop conviction in that and for the lama to guide a person in relying on the spiritual teacher if the disciple does not first have a correct assumption that the kind teacher is incredibly important, even if they have not gained solid ascertainment through reasoning of what a buddha or the Buddhadharma is.

Likewise, using the example of leisures and freedoms, with respect to meditation on the difficulty in finding a meaningful human rebirth having leisures and freedoms, it would be difficult to explain how to identify one's own leisures and freedoms to someone who does not believe in Buddhism. If someone has thus not fully understood the topics of leisures and freedoms, then since meditation on death and impermanence is not just about the statement, "You are going to die," but in fact to do with how terrible it would be if one died without having time to practice Dharma, it would be difficult to guide someone without any refuge whatsoever on the topic of impermanence. [107]

Thus, for the time being, it is not important whether a first-time listener to the stages of the path is a refined person or not. It is obvious that it is guidance for those who consider themselves Buddhists and those who have an affinity for Buddhism. That is why the mind of refuge is first explained briefly in this context. Following that is the way to rely on a spiritual teacher, the leisure and freedoms, death and impermanence, the suffering of lower realms, through to an extensive presentation on the mind of refuge, completely covering the nature of Buddha, Dharma, and Sangha.

This being the case, **my exceptional holy guru,** the glorious Khöntön Paljor Lhundrup, used the omniscient Sönam Gyatso's stages of path treatise, *Essence of Refined Gold,* **as a basis and presented an annotated supplement to the two stages of the path treatises** of the gentle protector Lama Tsongkhapa, and **therefore the mind of refuge is thus clarified within** *Essence of Refined Gold.* **Since there is no clarification of the mind of refuge within the greater treatises,** such as the *Middle-Length* and *Great Stages of the Path* treatises, **those charlatans who explain this without having heard the oral lineage, or having knowledge of the practices might boast, but they should acknowledge their faults.**

Therefore, going for refuge from the outset is as said in *Praise in Honor of One Worthy of Honor*:

> What trouble is there away from which
> you cannot lead migrating beings?
> What excellent thing is there
> that you cannot bestow on the world?

There is not another single cause that has not arisen through the power of the Buddha that frees beings from the troubles of cyclic existence and peace, or that affords enjoyment in temporary and ultimate happiness. Therefore, whether one is listening to or explaining the Dharma, or doing either of the three acts of listening, contemplating, and meditating, they must be conjoined with the spirit of refuge and mind generation.

Well, then, what is the way to go for refuge? The three objects of infallible refuge—Buddha, Dharma, and Sangha—were never taught as refuges for the sake of temporary, lesser purposes such as longevity, wealth, and so forth. [108] For those ends one can even place their hopes in worldly gods, nāgas, and so forth to offer some minor assistance. If one takes refuge in non-Buddhist gods such as Īśvara,

Brahmā, Viṣṇu, and so forth, one may occasionally accomplish their desired aims. Only if one depends on refuge in the Three Jewels is one able to attain ultimate liberation and the state of eternal happiness of an omniscience one, which is greater than the temporary happiness of higher rebirths. The purpose of calling the Three Jewels an "infallible refuge," and so forth, is as it is explained in greater detail in the later section on refuge.

Our teacher of refuge, **the Buddha who has exceptional qualities**, is not a buddha who from the outset was free from all faults and possessed all qualities; rather, he was like us, possessing many faults. If our continuum of consciousness meets with the right conditions, the afflictions of attachment and aversion will generate. Yet through the power of a true path that sees reality directly—a new antidote—arising in our continuum, even though its opposing class of contradictory factors might meet with the right conditions, it will make them unable to generate. Due to that one attains cessations, or "true cessations," of phenomena that are destroyed through the power of the antidote that is known as the *qualities of separation*, or *qualities of abandonment*. Having actualized such a cessation, however much the strength of the true path increases, it will result in the objects of abandonment of the opposing class of contradictory factors—objects of abandonment of the path of seeing, and objects of abandonment of the path of meditation—being abandoned in stages. Once they have all been abandoned, the ultimate cessation that is the destruction of two obscurations together with their imprints—a buddha's quality of abandonment—is actualized. Thus the Buddha who has exhausted all faults and possesses all qualities **arose** only **through** the power of practicing the Dharma Jewel that includes the two **holy dharmas of true cessations and paths**. [109]

Based on that, the Dharma Jewel is the most important, and more important than even the Buddha. **Since correctly accomplishing that Dharma too depends on trainee and nontrainee sangha, first prepare yourself with the vivid thought, "From this day on until I become a** buddha, I request the holy objects of refuge to be my protectors and defenders." Through the power of a yearning conviction that they have visibly come as my protector in a pleased manner, since they are endowed with the exceptional qualities of omniscience, compassion, and power, they come for the sake of looking after disciples, like a bird soaring through the sky. This is the nature of dependent origination, and it was therefore said:

> Whoever places foremost importance in conviction,
> in front of them the sage remains.

This indicates that one should definitely have a factually concordant, nonsuperficial conviction.

Having recognized this, in order to visualize the object of refuge, although an elaborate session as contained within secret tantric texts was not written, a mere practice related to the sutric tradition of many recitations of refuge verses become a way to prevent idle chatter.

When applying the system of visualization in which a pledge being is first generated in front of oneself and then the wisdom beings are invoked and become inseparable (as described in Panchen Losang Chökyi Gyaltsen's *Easy Stages of the Path*) from the ritual of generating the merit field of inseparable bliss and emptiness (as contained in his *Guru Pūjā*) one takes refuge in that merit field and purifies negativities and obscurations by way of the descending ambrosia. One then visualizes oneself and others—all sentient beings—as coming under the protection of the Three Jewels. Such tantric methods of meditation were taught for those people who have taken not only a general tantric empowerment, but a highest yoga tantra empowerment, and who also maintain lamrim meditations. [110]

However, when a person who has not entered into tantra meditates on the stages of the path, if general tantric practices such as purification

within emptiness through the *svabhāva-śuddhāḥ* mantra,[52] or purification through descending ambrosia, and so forth, or particularly highest yoga tantra meditations on the merit field are taught, then there is
a danger of it becoming a case of divulging secrets to an unripened
recipient. Therefore, the visualizations contained within *Oral Transmission of Mañjuśrī* are in accordance with the sutric presentation for the
common trainee. Thus, one recites invocation verses such as "You are
the protector of all beings without exception," and so forth,[53] or, alternatively, instead of invoking them, one visualizes them oneself—since
the objects of refuge are of course there already—and one remembers
the Teacher's body, speech and mind, remembers his kindness, and
sees the reasons for the Dharma Jewel being the pure path, and thus
generates from the heart an unwavering faith and a firm aspiration to
actualize that. One then concludes the refuge by generating admiration and respect for those ārya trainees.

Alternatively, for those who wish to visualize the objects of refuge
for the sake of quickly subjugating their minds: visualize the guru,
the victorious ones and their spiritual heirs—the buddhas and bodhisattvas. If one contemplates all sentient beings surrounding oneself,
experiencing their individuated suffering of the six types of rebirths,
one's compassion increases. If one visualizes them in the aspect of
human beings who can speak and understand meaning, there is an
oral lineage that explains there to be a distinguishing feature of auspicious interdependence that enables them, before long, to practice
extensive vast and profound Dharma just like the Dharma one practices oneself.

Therefore, if one accumulates recitations of refuge prayers, such as
"I go for refuge to the guru; I go for refuge to the Buddha," and so
on, without having the slightest idea of what taking refuge means, it
might help to slightly diminish pride, but is said to not have extensive benefits. [111] Occasionally some people ask me to give them the
oral transmission for refuge, which is slightly uncomfortable. One can

recite something similar to an oral transmission of the refuge verse, but "refuge" is something that must be thought about through its meaning. Rather than reciting "I go for refuge to the Buddha, Dharma, and Sangha . . ." and so forth, and pretending that this by itself is refuge or mind generation, instead, bring to mind the qualities of the noble ones and the Dharma—the particularities of the objects of refuge—and from the core of one's heart pray, "Guru and the Three Jewels, think of me!" Being moved with a strong mental feeling, the verse of refuge "I go for refuge to the Buddha," and so forth, should then slip without control from one's lips.

As was explained prior, **if one takes refuge in the objects of refuge identified thus in the manner that the preceptors of refuge themselves do, then one will generate fear of the torment of the three types of suffering experienced in this vast ocean of suffering, which is the deep and beginningless samsara we enter into through the power of karma and afflictions; a fear like that toward a deadly enemy coming to murder oneself. Understanding that only the Three Jewels have the power to protect us from such fear, one generates a** strong, clearheaded faith **wishing to actualize that faith** of conviction **and those exceptional qualities** that they possess **in one's own continuum. Furthermore,** one needs to have **an attitude of surrender, thinking, "Whatever happens—good or bad, happiness or sadness—you know best!"** Requiring such a mindset is due to the fact that the two causes of refuge in the common Mahāyāna presentation are fear and faith; it is said that whether or not something becomes pure refuge relies on whether those two causes of refuge are present.

Thus, whatever verses of refuge one may recite—whether extensive verses from this lamrim text, or other short or extensive verses—it does not become actual refuge without such a feeling accompanying it if one merely recites the words [112]. In this context, a Mahāyāna practitioner meditates on the paths of the small and middle scope persons as common paths, in the manner of preliminaries to the Mahāyāna path.

Therefore, since the uncommon Mahāyāna cause of refuge must be present when they go for refuge, on top of faith and fear, **through the power of compassion observing sentient beings, one recognizes that even though one does not have the power to liberate them from suffering, one supplicates the Three Jewels, understanding that they do.**

In brief, with compassion observing other sentient beings to be tormented by suffering in the same way as oneself, the three causes of faith, fear, and compassion are complete. With a strong transformation of mind, one audibly voices the words, **"From this day forth, until I and all sentient beings equal to the limits of space attain the essence of enlightenment, I go for refuge to the holy gurus; I go for refuge to the Buddha Bhagavān; I go for refuge to the holy Dharma; I go for refuge to the ārya assembly." Taking count with a mala, recitation of a minimum of twenty-one times, up to a maximum of around three hundred, is a suitable amount. Pretending to be strict in spiritual practice from the beginning**—strict meaning tight, and therefore acting extremely uptight with spiritual practice—**is a sign one does not know how to practice. As it is said** in the *Great Treatise on the Stages of the Path*:

> Furthermore, in the beginning you will be readily susceptible to laxity and excitement. If this becomes your habit, it will become difficult to correct your mind. Therefore, create many short sessions. If you end your session while still wanting to meditate, you will be eager to reenter each future session. Otherwise, it is said that you will feel nauseous when you see the cushion.

It is important not to become a jaded Dharma practitioner who falls flat on their nose from the outset. When practicing Dharma, one might generate, for a few days, unstable renunciation, and bolster it with an energetic feeling [113]; however, later one becomes tired and exhausted, and despondently thinks, "Why is it that however much I meditate, I do not generate realizations?" Other than engaging oneself in misery, there is no benefit in that; therefore, maintain a relaxed continuity of a natural state. If one makes effort correctly in this way, results will undoubtedly arise eventually.

Through making such supplications, the victorious ones together with their spiritual heirs (bodhisattvas) become pleased, and light and ambrosia descend from their bodies, which transform the continuum of oneself and all other sentient beings through blessings. Through this, prior negative actions or obstructions such as lack of faith and two-sided doubt in the Three Supreme Ones, misdeeds performed, and so forth, are purified. Generate belief that one enters under the protection of the guru and Three Jewels.

After having completed the practice of refuge, repeat the following words seven or twenty-one times according to context, with a strong sense of anguish: "I go for refuge to the precious guru and Three Jewels. I beseech you to please bless my continuum. In particular, please bless me to generate the stages of the path of the persons of three scopes in my continuum." There is an exceptional purpose of generating the later-mentioned meditation rounds in one's continuum through the power of supplicating an exceptional field of merit—the Three Jewels, and therefore it is said in the *Great Treatise on the Stages of the Path*:

> **When our mind's power is so weak that we cannot retain the words that we memorize, understand the meaning when we reflect, or generate results when we meditate, we should rely on the power of the merit field.**

In the beginning, sources for why refuge is necessary are very important. Since from now on one must train in merely the abbreviated precepts of refuge, exert oneself strongly in collecting merit

through making offerings. Like a single slingshot that drives away a hundred birds at once, through supplicating and going for refuge in the beginning, the power of the exceptional merit field leads to the paths generating in one's continuum, but one need not recite the supplicating verses at the conclusion of each meditation round [114].

Mind generation follows that. Generating the mind of enlightenment, recite three or seven times, whichever is suitable, "I will attain the state of a perfect buddha for the sake of all sentient beings. For that end, I will practice the stages of the path of the persons of three scopes," while remembering the meaning. This has the exceptional purpose of transforming all later virtues into the cause for attaining buddhahood.

Relying on the Spiritual Teacher: The Root of the Path

[Regarding] the actual practice of the path of relying on the spiritual teacher, relying on a spiritual teacher is the foundation of all Mahāyāna and Hīnayāna paths, and therefore it is termed "the root of the path." Since one must sustain the later lamrim meditation rounds and traverse the grounds and paths in light of this, the incomparable Jowo Jé Atiśa said:

> All greater and lesser qualities of the Mahāyāna arise from relying on a guru. You Tibetans only view gurus as ordinary, so how can qualities arise?

In the words of Potowa:

> There is nothing more important for achieving liberation than the guru. Considering that the actions of this life cannot be carried out satisfactorily without a teacher, how could it be

possible that those who have just come from the lower realms
go to a place they have never been before without a guru?

It is the same even with respect to studying subjects pertaining to
worldly affairs: if you do not learn the finer points of information through
an experienced tutor you cannot understand them perfectly. [115]

In Sanskrit, "guru" literally means heavy or weighted. It was translated as "lama" (*bla ma*) in Tibetan, meaning someone who bestows
knowledge. Furthermore, the syllable "la" is explained to mean "superior," as in there is no one more superior in terms of kindness, and
heavy with qualities. "Ma" is a possessive particle, indicating that
someone who possesses those attributes is a "lama."

Therefore, one must rely on a fully qualified spiritual teacher. Furthermore, practicing Dharma on the basis of their advice is unlike
outer trainings in a craft. As the qualities of mind must increase
through progressively subduing one's continuum, one must also have
the stream of blessings transmitted sequentially and in an unbroken
manner from our Teacher the Buddha to one's root gurus that then
enter one's continuum and allow for the generation of realizations of
the grounds and paths. Therefore, without relying on a fully qualified
lineage guru, it is not possible.

The preliminary of relying on the spiritual teacher, the root of the
path, has two parts:

1. A slightly elaborated explanation for the sake of certainty
2. A brief instruction on how to sustain the meditation

The first of these, "a slightly elaborated explanation for the sake of
certainty," relates to the definitions of guru, student, and so forth, and
is comprised of six topics:

a. The definition of the spiritual teacher—the object of reliance—together with the method of investigating them
b. The definition of the disciple who relies on them, together with the method of investigating them
c. How the disciple relies upon the guru
d. The benefits of relying on a guru
e. The disadvantages of not relying on the guru
f. A summary of the above points

The Definition of the Spiritual Teacher— the Object of Reliance—Together with the Method of Investigating Them

Regarding this topic, it says in the *Great Treatise on the Stages of the Path* that there is an important purpose for explaining the definitions of the object of reliance—the guru—and the one who relies on the guru—the disciple—in two dedicated sections. What are the characteristics or qualifications a spiritual teacher must have according to the explanations of the definitions of guru and disciple? Regarding this, the benevolent teacher gave individual explanations in the context of Vinaya, in the context of the sutras, and in the context of secret tantra wherein the characteristics of a vajra master were taught. [116]

How was it taught in the sutric system? **From Maitreya's *Ornament for the Mahāyāna Sūtras*:**

> **Rely on a spiritual teacher who is disciplined, peaceful, thoroughly pacified,**
> **has superior qualities, joyous effort, is rich in scripture,**
> **has realized suchness, is a skilled speaker,**
> **has a loving nature, and has eliminated dispiritedness.**

The object of reliance—the spiritual teacher—should also have

THE STAGES OF GUIDING DISCIPLES

tamed their own continuum through the three higher trainings; have the quality of being well-studied and learned in scripture; an exceptional training of the wisdom realizing suchness; has superior qualities exceeding those of the disciple; skilled in guiding disciples on a path that is correct and pleasant to listen to through intelligence that differentiates the meaning of the scriptures with logic; has loving compassion toward destitute living beings without regard for gain or respect; has joyous effort endeavoring to accomplish the welfare of others; and has the quality of enduring the difficult act of constantly repeating explanations without weariness.

Out of the ten qualities that a Mahāyāna teacher must possess, the first, *discipline*, refers to subduing one's own continuum with the training of ethics that restrains negative actions of body, speech and mind. As it says in the *Great Treatise on the Stages of the Path*:

> It is unwarranted to discipline others without disciplining oneself; therefore, take great care in this respect!

Since the guru who tames others tames them through teaching that which is to be adopted and that which is to be discarded, stating that they must first tame themselves is quite significant. Furthermore, it is not helpful if one engages in all sorts of practices to tame one's continuum as mentioned, resulting in a few so-called qualities of realization; rather, one requires a method of discipline that accords with the Buddha's general teachings. That method is said to be as definitive as the three precious trainings and thus included within those; thus, one must possess the qualities of the three trainings. [117] Moreover, since the method for achieving liberation is the three trainings, the guru who teaches liberation must have the three trainings, and the teacher of the path to achieve the state of definite goodness and omniscience must have love, compassion, and bodhicitta, and therefore "a loving nature." In general, even if it is a guru who is temporarily teaching the path to liberation, they should have love for the student in their heart.

The meaning of the words of the precious lord Tsongkhapa are incredibly reliable, and the words themselves have a great, unsurpassed power that sets them apart from others; in particular, his *Great Treatise on the Stages of the Path* is like a charter for those of Mount Ganden, the Gelukpas.

The second quality, *peacefulness*, refers to possessing the training in meditative concentration that abides peacefully on the current focal object of mind, not distracted by external objects. The third, *thoroughly pacified* applies to the wisdom realizing selflessness; thus the spiritual teacher possesses the qualities of the training in wisdom, too. It is not enough that these three ways of taming our mind merely be called qualities of realization. Rather, it is taught that through these three trainings that accord with the general teachings of the Buddha one must tame one's mind.

With respect to taking care of others: the fourth, *superior qualities*, refers to possessing more of the qualities taught in the triple basket than the disciple; and when one teaches others what is to be adopted and discarded one does not become discouraged, but rather has the fifth quality, the *joyous effort* that enables one to teach. One furthermore is *rich in scripture*—the sixth quality of being learned in the explanatory treatises. The seventh, *a realization of suchness*, refers to [either] a realization of selflessness of phenomena or a profound understanding of that.

In the context of teaching others, one needs the eighth quality, to be *a skilled speaker*, one who is adept at teaching what is timely according to the listener's disposition and mental continuum, appropriate to the time and place. [118] The primary characteristic of a guru is the ninth, *a loving nature*; having a kind heart is very important. Likewise, they should prioritize the next life over this life, others over themselves, have a special pure altruistic attitude and be someone on whom we can trust and rely. Even for an ordinary person to become a trustworthy friend, while it is possible they become a friend due to their education or wealth, to become a true friend requires that no matter how much we trust them they never deceive us, and that they create happiness and well-being through pure intentions.

The tenth quality, the *elimination of dispiritedness*, means that one does not shy away from the weariness that comes from having to explain things to disciples again and again, and that one can fulfill the aims of the disciple.

Maitreya's *Ornament for the Mahāyāna Sūtras*, which is a text primarily adhering to Yogācāra tenets, posits grasping at a self of persons as the root of existence, and grasping at a self of phenomena as an obstruction to omniscience. In the context of the defining characteristics of a spiritual teacher, the training in wisdom—out of the three trainings—refers to the wisdom realizing selflessness of persons, and since one must realize selflessness of phenomena as an antidote to obscurations to omniscience, "has realized suchness" was stated separately.

As Nāgārjuna said:

Rely on one with twelve qualities
who is well studied and has great wisdom,
who does not seek material things,
who has bodhicitta and great compassion,
has patience to endure hardship, little discouragement,
a wealth of instructions, is liberated through the path,
is skilled in different lineages of beings, and knows levels of
    spiritual maturity.

From Śāntideva's *Way of the Bodhisattva*:

Never, even at the cost of one's life,
should one forsake the spiritual teacher

who observes the vows of the bodhisattva
and who is well versed in the Mahāyāna. [119]

From that renowned as the incomparable Jowo Atiśa's autocommentary of *The Lamp for the Path to Enlightenment*:

[What qualities make a bodhisattva a spiritual friend?] They abide in pure ethics; are well studied; have realizations; have loving compassion; apply themselves to the welfare of others; are fearless; have patience; and are without discouragement. Understand that if they possess these eight qualities, they have the complete aspects of a bodhisattva virtuous friend. Since they abide in the ethics of the bodhisattva vows and prevent faults, they abide in pure ethics. They are well studied because they do not have untrained minds. They have attained virtues arisen through meditation and possess realizations. Since they have compassion, they have loving compassion. They have cast away their own happiness and apply themselves to the welfare of others. When they teach others, their memory and courage are not reduced through fearful anxiety, thus they are fearless. They have patience for the contempt, blame, criticism, condemnation, undesirable speech of others, and for sentient beings with distorted perspectives. They lack weariness and discouragement and have great vigor for teaching pure Dharma to the fourfold assembly.

Furthermore, lord Atiśa said one should rely on a guru possessing four attributes: (1) being wise and thus not disregarding the view, (2) being venerable and thus not disregarding ethical conduct, (3) not striving for this life, and (4) striving for enlightenment.

Lord Gampopa said the guru must possess three attributes: (1) they lead others on the path through great wisdom, (2) they are unable to

bear the suffering of others due to their compassion, and (3) they do
not live for this life. [120]

A guru becomes a guru through having disciples. Without disciples,
there is no "guru." Gurus and disciples are only mutually designated
in dependence upon one another, yet these days being a guru is considered a status. Maintaining lama estates without any disciples is not
a quality of a lama. In Tibetan society, there might be a virtuous friend
having all the qualifications necessary to perform the activities of a
guru, but because they are not "so-and-so geshé" or "so-and-so lama,"
or do not have the title of tulku, they are not considered as important.
Furthermore, without considering whether such a tulku has any qualities, or if they have tamed their mind, we consider the title "rinpoché"
incredibly holy and think it's necessary they have an elaborate lama
estate. This is a terrible model.

Personally, I posit four possibilities between lamas and tulkus.[54]
Someone who is a lama but not a tulku would be the majority of the
Ganden throne holders throughout history, who mostly came to the
monasteries from far away villages with nothing but a rucksack. For
around thirty years, intermittently running out of tsampa, or roasted
barley flour, each endures great hardships to study the five great treatises year after year without a sabbatical. They follow a path of study
for their entire lives and thus are incredibly precious. For the sake
of the large offering ceremony that they must conduct before they
complete their geshé degree, they must put great effort into attaining
the means for that, which may end up slightly tainted by the wrong
livelihoods of flattery and hinting [for requisites]. However, as they
do possess the appropriate level of knowledge, they sit for their *geshé
lharam* examination and then enter into a tantric college wherein they
sit for another tantric examination on Dharma and the topics of the
teacher and the listener within secret tantric texts. After that, they
sequentially become the disciplinarian, deputy abbot, and abbot of
a tantric college, and then either the Shartsé Chöjé or Jangtsé Chöjé.

Those who have ascended to the golden throne of Ganden through progressing through the vehicles in this way are real lamas; they are holy beings arisen from the complete perfection of the power of karma, aspirational prayers, merit and bodhicitta. [121] Furthermore, since the golden throne of Ganden is the throne of Jé Rinpoché Tsongkhapa, the Ganden *tripas* who sit on it are representatives of Jé Rinpoché, and the holders of the Geluk tradition.

Following on from that, someone who is a tulku but not a lama would be someone with the title of tulku, who has a lama estate, but does not care for qualities such as Dharma knowledge or the taming of one's mind. They have a multitude of plans and activities, are arrogant, misbehave, and deceive others through lies. Such a person is not a lama, yet they carry the name of tulku within society. It is not impossible that some of them have biographies of inconceivable concealed activities, and that some have strong imprints from their past lives, but from the perspective of general Buddhist teachings, those manifest qualities accepted by general consensus of being learned, morally pure, wise and skilled in explanation, debate, and composition should be the basis upon which we designate lamas. Otherwise, if we talk from the perspective of inconceivable concealed activities, who is to say whether autocratic tyrants such as Russia's Stalin, Germany's Hitler, or China's Mao Zedong were good or bad people, or wicked Māra or not in reality?

As for someone who is both a lama and a tulku, my tutors Kyabjé Ling Rinpoché and Kyabjé Trijang Rinpoché (1901–81), for example, were fully qualified tulkus and inconceivably precious lamas who were both learned and realized. Sometimes in our society the general public will have great devotion for a lama in the beginning, but eventually border on criticizing them. This is improper, and therefore before one relies on a guru one should investigate if they possess the characteristics of a guru, and whether they are to be trusted. [122]

As such, regarding the way to investigate the guru and disciple, first comes the manner of investigating the guru and the way to rely on them. It is said that one should not rely too swiftly on a guru, like how a dog reacts when thrown a piece of meat. Thus, even with respect to the means of investigating whether the guru is worthy, if one does not have clairvoyance, it is difficult to determine their level of realizations. However, since it is suitable to investigate at the very least whether the guru is a good person or not through their conduct, character, level of knowledge, level of greed, actions of body and speech, and so forth, regarding this, the Dharma king Songtsen Gampo says in his *Maṇi Kabum*:

> There are three types of guru: the guru to be investigated; the guru to be relied upon; and the guru to accomplish.
>
> The guru to investigate is of three: those to investigate from afar; those to investigate from close proximity; and those to investigate through keeping close company.
>
> The guru to investigate from afar has greater fame, is learned and righteous, and is esteemed by all as like a bodhisattva. Exert yourself to seek and take up such a person.
>
> The guru to investigate from close proximity is of two types: that to reject, and that to adopt. There are three gurus to reject: a "fire-like guru" is to be rejected because of their words at the time one gets too close to their heavy afflictions of the three poisons; reject gurus similar to a chained dog that is greedy and crude with food; and reject gurus who are like businessmen, who do not give Dharma without having money or flowers.
>
> There are three gurus to be accepted: rely on a father-like guru with profound instructions, who is wise in Dharma, and has extensive advice; rely on a mother-like guru who keeps one in mind, is compassionate and loving; and rely on a jewel-like guru who has great blessings, is greatly considerate of the welfare of beings, and is an accomplished being.

With respect to the guru to investigate through keeping close company, rely on one who is not fickle with new company, is highly altruistic, equanimous, and who gives instructions, and in so doing, exert yourself in Dharma.

There are three ways to rely on the guru: through faith, through wisdom, and through requisites.

There are three ways to rely on the guru through faith: [123] reliance through perceiving the guru as a sacred personal deity; reliance through listening to the teachings with keen interest and being polite; and reliance through respectfully venerating them with body, speech, and mind.

There are three ways to rely on the guru through wisdom: retaining the words taught by the guru through the wisdom of listening; contemplating the meaning of the words heard correctly from memory through the wisdom of contemplation; and meditating on all phenomena as inconceivable, unobservable, and uncompounded through the wisdom of meditation.

There are two ways to rely on the guru through providing requisites: reliance through one's own requisites is to offer all of your requisites, including foodstuffs, and so forth, to the guru; reliance through others' requisites is to encourage others to be faithful and respectful toward the guru, thus increasing the merit of the guru[55] through the requisites of body, speech, and mind: prostrating to and making circumambulations around the guru with body; praising the guru and using respectful speech; and making mental supplications and having conviction.

What is a suitable number of gurus to rely on? The omniscient Gendun Drup says in his *Song of the Eastern Snow Mountain*:

Spiritual teachers have gratitude toward the kindness of all
    living beings
and train in pure appearance of every detail and action,
they seek to harm only the enemy within themselves,
the enemy of delusion.

According to Geshé Sangphuwa Ngok Lekpé Sherab, one can rely on as many gurus as necessary; if one remembers the kindness of all sentient beings, one can maintain the perception of pure appearance and suppress one's inner enemy of discursive thoughts. Otherwise, it is a significant statement that it is better to have fewer gurus, as we can see in Geshé Dromtönpa's biography, and that it is more important to rely on those few properly.

In prior times, it was the status quo in Tibetan and Indian society to differentiate between men and women as superior and inferior. [124] Due to this, women were habituated to being timid in thought and behavior, and for that reason there were very few female gurus. However, there were many fully qualified, great beings of India and Tibet in female bodies who upheld, preserved, and spread the continuum of the Buddha's system of instructions, such as Gelongma Palmo; Niguma, the singular queen mother of the siddhas; Machik Labdrön (1055–1149), Machik Shama (1062–1149), Simrak Shaki Semo, [who was the prominent figure from central Tibet named] Khandro Kunsang Dekyong Wangmo (1892–1940), among others. Likewise, in more recent times, the lineage of Samding Dorjé Phakmo, the former and latter Sakya Jetsunmas, Shuksep Jetsunma, and so forth, upheld, preserved, and spread the Buddha's teachings through explanation and accomplishment as explained in volume 1 of the present work. Therefore, it is unacceptable to differentiate such figures as a basis of reliance if they possess the qualities of a spiritual teacher.

The Definition of the Disciple Who Relies on Them, Together with the Method of Investigating Them

Even if the guru possesses all necessary defining characteristics, if the student does not, whatever excellent Dharma is received might not be beneficial. We need to ask which defining characteristics the student who is a suitable vessel for the holy Dharma must possess. **The trainee who is a suitable vessel for the holy Dharma taught by the sublime guru is as said in Āryadeva's** *Four Hundred Verses*:

> **A listener who is impartial, intelligent, and interested**
> **is called a suitable vessel.**
> **Neither the teacher's nor the student's**
> **qualities will be otherwise. [125]**

One should be free from the partiality of attachment to one's own position and disdain toward the position of others; intelligent with respect to differentiating that which is to be adopted and that which is to be discarded, between faulty and excellent speech; thoroughly interested in the holy Dharma, respectful of the teacher and fully concentrated. These are the five qualities a student must possess. If such a teacher and student work in tandem, it is much less difficult to achieve liberation, just as a two-winged bird soars in the sky without hindrance.

The first characteristic, being *impartial*, or honest, is required, since it is extremely pertinent that one remains impartial with respect to understanding reality. Impartiality requires that one not fall into preferential bias; rather, being able to see the reality of the thing in question as it is. To view things according to one's preferences is an obstacle to seeing the truth.

The second, *intelligence*, is knowing to discard faulty speech and adopt excellent speech. Furthermore, if the guru offers an alternative explanation on a topic out of necessity, one should possess an analytical intelligence able to realize the difference between definitive and interpretable meaning, thinking, "The intention and purpose for saying that was such and such." Moreover, in this context, one should have doubt with respect to the meaning, since doubt leads to questions, and questions lead to investigation. Investigation benefits one's understanding of the actuality of the topic, and thus one must investigate and analyze whether something is an excellent or faulty explanation. Therefore, for there to be an investigative process, one must not be completely faith-based from the outset; rather, operating within doubt is important. For example, it is said that the majority of classical Indian treatises possess four interrelated aspects—[a topic], a purpose, [an ultimate purpose, and the relationship between them]. The intended disciple who is of sharp faculty, has keen interest, and an investigative nature, first investigates the topic of the text; having understood the topic, they then investigate the purpose; then the ultimate purpose, as opposed to the temporary purpose, of the text. Only after having investigated these do they see a purpose in studying and contemplating the text due to this process. Therefore, the fact that such texts are said to have the four attributes of a purpose and so forth is quite significant. [126]

Even if one possesses such a mindset, if one relies on a Dharma teacher as a guru without the motivation to listen to genuine Dharma, simply maintaining the facade of listening while sitting in the teaching, then the relationship between guru and disciple will not develop. It is said such people are called "listeners to visual Dharma." Therefore the third characteristic, *interest,* is indispensable. If one has deep respect and admiration for the teachings and the guru, and a desire to listen to Dharma from them, then one is said to be a suitable vessel. Thus, a disciple who possesses such qualities should, at the very least, rely on someone who has few faults and many qualities.

The Way to Investigate, Cultivate, and
Advance the Student

The way to check, cultivate, and advance the student is as found in Songtsen Gampo's *Mani Kabum*:

> WAM. The discussion of the disciple to be sought out is divided into three sections: the disciple to be investigated; the disciple to be cultivated; and the disciple to be advanced.
>
> The topic of the disciple to investigate is in three sections: that to investigate from afar, that to investigate from close proximity, and that to investigate through cultivating the disciple.
>
> Those investigated from afar are of three types: those who are from a noble family and who abide by Dharma, those who have great faith and maintain their samaya, and those who have great wisdom and are diligent. Form a Dharma connection with those and take them as students.
>
> Those investigated from close proximity are of two types: those to be rejected and those to be accepted. Those to be rejected are of three types: a "disciple fired like an arrow" is one who has neither faith nor respect for the guru, and no love for their friends. Cast them far away! The "disciple who is fled from like an enemy" is one who has neither commitments nor concern for decency, and who hides their faults while criticizing the spiritual master. Make no Dharma connections with such people and flee from them! [127] "The poisonous disciple" is one who is defiled by corrupted samaya and who resents the master for their degenerated samaya. Such people create obstacles to the life force; therefore do not cultivate them.
>
> There are three kinds of disciples to accept: a disciple who is

like a fertile field—faithful, respectful, and compassionate—should be cultivated through Dharma blessings; cultivate a disciple who has behaved like one's shadow, who has attended one long term with respect to body, speech, and mind; cultivate a disciple who is like a jewel—compassionate and altruistic, and unattached to the retinue of the guru.

The disciple to cultivate is of two types: those cultivated through Dharma and those cultivated through material things. Those cultivated through Dharma are encouraged to practice offering what they desire for the teachings. Those cultivated through material things are encouraged to engage in the Dharma of offering food, clothing, and so forth, to the faithful who are without provisions for practice.

The disciple to be advanced is of two kinds: those learned ones spiritually reared through explanation who are then promoted to the level of a great teacher and those diligent meditators spiritually reared through practices who are made to meditate in forests and mountain hermitages and then promoted to the level of a great meditator.

How the Disciple Relies upon the Guru

The actual way a student with such characteristics relies on a guru has two parts:

1) **The way to rely in thought**
2) **The way to rely in action** [128]

The first has three respective sections in the *Great Treatise on the Stages of the Path*:

a) A discussion on how to view the guru while relying on
   them in general
b) Cultivating the root of faith in particular
c) Recollecting their great kindness and generating devotion

The first of these is not listed separately in other lamrim texts, [including the Great Fifth's treatise]. In the *Great Treatise on the Stages of the Path*, Tsongkhapa explains veneration for the spiritual teacher through nine attitudes, and so forth. Thus, there are many things to be understood in that section which are also very important.

How should a disciple view their guru? It is natural that one's faith increases in relation to the degree to which one observes the qualities of the guru's three secrets of body, speech, and mind , and therefore doing so forms the foundation for building faith. However, many distinctions are made regarding the way one actually observes those, according to one's mental capacity, and therefore it was taught differently according to the higher and lower vehicles. Within the original lamrim text, Atiśa's *Lamp for the Path to Enlightenment*, and the autocommentary, it is not explicitly clear in the preliminary section, starting from mind training, that one must view the guru as a buddha.

Furthermore, from teachings of Geshé Potowa, as cited in the *Kadam Treasury of Gems*:

> From among the three—the spiritual teacher who is a buddha, the spiritual teacher who is an ārya, and the spiritual teacher who is an ordinary being—only the last is incredibly kind.

The incomparable Gampopa Dakpo Lhajé Sönam Rinchen says in his wish-fulfilling jewel of holy dharma, *The Jewel Ornament of Liberation*:

> There are four categories of spiritual teacher: spiritual teach-

ers who are ordinary beings; spiritual teachers who are
bodhisattvas abiding on the higher levels of the path; spiritual teachers who are emanation bodies (*nirmāṇakāya*) of
buddhas; and spiritual teachers who are supreme enjoyment
bodies (*saṃbhogakāya*) of buddhas. These are relevant to one's
personal situation. As one is unable to rely on buddhas or
bodhisattvas abiding on the higher grounds while one is a
beginner, rely on a spiritual teacher who is an ordinary being.
When the majority of karmic obscurations have been purified,
one is able to rely on high-level bodhisattvas. [129] When one
abides on the greater path of accumulation and above, one
is able to rely on the spiritual teacher in the emanation body
form of a buddha. Once one attains the higher grounds, one
can rely on the supreme enjoyment body form of a buddha.

Who of these four types of teachers is the most kind? In the beginning, while still in the dark chamber of karma and ignorance, if one
attempted to rely on the three latter spiritual teachers, one would not
even see their faces. However, through encountering the spiritual
teacher who is an ordinary being, the path is illuminated by the lamp
of his teachings and thus one comes to encounter the latter spiritual
teachers. Therefore, the kindest of all is the spiritual teacher who is an
ordinary being.

Furthermore, it says in the perfection of wisdom literature that the
boundaries for a guru who teaches Mahāyāna instructions are from
before entering the path up to the grounds of a buddha. The intention of
the scriptures was clarified with respect to the appropriate way to view
the guru according to the sutric system and the superiority of the disciple
themselves. Regarding that, in the biography of Trehor Kyorpön Rinpoché it says that Trehor Geshé Palden Drakpa from Drepung Monastery
asked the question, "I have heard that in the context of lamrim literature,
it is said the gurus merely display an ordinary aspect, and are all buddhas

in actuality. Is this the case?" The answer given by Rinpoché was, "This is not necessarily the case. In the context of the perfection of wisdom literature, the boundaries for gurus who teach Mahāyāna instructions are from before entering the path up until the grounds of a buddha."

Likewise, viewing the guru [as an emissary of the] buddha in the context of pratimokṣa discipline, viewing the guru as like a buddha in the context of bodhisattvas, and viewing the guru as an actual buddha in the context of tantra is the intention of the above citation from *Ornament for Liberation*. [130] Therefore, if one insists to mundane, ordinary beings who are unable to rely on anyone other than an ordinary guru that they must generate the perception of the guru as an actual buddha, and if as a result they cling to the idea of infinite pure appearances, then they will be led astray on the path. It is therefore appropriate to emulate teachings that teach different ways to view the guru according to the context.

From the gentle protector, the great Tsongkhapa's *Great Treatise on the Stages of the Path*:

> Regarding how the disciple should view the guru, the *Tantra Bestowing the Initiation of Vajrapāṇi* says:
>
> > O Lord of Secrets, if one asks how a disciple should view their master, they should view them just as they view the Buddha Bhagavān.

After citing tantric texts such as the *Tantra Bestowing the Initiation of Vajrapāṇi* and Aśvaghoṣa's *Fifty Verses on the Guru*, he says:

> In Mahāyāna sutras it is also taught that one must generate the discrimination of the guru as the Teacher; likewise, it says the same in the Vinaya.

Such teachings, from the beginning of the *Great Treatise on the Stages of the Path*, are all in the context of leading those uncommon, suitable vessels for tantric teachings on the path of highest yoga tantra. It can also be inferred based on the aforementioned citation from *Ornament to Liberation* that the intention is with respect to those abiding on the great path of accumulation onward.

Fifty Verses on Guru Devotion is a famous text regarding tantric practice composed by Ācārya Aśvaghoṣa, formerly known as Tīrthika Aśvaghoṣa, who later converted to Buddhism. It is quite clear that he aimed the text at those who had backgrounds in the traditional Indian and Hindu religious explanations of how to rely on a guru, picking out the beneficial aspects befitting Buddhism.

In the same way, Panchen Losang Chökyi Gyaltsen's *Easy Path* has a tantric style in which one makes supplications, purifies through descending ambrosia, and so forth, to be able to see the spiritual teachers as actual buddhas and Munīndra Vajradhara. The text thus applies visualizations from the tantric system. [131]

Panchen Losang Yeshe's *Naked Instructions for the Swift Path* furthermore comments on the need to view the guru as a buddha, the ability to view thus, and the manner of viewing in three separate sections. He gives as a reason for the guru being a buddha the fact that Vajradhara proclaimed such, and so forth. His sources are citations from the tantras, and from *Fifty Verses on Guru Devotion* the lines, "Never regard the master and Vajradhara as different," and "Offer flowers, mandala, and touch one's head to their feet." This being the case, such terms as "Munīndra Vajradhara" are not found in the context of solely the common path. Furthermore, following the pattern of the intention of tantric texts with respect to viewing the guru as a buddha or the guru-yidam as inseparable from one's mind, such must be understood in this context of the common path as authored for the sake of exceptional persons who are able to practice sutra and tantra in union.

In earlier times, being a follower of Tibetan Buddhism was not contingent upon whether one acquired faith through knowledge; rather, through prior habitual tendencies and environmental factors, irreversible, firm faith toward the Dharma arose naturally. Due to that and the heavy proliferation of secret tantra, eventually, no longer investigating whether a disciple was a suitable vessel, systems of explanations arose that assumed all would train entirely in the union of sutra and tantra. Thus, most latter commentaries on the stages of the path sequentially promulgated the fact of the guru as a buddha as a general feature of lamrim literature. [132]

It therefore became quite rare that explanations of initial foundational practices purely from the sutric path were given. A criticism appears later in *The Oral Transmission of Mañjuśrī*, reading, "As it has been corrupted through secret tantra, there are slight dissimilarities with the practices of this system." The mind training techniques in the preliminary stages of the path are not to be discarded in the context of tantric practices and are therefore in common with tantra; thus, the phrase "training in the common path" became well known. Most of these treatises, such as the *Great Treatise on the Stages of the Path*, are coming from a perspective of general training in conduct, and a teaching method related to training within Vajrayāna; therefore, the way to rely on a spiritual teacher is taught as a preliminary. Thus, in reality, it is a preliminary for tantra, and in the case of someone who is merely a person of small scope, I really wonder if it is necessary to teach the way of relying on a spiritual teacher in the very beginning. Tantric practices should not be shared in common with lamrim. Therefore, it is extremely unfortunate that a pure practice of entering into the tantric path only having trained in the common lamrim became lost—a relic of texts and mere advice. It is very important that such is revived.

In particular, the younger generation of people from Himalayan and Mongolian regions should go beyond merely following Tibetan Buddhism as a family tradition. Those that thoroughly train themselves in the three principal aspects of the path from the outset and later find conviction in tantra are rare. Furthermore, in this time when people of all different races, cultures, and creeds are showing great interest in Buddhism, there needs to be a means to establish a firm foundation through the reasoning of dependent arising, starting from the two truths and the order of cause and effect within the four noble truths, to guide them gradually through refuge and so forth.[56] [133]

Otherwise, if we advise those who are just on the cusp of directing their minds to the common path that they must view the guru as a buddha, then it becomes a forceful act of conversion for those who are interested in only the sutric path and those who only have the capacity to practice the sutric path for the time being. Furthermore, as it is temporarily incomprehensible for others, it is obvious that it leads to increased criticism. On top of that, how can one be certain that there is no fault of divulging secrets to the unripened if one explains the context of the guru needing to be taken as a buddha? Buddhism being renowned for withstanding logical scrutiny will become just talk, as there is a possibility that the obviously intimidating traditional explanations of falling to hell if one errs in the reliance on the guru, constituting a serious breach, can become similar to the explanations of having to go to hell if one goes against the will of God.

There is the danger of this becoming a basis of harm, not benefit, for those who have aversion toward religions that do not rely on reason, yet are newly interested in Buddhism; they will immediately have an erroneous perception and have the door to their conviction shut. Through the conditions of wrong thoughts and a lack of realizations, it is temporarily incompatible with their dispositions, and thus does not achieve benefit for others. As that is the case, the practice of lamrim from a purely sutric perspective and the practice of it combined with tantra should be separated, rendering an easier approach in which criticism does not arise from those who can train as they please in either the common or uncommon path. This accords with reality.

In the snowy land of Tibet, it is not astonishing to say that, from a young age, learned and accomplished holy beings such as the yogi Milarepa Shepé Dorjé (1040–1123) and the gentle protector, the great Tsongkhapa, or any other lama, are emanations of buddhas. [134] Other than that, from the perspective of ordinary trainees, they were born from their mother's womb just like any other ordinary person, and not arisen from an aura of light. In the footsteps of the benevolent teacher, they gradually engaged in listening, contemplation, meditation, and accomplishment, and with strong fortitude carried out the difficult deeds of accumulating merit and purifying obscurations. In accordance with the saying "Although having realizations equal to those of the gods, one's conduct must accord with that of men," they lived the same as the rest of us and achieved the indisputable and famous result of becoming learned, pure, and wise. These holy, inconceivable beings plain to see, who had perfected their own and other's welfare, are people we can be proud of. We should look up to them as examples, and persevere with the thought, "What is stopping me from achieving what they have?"

Cultivating the Root of Faith in Particular

[Regarding this section,] **cultivating the root of faith in particular**, if one sees the qualities in an object, one generates faith in that. For example, if one sees another person who has positive qualities, it does not matter if they are one's guru or not, one admires them and generates respect through recollecting their kindness. In general, the generation of faith through seeing the guru's qualities as admirable qualities has nothing to do with one being the student of that guru—anyone can generate that kind of faith. It is said that the faith of one who sees faults in the guru yet still generates faith is the uncommon faith of an authentic student. Therefore, one must deeply understand the system of the crucial points of this root of the path, and in particular the way guru and disciple must fulfill their defining characteristics. Otherwise, [one's devotion] can end up slightly tainted through being coerced into having conviction in someone because of others' counsel, [135] and thus, if one is not careful, there is a possibility that one will train in blind faith while saying that one should not have blind faith. Therefore, the word "root" in the phrase "train in the root of faith" shows that it is an extremely important unshakable faith based on conviction through reasoning.

From the *Dhāraṇī of the Blaze of the Three Jewels*:

> **Faith is generated as a preliminary for all good qualities,**
> **like a mother it protects and increases them.**
> **It clears away doubts and frees you from samsara's torrents;**
> **faith symbolizes the city of happiness and goodness.**
>
> **Faith clears the mind, cutting through the fog,**
> **it eliminates pride and is the root of respect.**
> **Faith is the supreme jewel, treasure, and footing,**
> **like hands, it is the root of gathering virtue.**

As stated, it is important that [the practices] are necessarily preceded by unshakable faith in the spiritual teacher.

Furthermore, from the *Sūtra of the Ten Teachings*:

> Positive qualities will not arise,
> in those who have no faith,
> just like a green sprout will not grow
> from a seed scorched by fire.

As it is said, faith is important as the basis for all good qualities. If one has single-pointed faith toward the guru from the depths of one's heart, there are great advantages: since we all desire happiness and do not want suffering, one generates unerring realizations for the sake of ending suffering, and our suffering decreases and perpetual happiness commences in relation to how much the strength of those realizations increase—the collection of good qualities will increase like the waxing moon. Therefore, if we look at historical accounts and the experiences of our Dharma friends in the present, one is really able to generate uncontrived faith in the guru, and it should be a rational faith, not just blind faith. If it is blind faith, then when one closely investigates the basis of one's faith, it becomes shaky, and, unable to find certainty, it vanishes. [136]

Therefore, do not have complete faith in the guru from the beginning; rather, investigate whether they are really worthy of faith. If there is a verified reason for placing one's trust in them which one can be sure about, faith arises naturally, and such faith is an unchanging faith.

Thus, when investigating the guru, one cannot come to a prior conclusion through guesswork regarding whether one can trust them and have conviction, whether they are good or bad, or the reality of their situation. One should remain with equal doubt, thinking that anything is possible; if there is no doubt, there is no basis for reasoning. The more one investigates through reasoning, the clearer one's ascertainment becomes regarding whether or not they will deceive you.

With respect to this, the great authoritative treatises mention two kinds of beings: sharp faculty beings who are followers of Dharma—those of keen intelligence who follow reasoning to analyze actual reality, who enter into something with faith once they see its value and that it has a trustworthy source—and those of dull faculty who are followers of faith do not investigate; rather, they follow what others say and take for granted that things are exactly as said. They merely go through the motions of a traditional-like path, and thus are without the basis of having acquired certainty.

Rather than having faith in the guru in the manner of a dull-faculty being of blind faith, if one can be deeply moved through strong feelings of faith, respect, and conviction that are based on well-thought-out reasoning, that is best. With respect to this, we have first-hand experience in our current generations wherein people generate extremely strong, single-pointed devotion toward a guru, which leads them to correct understanding in general, and in particular, many who have, generate tantric realizations. [137] We should investigate with our own reasoning these situations that continue to provide clear confirmation, and take examples from our spiritual brothers and sisters. Throughout hundreds and thousands of years of our history there have been holy beings who have unlocked the door to realizations through generating flawless faith from the depths of their hearts in their gurus. Through such accounts found in biographies, which are backed up by clear and authentic citations, we should find recourse to move our minds.

In such a way, having found certainty that any particular teacher is suitable to be relied upon as a guru, **with respect to that, the** one relied on as a **spiritual teacher should be seen as free of all faults and endowed with all qualities. As it is said, "Due to this age of strife, the guru's qualities and faults are mixed"—the qualities and faults appear as mixed to us disciples of impure karma; therefore, one must first stop the mind that looks for flaws.**

In order to further develop understanding with respect to relying on the spiritual teacher, it is crucial to train in not giving rise to thoughts that find fault in the guru. If, in general, developing uncontrived faith and respect toward the guru merely through contemplation sessions related to reliance on the spiritual teacher seems to be difficult due to taking so much time, for some people it is permissible to occasionally perform brief contemplation sessions related to that instead of strictly adhering to them. Starting from the contemplation rounds of persons of small scope up to and including leisure and opportunities, continuing from the topic of four noble truths with respect to the middle scope, and in particular those topics of persons of great scope, if we relate the higher stages of mind training to renunciation, right view, and bodhicitta, our faith in the guru will increase in relation to the degree that our understanding deepens. Through the power of that, eventually firm faith will arise toward the guru who taught us bodhicitta, the view of emptiness, and so forth. In dependence on that, we can prevent the mind that finds fault in the guru. **If that is stopped, it can only be the case that as a matter of course they will be one endowed with all qualities.** [138]

With respect to eliminating the mind that finds faults, take for example an expert physician who administers potent medicine: underlying illnesses manifest themselves again, causing some pain, but are eventually pacified. There is a similar purpose in intentionally visualizing the actions of the guru one sees as faulty. When we do not purposefully scrutinize the actions of our friends, enemies, and neutral people whom we have known a long time, our minds are simply clear—the three poisons do not arise in relation to them. When we examine those people with conceptual thought, we see their good or bad actions not as something of the past, but something happening right now, and feelings of joy or suffering naturally arise in relation to that. In the same way, one should repeatedly bring to mind all of the holy guru's good, bad, and middling activities together with the subtleties their body shape, tone of voice, openness of mind, even down to the style of clothes worn when coming and going, and so forth. And when you allow them—all faults and qualities from when you saw the guru—**to arise naturally,** without addition or fabrication, **all good and bad appearances appear** clearly as if they are happening now. Contemplate until this occurs.

Then, when the doubt arises regarding whether such a mode of appearance is due to faults that actually exist in the guru, or are an appearance even though there are no faults, ask yourself where are these bad faults in this holy guru? You have had appearances of things that do not exist due to extreme defilement from karmic and afflictive obscurations since beginningless time. What is the difference between that and a mistaken sense consciousness that sees an incredibly white snow mountain as blue, or an eye consciousness affected by jaundice seeing a conch shell as yellow? In order to act for the benefit of others in a way that accords with those of us who are totally under the influence of the three poisons, how can we be certain that such impure appearances were not intentionally shown? We should constantly reflect in this manner. [139]

At that point, when the thought arises, "Even though it is possible that this guru is one who has more qualities and less faults than that one, my guru has such and such faults and does not have such and such qualities," one has logically justified seeing the guru as faulty. This is obviously only a result of one's own perceptions. If everything that appears to us must be true, all phenomena must be truly established, and therefore it is logically absurd if we claim that all appearances are true while they actually are not true. Therefore, using this as the reason for why there is no certainty in what appears to us, when we perceive faults in the guru, that perception of faults becomes an aide to faith, and the mind which sees qualities overpowers the mind seeing faults.

If we reflect in this way, our faith in the guru increases naturally. With respect to the ability of the mind that sees their qualities to overpower seeing the faults, if we look at our own experience within a twenty-four-hour day, we see others' faults immediately, but find it difficult to see our own. This is not because we are without faults—we are a pile of faults. However, through the pure perception of our own selves, excessive pride arises. Furthermore, our faithful friends and relatives most dear to us, who may have huge faults, are given a free pass without a second thought. This is due to our seeing them in an excellent manner from the depths of our minds. The mind that sees their small qualities as huge suppresses even their greater faults. Opposite to that, as soon as we see a small fault in someone we do not like, we see it as completely exaggerated. Because of this overpowering mind, even their great qualities are not seen. In this way, whatever seems suitable from our own perspective greatly affects how we perceive things. [140]

Likewise, when one becomes emotionally agitated from a plethora of immediate conditions, like disturbed dreams and so forth, we have disdain for whomever we meet, and however we look at them everything appears negatively. On the other hand, even if something goes wrong when we are having a happy day, we brush it aside, thinking, "Oh it's not so bad," and only slight anxiety and unhappiness arises— this is obviously dependent on our state of mind. Therefore, trainees striving to view things correctly should recollect the kindness of the guru and their qualities of body, speech, and mind through primarily reflecting on reasoning. Particularly, however much certainty we gain in the Buddha Bhagavān's Dharma, starting from the two truths and four noble truths, that is how much our faith increases in the teacher of those and the Sangha who practice those teachings correctly. Based on this we are able to develop devotion toward the guru who teaches the scriptures and instructions related to that.

In the case that one is not able to find certainty from the depths of one's heart in the teachings of the Buddha, showing faith and devotion toward the guru feels more like an obligation that must be met. Thus, exert yourself in transforming seeing faults into an aide for your faith, as said. If we do this in conjunction with creating merit and purifying obstacles, and investigate with an unbiased mind, it is certain that we will give rise to a mind that does not look for faults in the guru.

Meditation that is merely faith-based—foolish meditation—is insufficient as a condition; therefore one must find certainty through logical proofs and examples.

The perfect and completely enlightened Buddha who is free of all faults and endowed with all qualities was seen by Sunakṣatra, Devadatta, and other non-Buddhists as a mass of faults and defects. [141] Ārya Asaṅga saw venerable Maitreya as a female dog whose lower body was heavily affected by maggots; Buddhajñānapāda

saw Ācārya Mañjuśrīmitra as an old layman who was wrapped in a Dharma robe plowing a field and then boiling the sentient beings from the furrows of the plowed field in hot water; Nāropa saw Tilopa killing and roasting fish; the novice Kantalipa saw Vajravārāhī as a leper woman. Furthermore, it is explained in the *Sūtra of the Meeting of Father and Son* that the Tathāgata accomplished the welfare of sentient beings through emanating as a demon. When one contemplates that there is no difference between one's own perspective and these attestations, it is said that unpleasant, negative aspects of the guru's prior actions are transformed through the practice of these analytical meditations into utterly lucid aspects in which the guru is free of faults, like a beam of light piercing through a small hole into darkness. Even beginners are certain to experience this if they meditate on it.

Having gained conviction that the guru is free of faults, one implicitly realizes that the guru is replete with all qualities. Even so, it is natural that the capacity of whatever stronger mentality we have will overcome its opposite, be it a fault or a quality.

Whatever qualities the spiritual teacher may have, whether they be expertise, accomplishments, righteousness, and so forth, or simply slight attachment to objects or good reading skills—whatever small qualities there are—if one intensely contemplates that the guru has such and such supreme qualities, when they have faults such as a lack of education or miserliness that holds onto things, one can overcome these to the point they become similar to being nonmanifest. Just as on the day the new moon rises into the sky but cannot be seen due to the brightness of the sun, in the same way, blocking out the more subtle faults and increasing our faith in the minor qualities is the root of all of one's spiritual accomplishments and goodness, and therefore a significant point. [142]

To furthermore block the perception of faults, contemplate the general reasons for needing to rely on the guru. If one still has a mind that finds faults with the guru, there is no difference for the guru, but since the disciple desires gain and not loss, if one focuses on the faults of the guru one only incurs a loss. If one focuses on their qualities there is great gain to be had, and therefore why does one not intentionally focus on their qualities? Moreover, whether the guru has greater or lesser experience and realizations, in this time when one has finally taken a human rebirth twenty-five hundred years after the Buddha passed into nirvana, bereft of the good fortune to see the him directly and listen to his instructions, the enlightened speech of the kind Teacher, which lays the foundation for accomplishing the great welfare of oneself and others, is directly made known to us by the spiritual teachers.

Therefore, meeting with the spiritual teachers is no different than meeting the Buddha directly; the ordinary guru whom we can see as often as we like lives an ordinary life, just as we do, yet accomplishes vast benefit. Therefore, they are by nature more kind and compassionate to us than the Buddha, too. This is due to the fact that they make every effort for us to progressively enter the Buddhist path, to help us understand what to adopt and what to discard, and to encourage our interest and effort. Thus, through understanding the subtleties of the nature of Dharma, one can discern right from wrong, and from the beginning stage of the way to rely on a spiritual teacher up to the union of no more learning at the end, all stages of the path—the Dharma of what is to be adopted and what is to be discarded—transmitted in detail from the Buddha, is introduced to us by the spiritual friend. Through this, having been able to bring them into focus of one's glance meditation, one relies on the three wheels in relation to the treatises of the three baskets—the study wheel of listening and contemplation; the renunciation wheel of meditative stabilization; and the action wheel of Dharma activity. In dependence on whose kindness does one thus gain even a mere understanding of the three trainings? [143] It is due only to the power of the ordinary spiritual teacher, the guru in this fleshy human body; through one's own experience one can understand that there is no other way.

Furthermore, what is meant by "the aspect of the ordinary guru"? The distinction of ārya persons and ordinary, common beings is not one of social stratum or body stature, but an internal difference of mind based on whether one possesses the quality of a direct realization of emptiness or not. Therefore, a person who has such a quality is an "ārya" being, and all those who are bound by the three poisonous afflictions are "ordinary." A guru who has the three poisonous afflictions thus manifests an "ordinary aspect." From the perspective of being a peer, we should think of the guru who achieves enormous benefit as in the nature of compassion without contest. For example, when we are happy and satisfied, if someone offers us excellent food, clothing, and bedding we are very grateful. However if someone offers us a spoonful of tsampa when they are about to die of starvation, even though from a materialistic point of view the spoonful of tsampa is inferior to luxurious foods, clothing, and possessions, if one thinks in terms of benefit to oneself, that person giving a spoonful of tsampa when one is on the verge of death is vastly kinder. In the same way, when one is not self-reliant and is in a serious state of needing help, although the ordinary guru may be incapable in some ways, because they are a real, authentic teacher of the path they are thus not only more brilliant and precious, if we consider how we are under the influence of our mind now, and that we have strong karmic obscurations due to that mind being under the influence of the three poisonous afflictions, we can know that merely following a guru such as that is extremely fortunate, and meeting someone superior to them is incredibly rare. As Geshé Chen-ngawa Lodrö Gyaltsen says: [144]

> Since our karmic obscurations are so heavy,
> we should be happy to see the guru even in human form.

Our merit is great to not see them as a dog or donkey;
therefore, generate heartfelt respect, children of Śākyamuni.

This point can also be understood from the previous citations from the *Jewel Ornament of Liberation*. If one can generate an attitude of strong veneration from one's own side, even though it makes no difference to the guru, there are huge advantages to the student such as always receiving temporal and ultimate blessings. What does "blessing" (*chinlub*; *byin rlabs*) mean? The syllable *chin* carries a meaning of magnificence and potency, while *lub* has the meaning of transformation; therefore, it should be understood as the transformation of our thoroughly unpacified continuum, or intractable mind, into the potential for good qualities, or something magnificent. Receiving or not receiving the guru's blessings of course has some slight relation to the level of the guru's mind, their qualities, and capacity; however it is primarily not from the side of the guru, but rather it depends on the level of faith of the disciple. Therefore, it is certainly the case that a significant factor in the receiving of blessings is the strength of the disciple's devotion, as said by Geshé Potowa:

The great and small blessings of the guru
do not exist in reality—they depend on oneself.

One should, from the depths of one's heart, have the discernment that the guru is a representative of the Teacher, and that they do not waver from entirely beneficial activities and the intention of all the buddhas; furthermore, the activity of speech—the supreme of all activities—is bestowed on us only by the guru of ordinary appearance, and therefore they are far kinder than all the buddhas. Not only that, they are also the sole agent of the enlightened activities of all the victors, and the fact that the Buddha still continues to accomplish the welfare of all sentient beings in this day and age is only through the activities of the spiritual teachers. [145] In dependence on this and the other reasons we must realize that the guru is the foundation of all good qualities and the source of all that is excellent.

We might raise a few doubts with respect to this point. The explanation style of lamrim is primarily one taught in accordance with our shared experiences and entirely in accord with reality. Therefore, if the differing fundamental intentions behind the sutras and tantras are not commented upon with respect to this way of relying on the spiritual teacher in the context of merely the common path to those who are unable, in this day and age, to view everything solely with pure appearance, statements such as it being incorrect to revise one's approach after already having relied on the spiritual teacher, or that one must view the guru as a buddha, will not sit well with the majority of people who adhere to a common approach.

Thus, if the intention of the sutras is that the guru is an actual buddha, that seems to not accord with Maitreya's *Ornament for the Mahāyāna Sūtras*, which delineates the ten qualities of a guru—being disciplined, pacified, and so forth—or statements in other treatises that the guru needs to have the qualifying characteristics of compassion, abiding in ethical discipline, applying oneself to the welfare of others, patience, not being discouraged, and so forth. Furthermore, it does not accord with the statement that, at the very least, whether the guru be a good or bad person, it is appropriate to investigate them by way of their conduct, character, level of knowledge, level of desire, expressions of body and speech, and so forth. If they were a bodhisattva, let alone a buddha, there would be no need to mention that they would have such qualities, and we could appropriately assume that to be the case. The very intentional instructions on the necessity that they possess such qualities are clearly based on the assumption that the gurus are ordinary beings. [146].

Therefore, it is not impossible that one finds contradictory that, on the one hand, the guru has to possess the aforementioned qualities, and, on the other hand, that the guru is a buddha. For example, if a guru is a buddha in the perspective of their disciple, one must assert that even if the guru were ordinary before they established a guru-disciple relationship, from the moment the disciple listened to the Dharma the guru spontaneously became a buddha. Likewise, those in harmony with the guru consider them a friend, and those not in harmony may consider them a foe; therefore, even though from the perspective of a single person the guru cannot be simultaneously both a friend and foe, or both a buddha and sentient being, would it not entail they have a common locus?

If one must hold them as a guru after hearing only a verse of Dharma, and all such gurus are emanations of buddhas and bodhisattvas yet "show the aspect of an ordinary guru," then if the wicked Māra were to emanate as a guru and teach Dharma, one would have to view them as a display of a buddha and so forth. Thus, the passage "they do not exist in reality—they depend on oneself" holds true.

Likewise, even if the old men and women who are reading instructors in their villages or the astute monastics who have commenced their studies of the great treatises and are capable of teaching the new monks and nuns are to be viewed as buddhas by their students, then from their own side, even without the confidence to generate the manifest pride thinking oneself is a buddha, they might fall into the mistake of having the conviction that they are not controlled by the afflictions and that they have not run out of qualities. On top of that, even having reached the peak of scholasticism through extensive study of treatises, even famous geshés or lamas poised on top of Dharma thrones can have strong pride, jealously, attachment, and anger. [147] Therefore, if one places unrestricted confidence in "displays," the "showing of aspects," or "inconceivable secrets," and so forth, the advantages and drawbacks to be had are obvious when looking at history.

There are, of course, reasons why the guru is a buddha according to the tantric system; however, from the perspective of an ordinary being who has not tamed their continuum through training in the common path, I think it is still difficult for them to clear up their doubts. Many gurus who are renowned as emanations of different buddhas and bodhisattvas are not postulated as such based entirely on worldly conjecture; rather, they can be inferred to be such totally based on their qualities of scriptural knowledge and realization, and the activities of their three secrets of body, speech, and mind. These gurus follow the life stories of the Kadam masters and hide their qualities like a butter lamp hidden inside a vase. Their saying that they have no qualities of scripture and realization is due to their humility. However, since the majority of people these days take things as they hear them, they end up thinking, "If, as they say, they do not have qualities of scripture and realization how can they be an emanation of a buddha or bodhisattva?" Furthermore, people doubt whether bodhicitta is able to be developed in general, whether there is any proof of a person having bodhicitta, and whether the disciples' minds seriously viewing the guru as a buddha are factually concordant or not.

These questions keep arising. There might be no higher method for increasing faith in those who direct their minds according to the teaching that disciples should train in pure perception independent from the reality of whether the guru who teaches the Dharma is good or bad, or that there is only benefit and no disadvantages from the disciple seeing the guru as a buddha even if they see themselves as an ordinary being. Nevertheless, one still has to analyze the types of explanations given to others with a common mindset as to the reasons for engaging in the practice while ignoring that appearances and reality are contradictory, or that it is like training in factually discordant minds. [148]

RECOLLECTING THEIR GREAT KINDNESS AND GENERATING DEVOTION

Accordingly, exceptional unshakable faith can of course arise merely from hearing of the guru's fame even without benefiting

oneself directly through their kindness. However, the recollection of kindness is very important in order to generate great devotion, and even though buddhas whose nature is free of faults and possesses all qualities are equal in number to the grains of sand of the river Ganges, if one is not fortunate one cannot receive their kindness. In order for the holy guru to lead migrating beings who are unruly and difficult to tame, they have emanated as the ordinary form of all the sugatas of the three times. Thus, in terms of having exhausted faults and possessing qualities, they are no different than the buddhas, yet for us they are more superior than the buddhas. This is because the buddhas, while not wavering from the great bliss of the dharmakāya, emanate the aspect of the enjoyment body for the sake of ārya bodhisattvas who are uncommon disciples. Since that body is not perceptible to śrāvaka, pratyekabuddha, and ordinary beings, they establish beings into the path of ripening and liberation by displaying an emanation body in the world. Those buddhas do not intentionally forsake us out of partiality, but just like a cave facing north does not receive any sun, through one's own misfortune and poor karma, one has not become a vessel to experience the nectar of their teachings, nor to see the buddhas directly. [149] Due to that, one is cycling in this endless samsara and experiencing suffering. If we do not meet with the holy spiritual teachers in this time when we have attained a human body, one has to wander in this unfortunate state without freedoms in which one does not even hear the words "Three Jewels," and even if one met the Buddha directly, the Dharma, the profundity and depth of which cannot further increase, is already excellently taught by the spiritual teacher! If one is able to practice that, there is no doubt that one will attain liberation and omniscience, and that one will be protected from the fear of sickness and foes in this life. If one considers the gratitude we show toward those who give food, clothing, and possessions, how can we ever repay the kindness of bestowing the highest everlasting happiness and the clearing away of the general and specific sufferings of samsara, even if we filled the billion world systems with gold?

From our own side, we should contemplate from the depths of our hearts the devotion and respect that thinks that the guru is more kind and more superior to all the buddhas of the three times, and we should meditate on this until the hairs on our bodies rise up and tears fall from our eyes. If one wants to cultivate this, one can recite in a supplicating fashion the verses from the *Stem Array Sūtra*, starting with "This is my spiritual teacher who propounds the Dharma" and so forth, with a pleasing tune.

If one reflects on the kindness of one's spiritual teacher in this fashion, one generates devotion and knows that in terms of kindness, the guru is kinder than all the buddhas, kinder than our Teacher Buddha Śākyamuni, kind because of blessing our continuum, kind because of gathering disciples through material things, just as said in the *Guru Pūjā*:

> I supplicate the compassionate protector,
> who correctly teaches the path of the sugata
> to unruly migrators of this degenerate age,
> who were untamed by countless past buddhas. [150]

> I supplicate the compassionate protector,
> who enacts the deeds of the conqueror,
> for numerous protectorless migrators,
> after the sun of the subduer has set.

There have been countless past buddhas, but we were not suitable candidates to be tamed. During the time the Teacher Śākyamuni lived in India he established countless disciples on the path of ripening and liberation, but we were unable to be there during this time. Subsequently, the seven successors of the teachings, the seventeen pandits of Nālandā,[57] the eighty mahāsiddhas, and the inconceivable, great holy gurus of the Dharma lineages of the Sakya, Geluk, Kagyü, and Nyingma traditions, all accomplished the welfare of countless trainees, but we were unable to see them, listen to their teachings, or be their disciples. Therefore, realizing that only the compassion of the guru with whom we have a direct Dharma connection, who upholds the teachings, and who is a representative of the Buddha, is superior to that of others, we must now train our mind of devotion. Since we do not get to regularly see the spiritual teacher seated atop a high Dharma throne, it is as the saying goes, "The blessings of the guru are great from afar." This means that when we see them from a distance our faith and veneration strongly increases, but it is more difficult to generate faith and veneration toward the guru with whom we are in close contact. Therefore, with respect to the general spiritual teacher, and particularly the guru with whom we continually relate to on an equal level—those for whom it is easy to find fault—we must primarily strive to train faith and devotion specifically toward them.

Accordingly, the disciple should generate single-pointed faith and devotion toward the guru, but however much they show respect through prostrations, polite speech, and so forth, from the guru's own side they should remain as low and humble as if they were about to dissolve into the ground. As Dromtönpa said:

Even if everyone visualizes you on the crown of their heads,
sit on the floor and be amenable.

Likewise, as it says in the *Eight Verses of Mind Training*:

By thinking of all sentient beings
as more precious than a wish-fulfilling jewel,
for accomplishing the highest aim,
may I always hold them dear. [151]

Whenever I am in the company of others,
I will regard myself as the lowest among all,
and from the depths of my heart
may I cherish others as supreme.

Thus, from the guru's own side, they should think of themselves as at the end of the line of all sentient beings; it is a mistake for them to be haughty or have pride that thinks they have reached the front of the line, sitting tall with an arched back.

The Way to Rely in Action

With respect to reliance through practice, it says in *Fifty Verses on Guru Devotion*:

What need is there to say more?
Always strive to do whatever pleases the guru,
and avoid that which displeases them.

We must engage in what pleases the excellent spiritual teachers, and discard what displeases them. To this end, in prior times the Buddha, for the sake of hearing one verse of Dharma while on the path of training, stuck a thousand butter lamps and pierced a thousand nails on his body, gave up his son, princesses, subjects, and all his possessions. Furthermore, the way Sadāprarudita relied on Dharmodgata, Nāropa on Tilopa, Jowo Atiśa who faced hardship on the great ocean to receive bodhicitta from Dharmakīrtiśrī, the way Dromtönpa relied on Jowo Atiśa, Setön Künrik (1026–1116) on Drokmi Śākya Yeshé (992–1072), and how Milarepa relied on Marpa, and so forth, all facing hardship without concern for their bodies or possessions as indicated in their biographies, is inconceivable.

Even though those gurus were not interested in material possessions, they temporarily made out as if they depended on such things
with the intention of the disciple completing the collection of merit.
[152]. Therefore, it says in *Fifty Verses on Guru Devotion*:

> Giving to the guru is equal to giving
> to all the buddhas at all times.
> That offering is the collection of merit
> from which the supreme attainment comes.

One offers all of one's wealth for the sake of creating great waves
of merit, and even if told to do something difficult or inappropriate,
one should do so without any doubt, thinking, "This is only for my
benefit." However, if it is really something one could never do or is
inappropriate, one should thoroughly explain, as it says:

> If you lack the knowledge to do as told
> politely explain why you cannot.

It is not appropriate to simply put the task out of one's mind and
leave it at that. Since it is said that the most important thing is pleasing the guru through the offering of accomplishments, one should
reach a definitive conclusion of the Dharma they taught through
listening, contemplation, and meditation.

From among the points of offering material things, venerating, serving, and carrying out their instructions, with respect to reliance in
practice, making donations and giving items to the guru for the sake
of completing the collections is the best material offering. With respect
to venerating and serving the guru, if the guru lives close by and one
directly offers devoted assistance, or serves as an attendant or part of
the retinue with pure intention, this is the true guru yoga, and most

importantly one pleases the guru through the offering of carrying out their instruction.

As I always say, with respect to "devotion which sees all actions as excellent," it is not good if there is an absurd lack of judgment, and if one falls into the extreme of devotion, the guru also becomes negligent through being spoiled, which in turn becomes a cause for the disciple to rebel. Furthermore, it says in the *Great Treatise on the Stages of the Path*:

> If one must carry out the instructions of the guru, then what
> if through relying on that guru one is lead down a wrong
> path, or engages in an action that goes against the three vows,
> should one do it? With regard to this it says in Gunapra-
> bha's *Vinaya Sūtra*, "If non-Dharma is instructed, one should
> refuse." Also, the *Jewel Cloud* says, "If it is virtuous, act in
> accordance; if it is nonvirtuous, do not act in accordance."
> Therefore, do not listen to those nonvirtuous instructions. Not
> engaging in what is improper is clearly shown in the twelfth
> birth story. However, it is incorrect to take their wrong actions
> as a reason to disrespect, reproach, or despise the guru. [153]

And furthermore:

> Thoroughly excuse yourself and do not engage in the
> instruction.

Just as the great Lord Tsongkhapa has advised, if the guru instructs non-Dharma—that is, something incompatible—it should be refused. Likewise, "carrying out all instructions" presumes a fully qualified spiritual teacher; such a person would not suggest something unreasonable, and one must make distinctions with respect to the way to carry out all instructions, as the great Tsongkhapa says in his section titled "A General Indication of the Attitudes Needed to Rely on the Teacher." He begins with the teaching on respecting and serving the guru with nine attitudes: like a dutiful child, a diamond, the earth, a mountain, a servant, a sweeper, a vehicle, a dog, and a ferry. These are as taught in the *Array of Stalks Sūtra*, and importantly adds, "This refers to a fully qualified teacher; do not let just anyone lead you by the nose."

When Dromtönpa was about to leave this world, he lay his head in Geshé Potowa's lap and slept. [154] At this time, tears fell from the devastated Potowa's eyes onto Dromtönpa's face, and when Dromtönpa questioned why, Potowa said, "Until now, master, you have been someone I could trust and ask my questions to. If you now direct your mind elsewhere, I feel myself and others will be without the protection of a spiritual teacher." The great Dromtönpa then replied, "Make the scriptures!"

This is the most excellent advice; we do not necessarily need a person—if we study, contemplate, and meditate based on the instructions taught by the gurus and the excellent teachings in the Kangyur and Tengyur in an unbiased fashion, that is the highest offering of practice that pleases the gurus. If there are points one is doubtful about, then for the time being discuss these with a qualified, decent person without viewing them as a guru, just as a Dharma friend.

Sometimes what a fully qualified guru says may seem untimely or irrelevant, but there are definitely many reasons and purposes behind it. For example, each time Tilopa gave Nāropa instructions, from the outset they seemed to be without reason and unfitting, but the great pandita Nāropa fulfilled them without any hesitations, resulting in many stories of exceptional realizations arising in his mind.

Rather than offering thousands of items to such a guru, the main way to please them is to strive with great diligence to fulfill instructions they give regarding what to adopt and what to discard. It is an important point that the great lord Tsongkhapa taught both the heavy and light from the good and bad sides in this way. We Tibetans have maintained familiarity throughout generations and therefore do not have many faults in this regard. However, since Buddhism is newly spreading east and west to other countries where it did not exist prior, there is room for errors such as misunderstanding the full meaning contained within earlier and later Buddhist treatises, and not being able to compare them properly. [155]

The Benefits of Relying on a Guru

This text will not go into fine detail regarding the great benefits and advantages of relying on the guru in this way, nor regarding the faults and disadvantages of not relying; however, an explanation will be given following the order presented in the *Great Treatise on the Stages of the Path*.

PROXIMITY TO THE STATE OF BUDDHAHOOD

Through the instructions of the guru our smaller qualities gradually develop, and larger faults gradually decrease, leading to a transformation of mind through understanding what was not previously understood. A newfound conviction in the objects of our understanding becomes more and more stable. In this way we attain unsurpassed, complete enlightenment possessing all qualities and free of all faults. Therefore, if through the guru's instructions even one fault decreases, or one quality is increased, then we are that much closer to buddhahood. Moreover, since, in order to attain the state of buddhahood we must accumulate vast collections, and since the field through which we accumulate that merit is the guru themself, from that perspective, through relying on them there is the benefit of becoming closer to buddhahood.

Pleasing the Victorious Ones

Even though the victorious ones dedicated themselves to attaining enlightenment for all sentient beings and are now accomplishing the welfare of others without break, we ourselves cannot see the enjoyment bodies endowed with the major and minor marks, free of all faults and having all qualities, let alone the dharmakāya. Not only that, we also did not have the fortune to see the supreme emanation body that ordinary beings with pure karma were able to see. [156] Therefore, for us ordinary sentient beings with impure obscurations, those beings who look just like us and who train in the Dharma and teach the path are the spiritual teachers, and following their enlightened activities leads only to achieving buddhahood. For this reason, these spiritual teachers are the representatives of the bodies and speech of the victors and their spiritual heirs; thus, if we correctly rely on them and train ourselves, it is possible to please the victors.

Not Being Destitute of a Spiritual Teacher

Through correctly relying on the guru in this life, as a concordant result one will have the protection of spiritual teachers also in future lives.

Not Falling to Lower Realms

Through correctly relying on the spiritual teacher, one's karma for experiencing the lower realms is exhausted in this life with only very slight harm to one's body or through dream experiences.

Not Easily Overcome by Bad Karma or Afflictions

The degree to which the mind of the spiritual teacher who protects the student is tamed, that is how much their polite and gentle nature will rub off onto the student, and it will also lead to a natural decrease in bad behavior and in the creation of bad karma due to afflictions, and eventually to their cessation.

Not Transgressing Bodhisattva Conduct, and Growing the Collection of Qualities Through Being Mindful of These

The spiritual teacher instructs on the practices for maintaining the six perfections for ripening one's own mind, and the four ways of gathering disciples for ripening others' minds. If one trains correctly in these, one's conduct becomes completely in line with bodhisattva conduct, and through the power of that one completes all qualities for spontaneously accomplishing the two purposes in one's own continuum. [157]

Fulfilling All Temporary and Ultimate Aims

If our faith and devotion in the spiritual teacher increases, our minds temporarily turn to Dharma, establishing the roots of happiness. Through this our realizations on the grounds and paths increase, and ultimately we are able to become free of all faults and to possess all qualities.

Attaining the Virtue of Thought and Action Through Serving the Guru, thus Accomplishing One's Own and Others' Aims and Completing the Collections

One completes the two collections of merit as explained when relying in thought and when relying in action. It is said that there is no greater way to purify the two obscurations than to worship and serve the guru; thus, through worshipping the guru one attains great roots of virtue, quickly completing the two collections that benefit one's own and others' aims.

The Disadvantages of Not Relying on the Guru

If one's method of reliance is wrong after taking someone as a spiritual teacher, one will experience eight disadvantages. First, one will be afflicted by sickness and spirits in this lifetime, and second, in future lifetimes one will experience immeasurable suffering in miserable realms for an immeasurable period of time. Third, qualities that have not arisen will not arise, and fourth, those that have arisen will degenerate. Fifth, if one relies on nonvirtuous teachers and bad friends, one's qualities slowly diminish and sixth, all faults will increase, leading to everything undesirous. Seventh, by relying on nonvirtuous teachers, previously existent wrongdoings—deeds wrong by nature and deeds wrong by prohibition—do not diminish, and eighth, previously nonexistent ones newly increase. The disadvantages that fall on oneself—as opposed to those advantages one gains from relying on the guru—are as in the *Great Treatise on the Stages of the Path*. [158]

A Summary of the Above Points

Not relying correctly on the guru in this way is the root of all faults, and correct reliance is the source of all that is good, as said in the *Array of Stalks Sūtra*, the *Tantra Bestowing the Initiation of Vajrapāṇi*, and other discourses of the Buddha and their commentaries. Having found ascertainment in these teachings, from our reading teacher, or guru, in the beginning, we are sequentially taught the meaning of Buddhist treatises, then we train in immeasurable knowledge for attaining omniscience, our object of attainment. Only once we have reached the culmination of our experience and intellectual understanding of all things will we attain the omniscience that knows all modes and varieties of phenomena. If we do not train at all, we will not spontaneously come to know all modes and varieties. Thus it says in the *Ornament for the Mahāyāna Sūtras*:

> Without becoming erudite in the five fields of knowledge,
> supreme ārya beings will also not attain the all-knowing state.

Thus, even though the points of a spiritual teacher who is worthy of reliance should all be practiced at the level of mere words, freely giving up the body and one's life like the bodhisattva Sadāprarudita and so forth cannot be directly practiced by beginners, and therefore should be done in one's prayers; those people that are actually able should only do so taking into account the time, place, and situation. It is not the case that one should necessarily carry out their meditative practice in real life; act according to your ability. [159]

A BRIEF INSTRUCTION ON HOW TO
SUSTAIN THE MEDITATION

This has two parts:

a. The actual way to sustain the meditation
b. Refuting misconceptions with respect to the way to sustain the actual meditation

The first has two parts:

1) How to carry out the actual sessions
2) What to do during the breaks between the actual meditation sessions

The first has three parts:

a) The preparatory practices
b) How to sustain the meditation during the actual sessions
c) What to do at the conclusion of a session

The Preparatory Practices

With respect to the first, **the brief practice of those points comes under the section titled "A Brief Indication of the Way to Sustain the Meditation" in Tsongkhapa's** *Stages of the Path to Enlightenment* **in which he instructs that one must first identify the actual preparatory practices to carry out. In the older instruction manual** *Essence of Refined Gold*, the preparatory practices **first appeared under the title "The Preliminaries for Relying on the Spiritual Teacher." However, they were intended as preliminary accumulations of the collections of merit and wisdom in order to generate the aforementioned analytical meditations in one's continuum.** The present section, "A Brief Instruction on How to Sustain the Meditation" contains both the practices of the sessions and the breaks, and the subsection of the meditation session contains preparatory, actual, and concluding practices. Out of those, the preparatory practices were taught in six parts, **although they are not practiced in that order. Since this pertains to the life examples of Protector Dharmakīrtiśrī**, the first of the six preparatory practices is to **clean and sweep the abode and arrange representations of the body, speech, and mind of the Three Jewels.**

However much one cleans the place of virtuous practice, one's awareness becomes that much clearer. Through aspiration and conviction, one invites the victors and their spiritual heirs as a field of merit and, through the seven-limb ritual, thereby accumulates merit and purifies obscurations. Even though it is, for example, like the worldly norm of cleaning up before important guests arrive, one should completely purify the invitation area when inviting the victors and their heirs and accumulating merit. [160] It is a different matter if one is a yogin who has trampled course conceptuality through realizations and thus for whom good and bad have the same taste. However, since we lack the aptitude to be yogins, if we also paid no attention to cleanliness we would lack focus. For these reasons it is important to clean the place.

Then, with respect to arranging representations of body, speech, and mind, it is excellent if one has such representations, but otherwise one does not necessarily need them to practice Dharma. For example, Jetsun Milarepa is considered to have been one of the undisputed supreme Tibetan Dharma practitioners, yet he did not have any representations of body, speech, mind, and so forth while in his cave. There is a famous story of a thief who came one night and was feeling around the dark cave when Milarepa said, laughing, "What do you hope to find at night in my cave that is completely empty during the daytime?"

If one has the three representations, then place an image of the Buddha Bhagavān as the main representation, followed by Maitreya, Mañjuśrī, and the other great close disciples of the Teacher in the correct order. It is a mistake to order the statues or images according to their quality or age. Therefore, because the Buddha Bhagavān is the lord of the teachings, even if the statue is made of clay, it should be placed in the foremost position.

As for the representation of enlightened speech, one can place the *Prajñāpāramitā in 8000 Verses*, *Great* or *Middle-Length* lamrim treatises, or any text that one uses as a basis for practice of study, contemplation and meditation. For the representation of the enlightened mind one can place a stūpa, a stamped clay votive image (*tsa tsa*), or the like. [161]

The second preparatory element is making offerings. As it says [in the *Easy Path*] "use nondeceptive offerings and arrange them beautifully." **"Arrange whatever offerings one can afford"**—just like the widely used traditional offerings of water bowls, candles, flowers, incense and so forth. Whatever one arranges should be clean. In particular, the offerings should be free of dishonesty—dishonest substances and motivations. Items incorrectly accrued through trickery, intimidation, aggression—through any force or theft—are dishonest substances and are inappropriate. Likewise, any offering that is made as a beautifier or ornamentation to make things attractive to others, or to gain respect and esteem is an offering defiled by a dishonest motivation and thus inappropriate.

Once the eleventh-century Kadam master Geshé Bengung Gyal was expecting the visit of a sponsor and had arranged extensive offerings in his abode for the occasion. After doing so, he sat on his seat and examined his motivation and realized he had prepared the offerings so the sponsor would think well of him. Understanding his motivation was stained, he immediately arose and threw a handful of ashes over the offerings, as if throwing them on the demon of the eight worldly dharmas. In doing so, the story goes, those offerings became supreme.

In this way, one needs a pure motivation untainted by pretense or concern for superficial beauty, and thus one needs offerings untainted by those two faults. Furthermore, any item procured through flattery, hinting, bribery, coercion, or hypocrisy—the five wrong livelihoods— are unsuitable as offerings. [162]

As for the beautiful arrangement, when arranging the offering articles such as water bowls, one should first pour a small amount of water in one bowl that has been wiped clean, then initially use that to slightly fill the others. One should not arrange empty offerings, nor should they touch, or have a significant gap between them; they should be spaced approximately barely a grain's width apart. Water should be poured gently into the first and last bowls, like "grains of barley," and slightly stronger into the middle ones.

As said in the *Easy Path*, "Sit on a comfortable seat and assume the eight-point body posture or any other comfortable position." Although there is an oral tradition that necessitates finding an auspicious direction to face one's meditation seat, it does not make a big difference, and therefore place your seat as suits the layout of the room. Whatever the case, place the seat so it is the seat of samādhi—propping up one's back so that it is slightly higher can help one sit for longer with less discomfort. In this way **sit on a comfortable seat in a posture that is not careless—either cross-legged or with half-crossed legs.** If one is unwell and cannot cross the legs, in a good posture **and so forth, settle yourself suitably** and practice.

It is taught one should sit in the seven-point Vairocana posture, which, with counting the breath, makes eight points.

First, place your legs in the full-lotus posture, or however you normally sit. There does seem to be a clear benefit to sitting in the full-lotus posture: an Indian friend of mine who I requested to meditate immediately showed signs of having imprints of meditation, saying that if he meditated cross-legged he experienced his meditation went much better than if he used a chair. [163] It appears that through sitting in a crossed-legged posture the channels, winds and energies can be brought together, allowing for flow in the body and change in the mind. Furthermore, it is said that if one sits cross-legged one creates auspiciousness to accomplish the cross-legged pose with four attributes in future, but if one does not familiarize oneself with sitting cross-legged when one is young it is another matter.

Second, rest the hands evenly, placing the palm of the left hand underneath the right hand with the thumbs touching each other at the tip, and placed against the navel.

Third, "sit with the spine straight like an arrow." It is said one should not rock side to side but remain straight, resulting in the body's channels straightening, which in turn allows for even movement of the winds and drops. There is an oral tradition teaching that if the strength of fluctuation of the winds goes out of balance—for example if one leans too much to the right—the movement of the winds and constituents in the left channel becomes too strong, resulting in increased desire and attachment. Furthermore, if one leans too far to the left, the movements of the winds and drops in the right channel become too strong, resulting in increased anger and aversion. Therefore, there is importance in the body remaining straight.

Fourth, "the chin should be slightly tucked in." When looking forward, the head should be slightly bent to the point that the Adam's apple is not visible. Approximately, if one were to hang a string directly down from the tip of the nose, it should touch the navel.

Fifth, "the upper arms should extend like the wings of a vulture." The elbows should not touch the body; if they are placed loosely it is conducive for longer periods of meditation. The shoulders should fall naturally. [164]

Sixth, "the eyes fall to the tip of the nose." The eyes should be ever so slightly open in a relaxed manner, and one should look downward in the direction of the tip of the nose; it is not the case that one must look at the tip of the nose itself. If one deliberately closes one's eyes it is also unsuitable, but if the eyes close while focusing on the object of meditation it does not make a huge difference. Since we are primarily trying to establish concentration in our mind, we need to be nonreactive to the engagement of our sense consciousnesses. Therefore, whatever we see in front of us needs to not damage our concentration. There are differences according to particular instructions as to where to look; it is said when doing Kālacakra meditation one should look upward, but when doing dzogchen meditation one should look straight ahead, and likewise there is the manner of threefold motionlessness of body, speech, and mind.

Seventh, the teeth and lips should fall naturally, with the tip of the tongue touching the palate. In this way the mouth does not become dry during analytical and placement meditation, and saliva does not leak. Furthermore, it is said that the tongue should touch the palate to stop the throat becoming dry from breathing strongly through the mouth.

If one counts the breath in order to pacify a distracted mind, one should not breathe in a way that the inhalations and exhalations become noisy—that is, in a way that makes a strong sound. Breathing should not be uneven or disturbed, nor should one pant in a way that produces heat, and so forth. Rather, it is recommended that one count the breath slowly at the beginning of sessions. Thus, first placing one's undivided attention on the movement of the breath, one should count ten inner and outer breath cycles, up to one hundred, a thousand, and so forth. This is convenient as it is neither an extremely course nor subtle support for visualization. It is said that through observing one thousand coming and goings of the breath one's mental stability grows stronger. It says in tantric texts to first eliminate impure air nine times at the beginning of the actual meditation, thus when one's mind is continually disturbed, counting the breath acts as a peaceful method against distraction. [165] However, this only functions to temporarily relax the mind and does not have great potential. Thus once one's mind is relaxed it is more beneficial to contemplate the dependent arising and interdependence of cause and effect, bodhicitta, compassion and so forth with discriminating wisdom.

Bodhicitta undertaken with this physical posture is known as "the exceptional mind of virtue." The heart of Dharma practice can be synthesized into those two minds of refuge and bodhicitta. Just like there is no negative, nonvirtuous action that does not relate to either the Three Jewels or sentient beings, likewise our accumulation of the two types of merit, purification of the two obscurations, and subsequent attainment of buddhahood is the result of relying on either the Three Jewels or sentient beings. Śāntideva also says in his *Way of the Bodhisattva*:

> Just like one practices Dharma
> because of sentient beings and the Victor,
> why then are sentient beings not revered,
> like the Victor?

In this context, going for refuge in dependence on the Three Supreme Ones, generating bodhicitta in dependence on sentient beings, and meditating on the four immeasurables is very important. These must also be conjoined with a pure motivation. Therefore, think how one has attained a human birth, and, having met the Buddha's teachings, how it is in our own hands whether we go toward utter goodness or utter wrongdoing. With this in mind, contemplate dedicating all of your activities toward benefiting others, and to doing whatever it takes to have a meaningful life and achieve buddhahood for the sake of others. Thinking thus, visualize all sentient beings surrounding you as human beings who can speak and understand meaning, and experiencing their individual suffering within the six classes of beings. [166] If you want to further refine this contemplation, visualize in front of you your enemies, evil spirits, and antagonists; to the right all male sentient beings exemplified by your father; on the left all female sentient beings who are primarily your mother; and behind visualize friends of this life on whom you rely. In this way visualize all beings of the three realms filling all directions.

The reason for visualizing enemies, evil spirits, and antagonists in front is because we naturally want to forsake those we do not like, and thus you should intentionally visualize them clearly, and emphatically meditate on them in particular as objects of altruistic love, compassion, and bodhicitta. It says to meditate on the immeasurables through visualizing all sentient beings surrounding yourself and generating bodhicitta and thinking, "How great it would be if all sentient beings had happiness and the causes of happiness; may they have that! I will cause them to have that!" If you wish to meditate on special bodhicitta, the ways to do so are within the topics of refuge and bodhicitta.

THE WAY TO VISUALIZE THE MERIT FIELD, THE OBJECT OF REFUGE

In order to practice the field of accumulation, the object of refuge, in the older manuals, such as *Essence of Refined Gold*, it says to first purify through the svabhāva mantra, then generate the samaya being. With respect to this, in Jamyang Taklung Drakpa Lodro Gyatso's (1546–1615) oral commentary, he says to generate one's root guru as the protector Mañjuśrī then make supplications by way of repeating *dhīḥ*— the seed syllable of the mantra of Mañjuśrī—many times. Some manuals say to generate the guru as Vajradhara, then, creating many inner and outer lotus petals, place the gurus on top as with the deities of the mandala; then arrange them in lines from left to right, having the appearance of a congregation in a prayer assembly. Visualizations such as these contained in many practices have been adulterated by tantra and are thus slightly discordant with the practices of this tradition. [167] Here, as it is not mixed with the tantric tradition and an entirely sutric perspective, the merit fields related to guru yoga are invited as guests through blessing the abode and ritual tools according to the *Sūtra Ritual of Bhaiṣajyaguru*. Therefore, as a way of blessing the site, the throne, and so forth through the truth of the Three Jewels, the blessings of the buddhas and bodhisattvas, the completion of the two collections and the purity of the dharmadhātu, and the power of one's own faith and devotion, recite, "May the earth be pure everywhere"[58] and so forth, and visualize the abode and elements as transformed, within which is the even, jeweled ground, flat like the palm of one's hand, and on top is a beautiful jeweled throne held up by lions; surrounding are jeweled thrones equal to the number of root and lineage gurus beautifully arranged in the front and back, and high and low, in tiers.

These thrones have four tiers: the first tier is the Teacher, the Lord of Sages, and Mañjuśrī and Maitreya; in the second tier, Atiśa is seated in the middle, Dromtönpa on his right, and Ngok Lekpé Sherab on the left; on the third tier, the gentle protector Tsongkhapa is seated in the middle, Jetsun Sherab Sengé on his right, and the omniscient Gendun Drup on the left; in the fourth tier, either the Great Fifth or one's root guru is seated in the middle, with the Great Fifth on their right, and Jampa Chöden on the left. This visualization is according to an oral tradition, with the other root and lineage gurus visualized seated on the left and right.

In accordance with *Essence of Refined Gold,* invite them with the verse

> Even though they do not waver from the pure dharmakāya,
> they look upon limitless beings in the ten directions with compassion.
> Gurus of the three times who perform the vast activities of all victorious ones,
> please come to this place with your retinues. [168]

Together with the three verses beginning with, "You are the protector of all sentient beings without exception," visualize the kind root guru who teaches the Dharma and is inseparable with the king of the Śākyas, the unequaled teacher, surrounded by the lineage gurus of vast conduct and profound view. At their fringes are the trainee and nontrainee sangha of the three vehicles surrounding them like merging clouds. They arrive as in the *Account of Sumāgadhā,* and take their seats.

With the line, "The bath house has an extremely pleasant fragrance," and so forth, generate a bath house. Visualize one hundred, one thousand, ten thousand, or one hundred thousand—however much one is able—emanations of one's own body holding up jeweled vases filled with fragrant water. Then with the verse, "Just as the gods offered a bath," and so forth, and the verse, "Although the victor's body, speech, and mind do not have afflictions," and so forth, and the verses related to the six perfections, and so forth, as appropriate to the extensive and short rituals, perform the bathing ritual.

Even though in reality the fields of merit are not tainted by the unclean, from the perspective of beings with impure appearances they appear as tainted, and thus it is for the sake of clearing away those appearances. Bathing, performing oil massage, wiping away filth, nursing them when ill, and so forth, and expressing the qualities of the guru are what we should do if we are with the guru in person. These act as a substitute to that, and what follows are mostly methods for pleasing the guru through material offerings as explained previously.

With the verse that begins, "Fragrantly filling the billion universes," one anoints; with the verse, "Soft, smooth, and fine divine dress," one offers divine dress; and with the verse, "Out of your loving compassion for myself and migrating beings," one requests the merit field to remain firmly.

When performing the bathing ritual to those in the aspect of a monk—the Teacher Bhagavān, the seventeen pandits of India and so forth—the one visualized offering the bath should likewise be a monk. [169] Those in the aspect of male deities, such as Maitreya and Mañjuśrī, are offered the bath by female goddesses. The same applies to the oil massage and wiping away filth. When offering the cloth, Dharma robes and so forth are offered to monastics, and divine clothes are offered to deities.

ACCUMULATION, PURIFICATION, AND INCREASE THROUGH THE SEVEN-LIMBED PRACTICE

Following the fifth preparatory practice, one performs accumulation, purification, and increase by way of **the seven-limbed practice—a** condensed practice of accumulation and purification. Starting with prostrations, without forsaking the focus points of the objects of refuge, prostrate to them in their presence. Bow to the lowest point of the statue that is the object of prostration—the soles of the feet. Respectfully bowing in this way acts as an antidote to pride. The ways of prostrating include full-length prostrations, called "prostrations like a fallen tree," wherein all of one's body parts come to the floor like a tree that falls to the ground; the second way is bent prostrations, wherein five body parts—one's knees, palms of the hands, and forehead—touch the ground. These two are the most common ways of prostrating in the context of Vinaya, and unless one is unwell, one should touch the five body parts to the ground when making bent prostrations. Furthermore, an oral lineage says that if one completely outstretches one's arms when making full-length prostrations, however much one presses down on the ground with one's body, great merit equal in number to the particles of the pressed ground is accumulated.

The master Purchok Ngawang Jampa (1682–1762) was born in the Chamdo region, and it is said that his body was huge. He made hundreds of full-length prostrations every day, and because he was a huge Khampa it is said that he had a great advantage when prostrating. [170]

Whichever way one prostrates, there is a tradition of placing the pressed palms at the crown of one's head, then to the forehead, throat, and heart, or, alternately, first to either the crown of the head or forehead, then to the throat, and heart. In either case, when pressing one's hands together, do not leave the thumbs sticking out in the Indian manner of paying respect; rather, the thumbs should touch the palms of the hands, and the palms should form a hollow cavity. This is said to be the Buddhist way of joining the palms together. Furthermore, the external shape represents the rūpakāya, and the hollow cavity the dharmakāya of a buddha; touching the joined palms to the crown of the head is a means of accomplishing the crown protrusion;

to the forehead the means of accomplishing the hair coil; to the throat the means of accomplishing the Brahmā-like voice; and to the heart the means of accomplishing omniscience. Thus it is said this manner has the features of performing such symbolic representations and of placing their imprints.

One notes, however, that the Theravādin monks in other Buddhist countries are also seen pressing their palms flat together.

In general, prostrations can be of body, speech, or mind. Therefore, holding up one hand, pressing both hands together, or bowing with the body, are all prostrations of body; expressing and praising the qualities of enlightened body, speech, or mind is a verbal prostration; and making prayers or going for refuge with a pure mind are mental prostrations. To perform such a prostration, visualize the objects of refuge in the space in front of the point between the eyebrows however large you wish; in the case of a full-length prostration, visualize them within an arm span of the tips of the fingers. Together with the supplicating verses, **"Teacher Bhagavān, the incomparable guide,"** and so forth, of the individual vast conduct and profound view lineages, up to the revered guru. As an addendum, recite the following:

At the feet of the highly accomplished Sherab Sengé,
the genuine all-knowing Gendun Drup,
and Norbu Sang, who has manifested the state of the three
   bodies,
I make supplications to the three glorious gurus. [171]

Gendun Gyatso whose laughter is melodious,
Gelek Palsang, the sun of expounders,[59]
and the accomplished Lhatsun Sönam Palsang,
I supplicate the three holy spiritual teachers.

To the feet of Padmapāṇi, Sönam Gyatso,
Chöphel Sangpo, who received profound instructions,
and the lord of all families, Nangdzé Dorjé,
I make supplications to the three accomplished ones.

The incomparably kind Śrī Bhūti,
the lord of speech, Losang Gyatso,
those possessing a treasury of profound and vast Dharma,
to the personal and lineage tutors I make supplications.

(The lineage gurus of those after the supreme conqueror Sönam
Gyatso are in accordance with the teachings received by the incomparably kind protector of beings, His Holiness the Fourteenth Dalai
Lama, our guide within samsara and nirvana, and are as published in
the prayer booklet.)

At the feet of Padmapāṇi, Sönam Gyatso, Chöphel Sangpo who
    received the profound instructions,
the all-pervading lord, Khöntön Paljor Lhundrup,
I supplicate the three great accomplished ones.

The supreme victor, Ngawang Losang Gyatso,
the kind great abbot, the honorable Losang Chödrak,
the all-knowing Losang Gyaltsen,
and to Jamyang Shepé Dorjé, I make supplications.

To the spiritual teacher Jamyang Dewé Dorjé,
the incomparable great throne holder, Ngawang Chokden,
the supreme guide and victor, Kelsang Gyatso,
I supplicate the three holy and incomparable ones.

The great throne holder and lord, Longdöl Ngawang Losang,

the Panglung Tulku, Ngawang Nyendrak,
Ngawang Chözin, master of scripture and reasoning,
I supplicate the oceans of exalted wisdom.

Furthermore:

The regent of the conqueror, Darma Rinchen,
honorable Shakya Gyaltsen, the lamp for migrators,
erudite and accomplished Dönyö Palden,
I supplicate the three who illuminate the teachings. [172]

Chökyi Gyaltsen, supreme chief of expounders,
the honorable, great being, Namkha Gyaltsen,
and the learned Jetsun Chökyi Gyaltsen,
I supplicate the three unequaled gurus.

The lord of all accomplishments, Tsöndrü Gyaltsen,
the honorable guide of migrators, Damchö Gyaltsen,
Gelek Gyatso, holder of the treasury of heard transmissions,
I supplicate the three kind gurus.

Ngawang Jampa, who clarified the noble path,
the dance of Amitābha, honorable Palden Yeshé,
the great tutor, Yeshé Gyaltsen,
I supplicate the three who clarified the path to liberation.

The compassionate Losang Tenzin,
his principle heir, honorable Ngawang Chözin,
crown ornament of scholars, Yeshé Gyatso,
I supplicate the three holy guides.

Treasury of jewels of the noble tradition of the victor, the gentle
    protector,
lord of Dharma, the tutor whose memory cannot be matched,
to the great Losang Tsultrim Jampa Gyatso,
I respectfully make supplications through the three doors.

He who spread the teachings
like a vast summer lake, Ngawang Losang Thupten
fearless lord of the three realms,
I supplicate you, victorious over all.

Thupten Lungtok Namgyal Trinlé, like a second lord of subduers
    with respect to the Muni's teachings,
matchless holder of the holy teachings of scripture and
    realization,
whose victorious activities transform the three realms,
I supplicate the venerable guru.

With respect to Mañjuśrī's vajra speech he has attained mastery,
his excellent vase of intellect is filled with the nectar of exalted
    wisdom,
the beautiful ornament of upholders of the teachings [Tenzin] of
    which there is a vast ocean,
I supplicate to Jampal Ngawang Losang Yeshé, Padmapāṇi, the
    supreme ārya. [173]

Eyes to view all the countless teachings,
supreme gateway to liberation for the fortunate,
expert in loving skillful methods,
I supplicate the illuminating spiritual teachers. [173]

May I never be separated from perfect gurus in all lives,

and enjoy inseparably the glory of Dharma.

By completing the qualities of the grounds and paths,

may I quickly attain the state of Vajradhara.

Recite these supplications while prostrating. With the lines [from the *Samantabhadra Prayer*], "To all the buddhas in the ten directions of the universe," and so forth, make prostrations to the victors and spiritual heirs that were invited.

The second of the seven-branch practice is **the initial offering of the mandala. The material of the mandala can range from precious substances to a slab of stone if one cannot acquire the former. The heaps of grain and so forth, to be piled on that, are prepared beforehand. Offer the initial thirty-seven heaps as many times as one wishes, and then the seven-heap offerings are primarily performed. One offers these twenty-one to one hundred times, and so forth, according to the words and visualizations.**

Making offerings is the antidote to miserliness. Therefore, it is said the substances of the initial mandala offering should not be smaller than one's bowl. At best, the width of the mandala should measure approximately a cubit; if one places one's thumb in the middle, the circumference is measured by the ring finger. At the very least it should not be smaller than a finger span.

As for the substances, the best are gold and silver. At the very least they can be crafted from wood and stone. Whatever the case, if all of these are infused with the eight worldly Dharmas, instead of bringing benefit, there is a great danger of generating afflictions.

With respect to the extensive and short offerings of heaps using whatever one can acquire—whether a variety of precious substances, grains, or even sand—there is a tradition of reciting the single-stanza refuge prayer once, and then accumulating mandalas.

The mandala is strongly emphasized among the different offerings, yet the four continents, Mount Meru, and the sun and moon represented by the heaps that are set forth in Vasubandhu's *Treasury of Knowledge* contradict reality as established through the research of modern science. Therefore, it is possible one might be slightly uncomfortable offering what does not exist in reality; however, there is no need to be hesitant. [174] If the imagery of the "earth anointed with fragrant water," and so forth that is recited does not come easily to mind, then one can recite it as if the meaning refers to the objects of enjoyment of body, speech, and mind of oneself and others and all virtue accumulated in the three times. Whatever the case, everything excellent pertaining to the universe and its inhabitants—owned and unowned—are voluntarily offered. Therefore, it is simply the case that whatever was most renowned in prior times was represented in the mandala heaps and offered; it is not that the world is suitable to be offered as a mandala if it accords with Abhidharma literature, and should not be if it does not.

Some say that when accumulating merit the actually arranged offering contains not a single grain and requires no effort of body or speech, but is created entirely through visualization and meditative stabilization. In the words of Potowa:

This is akin to putting herbs into a smelly conch shell and reciting, "Water anointed with sandal and camphor," and so on, like a blind man trying to trick the sighted.

Furthermore, making inferior, few, and inconsistent offerings out of miserliness and indifference even though one can afford better is a sign that one has not found faith in Dharma and persons from the depths of one's heart.

Once when I was in Hunsur, India, I was looking out of the window from my room and saw that the assembled sangha were offered tea. Two old ladies who were making circumambulations were also given tea. The two old ladies placed their cups in front of themselves, not worrying about the tea becoming cold, and in no hurry to drink it. [175] Whatever prayers they were previously reciting took a long time to finish, and then they held their small cups raised while they made an extensive tea offering; they finally drank the tea after finishing very long prayers, and I strongly rejoiced in this. I felt those two old ladies took some courage to act so proper and disciplined—the monks next to them had huge bowls of tea, and quickly drank it without taking the time to offer it.

Also, once when I was giving the Kālacakra empowerment in Gangtok, Sikkim, the assembly of people were offered sweet rice, and I saw there was an old monk over ninety years old who had missed out. I sent someone to give him my cup of rice, and as soon as he received it he did not eat it. He divided it among the people around him, and put a tiny bit in a tissue for himself. Finally, he lifted it up and offered it to the direction in front, then presented it to the right where the sangha were seated and offered it again, and then recited the offering prayer as he faced each of the eight cardinal and intermediate directions. His eating it only after such extensive prayers was something to be inspired by, not something to laugh at. Sometimes we might think that is such an elderly thing to do, but we should rather view it as something to praise and rejoice in. Furthermore, it is not at all okay to estimate the level of someone's mind. I do not know how well such people understand the Dharma, but their actions were very impressive. [176]

One does not have to recite a short or long prayer when offering the first part of food or drink. It is correct to think, "I offer this to the buddhas and bodhisattvas," or pray to lead a life of benefit to others, or praying that one lives long for that purpose. As it is said:

Not to gain weight,
not to boast,
not for radiance,
only to sustain the body.

This does not allude to focusing on oneself alone and only wishing for one's own happiness in this lifetime. It shows how important it is to build habits of doing what is useful. If one becomes accustomed to offering food and drink before one partakes in it, then the thought arises naturally; if one does not habituate oneself, one only remembers after swallowing! If one becomes firmly accustomed to this, upon waking in the morning one is motivated, without obstacle, to perform virtue and discard negative actions and do one's prayers and practice.

These days, those who take up Dharma and genuinely practice it are as rare as stars during the day. Those rare ones who do practice are said to be like two-legged humans in the Land of Mango Trees (*Cūta*)—living on the fringes of society. Many people refuse to do consistent practice, and are incapable of listing their lineage masters, yet boast like Kāñcī princes who beat victory drums in celebration of having killed their father. Such shameless confidence is oft seen these days and is entirely inappropriate.

These points are highly significant for us. Genuine practitioners of Dharma are rare like stars during daytime, and those rare ones who do practice almost appear as if they are ghosts among regular people—like the two-legged humans in the Land of Mango Trees [which is inhabited largely by one-legged beings]. If someone meditates while reciting their prayers, or closes their eyes while praying, others will, instead of rejoicing, mock them by saying "Oh wow!" and so forth, as if they are not even considered a normal person. [177] If one has faith in the Dharma, then rejoice and make prayers for them. One should emulate their approach, not undermine them—that is only the cause for faults. Furthermore, when someone sees monks and nuns singing, dancing, or even doing operatic singing, it is certainly unacceptable, but no one is shocked! Instead, when they see somebody sitting up straight meditating they are perplexed and snicker at them. This behavior is improper. We should nurture even the smallest of good deeds and do what we can to make them proliferate. Otherwise we run the risk of practitioners becoming outcasts, much like a white crow.

Regarding the other offerings, the two waters among the general offerings should be offered with the lines, "The majority of drinking water is arranged in the shape of a canopy of drinking water," and so forth. Likewise, offer the five sense pleasures and seven precious royal emblems with the appropriate verses. When one is comfortable with an increased number of sessions and continuity of practice, offer the branches of offering simply with the verse, "With the finest flowers, the finest garlands," and so forth.[60] Think that the offerings—both actually arranged and mentally created—are thoroughly enjoyed by the recipients, even though they have no attachment to them, for the sake of oneself completing the collections.

Aside from the drinking water offering that was just laid out, the other offerings of flowers, incense, light, food, music, and so forth—whatever excellent things satisfy our senses—should be excellently offered in all respects.

The third limb of the seven-limb practice is confession. [178] Through the four opponent powers one must confess all negative deeds and obscurations accumulated through the three doors with the lines, "All negative deeds that I have done," and so forth.[61] The third branch of confession is said to be the antidote to all of these. The way to perform confession with the four opponent powers is as follows: (1) the power of the support is refuge and mind generation; (2) the power of remorse is the generation of strong regret such as one would feel if one were to ingest poison; (3) the power of abstention is to think, "I will refrain from committing the act again even at the cost of my life"; (4) the power of applying the antidote is all virtue done with confession in mind, for example reciting the *Sūtra of the Three Heaps*.

Milarepa said so far as one doubts whether misdeeds are purified through confession, there is still benefit if one regrets. In this way, regret is the most important factor. However, if we have regret toward the misdeeds of body, speech, and mind that we can remember we committed in this life yet we go on without confessing them, not only will unfortunate things happen in this life, but we run the risk of not having much hope for our future lives. Therefore, we should go over in our mind the misdeeds we have performed in this life and confess them with a strong mind of regret. Even if we cannot remember them now, the fact that we have accumulated so many misdeeds in our past life can be inferred when we look at our behavior in this life, which is dominated by afflictions in thought and misdeeds in action. Thus, we must confess our collection of faults, misdeeds, and downfalls from the depths of our hearts, and rely on a mind of restraint from carrying them out again even at the cost of our life. [179]

In reality, there will be times when we can refrain from misdeeds and times when we cannot. This being the case, we should confess by way of the four opponent powers, making a strong vow from the depths of our heart to refrain. In this way, any negativity will be purified. It is said that although in general there are no positive qualities within negative deeds, their quality is that they can be purified through confession.

The fourth aspect of the seven-limb practice is rejoicing in virtue. **Meditate on the joy of rejoicing in the roots of virtue of all ārya beings with the verse, "I rejoice in all the merits of buddhas and bodhisattvas," and so forth. Due to this, one can equally enjoy the merits of the virtue they created.**

Rejoicing in virtue is an antidote to jealousy and competitiveness. Furthermore, one can rejoice in both the virtue one has accumulated oneself, or in the virtue of others. Thus, this virtuous practice is praised as a way of making one's life meaningful, one that engenders confidence, and increases enthusiasm to strive harder. It is said that to rejoice in the merit of the five beings—buddhas, bodhisattvas, trainee and nontrainee śrāvakas and pratyekabuddhas, and beings not yet on the path. It is important to marvel at even the most subtle and inferior root of virtue and make aspirational prayers. It is said that if one rejoices in such virtue, one can also enjoy the same share of merit.

The fifth aspect of the seven-limb practice is requesting to turn the wheel of Dharma. **With the verse, "You who are like beacons of light in the worlds of the ten directions," and so forth,** make requests for **turning the wheel of Dharma, and** if one has a mandala set at this point, build up the nine heaps and visualize an eight-spoked wheel with a hub, then raise the mandala and make requests to turn the profound and vast wheel of Dharma. [180] This is the antidote to doubt.

The sixth aspect of the seven-limb practice is requesting the teacher to not pass into nirvana. **With the verse, "I earnestly request those who would pass into nirvana," and so forth, make supplications to the teacher to not pass into nirvana,** but to turn the wheel of Dharma. **It is said that with respect to these two requests, one should firmly visualize that the merit field accepts one's request as one makes supplications.** At this point, construct a mandala with five heaps, and establishing the guru on an indestructible vajra throne, make supplications for them not to pass into nirvana. This is an antidote to ignorance.

The seventh aspect of the seven-limb practice is the dedication. **With the verse, "Through prostrations, offerings, and confession," and so forth, one dedicates the virtue of all aforementioned limbs toward enlightenment. Therefore, as said in the** *Sūtra Requested by Sāgaramati*:

> Just as a drop of water fallen into the great ocean
> will not vanish until the ocean runs dry,
> virtue dedicated to enlightenment
> will not be exhausted until one achieves enlightenment.

This presents the profound point that virtue does not go to waste but actually increases. In older instruction manuals it says to perform the *General Confession* **and so forth, which would make the above perfectly complete limbs. However, since that comes extensively below, to keep things simple it is not practiced these days.**

Generating a mind of conviction that happiness—the result of virtue—arises through the limb of dedication is the antidote to the wrong view that karma and its results do not exist.

Occasionally verses of the seven-limb practice are slightly more extensive, such as in *Way of the Bodhisattva*. It is excellent if one recites, "That I might gain this precious attitude"[62] and so forth, since the meaning of the words of the confession and so forth are so powerful. [181] Correctly accumulating, purifying, and increasing in this way is an essential point.

Starting with the aforementioned preliminaries and the actual meditation rounds, up until that of special insight, the order of visualization should not be confused, and the extensive and abbreviated divisions and so forth that correlate to one another must rely on your direct experience of the oral lineage and practices.

Currently, some neglect relying on a guru's empirical explanation and try to practice by taking books as their gurus, which impairs their whole practice, and their efforts amount to nothing.

As such, if you skip parts of the practice as you wish, like some these days who adhere too strongly to the written commentaries of practice manuals, this makes all virtuous endeavors faulty as is stated in the *Greater* and *Middle-Length* lamrim treatises. The wise should thus pay special attention to this. Those in current times who say they practice by entrusting the texts as their guru instead of relying on the naked instructions of a spiritual teacher will have their faulty virtuous endeavors amount to nothing.

BLENDING SUPPLICATION WITH TANTRA
ACCORDING TO THE INSTRUCTIONS

With respect to blending the sixth preparatory practice, supplication, with tantra in accordance with the instructions, first bring to mind the qualities of body, speech, and mind of the guru, the victors, and their spiritual heirs. Then, make supplications as instructed in this text, or, if possible, recite *Opening the Gate to the Supreme Path: The Lamrim Supplication Prayer* [*to the Lamrim Lineage Gurus*]. When the great protector Tsongkhapa was staying at Reting Monastery and practicing the stages of the path, he had visions of all the lamrim lineage gurus. At the end of the vision, all other lineage gurus dissolved into Jowo Atiśa and his two principal disciples Geshé Dromtönpa and Ngok Lekpé Sherab. For one month he had visions of Jowo Jé and his two disciples, and at the end Jowo Jé placed his hand on Jé Rinpoché's head and said, "Contribute vastly to the Buddhist teachings. I will assist you." The *Lamrim Supplication Prayer* was authored at this time and thus carries considerable blessings. [182] When Tsongkhapa later authored the *Great Treatise on the Stages of the Path* there, he wrote in his aspirational prayer:

> May the stages of the path to enlightenment,
> excellently accomplished through the marvelous enlightened
>   activity of the victors and their heirs . . .

It is said that this is the source for the text coming into being through the power of the victors and their heirs. When reciting the prayer, it is customary to repeat the final line twice; the first time as a supplication, and the second time while visualizing receiving blessings. Next, offer another mandala and make supplications for the three great aims.

Making recitations speedily for the sake of finishing sooner, or thinking about other things while doing so is problematic. Ideally, those who study the great treatises should not have a lot of recitation commitments. If one recites the root verses of the treatises one is currently studying, it accomplishes both goals with one action. While reciting Maitreya's *Ornament for Clear Realization* and so forth, it is very beneficial to perform glance meditation. Drepung Loseling's Geshé Rigzin Tenpa Rinpoché from Kinnaur recited Maitreya's *Ornament* and Candrakīrti's *Entering the Middle Way* daily without interruption.

There are furthermore amazing life accounts of others who also recited a few chapters from the five main root treatises daily on a continual basis. If those are the actions of inconceivable beings, what could possibly be better?

Whatever the case, since you are studying, contemplating, and meditating on the instruction of this lamrim treatise, reciting the preparatory practices of *Oral Transmission of Mañjuśrī* is excellent; alternatively, recitation of the preparatory practices of any suitable text is sufficient. When reciting the preparatory practices make sure you understand the qualities of the body, speech, and mind of the victors and their heirs. [183] If one does not have deep faith based on contemplating reasoning, the recitation becomes a mere voicing of "Three Jewels think of me!" One has not developed the kind of faith that keeps one from sitting still through deep joy or profound sadness. Through identifying the Dharma jewel as paths and cessations from the outset, one is suitable to go for refuge, and a heart-felt refuge will arise.

How to Sustain the Meditation During the Actual Sessions

This has two parts:

i) The general way of sustaining it
ii) The way of sustaining it in this context

THE GENERAL WAY OF SUSTAINING IT

Meditation during daily sessions refers to sustaining meditational focal objects through focusing again and again on a virtuous object. Since the beginning of time, we have been under the control of our mind; our mind has not been under our control. The mind has also been led astray by obscurations such as the afflictions. However, if we can bring this mind that is the creator of all faults under our own control, we can focus on virtuous observations as much as we wish.

Furthermore, after sustaining the observations for some time, there is a risk that one will become complacent with respect to the number and order of the chosen objects of observation; this is a huge obstacle. If one falls into bad habits from the start, the virtuous activities of a whole lifetime become faulty. Thus, first find certainty with respect to the number and order of the observations, and precede your meditation with several propelling thoughts thinking, "I will not divert from that." Furthermore, sustain the meditation through being mindful of additions and omissions as stated in the *Great Treatise on the Stages of the Path*.

The Way of Sustaining it in this Context

With respect to sustaining the meditation in this context, contemplate the benefits of relying on a guru—the quick attainment of buddhahood—and the disadvantages of not doing so—suffering in all future lifetimes. Furthermore, restrain the mind that tries to find fault with the guru. [184] Recall whatever qualities you understand of the three trainings, and meditate on these until you generate clear faith. Recollect as presented in sūtra all their kind activities that have benefited you in the past and continue to benefit you now until you generate deep respect, as said in the *Great Treatise on the Stages of the Path*.

What to Do at the Conclusion of a Session

Make a strong dedication of the merit gained during the session toward temporary and ultimate aims with an appropriate extensive or abbreviated prayer such as the *Prayer of Samantabhadra*, Āryaśūra's *Seventy-Stanza Prayer*,[63] and so forth.

What to Do during the Breaks between the Actual Meditation Sessions, and Refuting Misconceptions with Respect to the Way to Sustain the Actual Meditation

Using the guard of introspection that makes sure one's behavior does not become lacking or excessive during the session, read in the *Great* and *Middle-Length* lamrim treatises the explanations regarding the actual focal objects of the actual session, and in accordance with that practice, about the session breaks. Aside from that, it is said that if one lets one's mind loose there is very little development of qualities.

Furthermore, the meditations from the topics of relying on a guru up through bodhicitta are mainly analytical meditation, and those on calm abiding are primarily placement meditation. For example, when meditating on the topics of relying on a guru, one uses analytical meditation to contemplate the qualities of the guru and so forth, and at the limit of that the other conceptions become dormant, and one abides in single-pointed faith—placement meditation. Likewise, repeatedly paying attention to the points of calm abiding is analytical meditation, and abiding single pointedly is placement meditation. Thus, without understanding those points, saying, "I only meditate without analysis!" and so forth clearly demonstrates your meditation is not correct. This is taught in the great treatises, as exemplified in *Ornament for the Mahāyāna Sūtras*:

> First, correct the mental attention that arises through hearing. Through correct mental attention exalted wisdom whose object is true reality arises. [185]

One familiarizes oneself with an object through conjoined analytical and placement meditation principally to transform the mind. Therefore, one needs to be entirely certain that the clarity of the object being familiarized with is growing stronger. Otherwise, if one proceeds with doubt, it merely turns into imagined meditation, and one's awareness cannot transform into any given virtue. To culminate the process and achieve clear appearance, the mind needs to gain experience, and for that practicing analytical meditation is important. The familiarization and changes effected on the mind during the session should be continuously increased through the practices of the session break, just like rain benefits the swelling of a river.

One should study and contemplate related teachings during the break, and primarily hold firm to methods of building faith in the spiritual teachers such as reading the biographies of previous holy gurus. Likewise, guarding the doors of your senses, engaging with introspection, knowing the limits with respect to food, applying yourself to yoga when not sleeping and the activities of sleep are the four trainings for easily accomplishing calm abiding and special insight.

Furthermore, performing prostrations while reciting the *Confession of Downfalls*,[64] making circumambulations, offering mandalas and so forth are certainly appropriate. Aside from unique modes of sustaining the meditation during the actual session, the activities of the preparation, actual session, conclusion, and breaks are likewise applicable up until the sustaining of the observations related to special insight.

Concluding Verses

Alas! If someone who helps the wretched, parched, and
   famished
by gifting food and clothing [186]
and protects people from the harm of their enemies
is considered kind and proclaimed as such,

Then how does one repay the kindness of the teacher

who presents the jewel of everlasting happiness in one's palm,
and liberates from the terrifying oppression
of the three types of suffering in unending samsara?

If it is hard enough to attain the state of mere peace,
then the one who establishes you into "faultless, complete
    buddhahood with all qualities"
renowned since eons as difficult to attain,
is the actual embodiment of the victors of the three times.

Within your own mistaken perspective,
all projections of your own faults onto the activities of the
    guru
are sure signs you are rotten to the core—
understand these as faults and abandon them like poison!

I have understood that the roots of well-being in which all
    wishes are fulfilled,
are the crucial points of pure appearance that sees the guru's
    activities as excellent,
the faithful respect that follows their words like commands,
and the [transformation] of all actions into Dharma.

An Exhortation to Take Full Advantage of a Life of Leisure and Opportunity

The actual practice—training the mind having relied on a guru—has two parts:

1. An exhortation to take full advantage of a life of leisure and opportunity
2. How to take full advantage of a life of leisure and opportunity

An exhortation to take full advantage of a life of leisure and opportunity has three parts:

a. Identifying leisure and opportunity
b. Contemplating the great importance of leisure and opportunity
c. Contemplating the difficulty of attaining leisure and opportunity

Identifying leisure and opportunity has two parts:

1) Leisure
2) Opportunity

Opportunity has two parts:

a) Opportunity pertaining to oneself
b) Opportunity pertaining to others

With respect to the leisure, Nāgārjuna, in *Letter to a Friend*, writes,

Born into wrong views, as an animal, [187]
a hungry ghost, or a hell being,
without the victor's teaching, born in border regions
as a barbarian, born with dull faculties,
or a long-living god
are the eight unfree states.
Having attained freedom from these,
strive to end rebirth.

First, we must identify leisure and opportunity. These are explained in relation to a human body, and not just with respect to consciousness. A life having leisure and opportunity refers to a human life that has the capability to analyze with wisdom that properly discriminates Dharma. What, then, are leisure and opportunity? Leisure refers to the freedom of being without adverse conditions with respect to practicing Dharma. Opportunity refers to being endowed with the special concordant conditions. There are eight states of leisure that pertain to not being born into the following conditions: **(1) having wrong views, (2–4) the three lower migrations, (5) where a buddha has not visited, (6) border lands, (7) dull faculties, (8) long-living gods. Separated from these eight states lacking freedom, one possesses the eight leisures.**

There are ten opportunities: five pertaining to the self, and five pertaining to others. **According to Asaṅga's *Śrāvaka Levels*:**

Being human, born in a central land, sense faculties complete,
having not done extreme actions, having faith in the source.

The five opportunities pertaining to oneself are (1) being born human, (2) being born in a central land, (3) having complete sense faculties, (4) not having done extreme actions—that is, those of immediate retribution, and (5) faith in the source, which is faith in the triple basket. With respect to the five opportunities pertaining to others, *Śrāvaka Levels* states:

A buddha has visited and taught the excellent dharma,
The teachings remain and there are followers of it
And there is compassion and love for others.

(6) That the buddha has come but not passed into nirvana, (7) that buddha or his śrāvakas continue to teach the Dharma, (8) the Dharma established during the time of a buddha has not degenerated, (9) there are followers because it is seen that inferior beings attain results through the Dharma as taught, (10) that others are loving and compassionate. [188]

Do not jump to conclusions thinking that you have attained a human body endowed with these eighteen states, however, and reflect inwardly. You can know that since you are born human you do not need to investigate whether you are in the three lower migrations or are a god. If you have conviction in the resultant Jewels through certainty in past and future lives, you do not have wrong views. If the teachings of the fourth buddha of the fortunate eon—Śākyamuni—who came to this world remain, then the teachings of the Victor are present. Even though the four-fold retinue are not complete in this snowy land of Tibet, since fully ordained monks are present, it is in effect a central land. If one can understand even a little bit of the teachings than one was not born with dull faculties. Thus, one has the eight leisures.

Investigate if you have attained a human body possessing the eighteen types of leisure and opportunities as follows: being born as a human, born in a central land defined through Dharmic boundaries, having all five sense powers, not having committed one of the five acts of immediate retribution, having faith in the triple basket, the first four of the five opportunities with respect to others being effectively fulfilled although not literally to the word, a buddha having visited, their teaching the holy Dharma, that Dharma not having degenerated, oneself having entered into those teachings, sponsors and so forth providing conducive conditions such as material support to yourself. If you have these, then meditate until your mind fills with joy. It is said that out of all the people who, having not investigated, proudly assume they are humans possessing leisure and opportunity, most do not actually possess them when analyzed and investigated.

Tibetans like us have grown up in households where our parents taught us about karmic cause and effect, the Three Jewels, and so forth, and it has stuck in our minds, and thus we do not have wrong views. We have not been born in the three lower migrations and have acquired a human body, [189] and out of the ten five-hundred-year phases of the Buddha's teachings, we are, according to the Theravada tradition, living in a time when the teachings remain. As of the year 2015, 2559 years have passed since the Buddha's parinirvāṇa, and thus approximately half of that time period has ended. Furthermore, Tibetans in particular are not only humans of this world, but have been born as humans in the snowy land of Tibet where the Dharma flourished and remains, the realm of Ārya Avalokiteśvara, and thus we were not born in border regions where there is no Buddhism.

Leisure and opportunities are thus not guaranteed for all humans, and should be posited by way of a distinguishing mindset. Having the intelligence that differentiates between right and wrong, and a consideration for the future, which is something animals lack, means that one does not have dull faculties. Likewise, if one is born into the body of a long-lived god one is enraptured with sense pleasures and does not think to practice Dharma. Thus, liberated from these eight states without freedom we possess the eight types of leisure, and based on that also the ten attributes of opportunities as explained.

Contemplating the Great Importance of Leisure and Opportunity

Having found joy in the fact that one possesses leisure and opportunity, if one does not contemplate the reason for that joy, it becomes like a miserly person overjoyed with a useless object. With respect to decisively turning it into something useful, Candragomin's *Letter to a Student* states:

> That powerful mind attained by humans,
> the basis for the path to the state of a sugata, which equips you
>   to guide beings,
> is neither attained by gods, nāgas, or demigods,
> nor by garuḍas, vidyādharas, kinnaras, or mahorāgas.

Think as follows: The three lower migrations are primarily an experience of the fruition of nonvirtuous karma. There is not much ability to accrue karma in those realms. Gods enjoy the fruition of virtuous karma but have little power to accumulate merit. [190] Humans have powerful potential to accrue both virtue and negativity, especially we residents of Jambudvīpa. Therefore, when we do not err with respect to what we should adopt and discard, we can accomplish excellent states of higher rebirth of gods and humans, the nirvana of śrāvakas and pratyekabuddhas, that which guides beings to the state of a sugata—mind generation—and also accom-

plish the marvelous state of buddhahood. Therefore, when you contemplate that you have attained something more precious than a
wish-fulfilling jewel, think that you will set out to make this greatly
meaningful. Meditate until you have the joy of the impoverished
obtaining treasure.

In this way it is highly important to have leisure and opportunity in
order to accomplish the temporal higher states of gods and humans.
Since it is easy to guard the morality of refraining from the ten nonvirtues, the eight fruitional qualities of a higher rebirth—long life,
bountiful resources, noble speech, great influence, strength, and so
forth—can all be accomplished using this body with its leisure and
opportunity.

Likewise, in order to accomplish the ultimate aim of definite goodness that is liberation, one must maintain a powerful and quality
practice of the three trainings with this body. Achieving the ultimate
state of omniscience all depends on whether one has the attitude of
bodhicitta. It is said that this powerful mind of bodhicitta that humans
can develop cannot be developed in the realms of gods or demigods
and so forth. Not only that, in Ācārya Nāgabodhi's *Understanding the
Explanation* and other unsurpassable secret mantra texts, it says those
abiding in the Sukhāvatī pure land aspire toward and make prayers to
be reborn as a human being of this world of Jambudvīpa, born from a
womb and possessing the six elements. [191]

Therefore, our Jambudvīpa body, born from a womb and possessing
the six elements, is the greatest path for achieving omniscience. Not
only is it simply good by nature, it also carries incredible potential, has
strength, and is useful. Thus, since we have the potential to practice
Dharma, it only comes down to whether we decide to or not. For example, highly accomplished Tibetan masters of the past who attained high
paths and grounds practiced Dharma with a human body having leisure
and opportunity just the same as our own—nothing special or superior.
Furthermore, the Dharma they practiced is the same as the Dharma we

have today—they did not have something superior. If we can focus our minds and exert ourselves, we will think that there is nothing we cannot do. In this way one should contemplate the great importance of leisure and opportunity and conclude that one is able to practice Dharma.

Contemplating the Difficulty of Attaining Leisure and Opportunity

You might think that having a body with leisure and opportunity is indeed nice, but that leisure and opportunity are also easily attained since they are in abundance, and even if you do not finish what you plan to do this time around, you can continue in your future lives. However, this life of leisure and opportunity is actually very difficult to attain. Contemplating this fact, one arrives at the thought that it is not certain that one will continue to do so unless one takes up this precious opportunity right now and focuses oneself. [192]

In this way, the thought will arise, "At this time when I have attained a single opportunity to accomplish a great purpose, I will do whatever I can to not let it go to waste."

Contemplating the difficulty of attaining leisure and opportunity has three points:

1) The difficulty of attaining it by way of **an analogy**
2) The difficulty of attaining it by way of **the cause**
3) The difficulty of attaining it by way of the result, or **nature**

With respect to the first, the *Way of the Bodhisattva* states:

Just as a sea turtle sticking its neck
through the hole of a yoke floating around the great ocean.

If a golden yoke with a single opening floats in all directions on the great ocean carried by the wind, it is barely possible for a blind turtle who only comes to the surface once every hundred years to put its neck through the yoke. An even clearer analogy we can see from direct experience would be like throwing a handful of lentils at a wall and one of them sticking; such a thing is extremely rare. The lentils falling to the ground are like the uncountable rebirths we have taken as a human without freedoms. A body having leisure and opportunity is like the rare lentil that sticks to the wall. Think that one's situation is like this. Upon applying the analogy and its meaning to oneself and meditating on it, uncontrived joy and fear arise in this time when if not for some good luck, one would be like a rock falling off a cliff.

The analogy in the *Way of the Bodhisattva* is analogous to cycling through rebirth in the three realms. The yoke is analogous to the world of humans, and the single hole in the yoke is analogous to the Buddha's teachings. The single hole not staying stationary but always moving is analogous to the difficulty of meeting with the teachings. The turtle is oneself, the blindness is ignorance, and its neck making its way through the single hole in the yoke is analogous to oneself attaining a life with leisure and opportunity that is difficult to find. Thinking of the difficulty of attaining it in this way is overwhelming. [193]

Regarding the difficulty of attaining it by way of the cause, to attain a mere happy migration, one needs to guard the ethics of a single conduct onward. In particular, to attain a human body with leisure and opportunity, one starts with a basis of pure ethics, as it is said:

From generosity, resources; from ethics, happiness.

Generosity and so forth must act as assistants in connection with stainless prayers. To give rise to any virtue in the three lower realms

is difficult. The gods are distracted by either meditative stabilization or the happinesses of the desire realm. Human beings in a land
where the Dharma has not spread do not even hear virtuous words.
If those lands where Dharma has not spread are represented by a
mass of grain, then the number of lands where Dharma has spread
would be represented by merely a single grain. Taking the case of
our land of Tibet, among tens of thousands of people very few have
committed to guarding ethical conduct. Among those few, those
who accomplish those three factors of ethics, generosity, and stainless prayers are as rare as stars in the daytime.

Thus, when one's outward-looking mind is redirected inside and
one takes a look at oneself, one sees that one barely has a mind of
devotion toward the practice of Dharma, and the causes of virtue
that are required to induce a mind of happiness are incredibly few.
Due to the cause of accumulating nonvirtue and misdeeds as a matter of course, if one does not take the opportunity to bring that into
control in this life then one will not attain a human body in the
future. Hoping for such a thing is like planting white mustard in the
spring and hoping to reap a harvest of barley in the fall. Meditate
until one experiences that this way of thinking is naive.

The outline of the manner of attaining leisure and opportunity being
difficult to attain by way of the cause is stated as the second outline in
this section in the *Great Treatise on the Stages on the Path* and also this
treatise; however when meditating it is more effective to place it as the
third, or last, outline. In this way, although a human body is difficult
to attain, in the back of one's mind one still has a hope of attaining one
because we think reciting daily prayers and performing prostrations
and circumambulations is enough. [194] However, thinking of the
difficulty of attaining a life of leisure and opportunity by way of the
cause, regardless of however many or few people there are in the world
who have attained it, the possibility of oneself attaining freedom and
opportunity in a future life comes down to the behavior of our three

doors of body, speech, and mind in this life. Therefore, if the complete collection of causes for attaining a human body with leisure and opportunity exists in one's own continuum without degeneration, it will not be difficult to attain. However, if one does not have the complete collection of causes without degeneration, even if leisure and opportunity are abundant in reality, they have become rare for oneself. Thinking in this way, one gains an intense certainty that leisure and opportunity are difficult to attain.

Regarding reflecting on the difficulty of attaining leisure and opportunity due to their nature, imagine yourself in the presence of an exposed area of earth completely covered with insects in the summertime. First consider that even more numerous than animals are hungry ghosts, and that hell beings outnumber hungry ghosts. Even though scattered animals in the depths of the dark oceans between continents may be few, the number of animals on that raised piece of earth are countless, yet no more than ten humans could fit there. Furthermore, however many people there may be in a village, the populace will not exceed hundreds of thousands. The fact that minuscule living beings are uncountable does not need to be proven by inferential valid cognition; it is obvious to fools and scholars alike. Within the happy migrations, humans are rare, especially those who have come into contact with the Dharma. Even among those who have come into contact with the Dharma, there are many who do not remember the words they hear, do not understand what they contemplate, and cannot generate anything through meditation. Many who actually do have the intelligence to study, contemplate, and meditate spend their time focusing only on the plans of this life. Thus, with respect to a body that is replete with all the concordant conditions for practicing the Dharma, meditate until you have an experience of a mind like that of a desirous person who has found a rare and priceless jewel. [195].

This way of contemplating the difficulty of attaining leisure and opportunity considers the myriad living beings visible to us, and the fact that within those, animals completely outnumber humans, and that furthermore, among humans, those possessing the complete list of leisure and opportunities are quite rare. At the end of this analysis one can conclude that those who practice the authentic Dharma of correctly accomplishing the welfare of others are even rarer. One can imagine it like a pile of grain—wide at the base but more and more narrow until the pinnacle, on which barely anything fits. The expanse of the base represents the vast amount of hell beings, then more narrow above that those few who have attained a happy migration as a human and so forth, and above that the extremely few who have attained a human body with leisure and opportunity. Thus, in this world of seven billion people at present, there may be at most a few hundred thousand fortunate people who have such leisure and opportunity, but if one further analyzes their quality more closely, there are probably no more than some tens of thousands—incredibly few. Even if one makes a realistic calculation, one can be certain that those who have a fortunate and purposeful human body with leisure and opportunity are extremely rare.

Concluding Verses

For many lifetimes you enjoyed the delights of samsara,
yet still you are destitute and miserable.
The food, riches, and luxuries of this life
are grasped at by you, fool, as if they were rare and real.

In prior times you behaved just as now.
The great demon of the black, white, and variegated

eight worldly Dharmas lived in your heart, believing suffering
   was happiness,
and throwing your future dreams to the wind.

Now, if your basis for accomplishing is excellent,
if this ship of leisure and opportunity that is found just once
is not used to reach the shores of the precious land of definite
   goodness,
but is hopelessly sailed into samsara—how depressing! [196]

How to Take Full Advantage of a Life of Leisure and Opportunity

How to take advantage has two points:

a. Generating certainty with respect to the general presentation of
the path
b. The actual way to take full advantage of a life of leisure and
opportunity

Generating certainty with respect to the general presentation of the
path has two points:

1) How the entirety of the Buddha's teachings are contained
within the paths of the three beings
2) The reason for teaching the paths of the three beings
sequentially

a) The purpose for teaching by way of the paths of the
three beings
b) The reason for that particular order

i) The actual reason
ii) The purpose as taught in the *Great Treatise on the
Stages of the Path*

To explain these first in brief, the foundation for training the mind on the graduated path to enlightenment is separated into three stages: that of persons of small scope, middle scope, and great scope. Furthermore, the stages of the path taught regarding persons of small and middle scope are not the independent stages of the path of those beings; what is taught is only the stages of the path of small and middle scope beings in common with that of the great scope. This is because they are taught as preliminaries to the path of the great scope being.

The first stage is like self-protection—it is the method for restraining afflicted misbehavior through understanding the cause and effect process of good and bad karma. The second stage is like engaging the enemy—it is the method for abandoning the root conditions for all bad behavior, the afflictions that make the mind unruly. Having abandoned those afflictions, the third stage is training in the deeds of the victors' spiritual children conjoined with the method, the mind of bodhicitta. This is for the sake of removing the imprints left behind by the afflictions that prevent one from becoming a buddha. [197] These are the instructions of the stages of the paths of the three beings.

The paths of the three beings can be explained in terms of their objects of accomplishment. The persons of small scope accomplish higher states of rebirth. We can divide the object of accomplishment that is definite goodness into two aspects: the definite goodness that is an abandonment of merely the afflictive obscurations is accomplished by persons of middle scope; the definite goodness that is also an abandonment of obscurations to omniscience—the ultimate victorious state of buddhahood—is accomplished by persons of great scope.

The paths can also be explained in terms of the discordant conditions they clear away, or the dissimilar classes they abandon. With respect to the first stage, before one even applies the antidotes to afflictions that are the obstacles to liberation, one first abandons the ten nonvirtues; this is the method of restraint against misdeeds powered by afflictions, which by nature harm others. This is the Dharma practice of small scope beings, as said in Āryadeva's *Four Hundred Verses*:

First eliminate nonmeritorious actions.

This states that the path of persons of small scope is eliminating nonmeritorious karma, which is the cause of the suffering of suffering. It continues:

In the middle, eliminate the self.

There are various interpretations of this line, but one tradition states that the path of persons of middle scope accomplishes the liberation that abandons the affliction of self-grasping through understanding the suchness of interdependence. Lastly, it states:

Finally, eliminate everything.

This indicates the path of the persons of great scope is to accomplish the state of omniscience through the complete abandonment of the obscurations to omniscience, which are the imprints left behind by the afflictions. These paths depend on the former as a working basis to accomplish their goals. One cannot skip the path of persons of small scope and go straight to the practice of that of the middle scope. The first stage of practice of the persons of small scope is to eliminate attachment to appearances of this life. Based on that, the second stage is to eliminate attachment to the appearances of future lives. By way of these two, one then uses the middle scope path to generate a mind striving toward liberation. [198] Then, through thoroughly contemplating the fact that if one does not achieve liberation one will remain in a state of suffering under the power of karma and afflictions, one applies this same fact to others and meditates on that, leading to a generation of compassion and bodhicitta. This is the progression of the path of persons of great scope and is the order for all levels of intelligence—sharp, middle, and dull.

The great Tsongkhapa, in his *Three Principal Aspects of the Path*, employs the instruction style based on renunciation that follows contemplation on the four thought transformations—difficulty of attaining leisure and opportunity, death and impermanence, karmic cause and effect, and the faults of samsara. He states:

> Having found leisure and opportunity there is no time to spare.
> By gaining familiarity with this, attachment to the appearances
> of this life is reversed.

Leisure and opportunity, and impermanence, are taught to reverse the attachment to appearances of this life. He next states:

> Frequently contemplating the infallibility of karma and its
> effects,
> and the suffering of samsara, attachment to the appearances of
> future lives is reversed.

These lines teach karma and its effects, and the suffering of samsara, to reverse the attachment to appearances of the next life. He continues:

> When, by having familiarized in this way, attraction to the
> marvels of samsara
> do not arise, even for a second, and the thought seeking
> liberation is present day and night.
> At that point one has generated renunciation.

This accords with the aforementioned explanation of achieving renunciation by way of the four thought transformations; furthermore, in this context of the lamrim, the topic of karma and its effects is included within the section on the persons of smaller scope.

The statement, "Those who have the mental capacity of smaller-scope beings strive for higher rebirths," refers to striving for higher rebirths free from the suffering of lower migrations mainly due to seeing the harm from the suffering of suffering. The four noble truths can be explained in this context from the perspective of this suffering of suffering. In this case, true suffering is the suffering of suffering itself; true origins are the causes of that, which is to say, nonmeritorious karma and the coarse motivating afflictions of covetousness, malice, wrong views, and so forth. [199] The substitute for true paths is the antidote to those—the ethical conduct abandoning the ten nonvirtues. True cessations in this context are the body of a higher rebirth that is a liberation from the suffering of the lower realms. All the causes for attaining a higher rebirth—their object of accomplishment—are thus taught within the stages of the path of persons of smaller scope.

TRAINING THE MIND IN THE STAGES OF THE PATH SHARED WITH PERSONS OF SMALL SCOPE

The actual way to take full advantage of a life of leisure and opportunity has three points:

1) Training the mind in the stages of the path shared with persons of small scope
2) Training the mind in the stages of the path shared with persons of medium scope
3) Training the mind in the stages of the path for persons of great scope

With respect to the first, training the mind in the stages of the path shared with persons of small scope, this has three parts:

a) The actual training in the attitude of small scope persons
b) The measure for generating that attitude
c) A summary of teachings on the misconceptions regarding that

The Actual Training in the Attitude of Small Scope Persons

It states in Atiśa's *Lamp for the Path*:

> **Those who by whatever means**
> **pursue for their own sake**
> **mere happiness in samsara**
> **are known as the lowest persons.**

The ordinary person of small scope simply pursues the happiness of this life and makes effort to remove suffering, similar to animals. That is not the person of small scope identified in this context. The person of small scope indicated here must be unique in that they pursue the methods for higher rebirth and **the happiness of future lives rather than that of this life; however, since this section discusses the path shared with them, before becoming repulsed by the whole of samsara, one must first be repulsed by the suffering of the three lower migrations. Therefore,** the stages of the path shared with persons of small scope taught here is not for guiding beings on the actual path of small scope, but rather functions as a preliminary for training in the path of middle and great scope beings so as to engender the mind that pursues future lives. [200]

The complete method for attaining happy future lives is taught for these people. The uncontrived mind of disgust toward the suffering of lower migrations induces the wish to attain a higher rebirth; the accomplishing agents of that which are refuge and its trainings—the general practice of accomplishing virtue and abandoning misdeeds, and the particular training of guarding the ethics of abandoning the ten nonvirtues—cover all the wishes of the ordinary person of small scope. Moreover, the mind repulsed by the suffering of lower migrations assists in the training of the mind repulsed by all of samsara, and is thus a method for training the mind in the paths shared with persons of middle scope. It is greatly beneficial for all levels of intelligence— whether sharp, mediocre, or dull.

This section on the actual training in the attitude of the persons of small scope **has two parts:**

   i. **Developing the mind intent on future lives**
  ii. **The method for achieving happiness in future lives**

Developing the mind intent on future lives has three parts:

   a′ **Contemplating death and impermanence**: the fact we will not remain long in this world
   b′ **Contemplating the sufferings of the lower realms**
   c′ Contemplating what will happen in your future lives: the happiness and suffering of the two types of beings

In order to explain the topic of death and impermanence, first it is important to give a brief summary of the foundational attitudes. The human body replete with the concordant conditions of leisure and opportunity for practicing Dharma is not by nature a permanent, stable entity. At the end of life comes death, and the time of that death has absolutely no certainty. Through recognizing this, one generates a mind striving for the sake of future lives. This is extremely important, and thus to develop such a mind first involves eliminating doubts with respect to the existence of future lives. [201] There is an incredible amount of Buddhist literature that expands on scriptural sources and reasonings to that effect and are worth studying.

To mention a few examples from direct experience: A young girl of the age of five living in the city of Kanpur, in India's state of Uttar Pradesh, recalled not only her former life in which she was a young girl on her way to school who suddenly died, but also recalled the names and history of her former family, such as that of her parents. She furthermore recalled the way to their house, what the house looked like, and the furniture inside. She was able to identify all of these herself without prior acquaintance or assistance. Having become completely convinced she had recognized her former parents, who were still alive, they likewise came to consider her their daughter. She now has four parents. The father from her previous life is a schoolteacher with a modern education who did not believe in past and future lives. However, through the child having such a clear recollection of former situations, he told me that he now has conviction in the existence of past and future lives.

Another similar story was told to me by a Sikh man from Punjab. His daughter, around three or four at the time, clearly recollected her previous life. I have likewise heard stories of past life recollection from people all over the globe.

In the Tibetan tradition there have been many tulkus unmistakenly identified based on their recollection of details from their past life. Many, although not clearly remembering their past life, had uncanny intellectual prowess and clear imprints of great deeds relating to the Dharma that were evident in this life. [202] For example, in the 1960s, Mrs. Freda Bedi, a Western woman who was living in India, took responsibility to establish the nonsectarian Young Lamas' Home School in Delhi. Later when it moved to Dalhousie in northern India, a few of the staff members told me that the young tulkus there were unlike other children.

These days there is an excessive amount of tulkus, of geshés, retreat masters, and so forth. With a bit too much pressure, before the [child] even speaks of their past lives the ceremonial arrow is already waved, and in this way the tulku population exploded. However, fundamentally, the tradition of identifying tulkus arose through the person showing clear imprints of remembering their past life, which in turn lead to the maintaining of the reincarnate lineage.

Likewise, a few of my Dharma friends who were practitioners from the older generations, upon ceasing the coarse consciousnesses that depend on the body through the force of yoga, were able to recollect their past lives through their subtle consciousness. This is easy to explain if one accepts past and future lives based on logical reasoning. Otherwise, it is very difficult to explain how such experiences occur. Whatever the case, verified accounts of past life recollection are possible through that life existing. That life becomes a "past life" in dependence on this current life, and it is therefore possible that there be a future life, too. At the time of death in one's previous life, the coarse body ceases, but the extremely subtle consciousness does not—instead it continues on, based on which one can recollect past lives. [203]

Moreover, when the coarse body of this life perishes, there is no reason why the extremely subtle consciousness should also perish. The fact that the extremely subtle consciousness that depended on the body continues even after that coarse body has ceased is proven by experience, and thus we can make a valid inference that it will likewise continue into the future. This reason, among others, constitute the many proofs for past and future lives. Another point is that there is no logical flaw that entails from the existence of past and future lives, and thus no one has thus far come up with a correct reason disproving the existence of past and future lives.

The assertion that past and future lives must exist is not based solely on faith; and while there are cases in our direct experience of real people recollecting their past lives, the existence of past and future lives is asserted by many classical Indian tenet systems—primarily Buddhist—through reasons and logic.

Thus, if one accepts future lives, one must rely on correct Dharma practice in order to exert oneself right now in the methods that bring about a happy existence in future lifetimes. Therefore, do not pursue only this life; rather, due to urgency and their greater importance, it is instructed that one should emphasize careful preparation for future lives.

It is said, "The first Dharma is to relinquish this life," but this does not mean one cannot accomplish happiness in this life. Rather, the Teacher Bhagavān, lord of the teachings, set forth four fulfillments pertaining to temporary and ultimate aims—riches, desires, Dharma, and liberation. Likewise, to temporarily obtain an excellent body in a higher rebirth, the well-being from riches and desires are required. Furthermore, the ultimate state of definite goodness that is liberation must be achieved through Dharma. These are realistic statements. [204] The Buddha did not say achieving liberation alone is sufficient and that well-being related to wealth and desires are unnecessary. Since he taught that all four fulfillments are necessary, in a Dharma context we require an ability to trust in the object of contemplation through our practice of study, reflection and meditation; at the same time, especially for the sake of benefiting others, we have a responsibility to consider society and the environment.

Putting effort into improving society is therefore a necessity—this is the fundamental point of the interconnectedness of human beings. Likewise, the state of our environment's flora and fauna—the wild animals, our forests and vegetation—the air, water, and so forth, are all connected to the temporary and long-term well-being of oneself and others. Bearing in mind that the advancement of not only our generation, but the future generations of individual villages and the world as a whole will depend entirely on people exerting themselves for the sake of the economy and resources, continually motivate yourself with an altruistic thought; whatever you set your mind toward for the sake of all sentient beings every morning, do not leave it on the level of mere words—carry it out in action throughout the day as much as possible and directly engage in action that helps others.

If one does this one has put mind generation into practice, and through abandoning the ten nonvirtues that bring harm to others, one encourages others to abandon them. All types of actions that help others are actions connected to Dharma and are extremely beneficial toward improving society. Therefore, if one can do that, one's actions really become Dharma.

Such beneficial acts do not come about through laziness and procrastination—effort is the defining factor. It says in the Seventh Dalai Lama's *Praise to the Noble Avalokiteśvara*:

> The world after this one is far from the one we are familiar with,
> and it is I alone who must wander in its dense darkness. [205]

We have no idea exactly when we will have to leave behind everyone we know and everything with which we are familiar to enter into the appearances of the bardo. That is when we begin the perilous journey to the next life, which we cannot even approximate based on our experiences in this life. Therefore, it is highly important that we start thinking about our future lives from now on. Just as it is considered naive to simply focus on day-to-day subsistence, and having a plan in case one lives long is considered prudent, foremost among all the religious traditions that accept future lives, the Buddhists established that one must implement a strategy for the sake of our future rebirths.

What is the Buddhist explanation of company that is always helpful to keep? If we develop qualities within the mind and extract positive potential, when we leave our body behind and only the extremely subtle consciousness continues into the next life, those qualities, or imprints, existing with that mind are what will help us. Therefore, in this time when we have leisure and opportunity, we have a perfect opportunity to accomplish the aims of not only this life, but all future lives. Thus, in order not to be unkind to oneself, one should make sure not to be complacent in placing virtuous imprints on the mind. In the case that you get distracted with the three mundane pursuits of food, clothing, and frivolous talk, it should naturally occur to you that this is an obstacle to pursuing future lives and considering them important. In order for that to naturally occur, it is important to meditate on death and impermanence—the recollection that we do not remain long in this world and will die. [206]

There are many stages to the meditation on impermanence. When the Bhagavān turned the first wheel of Dharma he taught the four noble truths, and he taught each noble truth to have four aspects— impermanence as the first, and so forth—totaling sixteen aspects. Likewise, in his teaching of the four summaries of Dharma, or four seals, he states:

All compounded phenomena are impermanent.
All contaminated phenomena are suffering.
All phenomena are empty and selfless.
Nirvana is peace.

The impermanence within the sixteen aspects and that taught first here are both subtle impermanence. In the context of the persons of small scope, the impermanence taught is the impermanence of the continua of things—coarse impermanence. Meditation on that is the primary cause of developing discontentment on the path of persons of small scope.

Persons of middle scope primarily meditate on subtle impermanence. In the context of the persons of great scope, when minds of favoritism and prejudice arise through the power of attachment and aversion, one generates a mind of equanimity toward all sentient beings. To achieve that one recollects that having attachment to some and aversion to others has no essence, and that oneself and others are the same in being in the nature of suffering and impermanence. Therefore, it is said:

> Why do impermanent people
> become attached to impermanent things?
> Why do impermanent people
> have aversion toward impermanent things?

In the same way, meditation on impermanence is important in all contexts of the paths common to the three beings. Furthermore, in Vajrayāna, the usage of bone ornaments and meditations in charnel grounds are methods to meditate on impermanence and representations of selflessness. Thus, in this time when we have the protection of a virtuous friend, a body enabling us to practice Dharma, and all special conditions are met, one must incite oneself to take full advantage and accomplish the ultimate aim. [207]

Contemplating Death and Impermanence: The Fact We Will Not Remain Long in This World

This has four parts:

1′ The disadvantages of not cultivating mindfulness of death
2′ The benefits of cultivating mindfulness of death and impermanence
3′ The kind of mindfulness of death you should develop
4′ How to cultivate mindfulness of death, or the actual recollection of death

The Disadvantages of Not Cultivating Mindfulness of Death

Some ignorant fools do not even consider whether death will come. Most people think death will come at some point, but in the days, months, and years leading up to old age one thinks one will not die. Due to this, whether one will succumb to a fatal disease or live to a hundred, for the time being we think we will keep living. It is like, for example, having a mentality of never wanting to go to another place—in such a case, one will never make preparations to do so. One will stay and prepare the fields and reinforce the stronghold walls. In this way we continue under the sway of the aims of this life alone. Reverse that mentality and think there is no certainty you will not die tomorrow. Even if you have prepared your monthly provisions, there is no certainty that at that time you will not already have taken on a different shape and grown horns. When you develop continuity in your awareness of that uncertainty, you will become like a person needing to get somewhere quickly who does not plan to settle down. In the same way the pack horse is meticulously prepared for the journey abroad, through reflecting on approaching death one does not toil for the affairs of this life; naturally engaging in means to benefit future lives becomes second nature. Thus, for those who wish to pursue this Dharma it is important to train the mind in the topics of death and impermanence. [208]

With respect to meditating on death and impermanence, there are six faults, or disadvantages, of not cultivating mindfulness of that.

The Disadvantage of Not Recollecting the Dharma
If One Is Not Mindful of Death

Becoming distracted with pursuing only food, clothing, and renown in this life leads to not accomplishing Dharma for the sake of future lives.

The Disadvantage of Not Engaging in Dharma even if You Recollect It

The great Tsongkhapa said, "We all have the thought that we will die in the end, but up until that point we think to ourselves every day, 'Today is not the day I will die. Today is not the day.'" We think we do not have time now because we have other things to do, and that we will have time for Dharma later. This thought renders us powerless, and we continually postpone Dharma practice.

The Disadvantage of Practicing Dharma but Not Practicing Purely

Virtue, study, contemplation, and meditation performed with attachment to this life are clearly done as external Dharma practices; they are not authentic inner practices of Dharma. For example, performing certain practices to live longer such as accumulating hundreds of millions of long life dhāraṇīs, making thousands of Amitāyus statues and so forth along with thousands of offerings, and performing any of the four actions of pacifying, increasing, magnetizing, and subjugating as a means for happiness in this life means they are not pure virtues. Therefore, Jé Gungthang Tsang Tenpai Drönmé states:

> If secret tantra is used only as a side practice in this life
> to dispel present obstacles, achieve long life and wealth,
> to magnetize and perform wrathful intervention,
> it is as if one has made charcoal of white sandalwood—
> do not use Dharma to send yourself to the lower realms!

As said, the teachings of the secret Vajrayāna are means to attain unsurpassed complete enlightenment, but if they are used under the sway of an untamed mind to accomplish one's long life, wealth, physical bliss, or power, it is like burning away the priceless soothing potential of white sandalwood. [209]. In this way the Dharma for achieving omniscience is rendered useless.

Furthermore, we as Dharma practitioners mostly take the pra-timokṣa, bodhisattva, and tantric vows and feign prayer recitation and other virtuous activities for the sake of accomplishing Dharma. How-ever, these are mere facades; the fact that they are not taming the mind is clear if, when we are in a good mood and give little Dharma sermons, or perform our prayers looking all holy, but if someone else criticizes us or we encounter difficulty, we act completely vulgar as if we have no Dharmic imprints whatsoever—full of pride, miserliness, jealously, and attachment, totally ready to get into a fight. Just like the saying goes, "When full-bellied and enjoying the sun, how easy it is to pretend one is a practitioner; as soon as something goes wrong, one turns vulgar."

Even though you may have conviction in the Dharma that accom-plishes the ultimate aim and strive for its sake, the fact that you cannot give up many other things and hold them dear in the back of your mind shows clearly that you are affected by the disadvantage of prac-ticing Dharma but not practicing purely.

The Disadvantage of Not Being Serious in Your Practice

Although it might appear that you are sustaining the meditations and accomplishing your practices, if you are unable to persevere and endure hardships to carry this out for months and years, you will grow weary and fed up with your virtuous practices when meeting the slightest of difficulties. [210] These are the faults of not being seri-ous in your practice.

Jetsun Milarepa's chief disciple, the incomparable sun-like Dakpo Lhajé who was prophesied, otherwise known as Gampopa Sönam Rinchen, the youthful Candraprabhā, once was receiving vast spir-itual advice and pith instructions from Milarepa and practicing the import of those teachings. When he went to leave, Milarepa said to him, "I have one pith instruction to give to you, but now is not the right time." Dakpo Lhajé made fervent requests to receive it, but Milarepa simply replied, "Now is not the time. You will see later." When Dakpo

Lhajé started walking away, Milarepa said to him, "Wait. You are my only son. The instruction I have for you I will give to you now." The incomparable Dakpo Lhajé was thrilled, and humbly requested the instruction. Jetsun Milarepa then showed him his buttocks, covered in cracked skin and calluses, and said, "I endured great hardship for my practice until my body became like this. You, too, must persevere with your practice and achieve enlightenment."

When reflecting on this story there is an aspect of sadness that arises, but I tell it to others as it is beneficial. Although the famous Dharma of achieving enlightenment in a single lifetime has great potential, whether you achieve it depends on how much you can willingly bear the hardships one meets through perseverance. Therefore, as it is said, "Liberation is difficult through comfortable Dharma." We must make sure that our manner of practicing Dharma does not become like this.

The Disadvantage of Letting Oneself Become an Uncultivated Person

If one does not recollect death, trivial pursuits of food, clothing, gossip, and overcoming our enemies and protecting our friends become the most important things in our life. They end up being our long-term preoccupations, and even take over our dreams. [211] Due to this, if we meet with an obstacle, we forget we are followers of the Buddha, and forget our vows and commitments. We end up lying to and deceiving others, and if they do not find out, we carry on completely fearlessly. Even if the situation does come to light, some remain completely confident, giving the impression they are completely clever and capable. This comes about from not recollecting death, leading one to forget that the road ahead in future lives is long. If one lives their life in this way, who knows when tragedy may befall this body of leisure and opportunity.

All of us are the same in having human bodies and similar brains, or intellects, but there are those who strived to use their potential for the sake of bringing peace and helping others. This is what we should aspire toward through praising, venerating, and lauding them. Such persons include Atiśa Dīpaṃkara; the lord of yogīs, Milarepa Shepé Dorje; the great and gentle protector Lama Tsongkhapa, and so on.

Completely opposite to these masters are those who use the potential of their intellect to cause great harm under the power of attachment and aversion. Such examples include Stalin and Hitler, whose murder of human beings is inconceivable in thought and action. The history of this world is replete with disgraceful acts that are considered vile and denigrated to this day. When such people were alive, due to their military might, ferocity, authoritative power, and so forth, they did not fear anyone. Whatever threat or opposition arose was eliminated by whatever means possible. [212] Although such figures lived ruthlessly and confidently, upon dying there are written accounts of them becoming seized with fear due to realizing their power and might was not something they could rely upon.

The Disadvantage of Having to Die with Regret

When we let ourselves become uncultivated by letting afflictions take over our mind, we end up dying with regret. Even someone who presents as a long-term cheerful Dharma practitioner, when it really comes to it, at the time of death will still go with regret. For example, there is a story of a religious figure whose many family members considered him an object of veneration. He himself behaved as a perfect practitioner, and always pretended that he was on the verge of going to a pure land in his next life. When he eventually came down with a terminal illness, his benefactors, hearts full of grief, beseeched him, "Guru, since you are about to depart to the pure land, please be a refuge and protector for us who are left behind!" To that their guru said in anguish, "I'd rather not die." Make sure you do not become like this.

THE BENEFITS OF CULTIVATING MINDFULNESS
OF DEATH AND IMPERMANENCE

This has six parts:

a" The benefit of there being great purpose
b" The benefit of it being powerful
c" The benefit of it being important in the beginning
d" The benefit of it being important in the middle
e" The benefit of it being important in the end
f" The benefit of dying joyfully

If one considers accomplishing the ultimate goal day and night through recollecting death, the most important of all endeavors, one can accomplish great purpose; it is powerful like a hammer that destroys afflictions and bad behavior in one go. [213] When we have to urge ourselves to practice in the beginning, or face difficulties in the middle, we might become discouraged or feel inadequate, but through recollecting the uncertainty of the time of death one thinks, "How is it okay for me to avoid small hardships or let myself become lazy and procrastinate?" Since we need to encourage ourselves daily in this way, recollecting impermanence is also important in the middle. In dependence on that one brings the Dharma to completion, and therefore it is also important in the end. If one sees the advantages of meditating on death and impermanence and the disadvantages of not doing so, one will not be affected by disinterest toward meditation on impermanence.

THE KIND OF MINDFULNESS OF DEATH
YOU SHOULD DEVELOP

It states in the *Great Treatise on the Stages of the Path*:

Through strong attachment to friends and relatives one is plagued by fear of separating from them—this is the fear of death of someone who has never practiced the path. This is not to be developed here. What, then, should be developed? All bodies taken on through karma and afflictions cannot escape death. This may be frightening, but for the time being this process cannot be stopped. You should, however, fear death if you have not ensured the interests of your future lives through stopping the causes of lower migrations and accomplishing the causes of higher rebirth and definite goodness. If you consider your fear of this, it is possible to accomplish those things, and thus you do not have to die in fear. If you do not secure your future interests, however, not only will you carry the fear that you will not be liberated from samsara in general, but you will also fear falling to the lower realms, and thus you will be tormented by regret at the time of death.

It furthermore states:

If one contemplates impermanence, thinking, "There is no doubt I will leave my body and belongings soon," one stops the craving that hopes not to separate from them. Therefore, the fear of death born from the mental torment of future separation from them does not arise.

We must train in this way. [214]

How to Cultivate Mindfulness of Death, or the Actual Recollection of Death

This has two parts:

a" The manifold contemplation of death

b" Meditation on the aspect of one's own death

The manifold contemplation of death has three parts:

1" Cultivation by way of the three roots

2" Cultivation by way of the nine reasons

3" Cultivation by way of the three decisions

Regarding the three roots: they are each proven by three reasons, which in the end serve as the meditation focal points of each decision.

The three roots are as follows:

(a) **Contemplation that death is certain**

(b) **Contemplation that the time of death is uncertain**

(c) **Contemplation that at the time of death nothing helps except Dharma**

Contemplation That Death Is Certain

Regarding contemplation that death is certain, it states in the *Sayings on Impermanence*:

If all the buddhas, pratyekabuddhas,
and śrāvaka disciples of the buddhas
abandoned their bodies,
what need to mention ordinary beings?

Furthermore, it states in the *Collection of Indicative Verses*:

Somewhere that death does not strike—
such a place does not exist.

Not in the sky, not in the sea,

not even if you live inside a mountain.

We are all certain to die. Even those completely enlightened buddhas of the past who had conquered birth and death passed into nirvana as an exhortation to those disciples grasping at permanence. Likewise, the Tibetan and Indian panditas and siddhas, kings and ministers, bodhisattvas and so forth—all countless supreme and ordinary beings in the history of religion, chronicles, legends and tales—are as if they are still present in a way, if one does not give it thought. Upon deep reflection, only accounts of their lives exist; they themselves are nowhere to be found in any place, time, or occasion, having already showed the aspect of passing into nirvana. Within a hundred years from now we are certain to die. If there has never been anybody who has escaped death in the past, how could we be the single exception that will do so?

All of my enemies, friends and persons neutral to me that I have known, including preceptors, students, my parents, friends, and so forth, have all gone to their next life. Even if tens of thousands of persons gathered now, everyone present is certain to die within the next hundred years. If there has been no one who escaped death and lived on, why would I be the exception who does not have to die?

The contemplation of the certainty of death is recollected by way of three reasons. [215] The first of these is that the lord of death will definitely come, and therefore cannot be avoided. The fact the lord of death will come for us is one hundred percent guaranteed. At the time of death, it does not matter what kind of body you have or where you live—death cannot be avoided by any means. Je Gungthang Tenpai Drönmé sums up the statements in *Oral Transmission of Mañjuśrī* in his *Verses of Advice for Meditating on Impermanence*:

The past victors and their spiritual heirs
who pervaded the three realms with enlightened activity
yet are no more, with only their names remaining,
are also teachers of the impermanence of all.

When recollecting the names and activities of the masters from the
kind teacher Śākyamuni up through those of our own gurus with
whom we shared a Dharma connection, they feel very much real. Upon
analysis, however, they have all passed away, and thus all that might
remain are relics—nothing else. A great being who had the marks and
signs of the emanation body of the incomparable lion among Śākyas
did exist once, but now all that remains is a feeling of intense sadness
when viewing holy pilgrimage sites containing relics, such as Sarnath,
India, which contains a small bone relic of the Bhagavān. It states in
the *Golden Light Sūtra*:

If his body has no flesh and bone,
how could there be relics?

Even though it states thus, from the perspective of ordinary disciples
there are relics to be seen. Likewise, Gungthang Tenpai Drönmé's
Verses of Advice for Meditating on Impermanence states:

Kings and statesmen so proud of their power and wealth,
who boasted of deeds that went down in history—
without much thought, it all seems so real,
but they have scattered within the three realms without a trace.

Whether such former kings or state leaders were good or bad people,
now they are mere objects of memory, relegated to history books. [216]
They are not people we can look at now, and many generations of their
descendants have already passed away.

More than four billion years have passed since Earth was formed. Creatures evolved within the past billion years, and modern *Homo sapiens* only over one hundred thousand years ago. Out of all the people that ever existed, there has never been a human—or insect— that avoided death and lived on forever. With respect to our parents, friends, enemies, and all people to whom we are neutral. It further states in *Verses of Advice for Meditating on Impermanence*:

> Our loved ones, helpers, and all those around us
> will scatter in an instant to distant mountains and valleys
> like a pile of leaves blown away in a storm,
> never to reunite again.

Within a hundred years there will not exist a single person who is alive now. Whether a new generation will be living here, or whether it turns to ruins, one day people will look back and only be able to tell stories of the Dalai Lama of Tibet spreading Buddhism here—nothing else will come of it.

No one can say who will die first. We act as if those who are older will die first and the young will die later, but clearly there is no certainty. Thus it further states:

> With white hair and body curved like a bow,
> the old parents, trembling,
> bury their child.
> Who, then, says it is the old who must go first?

We are all aware of cases in our lifetime of young children passing away and the parents having to perform funeral rites. Whether from history or our own experience, we know that life is certain to end with death. [217] As the saying goes:

Amitāyus bestows the siddhi of long life,
Vajrapāṇi, lord of secrets, safeguards against hindrances,
Bhaiṣajyaguru, king of physicians, bestows medicine,
but when death befalls oneself,
nothing can help you escape—
not Dharma, not might, not an army,
not wealth, and not cunning deception.

The second reason by which one contemplates certainty of death is that our lifetime cannot be extended, and constantly diminishes. Even though our lifespan is determined by karma, until that projected time our life must still depend on many other conditions. It is difficult to increase one's lifespan, although there is some effect on the lifespan through increasing merit by life-accomplishing practices, animal liberation, and so forth, and through taking care of one's health and seeking medical treatment. Take the example of someone who will live another forty years from now: they will not live their life with ease and leisure every second of every hour, day, week, month, and year, and as each second passes until the fortieth year, they are running out of time. Therefore, we should contemplate that from the point of view that the lifespan cannot be increased and that obstacles constantly arise, we are certain to die.

The third reason is the contemplation of the certainty of death such that even while you are alive there is little time to practice Dharma. Even if we live another forty or fifty years, unless we focus all our efforts and do not waste time, that lifespan does not guarantee an opportunity to practice Dharma. Since practicing Dharma does not come naturally, Jé Gungthang says in his *Mirror Illuminating Words of Truth*:

Twenty years pass not recollecting the Dharma,
another twenty pass repeating "I will practice! I will!"

Another ten in dismay, "I failed! I failed!"
Ah, the story of a wasted life. [218]

This has happened to most of us. When we are young, for twenty years it is difficult to recollect Dharma. For the next twenty years we go through life thinking, "I will get around to it." Once we reach around fifty years of age our faculties start to wane; we have less energy, and we apprehensively head toward the end of our life.

Using myself as an example, up until ten years of age the most important thing to me was getting distracted in fun and games. At that time my playmates were the sweepers around Norbulingka, they were very clever at games and extremely kind. There was one whose job was to sweep above the lama residence—he had learned some elementary debate from the subject of Collected Topics relating to colors. I was only seven or eight at the time and had not studied this topic, so I did not understand. It was at that point that I thought to myself with a little bit of pride and enthusiasm, "It is improper if I do not study philosophy."

It was when I was around fifteen or sixteen, on my way to the village of Dromo, that I thought a bit about the stages of the path. That was also when the Chinese started arriving in Tibet. Thus, until the age of twenty-four or twenty-five I was focusing on philosophical studies, but on the other hand found it difficult to engage in a pure practice of Dharma amid the troubles with the Chinese.

In 1959, at the age of twenty-five, I arrived as a refugee in India. After I had settled, I resumed philosophical studies, and reviewed the major treatises such as Tsongkhapa's *Golden Rosary* and so forth. Apart from that, my life goes on in a busy and turbulent way. Aside from the mere thought to engage in intense practice, I have not been able to follow up on that. However, there is something that puts my mind at ease. The omniscient Gendun Drup went to Tashi Lhunpo and not only constructed the monastery but taught the new monks

scriptures starting from Collected Topics, and put great effort into raising funds and bringing together the conditions for construction of a
new temple and its contents. [219] At that time, the students requested
to be excused from work, which thoroughly disappointed him. He
told them, "I lived in solitary retreat in the snow mountains with little
wants and few possessions and thus I was free from work, able to focus
all my time on meditation. If I had continued with that, I would have
developed realizations by now, but I gave up my meditation practice
to help whichever trainees were in need. With that thought I toiled to
establish Tashi Lhunpo Monastery and gave up my life for this cause.
How pitiful it is if you all decide not to collaborate." Likewise, I myself
have not been able to devote all of my energy to prayers and practice,
but since many exiled Tibetans are comforted by the thought that the
Dalai Lama is still around, merely living on with this title seems to be
helpful. If it brings general benefit, I think that too is Dharma, and this
encourages me to continue. Whatever the case, my life continues to
finish without having much time for anything.

Each day is made up of twenty-one thousand inhalations and exhalations, each month is thirty days, and each year in twelve months.
Twelve such years is called a "cycle," and when five of these cycles
are complete, it is said one has also reached one's lifespan of sixty
years. Thus, it says in the *Play in Full Sūtra*:

> The three spheres of existence are impermanent like an
>   autumn cloud.
> The birth and death of beings is like watching a performance.
> The passing of a lifetime is like a flash of lightning;
> it moves quickly like a waterfall.

As said, we do not remain for even a minute. It is not like our food
and wealth being consumed and replenished, for the lifespan cannot
be newly increased. Therefore, it says in the *Way of the Bodhisattva*:

Never stopping day or night,
my life constantly drains away.
If it cannot be increased in any way,
why should someone like me escape death? [220]

Contemplate this through examples and reasoning, and meditate until you have concluded you will certainly die. At the end of the analysis of the certainty of death by way of three reasons, one concludes it is necessary to practice Dharma.

Contemplation That the Time of Death Is Uncertain

Regarding the contemplation that the time of death is uncertain, having meditated in this way, if one thinks, "Although I cannot escape death, I have temporarily sought out the benefits of overcoming enemies and protecting loved ones, and also the benefits of practicing Dharma; in the end I will practice Dharma!" Even though it is said sentient beings of the three realms each have a lifespan, at the end of the day the conviction that they will reach it is only certain for persons of the northern continent Unpleasant Sound (*Uttarakuru*). There is especially no certainty for persons from Jambudvīpa, as it says in the *Treasury of Knowledge*:

Here the lifespan is indefinite—at the end
it will be ten years, in the beginning it was measureless.

As said we know from our own experience that many people younger than ourselves have died before us, and many people older than ourselves still live on. Therefore, how can you have any certainty you will not die before them? As it says in the *Collection of Indicative Verses*:

Tomorrow or the next life,

which comes first, nobody knows.

Do not seek for tomorrow.

It is better to concentrate on your next life.

Who can be so resolute as to whether tomorrow or the bardo will come first? [221]

Contemplating the uncertainty of the time of death can be divided into three points, the first of which is that the lifespan in this world is uncertain, especially during the degenerate era.

Therefore, contemplating of the uncertainty of the time of death can be divided into three:

(i)   The contemplation that the lifespan in this world is uncertain, especially during the degenerate era

(ii) The contemplation that the conditions for death are many and the conditions for life are few

(iii) The contemplation that the time of death is uncertain because the body is very fragile [221]

The Contemplation That the Lifespan in this World Is Uncertain, Especially during the Degenerate Era

During our limited time on Earth, the Dharma-related and worldly plans we devise are based only on the whim that we will live long enough to see them carried out. Since we see a few reasons why we would keep living, we do not think we will die today. Yet not one person alive in the morning can guarantee they will not be dead by the evening. We know this because of the many healthy people who have passed away suddenly. We constantly hear about people who have died, but we associate death with something that only happens to others. Even though we do not think about the fact death will befall us one day, the time of our death is uncertain all the same.

The Contemplation That the Conditions for Death
Are Many and the Conditions for Life Are Few

Some think the causes to go on living are many, like adjusting one's diet, receiving medical treatment, and so on. It states in *The Precious Garland*:

> The causes of death are many,
> those of staying alive, few.
> These, too, become the causes for death.
> Thus, always practice Dharma.

Conditions for life that have become causes of death are many, such as disagreeable food, wrong medication, collapsed housing, broken down ferries, being swindled by friends, and so on.

Even though life expectancy is edging closer to one hundred years of age through advancements in health care and so on, the many conditions we have set up for ourselves to live happily during this time often become a cause for our death instead. Take for example food: even though it is conducive for life and a unique cause for sustaining healthy bodily constituents, many illnesses are born from eating food that does not agree with us, leading to death. [222].

Additionally, in Western countries different foods and treatments will be strongly promoted as fantastic for your health and then a few years later it becomes necessary to announce they are, in fact, harmful. In modern times we are also presented with new paradoxes: cars, trains, planes—all designed to help us get to our destination quickly and with ease but often leading us quickly to our death instead. After the plane door is secured shut, one can only think that if something goes wrong, we are all finished, and there is nothing we can do about it. Even though these are all conditions for a comfortable life, they can be a main cause of our death. Thinking about the way we live now, the causes of life and the causes of death are intertwined, with causes of life often turning into the causes of our death.

The Contemplation That the Time of Death Is Uncertain Because the Body Is Very Fragile

If our body were made from a solid and indestructible metal, for example, it would be another matter. However, we are conceived in the womb from the joining of our parents' ovum and sperm. The explanation that a great number of substances exist at that initial stage is slightly akin to the non-Buddhist Sāṃkhya explanation of things.

When doctors explain the formation of every part of our body from head to toe, up to each individual hair, and the function of each substance in our body, they start from the origins—the sperm and the potential of the substances it contains. [223] Therefore, [from a Buddhist perspective], through the condition of karma acting as a foundation, those many bodily substances must aggregate together interdependently, and likewise through mutual dependence their capacities transform.

Just like a plant, for instance, has stages of growth based on substances from the stage of a seed up until it withers and dies, so too our body develops through the interdependence of the different substances that came from our parents' ovum and sperm, such as the four elements and so forth. Along with that we also have an experience of pleasure and pain in dependence on those substances, which is due to karma. Ultimately, this can only be thought about in terms of karma.

The elements and substances serve as a condition for the body to be alive, but those very things themselves are in opposition, as stated in Āryadeva's *Four Hundred Verses*. The fact that a living being must be posited onto a conglomerate of clashing substances is established by modern science. That we have to take so much care of our body is because it is by nature a feeble mass that depends on a collection of opposing substances. When the strength of the opposing substances finds balance, we are "healthy," and when a single element, for example, is out of balance, we are unhealthy. Without these opposing factors we cannot live, and yet they are always ready to fall into disorder. Therefore, the time of death is likewise uncertain due to this fact of the body being so fragile. [224]

It is, for example, like a butter lamp that has the conditions to burn for a long time, such as butter and a wick, but is extinguished suddenly by a gust of wind. In the same way, even though one's allotted lifespan has not run out, there is an extreme number of harmful spirits and other things that disturb the elements and interfere by creating obstacles. As it states in *Letter to a Friend*:

> If life is more impermanent than a water bubble
> battered by the winds of many perils,
> then the fact you can take another breath
> or awaken from sleep is amazing indeed.

Meditate until you experience the conviction that death is uncertain. With respect to this critical point, one thus takes heed, as if a relentless enemy is certain to come for you, but at what time is unknown.

This teaching on the uncertainty of the time of death is profound. What ultimately ruins us is not properly contemplating the uncertainty of the time of our death. For most of us, the thought occurs that we will die at some point, but we still think that we will not die today, and in this way, life passes us by. We also extend this into the future, thinking, "Nothing will befall me for now." We know we must not neglect working for the sake of our future lives, but we still insist we must do this and that beforehand. With respect to this pattern of behavior, Jé Gungthang says:

The activities of this life are like ripples on water.

As one fades the next appears.
We accomplish one after the other yet they still increase;
would it not be better to forcefully bring it to an end?

Along the same lines, the Seventh Dalai Lama, Kelsang Gyatso, states:

Once born, no one has the autonomy to remain for even a second,
we all race toward the lord of death.
We tell ourselves we are alive, but we are on death's highway.
What a miserable image this is, of the faulty being led to
slaughter.

Essentially, we are all certain to die, and we do not know when. It is
a scary event that is definite to happen to us within the next hundred
years. However, since you cannot accurately predict exactly when,
do not delay your preparations for even another day and remain
ready. [225] As it says in *Verses of Advice for Meditating on Impermanence*:

Before you get to tomorrow's Dharma practice
there's a danger death will come today.
As such, stop fooling yourself—
if you are to practice Dharma, do it now!

As said, contemplate the uncertainty of the time of death and decide
not to delay Dharma practice until tomorrow, and begin right now.

CONTEMPLATION THAT AT THE TIME OF DEATH NOTHING HELPS EXCEPT DHARMA

As it states in the *Way of the Bodhisattva*:

When seized by the servants of the lord of death,

what help are friends or family?
At that time meritorious deeds are my only savior,
yet those too I have forsaken.

When it comes time for the avalanche to crumble onto the treacherous path renowned for impermanence and death, at that time
substances, mantras, samādhi, and heroic weaponry cannot prevent
it. Likewise, neither bribery nor flattery can be used to get out of
it. There is no need to mention that death has the power to take
those who rival cakravartin kings in power and wealth; surrounded
by many loved ones, this body of ours, together with us since the
womb, must be completely discarded. Only our primary consciousness travels on, powerless and alone. At that time, the only benefit is
the previously accumulated virtue that follows after it. Thus, meditate until you experience that only Dharma can help at the time of
death.

It appears some fools are under the impression that, at the time
of death, the benefit of Dharma is immortality. In our own tradition that is not the case. However, the way one dies is influenced:
excellent practitioners are joyful toward death; average practitioners
do not fear death; and lesser practitioners die without regret. This
comes from the teachings of the previous Kadam masters.

When this thing called death finally arrives, only Dharma can help
us, not wealth nor belongings, friends nor family, and not even our
body will be of any use. [226] Our wealth can determine the level of
facilities and medical care we receive when we fall ill, but when it
comes to death itself, no material wealth can save our life. Above all,
we cannot take any of it with us when we die; even the most wealthy
on this planet will not be taking a single cent with them. When we
Tibetans left Tibet and went into exile in 1959, our money and possessions were of no use. In this way our wealth and possessions cause

additional stress and anxiety while we are alive, and it is quite clear they are not hugely beneficial.

Our reliable friends and our dear family members, partners, and so forth, cannot stop death happening to us—they are simply left behind weeping. They cannot go with us. They experience life's trials and tribulations together with us and help us when we are struggling, but when it is time for us to go to the next life, instead of them helping, we experience sadness and anxiety to have to leave them behind on top of going through fearing death itself. At this time, we anxiously wonder how their lives will play out and whether they can take care of themselves without us.

To take the example of monastics who have gone forth into homelessness, the monastery disciplinarians of the past would advise the assemblies, "If one stands, stand like an incense stick; if one falls, fall like incense," the point being to stay with ease and leave with ease. Furthermore, the Kadampa masters say, "With few wants and few possessions, whether staying or going, do so as a crow takes flight from a rock. [227]" As it is said:

> Searching just for the food he needs now, he is like a bird;
> He quickly rises, his entire estate complete.

Simply taking whatever you can carry and focusing on your immediate needs, without dillydallying and making calculations many months and years in advance, that person, as soon as he stands, has his entire estate with him; he leaves nothing behind. The monks and nuns of today who have great attachment to friends, relatives, and belongings are simply superficial practitioners.

Taking myself as an example, there have been many people who said they would give their life for the sake of the Dalai Lama, even boldly proclaiming how they would go about it. I do not know whether they actually would or not, but even if they were able to it is still absolutely of no benefit on the day I die. When it is time to go we can only rely on ourselves. Saying, "I am the Dalai Lama. I have disciples. I have supporters," achieves nothing. Powerful leaders of nations have body-guards with them wherever they go, stationed inside and outside—but no one can guard them from the frights of death. Likewise, however much power you have or armies you control, at the time of death they cannot help.

Not only that, even our own body is of no use. After the body is conceived in the womb and becomes a human being, it is then the basis of our mind. Our heart works like a servant to keep this body alive, but one day this body we have held so dear, clothed when it was cold, fed when it was hungry, hydrated when thirsty, slept so it could be relaxed—however much care was taken—on the day we die our body and mind separate. [228] This body we have held so dear becomes a corpse. Regarding this, Jetsun Milarepa says:

> This frightful thing called a "corpse"
> is present in the channels of the yogi's body.

That which is known as a corpse is veiled by misconception, and is considered dirty. It is not something that arises newly later; rather, when the relationship of dependence between our mind and body breaks down, that is exactly when it becomes a corpse. Then, that thing we held so dear all along is to be discarded. Even though one might think the dead body of a lama is precious, as it is said:

> Even if a corpse is wrapped in fine cloth,
> when placed in the cremation furnace it is destroyed.

In reality, most people end up cremated. Therefore, that which is taken with us to our future lives is only the virtue created in our mindstream; that is to say, the potential, or imprints, of previous good karma that was placed in our consciousness. If such potential or imprints of good karma have been placed in our continuum of consciousness, those are what we can rely on at death and what we can take with us. We can only relax if our bad karmic imprints are few; otherwise, having memorized all scriptural definitions, divisions, boundaries, and inter-pretations will not help if one has not applied the meaning to oneself. At that time, it is difficult to procure benefit from your expertise in semantics alone. Therefore, through understanding both the words and their meaning, thoroughly habituate your coarse mind by focus-ing on the meaning. If through that one can place imprints on the sub-tle mind, since that accompanies us when going to the next life, those are the only things that can be taken. Therefore, Gungthang Tenpai Drönmé states:

> The Dharma is your guide on a path unknown,
> the Dharma is your provision on a long journey,
> the Dharma is your protector on a treacherous path.
> From now on engage your three doors in Dharma. [229]

If we must walk an unknown path, at the very least we should ask someone who is familiar with it and consult a map to build under-standing. In the same way, our experiences in this life are not sufficient for the purpose of our future lives; when it comes time to embark on that unfathomable journey, only Dharma can help. Furthermore, that Dharma cannot be taken in the form of texts carried on our backs; our inner practice of taming the mind is what will guide us. Therefore, it is said that Dharma is the guide on a path unknown.

Furthermore, since the lamrim literature includes the stages of death, contemplations at the time of death, the establishment of the bardo, the experiences within it, the necessary mental attitude, and the process of the bardo finishing and one taking rebirth, the guide is therefore the lamrim itself.

With respect to "a long journey," take for example going on a long road trip and not knowing if there will be a gas station when needed, and how one must prepare life-saving provisions like spare fuel, drinking water, and food. Similarly, if one has undeteriorated qualities of mind due to Dharma practice, then the imprints in one's continuum will follow the stream of consciousness wherever it goes. Going from lifetime to lifetime those imprints are not wasted and are thus the unfailing refuge. Therefore, the Dharma is like your provisions on a long journey.

Moreover, the Dharma is our protector on a treacherous path. Whichever virtuous or nonvirtuous imprints in our mind are particularly strong are the ones that influence us. [230] Even within the context of a single lifetime, children that grow up together in very similar environments can display highly varying dispositions—some naturally trusting and compassionate from a young age, and others whose virtuous imprints are not as easily awakened. Not only that, some are noticeably drawn to nonvirtuous acts. Thus, if we put effort into depositing good imprints through actions that accord with Dharma, they become the protector who guides us without hardship on the treacherous path. We will then be able to guide ourselves on our own future journeys.

Generally speaking, there are biological factors that play a role in a child's personality due to genes inherited from the parents; however, the aforementioned imprints appear to be a dominant factor. Take for example sets of twins: even if they have had no contact for a long time and have lived far away from each other, due to their shared physicality a lot of broad similarities are observed between them, such as their state of health, mental disposition, and how they live their lives. However, there are cases where twins could not be more different from one another. The current self that is imputed onto the stream of consciousness is simply circumstantial and temporary, and did not exist in the lifetime before. Therefore, their way of thinking and the levels of their afflictions differ, resulting in different dispositions. Due to placing virtuous and nonvirtuous imprints in previous lives, when the slightest of conditions are met in this life, those good or bad potentials are naturally awakened.

Therefore, good or bad imprints from habituation in our past lives discretely influence us in our new life, as we can see in this life now. [231] Thus, for the great journey of our future lives to be more comfortable, we must practice Dharma in this life; in other words, placing virtuous imprints on our consciousness now is important.

Since our own mind is not obscured to us, it is not the case that we cannot understand our own being. Therefore, analyzing oneself, it is certainly difficult to say we have accomplished only virtue and are guaranteed a good rebirth. Future rebirths, whether good or bad, are entirely influenced by karma; even if we took refuge in a qualified guru it is highly unlikely that they could lead us to a rebirth through their compassion. Furthermore, things like reverence toward and offerings made to the sangha have some benefit; however, most importantly, if we cannot be careful ourselves, then transference to a good rebirth is incredibly unlikely.

If the blessings of compassion alone were a refuge, we would have been saved long ago by the myriad buddhas and bodhisattvas who fill space. Their inability to act as saviors comes down to Buddhists not accepting anything akin to a creator god, and thus not accepting that one being can liberate another through their omniscient wisdom, love, or power. Therefore, we can only liberate ourselves through newly developing qualities in our own continuum. Thus, the Bhagavān said:

You are your own protector.

Although brutal in a way, it highlights the profound fact that, fundamentally, Buddhism revolves around accomplishing things oneself. Furthermore, it states in a sutra:

Sages do not wash away sins with water.
Nor do they remove the suffering of beings with their hands.
They cannot transfer their realizations to others;
through their teaching the truth of reality beings are
    liberated. [232]

Furthermore:

I showed you the path to liberation;
however, understand that liberation depends on yourself.

Now we have attained a human body and understand and have some basic faith in the Buddha's Dharma. All relevant conditions have come together. Still, if we do not try to manage our current situation in which so much effort is required to direct our thoughts toward virtue, just like forcing water to flow uphill—and engaging in nonvirtue is as natural as water flowing downhill— that is, if we do not commit ourselves to engaging in virtue and disengaging in nonvirtue while we are alive, then liberation and buddhahood become further away. All the while we pray to achieve buddhahood for the sake of all sentient beings—just empty words. In brief, become completely determined to practice only the Dharma that is free from the binds of attachment to this life.

Meditation on the Aspect of One's Own Death

Contemplating the death of any other person and the occurrences at that time, and recollecting that one day it will happen to oneself, one cultivates a mental experience of it. The omniscient Panchen Losang Chökyi Gyaltsen states in his *Compassionate Refuge*:

One can meditate on whatever manifestation of death was taught. The main point is that everyone—whether old or young—will be seized by a final, fatal ailment, whether because their lifespan has finished, or whether due to a sudden obstacle, or because their merit depleted. At that point doctors will give up and religious ceremonies will not help, and the last hopes of your loved ones for you to live will fade. [233]

Along the same lines, that final illness can drag on to the point that medicine does not help and even your soft bedding becomes unbearable. The body emits a foul smell, becomes void of feeling, and your once sharp mind deteriorates to the point you cannot remember names or meanings. The illness continues until half of your living body is like a corpse, and you know the only avenue is death. Not only are you weary, but those around you too, as you wonder if the nurse will come, and so forth. Eventually you would rather be dead than alive. When the pain becomes unbearable day and night, even your continuous yogic practice is ineffective, and you must die with great difficulty at the end of your life. Such visualizations are also stated by Kyabjé Pabongkha (1878–1941) in his *Heart-Spoon: An Exhortation to Remember Impermanence*:

Worn out, you try hard to express
your final words—your testament and lamentations,
but your tongue has dried, and no one understands.
Weighted by great despair, you perish.

And:

Your final sustenance—blessed substances and relic pills—
are placed in your mouth with some water,
but you cannot even swallow.
They remain in the mouth of a corpse.

Such will befall oneself. The elements will also go through a process of dissolution, starting with the earth element. Upon its deterioration, one has an experience as if sinking into the ground, and the body becomes feeble. When the water element deteriorates, the eyes become sunken, one loses hearing, and the saliva dries up. When the fire element deteriorates, the body's warmth retracts. When the potency of the winds deteriorate, internal and external signs appear, such as a rasping sound in the throat. One's breathing suddenly becomes rapid, followed by the outer breath ceasing, and one's life comes to an end. Generally, one is considered dead once the breathing and heart have stopped along with brain function. Certain practitioners, however, still have consciousness in their body, and at this point abide in the clear light of death through yogic practice. [234]

For example, when Ling Rinpoché, Yongdzin Dorjé Chang (1903–83), passed away, he stayed in *tukdam* meditation for thirteen days after being pronounced clinically dead. His body stayed fresh without deteriorating as he remained in the clear light of death according to the path of secret mantra. Although the coarse connection between [body and mind] has ceased at this point, since consciousness has not yet left the body, the term is actually clear light of *dying* in Tibetan, and not clear light of *death*. As soon as that clear light has stopped, the consciousness leaves that body, which then becomes a corpse.

Afterward the body must be disposed of, and aside from the cases where the person died of a seriously contagious disease and had to be buried, the preferred method in Tibet was to cut up the body and feed it to the vultures. Gomang Khangsar Dorjé Chang requested sky burial after passing away, and likewise so did many other Kadampa masters. Incredibly, not only were they devoted to virtuous practice in life, but also in death, by offering their bodies to sentient beings.

Once I went to meet Baba Amte (1914–2008) in Anandwan, a place in India,[65] where he had settled long term to look after lepers and the disabled. I was deeply touched by the level of care he gave to them.

When we sit comfortably on a soft cushion, back straight, reciting, "May all sentient beings . . ." those are mere words; they do not translate into action like his. [235] When the people there passed away, instead of cremating them according to Hindu tradition (1200 BCE), it was considered better to bury them in consideration of the environmental impact of using so much wood. Furthermore, instead of using a fancy coffin, their bodies were wrapped in cloth, and once buried a tree would be planted on top as a memorial. I found the idea of growing a tree instead of burning one an admirable idea. I am not advocating that everyone adopt burial practices like these; I am simply sharing what I saw.

In brief, the body you cared for during your life will either be fed to animals, buried, sent down a river, or cremated. In the case it is cremated, once that is out of the way, those left behind might keep a handful of your ashes, and for a while look at them and lament what a great person you were. Before long, not only does your family lay claim to the funds you saved for retirement, but they start legal battles for them, breaking family bonds out of greed. In some cases, your loved ones start claiming your assets before you have even died! These are things to consider. If those surviving you have faith in Dharma, it is better if you pre-arrange for those with faith to make offerings on your behalf, donations made to those in need, recitation of dhāraṇī mantras, and contributions to social causes.

In brief, visualize the occasion of your own death, and the handling of your corpse afterward, whether in a cemetery or during the cremation process. [236]

Having contemplated the certainty of death, if you can sustain the meditation by integrating the visualization of your own death, it will enhance the efficacy of the following contemplation of the uncertainty of the time of death.

Concluding Verses

This existence projected by karma and affliction
has headed from the very start without pause
straight to death and impermanence.
What fool, then, would constantly prepare to live forever?

Upon seeing untimely and uncertain deaths,
and the young dying before the old,
still you think your time is fixed.
You are wide-eyed but blind!

Having turned away from your faithful companion of virtue,
without shame you thought that friends, servants, and wealth
would always be there for you, but now you start to fear
that you must traverse the perilous bardo alone.

Contemplating the Sufferings
of the Lower Realms

AMONG THE TWO TYPES of beings, contemplating the suffering of a being in a bad rebirth requires that one understand the possibility of bad rebirths in general, and rebirth as hell beings in particular. The underlying reasoning for those is that if future lives exist, whether good or bad, they are determined by one's own karma and one cannot choose one's rebirth. You did not control your rebirth into this life as it was also due to your karma, and therefore after you die you will go into your next life under the power of your karma.

How, then, does a good or bad rebirth come to be? If one has accumulated bad karma in this life under the power of the three poisonous afflictions, that karma has a bad rebirth as its result. If one's three poisonous afflictions were not particularly strong, especially hatred, then one can reasonably ascertain one can achieve a good rebirth. [237] On the other hand, if one does not accept past and future lives and asserts a creator god instead, many such theories of the universe become untenable.

Furthermore, let us consider the fact that a huge number of visible sentient beings, who experience happiness and suffering, have parents. Explaining how they come into being through their parents is simple enough, as in the case of a human being conceived through a sperm and ovum. However, if we try to trace their ancestors by going back one hundred thousand years, one million, ten million, or one hundred million years, there are no humans and life has not come into existence on Earth yet. Thus, at the beginning of the earliest eon there were no ancestors of humans or animals.

If one has to provide a solid reason to modern scientists as to how different life forms arose on a planet that started as an inconceivably hot molten rock, one must explain why the same type of matter resulted in animals on the one hand, and humans on the other. From our perspective this can only be explained on the basis of karma. Furthermore, through good and bad karma there will also be other kinds of places to take birth that will exist in future. Therefore, although at first glance the idea of hot hells, cold hells, adjoining hells, and occasional hells as found in the sutras and shastras might seem inconceivable at first, aside from our not seeing them and not believing in them, one cannot provide better proof for their nonexistence.

Many facets of the human body such as its atoms, sense powers, sources of perception, and likewise the individual substances of each sense power are not visible to us, but we cannot say they do not exist. However, if questioned exactly how or why they came into existence, we can only answer with, "Who knows!" [238] One only disbelieves the existence of hells and so forth because one cannot see them. However, giving it careful thought, we also cannot fully explain the complicated design of our body parts that form the basis for our feelings of happiness and suffering even though these parts are visible to the eye.

If we contemplate how the body arose through causal interdependence under the power of karma, from a negative perspective we can understand how it is possible it must be in the nature of suffering. From a positive perspective, we also arrive at the inconceivable idea that there must be an everlasting state of happiness. Through a tamed mind good results increase infinitely, and thus the qualities of enlightened body, speech, and mind, and likewise true cessations and true paths are feasible. If we ascertain that, we can also infer that an untamed mind leads to negative results that were once difficult to fathom.

If it were impossible that hot and cold hells, for example, could not result from an untamed mind, then how could it be possible that lib-

THE SUFFERINGS OF THE LOWER REALMS

eration and omniscience resulted from taming the mind? Therefore, if one does not accept that, one must hold to the notion that the mind is in the nature of the flawed defilements. If one holds to that, then it must be the case that the mind's nature is unchangeable, and that an angry person must be forever angry. But that is not the case—however bad tempered someone is, we know that they do not stay angry every month of every year.

Furthermore, even if someone does not have much familiarity with loving-kindness, the opponent of anger, it is still possible that they dearly love and have no anger toward their friends and relatives, but if the nature of their mind has become loving-kindness in that moment, it would mean that they could never become angry again. However, we know this is not the case, and we experience that the manifestations of the mind are always changing. [239] Thus, while the primary mental consciousness, experiencer of happiness and suffering, remains impartial, it can still be tainted by positive and negative conceptions. However, misconceptions like attachment and aversion cannot become the nature of our mind.

Thus, not taming our mind and creating the karma of harming others results in the suffering of bad rebirths.

To explain this suffering, we move onto the next outline under "developing the mind intent on future lives," the first of which is **contemplating the suffering of bad rebirths.**

CONTEMPLATING THE SUFFERING OF BAD REBIRTHS

1' **Contemplating the suffering of hell beings**
2' **Contemplating the suffering of animals**
3' **Contemplating the suffering of hungry ghosts**

Contemplating the Suffering of Hell Beings

I will first present a brief history of hell, or hells, and their makeup as described in various classical religious texts that explain cosmology, from different countries. The way that hell is described in terms of its layout and content is not something that newly originated in Buddhism; rather, the various depictions from other classical religious traditions had an evident influence within Buddhism. I aim to give a basic idea of a few classical explanations. [240]

1. To give brief summations of the versions of hell, let us start with the **ancient Greeks** (eighth century BCE). The abode of the dead is called Hades by the ancient Greeks. Hades is both the underworld and the god himself. In the rare depictions of him, he is ashen in color, and portrayed as passive rather than a deliverer of punishment. He guards the underworld with his multi-headed, raw-flesh loving hound called Cerberus. The descriptions of his abode become clearer throughout history. Homer, for example, describes the Erinyes figures who live there as winged female humanoids having snakes for hair and brandishing scourges. Furthermore, they are described as oath-bound avengers, relentless, able to cause others to perform unusual acts through insidious means and are arisen from a curse. Additionally, esoteric liturgy describes ferocious beasts, demons, malicious spirits, and so forth in great detail. [241]

2. In the **ancient Egyptian religion**, the dead had to journey through the netherworld, which contained passages, each with individual gates. Some gates were guarded by avaricious demons including blood suckers, organ eaters, shadow eaters, bone crunchers, and so forth, all with different names. They could drink the soul (the Egyptians believed the person was made up of three souls, a heart, and a vital essence), or swallow the body whole. Thus, during this time, if their souls were not judged favorably, one underwent a second, definitive death. The final judgment of the soul takes place during the weighing

of the heart ceremony. The heart of the deceased, which contains evidence for or against its possessor, is weighed against a feather of Ma'at, god of truth, on a scale. Next to the scales waits the demoness Ammit, having the head of a crocodile, the forelegs and body of a lion and the hindquarters of a hippopotamus. If the heart tips the scale, the corpse of the deceased is immediately eaten. Thus, the actual punishment is to be reduced to nothingness, and they therefore do not accept eternal damnation.

3. In **Judaism** (1500 BCE) there are no flesh-eating spirits, unlike those found in the reference material for the aforementioned traditions. However, after a development of ideas in the books of the Old Testament, the abode of punishment became Gehenna, a hot hell. [242] Out of the two major Jewish traditions, the Ashkenazi tradition that spread in the Middle Ages adopted the depictions of hell from Christianity.

4. In **Islam** (seventh century CE), on top of a myriad of sufferings, there are explanations of a hell beast who ravenously eats sinners.

Some other points of interest are the following: It is possible for there to be temporary hell-like suffering for people on Earth; the dead have wants but are never satisfied; there is an assertion that the experience of hell is not eternal for the mind, and God is not aware of it; it is accepted that the servants of death are the ones who inflict punishment and torture on the dead.

5. In some histories of **Christianity**, early Christians, up to the third century CE, placed greater emphasis on the positive aspects of the New Testament, and hell fell slightly out of focus.

Regarding hell in the Orthodox tradition of Christianity as per the teachings of Origen and so forth, punishment is undergone in purgatory through the cleansing of one's soul by a flame before the final judgment. [243] This flame, which exists within the domain of one's mind, was said to also protect against ghosts and demons. Around 550 CE, after the ecumenical council during the time of the Eastern

Roman emperor Justinian I, the [Nicaean Orthodoxy] became the official religion of the empire. After its adoption [the earlier views on purgatory] began to be seen as a heretical position.

Saint Augustine (354–430), a father of the Church, stated that on the one hand, one must experience punishment similar to the sin, and on the other hand, one will undergo eternal punishment due to all of man inheriting "original sin" through the great sin of Adam.

The theme of depicting the suffering of hell in paintings during the Middle Ages relates to this. In order to propagate the system of penance, the torments of hell were depicted to frighten people against committing sins.

In those images, demons take various forms, including reptilian, such as dragons and snakes; likewise of different beasts and of cannibal demons, or humanoid beasts, and so forth. There are also writings of beasts that drag down sinners, insects that eat them, and so forth.

Furthermore, there are depictions of a fearsome lord of darkness having a human body and a beast's head, who "departs with, or eats," the souls of the cursed. [244]

A few ancillary comments: Demons disguise themselves through deception among the religious, not only among regular people. Hell as an inferno is a common conception; however, Dante asserts the last circle of hell to be eternally frozen. Around the High Middle Ages, new ideas emerged about purgatory as an intermittent state to purify sin. It was deemed possible to gain entrance to heaven if one underwent suffering in hell for a certain period of time.

Martin Luther, the Protestant reformer, rejected the explanations of purgatory and the excessive torment of hell, considering them to exist only for the sake of intimidating people. According to him, if anything must be said about hell, it should only be to encourage repentance. Luther's opinion was that man is beset on all sides at once by the danger of being deceived, and that itself is a form of hell. Furthermore, he believed that the hope of purifying sins through the benevolence of the creator, an instruction on the path to salvation (Christ's act of salvation was to overcome death, hell, and the power of our sins against the creator), should be greater than the fear of negative consequences. Without fear, he believed, people are better able to love and act righteously.

During the Age of Enlightenment that started at the end of the seventeenth century, new perspectives on Christianity emerged in which hell was likened to a malediction brought upon oneself. [245] However, in modern exegeses more fundamentalist Christians reject that idea.

In Buddhism (sixth century BCE), the traditional presentation of hell divides it into four: **the hot and cold hells**, the adjoining hells, and the occasional hells. **The first** has eight: the Reviving Hell, the Black Line Hell, the Crushing Hell, the Howling Hell, the Great Howling Hell, the Hot Hell, the Extremely Hot Hell, and the Unrelenting Hell. An explanation now follows on how to contemplate their suffering.

The aforementioned topics of death and impermanence are meditated on because we do not cease to exist after death like the extinguishing of a flame, or combustion of a pile of dry grass. Our latter continuum of similar type is not cut. There is no choice but to take rebirth. That rebirth can only be in a good or bad migration. I cannot know if I have accumulated enough virtue to cause rebirth in a good migration, and I cannot be sure if virtue was even accumulated in previous lives. Nonvirtuous karma is like a royal storeroom— wherever I look it is full. If I have to undergo the sufferings of bad migrations as a result of that, it makes no difference whether it is experienced on the basis of this body or the body of the next life.

Not giving it much thought, although it would seem that the experience of an infection is felt by our flesh and bone, the actual experiencer is the mind. If it were not, then after death if one pressed hard on a corpse it must feel pain, but it definitely does not. How can I be so certain that my present mind that revels in the prosperity of gods and humans will not have to undergo the torment of the

Unrelenting Hell tomorrow? Nāgārjuna states on detaching from those experiences:

> Reflect daily on the hells,
>   both the extremely hot and cold.

One should contemplate thus on the suffering of hells. [246] The way most people approach this is to recite that quote and subsequent verses and focus outward as if viewing the suffering of others, never applying it to oneself. For example, when seeing a criminal being dealt multiple sentences in the king's court, virtuous people will have compassion and renunciation in this situation, but most see it as a show and get excited. However, if those people themselves were to be brought into court and bound in chains, their glee would quickly turn to suffering, unable to bear a second of it. All they would be able to think of is getting out of the situation. In the same way, most of the meditations in this context should be done by visualizing oneself taking rebirth in one of the six migrations and refocusing the mind on oneself undergoing that suffering.

First, the eight hot hells. When one has entered the bardo of hell as a result of nonvirtue accumulated through hatred, the body feels cold, one therefore seeks warmth and at that moment the bardo ceases and you are born in hell. The ground is completely covered in burning iron. The place is encompassed by a burning iron fence. Above and below flames perpetually blaze.

The first of the hot hells is the Reviving Hell. Strive to meditate on yourself as actually being born into the state just described. You will start to shake, and fear will swell up. When that happens, contemplate the beings born there gathering and, out of hatred, attacking each other with all sorts of weapons. Visualize your body rendered into thousands of pieces, others losing consciousness, and so forth, until it is as if you are experiencing it yourself. Then, continuously meditate on their suffering as a voice from the sky commands, "All of you, revive!" and they attack each other as before. [247]

Practicing in this intensive manner, you feel your appetite is lost, your mind does not wander to entertaining conversation and preoccupations, and in all activities you will effortlessly give up misdeeds and engage in virtue. When you fall back into old ways of thinking and behavior, the Dharma and the person have separated.

The second is the Black Line Hell. Here the hell guardians draw eight lines on the body and cleave it into pieces with weapons. The third is the Crushing Hell. One does not have to be born into all eight hells in order; however, taking this as a guided meditation, visualize that you escape the previous torment. As soon as you have, you find yourself squeezed between goat-faced, sheep-faced, elephant-faced, and lion-faced mountains. Blood then gushes out from every orifice.

The fourth is the Howling Hell. You escape again. Now you have found yourself in an iron chamber. The door has been built inseparable from the wall, and from every direction fire blazes and you start to burn. You cry out sharply as you see there is no escape. The fifth is the Great Howling Hell. It is explained that one should meditate that the exact same iron chamber is now within another iron chamber that surrounds it; however, my guru's position is that as you escape the first iron chamber and enter into the second, you experience twice as much suffering as before. The difference in the contemplation is that it is possible to exit from the first iron chamber, but that you cannot leave from the second. For example, if a prison has two outer containment walls, one would suffer from the suspicion that first is penetrable but the second is not.

The sixth is the Hot Hell. You are impaled with a blazing iron skewer into your anus which then emerges from the crown of your head. Flames shoot forth from your orifices. Your shriveled body is then cooked in molten iron. The seventh is the Extremely Hot Hell.

You are impaled by a trident, the middle prong exiting through your head, and the left and right prongs through your shoulders. Your body is then wrapped in red-hot iron as like cloth. You are cooked in molten iron until your flesh and blood fall away and you are left a skeleton. [248] The eighth is the Unrelenting Hell. Fire blazes in all directions and the body is as if inseparable from fire. Due to this one only hears the wailing of the beings there. The suffering also does not end quickly.

The *Treasury of Knowledge* states that fifty human years is a single day for desire realm deities, and so on, although it is unclear and slightly difficult to understand. Regardless, out of the eight hells, the shortest lifespan is in the Reviving Hell, and is equivalent to one trillion six hundred and twenty billion human years. Thus, if we think that the lifespans of the other hells only increase from there, our heart can only break. In Nāgārjuna's *Letter to a Friend* it states:

> Until your nonvirtue has exhausted
> you cannot die.

As such, looking at how we behave now, how can we be sure we will not have to stay even longer. Meditate on this until you are overwhelmed.

Second, the cold hells. These are the Blistering Hell, Bursting Blisters Hell, Chattering-Teeth Hell, Weeping Hell, *Brrr* Hell, Splitting-Like-a-Water-Lily Hell, Splitting-Like-a-Lotus Hell, and lastly the Great Splitting-Like-a-Lotus Hell.

The hell beings feel hot and then think longingly for the cold. That causes the bardo to instantly cease and them to be born in a place surrounded entirely by a snowy mountain range. The bottom is a snow-covered land with deep frozen chasms, above which a blizzard rages. A piercing wind blows in the darkness. Aside from a difference in temperature, the general place and rebirth within are as before, with some specifics. In the Blistering Hell the wind blasts your body with a snow blizzard from each direction. As it hits you, you develop blisters and shrivel up. In the Bursting Blisters Hell blood and pus ooze from those blisters. In the Weeping Hell suffering becomes so strong that you let out an intense noise. In the *Brrr* Hell suffering intensifies further until your voice breaks and a "brrr" sound comes from your palate. [249] In the Chattering Teeth Hell the suffering is even more intense than before. The teeth chatter so you can no longer voice a sound. In the Splitting-Like-a-Water-Lily Hell you are blasted with a strong wind, turning you blue. You then split along six fine lines. In the Splitting-Like-a-Lotus Hell your blue skin peels off revealing the bright red flesh underneath. You then split into ten pieces. Finally, in the Great Splitting-Like-a-Lotus Hell, your color is as before, and you split along one hundred or more lines.

It states in the *Garland of Birth Stories*:

> In their future life the nihilist
> finds themself in the dark, a cold wind blowing.
> It makes them so ill even their bones shatter.
> Who with a desire to help would enter in there?

[Paraphrasing sutra:]

> If a granary heaped with eighty large measures of sesame
> as it is measured here in Magadha were to have a single sesame seed removed from it every eight hundred years, when
> it finally empties that would be the measure of a lifespan
> in Blistering Hell.

Recollecting thus one trembles. Generate an intense feeling of sorrow. Thus, if one becomes dispirited with respect to the suffering through knowing that the torment of the sixteen hells will certainly befall oneself, one implicitly becomes dispirited with respect to the adjoining and occasional hells contained in the extensive explanation. One need not elaborate on this topic extensively—this much is sufficient in itself. If one has around two months' time, one can elaborate the meditational topics to include the adjoining and occasional hells. As I have not included them here fearing too many words, they can be understood from other texts.

The Great Fifth indicates here that one can fill in the remaining topics of the occasional and adjoining hells from the *Great* and *Middle-Length* lamrim treatises.

The Occasional Hell is something that can exist in the realm of humans. It is said that there are hell beings who have the appearance of a broom, or like a tree. [250]

In Tibetan, the word "hell" (*dmyal ba*, pronounced "nyelwa") comes from the verb meaning "to suffer," and thus "hell" has the meaning of a place of unbearable suffering. Although different Buddhist and non-Buddhist texts have a variety of explanations about hell, it need not appear exactly the same to everyone based on any one of those explanations with respect to the place, the timing, and the occasion. It depends how it is established through karma, as it says in the *Treasury of Knowledge*:

The various worlds are arisen from karma.

Furthermore, in the chapter "Guarding Introspection" in the **Way of the Bodhisattva** it also states:

The weapons to torture living beings—
who made them for such purpose?
Who forged the flaming iron ground?
Whence have these women emerged?

All are likewise born from the sinful mind.
This the Sage has said.

It is certainly possible that there could come a time where we are tormented by suffering even greater than that mentioned in the texts due
to heavy karma, totally inexpressible and unbearable to experience on
a mental level.

Contemplating the Suffering of Animals

With respect to the suffering of animals, it says in *Letter to a Friend*:

In an animal birth there are multitudes of sufferings—
being killed, bound, beaten, and more.
Those who have abandoned virtue that brings peace,
will horribly eat each other.

There are animals who live in the depths and those who are scattered. Asaṅga's treatises on yogic levels states that animals who
live in the depths exist under the waters surrounding Mount
Meru. [251] Their bodies vary in size; those grouped like a pile
of grain are larger and swallow up the smaller. The smaller bore
holes into the larger ones. Others live in such pitch-black darkness that they cannot see the movement of their own limbs. Marine
ocean dwellers have no certainty with respect to housing, food, and
companions.

Scattered wild animals are chased by hunters, dogs, leopards,
and other carnivores. Domesticated animals are killed, beaten, and
boiled.

Nāgas are afraid of hot sand and garuḍa birds. Tiny creatures die
from the slightest of conditions. None know what actions to adopt
and discard. Meditate on being born as any of the aforementioned

animals and their suffering until you definitely generate experience in your practice.

The lifespans of animals are indefinite and vary from an eon at the longest to a day at the shortest.

Furthermore, the multitude of animals that exist range from those we can perceive with the ordinary eye to those invisible to us. Animals may be confused with respect to general suffering, unable to think as humans do, helpless, vulnerable, and incredibly unresourceful. However, whether domesticated or undomesticated, no matter how depressing their birth and life was, the care they give to their own young is akin to how human parents raise their own children. The birds, wild animals, and so forth in our world lovingly take care of their offspring in accordance with their resources. After reaching maturity, no matter night or day, rain, hail, or shine, they live in constant fear of being killed by the people and other animals moving around them. Therefore, one should pray, following *Way of the Bodhisattva*:

> May animals be free from the fear
> of being eaten by one another. [252]

Animals live their lives seeing each other as food. They face unimaginable suffering due to heat and cold, fatigue, being exploited, and so forth. In particular, animals are utilized by people and eaten indiscriminately almost like a vegetable, as if they are not sentient beings with a life and feelings of happiness and suffering. Therefore, not only do they face endless difficulties while alive, ultimately so many of them end up being used for their meat, bones, and skin. Domesticated animals like chickens, pigs, goats, sheep, cattle, and so forth, are mostly slaughtered in the end, and even if we do not do it ourselves, they are led to the slaughterhouse and handed over to be killed. If we give thought to that process, eating meat should become inconceivable and repulsive.

The most terrible example of this process, still practiced today, is that of "live food," in which animals are skinned, boiled, or fried alive. Many atrocious methods are employed to make "delicacies," and people even watch excitedly and laugh as if watching a show. Such indifference is a sign of a cold heart. Right now, we are like spectators watching from afar, but what would happen if we took rebirth as one of those animals?

In brief, it is clear that animals are powerless over their lives and are given no right to live out their lives happily. We need to ask ourselves how we as humans have the right to take the life of such destitute animals. [253]

What if there existed beings more powerful than humans who came along and traded us, exploited us and took our lives just as we do to animals? Some might arrogantly argue that we have a right to exploit all others because human society is more developed, has education, medical advancements, and so on, but however much we exploit animals, they are the ones helpless without a voice to argue for their rights and fend for themselves.

A lot of animal activist groups have formed in more progressive, free countries. Their campaigns are something to rejoice in. Still, even those animals that do not have to endure the suffering of exploitation would not go on to live a life of virtue from birth until death. They have the full range of afflictions, such as attachment and aversion, and under the power of those they would fight, kill, and live a life of constant nonvirtue. Thus, we can probably infer they would not only suffer now, there would be little chance of them taking a better rebirth next life. Thus, it is presumptuous to talk of them achieving liberation and omniscience. It is fortunate that we have not taken rebirth as such animals and have attained this precious human rebirth. If we recognize this good fortune, with great joy from the depths of our heart we can make the rest of our life meaningful.

Contemplating the Suffering of Hungry Ghosts

The contemplation of the third suffering, that of hungry ghosts, has three parts:

a" Hungry ghosts who have external obstacles for obtaining food and drink [254]

b" Hungry ghosts who have internal obstacles for obtaining food and drink

c" Hungry ghosts who have obstacles toward food and drink itself

It states in *Letter to a Friend*:

The suffering of disappointment
is an endless stream for hungry ghosts.
They undergo unbearable suffering
due to thirst and hunger, heat and cold, exhaustion and fear.

Of the three kinds of hungry ghosts, those with external obstacles for obtaining food and drink see the fruits of trees and running water, but when they go to partake of them, guardians either brandish swords or they perceive them as blood and pus.

In the land of Kapila, devoid of anything desirable such as water and vegetation, those with internal obstacles do not find water and food there, and if they find a little, their needle-eye shaped mouths, tiny throats, mountainous bellies, and grass-like limbs prevent them from eating. Whatever food manages to get into their mouths cannot be swallowed. Whatever they manage to swallow does not fill their huge bellies. Such is their suffering.

Those with obstacles toward food and water burn their bodies from food and drink that ignites in flames. They are decrepit beings who eat feces, urine, and their own flesh. The summer moon burns and the winter sun is cold. Just by looking at it a flowing river appears as a dried-up gully.

They undergo this suffering of hunger and thirst among other things. Imagine that you are born as these hungry ghosts and meditate on the understanding that it will definitely happen to you. That suffering is furthermore not short-lived; it is explained that it must be experienced for fifteen thousand human years. Contemplating these things, it is as if one achieves uncontrived renunciation.

In a nutshell, if we had to stick our hand in a fire pit for the length of time it takes us to drink a cup of tea, or go naked for even one day in winter, or go without food and water for three or four days, or remain under a pile of rubble unable to move, we could not bear it. How then could we tolerate the suffering of the three lower migrations? [255]

Nāgārjuna states:

> This human body, difficult to attain,
> must be utilized to eliminate the causes of lower rebirth
> as soon as it is attained.

Whip yourself on at the thought that at this present time when you are distinguished as a human from an animal you must persevere.

The class of beings who are tormented by some of the stronger sufferings of hunger and thirst are known as "hungry ghosts." Included in this class of beings are those who directly experience the intense pain of hunger and thirst, such as worldly guardian deities, and humans reborn as wrathful spirits like gods, nāgas, and local deities who have weaker abilities to help or harm, and even many types of benign intermediate beings.

There are accounts of people seeing ghosts with their own eyes. One example is from Namgyal Monastery in the top section of the Potala in Tibet: A monk nicknamed "Shorty" with whom I used to play went into Lhasa one day and met an accomplished practitioner who claimed to see ghosts. The naughty monk half-jokingly told the practitioner that he too wanted to see ghosts, and the practitioner agreed to help him. The monk returned to the monastery that night and waited up in the dark to see something, with no success. He did the same thing for a few nights and still saw nothing, so he returned to the practitioner in Lhasa.

He told him, "I did not see anything at all! I want to see a ghost!" To which the practitioner replied, "Fine. Take this," and handed him a hat.

That night the monk put the hat on and started waiting. Soon after a wretched face appeared in the window, staring at him. Freaked out, the monk immediately threw off the hat. This actually happened!

Likewise, we have ourselves seen or heard about those who have died and gone to the bardo entering into the body of another and telling of their suffering. [256] When I was younger Kyabjé Trijang Rinpoché took the role of my debate partner and was residing at Norbulingka one summer. At that time, a Namgyal Monastery monk who had received teachings from Kyabjé Rinpoché and with whom he was familiar passed away. It so happened that the deceased monk was roaming the bardo, unable to take another rebirth, and had joined the company of a powerful spirit. One day he entered the body of another Namgyal monk who immediately said that he must see Kyabjé Rinpoché. This was recounted to me by a monk who was the temple keeper for the House of Sixty, Thupten Sönam, who later became the ritual master. When the possessed monk was taken to Kyabjé Trijang Rinpoché, the powerful spirit then entered him and went straight to Kyabjé Rinpoché. Rinpoché instructed him in Dharma to contemplate. Later, when the powerful spirit left, the ghost of the deceased monk who had died then entered the monk's body and immediately started crying. When they tried to take him into Kyabjé Rinpoché's presence, he absolutely would not go further because the light from the butter lamps was shining on Kyabjé Rinpoché's face. The ghost of the diseased monk then left, but when the monk was in darkness, the ghost entered him again and wailed in torment for protection. At this point Kyabjé Trijang was able to guide him.

The ghost of the diseased monk was either wandering in the bardo under the control of the powerful spirit, or he had already taken birth as a nonhuman spirit. Either way, a formless being entered into the body of a human and recounted their great suffering of hunger and thirst while they cried. A burnt offering was made for him, but when the smoke rose to his nostrils he was unable to even notice it. From within his room, Kyabjé Trijang Rinpoché performed a burnt offering together with blessings through the six mantras and six mudrās. Very suddenly it was as if the possessed monk became ravenous for food and drink, and through great fear almost snuffed the flame of the burnt offering. After inhaling its smell, he proclaimed he was full and satiated, and then departed. Such accounts as this one retold by the ritual master in such detail must definitely be real. [257]

In his previous life the spirit had attained a human body with leisure and opportunity, took ordination and was a devout practitioner. Unfortunately, a negative condition at the time of death caused him to take rebirth into the circle of a powerful spirit. Kyabjé Rinpoché was able to help him transfer his rebirth through advising him. This candid account is fairly recent, and not a tale passed down from a thousand years ago. Since the ritual master also had no reason to lie about it, this hands-on account indicates that similar things also happen to others.

Those who are conduits for deities and spirits are able to directly verify the existence of nonhuman beings. Those include formless beings within the same class of hungry ghosts. At the peak, the haughty ones such as the dharmapāla Nechung, and so forth, are powerful among the society of the formless, just as a powerful person in a human society. They have various minor abilities, and a few qualities.

At the worst, there seem to be a variety of beings greatly tormented by hunger and thirst or the exploitation of other variously ranked spirits.

Within Christianity there are neither the six classes of beings nor the division into three realms. People have, however, recounted to me stories of doors within churches suddenly opening and closing while no one was seen, and I have listened to audio recordings of it happening.

Through meditating on the suffering of the six classes of beings, if one can effect an experience of taking rebirth into such bodies, it emotionally moves the mind and makes realizations come more easily. There are accounts of Trungpa Taphu saying these instructions helped him greatly.

The result of Dharma practice should not just be an acquisition of knowledge. One's temperament should become more tame, and one's thoughts more peaceful. [258] It is said, "The sign of listening is peacefulness and discipline; the sign of meditation is less afflictions." If one becomes like that then one has achieved a result in the practice of Dharma. Therefore, to make a self-assessment, if you see your temperament is not improving however much you read lamrim, for example, and apply yourself to Dharma, it is a sign you have missed the point in your practice.

If you check for a difference in your temperament from one day to the next, you will not be able to see an obvious improvement, so evaluate improvement based on a span of a few years, or ten, or twenty. In the case that you compare yourself to how you were ten years ago and find your thoughts are even more wild, the teachings and the person have become separate. As such it seems important to blame oneself and lower one's pride in that case.

Of course, it is true that when comparing oneself to how one used to be ten years ago maturity plays a role in the slight changes within us. Even if we have not developed a genuine practice of lamrim mind training and so forth during this time, we are still checking and correcting our minds as we read Dharma texts. Thus, when reading the texts, it can often be quite depressing for us. Even if we are unable to develop a strong meditation practice, since we have become familiar with the Dharma, if we take whatever Dharma we practice simply as a technique for disciplining the mind, then it is still helpful. Likewise, since you can now explain Dharma to others with an understanding of your own mind it is even more helpful, and thus one must still try to persist by being joyful and rejoicing in this.

Concluding Verses

Inside an iron chamber a fire rages acutely hot,
a torrent of blood flows from being hacked and crushed,
and fire erupts from the doors of your senses.
Those unafraid of this are possessed by demons. [259]

Between snow mountains it is pitch black amid ferocious
    winds,
The piercing weapon of cold splits your fragile body
hundreds and thousands of times, but you still do not die.
This is afflicted unto you endlessly by the enemy of your
    nonvirtue.

While you cannot bear the small pain
of infected wounds—you would have to be an inanimate
    object
to not tremble at the endless suffering
of beings slain and eaten for your flesh and bones.

If you get exhausted pursuing food and drink in this short life,
what about fifteen thousand years' worth of trying to
    overcome hunger and thirst?

To that end one might muster the courage
to sacrifice life and limb, but it is too weak.

One might not have the fear of the unbearable abyss of bad
  migrations
that moves even the tip of a single hair,
but who is more foolish than you,
who cunningly takes responsibility to uphold the eight
  worldly Dharmas
By protecting friends and overcoming enemies?

The Method for Achieving Happiness
in Future Lives

The method for achieving happiness in future lives [has two parts:]

   a′ **Taking refuge, the door for entering the teachings**
   b′ **Cultivating conviction in karmic causality: the root of all
      happiness and good**

The methods for achieving happiness in the next life primarily relate to karmic causality. Instead of having blind faith in the presentation of subtle karmic causes and effects and simply believing what people tell us, we should use our intelligence to understand the reasonings behind these teachings and base our conviction on that. For our ethics of abandoning the ten nonvirtues to become Buddhist Dharma it requires refuge, since there are non-Buddhists who merely abandon the ten nonvirtues outside of this context. Therefore, we say that refuge—the most excellent door for entering the teachings—and training in the faith of conviction in karmic causality, the root of all happiness and good, are the two main methods for achieving happiness in future lives. [260]

The means for protection against the fear that relates to one's stages of practice involving the aforementioned suffering of lower migrations and the later mentioned suffering of samsara in our future lives is faith gained through understanding reasonings related to the infallible Three Jewels, and going for refuge in them as perfect sources of refuge.

The correct approach to that is engaging in the practice of the conduct of proper adopting and discarding with respect to karmic causality.

In order to contemplate refuge so that we can have a pure refuge, one must reflect on the way to achieve liberation as set forth in the second chapter of Dharmakīrti's *Commentary on the "Compendium of Valid Cognition."* The principal is the Dharma Jewel, which is the two—paths and cessations—and it is the root of what must be proven. Ultimately, the reasoning proving paths and cessations is found in Candrakīrti's *Clear Words*, the commentary to Nāgārjuna's *Fundamental Wisdom of the Middle Way*. It states in chapter 24:

> For whom emptiness is possible
> everything is possible.
> For whom emptiness is impossible
> everything is impossible.

In this context, he argues and proves that if phenomena were inherently existent, the Dharma Jewel would be untenable. Likewise, if the Dharma Jewel were untenable, the Three Jewels and four results would be untenable.

Furthermore, philosophical systems that do not accept the emptiness of inherent existence of phenomena object that if something were empty of inherent existence, one could not posit cause and effect, nor agent and action. Nāgārjuna's logic is the opposite of theirs: If it exists inherently, emptiness is untenable; if emptiness is untenable, dependent origination is also untenable. And therefore, he presents the absurd consequence that anything—the three refuges, karmic causality, and so on—would be untenable, and thus he refutes inherent existence.

Generally, emptiness is understood as the emptiness of existing inherently or by way of its own nature; it is not nothingness. [261] Whatever exists does so in dependence on other phenomena and therefore is empty of existing by way of its own entity. Since this is proven, if emptiness is tenable, dependent origination is tenable; and if that is tenable, then paths and cessations are tenable. If dependent arising were not tenable, then paths and cessations would not be tenable. Thus, in general we must prove the Dharma Jewel that is a true cessation exists, and in particular that it is possible to achieve it within our own continuum.

True cessation is the purification within the dharmadhātu of the stains of the objects to be abandoned. To manifest that one must realize the dharmadhātu and manifest the dharmadhātu. Since that is the case, when explaining true paths and true cessations ultimately the explanation meets back to emptiness.

With respect to this, selflessness of persons and phenomena can be posited with different subtlety, and therefore ignorance is also differentiated by way of subtlety.

Likewise, getting to the bottom of the most subtle true origins requires that one understand the true nature of reality. Furthermore, the presentation of true sufferings includes both coarse and subtle true sufferings, and thus to understand the presentation of subtle true sufferings one must understand the presentation of subtle ignorance. For that, one must understand the subtle mode of being.

Thus, it is incredibly important to have an understanding of emptiness in order to have a correct understanding of the presentation of the four truths. Likewise, authentic refuge is helped by an understanding of the view of emptiness in the same way.

If one analyzes these principles well in connection with the second chapter of the *Compendium of Valid Cognition* and the *Clear Words* commentary to Nāgārjuna's *Fundamental Wisdom of the Middle Way*, it becomes much clearer, and thus is essential.

The Three Jewels are well-known as (1) the Buddha, supreme or principal among bipeds; (2) the Dharma, the peacefulness separated from attachment; (3) the Sangha, the assistants who are the supreme among assemblies. However, I think that much can probably be asserted by other traditions insofar as they accept their respective prophets as the best among bipeds, and most likely within their teachings they teach freedom from attachment. Likewise, their groups of religious practitioners are probably considered the supreme among assemblies. [262]

With respect to the differences between the Buddha, Dharma, and Sangha within Buddhism itself, there are different positions as to whether there are four bodies of a buddha, or whether the continuum ceases after attaining nirvana without remainder. Nāgārjuna, in his *Sixty Stanzas of Logic*, explains how the continuum cannot be cut, and that if one asserts it can, there would be no person who manifests nirvana without remainder. This is because the aggregates exist so long as the person exist, and if the aggregates ceased then no remainder of aggregates would be left, and thus the person too would cease to exist. If that were the case, there could be no nirvana without remainder.

Not only that, since every erroneous consciousness has a powerful opposite, it is natural that the causes for those erroneous consciousnesses to persist will be exhausted. Thus, he emphatically proves the continuum of consciousness that is simply clear and knowing cannot cease.

If one asserts that "the Bhagavān," the prolific teacher and holy being, manifested buddhahood through the path of the thirty-seven limbs of enlightenment alone, then it would be a case of the result not corresponding to the cause. The Buddha taught the particulars of the path of the six perfections in order to achieve the state of omniscience, which is not merely the thirty-seven limbs of enlightenment. Through the power of the special mind generation that is the thought to accomplish the aims of beings until the end of space, the result one aspires toward will also last until the end of space. Thinking very well about this, the "resultant state of buddhahood" must be achieved by way of the continuum of consciousness itself, and if one closely analyzes the mental continuum, it is imputed dependently and arises dependently. Thus, consciousness is empty of existing by way of its own nature. [263]

The tantric system teaches that not only are there many different subtleties of consciousness, there are also winds that move consciousness, similar to energy. Our current ordinary mental continuum that is empty of inherent existence together with the accompanying winds form the basis for the presentation of the four buddha bodies at the stage where they are purified of stains.

When the nature of mind—its natural purity—is free from adventitious stains, it becomes the nature body of a buddha. The mental consciousness possessing that nature transforms into the wisdom truth body, or mind of a victor. The wind-energy accompanying that wisdom truth body is the rūpakāya, and the speech of a victor comes from that. In brief, the body, speech, and mind of a buddha appear out of the basic indivisible and extremely subtle wind and mind that are a single entity but different isolates. Thus, the three secrets of body, speech, and mind are established as indivisible.

Our fundamental consciousness has nothing that interrupts its constant continuation as a similar type. Therefore, from the point of view of abiding without ever ceasing, they are the inexhaustible adornment wheels of buddha body, speech, and mind. These are the "inexhaustible adornment wheels of the three secrets."

The *Sublime Continuum* states:

> Uncompounded, spontaneous,
> not realized through other conditions,
> buddhahood possessing the two purposes
> is endowed with knowledge, compassion, and power.

The Buddha Jewel is characterized by eight qualities. The first four are (1) being uncompounded, the quality of natural purity; (2) being spontaneous, the quality of purity from the adventitious stains; (3) the quality of the qualities themselves not being able to be completely realized through name and conception; (4) and the quality of fulfilling one's own purpose. The second four qualities are (5) the quality of exalted knowledge; (6) the quality of love; (7) the quality of power; (8) and the quality of fulfilling the purpose of others. [264]

The *Sublime Continuum* continues:

> The Dharma is inconceivable, nondual, without
>   conceptualization,
> Pure, clarifying, counteracting,
> free from desire, and by which one becomes free from desire;
> it is characterized by the two truths.
> These are the eight qualities of the Dharma Jewel.

And:

> Because the perception of modes and varieties
> by their inner wisdom is pure,
> the intelligent, irreversible assembly
> Is endowed with the highest qualities.

Persons possessing the eight qualities, who through practicing such Dharma have generated the Dharma Jewel within themselves that comprises paths and cessations, are the supreme assembly of ārya beings, identified as the Sangha Jewel.

These do not exactly accord with the aforementioned explanations from tantra, but the basic intended meaning is the same.

If one correctly understands going for refuge, one becomes a person who accepts the four seals that distinguish the Buddhist view. Thus, the statement "Buddhists and non-Buddhists are distinguished by their refuge" is said in the context of common refuge. Therefore, determining whether one is Buddhist or non-Buddhist on the basis of the four seals that distinguish the Buddhist view is said in the context of superior refuge.

TAKING REFUGE

Taking refuge, the door for entering the teachings, has two parts:

- **Actual [going for refuge]**
- **[Refuge] precepts**

In the *Great Treatise on the Stages of the Path*, training in refuge, the excellent door to the teachings, has four parts:

> 1' The causes of going for refuge
> 2' Based on that, the objects to which you go for refuge
> 3' The way you go for refuge
> 4' Having gone for refuge, the stages of the precepts

The meaning of these is fully covered in this text. [265]

With respect to the first, it states in the *Way of the Bodhisattva*:

> **Just as in a dark night dense with clouds**
> **lightning strikes and briefly illuminates,**
> **likewise, rarely, through the Buddha's power,**
> **thoughts of virtue briefly arise in the world.**
>
> **Thus, virtue is always weak,**
> **and sin overwhelmingly powerful.**

We contemplate refuge with three considerations: fear of the drawbacks; faith in the qualities; and compassion for beings like ourselves. The dark eon of not hearing the mere words of holy Dharma is like the pitch-black darkness of dense clouds at night. From within that, the bright eon in which one meets the Dharma is rare, like a flash of lightning in the darkness. Thus, within the ocean of previous misdeeds, with the virtue that is incredibly weak, like a drop of water collected on the tip of a blade of kuśa grass, we trick others with our beguiling Dharma façade. If we reviewed the scriptures and our mind and conduct, we would see that the nonvirtuous class dominates by far.

Furthermore, aside from suspecting you have a dangerous enemy, if you have not heard talk of when they will show up, or their strength, or the reasons for their harming your body, possessions, or life, you will not know to fear them or take heed. If that enemy shows up, they will destroy you; if they are certain to come within a year, but you do not know exactly when, you cannot relax for even a second. Whether you befriend an official who has more power and might, build a strong fort, or leave for a distant land where they have not reached, whatever preparations you make the enemy that is the suffering of the lower realms will always find you within one hundred years. Understanding this, you cannot know whether next month or the unrelenting torment of hell will come first.

Thus, having previously effected experience with respect to death and impermanence, and the state of the miserable rebirths, there is nothing more worthwhile than seeking refuge.

With respect to the objects of refuge Dignāga states:

In the ocean of bottomless cyclic existence, [266]
one's body is devoured by the horrifying sea monsters

of attachment and so forth.

Where should I go for refuge today?

Dignāga puts the question to us: This cyclic existence is deep like the ocean, so where should we, who are plagued by the dangers of the terrifying sea monsters of attachment and other nonvirtues, go for refuge?

In brief, the cause of refuge from the perspective of persons of small scope alone is fear of lower rebirths. For persons of middle scope, it is, on top of that, fear of cyclic existence. For persons of great scope, it is the three causes along with the loving compassion that cannot bear others tormented by suffering in cyclic existence, as well as the faith of conviction that the Jewels can protect from those.

The Objects to Which You Go for Refuge

    a" Identifying the objects to which you go for refuge

    b" The reasons why they are worthy to be a refuge

IDENTIFYING THE OBJECTS TO WHICH YOU GO FOR REFUGE

As if answering the above question, it states in *Praise in One Hundred and Fifty Verses*:

In whom there can never exist
any fault,
and in whom there exists
all qualities—

if one has intelligence,
it is proper to take refuge in them alone,

praise them, respect them,
and live in their teaching.

Just as someone with less might and strength than your adversary cannot protect you from them, even if you relied upon humans and gods like Brahmā, Viṣṇu, Īśvara and so forth, since they are not liberated from samsara and are afflicted by samsaric faults, they are not suitable as a final refuge. Regarding who is worthy, Candrakīrti's *Seventy Verses on Refuge* states:

Buddha, Dharma, and Sangha
are the refuge for those desiring liberation.

These words are incredibly profound in the sense that they do not merely state that the Three Supreme Ones are refuges, but **that the Three Jewels are final refuges** for those desiring liberation. [267]

Sangyé, the Tibetan word for the Sanskrit word *buddha*, means "awakened," but also has two broader meanings: "cleansed (*sang*) from the stains of the two obscurations including their imprints," and "fully unfolded (*gyé*) intelligence realizing modes and varieties."

From this one can understand the meaning of the two syllables of the word for "enlightenment," *jangchup*. In order to realize all objects of knowledge through having abandoned all objects of abandonment, one does not need to individually ascertain and understand each object, nor does one need to establish a new capacity in the mind for knowing objects. The capacity for knowing the modes and varieties of objects is present within our consciousness, but so long as there are obscurations blocking our access to objects we are unable to know them. Thus, without the preceding *jang*, meaning "purification," there can be no *chub*, or "perfect comprehension." Therefore, the word for enlightenment is *jangchup*, and not *chupjang*; and the word for buddha is *sangyé* and not *gyésang*.

To have a perfect understanding of *jangchup* and *sangyé*, one must ascertain exactly how to purify the stains of obscurations within the dharmadhātu. Comprehending "purification of stains" requires understanding samsara and nirvana, which depends on whether you understand reality, or suchness. Thus, pure refuge is highly contingent upon an understanding of emptiness.

The Sanskrit word *dharma* can mean "to hold," or "to preserve." Thus, true cessations are the nature of protection, and the protectors are true paths, and these too must be thought of based on emptiness.

Since the Tibetan word for "sangha," *gendun*, means "those who aspire (*dun*) toward the virtue (*ge*) of liberation," and furthermore since true cessations must thus be understood based on emptiness, the Three Jewels are taught as the refuge for those desiring liberation. [268]

To briefly introduce the way to identify liberation, as explained in Buddhist treatises, it is liberation from being uncontrollably bound by karma and afflictions. That which hinders our achievement of liberation are the afflictive obscurations. Ignorance is the root of afflictive obscurations. Out of the two kinds of ignorance—ignorance of karmic causality and ignorance that apprehends a self through confusion about reality—it is the latter. As this ignorance apprehending a self is what interferes with attaining liberation, then through generating the opposing antidote to it—the wisdom realizing selflessness—it destroys the ignorance apprehending a self, and thus one attains the liberation that is freed from that.

The fact that no other tradition has a teacher of the complete path to achieve liberation can be proved by reasoning. In Buddhist texts, the skillful and compassionate Teacher first taught an approximate presentation of liberation and the steps of the path in order to give a rough understanding based on the mental capacities of his disciples. Eventually, in other treatises, more subtle meanings of paths were taught. All these varying explanations were taught by one teacher, and ultimately a real presentation of liberation and the nonerroneous paths to achieve it were given in those Buddhist treatises. Through this we can deduce that the Buddha, Dharma, and Sangha are the only infallible refuges for all those seeking the authentic liberation of everlasting happiness.

The Buddha arose entirely in dependence on causes and conditions, and thus is not a permanent self-arisen being. Dignāga conveys this in the verse of homage in his *Compendium of Valid Cognition*. Likewise, Dharmakīrti comments on that in the root verses of his *Commentary on the "Compendium of Valid Cognition,"* stating:

> In order to refute that [the Bhagavān] was not [already] arisen
> [as an authority],
> he taught that he has "become" [an authority]. [269]

The Tathāgata became an authoritative being through causes and conditions. Furthermore, it is stated in pāramitā literature and Nāgārjuna's *Jewel Rosary* that he did so based on a limitless collection of causes. Thus, even the Buddha himself was an ordinary being like us while on the path, but through the limitless collection of causes he gradually became a buddha having the nature of the dharmakāya fulfilling his own aims, and the rūpakāya fulfilling others' aims. Thus, Tsongkhapa states in his *Praise of Dependent Origination*:

> May the world always be filled by those who find conviction
> in the teacher by understanding the teachings' true nature.

Thus, when thoroughly analyzing the lion of the Śākya's teachings by way of the three analyses, not only are they without logical flaws, they also only contain accurate logical proofs. Therefore, one can gain firm ascertainment that the teacher of that Dharma is also a valid being. Whether a teacher is a valid being and one that can be trusted must be determined by analyzing their teachings. For example, if an ordinary person is appointed as a teacher, it is not on the basis of their body shape or appearance, but on the basis of their knowledge. After interviewing them about topics from the beginning, middle, and latter parts of their studies and evaluating their answers, if they seem qualified then they are appointed as a teacher. In the same way, one does not accept the Buddha to be free from all faults and endowed with all qualities simply by finding his marks and signs agreeable.

Out of all the teachers of the different traditions in the world, the only one to teach the mode of dependent establishment and the dependent origination of causes and conditions, and the view of selflessness as the path to liberation was our teacher, the Buddha Bhagavān. [270] Therefore, it is best to gain ascertainment that the Buddha is valid based on the reason that he taught selflessness, the nonerroneous method to achieve liberation.

The Reasons Why They Are Worthy to Be a Refuge

Having ascertained the infallibility of the one who taught the nonerroneous path **due to his being free from all faults and endowed with all qualities as just mentioned, one goes for refuge. The meditations for going for refuge are many; however, our tradition asserts Dharma that is not made up by fabricating or omitting extensive points.** Since it is a practice of increasing the three faiths that we have by expressing the greatness of the Three Supreme Ones, one must recollect the qualities of the Bhagavān Teacher's three secrets.

Going for refuge to the Three Supreme Ones in this manner demonstrates the difference between the way one takes refuge in a creator god and so forth in other traditions and the way Buddhists take refuge in the Three Supreme Ones. In religions like Christianity and Islam that accept a creator god, one goes for refuge on the basis of belief alone to one's respective source of refuge, bowing down and showing respect out of single-pointed faith, entrusting oneself to be cared for by them. Ultimately, their reasoning comes down to everything being made by the creator, and since all is his plan, one does not require insight into that.

Buddhists must use discriminating wisdom to thoroughly analyze topics the Buddha taught such as how all happiness and suffering arises on the basis of a tamed or untamed mind, and the presentation of causality related to that. Then, taking as a basis the experience of the result of that analysis, only through one's own effort in pursuing that to be adopted and disengaging from what is to be discarded do we achieve our object of attainment. There is absolutely no means by which others such as the Three Jewels, buddhas or bodhisattvas, can give that achievement to us. [271] As it states in the sutra,

You are your own protector.

Through Buddhism's impressive framework of self-reliance, one understands the characteristics and reasonings supporting the Three Jewels that are one's own causal refuge and resultant refuge, and since one goes for refuge based on faith and respect assisted by wisdom, it is known as "refuge based on faith gained through wisdom." In brief, it must be approached through the interdependence of causality.

Generally, Buddhist trainees comprise two types: those of dull faculty who are followers of faith, who say, "I take refuge!" without a deeper understanding of the reasons, and those followers of Dharma with sharp faculties who find conviction in Dharma based on seeing correct reasons. However, taking a faith-based approach by imitating the customs of one's parents and so forth, without identifying the Three Jewels, is a truly backward approach to refuge. Those who are quasi-Buddhist, who go for refuge with an undecided mind, remind me of how fruit comes in different varieties: ripe, unripe, or quasi-ripe. Thus, if one is not Buddhist then that is one thing, but instead of being undecidedly neither Buddhist nor non-Buddhist, one should be a Buddhist who meets the standard of going for refuge with single-pointed faith based on understanding.

No one is saying you have to practice Dharma, and no one can tell you to be a Buddhist. During the time of the Buddha, he only taught by saying, "This is my philosophy," he never said that all of India should practice the Buddha's Dharma, nor did he tell everyone to follow a Buddhist lifestyle. [272]

Likewise, when Nāgārjuna and others delineated Buddhist texts, views, or tenets, they refuted other contradictory positions only through logic, and never tried to forcefully defeat their adherents by the sword, or with guns, sticks, and so forth.

In prior times the Tibetan population was smaller, but Muslims and Christians who were present had total freedom to practice their religion. There were those who did not believe in religion, and they were also totally free to do so. If one does believe in Dharma, however, it should be practiced based on an understanding of how things are taught in Buddhism. With respect to gaining such understanding, Sakya Pandita in his *Treasury of Good Advice* states:

> Educate yourself, even if you will die tomorrow.
> Though you may not become an expert in this life,
> it is like a jewel entrusted to your next life—
> yours to be reclaimed.

This is the reason why it is constantly repeated that everyone—young and old—should study. When I say we must behave like twenty-first-century Buddhists, I mean that we should use our modern education to analyze and investigate the Buddhist teachings, bringing them into our experience and developing faith based on reason. I think such a Buddhist is one whose faith is balanced by wisdom, and I have previously explained this in detail.

The Way You Go for Refuge

This has four parts:

    a″ Going for refuge by knowing the good qualities
    b″ Going for refuge by knowing the distinctions
    c″ Going for refuge through commitment
    d″ Going for refuge by refusing to acknowledge other refuges[66]

Going for refuge by knowing the good qualities has three parts:

    1″ The qualities of the Buddha
    2″ The qualities of the Dharma
    3″ The qualities of the Sangha

The qualities of the Buddha has four parts:

    (a) The qualities of body
    (b) The qualities of speech
    (c) The qualities of mind

        (i) The qualities of exalted knowledge
        (ii) The qualities of love

    (d) The qualities of enlightened activity

The Qualities of Body

It states in *Praise by Example* [273]:

    Your body, adorned with the signs,
    is beautiful, a nectar for the eyes,

like the sky ornamented by star clusters
on a cloudless autumn night.

One should contemplate as explained. The way of meditating on the
Buddha's body, however, is not like the visualization of a pledge
being (*samayasattva*) generated in front, as in secret mantra. For
example, when going to a market or bazaar one sees various per-
formers singing and dancing, people beautified by their ornaments,
retinue, and so forth, and when one arrives at another place and
recollects those people, the shape of their face, their ornaments,
behavior and so on vividly appear as if seeing it with one's own
eyes. However, just like they do not appear if one intentionally tries
to meditate on them in the field in front, for instance, so too in this
case if one repeatedly looks at images or statues of the Tathāgata
then fosters that by thinking "I cannot get enough of looking at the
Tathāgata's body golden in color, wearing the three Dharma robes,
ornamented by marks and signs," then the visualizations become
vivid from the previous object of one's eye consciousness acting as
the condition. Thus, at this time, generate energetic faith, thinking,
"There is nothing disagreeable upon seeing it, and merely seeing it
is meaningful; such are the supreme qualities of the body of the Buddha that bodhisattvas and below do not have." On top of that, generate the longing of thinking "If only I could see the Buddha's body
directly," and the joy in thinking how great the merit is from recollecting the Buddha. Meditate until you strongly experience these.

The Qualities of Speech

The qualities of speech are as stated in the *Chapter of Satyaka*:

If all sentient beings were to ask questions
in different ways and all at once,

in an instant he would comprehend them,
and with a single voice provide an answer to each.

Therefore, know that in the world the Guide
teaches with a melodious Brahmā voice. [274]
This is the wheel of Dharma turned
that eradicates the suffering of gods and men.

It must be contemplated as such; however, since it is rare to directly hear something similar to the Buddha's speech, or even something worthy of comparison, for now infer it from a sound you find pleasant, like that of a lute that attracts one's attention. From the throat of the Buddha pleasant speech, having sixty-four melodious branches, issues forth. If all sentient beings of the three realms were to simultaneously ask questions, a single answer in the language of Sanskrit, for example, would be heard by beings in their own respective languages, eliminating their doubts all at once. As before, being about experience through the three: faith, longing, and joy.

Speaking tangentially, when a Western acquaintance of mine was on pilgrimage in Tibet, they went to the prophetic lake of Lhamo Latso and saw English words. I do not know if Palden Lhamo knows English, but "engaging in spontaneous and effortless enlightened activity" in accordance with the disposition and inclinations of that disciple is probably something akin to this. When the Bhagavān teaches Dharma, whatever he speaks is understood simultaneously by the listeners in accordance with their individual dispositions and inclinations. Not only that, but they also receive answers to the questions they have in their minds. Such modes of speech are to be understood from the perspective of total infinite purity (dag pa rab 'byams 'ba' zhig).

The Qualities of Mind

Regarding the **qualities of mind**, which are exalted knowledge and love, **it states in the** *Praise in Honor of One Worthy of Honor*:

> Only your pristine wisdom
> comprehends all objects of knowledge.
> For everyone else, however,
> there remain objects yet to be known.

The quality of exalted knowledge is that all phenomena are not concealed. [275] Thus, with pristine wisdom knowing all aspects, he is skillful in caring for disciples according to their faculties. It states in *Praise in One Hundred and Fifty Verses*:

> All of these beings
> are bound by afflictions without exception.
> You, in order to free them from afflictions,
> are perpetually bound by compassion.
>
> Should I first pay homage to you,
> or to the compassion that causes you to remain
> perpetually in cyclic existence,
> despite knowing its faults.

Since he is bound by loving compassion for all sentient beings, he does not have partiality toward those who anoint him with sandalwood perfume on his right hand and those who hack at him with an axe from his left. Therefore, contemplate as before on how he possesses love for all sentient beings like that of a mother for her only child, and so forth.

The Qualities of Enlightened Activity

Regarding the qualities of **enlightened activity**, it states in *Praise in One Hundred and Fifty Verses*:

> You explain the destruction of afflictions,
> teach the deception of Māra,
> proclaim the unbearable nature of cyclic existence,
> and also teach the side of fearlessness.

> Compassionate One wishing to benefit,
> who acts for the sake of sentient beings,
> how could there be anything
> that you have not done for the sake of beings?

With respect to that, of course śrāvakas and pratyekabuddhas have mere love for sentient beings, but having that alone does not help. For example, it is like the child of a mother with crippled arms being carried away by a river and her having to call on a friend for help to get them out. The Buddha has the complete ability to liberate beings, and therefore if it is for the benefit of beings, he enters the fiery pits of hell joyfully and unimpeded, just as he would the pleasant groves of the desirous higher realms. Contemplate it in this way.

Four other reasons taught as to why the Buddha is worthy of refuge are as follows: (1) he is free from all fear, (2) he is skilled in the means of liberating others from fear, (3) his compassion encompasses everyone without partiality, and (4) he accomplishes the aims of all, whether or not they have benefited him. [276] Thus, induce ascertainment of these by analyzing them in detail and thoroughly contemplating them.

The Qualities of the Dharma

Such qualities of the Buddha's body, speech, and mind are neither **causeless nor arisen from incompatible causes. Through listening** to and contemplating the Dharma Jewel of scripture that teach true paths and true cessations as their main subject matter, he manifested the Dharma jewel of realization—the purified class of the two truths that are the qualities of realization and abandonment. Having found ascertainment in this, meditate until uncontrived faith in the Dharma Jewel arises.

Out of the Three Jewels, the Dharma Jewel has the qualities in the mental continuum comprising paths and cessations. It is therefore important to understand such qualities. For the time being, thinking, "They are probably the Dharma Jewel qualities of the high grounds and paths extensively taught in treatises" leads one to take the bodhisattva path of accumulation, preparation, and so forth as something to look up to, but it is hard to immediately tame our minds by doing that.

Therefore, at present, by incorporating a little bit of Dharma-influenced thinking into our everyday life, even though the thoughts may be weak, they still help our mind to be calm, and give us strength. We can see this makes our lives happier. As the saying goes about the beer thief, "If this is what it's like drinking from the mouth of the chang[67] barrel [where it is not so rich], I wonder what it's like to drink from the bottom [where it is very concentrated]!" Even if one gains a slight understanding of renunciation, bodhicitta, and the correct view while a beginner, it is commonly experienced to bring more peace within our mind and influence our thinking. Therefore, if one is able to give rise to high realizations of the paths and grounds, one can infer that the effects of that would be even more powerful.

Thus, one can conclude that the Dharma Jewel is an infallible mental quality, and it becomes easy to see that it is the nonerroneous means for achieving temporary and ultimate happiness—the source of present and everlasting peace. [277] Based on that one comes to identify the Teacher of that Dharma as an excellent friend to look up to, greatly kind, himself infallible, and a holy being who has accomplished the Dharma correctly. Therefore, through the qualities of the Dharma one comes to see the qualities of the Buddha who taught that Dharma, and of the Sangha who correctly train in that Dharma. For that reason, one finds conviction in them. Based on that, in this context of the person of small scope, if one unites the fear from contemplating the suffering of lower rebirths with the faith of conviction gained from seeing the Three Jewels it can protect from that suffering. Then, from the depths of one's heart one gives rise to single-pointed devotion and faith thinking, "Care for me!"

The Qualities of the Sangha

The Sangha Jewels are bodhisattvas such as Maitreya, Mañjuśrī, Avalokiteśvara, and so forth, and śrāvaka Sangha Jewels are those such as Mahākāśyapa and the supreme pair of Śāriputra and Maudgalyāyana. As before, thoroughly reflect on the activities of body, speech, and mind with respect to them. Although they have not attained the qualities of a buddha, contemplate the fact they practice the pure class of the two truths, and act as assistants for accomplishing refuge.

GOING FOR REFUGE BY KNOWING THE DISTINCTIONS

1" The distinction based on their defining characteristics
2" The distinction based on their enlightened activities
3" The distinction based on devotion
4" The distinction based on practice
5" The distinction based on recollection
6" The distinction based on how merit is increased

These should be understood in more detail from the *Great* and *Middle-Length* lamrim treatises and so forth. [278] Going for refuge through conviction based on those superior distinctions, accepting them as refuges through ascertaining the Buddha as the teacher of refuge, the Dharma as the actual refuge, and the Sangha as those who help us achieve that refuge, one comes to accept them as such, and holding the Three Jewels to be the only refuge for those seeking liberation is based on analytical intelligence alone. Giving up adherence to multiple refuges—because liberation cannot be achieved through another refuge—is to go for refuge by not acknowledging other refuges.

These days there are increasingly more Christian people who are becoming interested in Buddhism, especially in Tibetan Buddhism. Since some of them have faith in both Buddhism and Christianity, I am often asked what the best thing to do is. I answer that, while a beginner, it is fine to have admiration and respect toward both one's heritage tradition and the Teacher Bhagavān. Furthermore, the good principles in common with both traditions such as love, compassion, patience, and so forth have greatly benefited countless people across the world since long ago and continue to benefit people to this day. If respecting and admiring these inspirational traditions leads to practical change in our daily behavior wherein we help others and become better people, then our life becomes meaningful, just as explained before.

However, to gradually get to the bottom of and deeply practice each religion requires taking their standalone views, meditations, and conduct as a basis, and therefore one has no choice but to adhere strictly to a single path. [279] If at that point one chooses to adhere strictly to the Buddhist path, one needs to meditate on bodhicitta and emptiness by adhering to them as taught in Buddhism. The very foundation of taking refuge in the respective traditions is mutually exclusive—one accepting interdependence of the lack of true existence, the dependent arising of emptiness, and the other necessarily accepting a creator who is real, permanent, stable, and changeless. Their views on following their respective paths also differ. Due to this, there is no way to unite the practice of both traditions. The way of accomplishing what we wish to achieve—liberation and omniscience—on the basis of one's mind can only be achieved through the Buddhist path.

If one gains ascertainment based on understanding through a mere correct assumption of this mode of distinguishing Buddhists from non-Buddhists based on refuge, and likewise distinguishing them on the basis of whether they accept the four seals of Buddhist doctrine, then based on a clear understanding of this, going for refuge by not acknowledging other refuges is for such reasons, not because of sectarianism and aversion toward others. This can withstand all impartial scrutiny.

Therefore, having seen the superior distinguishing features of the Three Supreme Ones and their highest qualities, the way one must go for refuge is as follows: **It is important not only to have special faith of clarity, but also to have intense longing. For example, even though a world leader can protect one from enemies, and an expert physician can eliminate physical disturbances, one cannot achieve their level; but who is to say that one will not be merely captivated by their powerful speeches and curative therapies, thinking, "Imagine if I could be like them."**

Although a lower scope being alone has not achieved the state of a Supreme One, [280] through their exalted compassion they are protected from temporary suffering and established in samsaric happiness, like being protected by a limited refuge.

Furthermore, in the context of middle-scope persons, they must protect themselves by manifesting the qualities of realization of learner or nonlearner śrāvaka and pratyekabuddhas. For persons of great scope, they must hold as a source of refuge one who has manifested the temporary refuge of a bodhisattva path, or the ultimate refuge of omniscience. As it explains in [Dharmamitra's] _Vinaya Commentary_, the Buddha is the teacher of refuge, the Dharma the actual refuge, and the Sangha are those who assist us in attaining refuge. Thus, repeatedly contemplate that one must also manifest such states.

One might think, "Since this context primarily regards persons of great scope, if one takes nonabiding nirvana as an actual refuge what is the point in taking the nirvana and sangha of śrāvaka and pratyekabuddhas as a refuge?" There is an exception to this. A bodhisattva

who has attained the second ground does not have to take refuge in first-ground sangha or Dharmas of realization and abandonment in the sense of taking refuge in them while wishing to achieve them. These are causal refuges, acting similar to a bridge that saves one from a formidable river. This being so, we who have not entered the path must take refuge in the objects of refuge of the three vehicles. Therefore, do not adhere to senseless talk that misses the essential points of the Buddha's teachings.

If you do not have devotional conviction that surrenders as a result of your faith in the qualities of the Three Jewels and your wish to achieve them, thinking, "Whatever happens—good or bad—I trust in you!" then it is like a hook without a ring to latch onto. Even though the supreme ones are greatly compassionate they become devoid of a means to help. Thus, recollect their qualities, i.e., the qualities of the Buddha who has exhausted all faults and possesses all qualities, the Dharma through which he achieved that—the Mahāyāna Dharma Jewel—and the Sangha who correctly practice that. [281] As one recollects the qualities of those objects of refuge, go for refuge in the resultant refuge with strong, clear conviction by thinking, "May I come to possess such qualities."

Those aspiring to achieve such qualities, together with a motivation of great compassion for sentient beings, should contemplate that they will come to the aid of sentient beings under the power of great compassion, like a bird taking flight, and repeat the following: "I take refuge in the Buddha, supreme among humans. Please be my guide for liberation from cyclic existence and the suffering of bad migrations. I take refuge in the Dharma, supreme among all that is free from attachment. Please act as my actual refuge that liberates from the terrors of cyclic existence and bad migrations. I take refuge in the Sangha, the supreme among assemblies. Please be my friends in becoming free from the suffering of cyclic existence and bad migrations." Recite these phrases in sequence like a rosary, one hundred times each session or however many you can manage. Of course, it is acceptable to recite the refuge verses mentioned prior: however these were performed definitively by my lama in accordance with *Essence of Refined Gold.*

Thus, you can recite a particular refuge verse or the normally recited four-fold refuge, or the following verse,

> I prostrate to Gautama
> who out of his compassion
> taught the holy Dharma
> in order to eliminate all views.

Or:

> I prostrate to the one who has become an authority, the
>   Compassionate One,
> the Teacher, the Sugata, the Protector,

One may recite these two lines from the *Commentary on the* "Compendium of Valid Cognition" with a full stop instead of continuing with the entire verse. Whichever it is, there are waves of benefit from reciting such words repeatedly. It is like how there is more taste if we change what we eat; it also helps maintain a good appetite. [282] Otherwise, it is also good if one goes for refuge with the two lines,

> I go for refuge, until I am enlightened,
> to the Buddha, the Dharma, and the highest assembly.

Through these words one goes for refuge to the Three Jewels until one achieves enlightenment, and the way of going for refuge is also explained as Mahāyāna refuge.

Thus, it has the following features as stated in the *Ornament for the Mahāyāna Sūtras*:

Migrators, a promise, realization, and surpassing.

The feature of the observed object, every migrating sentient being; the feature of the promise to attain buddhahood; the feature of realizing enlightenment, in which enlightenment is understood in the ultimate sense of being the mix of the wisdoms of equipoise and subsequent attainment that are one taste with the dharmadhātu. Thus, refuge in which one realizes that mode of enlightenment correctly has the feature of surpassing other refuge practices of śrāvaka and pratyeka-buddhas. The refuge practice must have these four attributes.

Since this context relates to mind generation, I will briefly explain that as an ancillary topic. The purpose of going for refuge pertains to the two aspirations that have as their observed object the accomplishment of one's own welfare, and the accomplishment of others' welfare. To accomplish these, one generates the mind of enlightenment by way of the two lines,

Through my practice of giving and so forth,
may I attain buddhahood to benefit sentient beings.

Whatever roots of virtue one accumulates are not solely for one's own comfort and happiness alone; their purpose is for happiness and well-being to come to limitless sentient beings. Contemplating this, make the following prayer: "For their sake may I become a buddha, an excellent being who can accomplish their happiness and well-being."

When saying, "Through my practice of giving and so forth," contemplate the "I." Is it an "I" that is something other than the aggregates? Or is it within the aggregates? Where is it? Search for the "I." [283] In brief, the "I" exists nominally, as a mere imputation. Recognize it as an "I" merely imputed onto the aggregates. Contemplate that this "I" goes for refuge until enlightenment, thinking, "May this 'I' achieve buddhahood for all sentient beings." Since our self is a mere dependently imputed self, ārya buddhas and the Sangha Jewel are likewise merely dependently imputed and empty of inherent existence. The awareness that actualizes the direct realization of that is the Dharma Jewel. If one keeps these things in mind while reciting the refuge verse even once then it will also include the collection of pristine wisdom, and thus thoroughly encapsulate the essence of Dharma.

In this way one can substitute the line "by the merit from practicing generosity and so forth" with "by the collections from practicing generosity and so forth." Doing so expands our understanding to include both the collection of merit and the collection of wisdom.

Having Gone for Refuge, the Stages of the Precepts

a" Those from the *Compendium of Determinations*
b" How they are in the oral instructions

From the *Compendium of Determinations* there are two four-fold sets of precepts. The first four-fold set is as follows:

(a) Rely on excellent persons
(b) Listen to the excellent Dharma
(c) Correct mental attention
(d) Practicing Dharma that accords with the teachings

The second four-fold set is:

(a) Do not excite your senses
(b) Train correctly in the basis of the precepts

(c) Be compassionate toward sentient beings

(d) Strive to make periodic offerings to the Three Jewels

Regarding how they are in the oral instructions, **it is not enough to have gone for refuge in the actual session—one must also maintain the precepts in the session breaks.** [284]

This has two parts:

1" Individual precepts

(a) Proscriptive precepts

(b) Prescriptive precepts

2" Common precepts

Proscriptive Precepts

Having gone for refuge in the Buddha, do not seek final refuge in powerful worldly gods. Gyalsé Thokmé Sangpo states in his *Thirty-Seven Practices of Bodhisattvas*:

How could a worldly god protect anyone
if they are also trapped in the same samsaric prison?

Regardless of whichever kind of powerful haughty worldly deity they are, or whatever they may be in reality, those that present as haughty beings to the average person have not even abandoned afflictions, let alone cognitive obscurations. Therefore, it is entirely unacceptable to place total trust in them as a final refuge.

In general, the merit field comprises gurus, meditation deities, buddhas, bodhisattvas, śrāvakas and pratyekabuddhas, ḍākas and ḍākinīs, and Dharma protectors. In accordance with Dharma protectors being last, Je Pabongkha does not include worldly protectors in his instructed merit field for the *Guru Pūjā*, thus there is no need to mention one like Dogyal, also known as Shugden. The five forms of the king-like spirit [Pehar] are also not included. With respect to those five, Kyabjé Trijang Rinpoché said, "Supramundane deities do not enter and possess people; it is the worldly deities that enter and possess people."

Some people ask me what I think about some of the Nechung monastery monks taking "Nechung Dharmapāla," as they call him, as an object of refuge. My answer is that it is irrelevant what Nechung is in reality: since he presents as a haughty and worldly class of deity to ordinary perception one should not take refuge in him as a Sangha Jewel, let alone a buddha.

The haughty class of deities are worldly, and whether they can be of assistance I do not know, but it is wrong to rely on them from the depths of one's heart, thinking, "Please take care of me!" [285] That would furthermore exclude oneself from being a Buddhist. If one has realizations such as stable clear appearance and divine pride of a meditation deity who is able to exhort haughty deities to perform actions for the sake of removing temporary obstacles and achieving minor siddhis, it is acceptable to entrust them with such tasks. However, you can have compassion and dedicate your virtue toward the class of worldly deities that harm the doctrine and living beings, but it is inappropriate to merely rely on or propitiate them, let alone take refuge in them.

In recent times, due to the harmful influence of Dogyal Shugden, I have had no choice but to become strict on the matter. The reasons for this are as follows:

1. Breaking samaya with the Great Fifth Dalai Lama
2. Harm done to the Geluk teachings
3. Hindrance to Dharma traditions keeping their samaya purely
4. My general responsibility toward the well-being of Tibet's religion and politics
5. Stopping the propitiation of gods and nāgas

With respect to the first point, the tutor of the Third Dalai Lama, Sönam Gyatso, was the fifteenth Ganden throne holder Panchen Sönam Drakpa. His reincarnation, the tulku of the Upper Chamber, Sönam Gelek Palsang, was followed by Tulku Drakpa Gyaltsen. However, he was a fake reincarnation, who was later reborn as an oath breaker through distorted prayers. Therefore, at the time when the Great Fifth Dalai Lama used wrathful direct means to exorcize him, he authored the following clear declaration as testimony:

The unholy Drakpa Gyaltsen whose samaya is false,
is an oath-breaking spirit born out of distorted prayers.
Since he harms the teachings and all living beings,
do not take him as an ally, protector, or refuge, and turn him to ashes!

This clearly states his cause being distorted prayers, his nature an oath breaker, and his function as harming the teachings and living beings. [286] Preceding this, in the author's colophon, he states, "Through the opportunistic deception of his mother Agyal from his birthplace Gekhasa, he was a fake reincarnation of Tulku Sönam Gelek Palsang, and through distorted prayers became an oath breaker who greatly harmed many living beings."

Second, the excellent and marvelous collection of teachings of Tsongkhapa comprising eighteen volumes are of course something for those outside of the Geluk tradition to praise, and are indeed the heart jewel within the tradition itself. However, putting those eighteen important volumes aside and taking this haughty deity—who is the basis of contention—as a heart jewel, proudly proclaiming him as "the protector of the gentle lord's teachings," is shameful and a disgrace to the Geluk tradition.

Third, through Dogyal's deception there have been many statements made back and forth between the different traditions and tenet holders based on misconceptions and wrong views that tarnish samaya. Discussions still continue regarding the great hindrances caused during the earlier, middle, and latter periods, and that still continue to this day, toward the permeating of the light of the jewel of pure appearance between Tibet's Sakya, Geluk, Kagyü, Nyingma, and Jonang traditions, which are the same in being teachings of Śākyamuni.

Fourth, with respect to the well-being of Tibet's religious and political matters, if I were to turn my back on the kindness of the Great Fifth Dalai Lama, and the responsibilities he undertook establishing the foundation of the religious and political elements of the Ganden Phodrang government that greatly helped Tibet, and take a wrong path in contradiction to his intentions, that would be distastefully unappreciative of me. Therefore, it is my responsibility to advise a clear path forward without regrets and blame regarding those mistakes. While giving such guidance, whether one accepts or rejects it depends on how much universal responsibility one takes, and this is one's personal choice. [287]

Fifth, the proliferation of god and spirit worship within Tibetan society is a tradition, mixed with Buddhism, of loyally petitioning worldly powerful spirits with offerings. This is an extremely big mistake, and shamefully misses the point of the teachings. The reasons for this being so are as I briefly explained in the section on secret mantra in volume 1.

Based on these reasons and my thorough analysis—not on hasty indiscretion—and principally guided by Kyabjé Trijang Rinpoché's answers to my inquiries, I try to follow in the footsteps of many qualified, nonsectarian Tibetan masters of the past who objected to Dogyal, and likewise of the firm decisions made by the incomparably kind Great Fifth Dalai Lama, and the Great Thirteenth.

If it were the case that new proof came to light, either scripture or reasoning, proving that the Great Fifth's words were untrue, then it would be a different matter. However, only a lama equal to the Great Fifth in realization, knowledge, compassion, and ability would be able to draw such a conclusion on the supposed hidden meaning of the words of a master composer. Aside from that, a haphazard approach does not suffice. Those who do not understand the overall and specific ways the situation has affected the teachings and sentient beings until now have used opportunism and their own sectarian agendas to damage the unity among the laity, monastics, the public and private lives of Tibetans in Tibet and in exile in whatever way they can. [288] In this way they have merely turned religion into politics, and there has not been a single person thus far who has presented any solid proof of scripture or reasoning supporting their case. Further reading on this can be found in *Clouds of Offerings to Please the Impartial on the Origins of Dogyal*, *Advice Regarding Dogyal: Part One*, and *Advice Regarding Dogyal: Part Two*.

Since one has taken refuge in the Dharma, one stops harming sentient beings. Dharma, consisting of paths and cessations, is rooted in compassion. Therefore, not only is it unacceptable to harm sentient beings at all, one also should do as much as possible to help them.

If we generally consider our own taking of refuge: the religious traditions have many different ways of taking refuge, but the common refuge precepts remain mostly the same, whether they emerged out of the context of the non-Buddhist tenets or within the religions of today. For example, among the ten nonvirtues that we propound, giving up killing, stealing, sexual misconduct, lying, divisive speech, harsh speech, idle talk, covetousness, and malice is common to all religious traditions.

Moreover, covetousness and malice, for instance, can be attachment, aversion, or ignorance in the context of persons of middle scope, whereas in the context of persons of small scope, covetousness is an instance of attachment, and malice is an instance of aversion, just as they are in all religious traditions.

Since there can be many degrees of wrong views, the wrong views of this context appear to be, for example, thinking that killing is without fault. What are the particular wrong views as explained in Buddhism? Liberation is not like a pure realm, but a quality of mind—a factor of separation in which one has abandoned the stains in the mind of the apprehension of a self. [289] To achieve that one meditates on the stages of the path starting from the leisure and opportunity being greatly meaningful yet difficult to find, to impermanence and so forth. When one contemplates those things with that goal in mind it becomes a Buddhist practice, and therefore viewing that kind of liberation as nonexistent, or karmic causality as nonexistent—that is, not accepting the many presentations of such hidden phenomena—are taught as wrong views in Buddhism.

In general there are a variety of reasons why people engage in those kinds of actions of adopting and discarding certain behaviors, whether it be because they are at odds with the intention of one's teacher or prophet, or because of understanding one will have to experience the unbearable result of that negative karma, or out of fear of being punished by the law without considering a religious aspect, or because one considers it poor behavior, or out of consideration for the happiness and suffering of others.

Having taken refuge in the Sangha one does not seek out perpetual friendship as a very close best friend **with people who have no conviction in the Three Jewels** even though it is unacceptable to reject them due to loving compassion. **These are the three precepts** one must train in.

Prescriptive Precepts

Regarding the **prescriptive precepts,** one must **train in visualizing even poorly manufactured Buddha images and those made of lesser quality materials as the Buddha.** Thus, whatever image of the Buddha it may be, whether excellently crafted or not, made of good or bad quality materials, old or new and so forth, one must hold discrimination of them as the actual Buddha. It is unacceptable to view them as merchandise. However, since it would make it difficult to acquire the three supports (stupa, image, and scripture) for the sake of hearing, contemplation, and accumulating merit, if there were no one setting up Dharma bookshops or statue shops, then I think there is no choice but to make an exception for those sellers who are well motivated to provide conditions for Dharma activities, and who put a reasonable price on those three objects. [290] Aside from that, it was taught to be entirely unacceptable to view such objects as merchandise and selling them for a high price, and so forth.

Imagine that any teaching comprising even four words is the Dharma Jewel. Thus, having gone for refuge in the Dharma, it is never acceptable to place any teaching directly on the ground, a seat, or a bare table, and so forth. One should not step over them, nor ever place objects such as one's eyeglasses and so forth on top of them. It is therefore very important to respect them.

As for spending the proceeds from publishing and selling scriptures, if one puts all that money back into further printing of the texts, then there is the advantage of many people being able to acquire copies of the texts, and thus it is a service to the teachings. However, if instead of doing that one sells Dharma texts to make a living, it is extremely precarious and thus should not be pursued at all. Thus, as the worldly saying goes, "The closer you are to a dog, the closer you are to a wound." Those who have a lot of contact with scriptures are definitely at greater risk of incurring faults with respect to the Dharma.

Through holding those who maintain the mere marks of a monastic to be the Sangha Jewel, abandon disrespect of body, speech, and mind, and esteem them with offerings and praise.

It is taught that, having gone for refuge to the Sangha, one must view anyone who wears the maroon patched cloth as the actual Sangha Jewel and pay respect to them. For example, in Thai society the laity pay great respect toward those who wear the robes of a monastic. When I went to Thailand, the lay men and women paid respect to us monastics, but the custom is such that monastics must receive respect but not reciprocate it with a respectful gesture; however, since I was not accustomed to this, I felt uncomfortable. [291]

In that country monastics are also not allowed to touch lay men or women with their hands, so when I went to see the king I could not shake his hand from the point of view of him being a lay person, but from the point of view of him being a king I must, so at the end of our talk I shook his hand as was appropriate. Furthermore, if a woman offers something to a monk, she must first place it on a cloth; the monk does not take it directly by hand. Monastics generally do not mingle with the laity, and thus they avoid a lay person going first while a monastic is left behind in a crowd—such are the customs of their country.

There are accounts of the king of Dharma, King Dromtönpa, a celibate lay vow-holder, where upon seeing maroon cloth he would pick it up, saying "It is impossible that someone who bears such cloth is without a single quality," then pat the dust off it, touch it to the top of his head, and place it in a clean place.

Our [Tibetan Buddhist] laity should respect those who wear the robes of a monastic, instead of interacting with them as if they are in the same social standing and refraining from using honorifics and respectful gestures, and monks and nuns from their side should not casually mingle and socialize with the laity. From the day one follows in the footsteps of the Buddha and goes forth from the home into homelessness, one voluntarily commits to make the *three changes*: changing one's attitude, name, and clothing. One's mental outlook and conduct must all be dissimilar to a lay person, and it is through this that one must make oneself worthy of respect from others.

If it comes to be known that monks or nuns bearing the marks of the ordained are behaving in a depraved manner that would damage the reputation of monastics and the community, we should try to bring an end to the inappropriate conduct of those few monastics who are obstacles to everyone's faith and respect. For the sake of good quality monastics, virtues should be strengthened and faults eradicated, like lancing pus, through collective concern from both the lay and ordained communities. [292] Taking refuge in misbehaving monastics because of believing one must be devoted to the Sangha Jewel is incorrect.

Therefore, **the three prescriptive precepts** are to be carried out with faith based on reasoning and are adopted voluntarily.

Common Precepts

There are six common precepts:

(a) Going for refuge again and again through recollecting the distinctions and qualities of the Three Jewels

(b) Through recollecting their kindness, always striving to make offerings and offer the first portion of food and drink

(c) Through considering them with compassion, also encouraging others in this manner of taking refuge

(d) Whatever you may do and whatever your purpose, making offerings to and supplicating the Three Jewels, forsaking other worldly means

(e) Taking refuge three times during the day and three times at night while understanding the benefits

(f) Whatever activity you do, doing so by trusting in the Three Jewels, and not giving up the Three Jewels whether in jest or at the cost of your life, but guarding your refuge in them

Taking refuge three times during the day and three times at night while understanding the benefits has two parts:

(i) The benefits according to the *Compendium of Determinations*

(ii) The benefits according to the personal instructions

The benefits according to the *Compendium of Determinations* are explained in two sets of four:

The first set of four is:

(1') Attaining vast merit
(2') Attaining joy and supreme joy
(3') Attaining meditative stabilization (*samādhi*)
(4') Attaining purity

The second set of four is:

(1') Having great protection
(2') Achieve reduction, extinguishment, and total eradication of all obscurations derived from incorrect beliefs
(3') You have become supreme and are counted among excellent persons
(4') You delight and please the gods whose conduct accords with the Teacher and Brahmā, and who favor the teachings [293]

The benefits according to the personal instructions has eight:

You Are Included among Buddhists

If one can sincerely accept the manner in which the Three Jewels are an infallible refuge in accordance with the above explanation that distinguishes Buddhists from non-Buddhists by their manner of taking refuge, then one is a Buddhist. Therefore, even if you live in a place without a single Buddhist, you are counted among Buddhists. Moreover, there are many levels within this, such as coming to perceive the Three Jewels as an infallible refuge through a mere understanding based on correct assumption, or following that, having conviction within going for refuge from the bottom of one's heart due to gaining ascertainment from valid cognition.

However, if through a spontaneous condition one thinks, "What is the Buddha *really*?" and loses one's refuge through strong disbelief, then from that point on even if you are within a Buddhist congregation, you are not Buddhist. Thus, one does not become a Buddhist because a lama states that "from this day onward you are a Buddhist."

Becoming a Basis for All the Vows

Whether it be the Buddhist lay or monastic vows, one must take vows having started with refuge, and therefore refuge acts as the support for all vows.

Reducing and Exhausting Previously Accumulated Karmic Obscurations

If one has pure refuge, then through relying on paths and cessations as one's refuge one can progress gradually through the grounds and paths without hindrance.

Accumulation of Vast Merit

Not Falling to Lower Migrations

Not Being Thwarted by Human and Nonhuman Interferences

Accomplishing All of One's Wishes [294]

Quickly Achieving Buddhahood

These can be easily understood if one firmly grasps the meaning of the above discussion. Refuge in the Three Jewels from the depths of one's heart **practiced correctly leads to eliminating the problems of this** and all future lives. Moreover, it becomes the source of all wealth of happiness and good.

Concluding Verses

Upon seeing those who strive for might, leadership, and
  respect
for the happiness of this life, which is short-lived like
  lightning,
and who aspire for the pinnacle of joys
of their future plans,
my encountering the protector from the frights of the
  unbearable lower rebirths,
the delighted smile of the infallible Three Jewels,
and these extensively explained crucial points,
have been created by the multitude of merit I accumulated
  previously.

It was enough that I experienced unbearable suffering in
  lower rebirths
due to the power of previous nonvirtue.
Now I will steel myself well, O Wise One,
and achieve the excellent basis of a good rebirth!

Cultivating Conviction in Karmic Causality: The Root of All Happiness and Good

REGARDING meditating on karmic causality, the root of all happiness and good, in accordance with the way to go for refuge explained above, the essence is to make it your practice to correctly cast aside and adopt what is necessary in relation to karma and its effects, which is the basis for actual refuge—the Dharma comprised of paths and cessations. "Karma and its effects" indicates a dependent origination of cause and effect. The meaning of the Sanskrit word *karma* in this context is "deeds." Thus, an action refers to a produced exertion that was motivated by an agent's intention, and the effect arisen from that is a feeling of happiness or suffering. Since those feelings are something that arises within consciousness itself, then it is on the basis of consciousness that karma is posited. [295] Furthermore, the Vaibhāṣikas explain it to be the mental factor of intention; the Madhyamaka Prāsaṅgikas explain karma of body and speech as something physical, and mental karma as the karma of intention (*sems pa'i las*).

With respect to karma and effect, the great lord Tsongkhapa in his *Great Treatise on the Stages of the Path* explains this topic under the heading "The Root of All Happiness and Good." These few words pack in great meaning, making this an extremely vital point. Therefore, I will first give an explanation summarizing the essentials of foundational attitudes toward karma and effect. The source, or basis, for karma and effect is the interdependence of cause and effect as explained before. The interdependence of cause and effect is a law, or natural mode or process, and can be understood empirically without needing to be proved by logic. Through our own multiple experiences we can say that varying expressions of effects arise in dependence on this or that cause and condition. Karma, or action, has an object of the action, an agent of the action, and an action they performed; since there can be no such action without an agent, that action is called a deed (or "karma"). Therefore, since all things arise in dependence on causes and conditions, a subcategory of that process is karma and effect—in which an agent accumulates karma that then produces an effect.

Moreover, there are varying subtleties of karma based on the particular motivation of the agent. Among those, the coarse can be explained, but there are many extremely subtle ones that cannot even be inferred through reasoning. In Buddhist treatises, objects of knowledge are divided into three—manifest, hidden, and extremely hidden. The extremely subtle presentation of karma and effect that cannot be proved through reasoning is included within the extremely hidden. [296]

For example, if many people are congregated in a meeting hall, they will all be experiencing different mental and physical feelings of happiness and suffering at the same time. They will be able to identify that the external environment of that place, the air, the temperature and so forth act as the temporary conditions for their feelings, but only be able to merely state that the primary cause of their happiness and suffering meets back to their karma. Aside from that, the presentation of exactly what that karma was, when it was accumulated, and in which context, as well as which specific karma led to which specific feeling is difficult for even ārya bodhisattvas abiding on the higher grounds to understand. Thus, the subtle presentations of karmic causality in which such and such karma accumulated at such-and-such time in such-and-such place, in such-and-such eon gave rise to this particular ripened result can only be understood directly by a buddha who has abandoned cognitive obscurations (shes sgrib) and achieved the pristine wisdom of omniscience. There is a huge amount of such extremely hidden presentations.

Although generosity resulting in resources and guarding ethics resulting in a good rebirth themselves are not extremely hidden phenomena, the specificity of which particular act of generosity leads to which particular result is what is extremely hidden. As stated by Potowa:

> Even emptiness can be understood through logic;
> treat karma and effect with the utmost caution.

The meaning of emptiness is difficult to understand and therefore it is a hidden phenomenon, but if analyzed with logic it can be realized. Extremely hidden phenomena cannot be ascertained through analyzing them with reasoning by the power of the fact. Therefore, in order to understand such a presentation of karma and effect one must rely on scripture, and if one does not have heart-felt faith in the Teacher of that scripture, one will doubt their teaching. [297]

Thus, it is not enough to believe the preciousness of the Teacher because other people say so and so forth—one must prove why it is suitable to trust that the Teacher is infallible from the outset. This is possible to prove because one can realize with respect to any teaching of the Buddha that: (1) the portion of perceptible manifest phenomena taught are not contradicted by direct valid cognition, (2) the portion of slightly hidden phenomena taught are not contradicted by inference through the power of the fact, (3) the portion of extremely hidden phenomena taught are not contradicted by inference of belief, and (4) the explicit and implicit and former and latter statements are not contradictory. We can also infer such since we can also ascertain what the Teacher said about directly perceptible phenomena being infallible. Moreover, due to the Teacher having no reason to lie, the critiques of other opponents fail, and however much one analyzes the word of the Teacher, to that extent one's ascertainment becomes clearer and deeper, thus they withstand analysis.

The main point that can be analyzed starts from the way to achieve liberation, and within that what to adopt and discard relating to the four noble truths. When analyzing that, one can find even more ascertainment, through which one ascertains that the Teacher is infallible and finds conviction. Through that one is able to infer that his teachings on what to adopt and give up with respect to karma and effect are also true.

The very subtle presentations of karma and effect that are extremely hidden to us, starting from the way to achieve the body of a higher rebirth, are secondary points when compared to definite goodness. We cannot infer through logic that he knew how to teach those secondary matters of what to adopt and discard starting in relation to higher rebirths. However, since he was not misleading with respect to the principal matters, we can infer he was not at all misleading with respect to those secondary matters, and thus it is permissible to have conviction in those. Based on this, the most important factor is that we can induce ascertainment of the primary matters—the presentation of the true cessation of definite goodness—through analyzing the infallibility of how it was taught.

Having contemplated the relationship between taking refuge and karma and effect—and particularly karma and effect—we will understand the faults incurred in dependence on karmic misdeeds, and what benefit there is to be had from refraining from those. [298]

Having understood this, you develop great enthusiasm for persevering in virtuous deeds, and through conviction from the depths of your heart you strive in correctly engaging and refraining in virtue and nonvirtue in relation to the presentation on karma and its effects. In this way ascertainment of how to achieve what we desire in future lives and so forth arises naturally.

Even though you recollect the difficulty in finding freedom and

opportunity, death and impermanence, and the suffering of lower rebirths, and fret, thinking, "I will practice," up until now you put the priorities of your future lives on the back burner and focused primarily on this life as more important. In focusing your attention on the matters of this life alone, you have not been able to put genuine Dharma into practice, which would help you in all future lives. Therefore, seeing the reasons of this life working out no matter what you do and distant future lives being more important, as well as the reasoning within the presentation of profound cause and effect, if you correctly put into practice karmic causality in conjunction with an attitude directed to the well-being of future lives, you will definitely achieve a human body in your next life too.

Moreover, since you strive for our object of achievement—the state of liberation and omniscience—even though the ultimate aim is omniscience, it still takes many lifetimes to accomplish; thus if you are not well-prepared to achieve a human body in the next life by having the collection of causes complete, there is the danger that you will take on an animal's body and so forth and become bereft of the good fortune to achieve liberation and omniscience. Therefore, with great foresight retain the state of omniscience as your ultimate goal, and temporarily strive to acquire a garland of good rebirths in which you can easily progress along the grounds and paths. This is most important.

For example, since the day in 1959 that we Tibetans arrived in exile in India we have never lost sight of achieving autonomy for the common good of Tibet. [299] Since that requires years and years of effort, then for the sake of achieving autonomy we have had to remain waiting in India for a long time. With no choice but to rely on aid, and in order to properly prepare for our goal of autonomy for Tibet, we created a constitution for the future in line with democracy. Furthermore, the real foundation we have been able to lay for subsistence and education are the settlements, schools, nurseries, and monastic educational institutes. The establishment of these is the implementation of a plan in which we will likely settle long term in India.

Even though our root goal is not to stay in India, if we do not act like it will take years and years to take the many, gradual steps necessary to achieve autonomy, then leave aside uneducated, jobless beggars achieving the autonomy of any country, it is entirely possible that we have to remain here without being able to support ourselves. In line with this example, strive to accumulate the complete collection of causes to gradually achieve both the short- and long-term goals: the ultimate goal of omniscience and the temporary goal of a support having freedoms. If you are able to get to higher grounds and paths in this life, that is best, but even if you cannot, then in order to execute a perfect plan in which the progress you achieve from continuing life to life as a human preparing for omniscience can be continued in your next life it is a vital point that you train in the stages not shared with persons of lower scope; such is the progression of this path, too.

What, then, is the measure for a perfected attitude of one who has trained in stages of the path in common with persons of lower scope? When one gives rise to a mind strongly intent on achieving the objectives of future lives and not just paying lip service to the idea, then one has achieved the result of training the mind in that. At present, **if we do not understand a vital point of how to practice Dharma, then we will not be content with those things we label "conditions for practice" such as food, clothing, and belongings. For that end we will accumulate a variety of misdeeds, passing time with the variegated eight dharmas.** [300]

Those who consider food, clothing, and chatter as disadvantageous might suppress the three nonvirtues of body, but under the power of the other seven alone, they will pass their time solely with the eight white dharmas, and thus not without being saturated by the downfalls of the misdeeds of the three doors.

The way to posit the white, black, and variegated eight dharmas is made clear in this context. The black eight dharmas are thoughts and deeds performed devoid of virtuous thought, completely for one's own sake in this life alone.

We who are not without an attitude of Dharma, who mostly think that which benefits after death is the Dharma and who through some minor conviction hold the deep aspiration to practice sublime Dharma, might suppress the three nonvirtues of body out of the ten nonvirtues that will be mentioned later, but through not knowing the correct way to practice Dharma, we become completely caught up in business, or gathering offerings, or collecting food, clothing and resources—all as supposed "conditions for Dharma practice." Such people who live out their lives in that way engage in the eight variegated worldly dharmas.

When becoming acquainted with so many people, the four nonvirtues of speech—lying, divisive speech, harsh words, and idle chatter are dangerously likely to occur. In particular, even when we are alone, the three nonvirtues of covetousness, malice, and wrong views easily arise in our minds through our ways of thinking. Those thoughts and conduct that suppress the coarser among the ten nonvirtues while unable to apply antidotes correctly to the subtler ones are taught as the eight white dharmas. Whichever black, white, or variegated eight dharmas you pass your time with, **after your death black and white karma will follow you like your shadow. Thus it states in the** *Precious Garland*:

> **From nonvirtue comes all suffering**
> **and likewise all bad migrations.**
> **From virtue comes all good migrations**
> **and the happiness in all rebirths.** [301]

This teaches the infallibility of black and white karma, and since it was taught by the Buddha, the speaker in whom one generated a valid experience of faith in the context of refuge, the *King of Concentrations Sūtra* **thus states:**

The moon and the stars may fall from their place,
the earth together with its mountains and towns may be
    destroyed,
the element of space may change into something else,
but you will never speak an untrue word.

You should contemplate, thinking, "It is totally impossible that the Buddha tells lies," until you give rise to undivided faith in karma and effect. Whether you have good conditions in which you are not physically ill or have mental difficulties, or harm from enemies and spirits, or whether you have the opposite of that, or whether you alternate between them—since you must be in one of those situations, visualize whatever is happening for you and meditate until you have a vivid appearance of happiness and suffering. Next, it says in the *Sūtra on the Basis of Discipline*:

Karma of beings does not go to waste,
even in a hundred eons.
When conditions gather and the time has come,
it will surely ripen as a result.

Happiness starting from a cool breeze blowing on your body while being scorched by heat, or suffering starting from a tiny splinter causing a wound, are both entirely the result of one's own past virtue and misdeeds. Thus, you should contemplate that karmic cause and effect cannot be blocked by any condition until you give rise to undivided faith that has found conviction in this point.

Undivided faith in karma and effect means unchangeable faith. Through strongly habituating one's behavior of body, speech, and mind at all times throughout the day and night through inseparable practice to be in line with what to adopt and give up, you accomplish extremely powerful virtue. Furthermore, if you can deposit virtuous imprints in your mindstream, then when dying a strong mind of virtue will effortlessly arise by which you can definitely take a good rebirth in your next life. [302]

As it is said:

> Karma by which we cycle in existence is either the heavy,
> or the recent, or that which we are habituated to,
> or that which was committed first in this life. From these,
> they ripen from former to latter.

Thus, out of all the millions of karmas we have in our continuum that lead to taking rebirth, whichever of those is activated at death is that with the strongest influence, and thus what mind we have at the time of death is extremely important. If we have strong habituation with and imprints of virtue while we are alive, there is a stronger chance a virtuous mind will arise while dying. If so, then at the end of manifesting the clear light mind of death good karma will be activated. In order to definitely achieve a good rebirth in the next life, being able to connect to an intermediate existence of that type of rebirth is heavily contingent upon the potential of your thoughts, deeds, and habituations in this life.

Regarding the explanation of the topic of karma and effect, the root outlines in the *Great Treatise on the Stages of the Path* are as follows:

> b' Cultivating conviction in karmic causality: the root of all happiness and good

This has three parts:

> 1' Contemplating karma and its effects in general
> 2' Contemplating karma and its effects in detail

3' How to engage in virtue and disengage from nonvirtue
having contemplated karma and its effects in general and
in detail

Contemplating karma and its effects in general has two parts:

a" The actual way to contemplate karma in general
b" Contemplating the distinctions among different karma

The actual way to contemplate karma in general has four parts:

1" The certainty of karma
2" The magnification of karma
3" Not meeting with [the effects of] karma you did
not perform
4" Actions performed not going to waste

The Certainty of Karma

Having accumulated a virtue, its result of happiness is certain to
emerge. As a result of a karmic misdeed, you will definitely experience
suffering. This certainty is unchanging.

The Magnification of Karma

Since even a small cause has a huge effect, one should not wait patiently
having accumulated small virtues, but emphatically accomplish them.
Likewise, even a slight misdeed should be avoided without being complacent, and if you are tainted by faults, you should confess and refrain
from them, and not keep company with them for even a day. [303]

Not Meeting with [the Effects of] Karma You Did Not Perform, and Actions Performed Not Going to Waste

With regard to not meeting with the effects of karma not performed and that performed not going to waste: If you have not accumulated a particular karmic debt, it does not matter what conditions you meet with—a result of suffering will not be experienced. For example, there are cases where a few people are traveling together in a car and the companions are killed yet one person survives; or in wars or environmental disasters where many beings die yet some survive, or when a great calamity occurs through a sudden cause. These are, respectively, clear indications of not meeting with the effects of karma not done, and karma done not going to waste.

Similarly, it is normal to say, "He had luck yesterday, but today he was unlucky." This "luck" is backed by many strong causes and conditions, and success cannot be determined through good and bad fortune alone. Likewise, sometimes we have the thought of, "Today I was deceived!" when actually there was no harm done, and other times our mind is at ease and we think, "Nothing is amiss today," when actually things are not okay. These common occurrences are the ripened results of their respective good and bad karma, and not just everything going wrong that day, or to do with whether or not you wish to succeed. These are signs that karma not done is not met with, and that done does not go to waste.

When the effects of karma ripen, one experiences feelings of either happiness, suffering, or equanimous feelings; thus the corresponding karmic causes for those are virtue, nonvirtue, or the unspecified.

As we do not desire suffering, its cause of nonvirtue is to be discarded, and since we desire happiness, its cause of virtue is to be accomplished. If the karma of virtue and misdeeds are further divided, there are those that are singularly white, singularly black, and a mix of black and white.

Furthermore, contemplate with respect to oneself that, "Even though I have attained this human body through the power of accumulating a virtue in my former life, due to nonvirtue I accumulated previously I have such and such completed suffering. [304] Likewise, when looking outwardly at the situation of an animal that is happy, consider, through your direct experience, that although they have attained such a projected body through projecting nonvirtue, their completed body is attained through completing virtue.

Induce the certainty of belief through your own inference about the way one strong karma can project multiple bodies, and how many weak karmas can project a single body, for example how one rich person can provide for many officiating clergy, and many poor people can provide for one officiating clergy member. If we had the choice, even if we could enjoy the mere bliss of the gods, we would not know satisfaction, nor would we be able to bear the slightest suffering. This being the case, we must recognize that the cause for experiencing unbearable suffering of past lower rebirths is nonvirtue, that if we do not abandon nonvirtue it is only suitable that we continue to experience the unwished for result of suffering, and that to abandon suffering it is not enough to recognize its cause— misdeeds—in the manner of saying, "The burglar was a person!" but we must identify them closely.

To explain this:

Contemplating the distinctions among different karma has two parts:

1″ An exposition primarily on the ten paths of action
2″ Teaching karma and effects

Teaching karma and effects has three parts:

CULTIVATING CONVICTION IN KARMIC CAUSALITY   331

(a) Black karma and its effects
(b) Contemplating white karma and its effects
(c) A presentation of other classifications of karma

Black karma and its effects has three parts:

(i)   The actual paths of nonvirtuous karma
(ii) Distinctions of weight
(iii) An exposition of the effects

The Actual Paths of Nonvirtuous Karma

The *Treasury of Knowledge* states:

Making a coarse summary among them,
the paths of action—
virtuous and nonvirtuous—are ten.

The nonvirtuous misdeeds are subsumed into ten: karma of body that is killing, stealing, and sexual misconduct; karma of speech that is lying, divisive speech, harsh words, and idle talk; and karma of mind that is covetousness, malice, and wrong views. This being so, if, from among those ten, someone kills any kind of sentient being, it is a nonvirtue of killing.

With respect to a basis such as Devadatta, for example, if one perceives them to be Devadatta, is motivated by any of the three poisons to kill them, and engages in that either by oneself or makes another do it by stabbing them with a weapon, for instance, then at the conclusion when the other person has died the nonvirtue of killing is complete. [305]

However, with respect to someone dying under one's foot while one's perception was mistaken or there was no intent to kill, or oneself dying before the other person, although it has not become a virtue where the four factors of (1) basis, (2) intention, (3) application, and (4) conclusion are complete, it still belongs to the category of the nonvirtue of killing.

Through contemplating karma and effect in general, and by way of reflecting that virtuous and nonvirtuous causes are certain to have a result of happiness and suffering respectively, one resolves to accomplish virtue. Through reflecting on the magnification of karma, one should not disregard even a small virtue and accomplish them with great effort. Likewise, one should not be indifferent toward small negativities but should give them up.

We need to have a precise understanding of what a "misdeed" refers to in general. Not all misdeeds are included in the ten nonvirtues; however if we subsume the main or generic misdeeds, they would mostly fall under those ten. Likewise, the main virtuous deeds are included among the virtues of abandoning the ten nonvirtues, thus we must practice the ethics of abandoning the ten nonvirtues. For a correct practice of that we must know what the faults are in engaging in the ten nonvirtues, and what the benefits of refraining from them are. To find heartfelt ascertainment in that, one needs reasoned conviction through an understanding of the presentation of the ten nonvirtues. Therefore, it is pertinent to elaborate a bit more on the ten nonvirtues.

Killing

To have a complete path of action of killing—the first among the three karmas of body—there are four factors that must be complete: basis, intention, performance, and conclusion. The basis of killing must be someone other than oneself. The intention has three parts: perception, motivation, and the three afflictions. Among those, one's perception must be unmistaken. If someone who wants to kill Tashi perceives Tsering as Tashi and kills them instead, then because the perception was mistaken the actual path of action is incomplete. [306]

With respect to the affliction, one can be motivated by any of the three poisons to kill. Out of attachment, when an animal one owns becomes unbearably ill, one might kill them thinking they would be better off dead than suffering from the illness, or one might kill them out of desire for meat, skin, bones, and so forth. Killing one's enemies, mosquitoes, or bedbugs and so on out of anger is to be motivated by aversion. Killing an animal as a sacrificial offering thinking it is a virtuous activity is to do so out of ignorance.

The required motivation is an unceasing desire to kill. The performance can be through any harsh or gentle means such as using a weapon, poison, or black magic, and is carried out by oneself or another you have made to do it. The conclusion is the death of that being who was to be killed before oneself dies, and at that point the path of action of killing is complete.

If monasteries or organizations order a certain quantity of meat from a butcher, even though the direct killer is the butcher, whoever ordered the meat has a complete path of action of killing. If, in a city with a huge population, a few people do not eat meat, then it might seem like it does not make much of a difference to the lives of sentient beings. However, it is unacceptable to forget the relationship of a seller existing if there is a consumer. As it says in Bhāvaviveka's *Heart of the Middle Way*:

Since, at that time, there is no harm toward it . . .

If you say that animals are not harmed when you eat the meat because the harm has already transpired, even though there is a convention that one may eat meat that is free from you seeing, hearing, or doubting that it was killed especially for you, still, however many meat eaters there are, to that extent animals' lives are preyed on, and so it is important to avoid meat as much as possible. [307] Especially these days when there are so many methods to kill an animal to make its meat taste better, or huge populations of animals confined together in small spaces. These are horrifying situations.

Moreover, killing others through cursing them with black magic and similar is comparable to slaughter.

Stealing

Taking what is not given involves a basis that does not belong to oneself and is owned by another, such as gold, that one has perception of it as that and, motivated by any affliction, wishes to seize it. The performance is taking it through various means, and concluding it with the thought, "I have acquired it."

The basis is something that meets a certain value, does not belong to oneself, and is owned by another. The intention is an unmistaken perception of the object as that. With respect to the affliction, one can steal because of attachment that sees the object to be stolen as attractive; one can steal through aversion through wanting to separate one's enemy from their prized possession; and one can steal through ignorance, as in the proverb, "When the Brahmin is in trouble he proclaims stealing to be dharma." Thus, the affliction can be any of the three poisons. The motivation must be an unceasing desire to steal. The performance is taking it through force, or sneakily, or through deception. The conclusion is the thought, "I have acquired it." At that point the path of action of stealing is complete. Workers in societies who use public property for private purposes and are obliged to pay taxes but do not do so are in fact stealing.

Sexual Misconduct

Sexual misconduct involves a basis that is either (1) that which one should not have intercourse with—someone who belongs to another, one's close relative, the mouth, the anus, and so forth, or (2) one's spouse who one can have intercourse with, yet near a holy object, or while pregnant, or when abiding in the one-day precepts.

One perceives them as such and, motivated by any affliction and a wish to have intercourse, endeavors to engage in it. The conclusion is when the two sexual organs meet.

The bases of sexual misconduct are four: inappropriate objects of engagement, inappropriate body parts, inappropriate places, and inappropriate times. [308] Regarding inappropriate objects of engagement, they are the spouses claimed by another, ordained people, persons without willingness,[68] close relatives, a prostitute paid for by another, members of one's own sex, and eunuchs.[69]

Inappropriate body parts are everything except the vagina. Inappropriate places are near objects of refuge, in the presence of other people, or in uncomfortable places and so forth that hurt the person you are having intercourse with. Inappropriate times are during the day, during menstruation, while pregnant, during an illness or disease that makes intercourse unsuitable, more than five times in one day, during the one-day precepts, and so forth.

The intention requires an unmistaken perception. The affliction can be desirous attachment, or hatred such as when raping an enemy, or ignorance such as engaging in a sexual ritual as a pretext [for sex]. The performance is the touching together of the two organs, and so forth, and the conclusion is experiencing pleasure. At that point the actual path of action is complete.

Lying

Out of the four nonvirtues of speech, the first, lying, involves a basis to whom you state that you have clairvoyance, for example, when you do not have it, and whose perception is converted to thinking that is the case. One is motivated by any affliction to desire to say such, and the performance is either a physical or verbal expression indicating that. The conclusion is when the meaning is understood.

The basis of lying requires another person who can speak and understands meaning. The intention is a desire to change their perception so that they think they did not see what they saw, and so forth. The affliction can be any of the three poisons, and the motivation is an unceasing desire to tell [the lie] and change their perception. The performance is their accepting it through you verbalizing it or not—that is, their understanding it through your physical gestures. The conclusion is their comprehension, and at that point the path of action is complete.

However, as for telling truths that would become a cause for nonvirtue, it is taught that when answering one should try to change the topic, getting them to forget the original point.

Divisive Speech

The second nonvirtue of speech is **divisive speech. The bases are two people, for example. One perceives them as such, and, motivated by any affliction, desires to split them up. The performance is telling them things that have the potential to divide them, and the conclusion is up to their understanding of the meaning.** [309]

The bases of divisive speech are any harmonious or disharmonious people. The intention is an unmistaken perception. The affliction is any of the three poisons. The motivation is an unceasing desire to split them up. The performance is telling either truth or lies to divide the harmonious, or to not allow the disharmonious to reconcile. The conclusion is discord among them through understanding your words. When this happens the path of action is complete.

Harsh Speech

The third of nonvirtues of speech is **harsh speech. The basis is a person you find unpleasant, whom you perceive as such, and, motivated by any affliction you desire to say harsh words to them. The performance is saying something unpleasant that hurts their feelings. The conclusion is their understanding your words.**

The basis of harsh speech is someone to whom you have a vindictive attitude. The intention is an unmistaken perception. The affliction can be any of the three poisons. The motivation is an unceasing desire to say harsh words. The performance is saying harsh words to them whether true or false. The conclusion is their understanding your words. At that point the path of action is complete, and therefore saying such words to an inanimate object does not complete the path of action.

Idle Talk

The fourth nonvirtue of speech is **idle talk. The basis is any pointless speech that does not fall under the previous three categories of nonvirtuous speech that one perceives as such. Motivated by any affliction, one wishes to say something arbitrarily. The performance is to commence reciting non-Buddhist scriptures or secret mantras of Brahmins, telling stories for entertainment about the king, his ministers, war, thieves and so forth, or singing out of attachment, reciting the words of a play, or practitioners of virtue flattering others to obtain their requisites. The conclusion is when one has finished talking.**

The bases of idle talk are senseless topics that are a condition for distraction. The intention is unmistaken perception. The affliction can be any of the three poisons. The motivation is an unceasing desire to speak. The performance is commencing to say such things. [310] The conclusion is upon having spoken. From among karmas of speech, idle talk is the lightest, yet because it is most likely to occur it is the most harmful.

Covetousness

Out of the three nonvirtues of mind, the first is **covetousness. The bases are the possessions of another. One is motivated by a mind of greed, thinking, "If only I had that!" by way of any affliction possessing any of the five factors: (1) any mind attached to one's own** possessions, (2) malice, (3) a mind wanting to experience having the possessions of another, (4) an envious mentality, and (5) an attitude that has suppressed the shame and the faults associated with greed. The performance is mental exertion toward acquiring it. The conclusion is upon wishing for it.

The basis of covetousness is an object that one has no influence over and is owned by another. The intention is an unmistaken perception. The affliction can be any of the three poisons, including a mind of attachment, an intent to accumulate the items, malice, and so forth. The motivation is an unceasing desire to acquire that object. The performance is mental exertion, even without physical or verbal effort, that intensifies the desire to acquire the object. The conclusion is upon being decided that one will try to acquire it. At that point the path of action for covetousness is complete.

A mind fretting about one's wealth diminishing, or a hoarding mentality, holding on tightly to things as dear through the desire not to be separated from them are similar to covetousness.

Regarding **malice, the basis is a sentient being one finds unpleasant, which one perceives as such. The motivation is a mind wishing to kill them, bind them, and so forth due to any affliction that has one of the following five characteristics: (1) hostility that characterizes them as a cause of harm; (2) impatience with those being harmful; (3) resentment through constant recollection of improper mental engagement; (4) hatred that thinks, "How nice it would be if they were beaten or died"; (5) and an attitude that has suppressed associated shame or faults.**

The performance is mentally seeking to do those things. The conclusion is resolving to carry out those actions when you have the ability. [311] It is said that thinking, "It would be great if I were Brahmā!" and thoughts such as, "If only this person would die," are similitudes of covetousness and malice.

The basis of malice is another person to whom you have ill will. The intention is an unmistaken perception. The affliction can be any of the three poisons. The motivation is an unceasing desire to harm another physically or verbally. The performance is that thought of engaging in the physical or verbal action. The conclusion is upon resolving to beat them and so forth. At that point the path of action of malice is complete.

Wrong Views

The third misdeed of the mind is wrong **views. The basis is, for instance, karma and effect. One perceives it as nonexistent, and, motivated by any affliction, desires to deny it. The performance is thinking it to not exist, and the conclusion is being decisive about that.**

The bases of wrong views are existent objects such as karma and effect. The perception is perceiving your false view as true. The affliction is any of the three poisons. The motivation is an unceasing desire to deny [their existence]. The performance is to begin to deny causes, effects, actions, and things that exist. The conclusion is the certainty or resolve that you have denied [their existence]. At that time the path of action of wrong views is complete. It is said that from among the ten nonvirtues, wrong views are the heaviest.

Distinctions of weight has two parts:

(a') The weights of the ten paths of nonvirtuous action
(b') A brief discussion of the doors to powerful karma

The weights of the ten paths of nonvirtuous action has five parts:

(1') Heavy due to attitude
(2') Heavy due to performance
(3') Heavy due to lacking an antidote
(4') Heavy due to clinging to what is wrong
(5') Heavy due to the basis

The ten nonvirtues **also have differences in heaviness among them,** and therefore **those motivated by strong affliction** are *heavy due to attitude.* Whatever misdeed you delight in and perform yourself or make others perform, do repetitively, or engage in to bring about maximum suffering to the object are *heavy due to performance* [312]. Those *heavy due to lacking an antidote* are done (1) without performing rites of confession and vowing not to repeat them at the appropriate times, and not striving in virtuous practice; (2) without an attitude of shame or embarrassment; (3) without strong regret for misdeeds done, and so forth.

Engaging in thoughts and deeds based on wrong views that take nonvirtuous sacrificial offerings and so forth to be correct are *heavy due to clinging to what is wrong.* Those that are *heavy due to the basis* are **killing one's guru or parents,** killing those with qualities, exalted beings, and persons who contribute to the common good, **stealing their offerings** or property, **deceiving, dividing, using harsh words, being covetous or malicious,** and so forth; **furthermore, killing animals, for instance, that are big-bodied is** explained as a heavy misdeed due to the extra pain inflicted; **stealing valuable or many objects; having intercourse with those one should not, such as with those who are celibate;** lying because you wish to deceive and cheat another; **telling a lie that splits the sangha;** splitting up long-term friends, spiritual teachers, harmonious relatives; using harsh words against them; harboring malice at the thought of performing heartfelt confession for harm one has done to them, to the destitute, and to those without fault; and wrong views **asserting that there cannot be any arhats,** and so forth.

One can infer that perpetuating such **misdeeds joyfully, without confession and vowing to restrain, makes them extremely heavy. On the other hand, their opposites**—such as those performed merely without strong affliction—**are relatively lighter.**

A brief discussion of the doors to powerful karma has four parts:

(1') Powerful in terms of recipient

(2') Powerful in terms of support

(3') Powerful in terms of objects

(4') Powerful in terms of attitude [313]

There are four doors to powerful karma. The first is "powerful in terms of recipient." Vast merit comes from slightly helping an exceptional object, even without strong intention, and even through slight harm toward them you accrue huge faults. The second is "powerful in terms of support." Those who are knowledgeable, not knowledgeable, ordained, lay, ordinary beings, ārya bodhisattvas, and so forth, have differences with respect to the strength of benefit and harm from their misdeeds and virtue due to the influence of their own support. The third is "powerful in terms of objects." Generosity of Dharma and offering of one's practice are superior to material generosity and offerings. Using this as an illustration, apply it to other instances. The fourth is "powerful in terms of attitude." In comparison to all sentient beings making vast offering until the end of the eon, a bodhisattva's offering of a single flower with a mind wishing to achieving buddhahood has greater merit. Likewise, just as there is a difference in the strength, duration, and so forth of attitudes, such as those focusing on superior and inferior objects of attainment, or focusing on one's own or others' interests, so too with regard to wrongdoing, the strength of the afflicted attitude and duration of it influence the difference in fault that comes from it.

An exposition of the effects has three parts:

(a') Fruitional effects

(b') Causally concordant effects

(c') Environmental effects

Moreover, just as sprouts will not deviate [from their seed] even if a variety of seeds have been planted, so too from an extremely heavy misdeed one is born into the fruitional effect of a hell being; from a medium misdeed as a hungry ghost; and from a lesser misdeed as an animal.

Killing has the causally concordant effect of a short life; of stealing, a lack of resources; of sexual misconduct, an unfaithful spouse; of lying, slander; of divisive speech, few friends; of harsh words, hearing many unpleasant things; of idle talk, others not taking your words seriously; of covetousness, not accomplishing your wishes; of malice, great fear; and of wrong views, confusion with respect to correct views. [314]

Environment effects are karmic effects that ripen commonly for sentient beings. From killing, food, drink, and medicine have little potency; from stealing, crops become fewer; from sexual misconduct, living where there is much filth; from lying, great fear and deception in that place; from divisive speech, a place that is uneven and difficult to traverse; from harsh speech, an unpleasant place having logs, thorns, and so forth; from idle talk, trees not bearing fruit; from covetousness, the gradual diminishing of excellent things; from malice, internal conflict [with family and so forth], and human and nonhuman violence; and from wrong views, misperception of what is right and wrong.

Due to these, fruitional and causally concordant effects ripen upon the person, and environment effects arise in the place or area that person lives.

Contemplating white karma and its effects has two parts:

(i)   White karma
(ii) The effects of white karma

These topics include the karmas starting with applying yourself to correctly refraining from the paths of actions of the ten nonvirtues due to a virtuous mind that sees them as faults, and continues through to the subject of the karmas of body, speech, or mind from having ulti- mately refrained from them, and their respective fruitional effects of attaining a body support of a higher rebirth, and attaining the good results that are opposite from the aforementioned causally concordant and environmental effects of the ten nonvirtues.

A presentation of other classifications of karma has two parts:

(i) The distinction between (1) projecting and (2) complet- ing karma

(ii) Karmas whose effects are (3) definite or (4) not definite to be experienced

Thus, there are four types of karma.

The Distinction between Projecting and Completing Karma

Even though one may attain the body support of a human, a high rebirth that is projected by virtuous projecting karma, due to that sup- port being completed by nonvirtuous completing karma, either body, speech, or mind could be debilitated, or in that lifetime one could face adverse circumstances such illnesses, calamities, or many misfortunes.

On the other hand, despite having attained an animal's body, such as a dog's, for instance, projected by nonvirtuous projecting karma, it can be completed by virtuous completing karma so that the dog has loving owners who take care of it, for instance.

There are also situations where both the projecting and completing karmas are virtuous, or both nonvirtuous—thus there are four possi- bilities altogether. [315]

Karmas Whose Effects Are Definite
or Not Definite to Be Experienced

There are karmas whose effects are definite or not definite to be experienced. Out of the two—those definite and not definite to be experienced—the indefinite can indeed also be explained as those that will not yield a fruition if one does not meet with the conditions, and will yield such if the conditions are met with. However, most of the karma we have accumulated was motivated by the three poisons in an intense manner, were misdeeds performed continuously, or were accumulated with respect to an extraordinary object and so forth, and thus we have many that are definite to be experienced. Ācārya Vasubandhu, in his *Treasury of Knowledge*, states that there are three that are definite:

> The definite are of three, those whose results are to be
>   experienced, and so forth,
> in this life, and so forth.

There is a difference in time they will be experienced: (1) karma that will be experienced in this life, (2) that which will be experienced in the next life, and (3) that which will be experienced in distant lifetimes. Karma that will be experienced in this life is karma accumulated in the earlier part of our lifetime that is experienced later in life. For example, in an account from the past, someone who verbally abused the sangha by calling them "women"[70] experienced in that very lifetime their genitals transforming, and for one hundred lifetimes was born with a female body, thus having both those to be experienced in the next life and distant lifetimes.

Moreover, if one has a karma to be reborn in a bad rebirth, one will not be able to attain even the forbearance level of the path of preparation in this lifetime; if one has a karma to definitely be reborn in the desire realm, then one will not be able to attain the result of freedom from attachment; if one has a single karma that leads to definite rebirth in cyclic existence, then one will be unable to become liberated from cyclic existence in that lifetime, and so forth.

Having ascertained this presentation of karma and its effects as just explained, investigate your own three poisons and the killing, stealing, and so forth motivated by those and see which one you have an obvious liking for. Make those appear in your mind, from the basis up to the conclusion. When intense aversion toward your enemy, or overwhelming emotional attachment toward a sentient being or an object arises, focus on it very tightly with mindfulness and introspection. Although so many misdeeds have been accumulated prior that were not caught by introspection, those accumulated have not been identified as accumulated. [316] As [introspection] is catching them now, make sure to apply the antidote as soon as they arise. Merely that is not enough, however, as one should strive to accomplish the ten virtues.

Since they must be identified, the opposites of the ten nonvirtues are the ten virtues. To illustrate their results: from abandoning killing by way of powerful virtue, one achieves the fruitional result of a human body, the causally concordant result of a long life, and the environmental result of potent medicine, and so forth. Contemplate these well as being opposites of the results of the nonvirtues, then meditate on these until aspiration and joy arises.

If one finely analyzes the crucial points of the system of virtue and nonvirtue, then generosity, for instance, that is conjoined entirely with a virtuous mind with respect to the aforementioned basis, intention, performance, and conclusion, is solely white karma. Killing, for instance, done for oneself and conjoined only with a wicked mind with respect to the entirety—from basis to conclusion—is solely black karma.

Killing one person to save the lives of many, for instance—a performance that is the cause of their death—is a weak nonvirtuous karma that gives rise to a causally concordant effect of suffering. However, since the distinction of the intention is a powerful causal virtue, it yields a happy fruitional and environmental effect. Thus, it is a black karma whose white fruition is that which is to be adopted. Furthermore, performing generosity without attachment but with an intention to kill many beings, for instance, has (1) a distinction of intention that is a powerful nonvirtue, which yields fruitional and environmental results that are only suffering, and a causally concordant result of a short life; and (2) a result of prosperity in resources, thus a mix of black and white results; therefore, since it is a white karma with a black fruition, it must be abandoned. It is vital to also contemplate the subtleties of karma and effect involving these situations and to adopt and discard as necessary.

Those with meditation hats, belts, and invisibility sticks in their webbed pouches who keep a fixed expression with raised eyebrows, however, mostly adopt and discard through having only a rough idea of the ten nonvirtues, yet that is already quite astute for them! [317]

Contemplating karma and its effects in detail has three parts:

 a" The qualities of the fruitions
 b" The effects of fruitions
 c" The causes of fruitions

There are eight qualities of the fruition of karma: excellent lifespan, excellent complexion, excellent family lineage, excellent privilege, authoritative words, renown as a great power, being a male, and having strength. The other two outlines likewise have eight.

In particular, the causally concordant methods for acquiring a body support endowed with these eight qualities of fruitions are saving others' lives; offering butter lamps to representations [of the Three Jewels]; respecting others as a servant would; striving in generosity; being careful with one's speech; making aspirational prayers to have a multitude of qualities; not performing castrations and perceiving being a woman who is more easily harmed, as disadvantageous[71]— being a male enables one to have less fear when staying in crowded places, and so forth, and to practice Dharma in isolated places, thus the intention here is that there are less obstacles if one is a male; and striving oneself to accomplish what others are unable to do, and so forth. In order for these to accomplish the qualities of lifespan, color, family lineage, excellent privilege, authoritative words, great power, being a male, and power, you must seriously contemplate them with aspirational joy as before.

The ten virtues are not a mere abstention from the ten nonvirtues, and thus, for example, merely not killing is not the abandonment of killing. The ethics of abandoning killing is to commit to properly refraining from the action of killing while viewing it as a fault and applying the antidotes with mindfulness and introspection. That kind of powerful virtue is conjoined with an intense virtuous mind during the initial motivation, in-between performance, and conclusion, and is ornamented at the end with pure dedication. If you practice the ethics of the ten white virtues that are pure in the preparation, actual act, and conclusion, then not only will you achieve a high rebirth next life, you will also achieve one with the eight qualities of a fruition—the consummate concordant conditions to easily achieve the state of omniscience, and strongly effective in accomplishing virtue. [318]

How to Engage in Virtue and Disengage from Nonvirtue Having Contemplated Karma and Its Effects in General and in Detail

This has two parts:

a" General explanation
b" Purification through the four powers in particular

Purification through the four powers in particular has four parts:

  1" The power of remorse
  2" The power of applying antidotes
  3" The power of turning away from faults
  4" The power of the support

At the end of both analysis and placement meditation on the nature of virtue, nonvirtue, and their effects, in order to accomplish the aforementioned ten virtues and achieve a good basis for accomplishing omniscience, you must definitely not be tainted by the aforementioned nonvirtues nor newly accumulate them. However, you have accumulated only a mere quantity of misdeeds in this lifetime which you directly perceive. That cannot compare in the slightest to the countless misdeeds you have accumulated in many lifetimes not only for yourself but for the sake of leaders, friends, children, relatives, women, servants, monastic communities, and so forth, as it states in *Letter to a Friend*:

> Do not commit misdeeds,
> even for Brahmans, bhikṣus, gods, guests,
> your father, mother, child, queen, or your retinue,
> for there is no co-sharer of the fruition of hell.

When experiencing the fruition of committing a misdeed for the sake of someone else, it comes to oneself alone, and is not divided up among them. Moreover, since karma that is definite to be experienced has been explained in Abhidharma literature as irreversible, when you start to panic from thinking that whatever you do you most likely will not become free from cyclic existence, know that our teacher, skillful and compassionate, explained it thus to the lower vehicles, to whom he taught many interpretable and definitive teachings; how-

CULTIVATING CONVICTION IN KARMIC CAUSALITY 349

ever, he taught as the definitive meaning that even extremely serious misdeeds of the heinous crimes can be purified through confession and vowing to refrain. Thus, it states in *Letter to a Friend*:

Whoever was careless before,
upon becoming conscientious at a later point,
is beautiful like the moon without clouds,
like Nanda, Aṅgulimāla, Ajātaśatru and Udayana.

The Buddha's younger brother Nanda was extremely attached to his wife; Aṅgulimāla was one person shy of killing one thousand people, and Ajātaśatru killed his father Bimbisāra; yet through confession and vowing to refrain, they became purified. [319] The former two achieved arhatship. Although Udayana killed his mother, it is said that through regret and correct adopting and discarding he was born in hell only [quickly, like] the bounce of a silk ball, then achieved the result of stream entry in front of the Bhagavān.

Thus, move your mind with strong renunciation, thinking, "Even if I cannot achieve as much as that, I will close the door to lower rebirths." Place representations of enlightened body, speech, and mind, the objects to whom you will confess, and firmly visualize them as the actual jewels. Start with a mind of strong regret toward previous misdeeds, revolted like having swallowed poison, and a mind of restraint that vows to never commit the acts again, even at the cost of one's life. Then, just like one relies on white panacea medicine to overcome poison, the actual practice is to make prostrations together with reciting the *Confession through the Four Powers* authored by the great lord Tsongkhapa, and furthermore the *Sūtra of the Three Heaps*, exceptional dhāraṇīs that purify bad rebirths and misdeeds, chant the names of the tathāgatas, and so forth. This is the actual practice [of confession] and is like taking the [universal remedy] *karpo chikthup* to fight poison.

The power of applying antidotes has six parts:

(a) Reading the profound sutras
(b) Meditating on emptiness
(c) Relying on dhāraṇī mantras
(d) Constructing representations
(e) Relying on making offerings
(f) Relying on names [of the buddhas]

The confession rite from the *Golden Light Sūtra* taught in the context of remorse in the great treatises is intended as a review of one's faults. Moreover, in the context of applying the antidotes: reading sutras, constructing holy bodies, making offerings, and so forth, are from the perspective of activities normally performed in session breaks. Sealing with suchness is not fixed with respect to actual sessions or breaks, but depends on the level of sharpness of the person. Furthermore, it is explained that a monastic, for example, repairs downfalls during the actual session, and thus these must be practiced by way of distinguishing general approaches from exceptions. [320]

Thus, ideally, you would never be tainted by faults, and if you happen to be tainted then you should make sure that they are as weak as possible. Moreover, strive to make your white virtues complete with respect to preparation, actual act, and conclusion, and as powerful as possible.

Concluding Verses

The blind who view adopting and discarding
through the cataracts of thick ignorance toward rebirth,
still boast of the importance of washing off the black smudges
   and stains
on one's own face and clothes.

For the sake of wealth that, although accumulated, will
　　disappear
without a trace like a bird's flight path and patterns in water,
some toil with intense, overwhelming effort
with their three doors for that end.

They protect friends and overcome enemies in this short life,
slaving away to the distraction of the eight worldly dharmas,
which are like the joys and sorrows in dreams,
but I fear these will become the kindlewood for the flames of
　　Unrelenting Hell.

It is true that ignorant fools engage in nonvirtuous deeds
for the sake of this life,
but how embarrassing that I cast off my ultimate goal to
　　the wind
while I myself listen to many holy teachings.

Woe! Just as the autumn fruit ripens
from whatever seeds were planted in spring,
cherish these vital points of adopting and discarding,
having contemplated how white and black karmic causes yield
　　happiness and suffering.

With regret and restraint in front of the Three Jewels,
through the four opponent powers that enable me to confess
　　my collection of misdeeds,
the collection of causes for the terrible places of lower births
　　to which I am long accustomed
can be uprooted and cast away.[72] [321]

Training the Mind in the Stages of the Path Shared with Persons of Medium Scope

TRAINING THE MIND in the stages of the path shared with persons of medium scope has four parts:

a) The actual attitude training
b) The measure for having generated the attitude of training the mind in the stages of the path shared with persons of medium scope
c) Dispelling doubts with respect to mind training in the stages of the path shared with persons of medium scope
d) Determining the nature of the path leading to liberation

The actual attitude training has two parts:

i) Identifying the mind intent on liberation
ii) The methods for developing the mind intent on liberation

Identifying the Mind Intent on Liberation

What is the essence of the path for a person of medium scope in this context? It is very clear that so long as we have the confusion that is ignorance that grasps to true existence in our continuum, we will continue to accumulate the karma that creates our aggregates within existence. Moreover, if we give thought to the origins of suffering by

way of the twelve links of dependent origination, we can understand
how the suffering of birth, old age, sickness, and death are created by
their roots of karmic origins, how those karmic origins, furthermore,
meet back to ignorance, and thus how we cycle in samsara through the
group of causes and conditions of the thoroughly afflicted class within
the four noble truths. In addition, we can realize that one can exhaust
and abandon ignorance, and thus that samsara has an end. Thus, we
need to train in methods to abandon that, which involves progressively generating the three trainings one after the other.

So, what is it that we need to put into practice at present? First, we
must value and give importance to the training in ethical conduct as
the foundation. We should consider whichever set of vows we keep—
pratimokṣa, bodhisattva, or mantra vows—as our prestige, and in that
way guard our training without hypocrisy.

In this dark age wherein the teachings degenerate there is inconceivable benefit from properly guarding even a single training of the
Bhagavān. Therefore, it is important that Buddhist practitioners in
general, and particularly males and females who have gone forth from
the home into homelessness, confidently cherish their vows. [322]

Within the path to liberation—made up of the three trainings—one
must rely on the important topics of the practices of the paths of the
thirty-seven factors of enlightenment, principally taught in the context
of the training in wisdom. This is because ignorance acts as the root
of cyclic existence, and that ignorance is the apprehension of a self of
persons. Proponents of a lack of inherent existence posit both apprehension of a self of persons and apprehension of a self of phenomena
as the root of existence since their mode of apprehension is the same
despite their objects being different.

Furthermore, the apprehension of a self of persons becomes the
view of the transitory collection due to the apprehension of a self of
phenomena. Having brought the aggregates to mind, the awareness
that apprehends the true existence of the aggregates and conceives of

"I" forms the basis, and the thought, "I," imputed in dependence on those arises, which is the apprehension of a self of persons and view of the transitory collection apprehending "I." The antidote to that is as stated in the *Commentary on the "Compendium of Valid Cognition"*:

Love and so forth are not in contradiction with ignorance.
Therefore, they cannot annihilate the thoroughly faulted.

Meditation on love and compassion, for instance, does not directly uproot ignorance. Only the wisdom realizing selflessness that observes the same object of observation and has a directly contradictory manner of apprehension directly counters ignorance. Therefore, out of the three trainings, the training in wisdom is special insight (*vipaśyanā*) realizing modes [reality]. Generally, calm abiding (*śamatha*) and special insight that has the aspect of the coarse and subtle are common to both Buddhists and non-Buddhists; however, special insight realizing suchness is a special insight unique to Buddhism.

A mere realization of emptiness is not sufficient to generate that—it requires a clear appearance of [emptiness]. Therefore, there is no choice but to rely on the assistance of calm abiding. The way to accomplish this is the mode of sustaining mindfulness and introspection. Therefore, since pacifying subtle internal distractions relies on a previous cessation of coarse external fruitions, you must first train in the ethical conduct of stopping coarse distractions of body and speech. [323] Then you must train in calm abiding that restrains from subtle mental distractions. In dependence on that you then generate special insight realizing suchness, and then you generate an ārya path in your continuum that realizes emptiness directly. This is the practice of persons of medium scope.

In the context of persons of small scope it was taught that one takes as their goal a body of a high rebirth having freedoms and opportunities, and one engaged in ethical conduct to achieve that. Now, one has

356 THE FOURTEENTH DALAI LAMA'S STAGES OF THE PATH

already accumulated the collection of causes needed to accomplish such a body of a high rebirth, and at this time where one's mental faculties are at the level capable of training in the practices of persons of medium scope, what goal should one hold onto? Since the body of a high rebirth is also arisen from karma and affliction, it is a contaminated appropriated aggregate. Whatever is under the power of karma and affliction cannot possess ultimate happiness, nor has it reached the limit of purity and power. Therefore, you are still yet to achieve what goes beyond that—liberation that is eternal happiness and an exhaustion of suffering from the root. Thus, you must achieve that, **as it states in** *Lamp for the Path*:

> **Those who seek pacification of oneself alone,**
> **turning their back on the pleasures of existence,**
> **and reversed from negative actions,**
> **are said to be persons of middle scope.**

Knowing that all marvels of existence are deceptions, influenced by afflictions, in the nature of suffering of conditioning, and so forth, they turn their back on their happiness. Here, one can interpret "negative actions" not as the misdeeds of "virtue and misdeeds," or "meritorious and nonmeritorious actions," but rather as afflictions. Thus, you could say they reverse from the karma arisen from affliction that projects one into samsara. [324] Therefore, a being who strives to pacify afflictions together with their seeds and achieve the mere liberation of everlasting happiness by training in that way is of "middle scope."

Persons of small scope only strive for the mere state of a high rebirth as a god, human, and so forth, and those who do not hold that alone as their goal but strive for the mere happiness and peace of liberation from samsara in dependence on the three trainings are persons of medium scope. Thus, even though in this context one does not strive to attain mere peace alone, in order to accomplish

omniscience, you must definitely attain liberation before it. Therefore, with respect to training in the stages of the path shared with
persons of medium scope, a person who trains solely in the path
of persons of medium scope strives for partial peace, and therefore
their goal is only the peace of nirvana—the state of an arhat. Even
though that is the case, in this context one is only guided through
the stages of the path shared with persons of medium scope, and
not guided through the path of medium scope in its own right [as a
standalone path].

What is the purpose of being guided on the path shared with them?
Obscurations to knowledge are what obstruct us from achieving the
state of omniscience, and afflictive obscurations are what primarily
obstruct us from achieving liberation. If it were the case that we could
abandon obscurations to knowledge without having abandoned afflictive obscurations, then bodhisattvas would primarily engage in abandoning obscurations to knowledge. However, in actuality, knowledge
obscurations are the imprints placed by the afflictive obscurations.
Therefore, until that which places the imprints is exhausted, there is
no way to exhaust the imprints placed by it.

Thus, to enact the welfare of sentient beings requires having the pristine wisdom that knows exactly all aspects of their dispositions and
inclinations. For that one must exhaust the obscurations to knowledge
that obstruct understanding objects of knowledge, and there is no way
to achieve that without having abandoned afflictive obscurations that
deposit knowledge obscurations. [325] Therefore, even though striving
for nirvana that is peace—the goal that persons of medium capacity
strive for—is not the ultimate objective of those who seek highest, complete enlightenment, only through traversing that path can one achieve
omniscience. There is no alternative way. Thus, it is taught that one must
train in the path shared with persons of medium scope.

With respect to this, in order to train in that path, **having already
done the previous practices within the context of persons of small**

scope without getting the order wrong, one will not have to experience the suffering of suffering from being born into the three
lower migrations for the time being. Just like a person freed from
a dungeon is overjoyed but has no confidence they will not be put
back into prison, in the same way even if you will attain the body
of a happy migration in your next life through the power of purifying your past misdeeds by means of the four opponent powers, not
newly accumulating any misdeeds, and practicing the ten virtues in
this life, since you have not abandoned afflictions, how can you be
sure that you will not newly accumulate nonvirtue if your fear of
the suffering in your past lower migrations does not remain? If you
accumulate new misdeeds, then you will return to bad migrations
again. Thus, it says in the *Way of the Bodhisattva*:

> Having come to happy migrations so many times
> you enjoy the many pleasures,
> and after you die you fall down to bad migrations
> where the suffering is unbearable and long.

It is like, for example, when you are tormented by heat and you let
a cool breeze or running water fall on your body: some temporary
happiness arises, but after a while you suffer from the cold. In the
same way, every contaminated happiness is only the suffering of
change. Therefore, it is not suitable to trust in temporary happiness.
Right now, our obvious state of being is bound in samsara through
being forced to take continuous rebirth due to karma and afflictions.
Together with the mindset wanting to discard that through a mind
of renunciation, if you put in effort and become liberated from that
bondage, that is the state of peace.

Therefore, even while you suppress afflictions, which are the causes
for accumulating karma, and temporarily stop the misconduct arisen
from them, there is still no firm guarantee. [326] Thus, while you still

have afflictions in your continuum, you are absolutely at risk of newly accumulating bad karma if you meet with sudden conditions. Through your experience you can determine that your future is not secure until you have abandoned afflictions, and thus it becomes important to contemplate whether it is possible to have a separation that is the abandonment of those afflictions.

Even if afflictions such as attachment and aversion are in your mental continuum, consciousness in its entirety is not an afflicted awareness. Moreover, it is clear that if afflictions are absent your consciousness does not cease to exist. While the mind of our dual "psycho-physical" [organism] exists, awarenesses that are attachment and aversion are not always manifest. Furthermore, the clear and knowing mind and the afflictions do not exist in the manner of being forever unsuitable to be separated. Thus, the mind is like a king or president, and afflictions like their high ministers or trustworthy friends. It is like when a wicked minister gives a president malicious advice and a huge problem develops later, or an excellent advisor recommends a good way forward and they gain advantages from that; in the same way if strong attachment and aversion arise in our principal consciousness that is a clear and knowing awareness, then it is corrupted by those and one accumulates bad karma, like a good individual led astray by a wicked person. Or the opposite can happen—through an increase in faith and compassion one could accumulate good karma, and thus our root awareness is liable to transform, whether into good or evil.

Moreover, among the many mental factors that influence the mind, noble awarenesses such as compassion and altruism have backing supports. [327] If you analyze these awarenesses you can induce certainty with respect to multiple reasons for their dependability. Even though awarenesses such as attachment and aversion are quite strong when they arise, if you analyze the exact mode of attachment or aversion that it has toward its object, it becomes baseless, and thus you can infer it as such.

To briefly analyze the reasons for this: When compassion and faith arise, for example, their objects also seem temporarily self-supporting; however the infinite development of awarenesses such as faith does not in any way depend on the awareness apprehending a self. Negative awarenesses such as attachment, however, are necessarily dependent on apprehending a self, and thus must come into existence in dependence on the assistance of other misconceptions such as the ignorance apprehending a self and so on. Moreover, the object of the awareness apprehending true existence appears as real and self-supporting, and those that grasp at it as such are erroneously engaging the object. Therefore, when analyzing whether the way the object is apprehended is how it exists in reality, one can prove through reasoning that since the awareness apprehending true or inherent existence is mistaken, then true existence does not exist, and that it is possible to gain firm certainty of this.

Contemplating these and other things clearly indicative of such awarenesses being baseless, you can understand that so-called afflictions are suitable to be separated from the mindstream and in fact can be separated. Therefore, just as it is said in the *Great Treatise on the Stages of the Path*, "liberation" is freedom from bondage. What are we bound by? Both karma that propels us into samsara and afflictions bind us to this burden of our appropriated aggregates. This existence is other-powered and suffering. The bearer of the burden of those aggregates is the "I," or person, who is imputed in dependence upon the continuum of consciousness and is the experiencer of happiness and suffering.

When we become free of the karma and affliction that constantly oppress us with this burden of unwanted suffering, then we will be free of the burden of the aggregates, liberated from being other-powered, and released. [328] Therefore, if you are released from birth due to karma and affliction, you are *liberated* from such a birth, and thus it is called "liberation." [As Nāgārjuna states:]

Through exhausting karma and affliction, there is liberation.
Karma and affliction come through conceptual thought,
they come from mental fabrications,
and fabrications cease through emptiness.

Together with the mind of renunciation wishing to discard this situation of having to take rebirth and be thoroughly bound in samsara due to karma and affliction, liberation from these binds that is accomplished by effort is the state of peace. Therefore, liberation from being bound by the burden of the aggregates of karma and affliction is called "the state of peace," or "the state of liberation that is definite goodness."

When you realize that liberation not only exists, but is possible to achieve for yourself, in order to strive toward it having seen it as an excellent, reasonable, and worthwhile goal, first contemplate in fine detail what the faults are of being in the nature of suffering while existing under the power of karma and affliction. Having done this, then from merely seeing that we are afflicted by suffering we will give rise to the uncontrived awareness striving for liberation.

Therefore, [the mind] intent on that, the first root outline, "identifying the mind intent on liberation," has two sub-outlines in this text [of the Fifth Dalai Lama]:

- **Contemplating the suffering of cyclic existence**
- **Explaining the stages of practicing the path that liberates from that**

The *Great Treatise on the Stages of the Path* does not have these two outlines, but rather gives the following outlines [for "the method for developing the mind intent on liberation"]:

    a' Contemplating from the viewpoint of suffering and its
       origins
    b' Contemplating from the viewpoint of the twelve links of
       dependent origination

The first, [contemplating from the viewpoint of suffering and its origins], has two:

    1' Contemplating true sufferings: the drawbacks of cyclic
       existence
    2' Contemplating origins: the stages of entering into cyclic
       existence [329]

CONTEMPLATING TRUE SUFFERINGS: THE DRAWBACKS OF CYCLIC EXISTENCE

    a" The intention behind teaching true sufferings as the
       first of the four truths
    b" The actual meditation on suffering

The Intention Behind Teaching True Sufferings as the First of the Four Truths

I will first give a brief explanation as to how there came to be four truths in dependence on there being two truths that have discordant modes of how they appear and how they actually exist in reality, and then introduce the intention behind true sufferings being taught first.

Through the nature of meeting with conditions in our life whose way of appearance and mode of existence are discordant, our experience is such that even things that seemed like a good idea at first but later turned out to be mistaken can lead to many misunderstandings.

In our life we meet with conditions whose appearance and reality are inconsistent. Sometimes even wrong behavior leads to a good result, which gives rise to many understandings. Regarding this, it is not that we see an action would have a negative outcome and do it anyway, instead we assume an action to have a positive outcome through taking the reality of appearances for granted. In this way our hopes are dashed. Since the way things exist in reality is discordant from their appearance, when we actually go to carry out an action we most often end up with unanticipated repercussions.

Discordant modes of appearing and existing generally pervade all phenomena within samsara. For us, the root of our attachment and aversion—that awareness called "grasping at true existence"—is confused with respect to modes of appearing and modes of existing. Through that, many strong mistaken awarenesses—the "afflictions"— arise in our mind every day. Due to those, we accumulate bad karma, which in turn leads to all suffering that may arise. Therefore, the fundamental point is to understand reality as it is in order to eliminate those mistaken awarenesses. [330]

For that sake we must engage in adopting and discarding after having clarified how things appear and how they exist. Therefore, the Bhagavān taught the presentation of the two truths that are based on appearance and reality: a presentation from the perspective of temporary appearances, and a presentation from the perspective of the innermost nature, or state of existence, of all of those [appearances].

Ultimately, all Buddhist tenet systems present the two truths in terms of (1) the infallible dependent origination of appearances, and (2) their ultimate mode of existence—emptiness of inherent existence. These two must be proven as empty of inherent existence by reason of emptiness of inherent existence itself being the infallible dependent origination of appearances. Therefore, they are not the same two truths that are presented in non-Buddhist treatises.

Essentially, the four truths—true sufferings, true origins, true ces-

sations, and true paths—arose based on all phenomena having the
nature of dependent origination and changeability through a variety
of causes and conditions. If it were the case that all things, good or
bad, were not mutually arisen in dependence on causes and conditions, then true origins giving rise to true sufferings and true paths
establishing true cessations would not be possible. The relationship
between cause and effect exists through that principle of dependent
origination and interdependence. Furthermore, even suffering is a
result, a changeable phenomenon, and it also depends on causes and
conditions. Therefore the everlasting happiness that is the exhaustion
of suffering can be achieved through the power of skillful means, or
the power of conditions. Therefore, it was in dependence on this principle of dependent origination and interdependence that the stages of
engaging and disengaging with respect to the four truths was taught.

As Ācārya Āryadeva stated:

> How can anyone who has no aversion to this
> have dedication toward pacification? [331]

If a person does not have aversion toward cyclic existence, or strong
renunciation through being deeply fed up with it from seeing the
faults of suffering, then how can they be dedicated toward the sphere
of total pacification of the suffering of cyclic existence together with
its causes—that is, how can they have a genuine pursuit of liberation?
They cannot. Take for example our situation in exile: however much
we see the intensity of our hardship, that is how much stronger our
aspiration for achieving an autonomous homeland becomes. In the
case that we view this exile experience as a pleasant event then there
is no way that we would fervently think to become free of this and
return to an autonomous homeland. In line with this, the great gentle
protector Lama Tsongkhapa stated in his *Abbreviated Stages of the Path*:

Without making effort to contemplate the drawbacks of true
    sufferings,
a proper aspiration toward liberation will not arise,
and without contemplation of the stages of entering samsara
    through origins,
one will not know how to cut the root of samsara.

Therefore, it is vital to cultivate the disenchantment that is renunciation from existence and understand what binds you to samsara.

When the compassionate Teacher turned the first wheel of
Dharma starting with the four truths, he taught that all aggregated
and compounded phenomena are in the nature of the interdependence of causality of being arisen through mere causes and conditions. This is not a fabrication through the enlightened deeds of
the Buddha, and nor is it established through the karma of sentient beings, it is just the nature of things. Therefore, since both our
unwanted suffering and desired happiness are also among phenomena of that same nature, happiness and suffering must also arise
through mere causes and conditions. Thus, in terms the class of
suffering which we do not want, the Bhagavān taught "true sufferings" and their causes "true origins"—a pair of cause and effect of
the thoroughly afflicted class; in terms of the happiness we desire,
he taught "true cessations" and their causes, "true paths," a pair of
cause and effect of the thoroughly purified class, and thus there are
four truths. [332]

In summary, having contemplated the drawbacks of true suffering,
if you no longer desire suffering then you will want to seek out the
causes, or origins, of that suffering, and the need to investigate that
becomes important. Having made this inquiry, you must check if the
causes can be eliminated or not. If there is no way to eliminate them,
then there would also be no point contemplating suffering, and it
would be easier to try and be happy by pretending the suffering of

samsara is enjoyable. However, if there is a way that the causes of suffering can be eliminated, then it becomes imperative that we do not waste this opportunity to do so, and investigate it and destroy it no matter what. This is the way of the first two truths.

Having identified the causes of that suffering through your seeking, once you see that they can be eliminated, you understand that there exists the so-called "true cessation" that is the total pacification of all suffering—a separation from their causes. Thus, you will wish to achieve that, and not just casually wish for it, but you will develop a decisive mind that sees it as what is to be attained, as attainable, as necessary to attain, and endeavor at all costs to strive in the methods to attain it.

Thus, if the reasons behind why suffering is undesirable and that its causes can be abandoned convince you, and you become confident to take on the means to abandon them, then even though there will be temporary difficulties in striving in the methods to accomplish that, you will come to willingly face those hardships and continuously endeavor toward achieving this great purpose. This is the way of the latter two truths. [333]

The fact that when the kind Teacher first turned the three wheels of Dharma he used the four truths as the framework for the first Buddhist teachings is incredibly important, and I continue to explain that importance as I understand it to others.

As such, the Buddha taught modes of phenomena commencing from the teachings of noninherent existence in the middle turning of the wheel of the absence of characteristics on the basis of the first wheel of Dharma of the four truths, which is accepted by both Great and Lesser Vehicles. The teachings of emptiness concluded in a vast manner in the perfection of wisdom sutras—which teach emptiness explicitly and the hidden stages of clear realization implicitly—clearly indicate that whether or not true cessations, the third of the four truths, can be understood in detail, how one should achieve it, and if it can be attained, all depend on whether you understand the reality of the emptiness that is the lack of inherent existence of all phenomena. Thus these teachings thoroughly delineate the third truth. If you do not understand the topic of emptiness, you can make a mere guess as to whether liberation is actually achievable, but you will not be able to come to a definitive, precise conclusion.

According to the order of cause and effect within the four truths, true origins and paths are causes, and their respective results are true sufferings and true cessations. However, as it is said that teaching them in the reverse order is an essential point of practice; thus it is an important point that true sufferings were taught first.

Since the four truths start with suffering, and the way we are made to suffer is presented so extensively, some people get the impression that this is a depressing philosophy. [334] However, this is due to not understanding the manner of the path. In actuality, this very clear presentation of suffering itself is explained from the perspective of suffering not being the natural disposition of our mind and that the mind can be separated from it. Thus, leave aside this being depressing; it can only give us confidence.

There are many ways to contemplate suffering. In accordance with the intention of the omniscient [Panchen Lama] Losang Chökyi Gyaltsen's statements in his *Melody of Laughter of the Intelligent— Answers to Your Questions*: Even livestock have the wish to be free from the suffering of suffering, and furthermore even non-Buddhists have renunciation of the so-called suffering of change; that is, contaminated feelings of happiness which we normally assume are enjoyable.

Therefore, we must be able to perceive that compositional suffering, which is the nature of suffering of being composed of the appropriated aggregates, is the root of all faults. Our aggregates— the "appropriated aggregates"—have arisen through the power of karma and affliction and still act as a support for suffering in that they assist in the generation of affliction. Moreover, if you can understand how these aggregates that create even future suffering are in the nature of suffering, you will become free of the trap of the appropriated aggregates having given rise to a genuine interest in liberation.

If you do not have an understanding of that, you will not perceive the faults of cyclic existence—true sufferings—and therefore you will not desire to abandon their causes, you will not desire to achieve liberation, and you will not seek out the methods to abandon suffering. Due to this, there is no way you can attain the separation that is the total abandonment of resultant suffering together with its seeds. Therefore, it is a crucial point that you must strive for paths and cessations after having understood the nature of suffering and its origins—how karmic origins and afflictive origins that are the two causes for suffering actually give rise to a variety of suffering. In this way there is not a single one among all Buddhist teachings that is not summed up by the four truths. [335]

The Actual Meditation on Suffering

With respect to that, since it is of great importance to first contemplate true sufferings, the teaching on the first truth of suffering within the presentation of the four truths that are emphasized in this context of persons of middle scope has two sections:

1" Contemplating the general suffering of cyclic existence
2" Contemplating specific suffering

CONTEMPLATING THE GENERAL SUFFERING OF CYCLIC EXISTENCE

With respect to the first, in sutra it states:

Bhikṣus, this is the noble truth of suffering; this is the noble truth of origins.

This teaching of resultant true sufferings first and causal true origins subsequent to that may appear contrary to cause and effect; however it was intended for a specific purpose as shown in the *Four Hundred Verses*:

> If there is no end at all
> to this ocean of suffering,
> then why are you, O child,
> not afraid to sink into it?

If you apprehend resultant suffering as happiness, you will not fear or wish to abandon its causes—karma and afflictions. Thus, opposite to that, you stop the causes by not wanting their results. For example, if you are on top of dry ground and water suddenly appears and saturates you and your belongings, thus making you cold, that is true suffering; analyzing whence the water originated and ascertaining "it is from this direction!" is to ascertain the true origin; your body being free from cold is the true cessation, and diverting the passage of the water as a solution is the true path. As it states in the *Sublime Continuum*:

> Just as an illness is to be understood, its causes eliminated,
> well-being achieved, and the remedy relied upon,
> likewise suffering, its causes, their cessation, and the path
> are to be understood, eliminated, known, and relied upon.

If you do not recognize the suffering that comes from being saturated with water, you will not wish to stop the flow of water. If you do not understand the absence of being wet as happiness, you will not give rise to the wish to build a dike to stop the water. [336]

Having identified that any kind of happiness or suffering is a result, one then engages in adopting or discarding their causes; this is a crucial point. Having understood this well, one starts with contemplating true sufferings.

[Tsongkhapa's] lamrim discusses general and specific sufferings. His [eight] sufferings of birth, old age and so forth to the general [sufferings of cyclic existence] was done within the context of a highly elaborated presentation.

To extract the essence of this topic: As one has already finished meditating the three lower rebirths in the context of persons of small capacity and effected a genuine experience, then it is like someone who has vomited from alcohol poisoning being repulsed just from seeing alcohol: they do not need to intentionally think of the specific sour flavor or unpleasantness. This now comes as a side effect, just as flowers are naturally cut up as a horse gallops. Therefore, it is no longer a fault if one does not deliberately meditate on the suffering of lower rebirths.

With respect to contemplating [specific sufferings] primarily in connection to the suffering of happy rebirths—the crux of the matter—there are three points: The suffering of human beings; the suffering of the other two happy rebirths; and the ancillary meditation on the shared suffering of the six types of beings.

With respect to contemplating suffering—the drawbacks of cyclic existence—the first stage is to engage in methods to (1) reverse attachment to the experiences of this life by contemplating the suffering of lower rebirths, and (2) engage in methods to reverse attachment to the next life through contemplating the suffering of happy rebirths. Contemplation of the suffering of lower rebirths has not only been covered in the context of persons of small capacity, but when it comes to explaining the unseen sufferings of the hell beings, hungry ghosts, gods, and demigods, it also is very difficult without belief in the scriptures. Therefore, in this context the suffering of good rebirths is to be contemplated, and furthermore the contemplation of the suffering of the higher rebirth of a human is something we can perceive directly and can be understood relative to our own experience.

Contemplating the general suffering of cyclic existence has three parts:

(a) Contemplating the eight sufferings
(b) Contemplating the six sufferings
(c) Contemplating the three sufferings

The eight sufferings are

(i)   The suffering of birth
(ii) The suffering of old age
(iii) The suffering of sickness
(iv) The suffering of death [337]
(v)   The suffering of encountering the unpleasant
(vi) The suffering of parting from the pleasant
(vii) The suffering of not getting what you want
(viii) The suffering of the five appropriated aggregates

The Suffering of Birth

With respect to the first, those who have taken rebirth under the power of karma and affliction are a basis for the multitude of sufferings of aging, death, and so forth. Since their minds are thoroughly disturbed by the three poisons, they are of course ultimately not beyond dying with physical and mental difficulty. Although four types of birth are taught, this is principally from the perspective of those born from a womb.

Out of the four sufferings—birth, aging, sickness, and death—our human life begins with the suffering of birth. Thus, at the time of birth, since it is a womb birth, we are born with intense feelings of suffering. The five sufferings of birth were thus taught: (1) birth is suffering because it is painful, (2) birth is suffering because it is associated with negative tendencies, (3) birth is suffering because it is a basis for suffering, (4) birth is suffering because it is a basis for the afflictions, and (5) birth is suffering because it is in the nature of leading to unwanted separation.

Generally there are four types of birth: birth from a womb, miraculous birth, birth from warmth, and birth from an egg. However, it is not that birth through compassion and prayers does not exist, but rather the majority of births are without control and projected by karma and affliction, and thus one is born with intense feelings of suffering at the time of birth. Thus, birth is suffering.

Since these appropriated aggregates are the projected result of one's previously accumulated karma and afflictions, they are a continuation of the seeds that proliferate negative tendencies, and also are not suitable to employ toward virtue of body and mind. Therefore, they are associated with negative tendencies.

As soon as we take rebirth with appropriated aggregates projected by karma and affliction they act as the condition to definitely bring forth a further variety of suffering such as aging, sickness, and death. [338] Of course a situation is feasible in which birth only creates a support for suffering and does not assist in the further arising of affliction, but aside from such a case it assists in the arising of the three poisonous afflictions that thoroughly disturb the mind, and thus birth is a basis for affliction.

At the end of birth there is no avoiding death, and thus these appropriated aggregates that are the basis of suffering and affliction—not permanent or stable in the slightest—must die despite us not wishing it. Therefore, birth is in the nature of leading to unwanted separation.

Thus, when such aggregates are first born, they must experience intense feelings of suffering, as it says in [Candragomin's] *Letter to a Disciple*:

> Having entered the womb, which is like hell,
> you are obstructed by foul-smelling filth
> and thoroughly confined in pitch-black darkness.
> Your body is cramped up, and you must endure intense
>   suffering.

Under the stomach and above the intestines, you face the spine, and amid a foul smelling and unclean slurry you develop gradually from an oval shaped [embryo] to having arms and legs. During this time, if your mother eats or drinks something hot, you enter a fiery pit, and if she takes something cold you dwell in an icy cavity. When jumping, running and so forth you have a visionary experience similar to falling in an abyss, and so on—in this way the respective suffering of all of your mother's incautious actions befall you until you reach the 266th day, upon which the winds of karma face your head downward and you emerge out from between the extremely narrow pelvic bones at the door of the womb. At that time, you are born with the intensely painful feeling like that of insects eating the exposed raw flesh of an ox. Even for a while after birth if you are placed on soft bedding it is like being forced into a thorny pit in which the slightest sufferings of cold and heat are hard to bear. [339]

Even though you have already gone through these experiences in your past and present lifetimes, you cannot remember them due to the obscurations of the womb and your young age. Thus, meditate by way of inference as was done in the context of persons of small scope, contemplating the abovementioned sufferings happening to oneself. Having done this, if you were to at present enter into a pot that fits you for a day and it were filled up with filth such as urine and feces you would directly perceive how unbearable it is, and yet that would not even constitute a fraction of the suffering [explained] above. Therefore, it was taught that you meditate until you are revolted by taking even a happy rebirth, like seeing poisonous food that induces vomiting.

Whether or not such feelings are present at the time of birth, when first reincarnated in the womb and the body is first formed, either way it is clear that however much the body progressively becomes grosser the feelings of suffering become that much stronger. Moreover, while one is being born [from the womb] there is intense fear, as such most babies are born crying rather than coming out joyfully. Furthermore, if there is not someone properly supervising the birth and something irregular happens, the child can end up physically disabled or unable to survive, or the mother could lose her life. These and other difficulties that occur are the sufferings of birth.

Physicians currently state the degree to which the mother's mind is peaceful and relaxed while her child is in the womb can positively affect its development. Since this is explained from the perspective of the physical health of babies being observed directly, it would appear that due to the mother's thoughts the child also experiences mental feelings of happiness and suffering. [340]

The Suffering of Old Age

Likewise, also the suffering of old age has two levels of subtlety. The subtle suffering of old is the aggregates' being in the nature of change, moving toward old age moment by moment from the day one is born. With regard to the coarse [suffering of old age], *The Play in Full Sūtra* says:

Age makes attractive forms unattractive.

Age steals valor and strength.

Age steals happiness and belittles us.

Age also takes radiance and brings death.

Let us first take the examples of the ways the body degenerates: white hair, bent body, forehead covered in wrinkles, and so forth. The body you had when you were young that was straight-backed with black hair, that had skin that was wrinkle-free, youthful and so forth, although not swapped out for the body you have now, it has become what it is now with no difference to having been swapped. Again, as more days, months, years pass you will eventually diminish like the waning moon and enter into the mouth of the lord of death. Contemplate this until a strong sense of sadness arises.

Second, your body's degeneration is indicated by your inability to sit or stand well. When you walk, you are unsteady. When you talk the words do not come out clearly.

Third, due to your faculties deteriorating, your eyes, ears, and so on cannot see, hear, and so forth, as they did before. Your unclear memory leads you to inevitably forget things. If you eat and drink as much as you did before it gives you a variety of illnesses. Meditate on these as before. Of course, a young practitioner will not be able to comprehend the majority of the drawbacks such as white hair and so forth through inferring these based on their own experience. However, contemplate by observing an old person and concluding that they also were definitely not old and frail like this when they were born from the womb, and yet at some point this person who was young like me has become like this! It is taught to meditate in this way.

There are five sufferings of aging: (1) complete physical deterioration, (2) complete deterioration of strength, (3) complete deterioration of senses, (4) complete deterioration of enjoyment of objects; and (5) complete deterioration of life force. [341]

In brief, on top of bearing the burden of aging in which even oneself is unhappy and repulsed by the attractive youthfulness of the body deteriorating, one might rather choose to die than still live on in a feeble condition. That these and other sufferings of aging as found in Gungthang Rinpoché's teachings happen to ourselves is a firsthand observation for us.

In Tibetan society there is an excellent level of respect and compassionate care shown toward the elderly by younger relatives. Although in more developed countries the general populace might seem more impressive and held in high esteem, after they have retired from work and become old, they become unseen and forgotten, which is often a cause of depression. Some live in nursing homes like they are waiting for death, some are not respected by even their children, and on top of that suffer from not dying quickly enough.

When how we excelled in this life fades away and our life finishes with sad longing, that is the suffering of old age.

The Suffering of Sickness

With respect to the sufferings of illness, [use your own] experience of being affected by a strong illness in the past, or if one has not [experienced that], then use others to infer [this suffering], the way they are tormented by long-term imbalance of the [body's] elements or sudden torment from harmful spirits, weapons, and so forth is as stated in the *Play in Full Sūtra*:

> In the deep of winter, the harsh winds and blizzards
> steal the vitality from the grasses, shrubs, trees, and herbs.
> Likewise, disease takes the vitality from beings,
> and deteriorates their faculties, energy, and strength.

Contemplate how, due to being helpless through various torments such as the agony of extreme hot and cold and so forth, one's flesh and skin dries up and it is hard to move. Suspicious that one's favorite foods will negatively affect one's illness, doctors and so forth do not permit one to eat them, and unpleasant foods, multiple medicines, bloodletting, and moxibustion must be undertaken. [342]

In the *Great Treatise on the Stages of the Path* this topic is addressed in five points: (1) the nature of the body changing, (2) suffering and anguish increasing, (3) being unable to enjoy pleasant objects, (4) having to engage with unpleasant things despite not wanting to, and (5) losing your life force.

Some types of illness involve having to live with unrelenting, intense pain day and night, and even when the pain is not intense, the chronic aspect of it means one is never comfortable. Some are afflicted by a contagious illness or vomiting sickness, having to endure life like outcasts of society. The way in which all such unwanted things befall us is the way to contemplate the suffering of sickness.

The Suffering of Death

Regarding the suffering of death, the *Play in Full Sūtra* states:

> When it is time to die and pass on,
> one is forever separated from beloved people and possessions.
> There will be no returning or meeting again,
> just as the leaves fall from a tree, or the current of a river.

If one recovered from an illness then that amount of hardship was acceptable while endured. However, in most cases even though trying a variety of remedies the illness deteriorates and the doctors give up, a Bön ransom ritual is performed, loved ones surround oneself and lament, and the place is arranged for virtuous practices for the

378 THE FOURTEENTH DALAI LAMA'S STAGES OF THE PATH

dead and burial. You yourself have gone pale. Your mouth has dried. Your lips have shriveled. Your nose has shrunk. Your eyes have sunk. Your breathing is rushed. You regret your past misdeeds. You are separated from all excellences—relatives, friends, helpers, wealth, and possessions. The body you lovingly cared for is laid to rest on the bed and you must go to your next life under the power of strong attachment. Contemplate these ways you are tormented by strong suffering.

This topic also has five points in the *Great Treatise on the Stages of the Path*: (1) you are separated from pleasant possessions, (2) you are separated from beloved relatives, (3) you are separated from pleasant companions, (4) you are separated from your pleasant body, and (5) as you die you undergo terrible suffering and anguish. [343]

Recollect these sufferings in the same way you meditated on the aspects of death mentioned prior in the context of persons of small scope. Our lives started with the suffering of birth, at which point this new burden of appropriated aggregates that are other-powered by karma and affliction and the perfect material cause for a lifetime of calamity were created. Thus, in brief, since we have such a body of a living being, the sufferings of birth, aging, sickness, and death must occur. Moreover, everyone, whether a king, president, army general, scholar, fool, rich, poor, Eastern, Western, non-Buddhist, Buddhist, having faith in Dharma or lacking it, and so on, must unavoidably walk the path sufferings in the manner of those from that of birth up to that of death.

The Suffering of Encountering the Unpleasant

This is the suffering related to one's enemies as taught [in the *Great Treatise on the Stages of the Path*]. Regarding this, there is no need to mention the suffering of suspicion that your unpleasant enemy has armed one's body, life, or reputation. Even if you had to share a living space with your actual enemy or an unfriendly person you would be distressed and imagine shadowy figures [in the dark]. If that person were to go somewhere else, you would be joyous as if dawn had come. Thus, in this way contemplate the suffering of suspecting you will encounter a hostile enemy. Just as this should be contemplated, likewise make sure you are able to identify the real unpleasant enemy that makes us experience suffering without end—afflictions. Having done that, it is you alone who must free yourself from the suffering of encountering the real unpleasant enemy.

The Suffering of Parting from the Pleasant

One might also think of this as "the suffering related to loved ones." This is the intense suffering of the three doors that occurs when your relatives, friends, and especially your dearly beloved depart for another place and you recollect their qualities and excellent features. [344] If they return you are filled with great joy. Contemplate in this way the suffering of suspecting you will be separated from dear ones.

The Suffering of Not Getting What You Want

Also called "the suffering related to wanting," this is the suffering of businessmen, farmers, and so forth who work so hard but have their stock destroyed or crops ruined by hail; it is of leaders and maternal ministers—a ministerial position appointed to a family member of the king's wife when past monarchies existed—who could not overcome foes or retain allies; it is of some monastics—male and female—who cannot manage their ethical discipline due to their antidotes being weak, and their activities of hearing and reflection being unaccomplished due to inferior wisdom. These and so forth are the sufferings of not getting what is wished for. Moreover, the haughty, or strong, becoming weak, rich becoming poor, only one remaining from many people, or nothing remaining from an empire, and so forth.

In brief, through a multitude of undesirable factors such as hunger, thirst, heat, and cold, meditate on this very body itself being in the nature of suffering until experience arises from the depths of your heart.

In the *Great Treatise on the Stages of the Path*, the contemplation of eight and six types of suffering and so forth were taught in a general sense. However, the guiding instructions make this more practical: one first contemplates the seven main types of suffering as applied to humans, then after that the suffering of the two other happy states of rebirth and the three, six, and eight types of suffering are taught generally.

The Suffering of the Five Appropriated Aggregates

Accordingly, from among the eight types of suffering, both the first and the last are the most important. Thus, the Buddha's concise teaching of the eighth type with the phrase, "In brief, the five appropriated aggregates are suffering," was taught for the purpose of clearly indicating the following: The appropriated aggregates were established through karma and affliction and the body, furthermore, is connected to the appropriation of further bad states through karma and affliction; thus [345] in dependence upon its appropriation it induces suffering in further rebirths, too. Since you have appropriated this body controlled by karma and affliction it will induce suffering even in future lives, and thus is a "vessel for suffering." You have taken up an aggregate that is under the power of karma and affliction—the root of all that is unpleasant and all that goes wrong in the world—and thus exist in a state without self-control. Therefore, the Buddha taught this to clearly show that through their mere existence these appropriated aggregates are of the nature of suffering.

In the *Great Treatise on the Stages of the Path*, this section is followed by:

(b) Contemplating the six sufferings

(i)   The fault of uncertainty

(ii) The fault of insatiability

(iii) The fault of casting off bodies repeatedly

(iv) The fault of repeated rebirth

(v)   The fault of repeatedly changing from high to low
      status

(vi) The fault of having no companions

This is then followed by the contemplation on the three types of suffering. However, in this treatise, *Oral Transmission of Mañjuśrī*, the order is reversed, giving the contemplation of the three sufferings first and the six sufferings subsequent to that. The outlines will be explained in accordance with the outlines in the *Great Treatise on the Stages of the Path*:

2" Contemplating the specific sufferings

(a) The suffering of hell beings

(b) The suffering of hungry ghosts

(c) The suffering of animals

(d) The suffering of humans

(e) The suffering of demigods

(f) The suffering of gods

The suffering of the three lower rebirths have already been covered in the context of the person of small scope, and the suffering of humans has just been explained. Therefore, in this treatise only the contemplation of the suffering of the two other good rebirths—that of gods and demigods—is given.

Contemplating the suffering of the two other good rebirths has two:

(i) The suffering of desire realm gods

(ii) The suffering of the gods in the higher realms

The suffering of desire realm gods has three parts:

> (a') The suffering of dying and falling
> (b') The suffering of anxiety
> (c') The suffering of being cut, gashed, killed, and banished

The suffering of dying and falling has two parts:

> (1') The suffering of dying
> (2') The suffering of falling into lower realms [346]

Regarding these, *Letter to a Friend* states:

> **Their bodies turn an ugly color,**
> **they no longer like their cushions,**
> **their flower garlands wilt, and their clothing smells,**
> **an unfamiliar sweat breaks out over their bodies.**

> **These are the five signs that foretell the death of celestial ones.**

Although desire realm gods do not have the suffering of birth, old age, and so forth like humans, when death approaches they experience five signs of death: (1) their body suddenly loses its brilliant hue, (2) they no longer feel like sitting on their comfortable cushions, (3) their flower garlands wilt, (4) their clothes become filthy, and (5) an unfamiliar sweat breaks out on their body. They furthermore undergo the five close signs of death: (6) their body's light diminishes, (7) their bathing water adheres to their body, (8) their clothing and ornaments make unpleasant sounds, (9) they begin to blink, and (10) they become attached to a single object. They suffer through understanding that these are signs of death, and in particular these so-called "seers of the three times"—that is, gods with basic clairvoyance knowing past, present, and future occasions—also know where they will take rebirth if they check. Therefore, if it is the case that they will immediately take rebirth in hell, then they undergo unbearable, intense suffering as if they were already reborn in hell. Humans only have a doubt they might be born in hell while lacking absolute certainty, and for that reason it is said that the suffering of gods is considerably greater.

Furthermore, when they see gods with great merit, those with less become frightened. More powerful gods banish the weaker ones to other places. When they fight with the demigods they kill each other and cut and slice through each other's limbs and bodies. The suffering of the desire realm gods is indicated through these various forms of suffering. Even though gods of the [form and] formless realm do not have those manifest sufferings, just like a ship's pigeon eventually returns back to the ship, the impetus of their meditative stabilization eventually runs out, and, after they die, they have to undergo the manifest suffering of the desire realm again. Meditate well on these things. [347]

Demigods are miserable because of their overwhelming jealousy of the wealth of the gods. This leads them to battle the gods, and in doing so they experience much suffering, such as their bodies getting slashed and split apart. As it says in the *Great Treatise on the Stages of the Path*:

They are intelligent, but they have fruitional obscurations; therefore, their basis is unsuitable for seeing the truth.

Contemplating the Three Sufferings

(i) The suffering of suffering

(i) The suffering of change

(iii) The pervasive suffering of conditioning

With respect to the contemplation of the suffering common to the six types of beings, whoever is not free from cyclic existence could become a universal monarch or Brahmā through the power of their merit and still become a slave again. Such is the suffering of becoming.

When Tsongkhapa taught the eight types of suffering in his *Great Treatise on the Stages of the Path*, he applied the Buddha's statement, "In brief, the five appropriated aggregates are suffering" to the eighth type, and then taught the three types of suffering in relation to the appropriated aggregates. He used the term "the suffering of certain becoming" to describe a situation in which persons not free from cyclic existence, although already having become Brahmā or a universal monarch at present, again become a slave, for instance. Appropriating those aggregates acts as a condition to induce continual future suffering yet again; therefore, from that perspective, the multiple sufferings of birth, old age, sickness, and death that happen to one's current aggregates are taught as "suffering based on that already created."

The suffering of birth, old age, sickness, and death in this life is suffering that has already been created. The suffering of suffering is, for example, the increase in pain from a painfully inflamed boil coming into contact with an irritant such as a saline solution.

The feelings of suffering, together with their internal and external conditions, and concomitant mental factors in dependence upon which feelings of suffering arise are all the suffering of suffering. [348]

When you get tired from walking, sitting seems pleasurable, but then after a while your limbs and waist start hurting. This is the suffering of change. Likewise, the food you eat when you are hungry is delicious, but if you eat too much you feel sick and no longer wish to even smell the same food. In brief, whichever contaminated happiness you overindulge in leads to suffering again, and thus they are all said to be the suffering of change. The pleasurable feelings of beings in cyclic existence—what we normally perceive as pleasurable—eventually give rise to suffering, and thus they are given that name.

As it states in the second chapter of Dharmakīrti's *Commentary on the "Compendium of Valid Cognition"*:

> Because of being impermanent it is suffering.

This powerful statement indicates that because something is impermanent, it changes moment to moment, and even though it changes in this way, its disintegration does not depend on any other causes, but rather the very cause that gave rise to it has created it in the nature of disintegration. Therefore, this appropriated aggregate is powered by causes. Its cause is the unfortunate "ignorance that is first among the twelve links of dependent origination." Without a basis for mental peace, there is only suffering.

Pervasive suffering of conditionality is like someone stuck in an icy cave having no opportunity to be warm until freed. It is the basis of all suffering. Since those aggregates arise as suffering of conditioning from their mere establishment, the Buddha thus taught, "The five appropriated aggregates are suffering." **To summarize, it is only suitable that anyone who has taken up these contaminated appropriated aggregates experience** the **suffering** of birth, old age, sickness, and death **of the current aggregates** of this life, **and that** through these aggregates much **future suffering is** naturally **induced**. These appropriated aggregates are like a mountain made of a heap of many parts.

Furthermore, with respect to "appropriated aggregates," **the meaning of "appropriated" is that of aspiration and attachment.** [349] **Thus, for example, just like a fire created from wood is called a "wood fire," so too the aggregates that will be established due to the wish to have a future body and attachment to the present body are named based on their causes. Likewise, just as a tree that grows** fruit is called a "fruit tree," so too the aggregates already established giving rise to aspiration and attachment are named by way of their result. Since one is arisen from the other, cycling in cyclic existence occurs.

At this point the contemplation of the six types of suffering is presented in this treatise. The first is uncertainty. **There is not only the aforementioned suffering, but furthermore the lack of reliability, as stated in** *Letter to a Friend*:

> **Fathers become sons, mothers become wives,**
> **enemies become friends,**
> **and the reverse happens as well.**
> **Nothing is certain in cyclic existence.**

Not only do parents, friends, and enemies reverse their roles over lifetimes, but even in this very life those who were so close to us in the beginning become our enemies in the latter part of life. Moreover, those who vowed to kill each other the previous year can end up being the best of friends by the next year. We can perceive these ourselves. Therefore, since it is not possible to have solid conviction regarding friends and enemies, contemplate the suffering of uncertainty.

The second type of suffering, insatiability, **or dissatisfaction, is as stated in** *Letter to a Friend*:

> **Just as a leper tormented by maggots**
> **turns entirely to fire for relief**
> **yet still finds no peace, in the same way**
> **understand attachment to sensual pleasures.**

You have previously drunk more than infinite great oceans' worth of the excellent nectar of the gods, ordinary mother's milk, and hor-

rible dirty fluids and boiling molten liquids, yet you are still not satiated by those. Understand that there is no satiation to be had from sensual enjoyments as like the example of a leper turning to fire [for relief].

Whatever joy or comfort you turn to for satisfaction will not satisfy you, but instead turn into suffering. [350] However much fame, fortune and so on you accrue will not lead to contentment, but rather, just as someone who is hungry remains craving to eat food, however many marvelous things in samsara you acquire, there is no right amount nor contentment found. This is one of the greatest sufferings.

The third type of suffering is casting off bodies repeatedly. Your various attempts motivated by that lack of contentment bring about even more countless other sufferings. Therefore, **the uncountable bodies are as stated in** [Aśvaghoṣa's] *Eradicating Suffering*:

> If the heads that were cut off
> because of fighting and disputes,
> were made into a pile,
> the height would surpass even the Abode of Brahmā.

Leaving aside the bodies lost to different illnesses, if the heads of those who died through being slashed by weapons were piled up, it would reach higher than the abode of Brahmā. Thus, contemplate that if you are not free from cyclic existence then you will not escape this apparent situation of discarding your body again and again.

Even though we might fancy the body being reliable and something to be attached to, not only must it be discarded again and again, but also none of the suffering or happiness experienced until now has sufficed. Therefore, while we are not free from the binding ropes of karma and afflictions, we cannot escape this status quo. Contemplate this and give rise to a sense of weariness.

The fourth type of suffering is repeatedly taking rebirth. With respect to traveling through countless wombs, [*Letter to a Friend*] states:

> Even if you counted the limit of mothers with little earthen
>   pellets
> the size of juniper berries, you would run out of earth.

If you were to take this great earth and make it into little pellets to count, "my mother, her mother, her mother's mother," and so on, there would not be enough earth to do so. This is what is explicitly conveyed by the word "limit." Since we cannot count even our own mothers, we must become disenchanted by rebirths already taken and at having to take them again. [351]

The fifth type of suffering is repeatedly falling from higher to lower [status]. **The uncertainty of high and low status** [is as stated in *Letter to a Friend*]:

> Having become Indra, worthy of the world's veneration,
> you fall back to earth through karma.
> Even having become a universal monarch
> you will once again become a servant of servants in cyclic
>   existences.

Contemplate how even if you achieve the state of Indra, the lord of the gods, or a universal monarch, through the power of your previous nonvirtue not having exhausted, if something activates it, then you will either be born into a lower status such as that of a servant, a bad migration, and so on, or you, once the deity of the sun or moon that lit up the world with your own radiance, will be born into thick darkness. Or contemplate how many of those intoxicated with arrogance about their might and wealth are eliminated through a king's punishment or defeated by their enemies, thus becoming lowly and devoid of power.

The sixth type of suffering is having no companions. One has already taken countless births while in samsara, and during those births one is without companions and continues alone. There is not a single trustworthy companion who you can count on. Furthermore, the fact that all will be left behind is as stated in the *Way of the Bodhisattva*:

> Even though this body emerged whole,
> Given that the flesh and bone that came with it
> will break down and disperse,
> what need to mention other loved ones?

Meditate on how one must journey on alone without friends at the time of death until you tremble with fear.

We have already experienced all of these sufferings, and one can infer based on the way we act now that it is only fitting that they will befall us again. From the holy mouth of Potowa:

> Whatever suffering, such as illness or death, that arises within rebirths in the six types of existence are all sicknesses to be undergone, and deaths to be undergone—it is not that something unsuitable suddenly befalls oneself. It is the character, or nature, of samsara. One cannot transcend that while one remains in samsara. If one is disheartened by that, then one must abandon rebirth. For that, one must abandon its causes.

Understand it also through these words. [352]

The gentle protector, the great Tsongkhapa, says [in *Foundation of All Good Qualities*]:

> The marvels of existence are unreliable.
> When they are indulged they never suffice, and are the door to
>   all suffering.
> Please bless me to understand their faults
> and earnestly strive for the bliss of liberation.

As stated, the root of suffering is taking for granted that the marvels of samsara are joys, yet not finding satiation or contentment however much you indulge in them. As Tsangpa Gyaré (1161–1211) states:

> At the door of the house of contentment,
> a rich man lies down.
> Those with desire do not feel that.

If you have contentment, you are effectively rich; if you do not have contentment, it does not matter how much wealth or assets you possess, because you will not be satisfied, and thus you are effectively poor. Therefore, not being satiated however much you indulge is the gateway to all suffering. Moreover, through not finding satisfaction we "destroy one hundred and summon a thousand," as the saying goes, doing many things that bring us worry, which negatively affects others to the degree we behave like this. Such conditions bring about that much suffering.

Whatever marvel of existence it may be, on the one hand not a single one is reliable or trustworthy in the long run, and therefore "after the rise there is the fall, after meeting there is departure, at the end of life there is death, at the end of stockpiling there is depletion." Ultimately everything deteriorates, and nothing is exempt from that. Therefore, having seen the drawbacks of samsara, which are under the sway of karma and

affliction, you must strive in methods to bring about an earnest pursuit
of the bliss of nonabiding nirvana—the freedom from those.

Concluding Verses

Amid the filth of an unclean womb,
a dark dungeon where no form could be seen,
in the piercing agony of intense suffering
a beautiful body is in the blossom of youth.

Hair once the color of kohl is white like snow,
a once radiant skin tone is black like darkness.
the body born straight is bent like a bow,
burdened by age, you no longer crave the desirable. [353]

Medicine, divination, Bön magic, and prayer ceremonies do
    not help.
As each day passes and you decline further,
your friends, relatives, and attendants become fed up and
    avoid you.
These are the messengers summoned by the Lord of Death.

Now this body that seemed inseparable from the mind
is laid on a bed, and the mental consciousness alone
traverses the long, perilous journey of the bardo,
wandering samsara.

Although destroying them through various means,
hostile, fierce enemies and demons descend like rain.
Although you made yourself strong, your dear ones and
    possessions
scatter into the ten directions like clouds in a drought.

As your body revels in the glory of the gods,
your mind directly experiences the anguish of hell
because of the signs of death of a god.
How could this suffering not break hearts made even of
    metal?

Just as a bird who has flown into the sky
must come back down to earth,
so too it saddens me that those who have gone to the peak of
    existence
must again cycle like a whirling firebrand throughout the
    three realms.

If even glorious, noble lords of gods and men
take bad rebirths, becoming the servants of servants,
and the gods of sun and moon are born into darkness,
the time has now come to bid farewell to cyclic existence.

Contemplating Origins: The Stages of Entering into Cyclic Existence

HAVING EXPLAINED true sufferings—the drawbacks of cyclic existence—above, it is very important to analyze whether there is a method to cut the continuum of a cyclic existence of misery, and whether cyclic existence itself can be brought to an end. Therefore, **with respect to contemplating the stages of entering into cyclic existence** by way of **its origins**, this has three parts:

a" The origin of the afflictions
b" How karma is accumulated by way of the afflictions
c" The manner of death, transmigration, and rebirth

The origin of the afflictions has four parts:

1" Identifying afflictions
2" The order in which the afflictions arise
3" The causes of afflictions
4" The faults of afflictions

Identifying afflictions has two parts:

(a) The general characteristics of afflictions
(b) The specific characteristics of afflictions [354]

The General Characteristics of Afflictions

Having understood the suffering of cyclic existence, if one does not desire it then one must abandon its causes. Abandoning its causes requires identifying them. What are they? True origins. They are of two types: karma and affliction. Of those, affliction is primary. Take the example of a seed planted in a dry field that does not receive water, fertilizer, and so forth: it will not bear fruit. In line with this, Dharmakīrti's *Commentary on the "Compendium of Valid Cognition"* states:

> The karma of one who has passed beyond the craving of
>   existence,
> is not able to project other [phenomena of samsara],
> since the cooperative condition has been exhausted.

If a human who has accumulated the karma to be born as an animal achieves the state of peace before meeting with that karma, that karma will never bear fruit through having gone to waste. Therefore, having applied the antidote to the craving of existence and having destroyed it, there are arhats who have overcome craving. The karma in their continua is unable to project other resultant samsaric phenomena through their application of an antidote to the afflictions that would otherwise activate that previously accumulated karma, thus destroying and exhausting those afflictions. "Afflictions" are defined in Ārya Asaṅga's *Compendium of Knowledge* as follows:

> An affliction is defined as a phenomenon that upon arising
> has the character of thorough disturbance; due to it arising it
> disturbs the mindstream.

As stated, an affliction is any awareness that, when it arises, agitates and involuntarily disturbs the relaxed state of our innate awareness when abiding in natural calmness.

It is possible that the arising of strong compassion disturbs the mind, but since that is voluntary it is not comparable. Moreover, upon having an uncontrived experience with respect to compassion, it does not disturb the mind. Hence, I wonder whether it is better to qualify the definition of affliction with "that which involuntarily disturbs the mind." [355]

From among proponents of Buddhist tenets, the way those who propound inherent existence posit afflictions accords with this. However, since systems that do not propound inherent existence set forth a subtle grasping at true existence, there also exist subtle afflictions such as attachment and anger related to that. Therefore, it is imperative to finely analyze the different subtleties of affliction. I think perhaps the definition of an affliction given in the *Compendium of Knowledge* should thus be applied to an affliction common to all systems, or a coarse affliction. For, aside from the Madhyamaka Prā-saṅgika, not all Madhyamaka adherents propound a lack of inherent existence.

In the context of identifying afflictions there are five views and five nonviews.[73] Afflictions that are nonviews are the mere modes of appearance occurring naturally to an awareness, but the five views are afflicted wisdoms that have a strong false ascertainment of their own mode of apprehension. Therefore, the antidote that eradicates those views must also be a wisdom. If the class of objects of abandonment are awarenesses that wrongly apprehend phenomena, then regarding their antidotes, too, they cannot be abandoned by an ordinary aware-ness that is not of the type of wisdom.

Regarding the antidotes to afflictions that are nonviews, not only does the antidote for attachment—meditation on unattractiveness—not act as an antidote for aversion, it can possibly serve to increase it, and likewise the antidote for anger—meditation on love—does not act as the antidote for attachment, but can also serve to increase it. Therefore, even though there is no one-size-fits-all single antidote for suppressing afflictions, since the root of all afflictions meets back to ignorance grasping at true existence, whatever is the antidote to ignorance counters all afflictions. We can get a small understanding of this through analyzing our own experience. When attachment, aversion, and so forth arise, their objects appear as true, self-supporting, and unfabricated, and upon understanding that the object is by nature fabricated and not self-supporting, attachment and aversion become weaker. [356] Therefore, it is clear that awarenesses such as attachment and aversion have a mode of apprehension of objects existing as self-supporting and truly established. Whatever kind of affliction it is, its root meets back to the ignorance apprehending true existence, and thus if one understands the mode of suchness of dependent origination, then the basis for attachment and aversion has been loosened, and the solidity of the grasping is broken.

Regarding the drawbacks of afflictions, *Way of the Bodhisattva* states:

> Even if all gods and demigods
> should rise against me as my enemy,
> they would be powerless to lead and force me
> into the fires of Unrelenting Hell.

> But my powerful enemy of afflictions
> throws me in an instant
> to where even Mount Meru would be consumed
> without even its ashes remaining.

Even if all sentient beings rose up as enemies, they could not make my future life one of suffering, but through meeting with the condition of afflictions it is only fitting that one be oppressed by immense suffering and turned to ash.

Therefore, it is important to understand that the so-called afflictions have been our fundamental, self-sabotaging enemy within beginningless samsara up until now. Even the renowned scourges of this earth, however unyielding and evil, may only harm us in this one lifetime, and an ordinary enemy, however strong, at the most can harm our life, but more than that they can never force us into suffering in a string of future lives. For example, during events such as the Chinese Cultural Revolution, those in power principally targeted the brave, noblehearted, and educated among the interconnected Tibetan, Chinese, and Mongolian ethnicities, who underwent struggle sessions, torture, and misery. [357] Among the countless many who died of starvation or were murdered, records up to 1980 indicate 1.2 million Tibetans lost their lives. The death of over one million people within a population of only six million was massively devastating, but it did not send them to the three lower realms or into happy rebirths within samsara.

Therefore, ordinary enemies have no way to harm us throughout all our lifetimes, yet it is evident that the enemy of affliction, through making us temporarily angry, attached, proud, jealous, and so forth, brings forth limitless events of unhappiness now and in the future for ourselves and others, up to even killing oneself out of self-loathing, being unable to cope, and so forth.

In a past anecdote that was recounted to Kyabjé Trijang Rinpoché, a person from Chatreng who was living in Lhasa became deeply distraught and decided to commit suicide by jumping into the [Yarlung] Tsangpo River. Knowing he would not be able to spontaneously jump in, he brought a bottle of alcohol with him and went toward the bank of the river. After arriving, he started drinking but was still unable to jump. In the end, he drank all the alcohol and returned home carrying the empty bottle. In the same way, we are liable to do anything when intense afflictions arise.

In general, having wealth and assets, kind friends and relatives, and good health are conducive conditions for living happily in this lifetime. However, even if you consider these the root of happiness, friends and relatives are only human, and while not seeing eye to eye, even siblings become enemies because of not being able to suppress afflictions of attachment, aversion, pride, jealously and so forth. [358] Subsequently, unable to live their lives with patience and tolerance for one another, their other relatives become fed up and intervene, leading to a further increase in afflictions. Thus, the conducive conditions for a happy life become impediments. Furthermore, not being able to be consistently happy through lack of contentment with however much wealth one has and so forth means that the afflictions also lead us into misery in this life, with no need to mention our future lives!

Moreover, those self-defeating minds of affliction deceive us by always appearing as our faithful friends and companions through the assistance of our own mind; their deception does not come from outside. For example, in Communist theory expressions such as "the exploited working class should have rights and well-being, and the exploiters should be overthrown" are valid ideas, yet when transformed into direct action they are not carried out with attitudes of loving-kindness, and the serious importance of loving-kindness is unable to be recognized. Afflictions are not seen as drawbacks, and thus attitudes of hatred and resentment are forcibly evoked toward the exploiting class, and even though they eliminated the lords and stewards who controlled the classes, many other enemies that needed to be eliminated still continued to crop up. Therefore, as much as they proclaimed slogans such as, "Dare to think, dare to speak, dare to act!," they removed freedom of speech for all, with zero tolerance for any criticism of the nation. Because the continuum of attachment and aversion was not cut, they were suspicious of everyone, and unable to trust anybody, so they planted spies internally and externally, leading to people having to live continuously in fear and terror. [359] All these factors are due to an inability to be suspicious of afflictions, and instead falling under their sway. Thus, their fundamental cause—although noble and reasonable—could not be carried out.

Along those lines, take religious communities, for example: it does not matter how good the religion that is the object of faith is, it can be misused in a way that gives rise to pride, jealously, attachment, and hatred rather than being used as a method to tame afflictions. Due to this a liking for some, hatred for others, and fighting still occur. Moreover, even someone who studies the qualities of the religion ruins it when their pride, jealously, and so forth increase together with their knowledge. As such, afflictions are not something external, but rather in one's own mind, and until now afflictions have taken control of us such that we uncontrollably pursue the imagination of the afflicted mind, like a cow being chased by a thief, and thus the waterwheel of samsara continues to turn.

Right now one must try to bring one's afflictions under one's own control, and for that there also exist methods to do so. For example, thoroughly check whether anger, for instance, is worth having in your life, and when you are convinced that it is destructive, then you should not only be strictly cautious about it, but through developing familiarization by way of verbalizing that again and again to others as well, your anger will gradually decrease. Furthermore, if someone who was very arrogant or proud during their youth comes to gradually see pride as a fault, and calm, disciplined behavior as well-mannered, and thus develops well-rounded behavior and reflects repeatedly on the faults of their other afflictions like attachment and so forth, through habituating oneself with the dissimilar class of those, one can gradually suppress those afflictions. [360]

We cannot speak extensively of having abandoned afflictions from our own direct experience. However, we know firsthand that when we strive in methods to bring about their opposites then afflictions do decrease. Therefore, it is certain that if you put effort in from your own side that negative mental states can be transformed. Afflictions of attachment and so forth appear, at present, as beneficial and self-preserving. This is because it is not generally considered inappropriate to respond with anger to offensive behavior toward oneself. While you may think there are situations that can be handled with anger or in which you can bring about a good outcome, although that might be possible occasionally, is there ever a situation in which you must necessarily be confrontational with another person, or which requires you to be absolutely riled up with anger? If you give it careful thought, not at all.

Not only that, but when anger is present it also upsets our state of mind, and it is seldom that a situation is then dealt with effectively. If a situation is handled with a calm attitude devoid of afflictions such as anger, it can be more helpful, impactful, and much more effective in resolving the issue. Regarding this, although the bodhisattvas have taken up the burden of accomplishing the welfare of others and love all sentient beings like a mother would her only child, it is not that they try to fulfill the individual wishes of beings, but rather with the purest of altruistic motivations they engage in various skillful means of peace, increase, control, and wrath as is appropriate. This being said, there are ways to face situations without even one's speech having to be motivated from the heart by afflictions such as anger, and therefore, for bodhisattvas, there are occasions where desire is permitted to help other beings, but never aversion. [361]

Therefore, in order to help both ourself and others, without a pure mind wishing to benefit all that is unstained by deceit and so forth, and without an attitude of loving-kindness and compassion, then one is bereft of the means to do so. Thus, if giving things to others, performing the four acts of generosity,[74] or praising others is done for one's own gain, those acts are totally phony and ultimately not beneficial. Thus, in brief, it is the factors of a subdued mind that are certainly needed over those of an unsubdued mind, and without them you cannot enact positive deeds that bear fruit. Thus, it is the basic nature of things that one must acknowledge and develop those awarenesses that are required to bring forth positivity, and to regard nonbeneficial afflicted awarenesses as faulty and discard them.

Furthermore, if one identifies afflictions, the mind becoming as if it is clouded once attachment, aversion, and so on have arisen is what is meant by "disturbed." Thus, it is on the basis of that kind of consciousness that thoroughly disturbs the mindstream that they should be identified. This manner [of disturbance] is as explained above.

The Specific Characteristics of Afflictions

There are ten afflictions: (1) attachment, (2) anger, (3) pride, (4) ignorance, (5) doubt, (6) the view of the transitory collection, (7) views holding to extremes, (8) holding views as supreme, (9) holding ethics and asceticism as supreme, and (10) wrong views.

The afflictions that lie dormant in our continuum are difficult to separate, like oil spilled on paper. Our situation is like someone with a chronic illness who is healthy at present, but who experiences fierce pangs upon eating food that triggers the illness. In the same way, when we see attractive men and women, horses and livestock, valuable silk clothing, and other such things, it activates the dormant attachment which then rises up as manifest. *Attachment* is an affliction which yearningly wishes to enjoy those through looking, touching, and so on. [362] Therefore, during your practice, visualize the object you are currently attached to whether it is present or not, and upon doing so, with your consciousness remaining as it was before—that is, neutral—immediately identify how other coarse conceptions have ceased due to manifest attachment and that attachment intolerant of forbearance has arisen.

While the attachment that afflicted our continuum before lies dormant, when it comes into contact with the condition of perceiving dear ones, fancy possessions, fame, or any object of attachment, a mind of manifest attachment to that arises repeatedly, and regardless of whether those things are actually appealing in reality, our awareness sees them as such from every perspective, and seeing that alone with a strong wish to indulge in them, it holds them dear and grasps at them as if absorbed into or mixed with them—this is attachment. Thus, having identified attachment not from mere words but drawing from one's own experience, **then it is taught that whenever it arises the antidote must be applied, for it is taught that a practice ruled by afflictions leads nowhere.**

Thus, the reason one must properly identify the afflictions is because, **for example, if Devadatta is to be killed, then you must be completely sure of his figure and so forth so as not to mix him up, and when he appears he must be taken down with a weapon. As Geshé Bengung Gyal stated, seemingly intended to this effect, "Hold ready the spear of the antidote at the door of the castle of affliction."**

Upon seeing an enemy or someone unfriendly, fierce aversion maliciously thinking, "By what means could I harm them?" is ignited like embers by the wind. This burning red affliction is *anger.* [363] The enemies we dislike and the various objects we get angry at can be either sentient or inanimate. Thus, it does not matter what they are in reality: when we see them, they appear as unappealing and disagreeable in every aspect, and all other perceptions of the present, future, and distant future are stopped while you contemplate with sinister, insuppressible aversion how you could harm them in various ways, even to the point you have shortness of breath. Thus, when this awareness arises all other appearances are halted, and the person becomes idiotic and crazy-like.

Influenced by apprehending a self, one thinks that because of being a higher caste, rich, educated, having physical prowess, and so

forth, that such-and-such person cannot harm a hair on one's body. This affliction having the aspect of haughtiness holding oneself as supreme is *pride*. Based on having a good family background, status, wealth, being highly educated, physically attractive, and so forth, one has an arrogance of superiority, which can even manifest as looking physically inflated. Regarding this, it is taught there are seven types: (1) pride, (2) exalted pride, (3) exaggerated pride, (4) egoistic pride, (5) presumptuous pride, (6) pride in modesty, and (7) perverted pride.

In a house without windows, even if there are all sorts of colorful objects present, one cannot distinguish their tone, quality, and so on because of the darkness. In the same way, the affliction that clouds and obscures the reality of things as they are and all that exists, such as karma and its effects, the four truths, and suchness, is *ignorance*. [364] There are many ways to identify ignorance, and in general there are two types: (1) the ignorance that is merely confused with respect to, or does not realize, an object, and (2) the ignorance that erroneously grasps at, or wrongly conceives, an object. The ignorance that is merely confused regarding objects and acts as an obscuration to seeing the nature and extent of phenomena also has two types: afflicted and nonafflicted. The nonafflicted ignorance that is merely confused with respect to an object can also exist in the continua of arhats.

The affliction that prevents one from generating ascertainment with respect to objects, such as the thought, "Are things such as the Three Jewels, karma, and so forth taught in the scriptures real or not?" is *doubt*. This has three kinds: (1) doubt leaning toward the fact, (2) doubt not leaning toward the fact, and (3) equal doubt.

The view of the transitory collection is the afflicted wisdom that holds to a self, thinking of "I" and "mine" in regard to a basis of designation of such as the five aggregates that disintegrate in their second moment due to their impermanence and are a collection of not one, but many. In dependence on the collection of the aggregates that are in the nature of disintegration, one thinks "I" and "mine," and apprehends an independent, or self-sufficient, substantial entity. In brief, the afflicted wisdom that apprehends a self-sufficient I or mine is the view of the transitory collection, the first of the five views.

The afflicted wisdom that views the self apprehended on the basis of the aggregates as either permanent and everlasting or that it does not continue to the next life and is annihilated are *views holding to extremes.* This also has two kinds: permanence and annihilation. These views holding to an extreme are (1) the extreme of permanence that apprehends the "I" as permanent, unitary, independent, and separate from the aggregates, and (2) the view of annihilation that views the independent "I" not coming here from a previous lifetime nor going from here to the next life. [365]

Holding views as supreme **refers to the afflicted wisdom that observes (1) either of the three—the view of the transitory collection, extreme views, wrong views—and (2) the aggregates that form the basis for those and holds them as supreme.**

Holding discipline and asceticism as supreme **refers to the afflicted wisdom that observes (1) the ethical discipline that has abandoned distorted ethics from one's own perspective, and (2) discipline such as cutting one's hair and wearing skins and skeletons, fasting, the practice of the five fires, standing on one leg while staring at the sun, rubbing ash on one's naked body and keeping silence, and (3) the aggregates that form the basis for those, and wishes to achieve liberation. This is not the arrogance holding to pure ethics as supreme; rather it is, for example, a case of an ordinary, non-ārya being who upon gaining clairvoyance sees their past life in which they maintained the ascetic practices of dogs and pigs and believes that cause led to their rebirth as a human, and so maintains those ascetic practices now. These and so forth are taught to necessarily be wrong views.**

It is explained as two types: the (1) deprecating wrong view that views an existent as nonexistent, and (2) the superimposing wrong view that views a nonexistent as existent. For example, deprecating **karma and its effects and past and future lives as nonexistent** is the deprecating wrong view, **and the afflicted wisdoms accepting that the creation and destruction of the universe is carried out by Brahmā, Īśvara, or Viṣṇu, and so forth are** superimposing **wrong views.**

In this context the ten afflictions consisting of the five views and five nonviews have been explained; **however it is not that one should relegate the other afflictions by merely skimming over the terms or reciting them from memory.** [366] **You should make each of them arise manifestly in your continuum so that later you do not need to put in effort to easily identify them as soon as they arise. If you do not get to a point where it is like recognizing a person within a crowd of ten thousand people as soon as you see them, it is taught to be like blindly shooting an arrow into a crowd without recognizing the enemy.**

Furthermore, even if it is easy to somewhat recognize any of the ten afflictions when they manifestly arise, just like it is slightly difficult for a doctor to identify a combination or compounded illness,[75] **so too if two or three afflictions manifest together, they are difficult to handle in one's practice. If you were to manifestly be attached to a chariot, for example, and then someone forcefully took it, you would develop aversion. The intensity of that aversion would be caused by the intensity of your attachment to the chariot. Furthermore, you would have a view of true existence that apprehends the collection of the mere seven parts of the chariot as a chariot existing from its own side. That view you might hold as supreme, and so forth. This is a situation in which only four afflictions manifestly arise, therefore you must finely analyze [afflictions] and recognize them.**

When attachment to our homeland emerges, afflictions such as aversion, jealously, pride, and so forth each enable the other, making it temporarily hard to clearly identify them individually. However, one must still finely analyze and recognize them.

The Order in Which the Afflictions Arise

If one were to take both ignorance—the root of all afflictions—and the view of the transitory collection to be the same thing, there would be no contradiction. However, when making a fine distinction they are taken separately. For example, the darkness obscuring the reality of a rope is ignorance, and the awareness that apprehends the rope as a snake in dependence on that is the view of the transitory collection. The awareness apprehending the rope as a snake although it is not, is apprehending it erroneously. Furthermore, the ignorance confused with respect to the object prior forms the basis, or the condition, and the erroneously apprehending view of the transitory collection is born. [367] Thus, both ignorance and the view of the transitory collection act as the root of all afflictions and then through attachment and aversion all faults are generated. As it states in the *Commentary on the "Compendium of Valid Cognition"*:

> If there is self, there is an understanding of other.
> From the perspective of self and other, one grasps and hates.
> All faults occur
> in total connection to these.

Having grasped strongly to an independent self, "others" are then conceived of as something to be forsaken. Having differentiated self from other and set them apart, one adheres and grasps to oneself and has aversion toward others. Under the power of that one accumulates a variety of karma through which all faults arise. Furthermore, Candrakīrti states in his *Entering the Middle Way*:

> First, there is grasping to a self, "I,"
> then attachment to objects arises, "mine."

I bow to compassion for powerless are those migrators
who cycle like a waterwheel.

Concerning the order afflictions arise, as indicated [by Candrakīrti],
when it comes to pinning down the apprehension thinking, "I," that
occurs to our nonanalytical, noninvestigative awareness, it is an awareness that grasps at an appearance of self-sufficiency, and there are multiple modes of apprehension that can occur, such as the apprehension
of a mere "I"; the apprehension of a true "I"; the apprehension of a
self-sufficient, substantially existent "I", within which there can be an
apprehension of a self-sufficient "I" having discordant characteristics, an
apprehension of a self-sufficient "I" having concordant characteristics,
or a mode of apprehension of a self-sufficient "I" similar to that of a lord
and servant. When such an awareness firmly increases in intensity, the
strong awareness apprehending mine, thinking, "my body," "my dear
ones," "my possessions" naturally occurs. From the fixated attachment
and apprehension to "mine" induced by that having become tighter, it
seems almost as if there is nothing for others to touch or reach for.

In general, one exists, and others exist, and since self and others exist,
actions and agents are logically acceptable, such as oneself developing
the intent for the sake of others. [368] In this context however, due to
apprehending a self-supporting self in opposition to a self-supporting
other, biased mindsets arise.

The Causes of Afflictions

There are six causes of afflictions: (1) support, (2) observation, (3) circumstantial distractions, (4) explanations, (5) habituation, and (6)
improper attention

**Thus, although at present you may have cast an impression of
having slightly suppressed these afflictions, the causes that give rise**

to all faults, if you fail to extract them from the root then just like a reflection in a mirror, those ones lying dormant (the imprints of the prior afflictions) will act as the *support* for increasing afflictions.

Just as when face and mirror meet, a reflection immediately appears, so too through the *observations* that manifestly arise in dependence on objects such as friends or enemies do the afflictions increase. Among the afflictions that are always on the verge of rising up within us, attachment arises when meeting an attractive object, anger arises when meeting an unpleasant object, and likewise pride, jealously, and so forth; the appropriate affliction arises according to the features of the observation, or object.

Through the *circumstantial distractions* of the conversations, lifestyles, and so on, of bad company who have tremendous afflictions, while being far from one's virtuous teachers and Dharma friends, afflictions are caused to increase. When continuously doing prayers, for example, the causes for afflictions to arise are of course present, but since an object is not encountered then one's afflictions lie dormant without being evident. It is rare in that situation to encounter conditions, so peaceful and relaxed minds increase. However, since the bases for generating attachment, aversion, and so forth—those multitudes of good and bad objects that are liable to agitate us, wherever they may be—will act as the condition to increase afflictions, and thus through social distractions—the basis for distraction—afflictions increase. [369]

Nonvirtuous spiritual teachers and so forth, who have not abandoned afflictions, give explanations of having achieved liberation, due to which one's afflictions increase. Here "explanations" include historical accounts and stories of human courage, bravery, battles, and so forth—actions arisen from afflictions—that give rise to aversion in our minds, or erotic material such as the *Kāma Sūtra*, and other compositions that serve to increase distraction. Through these explanations, or reading books, for example, the relevant afflictions increase.

These days we are able to keep up to date on current events broadcasted on television, and there are categories worth watching that develop our critical thinking; however, topics like historical recounts of victors defeating others, violence, murder, using various weapons, sexual themes, and furthermore violent and competitive computer games and so forth, are a basis to increase our aversion and attachment. Ways we are at risk of being misled through watching these is a topic currently being discussed within society too.

Particularly, if one does not have a mindset maintaining self-control, then interest and captivation with shooting guns, or craving for erotica and so on increase, corrupting us. Even if a person is normally mindful, introspected, and conscientious, these can still arouse one's afflictions and thus we should be careful. In particular, those who are celibate need to be even more careful.

Murder shown on television and in movies is prevalent in this day and age and thus children have become accustomed to the idea of toying with guns, and it is obviously becoming dangerous. [370]. In the same way awareness is increasing regarding a need for conscientiousness about what is being shown to people on television and in movies; an increase in murder rates in a heavily armed population can be linked to influence from such things. In a Tibetan story that goes back generations, some children saw a butcher slaughter a sheep, then one day when they were playing, they acted out the slaughter of the sheep, one pretending to be the sheep and another the butcher. The child acting as the butcher grabbed the one pretending to be the sheep and, holding him down, stabbed him with a real knife. He screamed, "Ow!" to which the other told him, "You're playing the sheep! You cannot say 'Ow'! You have to say 'Baa'!" Thus, the tale shows the dangers of falling under a bad influence.

In any case, this and so forth show how "explanations" cause the mind to become distracted.

Just like if you let your mind wander while reciting prayers they still flow unimpeded from your mouth, so too due to *familiarization*

from strong acquaintance in the past are our afflictions caused to increase. Thus, even as we contemplate that it is wrong to put energy into the afflicted side of things it is still hard to stop them, and on the virtuous side of things however much we analyze reasonings, cite scriptures, and recollect the guru's teachings and contemplate these, it is so difficult for the mind to change. This happens due to the intensity of our habituation.

Through the various superimpositions of attachment and aversion, thinking for example, "This person helped or harmed me in this way!" and through improper mental attention thinking, "This person committed such an atrocity yet they live happily now—karmic causality is not true!" one's afflictions increase. [371] Through analyzing the objects that give rise to attachment and aversion [one can understand that] in dependence on keeping attention on attitudes that superimpose or deprecate whatever qualities or faults that do not accord with reality, one increases the discursive thinking of *improper mental attention* that is interested in some objects and wants to be distant from others. This acts as the cause for afflictions to increase.

Having identified these six causes like so, if one falls under the sway of the afflictions while not having developed a practice, which is like lying in ambush waiting for the enemy, regarding the drawbacks of afflictions, while creating a multitude of negative deeds in this and all future lives one links oneself to the suffering of samsara. Moreover, since one has distanced oneself from nirvana, then through befriending [afflictions] up until now, one has become the root of all one's own misfortune. If you hold a grudge even against those who harm you slightly in this life, calling them enemies, then why do you not put any energy into the enemy of afflictions that have committed one to suffering since beginningless lifetimes until now? If you can overcome them through applying the destructive antidote again and again, they cannot strike again like any other type of enemy. Therefore [it says in *Way of the Bodhisattva*]:

The ordinary enemy, though banished from the state,
fortify and base themselves in other lands,
gathering strength. Afflictions, on the contrary,
are a different breed of enemy.

Since it is the afflictions that have acted as the root of ruin from beginningless time until now, how can we voluntarily welcome the enemy of afflictions that harms us? So, how is it that one can destroy them from the root by applying the antidote?

Afflictions, O afflictions, abandoned by the eye of wisdom,
where will you go, driven from my mind?
Where could you return from to do me harm?
Alas, I, weak minded, am without resolve.

With respect to the repetition in the phrase, "Afflictions, O afflictions," they can be explained from the perspective of the Tibetan language or original Sanskrit. Khunu Lama Rinpoché (1894–1977) takes these two words individually. [372] His explanation according to the Sanskrit gives the first instance of "afflictions" as having the meaning of weakness, explaining it as "Weak afflictions are abandoned by the eye of wisdom." How, then, are afflictions "weak"? Afflictions can be destroyed through the antidote of a certain way of thinking; one does not need to organize an army against them, nor are weapons required. You cannot face ordinary enemies yourself alone—they require armies of hundreds, if not thousands. In the face of this, afflictions are comparatively weak. Thus, Śāntideva taught that the weak afflictions can be eliminated by the eye of wisdom. When interpreting it from the perspective of the Tibetan language, "afflictions," which are the afflictions to be destroyed, are eliminated by the eye of wisdom that knows the nature of those very afflictions themselves.

How Karma Is Accumulated by way of the Afflictions

1" Identifying the karma that is thereby accumulated

(a) Karma that is intention
(b) Karma that is the intended action

2" How that karma is accumulated

(a) Accumulating karma for pleasant feelings
(b) Accumulating karma for neutral feelings

The topic of karma and effect has already been explained within the outlines of karma and effect in the context of persons of small scope. To state it very concisely: If you accumulate good karma, you will definitely experience a good result, and if you accumulate bad karma, you will definitely experience a bad result. However, one may doubt karmic cause and effect from witnessing certain people who have committed great atrocities and then live long lives or become highly successful, while seeing pious Dharma practitioners face a number of obstacles. Such is not as it seems. Through the force of good karma from putting great effort into practicing Dharma correctly, virtue increases, and by its power strong bad karma accumulated prior that would otherwise propel one into bad rebirths gradually weaken. [373] The fruitions of the strong misdeeds previously accumulated will ripen in a timely fashion, and any misfortune that befalls one's present human support will purify the results of the misdeeds.

In order to make karma have powerful potential one must develop renunciation having seen samsara as faulty from a manner of perspectives and having become fed up with the marvels of samsara with which one is habituated. Then, correctly analyzing the meaning of selflessness with individually discriminating wisdom again and again, one gains an understanding of emptiness that is the lack of inherent existence. Subsequently, the virtuous practice arisen through familiarization with both conventional bodhicitta and ultimate bodhicitta becomes karma possessing strength.

Our usual virtuous practices devoid of the essence of the three principal aspects of the path that mimic merit collection and purification of obscurations are weak—except in the few instances they rely on the power of the merit field—and turn the wheel of samsara just like origins among the four truths do. "Relying on the power of the [merit] field" is as said [in *The White Lotus of the Good Dharma*]:

> Even one who makes an offering with an agitated mind
> to the image of a sugata in a mural,
> will eventually see millions of buddhas.

Such is said to arise through the force of a powerful merit field. Thus, if even an ordinary being whose mind is disturbed is able to accumulate such merit from seeing a drawn image of the Buddha, then this point is able to be understood even more through the bodhisattvas who single-pointedly generate the strong special intent for the welfare of migrating beings until the end of space, by which they accumulate three countless eons worth of collections for the sake of sentient beings, and so on, through which they possess an incredibly powerful, unique potential. From that point onward, merely seeing, hearing, or touching them brings benefit.

[As it says in *Way of the Bodhisattva*:]

> I go for refuge to those sources of happiness
> who bring to bliss even those who harm them.

Such beings are arisen through the power of generating incredible courageousness. [374]

c″ The manner of death, transmigration, and rebirth

1″ Conditions for death
2″ The mind at death
3″ From where the heat gathers
4″ How the bardo is established after death
5″ How you are then born into the birth state

CONDITIONS FOR DEATH

Those who are born due to karma and affliction are not free from death, transmigration, and rebirth. Regarding this, there are nine causes of death taught in sutras, such as death from one's lifespan running out, death from one's merit exhausting, death from a lack of provisions, sudden death from disagreeable food or destructive behavior, and so on. There are many such factors, however, that help or harm you on the approach to death and afterward, which are the virtuous and nonvirtuous karma accumulated through afflictions. These are either karma of intention (*sems pa'i las*) or intended actions (*bsam pa'i las*), in dependence upon which happiness or suffering occur.

It is furthermore possible that someone who carried out powerful virtue in this lifetime might face problems with their dominion, harm to life and limb, or their life ending in terrible torment, while those who committed atrocities may experience magnificent happiness, due to which the foolish wrongly think karmic causality is false. How can one be so sure that such are not the ripening in this lifetime of the results of powerful virtue or misdeeds in their previous life?

As stated in *Way of the Bodhisattva*:

What is not great if, condemned to death,

a man is instead freed with his hand cut off?
What is not great if, through human suffering,
one avoids hell?

Just like a criminal escaping capital punishment by having their hand cut off instead, for someone who must be reborn in hell, experiencing suffering as a human can suffice. Moreover, because Śikhandin, king of Rauruka, threw dust on Ārya Kātyāyana, initially a shower of jewels and so forth fell [on the city], but later he was buried under [dirt from] a dust storm. One can understand it through these [examples]. [375]

THE MIND AT DEATH

- (a) Dying with a virtuous mind
- (b) Dying with a nonvirtuous mind
- (c) Dying with a neutral mind

The mind at death is what determines whether someone immediately about to take birth will be born in a happy migration or a bad migration is as stated in *The Treasury of Knowledge*:

> Within the cycle of karma, whatever is heavier,
> closer, more habituated, or done first—
> that will be the first to ripen.

As long as there is a variety of virtuous and nonvirtuous karma present in one's continuum, then while dying the thought most strongly habituated with whichever virtue or misdeed in that lifetime will arise. The mind of death is still coarse while the external breath is about to stop, and it is subtle while the external breath has stopped and the inner breath has not yet stopped. When the mind of death is coarse, one will automatically recollect either nonvirtuous minds of attachment, aversion, and so forth toward one's dear ones or enemies, or virtuous minds such as a recollection of the Three Jewels— depending on which one was more familiar with prior. For those who are dulled due to illness, these can be activated by a helper through a variety of virtuous speech.

For example, when [virtues] and misdeeds carry equal weight and it is uncertain which will [ripen] at the time of death, due to stronger habituation even a person who committed great misdeeds can take a good rebirth through manifesting a virtuous mind at the time of death. Likewise, even if one had accumulated powerful virtue during one's lifetime, one can be born in a bad migration if a nonvirtuous mind manifests at the time of death. This is a crucial point.

Since one's own mind is not hidden to oneself, one can recollect one's past actions, by which one has joy or regret. Thus, although a sinful person who does not know the difference between virtue and nonvirtue will only give rise to whichever sinful mind they were most accustomed to in their lifetime, there is great benefit in the capacity of the extraordinary names and dhāraṇī mantras of the tathāgatas to reverse them from birth in a bad migration.

Neither appearances of virtue nor nonvirtue dawn at the time of the subtle mind of death, thus it is a neutral mind. In general, if this is interpreted from a sutric point of view, the mind of death is divided into levels of subtlety, and while the mind of death is coarse, it can be any of the three—virtue, nonvirtue, or neutral—and thus this is considered a critical time. Someone who has generally performed very little nonvirtue, even though they may not be familiar with Dharma, very strong virtue can arise at the time of death through recollecting it either themselves or through being reminded by another. It is taught that at that point, if there is virtuous karma that has been previously accumulated in their continuum, it can be activated by their mind and

in future they are definitely able to take a good rebirth. Even someone who was a reasonably good Dharma practitioner can meet with
attachment or strong minds of nonvirtue at the time of death, and
through activating that [prior misdeed] there is the danger of taking
a bad rebirth.

Therefore, whatever kind of rebirth one will take in the next life
depends on the karma that is activated at the time of death; thus
through the mind being upset and so forth at that time it is possible
that it gains the powerful potential to propel one into a bad rebirth
through activating previously accumulated bad karma. As that is the
case, it is extremely critical that one be careful at the time of death and
employ means to give rise to a virtuous mind.

Generally, even if someone does not believe in virtue, nonvirtue,
and Dharma, or they are simply uninterested, it is still highly advantageous to try to allow them to remain peaceful without making their
minds disturbed. Whether it be hospital staff, doctors, family members
or whoever, if a person is approaching death, one must be careful as it
is not good if they become strongly attached or highly anxious leading
them to be upset.

The way happiness and suffering are experienced is taught to differ
greatly among those who continuously commit nonvirtue and those
who engage in virtue. [377] Regarding the way karma is activated, or
the way one connects to the next life at the time of death: Among the
various karma accumulated, the order in which they will activate is in
accordance with the *Treasury of Knowledge* citation whose meaning was
explained above in the section on karma and effect. This is the process
that occurs during the coarse mind of death. During the subtle mind of
death, an ordinary person will have no recollection, nor is there a way
another person could make them have recollection. After the external
breath stops, the mind can only be neutral. In the context of highest
yoga tantra, however, it is taught that the subtle mind of death can
transform into a virtuous mind.

Furthermore, those who generally engaged in virtue experience fewer death throes, they see pleasant forms as if in a dream, and they have the appearance of going from darkness into light. Those who were nonvirtuous experience the opposite. At this point visions caused by the disturbance of the elements occur. Some patients on the verge of death report a blissful vision with appearances of fire. Animal killers, such as butchers, see appearances of animals being murdered in the place they are to be born through the awakening of past imprints. At the time of death when the consciousness is dissolving it is likely one has visions of the place in which one is going to be born. Additionally, if one is about to take a bad rebirth it seems that one seeks out a feeling that is opposite to that.

One can hear accounts of those who practice virtue seeing pleasant appearances of a happy mind at the time of death, while those who committed negative actions see terrifying visions with an unsettled mind.

From Where the Heat Gathers

As it states in the *Great Treatise on the Stages on the Path to Enlightenment*:

> With respect to those who continuously cultivate nonvirtue, the consciousness discards the body starting from the upper part of the corpse. The corpse gradually becomes cold from the top down until reaching the heart, where it is then discarded. For those who continuously practice virtue, the body is discarded and becomes cold from the bottom up. In both cases the consciousness transfers out from the heart. [378]

How the Bardo Is Established after Death

The cessation of the subtle mind of death and the establishing of the bardo are simultaneous. **Whether one is virtuous or nonvirtuous,** when approaching death strong attachment to the body arises with the thought, "Now death is here!" and acts as a cause. Immediately upon the transference of consciousness—like the tipping of the balancing arm of a scale—the bardo body is established in the likeness of whoever you will be born as. The bardo for hell is like a charred log of wood; the bardo for animals is smokey; the bardo for hungry ghosts is watery; the bardo for desire realm gods and humans is golden; and the bardo for the form realm is white. The beings in the bardo for gods ascend in their movement; those in the bardo for humans move straight forward; those in the bardo for bad rebirths move downward. This is a tradition of explanation.

Furthermore, if someone is to be born as a human it is said they will establish a bardo that looks like a human. As for a bardo being's lifespan, according to the system of Vasubandhu's *Treasury of Knowledge* they can live for a few seconds up to approximately one week, and if at that point they do not find a rebirth they undergo a small death every seven days, becoming a bardo being again. This can happen seven times at most, and thus they can live up to forty-nine days, at which point it is taught they must necessarily find a birthplace no matter what. In the *Mahāparinirvāṇa Sūtra* it states that the son of King ·Roca passed away and remained in the bardo for three years. In other texts it says the duration [of the bardo] is indefinite. Afterward, in the case of someone who will take a womb birth upon their intermediate existence ceasing, they are conceived in the center of the mother and father's mixture of ovum and sperm. In brief, under the power of karma and afflictions the wheel of birth and death successively continues in this way.

Regarding how days are measured, they are mostly taken to be days of a human life, yet in some treatises there is an alternative system of measuring them in terms of a day in the life of whatever you will be born as. Therefore, if one claims the bardo being who will be born as a human actually looks like a human as said before, then not only should the bardo beings who will be born as gods and so forth also take on those appearances, I think the lifespan of such a bardo being should also be measured according to how long a "day" is in their future rebirth, and does not make sense that it would be measured in terms of human days. [379]

How You Are Then Born into the Birth State

In the case of someone who is womb-born, the bardo being observes living beings that are the same type as itself at its future birthplace. It then wishes to observe them, play with them, and so forth, and desires to go there as the place of its future birth. **Within forty-nine days it sees the parents lying together as if an illusion, and through either attachment or aversion toward them** the intermediate existence ceases and **they enter** the womb, **thus being conceived.**

This is the general explanation from the traditional treatises. In later times through scientific advancements a new method of conceiving children was made possible [by in vitro fertilization] in the English city of Manchester in 1978. A mother's egg and father's sperm were extracted and combined in a laboratory dish, and after twenty-four hours it had developed sufficiently that it could be transferred via a needle into the uterus. With further research it could be possible to store multiple embryos for many years. It might even be possible for those who wish to become pregnant to choose either a boy or a girl, their physical shape, stature, skin tone, hair type, or for them to be without detrimental health factors. Upon deciding the features they wish, the embryo would be taken from storage and genetically engineered. After collecting the desired embryo and inserting it into the woman's uterus she would become pregnant, and able to birth a child matching her wishes.

If the mother's uterus that the embryo is to be inserted in is healthy and other conditions are met, even a mature-aged sixty year old could hypothetically become pregnant, and therefore pregnancy does not require that one has not reached menopause. [380] Additionally, it is not required that the parents have sexual intercourse through mutual desire.

The fact that even identical twins who originated from the same egg and who become separated from each other to be raised in different environments within different countries and so forth end up with totally different personalities and so on, shows that the processes of the mind depend on one's environment, and not on one's ancestry. Such new and nontraditional presentations should be understood and analyzed well, and rather than leading us to disregard the presentation of karmic causality, we should try to use them to understand the subtleties within its vastness.

In any case, it is important to seriously contemplate the many levels of suffering that occur when one is conceived into the birth existence under the power of karma and affliction. For example, **someone who will be born in hell**—a being in the intermediate state for hell—**sees sentient beings that are objects of murder, which acts as a cause for birth. Meditate on this and so forth—the way one wanders in samsara like a whirling firebrand—until renunciation has developed.**

Concluding Verses

Since beginningless time your mind
has not been separated, for even a second,
from the companion of afflictions whom it constantly
   relies on,
due to which you have been cast into samsara's ocean with
   no clear end.

Churned by the unwanted winds of karma,
it forms the waves of the three sufferings.
Upon these you forever turn like a firebrand.
Thinking about this, afflictions are the quintessential enemy.

If you fancy yourself a hero capable of killing
an enemy of this lifetime,
then your time has definitely come
to subdue the perpetual enemy of afflictions.

At this time when you have excellently achieved a
    human body
with leisure and freedom, and have understood the
    crucial points of the path of the three trainings,
if you do not destroy the army of origins,
I fear you will again grow weary on the plain of birth and
    death. [381]

Contemplating the Suffering of Cyclic Existence from the Viewpoint of the Twelve Links of Dependent Origination

IN THE *Great Treatise on the Stages of the Path* four outlines are given in the section training the mind in the stages of the path shared with persons of medium scope, the first of which is the actual attitude training. This contains two further outlines:

i) Identifying the mind intent on liberation
ii) The methods for developing the mind intent on liberation

The latter contains the outline **contemplating [the suffering of cyclic existence] from the viewpoint of the twelve links of dependent origination.** This has four parts:

1′   The division into twelve links
2′   Summary of the links
3′   The number of lifetimes required to complete all twelve links
4′   How their significance is summarized

The Division into Twelve Links

When explaining the presentation of the four truths in extensive detail, the way the two origins of karma and affliction establish one's samsaric aggregates—true sufferings—is taught on the basis of aggregates that are exclusively characterized by birth, old age, sickness, and death, which give rise to all torment, wailing, and suffering. Accordingly, the manner those aggregates are established based on their root cause of beginningless ignorance is explained by way of the twelve links of dependent origination, up to old age and death.

Regarding this, when the Bhagavān commented in detail on the four truths, he taught the twelve links of dependent origination. He taught that under the power of the true origins of afflictions karma comes into being, and through that karma one establishes aggregates that act as the basis for the feeling of suffering; based on those there is old age and death, and the suffering of tormented wailing and so forth—thus teaching the set of cause and effect of the thoroughly afflicted class by which these arise. Moreover, via the reverse process whereupon if origins are stopped then suffering will stop, which is implicit through teaching the manner in which origins give rise to true sufferings, he taught the set of cause and effect of the thoroughly pure class, thus teaching two sets of cause and effect. [382]

Among the twelve links of dependent origination, Nāgārjuna states:

> The first, eighth, and ninth are afflictions.
> The second and tenth are karma.
> The other seven are suffering.

He thus divides the twelve links into three: afflictions, karma, and suffering, a presentation of propelling agents and projected results by which the twelve links require a minimum of two lifetimes to complete; thus many issues can be resolved, including even the relationship between past and future lifetimes.

The great Kadam master Phuchungwa practiced mind training solely with respect to the twelve links of dependent origination. Having made also the stages of the path of the three beings a reflection on the progression through and cessation of these links, he thus taught the lamrim by way of the twelve links of dependent origination. That is, regarding reflection on the progression through and cessation of the links of bad migrations, he explained the teachings of persons of small capacity through twelve links in which ignorance confused with respect to karma and effect leads to the accumulation of non-meritorious karma, which then projects rebirth in a bad migration. He explained the teachings for the persons of middling capacity to be the accumulation of meritorious karma, or unwavering karma motivated by ignorance confused with respect to suchness, which nevertheless results in a good migration. He explained the teachings for persons of great scope to be the generation of love and compassion toward all sentient beings—who, inferring from one's own experience, also wander in samsara by way of the twelve links—training in the path with a wish to achieve the state of buddhahood for their sakes.

Regarding the individual words in the term "dependent-related origination," "dependent" refers to things not having arisen without causes or conditions and that they arise in dependence upon causes and conditions. "Related" refers to such causes being concordant causes—that is, originating from related causes, and not being arisen from discordant causes. Thus, one can understand that they are not arisen without causes nor from discordant causes, as it states in the *Interwoven Praises*: [383]

> "Dependently" does not forsake their nature,
> and "arisen" demonstrates the way of the world.
> Like one who conquered all manner of reasoning,
> dependent-related origination is the authoritative word.

This teaches that "dependent related origination" clears away the two extremes.

What, then, are the natures of the twelve links of dependent origination, and how is it that the former ones produce the latter ones? Regarding this, there are two sequences of dependent origination: the system of the forward order and the system of the reverse order. When explaining it from the perspective of the thoroughly afflicted class, the stages of occurrence in the forward order system is as follows: from ignorance comes compositional action, from compositional action consciousness, from consciousness name and form, and so on.

There is a system of the reverse order in which old age and death are arisen from birth, and birth is arisen from existence, and so on.

The forward order is explained starting from the true origins of "ignorance and compositional action"—that is, karma and affliction—and thus explains the understanding of true origins. In the reverse order, old age and death are arisen from birth, and thus the way that the suffering of old age and death is arisen from the suffering of birth, and how that is arisen from the link of existence and so forth, explains the understanding of true sufferings.

When explaining the twelve links from the perspective of the thoroughly purified class, the principle that if ignorance ceases compositional action ceases, if compositional action ceases consciousness ceases, and so forth, gives one an understanding of the need to stop ignorance; and moreover, since it must be stopped by seeing the truth, one gains an understanding of true paths.

When explaining from the perspective of the stages of cessation—that if birth ceases old age and death cease, if existence ceases birth must cease, and so on—one develops an understanding from the perspective of the cessation of suffering. Each of the twelve links that are examined individually in the *Great Treatise on the Stages of the Path*, along with the ancillary explanation of projecting agents, actualizing agents, projected results, and actualized results with respect to those, are summarized in this treatise. [384]

Regarding the first, ignorance, which is like darkness that obscures external forms, it includes both confusion regarding karma and effect, and confusion regarding suchness. In general, *ignorance* is a lack of knowledge, or confusion. Since there are levels of subtlety in the positing of reality, there are thus levels of subtlety when positing ignorance. With respect to the initial ignorance within the twelve links, it of course can be an ignorance that is merely confused with respect to an object, but principally it is the erroneous awareness that is the ignorance confused regarding suchness. It is the opposite of the pristine wisdom that is the knower realizing selflessness; and there is no difference in pristine wisdom acting as the antidote to mere confusion as well.

According to the Prāsaṅgika system, the initial ignorance [among the twelve links] is necessarily the grasping at true existence, and thus, whatever karma is accumulated is under the power of the ignorance that is confused with respect to suchness. Since that is the case, in order to accumulate nonmeritorious karma it is taught that on top of ignorance confused with respect to suchness, ignorance confused with respect to karma and effect must act as the motivation during the action. The ignorance confused with respect to karma and effect also *arises under the power of the ignorance confused with respect to suchness.*

Summary of the Links

By way of either of those two types of ignorance, one accumulates black or white *compositional action*—the second of the twelve links— in dependence upon which one is projected to a result of a happy migration or a bad migration. Regarding the way one is projected, there is a projecting cause, actualizing cause, projected result, and actualized result.

To illustrate these with respect to a happy migration, [one starts] in a previous life with a link of *ignorance* that was confused with respect to suchness (but not with respect to karma and effect[76]), which acted as a motivation to perform a virtuous deed. This virtuous deed that was accumulated was a link of *compositional action* that belonged to the level of the desire realm among the three realms.

This link of composition action, having turned into a disintegratedness of karma, or a potential for projecting a future result, became infused as an imprint with the mere "I," or stream of consciousness, of that time. [385]

For example, the meritorious karma accumulated from being generous toward another person out of a good motivation becomes the nature of an imprint, or potential, once that karma ceases when one finishes giving the gift. Where are imprints, or potentials, deposited? The temporary basis of infusion is the consciousness of that occasion, and the perpetual basis of infusion is the mere "I." Separating that consciousness into the consciousness of the causal period and the consciousness of the resultant period, **the imprint infused by that very karma on the link of consciousness of the causal period is the projecting cause.**

The projecting cause that abides in the nature of a potential, or imprint, requires the eighth link of *craving* and ninth link of *grasping* to activate it into something that has the ability to definitely give rise to a result later. Craving is attachment regarding pleasant or painful feelings, and grasping is the attachment that regards the object from which those pleasant or painful feelings arose, such as forms or sounds; it is an attraction toward those objects. **Thus, to make manifest the infused imprints of karma, the link of craving that wishes to not be separated from happy feelings and be free from pain, and likewise the link of grasping that is attracted and attached** contains four types of attraction and attachment that are the link of grasping: grasping at desire, grasping at views, grasping at moral conduct and asceticism, and grasping at adherence to a self. **Through the two** links of craving and grasping, the imprint that was infused with the consciousness before **is activated, and the** tenth **link of** *existence* **that induces the next rebirth becomes powerful. Thus, the three** links of craving, grasping, and existence **are the actualizing causes.**

Thus, in dependence on that—the actualizing agents activating whatever was projected by the projecting agents—how many links that are projected results will be established? [386]

The third, *consciousness of the causal period,* **is conceived in the womb of one's mother in this life, and thus the aggregates of the resultant phase—consciousness, feeling, discrimination, and compositional action—are the link of name,** and thus the aggregates that are the basis of name are initially established. Then, the **blood and semen of the parents, or heat and moisture, for example, are the link of form. Since those two links are combined together,** the fourth link of name and form is established.

The tenth link of existence is the time at which the potential to establish the next rebirth has become powerful through being activated by craving and grasping. It has two divisions: *inclined existence,* and *entering existence.* Inclined existence occurs before the intermediate existence is established. Entering existence, if taken to be while in the bardo, refers to the time after the bardo is already established.

The second and tenth links are karma.

This is what is stated in the passage cited before. However, the compositional action that will be activated by the three—craving, grasping, and existence—is actually the state of disintegratedness of karma, or the imprints deposited on the consciousness at the time of the basis. Since it is an action—whether physical or an intention—that has already ceased, the continuum of disintegration, or the imprint, is given the name "existence." This is one manner of explanation.

Even though karma that projects a single birth is activated by a single existence, it is clear that an action that projects a hundred births requires activating agents of craving, grasping, and existence to establish that each lifetime.

Next, the establishment of the six sense sources of the eye and so forth is the link of the six sense sources. When these have developed,

the object, sense power, and consciousness gather together, and the contact and interaction with something pleasant, unpleasant, or neutral is the fifth link of *contact*. In dependence on the three kinds of contact with a pleasant, unpleasant, or neutral object, three types of feelings arise: pleasure, pain, or neutral feeling. [387] **Thus the three feelings of pleasure, pain, and neutral feeling that arise in dependence on that interaction are the** seventh link of *feeling*. These four [name and form, the six sense sources, contact, and feeling] are projected results.

Since the consciousness has already been conceived in any of the four places of birth, its being born is the eleventh link of *birth*. The born aggregates reaching a ripe age is old age, and the discarding of the aggregates is death, which together constitute the twelfth link of *aging and death*. Since those two links of aging and death are manifestly actualized results, those projected by the projecting factors that are results of actualizing causes are the link of birth and the link of aging and death.

Everything just mentioned was taken on the basis of the illustration of a virtuous karma included in the level of the desire realm. In the context of nonvirtuous karma the stages of establishing the twelve links would also be congruent with that.

The Number of Lifetimes Required to Complete All Twelve Links

Regarding the number of lifetimes required to complete all twelve links, in the *Great Treatise on the Stages of the Path* it states:

It is possible for even countless eons to intercede between the links that are projecting agents and projected [results]. It is also possible that they will be actualized in the next lifetime with no other lifetime in between. Since the actualizing links and the actualized links can occur without an intervening lifetime, it is possible, at the shortest, [for all twelve links] to be completed within two lifetimes. For example, if in a lifetime such as this you were to newly accumulate the karma to be born as a deity and experience [the life and resources of a deity], at that point you would complete the first two and a half links of ignorance, compositional action, and consciousness of the causal period. Up to the time of your death you would complete the three links of craving, grasping, and existence. In the next lifetime you would complete four and a half projected links [consciousness of the resultant period, name and form, the six sense sources, contact, and feeling], and the two actualized links [birth and aging and death].

Even at the longest, completion of all twelve factors will not be delayed more than three lifetimes, since the actualizing agents, the two actualized factors, and the three projecting agents each require their own lifetime, while the projected links are included [within the lifetime of] the actualized links. And, although many lifetimes may intervene between the projecting agents and actualizing agents, they are the lifetimes of other [cycles] of dependent origination and do not belong to that [cycle of] dependent origination. The time of the bardo is not counted among these. [388]

How Their Significance Is Summarized

Upon having meditated well on the way one cycles in happy rebirths and bad migrations through the twelve links of dependent origination, the crucial points of the Dharma topics for persons of both small and medium capacity are covered.

Regarding that, contemplation of the twelve links from accumulating nonmeritorious karma motivated by ignorance that projects a bad rebirth up until the link of old age and death of that cycle is related to topics of persons of small scope. On the other hand, having contemplated accumulating meritorious karma through ignorance and being projected into a good rebirth up to the link of old age and death of that cycle, thus averting attachment toward higher rebirths and training the mind in seeking liberation, is connected to the teachings of persons of middle scope. **Moreover, the great spiritual friend Phuchungwa engaged in the mind training involving the forward and reverse systems of the twelve links of dependent origination.**

My lama taught me that these days, when it comes to practice, once people are guided on the paths of small and medium persons just as explained prior, those who are broad-minded are taught meditative focal points that are a mere summary of the stages of the twelve links. Since this is not sufficient for those of middling faculties and below, these meditative focal points do not suit their level. Some persons are quite astute regarding the twelve links of dependent origination, and thus there is a tradition of experiential instructions wherein the manner of reliance on a teacher up to refuge is taught as per usual according to the small scope, then experiential instructions are given on the small scope in relation to the progression through and stopping of the twelve links of bad rebirths, and [likewise] on the middle scope in relation to the progression through and stopping of the twelve links of good rebirths. [389]

THE MEASURE OF HAVING GENERATED THE ATTITUDE OF TRAINING THE MIND IN THE STAGES OF THE PATH SHARED WITH PERSONS OF MEDIUM SCOPE

Regarding the measure of having generated the attitude of training the mind in the stages of the path shared with persons of medium scope, to give a brief summary as taught in the *Great Treatise on the Stages of the Path*: If you have understood in detail the characteristics of cyclic existence through both suffering and its origins, and the twelve links of dependent origination, then when you have naturally developed an uncontrived mind that wishes to be free from cyclic existence just as much as you would wish to escape a burning house or prison, then you have trained your mind in this path.

Otherwise, it is as Sharawa said: If [this attitude] is simply underwhelming like barley powder added to a weak beer, then your view of the causal origins of cyclic existence as undesirable will be no stronger than that. Your quest for liberation will become similar to that, as your intention to accomplish the path to liberation becomes just words. You also will not give rise to compassion that cannot bear the samsaric suffering of other sentient beings. Since you cannot give rise to uncontrived bodhicitta that is powerful enough to urge the mind on, your understanding of the Mahāyāna will also become merely a following of words.

It is thus taught that one must train by taking the topics of persons of medium capacity as the center of instructions.

Dispelling Doubts with Respect to Mind Training in the Stages of the Path Shared with Persons of Medium Scope

This third root outline should be understood from the *Great Treatise of the Stages of the Path* and so forth.

Concluding Verses

Having totally infused your consciousness in previous lives
with the imprints of karma and afflictions,
they are activated by both craving and grasping,
creating a potent future rebirth.

The aggregates of name and form are established,
diversified with constituents and sense spheres,
which experience contact and feeling from engaging in
    desired objects,
and through their birth, old age, and death you will cycle
    again. [390]

Still, these twelve links of dependent origination of existence
that appear in a manner of cause and effect,
I have experienced endless times in their forward progression;
would it not be better if I were to accomplish their reverse?

Determining the Nature of the
Path Leading to Liberation

REGARDING THE ROOT OUTLINE "determining the nature of the path leading to liberation," it is similar in meaning to the Great Fifth's outline "**the stages of practice for liberation from that**," which is his second main outline within the middle scope. [It will thus will be used here instead]. It has two parts:

   i) The type of support through which you halt cyclic existence
   ii) The type of path you cultivate to halt cyclic existence

The Type of Support through Which You Halt
Cyclic Existence

If you contemplate how you cycle in samsara under the power of the origins—karma and afflictions—and how you cycle in samsara through the twelve links of dependent origination that were taught, you will find that there is a method to free yourself from samsara, a method to halt samsara, and a method to liberate yourself from samsara. Then, when you see that liberation is most definitely an important goal or object of accomplishment worth striving for, you might ask through what kind of support can one halt samsara as a means to achieve that. The human body we have obtained that has leisure and opportunity is the supreme support for halting samsara! You are free from conditions that are counterproductive to benefiting yourself and others in this life, future lives, temporarily and ultimately. The way in which you have all conducive conditions for that have been covered in detail in the context of persons of small scope.

The Type of Path You Cultivate to Halt Cyclic Existence

This has three parts:

a′ The definitive enumeration of the three trainings
b′ The definitive order of the three trainings
c′ The nature of the three trainings [391]

In the context of mind training for persons of small scope it was taught that since a human support is highly precious and something to be achieved, for its sake one restrains faulty behavior arisen under the power of afflictions, and that a high-status physical support is to be accomplished in dependence upon the ethics of abandoning the ten nonvirtues.

Since these appropriated aggregates are currently a necessity to practice Dharma, they are helpful if utilized correctly, and thus it was taught that they must be depended on. Since in this context of persons of medium capacity we have reached a slightly higher level of mind training, appropriated aggregates that are a high-status support are not greatly treasured, but rather they are taught as an object of abandonment through viewing them as faulty, since they arise under the power of the root of all suffering itself. Thus, to be free from them not only does one need to refrain from faulty conduct arisen through afflictions, but the afflictions from which this faulty behavior arises must be made targets, besieged by the antidotes and destroyed. Therefore, one must meditate on the path that totally destroys afflictions by way of the practice of the three trainings.

If you are able to conquer the army of afflictions then you have stopped the causes that actualize the aggregates, which are appropriated through the force of having accumulated karma that actualizes existence, and thus the results also cease. This being so, the teachings for persons of middle scope have increased the level at which one counters one's mental afflictions, and raises the level of one's goal through the aspiration to achieve liberation by using a high status support.

The Definitive Enumeration of the Three Trainings

This has three parts:

> 1' There being a definitive enumeration from the perspective of the stages of taming the mind
> 2' There being a definitive enumeration of three trainings from the perspective of afflictions, the objects of abandonment
> 3' There being a definitive enumeration from the perspective of the result

What kind of path should one practice with a support having leisure and opportunity in order to halt samsara? **As it states in *Letter to a Friend*, you must train in the path of the three precious trainings:**

> **Even if your head or clothes suddenly caught fire,**
> **rather than attempting to put it out,**
> **it is better to direct your efforts to stopping rebirth,**
> **since nothing is more important!** [392]

> **Through ethics, wisdom, and meditative concentration,**
> **you must attain nirvana—pacified, tamed, stainless,**
> **without old age or death, and inexhaustible;**
> **parted from earth, water, fire, wind, sun and moon.**

This is the path to liberation that lacks nothing and is without error. Generally, non-Buddhists have practices of ethical discipline and concentration; however these are not paths through which one achieves liberation that is an abandonment of afflictive obscurations. That is why the three trainings taught by the Bhagavān are referred to as the "three superior trainings."

The three reasons given below for the definitive enumeration of the three trainings are presented as a brief identification of the three. **Through that which makes the distracted mind undistracted—the training in ethics—the manifest afflictions are undermined, and one enjoys the result of the bliss of gods and humans in the desire realm. Through that which sets the mind in equipoise which has not been set in equipoise—the training in meditative concentration— manifest afflictions are suppressed, and one enjoys the result of the bliss of gods in the form and formless realms. Through that which liberates an unliberated mind—the training in wisdom—the seeds of afflictions are eliminated from the root, and one achieves the result of liberation that has passed beyond sorrows.**

There Being a Definitive Enumeration from the Perspective of the Stages of Taming the Mind

Ethics eliminates the nature of the mind to be distracted, thus restraining coarse mental wandering. The training in mental stabilization stops the enslavement of the mind to distraction through mindfulness and introspection and sets minds that have not been placed in equipoise into equipoise. The training in wisdom liberates the mind that has not been liberated. From this perspective they are of a definitive enumeration.

There Being a Definitive Enumeration of Three Trainings from the Perspective of Afflictions, the Objects of Abandonment [393]

Through the training in ethics manifest coarse afflictions are stopped. Through the training in meditative concentration afflictions are suppressed. Through the training in wisdom the seeds of afflictions are cut from the root. From this perspective the enumeration is definitive.

There Being a Definitive Enumeration from the Perspective of the Result

Through the training in ethics, one achieves the result of guarding ethics that is the state of a god or human in the desire realm. Through the training in meditative concentration, one achieves the high status of a god in the form or formless realm. Through the training in wisdom, one achieves the state of liberation that is a passing beyond sorrow. From this perspective the enumeration is definitive.

THE DEFINITIVE ORDER OF THE THREE TRAININGS

Among the three trainings, **in order to give rise to the training in wisdom** that achieves the result of liberation and totally abandons afflictions together with their seeds, **a serviceable mind—that is, the training in meditative concentration—must precede it. Regarding that too, the training in ethics is a necessary prerequisite for an undistracted mind. Therefore, if these are practiced in the right order in the manner of cause and effect, one will become liberated from samsara. For this reason, the meaning of the Bhagavān's statement, "Actualize cessation. Meditate on the path," is that practicing true paths—the means of attainment—in order to actualize the goal of true cessations is in accordance with the mode of suffering and its origins that are prior to that.**

Contrary to that, hoping to accomplish the training in wisdom without a basis of ethics or meditative concentration ends merely in exhaustion.

The Nature of the Three Trainings

[It states in the *Sūtra Requested by Brahmā*:

Ethics] has six branches;
[Meditative concentration] is the four blissful abodes;
The four aspects of the four [noble truths
Are always pristine wisdoms.]

To summarize the intended meaning of the *Great Treatise on the Stages of the Path*, the training in ethics has six branches. (1) The possession of ethics and (2) restraint through the individual liberation vows both demonstrate pure ethical discipline that definitely leads to liberation. One's (3) religious rites and (4) range of activity both demonstrate impeccable, pure ethics. [394] (5) Dread of any misdeed—great or small—demonstrates uncorrupted, pure ethics. (6) Training having correctly adopted the bases of training demonstrates nonerroneous, pure ethics.

Regarding the training in meditative concentration, the four mental abodes are the four concentrations. They are blissful because the mind abides blissfully in this lifetime, and they are a training of the mind.

These four are the four truths having sixteen aspects. The training in wisdom is the wisdom realizing the sixteen aspects of the four noble truths.

Furthermore, a disciple of the middle scope alone who does not practice the path of persons of great scope would need to be taught all the aforementioned paths extensively. However, since we are in the context of paths *shared with* the middle scope, aside from the mere way to train in ethics, the other two trainings come up in the context of calm abiding and special insight, and therefore do not need to be elaborated on extensively **here.**

If you suppose, "Well, in that case the abandonment of the ten

nonvirtues in the context of the small scope and the ethics taught here are both included among the general training in conduct, so they do not need to be individuated!" they still do, because in Tsongkhapa's *Songs of Experience* it states:

> It is especially important that the three doors [of body, speech, and mind]
> that are defiled by misdeeds and downfalls are purified of karmic obscurations.

To give rise to either the paths of great or middle scope persons, it is essential to apply the methods to purify yourself of misdeeds and transgressions, such as the abandonment of the ten nonvirtues and so on. Some bodhisattvas have individual liberation vows and others do not. For those that do not have individual liberation vows, there is no substitute for them explicitly indicated in its entirety other than the abandonment of the ten nonvirtues, and thus that is suitable as the practice [of ethics] in this context.

Only mind training of the paths *shared* with persons of middle scope are presented here, not the standalone path for persons of middle scope. If the standalone path of persons of middle scope were to be taught and mere liberation were the goal, of course the trainings in meditative concentration and wisdom would need to be extensively explained here. [395] However, in this context the meditative focal points of the middle scope path are, like those of the small scope, presented briefly as prerequisites for the path of persons of great scope. Since the actual practices will be taught in the section of training in bodhicitta, here only the training in ethics is explained, and both the training of the mind and the training in wisdom are explained later within the context of the practices of the six perfections.

You might think it logically unnecessary, then, that the ethics of abandoning the ten nonvirtues and the training in ethics from three trainings relevant to this context be brought up when they will appear again later in the section of the bodhisattvas' training in ethics. There is no fault, however. The reason and purpose behind a division into three beings within the stages of the path is that it is more helpful for those of sharp, middling, and lower mental faculties, and furthermore, prior to small scope practitioners generating the aspiration for liberation of the middle scope, it is important that they have already prepared the collection of causes to achieve the support of a high-status rebirth. Thus, even though one is not guided on the standalone path of small scope in that context, the training in the ethics of abandoning the ten nonvirtues—the complete path for achieving the small scope goal of a high-status rebirth—must still be taught. There is no flaw of it being excessive if taught, and it would be a complete path for accomplishing the needs of those who temporarily can only meditate on that path.

Not only that, but if ethics are taught prior, even if one does not strive for mere liberation, during the extensive time it takes for one to develop an experience from training the mind in bodhicitta within the great scope, if one excellently practices the training in ethics, it will only help to achieve the higher paths and one will not be led on wrong paths. Therefore, it is helpful for those of excellent, medium, and lesser mental faculties.

Thus, **the training in ethics is as stated in the** *Letter to a Friend*:

> **Ethics, just like the ground under the animate and inanimate, was taught as the foundation of all good qualities.** [396]

Corresponding to the strength of the antidote, take upon yourself any of the seven types of individual liberation vows; that is, any of the three lay vows—the male, female, and the one-day vow—or any of the four vows of the ordained—the male and female novice vows, and male and female fully ordination vows. **It is not enough to simply take these vows; you must guard them, and thus** the four doors through which downfalls occur **were taught. The first door to downfalls is** *a* *lack of knowledge*. If you do not know what action leads to a downfall, you will be stained by faults. **Therefore, the antidote that stops** those **is making sure you understand the major and minor trainings. The [second door to downfalls is]** *carelessness*. **Its antidote is visualizing whatever is to be adopted or discarded through recollecting them. Let introspection analyzing right and wrong stand guard, and have shame, embarrassment, and trepidation for karmic fruitions.**

Even though you may understand the important distinction of having incurred a downfall or not, one can still become too lax due to carelessness. For example, if you have taken either lay or ordination vows, you must remember that you are a disciple of the Buddha, and whether you are practicing to achieve a high-status rebirth in the next life, or liberation, or omniscience, at the very least you must practice the ethics of abandoning the ten nonvirtues. Thus, through continuously being conscientious you will be mindful and introspective. The unique cause for introspection is thus constantly checking the state of one's mind and not letting it slip from one's mental awareness.

The third [door to downfalls] is *disrespect*, **and the antidote is respecting our Teacher, the rules he taught, and the companions that practice them with conviction.** Even though you may understand the presentation of downfalls and have respect toward the Teacher while being mindful, introspective, and conscientious, due to being habitu- ated to strong afflictions most of us naturally criticize and try to find fault as soon as there is a slight inadequacy. [397]

The fourth [door to downfalls] is *excessive afflictions*, **the antidote for which is to cut through the strongest of those as soon as they come to mind. Check day to day whether you have transgressed any trainings to which you have committed yourself and repair those you have transgressed and confess and restrain against those by way of the four opponent powers.** As it states in the *Sūtra Requested by Brahmā*:

> Rely on the trainings.
> Do so seriously, from your heart.
> Do not forsake them later on.
> Do not give them up even at the cost of your life.
> Always remain ardent.
> Subdue yourself.

Pure ethics are the root of all temporary and long-term happiness, and are especially helpful in this time when the five degenerations are rampant, according to the *King of Concentration Sūtra*, among others.

It is particularly important to contemplate the benefits from guarding ethics and the drawbacks from not guarding them. Since our eternal foes in all lifetimes are the afflictions, we must rely on that which directly opposes and cuts through them—the training in wisdom, which in turn depends on the training in meditative concentration. In order to have firm meditative concentration, the coarse physical and verbal deviations must first be restrained through the training in ethics. From there on, to develop in oneself the qualities of a totally pacified mind that has halted the subtle internal distractions, one must organize the very best preparations for achieving liberation—the adoption and guarding of the ethics of either the lay or ordained.

Since it is both mindfulness and introspection that pacify the subtle mental deviations, through practicing them again and again those [mental states] that are headed in the direction of a pernicious mind are thwarted, and mindfulness is placed on all behavior whether walking, moving around, lying down, or sitting—in brief, from the in and out breath onward. Thus, you stop the self-destructive situation in which you are controlled by your mind, which in turn is controlled by afflictions. [398] Then, the process of bringing your mind under your own control is simply to bring it under the control of mindfulness, nothing else. Thus, in brief, the initial instruction for generating mindfulness and introspection is via the training in ethics.

One must understand why so-called "ethics" are so important. For someone who has renounced the home life for homelessness, it is easier to engage in Dharma activities such as study, reflection, practice or retreats. Since one has gained control, there is the great advantage that one can go with ease and stay with ease in every facet and at all times, as the saying goes, "Rise like incense, fall like incense."

On the other hand, lay householders have many dependents such as spouses, children, relatives, and close friends whom they have to appease. One can end up having no choice but to get into verbal disputes through taking their sides. They are busy with work to ensure their livelihood, or otherwise preoccupied with all sorts of distractions that exhaust them beyond their control. Pondering this, male and female monastics have much greater opportunity to practice authentic Dharma. However, it is not appropriate to ordain for the sake of food and clothing, and there is also no point ordaining while you are incapable. Thus, because of being skilled in means and providing what is needed, the Teacher Bhagavān did not simply say guarding the monastic vows is the best and most impactful and leave it at that. Rather, for the many who are unable to guard such vows, he separately taught the way to guard lifelong vows and one-day vows for the laity as their own allotment. Thus, there are all levels of practice—great and small—to suit one's own ability.

There is no general rule that a Dharma teaching will be of benefit to all simply because it is profound. [399] The degree of profundity depends on one's inclinations, predispositions, and what one is ready for. A given Dharma might be profound, but if it does not accord with one's individual predisposition then it is not profound for oneself.

For someone who can excellently guard the monastic vows there is nothing greater; however, it is pointless if one pushes oneself to take monastic vows even though unable to guard them, and in such a situation it would be better to take up lay vows. Furthermore, with regard to lay vow holders, the best version is a celibate lay vow holder (*brahmacarya*), and if not that, it is still very important to guard the ethics of a lay vow holder having all five precepts, or at the very least guard a few, or a single precept.

In particular, it was the Jowo Kadampas who principally practiced pure ethics. In the holy words of Sharawa:

> Whatever good or bad happens, rely on the Dharma. Within the Dharma, if you rely on the teachings in the Vinaya you will not have to start again.

If from the outset you strive to have singularly pure ethics, you will not have to start over again from the preliminaries of the path. Otherwise, although you may concentrate your efforts in accomplishing approach retreats or achieving calm abiding, for authentic realizations to arise you must not have mixed up the stages in which ethics forms their foundation. If you do not have such a foundation, you simply cannot give rise to the realizations of the higher paths. For example, when practicing calm abiding (*śamatha*), if the collection of causes that are taught—such as abiding in an agreeable location, having pure ethics, and so forth—have not been well prepared, then calm abiding cannot be achieved. If you try to rush your progress you will not accomplish your desired result, and you will have to start over again with the prerequisites of the path. For this reason, if you strive hard in your ethical discipline and maintain purity, you need not be ashamed in front of anyone regarding your external or internal purity. In this sense Sharawa continues:

> You will have pure thoughts, stand up to scrutiny, be immediately joyfully content, and have an excellent long-term outcome.

As this statement appears to be completely true, I ask you to stop your search for branches that have no root and make this path alone the core of your practice. [400]

What, then, is the liberation from samsara that is reached in dependence upon the three trainings? Of course, a mere presentation of liberation can be found even in non-Buddhist treatises, but if one makes an unbiased, thorough analysis of that and the path to liberation taught by our Teacher, they are indeed dissimilar. Whether one believes in a creator God, or asserts that the cause of cycling in samsara is something permanent, then, due to the fact that a permanent cause cannot be stopped, samsara that has arisen from it could also never be brought to an end. This is because if any given cause abides permanently, its result must also abide permanently.

Alternatively, if one describes samsara as created by the preceding fluctuation of a motivating thought of a creator God, when stating such a creator of the universe is permanent and self-arisen, there is a contradiction in the assertion that a created universe could be momentarily fluctuating while its creator does not fluctuate moment by moment. If one then believes an explanation of the root of samsara being something that goes beyond the boundaries of the intrinsic law, or nature, of causality and that there is a way to leave that kind of existence, then one is merely a follower of religious proclamations since one does not have ascertainment based on reasoning nor a suitable basis for conviction.

Therefore, not only can one ascertain the infallibility of the theory of liberation and the way to achieve it taught in Buddhist treatises through one's own experience of mental development, but it also cannot be disproved through reasoning. This is because samsara is arisen from ignorance, that ignorance is an erroneous awareness, and there is a nonerroneous awareness that counteracts it. Since those two awarenesses oppose each other in the manner of one being harmed and the other acting as the harming agent, if one becomes powerful, the other becomes weak.

Moreover, since a nonerroneous awareness has a backing valid cognition, it develops further in relation to how much one meditates on it, and ascertainment becomes clearer however much it is analyzed. [401] On the other hand, its opposite, the erroneous awareness, may occasionally manifest a little strongly through prior habituation, but if it is analyzed well it is not self-supporting and is thoroughly disturbing. It furthermore has no supporting valid cognition, and the ignorance grasping at true existence that is the root of samsara itself is impermanent by nature—it arises and passes away. There are many such reasons for the state of our mind to have the potential to develop.

If there is a cause, it will have a result; if that cause is good, the result will likewise be good, and if the cause is bad, the result will also be bad. Moreover, if a cause is terminated, the result will likewise cease. As these are the facts of reality, then taking them as a working basis, external causality does not go beyond results being able to be inferred based on whether their causes are good or bad, or big or small, and therefore internal causality—the workings of different subtleties of mind—also have a respective result of happiness or suffering that they correlate to. This is the basic premise.

Take ice, for example: even if it becomes as hard as a rock, since it is fundamentally in the nature of water, when it meets the right conditions, it will melt. In the same way, we have currently become a mass of the three poisons to the point where our stream of consciousness has become like a glacier. Yet fundamentally it is in the nature of clear light that has existed without beginning, and therefore upon meeting the right conditions the adventitious obscurations clear away. Since the ultimate nature of mind—spontaneously arisen clear light—and its ultimate potential, the ability to realize of all objects of knowledge, naturally exist, from the perspective of the mind being clear and knowing by nature, the Dharmas of realization and so forth are able to be accomplished.

Moreover, through the above-mentioned reasons, or basis, of how mistaken awarenesses meet back to ignorance grasping at true existence, [402] the coarse continuum of aggregates belonging to childish, ordinary beings who are currently under the control of the three poisons will be completely terminated, at which point will emerge a body in the nature of mere wind and mind that can appear in a multitude of creative displays. Thus, one can find conviction that, in general, something called "liberation" exists as an object of knowledge, and that a special quality of mind—a separation that is an abandonment of afflictions—exists as an object of knowledge.

In particular, one can become convinced that it is possible to accomplish those within one's own mindstream, and that there comes a point of having achieved a state of separation that is an abandonment of afflictions in which, even if met with the right conditions, the afflictions could never arise again, and if such a state exists, then it is possible to be separated from the imprints of those afflictions also. Due to that, one can find conviction that so-called "omniscience" exists, and if we can gain an understanding of omniscience through our own continua, the Buddha, our object of faith, becomes as if nourished, through which one is able to find conviction in liberation and omniscience.

Concluding Verses

In the pure earth that is the foundation in ethical conduct,
the water and fertilizer of a pliable mind
ripen the harvest from the seedling of the path of special
    insight,
thus eradicating destitution within samsara.

Majestically atop [the elephant] of conscientiousness,
  Airavata,
[Indra], the one with a thousand eyes of mental equipoise,
destroys samsara's mountains, the foundation,
 with his hundred-spoked vajra of nonexistent self-grasping.

In the dense forests of the wilderness of endless samsara,
grows a wish-fulfilling tree that is the three trainings,
beautiful in the undying forest of eternal happiness,
and never singed by the flames of suffering. [403]

Training the Mind in the Stages of the Path for Persons of Great Scope

HAVING ALREADY EXPLAINED the topics of persons of middle scope, then in connection with the stages of the path for persons of great scope that will be explained now, the Great Fifth's promise to compose is as follows:

> The lama of all migrators in the three realms,
> Tsongkhapa, the illusory display of Mañjuvajra,
> cuts all webs of confusion without exception,
> with a subtle weapon that is pure and sharp.

> The jewel handle of renunciation from the drawbacks of
>   suffering and its origins
> holds up the canopy of the three trainings.
> [This parasol of] your excellent advice, beautified by the gem
>   tip of nirvana,
> has already twirled up to the peak of existence.

> Now will be explained how the four rivers of great conduct
> unceasingly flow down
> from the great Anavatapta lake of supreme compassion
> into the ocean of omniscience.

Regarding this it states in the glorious protector Nāgārjuna's *Precious Garland of the Middle Way*:

If you and the world
wish to achieve highest enlightenment,
its root is bodhicitta—
stable like the king of mountains.
It is compassion reaching the limits of space,
and pristine wisdom not dependent on duality.

As stated, as a cause for achieving our ultimate goal of the victorious state of omniscience in which the welfare of oneself and others is perfected, one must have the view realizing emptiness that is connected to precious bodhicitta, rooted in compassion—the unification of method and wisdom. This is the "perfection of wisdom" that is a wisdom directly realizing emptiness conjoined with bodhicitta. Therefore, bodhicitta has an indispensable relationship with enlightenment. [404] The wisdom directly realizing emptiness is the cause for enlightenment in all three vehicles, whereas bodhicitta is the root among causes for enlightenment in the Mahāyāna.

From one perspective, we have been born in a time where the five degenerations abound: (1) degenerate sentient beings, (2) degenerate afflictions, (3) degenerate times, (4) degenerate lifespan, and (5) degenerate views. Moreover, we exist during a time of many obstacles, such as inferior wisdom and inferior merit. However, looking at it from another perspective, we have been born during a time when the doctrine of the benevolent Teacher has not degenerated and we are able to meet with the path to omniscience—this method of training in precious bodhicitta. This is worthy of such joy as if a more valuable opportunity had never come our way. This situation did not come about without causes and conditions, but rather through the power of many outer and inner conditions including vast merit accumulated in previous lifetimes. This unparalleled opportunity achieved this once should not be wasted. In order to make it meaningful, first gain an understanding of the way to achieve omniscience. Then, through listening, contemplation, and meditation, it is of utmost importance to bring the practice of habituating our mind in that direction [of omniscience] to completion.

Even accomplishing each individual mark or sign of a buddha requires a vast collection of causes, as stated in the *Precious Garland of the Middle Way*, and as such, in brief, attaining the state of buddhahood requires accumulating the collections for three countless eons. Contemplating this in depth, you might get the feeling, "How am I able to do this?" However, just as it is taught that bodhisattvas are able to easily complete the collections through the four inconceivable aspects, upon seeing such an approach one finds self-confidence and despondency is cleared away. This all happens due to bodhicitta that cherishes others more than oneself. As it states in the gentle protector Tsongkhapa's *Great Treatise on the Stages of the Path* [405]:

> Thus, merely seeing, hearing, recollecting, or even touching upon the source of all excellence of oneself and others, the medicine that heals all fragility, the great path traversed by all great masters, it becomes the nourishment of all wandering beings. The fact that one is able to enter into the Mahāyāna which possesses the superbly skillful means of accomplishing the totality of one's own welfare as a byproduct of working for the sake of others, is incredible! KYE MA HO! Having thought, "What I have found has been excellently acquired," enter into this Mahāyāna with all the resourcefulness of a capable being.

This powerful advice given here is akin with that stated in *Way of the Bodhisattva*:

> Mounted on the horse of bodhicitta,
> which dispels all sorrows,

what sane person could become despondent,
proceeding in this way from joy to joy?

Bodhicitta accomplishes what is stated in the *King of Aspirational Prayers of Ārya Maitreya*:

> It turns one back from the road to the lower realms,
> perfectly revealing the path to higher status.
> It leads to the state without old age and death.
> To bodhicitta I prostrate.

The first two lines indicate the path of persons of small scope, and the third indicates the goal of persons of middle scope—liberation— thus teaching the special quality of bodhicitta being able to accomplish these also.

In brief, bodhicitta is the principal cause that lacks nothing for achieving higher status and definite goodness. When bodhicitta is born it is not that the small and medium scope paths are discarded and bodhicitta is generated separately from them. Rather, since bodhicitta must possess two aspirations—one awareness endeavoring for the welfare of others, and another seeking enlightenment—and since the root of the awareness endeavoring for the welfare of others meets back to renunciation, and because disillusionment with future lives has a causal relationship with being weary of this life, when the three beings were taught in the stages of the path it did not focus on stand-alone persons of small or middle scope, but rather on the stages of the path *shared with* persons of small and middle scope. [406] Through this one can understand that the lower paths are a collection of causes that must be fulfilled as a preliminary to bodhicitta, the path of persons of great scope.

So-called "mind generation" is not the mere noble thought, "May beings be happy and free from suffering." Rather, through seeing that suffering can be removed, it becomes a reality that an altruistic attitude is what one should develop, and thus in the treatises it states, "Compassion focuses on sentient beings; wisdom focuses on enlightenment." The two arise in conjunction.

Therefore, just as the Kadam lamas of the past also taught that the practice of bodhicitta must be held as the center of the path, how could this opportunity for us to meditate on such profound Dharma not be incredibly fortunate? Even hearing the mere mention of bodhicitta is the highest of good fortune, and thus developing an understanding of it, thinking, "Bodhicitta is like that," and on that basis simply being able to recollect its good qualities shows one has seriously great merit.

In order to cultivate the beneficial mind of bodhicitta, this section on the path of the persons of great scope first teaches the manner of training one's mind, and then, having trained it to the point of developing some small experience, the way to practice it by means of adopting it through the mind generation rite.

With respect to the third topic of training the mind in the stages of the path of persons of great scope, Atiśa's *Lamp for the Path* states:

> **Through an understanding of their own suffering,**
> **whoever deeply desires to correctly eradicate**
> **all suffering of others**
> **is a supreme being.**

Whichever being, gauging from their own experience, has an attitude of wishing to completely free all other sentient beings to the limits of space from suffering and its causes, and through this strives for the state of victorious omniscience, that being is supreme.

In the context of persons of middle scope, those who have become fearful of the suffering of cyclic existence and have given rise to an uncontrived aspiration for liberation from suffering, and who subsequently train their mind only in the path of medium scope are of

course only seeking pacification for themselves alone. [407] Whereas someone who trains their mind in the path shared with persons of middle scope in this context infers, based on their own suffering, that other sentient beings likewise cannot bear suffering, and wishing them to be free from suffering, accomplishes the method for that. Such a person is a being of great scope.

Thus, when meditating on the middle scope path as explained before, the goal of high status explained in the context of the small scope similarly without essence, arisen from the root of impure karma and affliction, and as a result lacks a state of peace, thus it is explained that liberation from the binds of karma and affliction is the sole goal to be achieved. Subsequent to that, here in the context of the great scope, liberation likewise is not the ultimate goal, for the peaceful state of nirvana is only partial peace. Therefore, only limited objects of abandonment have been abandoned, and the qualities of realization are likewise limited; abandonments and realizations have not been completed. There is still the dharmakāya—the completion of abandonments and realizations—that remains to be achieved. Thus, if you become totally entranced by the liberation of nirvana, you fall into the extreme of partial peace, and it is said that can become an obstacle to achieving omniscience for a long time.

As that is the case, if you contemplate the suffering of samsara—the three realms—applied to yourself, and, unable to bear it, give rise to an awareness seeking mere liberation from that, and then, upon seeing that other sentient beings are oppressed by suffering just as yourself, you become unable to bear their suffering as well. Just as you must end your own suffering, so too must the suffering of others be brought to an end. Upon clearly seeing that if you discard the welfare of others and merely seek the partial peace of nirvana for yourself alone it is incredibly rude, inappropriate, and cruel, then you become able to give rise to an uncontrived mind that can single-pointedly achieve the happiness and well-being of others. [408]

The way one correctly enacts the welfare of others is to teach the way sentient beings achieve omniscience through striving to purify their own afflictions together with the imprints of those afflictions through correctly putting into practice what is to be adopted and discarded. One must moreover guide sentient beings by teaching a path that accords with their individual dispositions and inclinations, and thus one must not only know their dispositions and inclinations, but one must know the unerring path, or Dharma, that is to be taught to them.

From that perspective, until one achieves the state of omniscience that knows all modes and varieties of Dharma, one can only accomplish a partial and limited welfare of others, rather than their everlasting, ultimate, and perfected welfare. Having understood how clear this is, then spurred on by the mind wishing to place all limitless old mother sentient beings in the ground of omniscience that is free from suffering and its causes, one thus seeks one's own enlightenment.

Thus, it is important to understand that, in general, enlightenment exists as an object of knowledge, while in particular it is suitable to be achieved in one's own mind, and likewise that all other sentient beings have the potential, or conditions, to achieve enlightenment within their minds.

Sometimes we might think to ourselves that if buddhas fill space, have their minds directed toward sentient beings, and only enact the welfare of others in such a way that they are always waiting in preparation to fulfill the welfare of others, then what difference does it make to sentient beings whether I achieve buddhahood to place them in the ground of buddhahood? What need is there for me to become enlightened? If sentient beings already have everything they need, then from the perspective of the one trying to help are they indeed destitute? [409]

That might deceptively seem true, yet we ourselves are left untamed by other buddhas, and as disciples of the Lion of the Śākyas, the Guide, it is with our Teacher, the Buddha, that we have a greater karmic

458 THE FOURTEENTH DALAI LAMA'S STAGES OF THE PATH

connection. As such, it is through that connection that we were able to take our first steps along the path to high status and definite goodness. For that reason, however much earlier a sentient being who has fostered unique connections of uncommon karma with others over many not-too-distant lifetimes ends up achieving the state of buddhahood, then to that degree they will be able to speed up the process of helping, at the very least, whomever becomes their disciple based on the extent of their karmic connection, and by all means are much more capable of doing so. It is worth considering it in terms of this reasoning.

Thus, if one understands the consideration that the happiness and suffering of many beings is dependent on whether one becomes enlightened or not, one is able to see that this directly concerns the welfare of others. Through this one is spurred on by the aspiration seeking the welfare of others, thinking, "Since there is no option but to obtain buddhahood, I will achieve omniscience with my focus on the objects of intent, sentient beings," and bodhicitta, a primary mental cognition concomitant with that aspiration is born.

Thus, here in the context of beings of great scope it is not enough to merely achieve liberation for oneself alone as was explained as the goal of the middle scope, but rather one must take it to a more profound level and expand one's point of view. One must thus strive for the state of buddhahood that is by nature the four bodies—the goal of nonabiding nirvana. There is no higher goal or achievement. Thus, although the three paths of small, middle, and great scope are equal in clearing away untamed minds through a person meditating on them and sequentially training and developing their mind, from among those it is the great scope path—the methods for omniscience—that is truly elevated, the highest, the ultimate, and the most noble. [410]

By which method is [this path] generated? According to [Āryaśūra's] *Compendium of the Perfections*:

Having totally given up both vehicles,
that are incapable of helping the world,
I will enter into the vehicle of the victorious sage,
taught out of compassion, and of one taste with altruism.

Even if one achieved liberation through the practice of engagement in [the third and fourth] and disengagement from the [first and second of the] four truths, one has still not fully completed one's own welfare, and thus no vast altruistic benefit has occurred. Since that is the case—that one is clouded with respect to how to achieve the welfare of the entire world—one should not enter into the two vehicles of śrāvakas and pratyekabuddhas that have no capacity for accomplishing vast altruistic benefit, but rather into the Mahāyāna, the way of the sage and king-like vehicle, the teaching of the Buddha rooted in compassion, that which is in the same nature and one taste with altruism that single-pointedly benefits others. Through this one must achieve the aims of sentient beings, as stated in [Candragomin's] *Letter to a Student*:

Even cattle eat grass that is easily found
or happily drink water when parched with thirst if they come
    across it.
The endeavor of great beings for the welfare of others,
    [however]
is their glory, their joy, and their superior skill.

The sun races on a chariot, illuminating all,
and the earth supports the world without a thought of burden.
The nature of great beings without any self-concern is similar
    to this—
they devote themselves to the happiness and benefit of world!

Since animals can also accomplish the mere happiness of this life, the thought of seeking mere happiness for oneself alone is nothing to be amazed at. Having achieved this precious human body, whoever puts this incredible human intellect to use for the benefit of others is truly impressive. Therefore, **the ability or prowess of supreme beings is taking on the burden of helping others with fortitude, like the sun and moon who vanquish darkness, and the great earth that holds up the world.** [411] Thus, perceive it as a responsibility fitting for intelligent beings, and do not be content with an attitude of seeking happiness for yourself alone. You must help others by developing the courage to take on the burden of the welfare of all sentient beings.

Such is indispensable, as it states in *Way of the Bodhisattva*:

> **Wretched beings chained in the prison of existence**
> **are suddenly proclaimed as the children of sugatas**
> **and become worthy of veneration in the world of gods**
>   **and men**
> **when they give rise to bodhicitta.**

[Śāntideva] teaches here that even a migrating being suffering within cyclic existence becomes a bodhisattva the moment they develop bodhicitta. Without bodhicitta, it matters not what other qualities you might have, such as a precious higher training—you are not included within the Mahāyāna.

In the lamrim text *Swift Path* (*Myur lam*) [the outlines in this section are as follows]:⁷⁷

a) Showing that bodhicitta is the only entrance to the Mahāyāna
b) The way to develop bodhicitta
c) How to train in the conduct having given rise to bodhicitta

The benefits of bodhicitta—the entrance into the Mahāyāna—are very important, so here I will present ten points. [412]

Bodhicitta as the only Entrance to the Mahāyāna

Whether you are a follower of the Mahāyāna—that is, someone with the courage to take on the great burden of the welfare of others, who has the exceptional resolve and bravery—depends on whether you have this mind. As soon as you develop this mind, you are a "great being" and member of the Mahāyāna. If that mind weakens, you are expelled from the Mahāyāna, hence why it is taught that "bodhicitta is the sole entrance to the Mahāyāna." In the gentle protector Tsongkhapa's *Great Treatise on the Stages of the Path* it states that it is not enough that their Dharma be a Mahāyāna Dharma, but the person themselves must enter the Mahāyāna.

One Receives the Name "Child of the Victors"

When bodhicitta has arisen in oneself, it does not matter whether one was born in samsara within the class of animals or hungry ghosts, destitute through being dominated solely by karma and affliction. Through the power of that mind arising one is proclaimed as a bodhisattva, a child of the sugatas who has overcome the enemy of the four māras. Even though one's own support is inferior, and one might lack any other qualities, one is worthy of veneration by all gods and mankind.

Likewise, without bodhicitta it does not matter if a person has directly realized emptiness or achieved the state of an arhat with the quality of having abandoned afflictive obscurations—the name "bodhisattva, child of the victors" will not apply to them.

One Surpasses Śrāvakas and Pratyekabuddhas in Lineage

Even though, occasionally, beginner bodhisattvas may not be able to surpass śrāvakas and pratyekabuddhas in terms of capacity of mind, once they achieve the qualities of the seventh ground they can surpass them. Although that may be so, it is said that through merely having bodhicitta in one's mind one surpasses śrāvakas and pratyekabuddhas in terms of the lineage of vast capacity of mind. [413]

One Becomes a Supreme Field of Offerings

In Candrakīrti's *Entering the Middle Way* it states:

> Śrāvakas and middling realizers [pratyekabuddhas] are born
>   from the lords of sages;
> buddhas are born from bodhisattvas.
> Compassion, nondual awareness, and
> bodhicitta are the causes for the children of victors.

As stated, buddhahood arises in dependence on bodhicitta, and thus it is a buddha's unique, close cause. Thus, it is taught that even buddhas pay their respects to the bodhisattvas. As such, since a being who possesses bodhicitta is the embodiment of astonishing bravery that takes on the vast welfare of oneself and others, they are worthy of veneration and homage from all beings, and have become a supreme, exceptional field for accumulating merit.

One Easily Completes the Vast Collections

It is as the eleventh-century Kadampa Geshé Nyugrumpa said:

> If you can give rise to bodhicitta once, initially the collections
> will complete themselves, the obscurations will also clear by
> themselves, and obstacles, too, will vanquish by themselves.

If you are embraced by the spirit of bodhicitta, then whatever virtue is performed for the sake of buddhahood with sentient beings as one's focus, you complete unimaginable collections equal to the number of sentient beings.

One Quickly Purifies Negativities and Obscurations

If you develop a noble mind intent on helping others, you will be able to purify exceptionally powerful misdeeds that could not be cleared away by other confessions [rites]. Not only that, but it is furthermore stated in *Way of the Bodhisattva* and other texts that cultivating this precious mind for a single session is superior to spending one hundred years exerting oneself in methods for purifying obscurations and misdeeds without embracing the spirit of bodhicitta. [414]

Your Intentions Are Fulfilled

Through generating this mind [of enlightenment], the temporary and ultimate aims of both yourself and others are spontaneously fulfilled according to your intentions. Therefore, it is due to lacking this mind that ordinary beings are unable to accomplish the collection of tantric activities. Of course, in that context one needs deity yoga and the view of emptiness, but if one has bodhicitta, all of the infinite activities are accomplished without effort, and it is for this reason that it is said to be the important heart of the path for any practice of sutra or tantra.

One Is Unaffected by Harm or Obstacles

Bodhicitta is solely a thought to benefit. It is the mind of the two aspirations having as its root the great love for all sentient beings like that of a mother for her only child. Thus, if anyone were to harm such a person with this mind, not only would the bodhisattva not perceive them as doing them harm, but they would have greater love for the one that harmed them than that person has for themselves. Thus, it is in every way like the supreme conqueror, the Seventh Dalai Lama, Losang Kelsang Gyatso said in his *Praise of the Noble One*:

The love I have for even myself does not make up a fraction
of your heart's compassion.

One Quickly Completes All Grounds and Paths

With such an altruistic thought there is nothing that can stop you,
and since all conducive conditions are excellently complete, it is only
natural that one's Dharma activities become increasingly successful.
Thus, without bodhicitta, the view of emptiness alone can only serve
to complete the collection of pristine wisdom, and not the collection of
merit. The easy completion of the collections and natural purification
of misdeeds and obscurations is primarily achieved through the power
of bodhicitta. [415]

One Becomes a Field That Is the Source of All Happiness of Beings

In line with all these qualities, bodhicitta is, in brief, the quintessential
holy Dharma that acts as a source of all goodness for all beings. With
respect to training in such a mind having many benefits and qualities,
it states in the *Sublime Continuum*:

> Those who have the seed of aspiration for the Supreme
>   Vehicle,
> whose mother is the wisdom that births the enlightened
>   qualities,
> who abide in the womb of blissful concentration, and whose
>   nurse is compassion,
> such a person is the child of the sages.

Water and fertilizer are the common cause for producing a variety
of grain, and a mother belonging to the merchant caste births sons
of various castes. The unique cause [for each of these, respectively,]
is a barley seed and a father of definite lineage such as a brahmin.
Planting a barley seed will not yield wheat, nor will a son of a brah-

min belong to the fisherman caste. In the same way, whichever vehicle, great or small, you use to free yourself from samsara, the mother needed for both is the wisdom realizing selflessness and so on. However, it is bodhicitta that is the unique father-like cause of buddhahood. It is akin to the precious vajra that eliminates all problems of existence and peace, and thus is the supreme path that surpasses all lesser ornaments.

The compassion that aspires toward the supreme vehicle and the bodhicitta rooted in that are like seeds, the creators of buddhahood that are its unique cause. The wisdom realizing selflessness is the mother that births all the Dharma of buddhas, pratyekabuddhas, and śrāvakas, and therefore is a shared cause. Special insight (vipaśyanā) assisted by calm abiding (śamatha), and likewise realizations that are a union of calm abiding and special insight are also akin to mothers. [416]

Regarding trainings in bodhicitta, **the stages of the path for persons of great scope**, i.e., the third outline within the stages of the path, there are three parts to the **practice**:

a) Showing that bodhicitta is the only entrance to the Mahāyāna
b) **The way to develop bodhicitta**
c) **How to train in the conduct having given rise to bodhicitta**

While [Tsongkhapa's] *Great Treatise on the Stages of the Path* gives three outlines, this treatise [of The Great Fifth] condenses them into the latter two.

To explain briefly why I have included the first outline "Showing that developing bodhicitta is the only entrance to the Mahāyāna" as Tsongkhapa has in his *Great Treatise on the Stages of the Path*: within the Mahāyāna the Buddha taught both a sutric and a mantric vehicle, and regardless of which one you choose to enter with, bodhicitta is the only gateway; there is no other. Therefore, even if no other qualities of realization arise, the moment bodhicitta is born that being has entered the Mahāyāna as explained before, and as soon as one loses bodhicitta, it does not matter whatever qualities one might have, be it a realization of emptiness or what not, it is proven through many scriptures and reasonings that one falls from the Mahāyāna. Therefore, whether you enter or exit the door of the Mahāyāna revolves around whether you have bodhicitta or not. It is not enough that your Dharma be that of the Mahāyāna; it was taught that it is more important for the person themselves to have entered into the Mahāyāna. Thus, if the wisdom realizing emptiness is not a unique path of the Mahāyāna, there is no need to mention the other paths.

THE WAY TO DEVELOP BODHICITTA

Regarding "the way to develop bodhicitta" (which is the second outline within the *Great Treatise on the Stages of the Path,* and the first outline within this treatise) there are two parts:

  i) The stages of training in bodhicitta
  ii) **How to adopt bodhicitta through its ritual** [417]

Here the *Great Treatise on the Stages of the Path* instead presents four parts as follows:

  i)   How bodhicitta depends on certain causes to arise
  ii) The stages of training in bodhicitta
  iii) The measure of producing bodhicitta
  iv) How to adopt bodhicitta through its ritual

The first, "how bodhicitta depends on certain causes to arise," has three further outlines:

   a' How it is arisen from the four conditions

b' How it is arisen from the four causes

c' How it is arisen from the four strengths

Regarding these, **generally the conditions for producing bodhicitta are, (1) directly witnessing the qualities of the buddhas and bodhisattvas; (2) listening to the scriptural collection of the bodhisattvas without witnessing them directly; (3) without having listened to them in great detail, having heard the rough reasonings of why** bodhicitta **is indispensable for achieving buddhahood, and one thus** gives rise to bodhicitta that **cannot bear the Buddhist doctrine disappearing; (4) one gives rise to bodhicitta wishing to achieve buddhahood while thinking, "Even though the teachings may not decline immediately, if, in these particularly depraved and degenerate times, it is rare for someone to set their mind on the enlightenment of śrāvakas and pratyekabuddhas, what need is there to mention highest enlightenment?"** These are the four conditions through which bodhicitta is generated.

Then there are the four causes by which bodhicitta arises: (1) lineage, (2) a spiritual teacher, (3) loving compassion, (4) not becoming disheartened.

Simply through being born into an excellent lineage one gives rise to bodhicitta through causes such as naturally arising strong compassion and great altruism. Through the power of relying upon spiritual teachers who are great bodhisattvas one trains in emulating their holy life examples and thus gives rise to bodhicitta through this cause. Regarding loving compassion, during the actual training in bodhicitta, the causal order is to first give rise to great compassion, then through that induce the special resolution, and that in turn induces bodhicitta; however, in this context there is no need to separately mention the special resolution to take on the burden oneself; instead one wishes to achieve buddhahood out of the loving compassion that thinks, "How wonderful if all sentient beings were free from suffering!" Thus, it is taught from the perspective of great compassion acting as the unique close cause for generating bodhicitta. [418]

Next, there are **four strengths**: (1) **one's own strength**, the power derived from concertedly developing commitment, by which one generates bodhicitta; **(2) the strength of others; (3) the strength of the cause—being habituated with the Mahāyāna in previous lifetimes; and (4) the strength of practice—having habituated with virtue in this life. Thus, many causes and conditions are presented for the generation of bodhicitta, including the four strengths and four causes, and so forth**. These must be understood in detail from the great treatises.

In brief, the cause for bodhicitta meets back to compassion, as it states in the *Ornament for the Mahāyāna Sūtras*:

> Its root is asserted to be compassion.

Compassion must fulfill two conditions: it must be an awareness that has love toward and feels devastated by someone tormented by suffering, and wishes to either free or protect them from that.

Within the introduction to suffering we saw in the context of persons of small scope the contemplation of the suffering of suffering together with its causes, and in the context of the middle scope the contemplation of the suffering of change, and in particular the suffering of conditioning. In these contexts, one contemplates how the suffering of conditioning affects oneself and thus gives rise to (1) a wish for oneself to be free from the suffering of conditioning, and (2) a pursuit of liberation that is free from that. The manner in which suffering is introduced in the contexts of persons of small and middle scope is converted into a focus on others in the context of the great scope. As it says in Maitreya's *Ornament for Clear Realization*:

> Mind generation is for the welfare of others.

It is taught that "the welfare of others is their own nirvana." One thus trains in the mind of compassion by contemplating an approximation of the nirvana of others based on one's own experience, and one thinks how they are either currently oppressed by the suffering of samsara— that is, controlled by karma and affliction—or if not directly oppressed by that right now then the fact they have all the causes for it to arise. One must then try to give rise to a mind wishing to free them from suffering and its causes. [419]

In the context of persons of middle scope, one contemplates "the suffering of conditioning"—that is, the faults of the root—afflictions. However much we view afflictions as faulty, to that degree we will wish to be free from (1) the imprints deposited by those afflictions, which continue to the tenth ground and end of a sentient being's continuum and act as obstacles to understanding the reality of objects, (2) the manner that they greatly prevent one from accomplishing the welfare of others, and (3) the fact that the negative tendencies of body and speech that remain for arhats is a fault of the imprints deposited by [their previous] afflictions.

In this context, that awareness that wishes to be free from those things must be redirected and transformed into an awareness that has a pleasant aspect: one that loves and cherishes all sentient beings who are oppressed by suffering. Therefore, regarding this, there are two topics to be explained: (1) training one's mind in the instructions on seven-fold cause and effect, and (2) training one's mind in the practice of equalizing and exchanging self and others.

Regarding the first, although it is common in textbooks to find the phrase "the seven-fold instructions on cause and effect" (rgyu 'bras man ngag bdun), since that is slightly unclear, it is better to employ the phrase "the seven-fold cause-and-effect instructions" (man ngag rgyu 'bras bdun). This mind training lineage comes from Maitreya, and the mind training in equalizing and exchanging self and others was passed down from Mañjuśrī. Later, the "tradition of powerful conduct"—that is, the practice of equalizing and exchanging self and others—was introduced in the protector Nāgārjuna's *Precious Garland of the Middle Way*. Nāgārjuna emphasizes the practice of equalizing and exchanging self and others in his *Commentary on Bodhicitta*. For these reasons this tradition is termed "tradition of vast conduct," which is highly significant. Since this is a practice for sharp-faculty bodhisattvas, Śāntideva states in *Way of the Bodhisattva*:

> Train in the secret vow
> of exchanging self and others.

Since there was a stronger emphasis on following the path of reasoning, then the manner of contemplation such in the context of equalizing and exchanging self and others did not involve visualizing loved ones such as one's mother initially, but rather contemplating straight away from the perspective of the "other side," like one's enemy, recollecting their kindness and how one is equal to them, and so forth. Since this is incredibly powerful, it is called the "tradition of vast conduct." [420]

When "understanding all beings to be one's mother and recollecting their great kindness" was taught in the context of the seven-fold cause-and-effect instructions, it is clear that the other person's behavior and expression are considered important in one's visualization and that there is a unique recollection of their kindness within that. That being said, in the context of equalizing and exchanging self and others there is no mention of the other person's demeanor [in one's meditation] due to the very fact that oneself and others are equal in wanting happiness and not wanting suffering. Normally our ordinary compassion depends heavily on the behavior of the other person; thus we have compassion for those counted as friends or loved ones who help us, and not for those who harm us.

I think that kind of compassion is distinguished through depending on another's behavior and demeanor. *Limitless* compassion is primarily only considerate of other sentient beings themselves, and thus is a different case in which the other person's nice or off-putting behavior and so forth is not important. Rather, because it is said that we are equal in wishing for happiness it appears to function in accordance with the agent.

With respect to the objects that a bodhisattva holds dearer than their own life, they are attached and yearn for them from the perspective of cherishing them; this is also required. Generally, there are those who teach that compassion can be afflicted compassion. If afflicted compassion existed then afflicted faith could, too. In some texts it also teaches that because faith is virtuous it does not arise in concomitance with the apprehension of true existence.[78]

If we look at how things appear to our own mind, when someone who has not understood the lack of true existence observes the Tathāgata, an apprehension of true existence most likely arises, and as it says [in Maitreya's *Ornament for Clear Realization*]:

It is the subtle attachment to the victors and so forth. [421]

I wonder if it is feasible whether single-pointed faith could occur together with grasping at true existence, and thus it is very important to make a distinction between such types. At a quick glance, the intense closeness of those two due to fondness is almost similar to closeness due to our afflicted attachment. However, there is a great difference in terms of the environs of that fundamental awareness, and there are also differences in disposition, faculties, and inclination. Thus, in reality, through these factors we protect our faith in the Dharma at our own volition.

Training through the Seven-Fold Cause-and-Effect Instructions Based on Jowo Atiśa's Works

With regard to a clear explanation of the two ways of training the mind like that, the second outline in the *Great Treatise on the Stages of the Path*, and the **first** outline within this text—"the stages of training in bodhicitta"—has two parts:

    a' Training through the seven-fold cause-and-effect instructions based on Jowo Atiśa's works

        1' Developing certainty about the order

            a" Teaching that compassion is the root of the Mahāyāna

                1" Compassion being important in the beginning
                2" Compassion being important in the middle
                3" Compassion being important in the end

            b" The way the six other causes and effects are either causes or effects of compassion

                1" How recognizing all beings as one's mother and so forth up until love are the causes
                2" How the special resolve and mind generation (bodhicitta) are the effects

        2' The actual gradual training

            a" Training the mind in striving for others' welfare [422]

                1" Establishing the basis for giving rise to that mind

      (a) Achieving impartiality toward sentient beings
      (b) Establishing all [beings] as having a pleasant
          aspect

        (i) Meditating on them as one's mother
        (ii) Meditating on recollecting their kindness
        (iii) Meditating on repaying their kindness

  2"   Actually giving rise to that mind

      (a) Meditating on love
      (b) Meditating on compassion
      (c) Meditating on the special resolve

  b"   Training the mind in striving for bodhicitta
  c"   Identifying the result of this training—bodhicitta

 b' Training through equalizing and exchanging self and others
based on ārya Śāntideva's works

To give a general summary of the above outlines, **these days the core
practices are the seven-fold instructions transmitted by Atiśa, and
the lineage of instructions** of equalizing and exchanging self and
others **from Śāntideva, the son of the victors.** Among those two traditions of mind training, **in terms of the reason for training in the
tradition of the great Atiśa, it is true that there is significance in their
order, in that the state of buddhahood arises from bodhicitta, which
itself arises from the special resolve, which arises from compassion,
which arises from love,** which is not the mere love that thinks, "May
beings be happy!" but rather is affectionate love that cherishes them
and is fond of beings without being mixed with attachment. **This** love
arises from [the thought of] repaying their kindness, which arises

from recollecting their kindness, which arises from recollecting all beings as one's mother—that is, as our dearest loved one such as one's mother—and so forth. However, there is no certainty that compassion arises between love and the special resolve rather than at another point, as it states in [Candrakīrti's] *Entering the Middle Way*:

> Kindness itself is like the seed of this excellent harvest
> of the conquerors, the water for its growth, and
> its ripening in a state of long enjoyment.
> I therefore praise compassion at the beginning. [423]

Compassion is thus the laying of a foundation in the beginning like a seed; it enhances potential in the middle, like water and so forth; and in the end is like the ripening of the fruit in that it brings long-term enjoyment. Compassion is thus important in the beginning, middle, and end. Therefore, **even the initial commitment to liberate beings from samsara relies on compassion. Not only that, but it is also necessary to not become despondent and fall to lesser paths due to difficulty in the middle. Even having become a buddha, working tirelessly for the sake of all sentient beings without abiding in a [state of] peace like śrāvakas or pratyekabuddhas relies on great compassion. Thus, for great compassion to arise, too, seeing beings as appealing is necessary.**

However much you cherish and are affectionate toward the object of your compassion, to that degree your wish for them to be free from suffering and have happiness will be stronger. Thus, for great compassion to arise, too, the object needs to be perceived as pleasant. For that reason, **one must know all sentient beings as one's mother**, then recollect their kindness, wish to repay their kindness, develop affectionate love, compassion, and the special resolution—the six causes in which the former act as the causes for the latter—and then give rise to the result of actual bodhicitta.

Regarding the topic of knowing all beings to be one's mother, it is not the case that one should only contemplate that all beings are one's mother, but it can be anyone who is very close to you, such as your mother and so forth.

Persons who have not trained in these paths can still recollect the kindness of their mothers and so forth, and through that recollection develop limited love and compassion, but they do not develop that toward their unfriendly enemies and so forth. Not only that, but they also wish them the opposite—that they meet with suffering and be parted from happiness. Therefore, if we, too, do not develop equanimity from the outset, even if we familiarize our mind with the path, our love and compassion will remain biased. The antidote for that is, therefore, to meditate on equanimity. [424]

One might thus think, "Well, if I need to accomplish affectionate love toward my mother and so forth, what about my current mind of affection I have for them?" The loving affection within the seven-fold cause-and-effect process cannot be mixed with attachment at all. The kind of love that we currently have in our minds is brought on by attachment. Therefore, just like it is uncomfortable to have a home built on uneven ground, love is not possible with greater and smaller degrees of attachment and aversion toward others.

For that reason, one must first level the mind with equanimity and only then move on to training the mind in gradually recognizing all beings as one's mother and so forth. Therefore, before giving rise to the wish to attain buddhahood for all sentient beings, if you do not already have a heart-felt, strong determination to achieve happiness and eliminate suffering for the sake of all sentient beings, which is the ultimate purpose, then one's wish to achieve buddhahood is nothing more than the words of a prayer. Striving for enlightenment must be induced by the aspiration of striving for the welfare of others, and it is therefore crucially important that one be sincere in one's thought for the welfare of others.

The welfare of others, moreover, is not the exhaustion of some faults and the gaining of a few qualities. Rather, it is the establishment in the state of omniscience in which all faults have been eradicated and all qualities are possessed, and thus this involves seeking the perfected welfare of others. For that reason, if one has affection and fondness for a particular being, one will be able to take on the burden, thinking, "I will be the one to free them from suffering and bring them happiness." This, therefore, is the purpose of developing affectionate love that cherishes and is fond of beings.

It is at present easy to apply this thought to those we like but not to those we do not, and thus to develop affectionate love it is crucial to start with an equanimous mind. If one has meditative experience with topics taught in the context of middle scope beings, such as *the fault of uncertainty* and *the fault of repeatedly descending from high to low*, then equanimity will be slightly easier to develop. [425]

Yet, one might think, "Would it not complicate things and cause delay by leaving aside the affection I have had, and still have, for my mother and so forth in this life, and instead start with the practice of equanimity?" Such is not the case, because the wish to help our loved ones that we as ordinary beings have is rooted in "me" when it comes to "*my* dear ones." This leads to cherishing that is biased through attachment associated with that. Likewise, putting this "me" who is so important at the center of everything is what results in "*my* enemy" to whom we are hostile. Such bias serves no purpose, and in this context, it is a loving mind free from prejudice, and which extends to all sentient beings, that is needed to induce bodhicitta.

Therefore, one does not take as one's reason for being kind out of love and compassion the fact that such persons are friends or relatives—that is, from valuing what is held as "I" and "mine"; rather, by reason of the other person not wishing for suffering and wanting happiness and having such rights it becomes a mind training in loving others like oneself. Thus, without getting caught up with whether such a person has helped me before or whether or not they like me, bodhicitta and the special resolve induced by unbiased love and compassion must arise. For this reason, our current biased love for friends and family serves no benefit and is only harmful; hence the purpose of meditating on equanimity from the outset.

Moreover, to meditate on limitless equanimity free from attachment and aversion to any sentient being, which is not itself a neutral feeling nor a neutral application,[79] first clearly visualize a sentient being who is neither friend nor foe—someone neutral. [426] Bring to mind their physical shape, behavior, and so on, and while observing these let aversion or love arise. If you find that neither your aversion that sees them as disagreeable or love that sees them as agreeable are very strong, yet one is still stronger than the other, then apply the antidote to the greater of the two, and meditate on it until your mind becomes equanimous.

The reason for meditating with respect to a neutral person in the beginning is because we have greater equanimity toward them and thus it is easier for it to arise. Then, balance your thoughts as much as possible through contemplating well the obvious thoughts of aversion toward our enemies who upset us, and attachment toward our loved ones so amicable to us. Even these enemies, whom we consider our foes right now in this life, have been our friends in past lives and helped us greatly, and have even given their lives for us countless times, among other acts, and they will become our friends again in the future. Along the same lines, thoroughly contemplate how our friends of this life were our enemies in past lives, harming us through murder and so forth, thus equalizing our thoughts of love and aversion toward them.

This is not only applicable to past and future lives; those who were our foes in the early part of our life can become the best of friends toward the end. Thus, if the tradition of cultivating equanimity based on the fact of total uncertainty is linked with the reasoning of visible reality—that is, **if one gains meditative experience in the middle scope topic of uncertainty regarding friends and foes—it is far easier to sustain this meditative focal object. Like scattering a flock of birds with one stone, if effortless equanimity toward beings arises through these three objects of meditation, that is sufficient. If you still struggle, it is crucial that you meditate by shifting to multiple different categories.**

Through initially expanding your attitude toward the three categories of persons—friends, foes, and neutral—in this way, first start by observing a group of amicable neighbors and a group of neighbors with whom you do not get along, and achieve equanimity toward them. [427] Then, if you gradually expand your focal objects to include persons from allied and unallied nations and achieve an equanimous mind with regard to them, in the end you will be able to achieve equanimity toward all sentient beings. Otherwise, contrary to that, if you observe an abstract generality of all sentient beings and have equanimity toward a big mass, you will still retain the nonequanimous mind that finely distinguishes between friends and foes. Therefore, first achieve equanimity based on the individual as above and then later expand it universally. Doing so ensures it will be stable and of good quality.

Having balanced one's mind that has aversion toward one and attachment toward another in regard to all sentient beings who are either friends, enemies, or neutral, you then first create the foundation of an altruistic intention. This involves recognizing all sentient beings as one's mother. For this purpose, contemplate as follows: (for the sake of viewing all sentient beings as one does the person closest to us in this life, among whom one's mother is foremost), **"Due to there being no limit to samsara how could there be a single being into whose womb I have not taken rebirth?" When contemplating this, you might imagine it, but it is difficult to induce certainty**

through meditating on this abstraction. Therefore, bring to mind your mother of this life in front of you, with all the realistic features of her age, stature, clothing, demeanor, and so forth. Similar to how she was one's mother in this life, she has been one's mother in many other lifetimes. It is as stated in the sutras how the mother of the Tathāgata in that lifetime had been his mother many times while he was a trainee. Moreover, he stated the same about the past and future lives of other beings. By thinking that these statements are the nondeceptive words of an authoritative being and inferring as such and meditating upon it, one will find exceptional and deep ascertainment. [428]

Then, meditate on this with respect to other beings such as your father, relatives, neutral persons, and enemies of this life as well as hell beings, and so forth. In the end, the mind knowing all beings to be one's mother will no longer be contrived, and you will see them as you do your mother of this life.

Since there is no limit to sentient beings, and because births are beginningless and so too are womb births, not only have all sentient beings been one's mother, every sentient being has been one's mother countless times. These and other topics related to knowing sentient beings as one's mother are of course difficult to conceive, yet one must make a concerted effort due to its incredible significance. If one does this mind training alongside merit accumulation and purification of obscurations, then upon seeing even an insect, one's mind that conceives how they have been one's mother naturally arises without having to think of other reasonings. Due to this, one will see that there cannot be found any being who has not been one's mother, and at that point, without requiring any focused effort, one will naturally cherish and respect them, and affection will arise spontaneously. Thus, you must train until this happens.

Once you have had an experience of this, then with regard to recollecting their kindness, bring to mind your mother's appearance as before. She carried you in her womb for up to ten months. She disregarded her own happiness, hunger, thirst, and so on. Every helpful or harmful course of action she did for her child, and thus offered her own life and body possessed of leisure and opportunities. She was therefore greatly kind in the beginning. Having given birth to you, she placed you on a soft bed, nurtured you with a mind of love, looked at you with eyes of tenderness, welcomed you with a joyful grin, called you with sweet words, suckled you with sweet milk, fed you by her tongue, wiped your nose with her mouth, cleaned your stool with her hand, pressed you close to the warmth of her body, protected you from crises related to fire, water, and huge falls. [429] From the depths of her heart she would have chosen that she got sick instead of you, to die instead of you, and so on. Since she protected you in these ways, she was greatly kind in the middle.

She taught you herself how to eat and how to walk, and what she did not know she had others teach you. She disregarded misdeeds, suffering, and scathing remarks and gave away all of her dearly prized estate and possessions that she acquired through hard work when she was fit and strong; thus, she was greatly kind in the end. Thinking of these things, do not stop meditating until tears fall from your eyes, your hairs stand on end, and your heart is completely moved.

Thus, from the perspective of being a mother of a single lifetime, when the mother in the context of a human being in this lifetime first gave birth to her child, this little child did not know the word "mother," yet they entrusted their heart, mind, and chest to their mother who was their sole protector of life and limb. In doing so there was no one dearer to them than their mother, and in dependence on her care they had to start their life's journey. From the mother's perspective, too, she saw her child as a part of her own body, and voluntarily took on and endured whatever pain or difficulty that arose. She only saw these as her responsibility. Without irritation over the difficulties, she had an intense desire to nurture you through her profound love and affection.

Scientists explain that generally, such a frame of mind even causes milk to flow naturally from the breast, and if she would not have had such strong love for her baby then the milk would not discharge. When milking cows or *dzo*, and so forth, occasionally leading a calf in front causes them to give more milk. These seem to relate even to loving instincts.

Whatever the case, we require supportive love starting from when we were born in order to survive. [430] Shabkar Tsokdruk Rangdröl (1781–1851) himself presents this clearly [in his *Repaying My Mother's Kindness*[80]]:

I entered into my mother's womb through karma.
My greatly kind mother, who carried me for ten months,
would not do activities involving jolting movements.
She could not eat random food from other people nor tighten
    her waistband.
My greatly kind mother, who worried about hurting her child.

When it was time for birth, the pain was as if her flesh and bone
    was splitting apart.
When I came out, she laid me upon a soft cushion.
Not concerned whether I was a boy or girl,
my greatly kind mother was delighted, as if she had found a
    jewel.

She lovingly took me in her gentle hands.
With affectionate eyes she welcomed me with a smile.
Calling me sweet names she suckled me at her breast.
My greatly kind mother, who enveloped me in her own warmth.

Cooked food would have sufficed,
but fearing for my health, she fed me from her tongue.
Thinking she might hurt me if she used her hand,
my greatly kind mother cleaned my nose with her soft mouth.

Fearing that using earth or stones might hurt me,
she used her own hand to clean up my filth without revulsion.
Scared she might crush me during the night,
my greatly kind mother gave up the bliss of her own sleep.

She protected me from all disasters of water, fire, and huge
    drops.
She gave me tasty food and called me sweet names.
She dressed me in soft clothes and taught me how to walk and
    talk.
My greatly kind mother, who kissed me on my forehead.

When her child had a headache or a simple cold,
she thought it better if she were sick instead.
She thought it better if she would die instead.
My greatly kind mother meant it from the depths of her heart.

When I would get up and take a few steps,
other people said she would prop me up from both sides
and tell them proudly, "Look at my child!"
My greatly kind mother whose heart was overjoyed.

When coming and going while drinking alcohol,
and when staying in the village I was cared for like a treasured
    possession.
When I went away, she worried if something had befallen me.
My greatly kind mother with no times of mental respite. [431]

When I had become physically active,
she fed me as much good food as my stomach could digest.
She dressed me in comfortable clothes and beautiful jewelry.
My greatly kind mother, her mind always joyful.

If she obtained some food, she thought to give it to her child.
If her child had gone away, she still would not eat it,
Instead, she would leave it until it would spoil.
My greatly kind mother who always loved me dearly.
When I was thirsty, she poured me the best sweet tea.
When hungry she piled food up in front of me.
When cold she wrapped me in warm, soft clothes.
My greatly kind mother who gladly gave me what I needed.

If, from her own side, my mother lacked this level of love and kindness toward me for even a day, it is clear that I never would have enjoyed the good fortune of living a comfortable life in this human body. For this reason, she was important in the beginning. In the middle period she reared and nurtured me by employing a variety of means according to each situation with great effort, teaching me manners starting from the proper way to eat, drink, dress, converse, and so on. Finally, she did all she could to ensure a good education when I was of schooling age so that I could have a good livelihood and be an upstanding person who has good food, clothes, and reputation. Not only that, but she was never lacking in fortitude or effort—factors that we as people of faith also require to get to the state of liberation and omniscience. Accordingly, she was integral in the beginning, middle, and end.

Even in the case of animals, whether it be birds or any other kind, although they lack intelligent resourcefulness, they lovingly rear their young to the best of their ability. Some species of birds form parental couples, much like in human households, where a mother and father bird will stay together year after year raising chicks until they are ready to leave the nest. [432] Others, while not staying together always, will share the care until the chicks are reared.

There are some species of bird where the father takes no responsibility, much like with dogs, where the mother must raise them by herself. This is the same too in the case of most womb births, not just merely with humans. If you think about the mother's care toward the offspring, it lends greater insight into the extraordinary kindness of mothers. In brief, you should view all sentient beings as like your dear ones who have cherished you from the heart throughout your life, exemplifying one's mother who is foremost.

Having thus trained your mind in recollecting the kindness of your mother, **then starting with your father and so on up to your enemies, contemplate that all the other six types of migrating beings who have been your mother countless times in past lives behaved much the same as your mother in this life. Although everything thus mentioned is not applicable with respect to animal [mothers] and so forth, it appears the intention is that there is not one of these acts they did not show you when they were your human mothers.**

Having developed experience in recollecting kindness, repaying that kindness is as stated in *Letter to a Student*:

> **While seeing that your loved ones have fallen into the ocean of**
>   **samsara**
> **as if into a whirlpool swirling around,**
> **there is nothing more shameless than liberating just yourself,**
> **while disregarding those who you no longer recognize due to**
>   **death and rebirth.**

Mother sentient beings are agitated by the demon of afflictions. Ignorance has blinded the eye that sees conduct to be adopted and

discarded. They are bereft of the staff of profound, holy Dharma. They are devoid of a virtuous friend who could lead them to the city of liberation, like a guide for the blind. Not being sure-footed, they have slipped on the resting place of higher rebirth and liberation and fallen into the abyss of samsara. [433] You no longer recognize these beings who wander in the prison of the three sufferings because you die and take rebirth, yet they are all your kind parents who helped you across many lifetimes. Therefore, think, "If these mothers do not put their hopes in me, their child, who will they put their hopes in? If the responsibility to carry this burden to protect them does not fall upon me, their child, who does it fall on?" For example, if you had a way to free your kind parents of this life from the horror of prison, or the wilderness, robbers, or dangerous predators, but you chose to ignore them and sit in comfort, what could be more shameless or embarrassing? As stated in the *Verses of the Nāga King Drum*:

> The ocean, mountains, and the earth,
> are not my burden to carry.
> But any deed left unrepaid,
> is indeed my great burden.

As such, if I were to abandon my kind mothers even while being able to protect them and enter into the lesser path seeking peace for myself alone, the holy ones would be ashamed from the depths of their being. Therefore, give up that pursuit and think, "I will help all beings."

What, then, is the way to help them? Think that you will give food to the hungry, drinks to the thirsty, medicine to the ill, material aid to the poor, and so forth, which eliminate temporary suffering, and which are causes for accumulating the collections and as such are not to be avoided. However, if you regard samsaric enrichment alone as the best way to help beings, remember that they have already been Brahmā, Kāmadeva, and cakravartin kings countless times yet not achieved stability, and they are now in a situation of suffering from destitution and heat and cold. If you principally enable them to have contaminated happiness, however much their wealth grows, that is how intensely their happiness will turn into suffering. It would be just like adding salt water to a wound that will not heal. Therefore, commit yourself to establishing them in either liberation or the state of omniscience. [434] Reflect on this to ensure you are stirred.

It is insufficient to have merely created a basis for generating the mind that seeks the welfare of others. Love, compassion, and the special resolve must be meditated on to give rise to the actual mind of bodhicitta. With respect to love and compassion, although there is no fixed order of cause and effect between the wish for others to be happy and the wish for them to be free from suffering, generally in one's practice love is generated first, as it says in the *Precious Garland*:

> Even offering hundreds of dishes
> of food three times a day
> does not match a portion of the merit
> from one instant of love.

Moreover, in relation to meditation on loving-kindness, there are the eight qualities of loving-kindness:

> Even if you are not liberated through love,
> you will attain the eight qualities of love:
> gods and humans will be friendly,
> they will also protect you,

You will have mental pleasures and much physical pleasure,
poison and weapons will not harm you,
without striving you will attain your aims,
and be reborn in the world of Brahmā.

With respect to meditation on love, whose benefits are limitless, contemplate your mother in this life. Whether or not she has the manifest sufferings of illness or poverty, she lacks happiness due to the suffering of change and pervasive compositional suffering. Generate a strong mind wishing to place your mother who lacks happiness into a state of happiness, and verbally repeat and contemplate the following many times: "How wonderful it would be if my old mothers, who are bereft of happiness, found happiness! May they find happiness! I will do what it takes to help them find happiness!"

You should similarly meditate by preceding as before with regard to all beings without bias—friends, enemies, and so forth. Apply it contextually as appropriate: in the three lower rebirths beings are undergoing manifest suffering, and in happy rebirths they may or may not be undergoing the suffering of suffering. [435] It is as taught in the *Way of the Bodhisattva* in the section on patience.

However, if you think that because of such-and-such harm they did to you they have not benefited you, consider whether the harm you did to them in a past life has come back to you as revenge, or if it is the case that they had no control and their afflictions made them do it. If your mother of this life or a close relative was possessed by a malevolent spirit and attacked you with a weapon or whatnot, instead of getting angry you would work hard to find a way to free her of the spirit. In the same way, the mothers of our past lives whom we labeled as enemies from the mistaken perspective of this life are also possessed by the demon of affliction. Thus, practicing as before by thinking, "It would be wonderful if they were free

488 THE FOURTEENTH DALAI LAMA'S STAGES OF THE PATH

from the demon of affliction and had happiness," and so forth is an essential point.

Just as you meditate on love by reflecting on how your dear mother and other loved ones of this life are oppressed by suffering and thinking, "How wonderful it would be if they were free from all suffering and had every happiness," in the same way, through reflecting on how your enemies of this life are the same as you in wishing for happiness and not wanting suffering, you must think, "May they have happiness," and "May they be free from suffering."

However, if you think it will be easy to cultivate love for your enemies since you have already meditated on them being your mothers then you have not given this proper thought. It is evident that some shameless people kill their mothers of this life, or see them as enemies and hurt them in different ways.

Having meditated on love for all sentient beings one moves on to compassion. Through observing one's mother of this life, as before, and their oppression by any of the three sufferings, you think, "Woe! My mother in this life is directly harmed by suffering, and indirectly harmed by its origins, and as such has no opportunity for happiness. If only she were free from this suffering!"

Verbally repeat the following many times while mentally reflecting on it: "How wonderful it would be if all these old mother sentient beings who are tormented by suffering were free from suffering. May they be free from suffering! I will do what it takes to free them from suffering!" [436] Furthermore, transition to your enemies, friends and neutral persons and contemplate this. If these, too, are grounded in the experience of the practices of small and middle scope beings then they will be easier to meditate on relative to your own personal experiences, as stated in the *Great Treatise on the Stages of the Path*.

Some might wonder whether the arising of strong compassion causes one to add to their own mental suffering. The fear would be that through thinking about the suffering of others one might feel as though one has taken on an extra burden when already one's own suffering is difficult to bear. Yet, training the mind that observes the suffering of others through compassion that contemplates reasoning is something that you take on voluntarily, and thus although it is obviously possible that it can disturb the mind on occasion, on the one hand it is assisted by wisdom, and on the other it is voluntary. This makes a significant difference, as stated in Śāntideva's *Way of the Bodhisattva*. If you thoroughly analyze this method, in dependence on your own suffering, although fear and terror are very intense, the awareness that arises through compassionate thoughts actually serves to increase your mental strength. Modern science currently states that a compassionate thought such as empathy arising in the brain leads to a proactive thought response. [437]

The love and compassion just explained are not the same as the mere wish that sentient beings be happy and be free from suffering that is cultivated by followers of the Hīnayāna. In this context **love and compassion are able to induce the perfect special resolve that thinks, "I will make that happen!" Therefore,** they are not posited as the mere wholesome thoughts of "May they be removed from suffering!" or "May they have happiness!" Rather, one must generate special, powerful love and compassion and think, "May I myself make them have every happiness and make them be removed from all suffering!" This is the special thought to take on the burden of accomplishing the welfare of others by oneself. In doing so, one creates the basis for generating the mind directed to full enlightenment. Since the bodhicitta possessing two aspirations is induced by this special resolve and born in one's continuum, **the perfect special resolve that is induced by both** love and compassion **is not merely a mind that wishes beings to be free from suffering and placed in happiness. One commits to do it oneself, thinking, "Woe! I myself will take on the responsibility of connecting these lovely sentient beings with happiness and freeing**

THE FOURTEENTH DALAI LAMA'S STAGES OF THE PATH

them from suffering!" Along with that thought, verbally repeat the
following multiple times: "I will be the one to bring happiness to
these old mother sentient beings who lack happiness. I will be the
one to free from suffering these sentient beings who are oppressed
by suffering."

Do not merely think, "How great it would be if they were free from
that," while observing their oppression from suffering, like a business-
person deciding on a sales price. **Through the force of generating a
mentally unfabricated perfect special resolve** in which you carry the
burden of the welfare of others, when you think of accomplishing the
welfare of others you see that you currently do not have the courage to
bring to completion the enormous welfare of others; nor do you have
the capacity to do so. [438] As the saying goes, "The fallen cannot lift
the fallen"—without being able to take care of yourself you cannot
help others take care of themselves. Through initially understanding
that, you give rise to an awareness seeking enlightenment for yourself
as a condition for accomplishing the welfare of others.

For such an awareness seeking enlightenment to arise, it is not
enough to merely think that there is something called a "state of
buddhahood." Instead, you must understand that it can be accomplished on the basis of your own continuum of consciousness. Therefore, make sure you employ the means to ascertain how liberation
exists, and how one abandons afflictions by means of analyzing the
four truths with reasonings for a long time.

Regarding this, it is most important to distinguish coarse and subtle
minds and come to an understanding based on explanations related
to highest yoga tantra. It is otherwise difficult to explain the concepts
decisively. When that literature explains the presentation of the four
bodies of a buddha, it imparts a way of thinking of them based on the
fundamental, innate clear light mind.

Thus, the statement "Compassion observes sentient beings; wisdom
observes enlightenment" carries significant meaning in the above con-

text and should therefore be considered carefully. Furthermore, with respect to the above, on the basis of having contemplated the statement "They cease within emptiness,"[81] the aspiration seeking the welfare of others acts as a cause, and the primary mind that is concomitant with the aspiration seeking enlightenment—that is, the "precious mind of bodhicitta that cherishes others more than oneself"—is generated in one's continuum.

Thus, **through remembering the qualities of enlightened body, speech, mind, and deeds explained in the context of going for refuge and thinking to yourself, "If I achieve this state that possesses these exceptional qualities then I will be able to guide sentient beings as well," you generate the aspiring mind directed to supreme enlightenment, and thus it is equal to the mind generation that starts the three incalculable eons.** [439]

One might wonder if, in the context of repaying their kindness, there is already the thought to establish sentient beings in the state of nirvana, and so whether there is anything particularly special about the perfect special resolve. The difference between the thought to repay kindness and the special resolve is like, for example, the difference between committing to buy an item and settling on the price. You therefore must make a careful distinction.

Training through Equalizing and Exchanging Self and Others Based on Arya Śāntideva's Works

This has three parts:

1' Contemplating the benefits of exchanging self and other and the faults of not exchanging self and other
2' The ability to exchange self and other if you habituate yourself with doing so
3' The stages of meditating on how to exchange self and other

If you have thus thoroughly trained your mind through the seven-fold cause-and-effect process you are able to generate actual bodhicitta, and therefore, aside from the difference in the manner of guidance, the essential meaning is covered in Śāntideva's tradition; thus both are not needed separately. However, both traditions are taught in the *Great* and *Middle-Length* lamrim treatises and these practices were set forth due to the various mindsets of trainees. The mind training method of Śāntideva's tradition is the tradition for brave bodhisattvas. In particular, its strength in analysis through reasoning is something we can establish through our own first-hand, direct experience of this life, and thus this tradition is important.

Regarding the explanation of this, the first section given in the *Great Treatise on the Stages of the Path* is the benefits of exchanging self and other and the disadvantages of not exchanging self and other; [however,] it would be advantageous if we expand these two in accordance with [Panchen Losang Yeshe's] *Naked Instructions for the Swift Path*, in which he creates five divisions for training the mind through exchanging self and other, namely: (1) contemplating equalizing oneself and others from many standpoints; (2) contemplating the faults of self-cherishing from many standpoints; [440] (3) contemplating the qualities of cherishing others from many standpoints; (4) the actual attitude of exchanging self and other; and (5) the way to meditate on giving and taking in dependence on that.

The way to equalize self and others in this context is not as it was before in the context of the seven-fold cause-and-effect process in which you merely equalize your mind so that you lack unequivocal hate toward "enemies" and absolute attachment toward "loved ones." Instead, here the division of self and other in which you hold yourself as more important and others as less valuable is totally nonexistent. Whether it be oneself or the limitless sentient beings, "oneself," "others," "friends," and "enemies" are all the same in not wanting suffering and desiring happiness. All are the same in having the right to rid themselves of suffering and achieve happiness, and all have the fundamental constituent of tathāgata essence. Thus we are by all means equal in that our state of being is such that we are able to eliminate suffering and achieve happiness. One should think that, "I, whatever the magnitude of my importance, am one person, whereas venerable sentient beings are limitless and uncountable." Thus, in terms of numbers, it is obvious that one should prioritize others. Therefore, if you can consistently carry out in thought and deed the wish to benefit others without different durations, it is greatly impactful. For this reason, you should first train your mind in this way in equalizing self and others.

Regarding this, Śāntideva states in his *Way of the Bodhisattva*:

> Both oneself and others
> are the same in not wanting suffering.
> So what difference is there,
> that makes you hold on to yourself and not others?

> Both oneself and others
> are the same in wanting happiness.
> So what difference is there from oneself,
> because of which you strive for the happiness of self alone? [441]

As said, taking your own suffering to be so important and trying to eradicate it while oneself and others are all the same in not wanting suffering is without reason. Moreover, since oneself and others—all sentient beings—are the same in wanting happiness, there is absolutely no reason why one's own happiness is particularly more important. The fact that all beings desire happiness in the same way is something we must understand. Just as we try through many avenues and a multitude of means to achieve our desired happiness and it *should* be achieved for oneself, so too we should strive for the happiness of others also by whatever means possible.

However, if you think that because one's own happiness is one's own welfare it must therefore be achieved by oneself, and since others' happiness is their own welfare and should be achieved by themselves, then it would have to be the case that since one's own happiness is one's own affair, one should not rely on any other person! Yet, that is not the case—we are highly dependent on others. It will never be the case that, for the sake of our happiness, we must only employ various means like showing outward expressions such as sticking our thumbs up pleadingly or feigning laughter in order to accomplish our own welfare, and that happiness will fall from the sky without having to depend on anyone else. The happiness of oneself and others is only created through mutual dependence. As such, having aroused concern for the welfare of others, it helps, for example, if you simply try to comfort someone who is going through a hard time, or even just showing a mere smile with a pure heart to someone who is sitting there sadly in a state of desperation. [442]

Therefore, just as one's happiness and suffering are connected to others, the happiness and suffering of others are also connected to oneself. This is the reality of the situation, and not a line of reasoning Buddhists pursue for a certain purpose. For example, the world as described by modern science cannot have been created by any one thing, but instead the entirety of its environs and beings therein have come into existence interdependently and depend on one another for survival. It is explained that when commenting on the presentation of the world, one can only do so by looking at it holistically, or in its totality, and that it cannot be explained using a single thing as proof. Such explanations by scientists are not through faith in a single religious principle, but instead based on reasonable inferences and demonstrations of reality founded in research performed for generations. A presentation in accordance with that is taught through Buddhism.

Training the Mind in the Manner of Contemplating the Faults of Self-Cherishing from Many Standpoints, and the Benefits of Cherishing Others from Many Standpoints

In regard to the manner of training the mind in the second outline of [Panchen Losang Yeshe's] *Swift Path* lamrim, contemplating equalizing oneself and others from many standpoints, and the third outline, contemplating the faults of self-cherishing from many standpoints, it is very important to be able to identify the faults of self-cherishing in the beginning.

Self-cherishing is to consider yourself as the most important and only think about yourself at all times and in all aspects, while seeing others as of little importance and disregarding them. [443] If you have a strong inclination to forsake others, you naturally will end up performing the ten nonvirtues and all that goes along with those. It would not matter who you needed to kill to temporarily get your way, you would do so without hesitation. You would rob others, rape and sexually abuse others, trick and deceive others. Without seeing anything wrong in hurting others you would lie, be divisive, use harsh speech, idly gossip, be covetous and malicious, and have wrong views.

We have seen people crush others' liberties without concern. Out of religious or political views, those who rule as dictators take part in systems of centralized power that make it so the majority have their freedoms removed and live in fear. This, also, is due to their self-cherishing. It comes from their pursuit of their own happiness, and in the quest for advantages of wealth, prestige, and so on, they disregard the lives of other beings and also destroy the environment without a care. Due to this, we are in an extreme situation on our earth in which we must experience the suffering of the upheaval of the elements, climate change, pandemics, famine, and so forth that make us question whether all life as we know it will survive. This is also a result of self-cherishing.

Even in the case of our own daily lives, if, from the moment you wake up, you make enemies of everyone around you including your neighbors by being rude to them, not only have you shown complete disregard for their well-being, but you will also end up friendless, alone, and having to talk to yourself, making it uncomfortable when you go here and there, and there will no longer be anyone for you to contact. When someone has become temporarily wealthy or powerful, those who always have their own self-interest at heart, suspicious that others might get to them first or whatnot, address them with respectful titles, and feign polite conversation. [444] In reality, everything up to their laughter is a short-lived act, and not at all heart-felt laughter. Since that person will be able to recognize the other wants something from them because of how they are smiling and acting friendly, but they will also stop thinking of them as a friend and thus be unable to trust them.

Leaving aside the question of such a person being happy throughout their lifetime—even when it comes time to die, at the end there will be no dear and faithful caregiver to look after them. On the day they die no one will feel a sense of loss and it will be hard to find someone who even mutters an empty prayer. Not only that, but they will also be sure to say, "Finally it happened. From tomorrow my ears can have some peace. If only they had died earlier—their death came too late."

There is absolutely nothing to admire in a person whose negative reputation outlives them and makes people spit at the mention of them. Thus, those who cherish themselves and forsake others will come to experience the result of unwanted suffering, as was taught in the section of karma and effect in the context of small scope beings.

From the perspective of practitioners of the path of great scope, the aspiration toward the goal of liberation for oneself alone as taught in the middle scope is similarly seen to be the inferior nirvana of one-sided peace that is arisen from cherishing oneself alone. Due to the view of emptiness they are not left in the lurch, and it has acted as the antidote to obscurations that are afflictions, yet even though [that view] is capable of being an antidote to knowledge obscurations, situationally it lacks the sufficient support of the method aspects of bodhicitta and so forth. Thus, as [the view of] emptiness cannot become an antidote to knowledge obscurations, being bereft of mind generation, too, is definitely because of cherishing oneself and forsaking others. [445]

If, on the other hand, through cherishing others you have recognized that others' lives are also important, even though you might not be able to hold their lives as dear as your own, still you have the thought that it is wrong to kill others out of a lack of affection, and through contemplating that others, too, have the wish to live happily just like oneself and that they have the right to do so, which is reflected by your adoption of concern for the lives of others and giving up of killing.

The practices of the ethics of abandoning the ten nonvirtues—that is, turning away from harming others and its causes, as mentioned in the section on persons of small scope—are not solely abandoned because it stops one being sullied by faults. They are also connected to the thought in the back of one's mind that would not dare to totally disregard the rights of others. Speaking from a religious perspective, one's engagement in applying antidotes through viewing the ten nonvirtues as faulty and practicing the ethics of abandonment for the sake of achieving a high status rebirth in the next life—and furthermore for it to have the conducive conditions of long life, wealth, and power, and ultimately the achieving of omniscience—are the advantages of cherishing others.

Even in the context of this temporary life, in a single day if you get up in the morning and greet whomever you meet—be it your townspeople, neighbors, and so forth—in a friendly way and with respect, then in general everyone will develop good relationships with joyful smiles. Thus, with the awareness cherishing others thinking, "If I do not, who will? I will try as much as I can," from the depths of one's heart if one not only refrains from harming others but also outwardly helps them, it will be returned in kind with sincere joy and closeness. [446]

When I was little, there was a small parrot and a few other birds at Norbulingka. My language tutor, Khenpo Dampa, would bring nuts with him and give them to the parrot, and so the parrot would display all sorts of delighted expressions upon seeing him. When he would cup his hands around the parrot and stroke its head, the parrot would sit so well. I wanted the parrot to show similar joy toward me, but how I went about it was to poke it with a stick when it was not happy with the minimal amount of nuts I had given it. This angered the parrot, and so it intended to bite me as soon I arrived and was never happy to see me. Just as when someone shows us sincere affection it is returned with fondness, so too all sentient beings have an innate desire for happiness and dislike for suffering. Regarding that desire for happiness, we can furthermore recognize if the kind person and the affection they have shown is genuine.

Even among our people, when Tibetans were endlessly tortured by the Chinese in prisons, despite being locked up and certainly terrified, it is said that if they had someone to trust in, there was some gladness to be found through being there for each other and being a shoulder to cry on for one another. In the same way, you accomplish benefit and happiness through mutual friendliness, affection, and sincere intention. This is the cherishing of others. As such, kindheartedness and affection are certainly the root of happiness.

Whether you are religious or not, or even if you object to religion, if you want a happy life, you must treat people with kindness no matter what. [447]

If you cherish others then whatever difficulties you encounter, such as if your financial situation is inadequate, those willing to help you, such as lend you money, will come from the left and right. Whomever you talk to will listen to you and respond, and in the end, all will be sad you are gone on the day of your death, saying, "Oh no! What a shame! They were such a good person." Even if they only have a single offering lamp, it will be lit, and even if only a single line of prayer, it will be said. Such are the benefits of cherishing others. Things such as future lives and understanding sentient beings as our mothers from beginningless cyclic existence are quite distant, so if we contemplate the possible drawbacks and advantages of the two types of cherishing within this life, whether we can do it from the depths of our heart is another story, but the noble thought of cherishing others itself cannot be faulted by anyone. Moreover, even someone who objects to religion cannot criticize cherishing others, and if birds could talk, they too would certainly support cherishing others! No one would attempt to explain how it is mistaken.

There is a lot of debate surrounding the view of emptiness, for example, due it being so hard to conceive and because of the misunderstandings that arise, yet in the three levels of existence there is no way to explain how this noble altruistic thought could be faulty or mistaken.

Between hatred and attachment, hatred is the total antithesis of altruism. Not only are there less instances of harming another through being directly motivated by attachment, but from time to time, out of attachment, one cares for others and benefits them. Hatred and anger only induce harm, and thus there is never a situation in which hatred is permitted within the bodhisattva scriptural collections and below. [448] Out of the two types of motivations—the causal motivation and the motivation during the action, secret mantra treatises permit one to have a wrathful motivation during the time of the action under special circumstances; however, the causal motivation must necessarily be compassion. As such, cherishing others is the root of all happiness, the source of all that is good in this life and the next, and the principal practice of the victors and their spiritual heirs. Thus, through this we are able to understand the statement made in Dharmakīrti's *Commentary on the "Compendium of Valid Cognition"* as incredibly true:

The establishing agent [came from] habituation with great compassion.

Regarding this, there emerged the so-called "exceptional recollection of kindness" among the traditions of recollecting the kindness of venerable sentient beings, as expressed in *Way of the Bodhisattva*:

> The qualities of buddhahood depend
> on sentient beings and on buddhas equally.
> What kind of practice is it, then,
> that honors buddhas but not sentient beings?

As said, achieving buddhahood comes from the kindness of venerable sentient beings, and moreover from the network of sentient beings who work hard to supply our amenities, such as all our delicious food and beverages, our accessories and beautiful clothing that protect us from the elements, and our housing including all furnishings. Take, for example, our homes that we live in comfortably thanks to the kindness and hard work of builders who ignored many hardships like heat, cold, thirst, and hunger to build them.

In brief, from the day we are born and until our deaths, our lives are entirely dependent on venerable sentient beings: we cannot survive from eating rocks, dirt, or grass, and thus the fact we have been able to keep this so-called "precious human body" alive that we consider so valuable is entirely due to the kindness of venerable sentient beings.

Accomplishing our aims and training in the path that will bring high-status rebirths and so forth, too, is due to the kindness of others. Ultimately, generating the mind directed toward full enlightenment for the sake of achieving omniscience also depends on focusing on all sentient beings, and thus their kindness is incredibly great. [449] Merely thinking of bodhicitta brings joy to the mind. Merely listening to its meaning bestows happiness to the heart. It has power, too, and likewise it has blessings; it is your companion, and the friend that will protect you during difficult times. This immeasurable, noble attitude of bodhicitta, compared to which there is nothing higher from the point of view of being a good quality integral to the beginning, middle, and end, is absolutely astonishing and the ultimate wish-fulfilling jewel.

THE ACTUAL ATTITUDE OF EQUALIZING AND EXCHANGING SELF WITH OTHERS BASED ON THE TRADITION OF ŚĀNTIDEVA, SON OF THE VICTORS

In accordance with the *Swift Path*'s fourth outline, the actual attitude of **equalizing and exchanging self with others based on the tradition of Śāntideva, son of the victors, is as taught in** *Way of the Bodhisattva*:

> Whoever wishes to protect
> both self and others,
> should engage in the secret vow
> to exchange self with others.

And moreover,

> Whatever happiness there is in the world
> all comes from wanting others to be happy.
> Whatever suffering there is in the world
> all comes from wanting oneself to be happy.

He thus gives quite a summary, and then supplies clear reasoning with the following illustration:

> What need is there to say more?
> The childish work for their own aims,

and the sage works for the aims of others.
Look at the difference between these two!

This indicates that we can understand the magnitude of difference between the buddhas' qualities of body, speech, and mind, and our own faults. Furthermore, regarding the Buddha Bhagavān becoming free of all faults and possessing all qualities, he became a great being by way of the practice of bodhicitta, which has at its center the cherishing of others through forsaking the cherishing of oneself. [450] We, however, do the opposite and cherish ourselves while forsaking others, and thus we can understand why we still remain with such a limited capacity.

On the other hand, if we cherish others and forsake ourselves, this does not mean we should not consider our own aims even for a moment. What is required is that we principally consider others so that we do not emphasize our own welfare while disregarding the welfare of others. It is clear that we ourselves also need happiness, and not only do we have a right to pursue our happiness, we should do so!

If it were the case that you considered the welfare of others as inferior to your own, Śāntideva continues:

If I do not exchange
my happiness with others' suffering
I will not achieve buddhahood,
and will not be happy even in cyclic existence.

Śāntideva indicates that self-cherishing is the basis for all misfortune, and cherishing others is the foundation for all happiness and good; hence practicing it is important.

If you do not exchange yourself with others, forget your ability to achieve buddhahood in the end, even at present you will not be happy in cyclic existence; whereas if you strive for others' welfare, for the time being samsaric happiness will gather unto you as if in mounds. This is because when you take on others' welfare as your burden and exert yourself with courage dispossessed of despondency, such a person cannot experience mental difficulty, as stated in the *Precious Garland of the Middle Way*, and which can be understood through experience.

It furthermore states in the *Guru Pūjā*:

> Even if I have to remain for the sake of each sentient being
> in the fires of the Unrelenting Hell for an ocean of eons,
> may I be blessed to complete the perfection of joyous effort,
> which is not miserable, because of compassion, and which
> strives for supreme enlightenment.

Through focusing on all desperate, venerable sentient beings we aspire to give rise to the mind that strives for omniscience for their sake. [451] Therefore, this beneficial and renowned mind depends on the kindness of those venerable sentient beings. Thus, all realizations of the grounds and paths, particularly those vast and profound realizations of the Mahāyāna grounds and paths, and all priceless systems that are beyond comprehension, come into being in dependence on the kindness of others. Upon thoroughly contemplating this, it is not simply because of their kindness when they were mothers or friends from the perspective of the seven-fold cause-and-effect process. Rather, all sentient beings—simply by virtue of existing—are greatly kind to us at the time of the basis and at the time of the path. Even at the time of the result, in order for the buddhas' spontaneous and effortless deeds to arise, there needs to be a basis for their enactment and a path through which they are performed. These come into existence in dependence upon sentient beings, and thus the greatness of buddhas, too, depends on sentient beings. Thus, sentient beings are highly important, whether it be at the time of the basis, path, or result.

When reflecting on enemies in particular, it is hatred and anger that are the adversaries in the accomplishment of the aforementioned altruistic intention. Anger is the most harmful within the three existences. It is unequivocally to be discarded and has absolutely no benefit whatsoever. Thus, it must be faced directly through the practice of patience. In order to do so, one must practice patience toward an enemy. Thus, although our enemies do not wish to benefit us, in reality our enemies are the causes and conditions for powerful Dharma practice. Therefore, if you desire the result—the practice of patience—it is justified to cherish your enemies. Such is the incredible advice given in *Way of the Bodhisattva*.

In brief, the enemies of those who meditate on bodhicitta are actually their spiritual teachers, and thus should be remembered as extremely kind; it is inappropriate to get angry at them. [452] If you analyze this advice, gradually it becomes possible to recollect the kindness of *all* beings. The biggest obstacle to generating the awareness that seeks to accomplish benefit for others is clinging to the view of others as enemies. Therefore, leave aside forsaking your enemies—if you can instead contemplate their kindness and worthiness of love, you will be able to benefit all sentient beings with ease. As such, this manner of recollecting kindness is said to be the "extraordinary recollection of kindness."

There is thus an eleven-fold practice that combines the aforementioned mind training by way of the seven-fold cause-and-effect process and the equalizing and exchanging self for others in this context:

1. The initial meditation on equanimity as taught in the seven-fold cause-and-effect process
2. Knowing sentient beings as one's mother
3. The recollection of kindness and the extraordinary recollection of kindness
4. Repaying the kindness

5. Meditation on the equality of self and others by way of the reasoning of both self and others wanting to be happy and not wanting to suffer, as taught in the context of training the mind in equalizing and exchanging self for others

6. Contemplation of the faults of self-cherishing from many angles

7. Contemplation of the qualities of cherishing others from many angles

8. The practice of taking [the suffering of others], with an emphasis on the focal object of compassion in relation to the actual attitude of exchanging self and others through combining mind training techniques

9. The practice of giving, with an emphasis on the focal object of love that wishes happiness for others

When analyzing whether or not what is observed in "giving and taking" meditation has transpired in reality, you come to the understanding that it is a mere visualization and does not directly benefit others; thus

10. You generate the special resolution to take on the burden of others, thinking, "I myself will make that transpire in reality no matter what!" [453]

11. For that end one generates the uncontrived mind that wishes to achieve unsurpassed enlightenment

Therefore, when you strive in the aspiration to train in the precious mind of enlightenment that holds others dearer than oneself and onward from that, you then go from happiness to happiness, and eternal happiness begins.

THE ABILITY TO EXCHANGE SELF AND OTHERS IF YOU HABITUATE YOURSELF WITH DOING SO

Do not think that because you are impatient with even the slightest inconvenience at present that you will never give rise to the thought of merely exchanging self with others. As it says:

> Do not shy away from difficulty.
> Once you were frightened upon hearing their name.
> Now through the power of habituation,
> you dislike their absence!

If you once again befriend an unkind enemy whom you previously feared and whose mere sight was repulsive, your prior disdain transforms into total attraction. In the same way, through habituation you are able to exchange self and others. Thus, in practice, having thought well about the faults and qualities of both cherishing oneself and others, even if you find certainty in the fact that cherishing others is incredibly noble in reality, and self-cherishing is like poisonous black wolfsbane that is the downfall of all, you might still sometimes feel despondent because in the corner of your mind you might wonder whether you could really give up even your life for the sake of others. Śāntideva states in *Way of the Bodhisattva*:

> There is nothing at all
> that does not become easier with familiarization.

And as Tsongkhapa says in the *Great Treatise on the Stages of the Path*:

> The mind being concomitant with habituation is the way of
> dependent arising. [454]

As such, if you utilize habituation, then those things that are difficult while you are not familiar with them become easy, and without struggle. It is just a matter of the degree of familiarization. Therefore, if we gradually habituate ourselves with the transformations that are the positive development of the mind that we cannot comprehend now, not only will we prevail eventually, but with joy we will see their brilliance and gain the fearless confidence to remain in the lower realms for eons for the benefit of each sentient being, without growing weary.

Nāgārjuna and Ārya Asaṅga, followers of the skillful and greatly compassionate Teacher to whom we owe gratitude, and likewise the great erudite and accomplished beings of the snowy land of Tibet, were all similar to us when they were beginners. They were in a mass of faults equal to our own; there was nothing that set them apart. Gradually they developed the power of effort and gradually traversed the realizations of the paths and grounds and became great ārya beings and achieved omniscience. Why would it not work for us? The austerities and so forth that the greatly kind Teacher underwent for six years also teach us to be self-confident. Even the Buddha himself did not become enlightened in an instant. Such acts were to instruct his followers to believe in themselves.

Furthermore, one thing to consider is that if we humans apply ourselves to love, compassion, and bodhicitta we can certainly accomplish them, because if we examine the nature of our lives since the time we were born up until our death, we prefer loving-kindness, [455] and therefore if someone is kind to us, our hearts become joyous and happy even without a particular reason. Moreover, if someone expresses dislike toward us, it does not matter whether they could or would actually harm us or not, it is simply mentally unpleasant. As such, oneself and all others desire and pursue a life lived happily until the end. However, we need to be able to see that the conducive conditions for that do not depend entirely on external factors such as fame, power, and wealth, but the huge difference the principal cause—our own attitudes—make.

In particular, as explained before, science has produced evidence that from the moment a child is born they grow up under the strong mental bond formed with their mother or primary caregiver. Thus, however much love is given to the child, to that degree it positively affects their physical well-being, and enables them to live a happy life with a relaxed mind, successful education and positive behavior. On the other hand, if the child grew up without receiving much love from their parents or guardian and on top of that there was constant fighting within the family that left them scared, then that has a negative impact on their physical well-being, and leads to a short temper and an impaired ability to display affection to others.

Moreover, increased mental well-being has a positive effect on blood and oxygen flow, but remaining in a negative mental space due to anger, pride, jealousy, malice, or holding grudges creates a proportionate imbalance in the flow of blood, oxygen, and so forth, thus adversely affecting physical well-being. [456] Thus, giving thought to a person's development throughout their life and their healthy or unhealthy physical state, it is clear kindness leads to healthy and balanced bodies, and thus there are many temporary benefits. Moreover, looking at the components of the body you can see that not only is there a relation to one's own and others' altruistic attitudes, but also that it is indeed important that the body should be raised with and grow through loving-kindness. Additionally, there are obvious and provable signs that arise in relation to the mind due to benefit or harm, and thus one should develop the conduct of nonviolence, and the root of a peaceful and happy mind—noble thoughts and an altruistic attitude.

If a person has an altruistic attitude toward others their mind automatically becomes relaxed and loses anxiety. For that reason, one can understand that, generally speaking, human nature is good, not evil. Even from the perspective of the ultimate reasoning that we are all pervaded by the constituent of the tathāgata essence, giving thought to this too leads to continuous conviction that we are all good by nature. I have spoken more about this in the discussion within the first volume.

If we can thus keep an open-minded and light-hearted approach in our daily lives it will not matter how people look at us. We will be free of regrets, and, having limited our overconceptualization, we will be free of anxiety. On the other hand, if we keep attachment, hatred, and grudges in the back of our mind, then, because we will be gripped by apprehensiveness whenever we encounter the various reactions of the people we meet, we will be overly suspicious to the point that we will make an unpleasant impression on others. Based on that you would be better off creating a protective barrier around yourself and living alone. [457]

If we did generate compassion that is unable to bear the suffering of others, some might wonder whether that would create added suffering on top of our own, whether we would be doubling our burden by focusing our thoughts on the suffering of others. Just as this was analyzed in *Way of the Bodhisattva*, the difference appears as follows: Generally, when we are oppressed by suffering, our strong dislike for it disturbs our mind, and due to various reactions, like deep-seated unhappiness or anger, we can feel destitute. When, motivated by compassion, an awareness arises that is overwhelmed from seeing others' suffering, mentally it can be quite heavy, but at the same time it came about through voluntarily taking the burden of others' happiness and suffering on oneself, based on seeing reasons to do so from the bottom of one's heart. For that reason, one's heart experiences neither destitution nor helplessness. Instead, because one's attitude is rooted in joyful conviction due to marvelous bravery, upon seeing the suffering of others one is not weighed down by a mental burden. As such there is a huge difference between this and your average person being weighed down by additional suffering. As it states in *Way of the Bodhisattva*:

If you do not genuinely exchange
your happiness with others' suffering,
you will not become a buddha,
and even in samsara you will not have happiness.

If one has analyzed and properly contemplated these reasons, then of course the mind can undergo transformation through familiarization and hope can increase, leading one to be able to exchange self with others. Therefore, **the meaning of "exchanging self with others" is not, for example, like if Devadatta were to think, "Yajñadatta is me." Rather, it is for Devadatta to substitute the cherishing of self for the cherishing of Yajñadatta, the other, and to substitute the forsaking of Yajñadatta, the other, with the forsaking of oneself, Devadatta.** [458] **This is called "exchanging self with others,"** and therefore exchanging self with others, or others with oneself, does not mean to apply your identity onto another and to transfer another's identity to oneself. Moreover, the self has been a self since beginningless time, and will remain a self after becoming a buddha. The self does not go to another, and others remain as themselves, too, without becoming us. Based on this fact, there is no fault that self and other exist.

Well, what *is* "exchanging self and others," then? Self and others are the same in wanting happiness and not wanting suffering, we are equal in our right to eradicate suffering, and we are the same in being worthy of eradicating suffering and achieving happiness. We have a bad mental habit of wanting to have the best for ourselves. If something bad is about to happen to us, we quickly deflect it to someone else, and if something good is about to happen to another we quickly try to secure it for ourselves. Reversing the roles of this bad habit and giving the best to others and taking on the worst for ourselves is what is known as exchanging self with others.

For example, even though there is not much gain to be had in banquets and performances and the like, if you tried to arrive early to get

in first, but once there you then let others ahead of you who had difficulties, you have given the advantage and the victory to others while
taking the drawbacks and defeat upon yourself—this is exchanging
self with others. [459]

THE STAGES OF MEDITATING ON HOW TO EXCHANGE SELF AND OTHER

**The actual meditative focus of exchanging self with others is to think
that up until now you have fulfilled your own purpose through cherishing yourself, which has only become a cause for suffering. Thus,
train in applying yourself to considering others. Having trained
yourself with transferring your self-cherishing to other beings, it is
said that with familiarization your two thoughts of forsaking others
and cherishing yourself can trade places.**

HOW TO MEDITATE ON GIVING AND TAKING ACCORDING TO THE SWIFT PATH

The way to meditate on giving and taking according to the fifth outline of the *Swift Path* is as follows: **to make this easier to imagine, it
is as explained in the** *Seven-Point Mind Training* **according to the**
Precious Garland:

> May their wrong deeds ripen on myself,
> and all my virtues ripen upon them.

**As indicated, focusing on both giving and taking has been the prac-
tice of past masters. Therefore, as before, visualize your mother in
front of you, and together with strong compassion focused on her,
think that as your breath exits your right nostril all your contaminated virtue and happiness ride the wind horse into the left nostril**

of your mother in front. It pervades her entire body and mind, giving her exceptional happiness. Again, as you breathe in through your left nostril think that all your mother's misdeeds, obscurations and suffering are drawn forth by your breath. They form a black mass within your heart and in doing so your mother experiences the bliss of being free from all suffering. Train by alternating between these two. Then do the same practice in relation to your father of this life, friends, neutral persons, enemies, and so forth, including the six types of beings. [460]

Although at present you lack such great mental capability, starting with food, clothing, and bedding, through familiarization you will fearlessly be able to give even your head, limbs, and so forth. In accordance with the practice of giving and taking upon the inner and outer breath asserted by the great child of the victors, Chekawa, the oral lineage of the lamas of the past posit the stages of mind training as follows: first compassion is emphasized by thinking that you take on the sufferings of others when you breathe in; then, love is emphasized on the outbreath by giving one's happiness and virtues to others.

Concluding Verses

Through diligence, deeply repulsed
by the great ocean of suffering within endless existence,
some have climbed the ladder of the three precious trainings
and entered the house of personal peace and happiness.

Yet upon seeing their mothers
who cared for them throughout lifetimes,
desperate and wailing while stuck in the prison of suffering of
    cyclic existence,
they are able to forsake them—who could be more shameless
    than them?

Through the strong winds of love and compassion,
due to the recollection of kindness that knows all beings as
    one's parents,
the ship of the altruistic special resolution that bears the load
    of others' welfare
sails unimpeded toward the jewel isle of omniscience.

With the noble mind that equalizes and exchanges self and
    others,
you come to recognize that even your enemies, who are like
    thorns in your heart,
are dear friends and relatives.
Cut the root of mistaken, biased thoughts!

Having forsaken self-cherishing,
the key that responds to harm with kindness
will instantly open the door to bliss that spontaneously
    accomplishes the two aims [of self and others].
How marvelous is this good fortune! [461]

How to Adopt Bodhicitta through Its Ritual

HAVING THUS TRAINED the mind in equalizing and exchanging self with others and gained some small experience, ultimate peacefulness arises in the mind. Wherever that person is, there is zero concern that they will cause unease for others through being harsh and so forth.

It does not matter what meaning you assign to our existence in this world. The fact that we have been born is established by valid cognition, and in the case that one lives a long life for around a hundred years, if you make the purpose of your existence to stir up trouble on this earth and disturb others then there was no value to your taking up a human body. For example, there are so many plants and trees that have grown in plain sight, yet it is because they are harmonious with their surroundings that they beautify the environment and also contribute to well-being of sentient beings.

As we humans are incredibly cunning and exceedingly intelligent, we do not like to remain as we are, and instead bring others to ruin and exploit them with our excessive greed, despite already knowing what we need to be happy. Considering this, it would be a great shame if someone was born to intentionally cause trouble on this earth. Thus, even if you cannot leave behind a positive impact on others, living out your life causing harm means it lacked any value. This is true whether you believe in religion or not, and whether or not you accept past and future lives. Since it is so important to live a positive life, if you can practice mind training, then even if outwardly things are turbulent, inwardly your mind is not going to be unhappy, with an endless stream of anxiety, expectations, and pleasant and unpleasant discursive thoughts. Therefore, it is said that wherever a person who practices mind training resides, that place becomes similar to a blissful pure land. Thus, mind training is known as the "City of Sukhākarā," which means the "Source of Happiness." [462]

Even if you are just able to hear about the practice of mind training, or simply imitate the practice because you are unable to do it extensively, you are still fortunate. If you practice this, even though the start of your life was ordinary, there is still hope that you can be a wholesome, faultless person in the latter part of your life. Thus, whether talking in religious or just worldly terms, this altruistic attitude is the great door revealing the root of all happiness, the source of everything good, and the noble path that benefits oneself and all others.

The outlines for how to adopt bodhicitta through its ritual are as given in the *Great Treatise on the Stages of the Path*:

iv) How to adopt bodhicitta through its ritual

    a'   Attaining that which you have not attained
    b'   Guarding that which you have attained from degenerating
    c'   The restoration method if it degenerates

Attaining that which you have not attained has three parts:

    1'   The person from whom you adopted bodhicitta
    2'   The person who adopts bodhicitta
    3'   The ritual for adoption

        a"   Preparatory ritual

          1"   Performing special refuge

(a) Arranging offerings after having beautified
the place and set up representations
(b) Supplication and going for refuge
(c) Stating the refuge precepts

2″ Accumulation of merit
3″ Purification of attitude

b″ Actual ritual
c″ Concluding ritual

Regarding this, it is said that if you adopt mind generation at the point where you have gained some minor experience, then there is the great advantage that the "aspiring mind possessing the commitment" fortifies mind generation and enhances it further. As that is the case, **having thoroughly trained in the awareness explained above that includes both the aspiration for others' welfare and the aspiration toward enlightenment, mere mind generation will still arise without relying on a ritual. However, a perfect ritual is important when entering an authentic path. [463] Therefore, the practices of (1) the preliminaries of refuge, merit accumulation, and mind training, (2) the actual practice of adopting aspiring bodhicitta through its ritual, and (3) the concluding statement of the refuge precepts for the purpose of not letting bodhicitta degenerate in this life and the next, should all be understood from the *Great* and *Middle-Length* lamrim treatises. Since all the fine details of practice depend on a direct transmission, avoid personal fabrication and oversimplification.**

Regarding the beings from which you adopt bodhicitta, visualize in front of you the lord of the teachings, the Bhagavān Teacher, his body ornamented with the marks and signs, who continues to accomplish the welfare of sentient beings through whatever enlightened activity suits the various dispositions, attitudes, and inclinations of trainees using his unceasing, Brahmā-like melodious voice. Surrounding him are the supreme beings of the ārya land who uphold the teachings including the eight great bodhisattvas,[82] the seven patriarchs of the teachings,[83] the seventeen pandits, and so on. There are also the lamas of the Nyingma tradition who spread the teachings during the earlier period—the lord and his twenty-four subjects.[84] It is good if, on top of those, you also visualize the Tibetan kings Nyathri Tsanpo and Lha Thothori Nyantsan, and the Dharma king Songtsen Gampo, the great beings who diligently devoted themselves to the flourishing of the teachings for the sake of their Tibetan subjects. Then, representing the old Kadam lamas, Jowo Atiśa, Ngok Lekpé Sherab, and Dromtön Gyalwé Jungné; the five great forefathers of the Sakya tradition representing the Lamdré lineage lamas;[85] The three—Marpa, Milarepa, and Gampopa—and so forth representing the Kagyü lineage lamas; Tsongkhapa, his spiritual sons, and so forth, representing those of the new Kadam (Geluk) tradition, and all lamas from the other traditions, too. Visualize them as your witness for bodhicitta, and the field of merit for your accumulation of the collections. Surrounding you are all sentient beings in the form of humans who can speak and can understand meaning. Visualize that they are experiencing the suffering of their respective birth among the six types. [464]

If you receive bodhicitta from a lama rather than a symbolic representation of the Buddha, such as a statue, then perceive the lama as similar to a translator of the Buddha's words. Think that surrounding them in all cardinal and intermediate directions are the four great kings[86] and so forth who guard from the interference of inner and outer obstructive conditions toward virtuous activities, principally mind generation.

Then, for your initial generation of bodhicitta, excellently adhere to the *Seven Limb Prayer* that originates from the *Samantabhadra Prayer* through recitation and aspiration for the purpose of accumulating the collections and purifying obscurations by way of the seven limbs.

Generally, if you are able, due to your faith, regardless of whether or not you invite the victors and their spiritual children you should think that they reside at all times in your field of merit accumulation.

Broadly speaking, during lamrim teachings the offering of bodhicitta seems to be aspiring bodhicitta possessing the commitment. The offering of bodhicitta itself has many extensive and abbreviated practices. Moreover, it is clear that the adoption of bodhicitta through its ritual was something even the incomparable Jowo Jé Atiśa performed. Then, taking that as his basis, in accordance with the same rituals taught in both of Jé Rinpoché Tsongkhapa's *Great* and *Middle-Length* lamrims, in order to receive bodhicitta initially from a lama one must supplicate them.

The way to do this is as follows. Repeat three times:

O Master, please pay heed to me. Just as the previous tathāgata arhats, perfect and complete buddhas, and great bodhisattvas abiding on the higher grounds first generated their minds toward unsurpassed, perfect, and complete enlightenment, please, O Master, help me, (insert your name), to also generate my mind toward unsurpassed, perfect and complete enlightenment.

Since you must first go for refuge in order to uphold bodhicitta, visualize well the objects of refuge as explained before, then go for refuge while recollecting their qualities of body, speech, and mind. [465] One must go for refuge with three unique causes of Mahāyāna refuge completed: (1) compassion that observes the sentient beings that surround oneself, (2) fright from recollecting the manner in which oneself and all other sentient beings are tortured by suffering and its causes, (3) faith that the victors and their spiritual children have the capacity, or qualities, to protect from those horrors.

The Purpose of Refuge

For the purpose of oneself and all other sentient beings to achieve the state of omniscience one requests protection in the pursuit of becoming the equal of the objects of refuge situated in front of oneself. In order to gradually activate your existent potential to accomplish the qualities of realization and so forth of the tathāgatas by way of receiving their blessings, one must generate bodhicitta while recollecting the meaning of the words below. If possible, place your right knee on the ground or squat. It is fine if you are not physically able to do so, as your inner motivation is more important than outward physical appearance; as such, be respectful in a manner that suits you.

The *distinct objects* of refuge are (a) the Buddha, (b) the Mahāyāna Dharma jewel that is his Dharma of realization and abandonment and so forth in his continuum, and (c) the ārya bodhisattvas that abide on the Mahāyāna grounds. On this occasion one must go for refuge to the Mahāyāna Dharma jewel since the Dharma by which one achieves the enlightenment of śrāvakas and pratyekabuddhas has a lesser capacity within its path to accomplish our goal of unsurpassed enlightenment, and thus does not serve our purpose. One needs to take refuge in ārya bodhisattvas who correctly accomplish goals that accord with that.

The *distinction of time* is that you express that you go for refuge until you achieve the state of unsurpassed, perfect buddhahood. Furthermore, regarding the *object of intent*, one does not go for refuge for the sake of oneself alone, but for all sentient beings. [465] Having made sure these focal objects and aspects of the unique Mahāyāna refuge are present, repeat the following three times:

> O Master, please pay heed to me. I, by the name of (insert your name), from this time on until I have achieved the essence of enlightenment, go for refuge to the buddha bhagavāns, supreme among humans.

O Master, please pay heed to me. I, by the name of (insert your name), from this time on until I achieve the essence of enlightenment, go for refuge to the Dharma of pacification, free from attachment, the supreme among all Dharmas.

O Master, please pay heed to me. I, by the name of (insert your name), from this time on until I achieve the essence of enlightenment, go for refuge to the ārya bodhisattvas, the irreversible sangha, the supreme among assemblies.

Next, for the purpose of generating bodhicitta, in the presence of the objects of refuge visualized prior, again recite the *Seven Limb Prayer* that originates from the *Samantabhadra Prayer* for the sake of accumulating the collections and purifying negativities. Recollect how all old mother sentient beings surrounding you are the same in wanting happiness and not wanting suffering, are equal in their right to achieve happiness and dispel suffering, and the same in possessing the cause for the eternal happiness of omniscience, the mind whose nature is clear light that exists intrinsically, yet still they are oppressed by suffering and bereft of happiness.

Think that in order for all of these mother sentient beings to ultimately achieve unsurpassed, perfect and complete buddhahood, you will generate the mind directed toward supreme enlightenment and gradually train in the conduct of the children of the victorious ones, through which you will progressively attain at all costs the victorious state of omniscience without impediment and in the not too distant future. [467] In this way, if you perform the confession and restraint rite by applying the four opponent powers for the sake of purifying accrued misdeeds and downfalls, then however much your continuum is purified, to that extent your bodhicitta will be stronger.

Moreover, the greater your wealth of merit the more powerful your bodhicitta. Thus, through taking the victorious ones and their spiritual children as your focal objects, you must do this practice that comprises the three important points of accumulation, purification, and increase.

During the actual generation of bodhicitta, having already trained your mind as explained prior, think the following: All the happiness of myself and others is interrelated, and must arise dependently. Until recently I have wanted happiness and not wanted suffering, yet being confused with respect to what to adopt and what to discard, I performed the opposite, and as such this has been the extent of my capabilities until now. At present I have attained a human body with leisure and opportunity and have met with the general teachings of the Buddha, and among those the Mahāyāna treatises, through which I have gained some small knowledge of the skillful path to eternal bliss in this and all future existences. At this point I can only request forgiveness through confessing the mistakes that have happened until now, and from this point on I will give up selfish thinking in accord with the Teacher Bhagavān's intent. In this way even a single prayer will be for the sake of all mother sentient beings. Whatever listening, contemplation, and meditation I perform will be done with limitless sentient beings in mind. From now on, I will make my life meaningful, accomplishing what the victorious ones and their spiritual children intend.

In this way, having brought to mind well the faults of self-cherishing and the advantages of cherishing others, take the victors and their children as your witness and make the resolution that, from now on, you will only think about the welfare of others, and only do what pleases the victors. [468] Make the following commitment, thinking, "How wonderful if I could achieve unsurpassed, complete enlightenment for the sake of all old mother sentient beings. I will attain it! I will do everything to attain it!"

Focusing on this mind thus generated and thinking, "I will never give this up," is the fervent aspiration for bodhicitta not to degenerate known as "adopting aspirational bodhicitta possessing the commitment." The "offering of bodhicitta" mentioned prior is also similar to this.

In the actual generation of bodhicitta, visualize the victorious ones and their spiritual children in front, along with all old mother sentient beings surrounding oneself as if actually present. Think that your faith focused on the victorious ones and your compassion for these sentient beings spur one another. The aspirational bodhicitta possessing the commitment is to think, "I alone will take on the responsibility of establishing all mother sentient beings on the ground of unsurpassed, complete enlightenment; however, in order to accomplish such welfare of sentient beings I first need the complete capability to do so, and that comes only from buddhahood alone; therefore, I will achieve that soon without delay." To adopt this, you must repeat the following lines three times:

> All buddhas and bodhisattvas who reside in the ten directions please pay heed to me. O Master, please pay heed to me. [469] By means of my roots of virtue in the nature of generosity, ethics, or meditation that I, (insert your name), have cultivated, caused others to cultivate, or rejoiced in the cultivation of in this and other lives, please help me, (insert your name), to generate the mind directed to unsurpassed, perfect, and complete enlightenment from now until I achieve the essence of enlightenment, just as the previous tathāgata arhats, perfect and complete buddhas, and great bodhisattvas abiding on the high grounds generated minds directed toward unsurpassed, perfect, and complete enlightenment. I will liberate beings who are not liberated. I will free all sentient beings who are not freed. I will give breath to those who cannot breathe. I will cause those who have not totally passed into nirvana to do so.

Repeat this three times, and on the third repetition think that you have given rise to mind generation in accordance with the words. This mind, along with the adoption of the strong commitment to never relinquish it, are known as "aspiring bodhicitta possessing the commitment."

Moreover, indeed it was taught in the *Sūtra of Maitreya's Liberation* that there is great benefit to be had in mind generation alone, even if one is unable to train in the conduct of the victors' children. However, it states in Dharmakīrti's *Commentary on the "Compendium of Valid Cognition"*:

> The compassionate one showed methods
> for the sake of overcoming suffering.
> Causes of the results of those methods that are obscured [for oneself]
> are difficult to explain [to others].

The purpose of generating aspirational bodhicitta by way of the special resolution induced by compassion is not merely to have a noble mind that thinks "may sentient beings be free from suffering." You must engage in the means to achieve that!

b' Guarding that which you have attained from degenerating

1' Training in the causes for bodhicitta not to degenerate in this lifetime

a" Training in recollecting the benefits of bodhicitta in order for your enthusiasm to increase

b" Training in mind generation six times daily so that actual bodhicitta increases

1" Not relinquishing aspirational bodhicitta [470]
2" Training to increase aspirational bodhicitta

c" Training in not mentally abandoning the beings for
     whose sake you developed bodhicitta
d" Training in the collections of merit and pristine
     wisdom

2' Training in the causes to not be separated from bodhicitta
     in future lives

a" Training in giving up the four dark practices that
     cause bodhicitta to decline
b" Training in adopting the four white practices that pre-
     vent the decline of bodhicitta

To summarize the essence of what is clarified within these outlines
from the *Great Treatise on the Stages of the Path*, **you must make the
bodhisattva trainings your essential practice as a means to achieve
buddhahood. It therefore states in *Way of the Bodhisattva*:**

> **Corresponding to the desire to go
> and to setting out,
> the wise should understand
> the difference that separates these two.**

The examples of desiring to go to a place and actively setting out
are used to illustrate the difference between aspiring bodhicitta
and engaging bodhicitta. In this regard, when an initial experience
from having trained well in aspiring bodhicitta has arisen in your
continuum, listen to the precepts of the bodhisattva vows and thoroughly understand the benefits of training in the six perfections,

the disadvantages of not doing so, root downfalls, infractions, and so forth. When you have given rise to strong, uncontrived joy in correctly adopting and discarding, you take on the vows of the victors' children, which combine the traditions of the two great charioteers, through a ritual.

The cause for mind generation to not decline is to recollect the benefits of generating your mind toward enlightenment again and again so as to increase your joyful inspiration. To enhance your actual mind generation, you should put effort into means that strengthen your habituation by practicing in six sessions—three times in the day and three times at night. For example, just as you would try to prevent a burning fire from extinguishing, then in order not to let the mind directed toward enlightenment cool from the day it is generated, bring it to mind and enhance it at the very least six times within the twenty-four hour period of each day. [471]

Most importantly, in addition to that, is "training in not mentally abandoning the beings for whose sake you developed bodhicitta." We say *all sentient beings* and not *my preferred sentient beings*, and thus when we generate the mind while saying, "I will engage in beneficial activities for the sake of *all* sentient beings," it is not acceptable to mentally relinquish even a single being.

Whether that person tortures us or harms the Buddha's teachings, when it comes to facing the situation righteously, it is still totally inappropriate to have deep-felt anger or genuinely forsake a person while thinking you cannot act for their welfare. It is therefore highly important to never mentally relinquish a single sentient being for whose sake you gave rise to the mind of enlightenment, and to never discard the mind that wishes to help all.

In particular, in the case of we Tibetans, in response to Chinese Communist authorities there come times when one needs to be defiant or remain tough, and thus Tibetans at home and abroad carry out various protests or expressions of struggle worthy of emboldening others, even going as far as sacrificing their own lives in acts of defiance, yet it is the virtue of Tibetans being followers of the Mahāyāna Dharma that we believe it is totally unbecoming to abandon others with a total lack of compassion even in such situations.

Next, train in giving up the four dark practices that cause bodhicitta to decline, and adopt the four white practices that prevent that decline: (1) In order to abandon the dark practice of deceiving through lies "those who wish to help—abbots, masters, gurus, and those worthy of offerings"—while knowing that they are such persons possessing qualities, then give up knowingly telling lies. [472] (2) In order to abandon the dark practice of making others regret what is not regrettable, cause sentient beings whom you are ripening to not desire the vehicle of limited actions, but exhort them into virtue and make them hold to full enlightenment instead. (3) In order to abandon the dark practice of angrily disparaging those sentient beings who have generated bodhicitta and entered the Mahāyāna, discern all bodhisattvas to be like the Buddha, and praise people with honesty wherever you may be. (4) In order to abandon the use of deceit and misrepresentation to manipulate or trick others instead of being sincere, be honest without deception or misrepresentation.

Properly practicing thus, it is as stated in the ritual for adopting the bodhisattva vows:

> Now my life has become fruitful.
> I have excellently attained a human existence.
> Today I was born into the buddha lineage.
> I have now become a child of the buddhas.

As said, in general we have attained this human body, and in particular we have met the Buddha's teachings. Among those we have heard the Mahāyāna teachings, and having preceded with refuge, merit accumulation and purification. We have, from the depths of our heart, given rise to the mind of enlightenment for the sake of all sentient beings, and have taken the victorious ones and their spiritual children as our witness. Thus, not only have we become a child of the buddhas, but it is also extremely fortunate that we have set in place the auspicious interdependence to achieve buddhahood without delay.

> Now, by all means,
> I will begin compatible activities,
> and will not do anything to tarnish
> this faultless, noble lineage.

Adopt this aspiration: Now I will categorically exert myself in activities compatible with the bodhisattva lineage—only altruism, without harming anyone at all. In this way I will abide in the noble lineage, free from the dirty fault of self-centeredness, and year after year sustain the focal points of this method of generating bodhicitta and correctly train in the conduct. [473]

In doing so you will enter into an experience initially, then gradually have experiences that require effort, and those that come without effort. It is in this way you must give rise to real bodhicitta. It is not impossible that it could arise within a few years, but it could also take a few lifetimes. Whatever the case, if you continuously recollect your commitment to never relinquish the mind directed toward full enlightenment and make strong prayers, you will ensure a special potential to give rise to uncontrived bodhicitta before too long.

The Restoration Method If It Degenerates

Having taken the vows of mind generation, **the way to guard against root downfalls and infractions, together with the practice of restoration are as explained extensively by the great lord Jé [Tsongkhapa] in his *Commentary on the "Ethics" Chapter of "Asanga's Bodhisattva***

Grounds," which is referenced in his *Great* and *Middle-Length* lam-rim treatises, and likewise in the [Third Dalai Lama's] *Essence of Refined Gold.* However, these days the practice is to defer the topic of taking the engaging bodhicitta vows and instead give the experiential guide on the six perfections and so forth. Still, through merely adopting aspiring bodhicitta via the ritual—that is, "adopting aspiring bodhicitta possessing the commitment"—one cannot attain omniscience. One must train in the conduct of bodhisattvas in order to put it into practice, and thus it is important to put effort into the conduct of the six perfections.

Moreover, it is not something that you can practice when you feel like it, and leave aside when you do not. The vow of the bodhisattva is the promise in which one has mentally committed to unequivocally put it into practice continuously. Thus, once you have taken the bodhisattva vow, you must guard it by recognizing that you must train in the conduct of bodhisattvas, and, having familiarized yourself with the wish to train in it, find certainty. If this happens, then you will be stable in your guarding of the vow and training in the conduct, since the situation will not be that you flip between wanting and not wanting to train, or being sometimes diligent and sometimes lazy.

There are differing views among the Indian scholars regarding how one trains in aspiring and engaging bodhicitta, [474] and there are also slight discrepancies between explanations of Tibetan scholars. Accordingly, Jé Rinpoché states in his *Great* and *Middle-Length* lamrim treatises that, having taken the vows, whoever trains in the practice of the six perfections included within the trainings of the engaging bodhicitta vows has engaged bodhicitta. Prior to that, regardless of whether one trains in conduct, one has merely aspirational bodhicitta. Gyaltsab Jé conveys a similar meaning in his *Ornament of the Essence: A Commentary on the Perfection of Wisdom,* although with slightly different wording.

Thus, you may wonder if there is a fault, since a contradictory order of aspiring and engaging bodhicitta and the six perfections

is presented in the great treatises. The intention behind it is that one can give rise to them in such an order, and not that this order is definite with respect to all persons. Someone who has not yet entered a path could take the vows of engaging bodhicitta, then aspirationally generate their mind toward full enlightenment and achieve the smaller path of accumulation. When they arrived at the middle path of accumulation, they would generate engaging bodhicitta because their aspirational bodhicitta transforms into engaging bodhicitta.

Alternatively, someone who has never taken engaging bodhicitta vows could generate aspiring bodhicitta and enter the path of accumulation. Upon arriving at the middle path of accumulation, they would generate engaging bodhicitta. Then, at the end of the middle [path of accumulation], they could take the engaging bodhicitta vows. Since this possibility also exists, there is no definitive order, and thus it states in the *Compendium of Trainings*:

> Therefore, in accordance with your capability, correctly
> take up even just one root of virtue and protect it!

Someone who has only recently generated aspiring bodhicitta may be unable to train in all of the precepts, and thus they should take on merely one root of virtue, and so forth, training gradually according to their mental capacity until ultimately they can train in all conduct. It is from this perspective that a person is guided in the six perfections after adopting aspiring bodhicitta through its ritual.

Since in this context all of the focal objects of meditation up to the topics of calm abiding and special insight are completely given, one might wonder whether it does not directly contradict the terms of the text to not adopt the vows of engaging bodhicitta. [475] All of the focal points one is guided through within the seven-fold cause-and-effect process and so forth are approximations of an experience that is the foundation of the genuine experience to be generated. As they are not the actual thing, the topics of the six perfections yet to be explained are likewise intended as a mere basis for laying imprints for the practice of training in the conduct of the victors' children. With this in mind, the spiritual teachers of the past gave the experiential guide of the persons of the three scopes sometimes for years, and sometimes only for a month. Otherwise, as illustrated by meditating until the actual great compassion that can induce the special resolve is generated in one's continuum, if you insist an experiential guide must involve doing that for all practices ranging from relying on the spiritual teacher up to calm abiding and special insight, it would be impossible for those who must practice for a considerable time with great difficulty to accomplish them effortlessly in one lifetime of the degenerate age.

Other than that, take the example of meditating until the actual great compassion that can induce the special resolve is generated in one's continuum. If you insist that an experiential guide must be done like that with respect to all of the practices ranging from relying on the spiritual teacher up to calm abiding and special insight, it would be impossible for those who must practice for a considerable time with great difficulty to accomplish them effortlessly in one lifetime of the degenerate age.

Hence, when I said above that the mind generated at the end of the seven-fold cause-and-effect is the generation of one's mind toward supreme enlightenment that marks the beginning of the three countless eons, I was referring to actual bodhicitta. If you confuse [actual bodhicitta] with [just having received] the introduction to meditation instructions according to the stages of the path and doing the meditations and adopting mind generation through its ritual and so forth, there would be nothing more deluded than proudly believing you are on the bodhisattva path of accumulation. Thus, inform yourself.

When giving the authentic experience and guide, the guru gives an introduction and the student meditates seriously, yet if you think that the minor mental change that occurs is an actual path, it is a huge mistake.

For these reasons, even if you rush into the engaging bodhicitta vows without having entered a path, in this time where afflictions are many and the antidotes weak, if you are unable to guard from root downfalls and so forth, you will deceive the entire universe including the buddhas and their spiritual children, along with the gods—such are the endless drawbacks that are explained. Since the objections outweigh the advantages, the direct and indirect holy lamas implement this in accordance with the mental dispositions of disciples. [476]

Concluding Verses

The sprouts that are initial experiences of emerged
  understanding
are matured through the moisture and warmth of enduring
  hardship
into a tree bowing with the fruits of valid realizations.
This is the same path traversed by ordinary and ārya beings of
  the three vehicles.

"Bodhisattvas" who have accomplished the undying special
  resolve
through the ambrosia of compassion,
yet whose life force of certainty that all beings are their parents
has been cut by the sharp knife of unfortunate circumstances,
are nonexistent, like a sky lotus.

The mode of traversing the Mahāyāna path is vast like space,
and the teachings of Indian and Tibetan scholars are deep like
   the ocean.
Nowadays the mental acumen of beings is black like darkness,
and the intelligence of most proud scholars is thin like grass.

Thus, the magic fingers of these excellent teachings
unravel the knots of difficulty for beings of inferior intellect,
and for the intelligent, this wellspring of words that is the
   treasury of the throat cakra,
contains all the inexhaustible wealth one could wish for.

How to Train in the Conduct Having Given Rise to Bodhicitta

THE THIRD OUTLINE from the *Great Treatise on the Stages of the Path* and this treatise's second outline, **how to train in the conduct having given rise to bodhicitta,** has three parts:

i) The reason why you must train in the precepts after developing the mind of enlightenment
ii) Revealing that you will not become a buddha by training in method or wisdom separately
iii) The order that one trains in the precepts

The order that one trains in the precepts has two parts:

a' How to train in the Mahāyāna in general

1' Cultivating the desire to train in the precepts of bodhicitta
2' Taking the bodhisattva vows after cultivating the desire to train in the precepts
3' How to train after taking the bodhisattva vows

a" The basis one trains in
b" How all the precepts are included in the six perfections
c" The order one trains in the six perfections

b'   How to train specifically in the Vajrayāna [477]

Within these outlines is taught the way to train in bodhisattva conduct. Since the goal of omniscience is a compounded phenomenon, not only does it arise through causes and conditions, but the collection of causes must be totally complete and without error, and practiced in the correct order. In brief, Nāgārjuna states in the dedication section of his *Sixty Stanzas on Reasoning*:

> Due to this virtue may all beings
> complete the collections of merit and pristine wisdom.
> May they achieve the two holy bodies
> arisen from merit and pristine wisdom.

The causes for achieving the two enlightened bodies—the dharmakāya and the rūpakāya—are the collection of merit and the collection of pristine wisdom. To briefly explain those two collections: in the context of maturing one's own continuum, there are the six perfections—generosity, ethics, patience, joyous effort, concentration, and wisdom. The perfection of wisdom has four subdivisions—namely, the perfection of skillful means, the perfection of power, the perfection of prayer, and the perfection of pristine wisdom, thus making ten perfections.

Regarding the perfection of skillful means, it is the endless, inexhaustible result of every root of virtue accumulated that is brought about due to their being dedicated toward unsurpassed, complete enlightenment on behalf of all sentient beings. The six skillful means that accomplish the qualities of buddhas and start with ripening sentient beings are as follows:

1. Making the small virtues of sentient beings become immeasurable
2. Accomplishing great virtue with little hardship

3. Quelling the anger of those who despise the Buddha
4. Causing those who are indifferent to engage in the teachings
5. Ripening those who have already engaged in the teachings
6. Liberating those who are already ripened [478]

Following that, in the context of maturing the continua of others, there are the four ways to gather disciples; namely:

1. Giving what is needed
2. Pleasant speech
3. Enacting welfare
4. Consistent behavior

The practices of bodhisattvas are taught through these. As such, if you do not practice in order to achieve the goals toward which you generated your mind, they will not be accomplished through the aspirational prayers of noble mind generation alone; "buddhahood" must be accomplished through training in conduct, not through noble prayers. The conduct to be trained in must furthermore be an inseparability of method and wisdom.

Moreover, out of the dharmakāya and rūpakāya within the result of buddhahood, the rūpakāya that directly accomplishes the welfare of others is achieved solely for the sake of sentient beings, the object of intent. It is furthermore not an aggregate fettered by flesh and bone, but rather a body in the nature of pristine wisdom. Without actualizing the pristine wisdom dharmakāya, a rūpakāya that is the same nature of pristine wisdom and that appears effortlessly and spontaneously to a variety of beings cannot exist. Thus, one must initially accomplish the dharmakāya for one's own purpose. Although it is achieved through being motivated by bodhicitta, when it is actualized it is unable to enact welfare through its qualities directly appearing to others, and thus is labeled "the dharmakāya for one's own welfare."

"The rūpakāya for others' welfare" is a body that enacts welfare through its qualities directly appearing to other disciples, and thus is labeled as such. These two bodies necessarily arise in dependence on causes and conditions, and not without cause or from discordant causes. Since they must be accomplished by way of a concordant cause, what, then, is their concordant cause? The rūpakāya for others' welfare appears in multiple natures to the disciples whose dispositions and aspirations are varied; thus the causes to achieve it, the "collection of merit," must be accumulated in a multitude of ways. [479] In brief, the true paths are contingent on a variety of phenomena, and the stages of the path are dependent on conventional truth. Their causes, furthermore, are separate in aspect from their results.

The dharmakāya is the "single taste of multiplicity," which refers to the general mode of existence, or reality of things, in which qualities of the multitude of varying objects are one taste in relation to suchness. Thus, from the perspective of an awareness that directly ascertains the dharmadhātu of this single taste of multiplicity, aside from the reality truth, all other appearances cease; therefore all the aspects of these variegated objects have become qualities of the sphere of pacification of all elaborations from the perspective of the meditative equipoise perceiving thusness.

Regarding the causes for accomplishing the pristine wisdom dharmakāya, during the time one is a trainee one comprehends the mode of a single taste of multiplicity, and because all objects that appear in a variety of pure and impure shifting displays are one taste in the sphere of reality, one settles the understanding of that sphere of reality and through the awareness that directly realizes the emptiness in which objects and object-possessors are of a single taste, and one achieves the pristine wisdom dharmakāya.

Both the causes and effects here are concordant in the sense that there exists the relationship of connection between causes and their effects, and it is in dependence on those that one must accomplish the two holy bodies that are one's goal—that is, the holy rūpakāya for others' welfare, and the holy dharmakāya for one's own welfare.

These causes contain method and wisdom, or the collections of merit and the collection of pristine wisdom. Moreover, the two truths are present in this basis—that is, conventionalities that are the variegated objects present in reality, and the ultimate truth of suchness, the dharmadhātu in which all of those are a single taste. Therefore, in connection to this, there exist paths of method and wisdom, and due to those the resultant dharmakāya and rūpakāya come into existence— arisen through relationships within reality. It is for this reason that the collection of merit and the collection of wisdom must be practiced without separation, in a conjoined manner. [480]

Since at the time of the result the two bodies are one nature, at the time of accomplishing the causes for those, method and wisdom must likewise be practiced inseparably. In this way, if the manner of conjoining method and wisdom is taken in the context of the mode of progression on the path according to sutra, then the general Mahāyāna system is an inseparability of method and wisdom in which wisdom is qualified by method, and method is qualified by wisdom.

In the *Great Treatise on the Stages of the Path*, the section on the reason why you must train in the precepts and the one regarding not training separately in method and wisdom but in a conjoined fashion are singled out and explained in brief. It moreover appears that things that fall under the category of method are mostly aspirations and their related practices, such as the practice of generosity which is posited as the mind of giving. Thus, generosity is seemingly approached through aspiration, and the increase in generosity is performed through wisdom that induces certainty. Moreover, since it is easier to give rise to the wisdom realizing emptiness if one's continuum has been ripened, then the need to perform accumulation and purification in order to give rise to the wisdom realizing emptiness is approached through method.

Thus, for someone who has never given rise to the view realizing emptiness to newly give rise to it, or to develop it further after having given rise to it, or particularly for that view realizing emptiness to become the antidote to cognitive obscurations to omniscience, then they must possess all aspects of method. Therefore, for wisdom to progress further it requires the assistance of method, and in order for method realizations to increase further they require the assistance of wisdom.

Transferring from one ground to the next is a transference from one meditative equipoise to another meditative equipoise, and since that is a point where one is in meditative equipoise on the wisdom realizing emptiness, then transferring to higher and higher realizations is primarily the accomplishment of wisdom. [481]

    b″   How all the precepts are included in the six perfections

        1″   The main topic of the fixed enumeration of perfections

           (a) The definitive enumeration of perfections based on high status

           (b) The definitive enumeration of perfections based on fulfilling the two types of welfare

           (c) The definitive enumeration of perfections based on completely fulfilling others' welfare in all aspects

           (d) The definitive enumeration of perfections based on subsuming the entirety of the Mahāyāna

           (e) The definitive enumeration of perfections in terms of completeness of aspects of paths or methods

           (f) The definitive enumeration of perfections based on the three trainings

        2″   The ancillary topic of the fixed order of the perfections

The categories of definitive enumeration such as "definitive enumeration in order to eliminate the presence of a third alternative," "definitive enumeration that has a purpose," "definitive enumeration in order to dispel doubts," "definitive enumeration in order to include certain types," and so forth have not come up in this book. The two truths are an example of a definitive enumeration in order to eliminate the presence of a third alternative, and the four truths and six perfections are definitive enumerations that have a purpose.

With respect to this, it states in the *Ornament for the Mahāyāna Sūtras*,

> High status possessed of superb resources and body,
> excellent companions and endeavors,
> never under the influence of afflictions,
> and never faulting in any activity.

Completion of the monumental deeds of the victors' children requires continuing throughout many lifetimes. Moreover, when these complete necessities—the perfect resources to be enjoyed, the perfect body with which one enjoys, the perfect companions together with which one enjoys, and the easily completed aims of actions that are undertaken—excellently assemble, one understands that they must never fall under the sway of afflictions. One understands the point of what to engage in or disengage from so as not to increase afflictions. Then all of these excellences—body, resources, companions, all undertakings of aims of actions being accomplished—become the compatible conditions for completing the two collections. Due to this the progression along the paths will be much more effective. Thus, in relation to high status rebirths the enumeration [of the perfections] is definitive. [482]

Taking these excellences within a higher status rebirth to be the goal, their causes are as follows: the excellent resources that are enjoyed arise through the cause of generosity; the cause of the excellent body that enjoys them is ethics; the cause of the excellent companions one enjoys them with is patience; the cause of excellently and easily achieving the aims of actions one undertakes is joyous effort; the reliance on mindfulness so that these excellent things do not become conditions to proliferate afflictions, and the understanding of what to engage in and disengage from to that effect arise respectively from concentration and wisdom. In this way achieving a high-status rebirth abundant with excellences and developing those further rely on the path of the six perfections.

Then, **that to be accomplished based on that support are generosity, ethics, and patience—the three perfections for others' welfare—and wisdom, concentration, and ethics—the three perfections for one's own welfare. Thus, the enumeration of the perfections is definitive based on fulfilling the two welfares.**

Through donating wealth **the poverty of material goods is eliminated; through giving up the harming of others** together with its basis **there is no violence;** due to patience **hurt is not returned with harm;** through joyous effort **there is no dismay in bearing hardship for the welfare of others;** through the power of meditative concentration, **miracles and so forth,** for example, **others are inspired;** wisdom clarifies, hastens, and deepens knowledge, and moreover, through the skill of the wisdom of explanation, debate, and composition **one provides excellent explanations, eliminating others' doubts. Thus the enumeration of the perfections is definitive based on completely fulfilling others' welfare.**

Through the practice of generosity, **one becomes devoid of attachment to resources, and therefore one respects the training** in ethics. **Through** patience one practices **tolerance toward the suffering connected to the faults of others'** unpleasant conduct and distasteful speech. If one lacks the patience of certitude about the teachings on the patience of taking on suffering, and the patience of disregarding harm done to oneself, then one will become upset from others' exaggerations and disparagement, and so forth. **Therefore, one has joy in** practicing **virtue. Through calm abiding one's body and mind become serviceable, leading to an increase in the wisdom of special insight. Thus, the enumeration of the perfections is fixed based on subsuming the entirety of the Mahāyāna.**

Next, **familiarity with generosity is the method for not being attached to possessions. Guarding from carelessness** through ethics **is the method for restraining the distractions of wishing to have** possessions. **Patience toward taking on suffering is the method for not forsaking sentient beings. Effort without sadness and weariness is the method to increase virtue.** The meditative concentration of calm abiding connected to the bliss of **physical and mental pliancy** that pacifies afflictions as soon as they become manifest is the method for eliminating afflictions. Analyzing fine details **is the method for purifying cognitive obscurations to omniscience. As such, the enumeration of the perfections is definitive in terms of all aspects of method.**

Following that, **ethics that is accompanied by generosity and patience is by nature of the training in ethics; the last two perfections are the entity of the other two trainings; and joyous effort is required for all three. Therefore, the enumeration of the perfections is fixed in terms of the three trainings.**

Within the causes of not passing beyond samsara, attachment to possessions and attachment to one's household are eliminated through generosity and ethical discipline; although tending toward liberation once, one is intermittently held back due to (1) the suffering from others' wrong actions and (2) the dismay due to fatigue from one's endeavors. Thus, in order to dispel these two, one must abide steadfastly in one's practice no matter how much others act wrongly against us, which is done through patience, and through the joyous effort that is not fatigued by weariness from the hardship of practice. Therefore, through these two, patience and joyous effort, one is not affected by the causes of not bringing Dharma to its completion. [484]

Even though you may single-pointedly strive in your practice year after year, if your mind becomes a slave to distractions, you risk your hardships going to waste. Therefore, the enumeration of the perfections is definitive in terms of the antidote for abandoning the discordant class since (1) by means of concentration one does not fall under the sway of distraction, and (2) by means of wisdom one is not tainted by the fault of confusion about the reality of knowable objects. Since the first four perfections are the accumulations required for meditative concentration, it is through those four that meditative concentration is achieved, and if one meditates on special insight in dependence on that one will come to realize suchness. For this reason the perfections are of fixed enumeration in terms of being the basis for accomplishing all qualities of a buddha. Their definitive enumeration in terms of being compatible with ripening sentient beings is similar in meaning to the third one listed prior. Although these three fixed enumerations are not given in the *Ornament for the Mahāyāna Sūtras*, they are taught in the *Great Treatise on the Stages of the Path* in accordance with Haribhadra's presentation of Asaṅga's intentions.

The Ancillary Topic of the Fixed Order of the Perfections

This has three parts:
  (a) The order of arising
  (b) The order in terms of inferior and superior
  (c) The order in terms of coarse and subtle

To show these briefly, their differing subtlety, difficulty, and order of cause and effect are explained as follows: **If one is generous without concern for possessions, from the cause of nonattachment ethical discipline arises. If one has ethical discipline, from the cause of**

HOW TO TRAIN IN THE CONDUCT 545

restraining from faulty conduct patience arises. If one has patience, from the cause of not despairing at hardship joyous effort arises. If one has joyous effort, from the cause of striving day and night concentration arises. If one has concentration, from the cause of physical and mental serviceability wisdom arises. Therefore, even the six perfections are such that the former are inferior and the latter superior. Their differing level of subtlety is also like that, as it states in the *Ornament for the Mahāyāna Sūtras*:

> Because the subsequent perfections arise contingent on the
>   preceding ones,
> because of their being inferior or superior,
> and because of their coarseness and subtlety,
> they are taught in order. [485]

Training in the conduct of bodhisattvas—the Mahāyāna path having fixed enumeration just mentioned—is as follows:

HOW TO TRAIN IN THE SIX PERFECTIONS THAT RIPEN ONE'S CONTINUUM

c" The order one trains in the six perfections

1" How to train in the bodhisattva deeds in general

(a) Training in the six perfections that ripen the buddha qualities in one's own continuum

(i) Training in the perfection of generosity
(ii) Training in the perfection of ethical discipline
(iii) Training in the perfection of patience

(iv) Training in the perfection of joyous effort
(v) Training in the perfection of concentrations
(vi) Training in the perfection of wisdom

(b) Training in the four ways to gather disciples that ripens others' continua

2″   How to train in the last two perfections in particular

Training in the Perfection of Generosity

TRAINING IN THE PERFECTION of generosity has four parts:

- (a') What generosity is
- (b') How to begin the development of generosity
- (c') The divisions of generosity
- (d') A summary of the meaning of these

Regarding the practice of generosity, **the first—the nature of generosity—is any intention accompanying a bodhisattva's disinterested nonattachment to one's body or possessions, and, motivated by that, the physical and verbal actions of giving an object of generosity. How does giving lead to the completion of generosity?**

How to Begin the Development of Generosity

Although the mind is principal over body and speech, it is not enough to have merely overcome miserliness toward possessions and so forth—even śrāvakas and pratyekabuddhas have done that! What is needed here is a sincere mind of giving based on contemplation of the advantages and drawbacks. To this effect it states in the *Garland of Birth Stories*:

> **If this body—without self, easily perishing, without essence, suffering, ungrateful, and always impure—**

could be of help to others,
only the unwise would not delight [in using it for that
    purpose]. [486]

In brief, through increasing habituation with the mind of giving that
gives one's body and possessions, together with one's roots of virtues,
to all sentient beings, upon finishing such habituation the perfection
of generosity is complete.

One might think that the perfection of generosity is an alleviation
of the poverty of all sentient beings through donating gifts, but *Way
of the Bodhisattva* states the following:

If the alleviation of poverty of sentient beings
were the perfection of generosity,
then since there are still wretched beings,
how did the previous protectors perfect it?

[Śāntideva argues here that] if that were the case, then since there
are still limitless sentient beings who are destitute, it would follow
that previous buddhas have not completed the perfection of generosity. Therefore, the perfection of generosity is the completion of
habituation with the mind of giving to others, along with the results
of having given sincerely all of one's possessions and virtues away
without miserliness. As stated in *Way of the Bodhisattva*:

Generosity is taught to be perfected
by the wish to give all beings
all one's possessions, along with the result [of giving].

Therefore, generosity is a state of mind.

(c′) The divisions of generosity

(1′) How everyone should practice it

(a″) Ensuring one has the six excellences

(1″) Excellent basis
(2″) Excellent objects
(3″) Excellent purpose
(4″) Excellent expertise in methods
(5″) Excellent dedication
(6″) Excellent purity

(b″) Ensuring one has the six perfections

(2′) Divisions of generosity relative to particular persons
(3′) Divisions of actual generosity

(a″) Generosity of Dharma
(b″) Generosity of fearlessness
(c″) Generosity of material things

(1″) Generosity of directly giving material things

(a)) How to give material things

(1)) The recipients of generosity
(2)) The attitude required for giving

(a′)) What kind of attitude is required
(b′)) What kind of attitude should be given up

(1')) [One should] lack an attitude that holds bad views to be supreme
(2')) Lack an attitude that is arrogant
(3')) Lack an attitude wanting support
(4')) Lack an attitude of discouragement
(5')) Lack an attitude in which you turn your back on someone
(6')) Lack an attitude of expecting something in return
(7')) Lack an attitude of expecting a fruition

(3)) How to give

(a')) How not to give
(b')) How to give

(4)) The objects given

(a')) Brief presentation of things given and not given
(b')) Detailed explanation [of things given and not given]

(1')) Detailed explanation of internal objects given and not given

(a")) That which is inappropriate to be given based on the timing
(b")) That which is inappropriate to be given in terms of necessity
(c")) That which is inappropriate to be given based on the recipient

(2')) Detailed explanation of external objects given and not given

(a")) How not to give away external things

(1")) That which is inappropriate to be given based on the timing
(2")) That which is inappropriate to be given based on the gift
(3")) That which is inappropriate to be given based on the person
(4")) That which is inappropriate to be given based on the material thing
(5")) That which is inappropriate to be given based on the necessity [488]

(b")) How to give away external things

(b)) What to do if you are unable to give
(c)) Antidotes to the hindrances toward generosity

(1)) Not being familiar
(2)) Being weak
(3)) Attachment
(4)) Not seeing the goal

(2") Generosity merely through an intention

To present a summary of these, **the spiritual friend Geshé Sharawa states the following about practicing the perfection of generosity:**

I do not talk about the advantages of giving; I talk about the
drawbacks of withholding!

In accordance with generosity being divided into three—generosity of
material things, generosity of Dharma, and generosity of fearlessness—
or four, with the generosity of love, **male and female ordained bodhisattvas** must have fewer objectives and less activities. Therefore, just
as doing business for money in order to make offerings to the Three
Jewels or give to the poor, or running here and there in order to gather
offerings for beggars **is a hindrance to study, contemplation, and
meditation,** even if you make offerings of your material goods that you
gained **through effort and exhaustion,** the benefit is not so vast, and
therefore it is inappropriate for those with meagre finances to go out of
their way to **perform generosity of mere material objects. Thus, they
must primarily focus on the generosity of Dharma,** the generosity of
fearlessness, and the generosity of love.

Even though one must give away without attachment surplus
wealth or **things acquired suddenly and without effort, generosity
of material things is a** more relevant **activity that bodhisattva householders should engage in. Therefore, having distinguished well the
general principles of generosity as well as the exceptions depending
on the giver,** act in accordance with the extensive explanation of how
to give and how not to give based on the giver as found in the *Great
Treatise on the Stages of the Path.*

**In order to put into practice the generosity of Dharma, material
wealth, and fearlessness,** one must give up the mistaken attitude **thinking, "There is no result from performing those three kinds of generosity."** [489] Moreover, **give up the attitude of holding wrong views as
supreme, such as wrong Dharma**—for example preaching violence as
Dharma—**forsaking limitless beings for the sake of one and protecting them, and thinking that flesh and blood offerings from murder
constitute Dharma.** Arrogant attitudes are likewise to be given up, and

thus it is inappropriate to **demean the person to whom you give offerings,** such as deprecating and looking down on the poor when giving to them. **Moreover,** an attitude of **desiring to compete with others** should be given up, **along with arrogance that thinks, "No one else except me speaks such good words of Dharma, protects the lives of as many sentient beings, or gives away as many special items."**

Likewise, give up the desire for fame, of wanting others to say, "They performed these three types of generosity"; the discouragement of thinking, "I cannot perform that much generosity"; the regret in having been generous; the bias that gives to dear ones but not to enemies and so forth: the attitude of turning one's back on others; the attitude that expects something in return, such as **hoping for thanks for teaching Dharma, saving lives, and so forth—like giving silver and hoping for gold in return; and likewise the hope for a fruition in the next life of being knowledgeable, being fearless, and having resources.**

The attitudes to adhere to are **as taught in the** *Compendium of the Perfections*:

> **When a beggar directly comes to ask for something,**
> **so as to increase the collections for complete enlightenment,**
> **bodhisattvas regard their [possessions] as belonging to others,**
> **and consider that person as their spiritual teacher.**

The way to focus on the purpose is to think, "May I complete the perfection of generosity in dependence on this sentient being who is the recipient of generosity." **The way to view your personal objects is to think, "Since from the outset I have already given the Dharma, my ability to protect others, and,** after first having generated bodhicitta, having **given all of my possessions to others, it is like returning an item that was entrusted [to me]."** [490] **The way to focus on the recipient is to think, "These are my spiritual friends with respect to whom I will complete the perfection of generosity."**

In brief, rather than focusing on the advantages for oneself, **one gives by way of an attitude possessing three features that focuses on** (1) the purpose, (2) the object, and (3) the recipient, through thinking, "I will complete the perfection of generosity in order to achieve full enlightenment for the sake of all sentient beings." **If done correctly in this way, one does not incur the faults of misdeeds such as hiding profound Dharma and teaching the nonprofound, protecting only a few even though one is able to eliminate all fears, and giving objects that are inferior, few, or stolen from the hands of others.**

Moreover, give with a radiant and smiling countenance, pleasant speech, without harming another, and with patience regarding the burden of one's undertaking. There are ten recipients of generosity: enemies, friends, neutral persons, those with qualities, those with faults, higher, lower, equals, happy, and the wretched. The reason for listing ten is to adapt to them individually by having love toward enemies, admiration for those with qualities—and so forth.

In brief, since all sentient beings are included in those ten types, then the generosity of Dharma is teaching according to your knowledge the holy Dharma of the Mahāyāna and Hīnayāna—that is, the Buddha's excellent speech along with the commentaries on its intention, and the general sciences of logic, arts and crafts, and so forth—with a pure motivation.

One must declare, "Having made the listener uphold the trainings and so forth according to their mental capacity, may they engage in listening, contemplation, and meditation by which they accomplish the vast aims of sentient beings!" Making dedications after teaching the Dharma is the practice of fully qualified spiritual teachers.

Furthermore, even though one might not have the title of a Dharma teacher, if friends and others are engaging in misdeeds and nonvirtue, have a conversation about what to adopt and discard, and to turn away from nonvirtue and engage in virtue, and so forth. In

**this way, strive directly in the generosity of Dharma through having
an attitude with the three special features.** [491]

Since this is the most beneficial, one should perform the generosity
of Dharma through teachings based on a guru-disciple relationship,
as well as the generosity of Dharma that is teaching the common and
uncommon sciences with a pure motivation together with dedication
of merit at the end. Likewise, the advice that schoolteachers and university professors give on qualities that are helpful for politeness and
good conduct of body, speech, and mind is most likely included in the
generosity of Dharma. Moreover, discussing Dharma while seeing the
other person as a spiritual peer without needing to be as guru and disciple, or indicating what to adopt and discard through discussing advice
that accords with Dharma with a motivation to be helpful in a way that
suits the other's ideas and manner are both generosity of Dharma.

Tselé Natsok Rangdröl observed the three commitments of not using
a horse as his mount when traveling, not eating meat, and not taking
offerings for his Dharma teachings. We should follow as much as we are
able such marvelous life accounts. Teaching Dharma for offerings is making business out of the Dharma, and as such is an incredibly grave fault.

As with "giving merely through an intention," **if you cannot find a
real recipient for your generosity, sincerely visualize yourself teaching the holy Dharma to all sentient beings and think that great benefit has come from the power of generosity of Dharma. For example,
make special aspirational prayers while visualizing that the hell
beings are freed from their bad state and suffering through hearing
the sound of the Dharma.**

Next, with respect to the generosity of fearlessness, **you should
protect sentient beings from the fears of being punished as crimi-
nals under the law, or having their body, life, or possessions come
under threat from wild animals or enemies, if you are able. If one is
unable to do that, then explain to them the way to be free from their**

situation. [492] As there are limitless beings tormented by suffering in other world systems, genuinely think that you give the generosity of fearlessness to them, and through its power they become free from fear. Through imagining yourself as having become possessed of the power of the mind directed toward supreme enlightenment, visualize and make prayers that you emanate out great rains that fall in the hot hells and extinguish the flames, and so forth.

This, along with similar observations of giving and taking, are like the many prayers of bodhisattvas that are impossible to achieve, as taught in the dedication chapter of *Way of the Bodhisattva*. If one has an exceptional motivation, then making an effort for the environment, or the actions of doctors and nurses, are also included within actions of the generosity of fearlessness.

The generosity of material things such as food and drink, shelter and bedding, medicine for illnesses, fine cloth and jewels, mounts such as horses and elephants, castles and land, head, eyes, arms, and legs—in other words, the body and all possessions—are given as before by way of an attitude possessing the three features.

I once knew a monk and a nun who both genuinely wished to donate their eyes out of a pure motivation, and they requested that I search for recipients for their gift. This was not a case of someone becoming an organ donor out of attachment to their loved ones or family, but rather it was purely out of altruism. In the beginning they wished to donate one eye each, then later determinedly said that if it were beneficial, they would donate the other eye. I was astonished when they told me this. However, later on, when they did a blood analysis, it turned out their blood was not suitable, and they were not able to actually carry out their wish. [493]

Furthermore, if one is hungry and impoverished and thus unable to do this, then mentally emanate limitless cooked and uncooked food and offer it to beings who are afflicted by hunger such as wild animals and so forth. Thus, think that they become free of that suffering. **Such vast emanations that are adapted to the recipient and items given are the [practices of] generosity of wise bodhisattvas; therefore, one should train this way.**

A Summary of the Meaning of These

Regarding the aforementioned three types of generosity, from now on one should, according to ability, directly teach at minimum a four-lined Dharma verse, give shelter to those suffering from heat, give food and clothing to poverty-stricken persons, and so on. Simply doing these through visualization while one is able to do so directly is to fool oneself.

We Tibetans have a good culture of giving to the poor, and as such we should correctly perform generosity while carrying a pure motivation of altruism without any disrespect or condescending behavior.

That being said, we are very generous toward projects for erecting monasteries, temples, and statues, but when it comes to issues such as health, environmental protection, schools, and education, Tibetans have not developed the custom of giving toward these things. This is a great fault, and as such it is paramount that our thought and behavior are reformed. We must engage in such ways that will benefit future communities and people through impactful actions that aid progress.

Restoration projects of monasteries, temples, and statues in Tibet these days are excellent, but it is of crucial importance to undertake action on the pressing needs that have the most immediate impact. Therefore, without any pretense or hope for fame or reward, if you genuinely focus on the bigger picture it is extremely beneficial and highly virtuous. [494]

In order to implement the antidotes to the obstacles to generosity, **having thoroughly ascertained what was explained prior, analyze well the miserliness that is attached to objects of generosity, the thought of not being able to give because one has no possessions, and the mind that is especially attached to beautiful objects. Curb**

558 THE FOURTEENTH DALAI LAMA'S STAGES OF THE PATH

discordant attitudes through contemplating repeatedly as follows: "Even though I have been born countless times into high and low status such as a hungry ghost or Vaiśravaṇa, this is the state I am in now. While I obtained objects more precious than those I have now, like wish-fulfilling jewels, I have parted from them all."

If you have given rise to a manifest desire to give yet you predominantly hope for reciprocity or the fruits of that generosity, then make a strong aspiration, thinking, "I have already made countless sacrifices through which I attained the state of Śakra, Brahmā, and so forth, yet those states have all been pointless. Therefore, I will now dedicate the giving of everything from a mere morsel of food to become the cause of supreme enlightenment."

With this aspiration, focus on giving the three types of generosity through mental emanation in the actual meditation session. Directly perform generosity between sessions, and strive to mentally familiarize yourself with giving.

One might wonder whether they should practice the three types of generosity as much as they are able. It is not completely definite that one should, as stated in *Way of the Bodhisattva*:

> Do not give away your body
> when lacking a pure motivation of compassion.
> Give so that it will become a cause
> to achieve great aims in this life and the next.

Until the hardship and repulsion toward cutting up one's body and so forth diminishes through your compassion, and through your practice of methods occasional anguish no longer arises in your mind, then eventually you will reach a high level at which you no longer experience bodily [suffering]. As such, until you have attained stability it is not good to immediately overdo it, and improper if untimely. [495] As such, it is inappropriate to give away one's body, for example, **for a small purpose,** and it is also inappropriate **to give away the body to harmful spirits, or because the mentally insane and so forth ask for it.** Thus, inappropriateness in terms of **time,** inappropriateness in terms of **purpose, and inappropriateness in terms of the recipient of generosity make the difference as to whether one gives or does not give one's body.**

That is to say, giving the gift of one's body without having stability in thought and practice is inappropriate in terms of time; giving one's body for a small purpose is inappropriate in terms of purpose; and giving to those who beg for the sake of harming others or seeking revenge, for example, is an inappropriate recipient.

Regarding outer factors, teaching the Mahāyāna Dharma to persons of extremely dull mental faculty, and giving food to monastics after midday are acts of giving that are inappropriate in terms of timing. In terms of the recipient, it is inappropriate to give **meat, alcohol, onion, garlic, or tainted leftovers to those observing precepts;** it is inappropriate to give away **living beings who are certain to be harmed by the other person;** it is inappropriate to give **food unfit for an ill person; and it is inappropriate to give a Dharma text, for example, to those who wish to make an assessment of it, or consider it in terms of its monetary value. In terms of the thing given, it is inappropriate to give away servants who would suffer due to not wanting to leave, for example.**

Giving that is inappropriate in terms of the purpose is to give protection from the fears of prison to someone who would cause suffering to countless persons if they left the incarceration of the king. Regarding the generosity of fearlessness, trying to secure the release of convicted persons from prison is a good form of the generosity of fearlessness; however it is certainly important to understand whether there are other greater arguments against that.

Moreover, giving poison, weapons, and so forth to those who ask with malintent is generosity that is inappropriate in terms of purpose. Thus, having thoroughly differentiated between the general

principles and the exceptions, think, "Since I, too, will also die soon, these things to be given away will also forsake me; and I, too, will forsake these things. As such none of these things have essence." In this way sincerely familiarize yourself with the mind of giving. [496]

Concluding Verses

By offering my body and resources with a powerful wish
   to give
countless times to sentient beings whose kindness cannot
   be repaid,
may the storehouse of inexhaustible treasures—
the jewel of eternal happiness—be attained.

This inexhaustible suffering of poverty
has not befallen me alone.
When looking at the state of all mother beings,
my mind cannot bear it.

If through the force of previously accumulated nonwhite
   karma,
my current situation is like this,
then through completing the perfection of generosity,
may I liberate endless sentient beings!

Training in the Perfection of Ethical Discipline

The training in the perfection of ethical discipline [has five parts:]

(a') What ethical discipline is
(b') How to begin meditating on ethical discipline
(c') The divisions of ethical discipline
(d') What to do when practicing
(e') A summary

What Ethical Discipline is

Way of the Bodhisattva states:

> Where can fish and so forth escape
> to avoid being killed?
> It is said that ethical discipline is perfected
> from the attainment of the mind of abstention.

Ethical discipline is the mind of abstention that turns away from harming others along with the basis for that.

How to Begin Meditating on Ethical Discipline

Since the perfection of ethical discipline is achieved through enhancing and completing familiarization with that intention, it does not depend on all sentient beings having been freed from harm.

The Divisions of Ethical Discipline

This outline has three parts:

(1') The ethical discipline of restraint
(2') The ethical discipline of gathering virtue
(3') The ethical discipline of enacting the welfare of beings

The Ethical Discipline of Restraint

Regarding the first, the ethical discipline of restraining from faulty behavior, it states in Atiśa's *Lamp for the Path*:

Those who maintain any of the seven kinds
of individual liberation vows
have the fortune to take
the bodhisattva vow, not others. [497]

Misunderstanding these words, some think it explains needing to possess any of the seven types of individual liberation vows to possess the bodhisattva vows, and thus assert this to be referring to the actual presentation of ethical discipline. However, since there are gods who are a basis for training in the bodhisattva trainings, this would contradict the fact that someone who possesses the individual liberation vows must be a human being.

Regarding this, it states in the *Commentary of "Lamp for the Path"*:

> Now I would like to teach the exceptional basis for the vows
> of ethical conduct.

Therefore, the support for bodhisattva vows in this context is not given from a universal perspective, but rather it explains an exceptional support. It is of course unsuitable that [Atiśa] is discussing a common, unexceptional support.

How should the ethical discipline be identified? If it is someone who possesses individual liberation vows who is training in the bodhisattva vows, their vows of abstention in common with the actual individual liberation vows would be identified as the ethical discipline of abstention in this context.

If it is not someone who possesses the individual liberation vows, the vows of abstention of abandoning the ten nonvirtues in common with the individual liberation vows would be identified as the ethical conduct of abstention from faulty behavior. Therefore, it states in the *Compendium of the Perfections*:

> Do not fall from these ten paths of action—
> the path to bliss of high status and liberation.
> Through abiding in these there comes the result
> of the exceptional thought of altruism toward living beings.

If one is ordained, one repeatedly analyzes with mindfulness and introspection whether one has incurred faults with respect to the root and branch [vows] one has taken in the presence of an abbot and preceptor. If one does not have individual liberation vows, one frequently analyzes with mindfulness whether one has fallen under the influence of the ten nonvirtues explained in the context of persons of small scope. Furthermore, in accordance with the practice of the previous Kadam masters, make a daily count of your virtue and nonvirtue with white and black pebbles—if there are more white ones, be joyful; if there are more black ones, have strong regret, and in your actual meditation session first perform restoration, confession, and restraint by way of the four opponent powers according to your misdeeds whose count is kept by the black pebbles and which you have held onto in your memory. [498]

Contemplate by thinking and verbalizing, "May I totally complete the perfection of ethics." Rather than letting strong attachment toward an object overcome you, suppress it and so forth by recollecting unattractiveness and the drawbacks of misdeeds, and thinking about the ripened results and so forth of whichever affliction is strongest. By applying the antidote and meditating in this way your ethical discipline will be pure.

Think about the approach of your own personal precepts. Lay householders who use mindfulness to engage in the way of positive behavior and restrain the doors to their senses are able to block the many potential avenues to making oneself and others suffer. As it says in the *Eight Verses of Mind Training*:

> Always analyze your own conduct,
> and as soon as afflictions arise,
> counter them with forceful means and stop them,
> since they are what make oneself and others vile.

Many afflictions such as pride, jealousy, attachment, competitiveness, and so forth come about through anger, and thus in the bodhisattva scriptural collections whether one is ordained or lay, male or female, they must absolutely be stopped. As soon as the types of awarenesses illustrated by those afflictions poke their head up even slightly, immediately recognize their faults and apply the antidotes and destroy them. Putting this into practice is extremely important.

As such, in brief, (1) the practice of the ethical conduct of abandoning the ten nonvirtues with an attitude that seeks higher status [rebirths] is taught in the context of beings of small scope; (2) the practice of the ethical conduct of abandoning the ten nonvirtues with an attitude that seeks liberation is taught in the context of beings of middle scope; and (3) in the context of the ethical conduct of bodhisattvas the practice of the ethical conduct of abandoning the ten nonvirtues by way of restraining from principally focusing on one's own aims with an attitude wishing to achieve enlightenment for the sake of others is a Dharma of great scope beings.

Thus, **although the ethical conduct of abandoning the ten nonvirtues that exist for all three beings are similar in nature, they are distinguished by differences in attitude.** [499]

THE ETHICAL DISCIPLINE OF GATHERING VIRTUE

The ethical discipline of gathering virtue is the virtue of body and speech performed by those possessing the ethical conduct of bodhisattvas. It is the three trainings, service offered to exceptional fields of merit such as gurus and so forth, praising the Three Jewels, verbally rejoicing in the virtue of others, seeing harm toward oneself as one's previous karma, sealing virtues with dedication prayers, making offerings to the Three Jewels, conscientiously not stemming the flow of virtue, guarding the doors to the senses from the afflictions, knowing your limit with food, striving in the yoga of the earlier and later parts of the night, applying the antidotes by relying on a spiritual teacher, or if you cannot find one, being your own spiritual teacher, and confessing faults to an exceptional basis. Among those, cultivating meditative concentration, for example, is [done] during the actual session. Preparations for making offerings to the Three Jewels and so forth are done in the session breaks. The watchmen of conscientiousness and introspec-

tion, and so on, are required for both the actual session and session breaks, while welcoming the lama and offering seats do not have determined times.

Nowadays the practice is to contextually apply analytical and placement meditation regarding everything thus mentioned and sustaining the focal object. Therefore, in brief, all virtue performed is subsumed in the ethical discipline of gathering virtue.

THE ETHICAL DISCIPLINE OF ENACTING THE WELFARE OF BEINGS

The ethical discipline of enacting the welfare of sentient beings is the assistance carried out by bodhisattvas toward sentient beings. This is, furthermore, explained as eleven beneficial activities. They are as taught in Tsongkhapa's *Commentary on the Ethics Chapter of Asanga's Bodhisattva Grounds*:

1. Assisting and helping those who suffer
2. Actions for those oblivious to [correct] methods
3. Acts for beneficial persons
4. Acts for those who are in danger
5. Acts for those overwhelmed by misery
6. Acts for those bereft of requisite items
7. Acts for those who wish to settle
8. Acts for those desiring likemindedness [500]
9. Acts for those who practice correctly
10. Acts for those who practice incorrectly
11. Enacting the welfare of beings through miraculous powers

The first, **assisting and helping those who suffer,** has two parts: preventing theft and aiding the sick. Regarding the first, **the method taught for preventing theft of one's belongings without wrongdoing**—that is, helping others in their activities through showing them how to guard wealth, and so forth, through interacting with others in a nonharmful manner—is **helping others through assistance.** The second part of the first is **giving medicine to the sick, and getting those with weak legs where they need to go by offering transportation, for example.**

Likewise, **indicating the way to turn away from faulty behavior by teaching the Dharma is to help people who are oblivious to correct methods.** This includes teaching the correct path to those who are confused as to what to adopt and discard by having a conversation with them, such as schoolteachers and so forth who have a personal duty, those who have become guides for others due to their title, or otherwise as stated in the context of generosity of Dharma. Thus, this concerns those who are able to meaningfully act by considering these types of deeds their duty while carrying a pure motivation.

Acts of service, veneration, and so forth, for example, help those persons who are **beneficial** through service, veneration, welcoming them, offering lodging, and so forth, thus supporting those who are focused on their own recipients.

Protecting persons from any kind **of harm from** animals **such as lions and tigers,** and that of humans and nonhumans **is to help those who are in danger.**

Helping those overwhelmed by misery is, for example, alleviating the misery currently **gripping** any sentient being **due to losing their parents** or other loved ones, **or because thieves have stolen their wealth by discussing impermanence with them.** [501] Even having supportive sympathy for those going through a hard time can offer solace. For example, when Atiśa was living in Tibet and Amé Jangchup Rinchen was serving as his cook, Amé lamented to Dromtönpa about only having time to serve Jowo Atiśa, and no time to meditate. Dromtönpa groaned in solidarity that he, too, had no time to meditate due to attending to Jowo Atiśa and serving as his translator. At the end, however, he told him that the opportunity to serve this holy guru simply surpasses meditation, and that if one is able to perfectly fulfill one's service now while the holy guru is still alive and remains, there is nothing to regret. Amé Jangchup Rinchen's mind was at ease having seen the truth in this.

To help those bereft of requisite items is to transfer one's equipment, job, transport, jewelry, and so forth—whatever the other person needs and when one is in a situation to give—or failing that, giving them advice and showing them how to acquire the thing they need. **Giving food to those who are without sustenance is an example.**

Taking destitute persons bereft of food, clothing, and shelter, under one's wing with a motivation of loving compassion and **helping them by giving religiously compatible clothing, pointing out unpleasantness to those experiencing attachment,** talking soothing words to calm the minds of angry persons, **and so forth, is to help those who wish to live [in a community].**

Upon seeing others who are unable to perform virtue, helping those who desire likemindedness is making them give up undesirable physical and verbal behavior and seek a skillful path that suits their dispositions and aspirations. For example, instead of insisting on explaining Dharma to those who do not believe in it, or Mahāyāna Dharma to those who cannot fathom it at present, [502] one should avoid the risk of it becoming detrimental rather than helpful despite one's best intentions, and persuade them **through benefiting their mind** in other skillful ways that better suit their disposition.

When someone is feeling disheartened about **qualities such as ethics,** faith, generosity, and wisdom, **praising** and making them joyful about **these qualities is helping those who practice correctly.**

Punishment for wrongdoing, for example—motivated by an attitude of compassion and being realistic with respect to the weight of the misdeed—**is to help those who practice incorrectly.** In this regard, one praises and takes under one's care those who do good to benefit others, advises people who have gone down the wrong path to change their ways, and puts effort into ways to stop those who have gone down a path of negative behavior through punishment if they have been unable to correct their behavior.

In order for authentic methods of taming disciples to be beneficial for others while not falsely claiming superhuman powers, those with the ability can **turn others away from misdeeds by conjuring [visions of] hell beings** through their actual miraculous powers, **for example, or display disfigured apparitions to make others believe. Doing so helps beings through miraculous powers.**

It varies whether you are actually able to perform these eleven acts or whether it is the right time for them. Despite this, it is a crucial point that you still bring them into your practice during the actual session using analytical and placement meditation, not leaving it on the level of mere words.

It says in the *Compendium of the Perfections*:

> If your own goals are not possible because your ethical
>   discipline has deteriorated,
> where will your power to help others come from?
> Thus, one who strives hard for others' welfare,
> should not relax their attention to ethics.

Since it is taught that ethical discipline is the root of accomplishing the welfare of oneself and others, one should engage in methods that further enhance one's ethical discipline of giving up harm toward others together with its basis. [503]

Concluding Verses

In the grove of a support with excellent freedoms and
    opportunities,
the wish-granting tree made up of the three ethical disciplines
bows down with the great weight of the fruits of nirvana,

its nectar of a hundred tastes of bliss and goodness all
   descending.

The good results of generosity
that are the resources accumulated for countless eons,
whether experienced as a human being or a god,
entirely depends upon the agent of ethical discipline.

Those who let this chariot—an excellent support attained
   once—
remain idly bogged down in the mud of careless downfalls
without fixing it and pulling it out onto the smooth flats of
   bliss
have been possessed by malevolent spirits.

Training in the Perfection of Patience

Training in the perfection of patience has five parts:

(a') What patience is
(b') How to begin the cultivation of patience
(c') The divisions of patience
(d') How to practice
(e') A summary

It states in *Way of the Bodhisattva*:

Intractable beings are like space—
they cannot all be overcome.
Yet through conquering this angry mind once,
it is as if all foes were overcome.

Where could I find enough hide
to cover the surface of the earth with leather?
Having the leather of my sandals alone
is like covering all the earth.

Similarly, I myself cannot control
what is external to me,
but if I restrain this mind,
what left is there to be restrained?

572 THE FOURTEENTH DALAI LAMA'S STAGES OF THE PATH

The completion of the perfection of patience is the total familiarization with a mind that has stopped anger and so forth toward sentient beings. It is not necessary that all beings become free of their
unruly mind states. In order to practice the perfection of patience
that is the culmination of the cessation of the faults of anger and so
forth in the depths of one's own mind, one must contemplate the benefits of becoming familiarized with patience, and the drawbacks of
anger. [504]

Concerning this, Śāntideva says:

Any and all good deeds
such as generosity and worship of the sugatas
accrued for a thousand eons
are destroyed in one moment of anger.

That roots of virtue are destroyed upon becoming angry with holy
beings is even stated in the treatises of the Mūlasarvāstivādins. In
particular, it states in Candrakīrti's *Entering the Middle Way*:

The virtue from generosity and ethics accrued over a
    hundred eons,
is destroyed in a single moment
of anger toward the victors' children.
Therefore, there is no greater evil than impatience.

It is taught that a weak bodhisattva's anger toward a powerful bodhisattva can destroy virtue accumulated for a hundred eons. Moreover,
ordinary non-bodhisattvas becoming angry at bodhisattvas renders
the virtue of a thousand eons fruitless, and so forth. Thus anger is
gravely heavy.

As such, since anger is the main opponent of those who practice the bodhisattva path, it is emphatically advised that "there is no evil like hatred."

We amass anger effortlessly over the slightest of conditions. An object of anger who is a bodhisattva is like a fire pit covered by ashes—one cannot be certain where they may be, and one's previous virtue is rendered totally ruined. It is definitely the root of all problems for this reason. As Śāntideva says:

> Whoever, having focused, has destroyed anger
> will be happy in this life and the next.

Having abandoned anger, not only are you without physical and mental torment in this life, it appears to be the cause of happiness in all lifetimes. As such, continuously commit to train in the perfection of patience.

If you practice the antidote of patience in order to abandon anger, there are infinite advantages such as a happy life, mental and physical ease in this life, and a relaxed society, which we know for a fact can be experienced even through a little hard work. [505] Likewise, through that condition one will have excellent fruits from lifetime to lifetime, including a nice body, beauty, and so on, as it states in *Entering the Middle Way*:

> Through patience one becomes beautiful,
> dear to holy beings, a knower of right and wrong,
> and after that born as god or human,
> with all negativities becoming exhausted.

In accordance with its inconceivable advantages, the way to practice it is taught as follows:

(c′) The divisions of patience

(1') The patience of disregarding harm done to you

  (a") Stopping impatience toward those who harm you

    (1") Stopping impatience with those who prevent your
    happiness and with those who cause you to suffer

      (a)) Showing that anger is unjustified

        (1)) Anger is unjustified when analyzing the object

          (a')) It is unjustified when analyzing if the
          object has self-control
          (b')) It is unjustified when analyzing if the object
          is adventitious or inherent
          (c')) It is unjustified when analyzing if the harm
          is direct or indirect
          (d')) It is unjustified when analyzing the cause
          that impels one's harmdoer

        (2)) Anger is unjustified when analyzing the subject
        (3)) Anger is unjustified when analyzing the basis

          (a')) Analyzing the cause of harm and whether
          it is faulty or not
          (b')) Anger being unjustified upon analyzing
          your commitment [506]

      (b)) Showing that love is justified

    (2") Stopping impatience with those who prevent you from
    being praised and so forth, and with those who behave

in three ways such as being contemptuous toward you
and so forth

(a)) Stopping impatience with those who block your
praise and so forth

(1)) Reflection on how praise and so forth lack good
qualities
(2)) Reflection on how praise and so forth have
faults
(3)) Delighting in those who prevent praise and so
forth

(b)) Stopping impatience with the three acts of disparagement and so forth

(b")) Stopping both dislike for the success of one's harmdoer,
and joy in their troubles

(2') The patience of accepting suffering
(3') The patience of certitude about the teachings

Anger Is Unjustified When Analyzing the Object

A suitable summary of these outlines is as follows: **first, whether or
not the harmdoer is actively hurting you, visualize** the harm **they
committed in the past** and perform analytical meditation. Analyze the
conditions that led to the other person harming you, and upon proper
recollection, **when furious anger has arisen, look at its nature.** You must
then reason with yourself that your anger toward them is unjustified.
To indicate the first step of meditating on anger being unjustified when
analyzing the object—that is, how anger is unjustified upon analyzing
whether they have self-control—**it says in Way of the Bodhisattva:**

If under the control of afflictions,
I would kill even my beloved self,
so how could I not harm
the bodies of others?

For instance, when some people develop the strong affliction of dislike for another and have come under the sway of affliction, there is simply no doubt about them harming others, and we know it can lead to committing suicide, self-harming, jumping off a cliff, overdosing on sleeping pills, and so forth. Thus, think, "While I cherish myself and so would not do myself any harm, it could happen under the sway of afflictions. Yet, I would not get angry with myself. So, when other beings have lost their self-control due to strong afflictions, why should I be angry when they harm me?"

Anger Is Unjustified When Analyzing If the Object Has Self-Control

If you think that a harmdoer has self-control since they would not hurt their loved ones and so forth, meditate on the fact that their helping others is done under the sway of attachment. [507] If sentient beings had self-control, then since all of them do not wish for suffering, there would be no beings tormented by suffering. Through this one comes to see sentient beings as powerless as someone forced to harm others by a king or the like.

Anger Is Unjustified When Analyzing If the
Object Is Adventitious or Inherent

Moreover, if it were the case that beings were inherently harmful by nature, then they would be unfixable like fire being hot and burning. If it is the case that it is an adventitious rather than inherent state, then it is taught that it is like how it is unjustified to be angry at the sky because the clouds block the sun. Whether it is inherent or adventitious, it is still unjustified to be angry.

Anger Is Unjustified When Analyzing If the
Harm Is Direct or Indirect

Likewise, that which directly harms you is the weapon, like a stick, for example, and the one carrying the stick has been incited by anger, so how can it be the person who has harmed you? Upon becoming angry when someone beats you with a stick, it is the stick that directly harms you. If you direct your anger at the one wielding it, since the stick has no self-control, then accordingly, they also lacked self-control and acted indirectly out of their anger. Therefore it is incorrect to overlook the actual harmdoer—that person's anger. It is therefore taught that it is senseless and unnecessary to put the blame of all the faults onto that person.

Anger Is Unjustified When Analyzing the Cause
That Impels One's Harmdoer

If you direct your anger at the root cause of harm, then you must get angry at yourself, since it is from your past actions of similarly harming others that have led to this. [508] As it states in *Way of the Bodhisattva*:

In the past it was I
who similarly harmed sentient beings.
Therefore it makes sense that I should be harmed
by the violence of sentient beings.

Anger Is Unjustified When Analyzing the Subject

Not only that, if you cannot even bear the minor harm caused by harsh words and wounds, you have now created more causes for lower rebirths. If you let yourself be angry without cultivating patience and continue to harm others it becomes negative karma; if you are born in hell as its result, how will you bear the pain? Give rise to deep shameful aversion by thinking in this way again and again.

It states in Candrakīrti's *Entering the Middle Way*:

> If you resent someone for the harm they have done
> does that resentment reverse what they did?

If you get angry at someone because they have hurt you, their harmful act has already passed—anger does not help you reverse it. If you continue to react to them out of anger it will end up as a cause for being burdened by suffering in the future. For this reason anger is unjustified.

Analyzing the Cause of Harm and Whether It Is Faulty or Not

This is the first outline from "analyzing the basis." **Moreover, just as when rain falls onto water both do not change from being wet, so too because both our body and the other person's weapon that harms it are causes for suffering, it is simply expected that one experiences pain.**

Anger Being Unjustified upon Analyzing Your Commitment

Meditate on the fact that if even śrāvakas who accomplish their own aims do not get angry at others, **then how is it appropriate that I, who know all sentient beings to be my mother, and who generated my mind toward accomplishing the well-being of others, should do so? It is taught that the mind and body become at ease through meditating on this.** [509]

Anger must be stopped by contemplating these and other reasons. Therefore, if you can meditate on this in steps, familiarization will lead to cultivation. For example, if someone immediately gets angry upon encountering someone they do not like, after continuous meditation on patience eventually they will get to a point where they are not fazed by the person they dislike looking meanly at them.

It is for this reason one should focus efforts on the smaller stages of practices, too, through which one enters into the training of virtue.

Through greater familiarization it comes without difficulty. Otherwise, if you start by thinking, "It would be nice to practice something that brings me joy," and immediately try to arrive at great results, it is just not realistic.

Eliminating our mental faults is a slow process, like the growth of a tree and its fruit. Trees cannot grow in a few days, and trees that have lived for one or two hundred years grew slowly. However much longer it took them to grow ensures that their fruits will be around for longer. As such, just like flowering plants that only last a few months will spring up in a few days, so too our roots of virtue that remain until the end of space take a longer time to grow, and our virtuous mind states induced by fleeting renunciation do not last long, and disappear quickly.

STOPPING IMPATIENCE

Stopping impatience with those who prevent you being praised and so forth, and with those who behave in three ways such as being contemptuous toward you and so forth [has the following outline]:

(a)) Stopping impatience with those who block your praise and so forth

(1)) Reflection on how praise and so forth lack good qualities
(2)) Reflection on how praise and so forth have faults
(3)) Delighting in those who prevent praise and so forth

(b)) Stopping impatience with the three acts of disparagement and so forth [510]

These are taught in an abbreviated fashion as follows: **If you are still delighted by others' praise, you will naturally detest slander. As such it says in** Way of the Bodhisattva:

> Praise and renown
> do not increase merit or lifespan,
> bestow neither health nor strength,
> and bring no comfort to the body.

Not only do praise and renown not serve to increase happiness in future lives, they do not do so even in this life! On top of that they have many faults, such as causing us to engage in meaningless distractions, and becoming a source of envy for others. These end up as a cause for losing one's renown. The praise of others or our fame will neither help in future lives nor in this life. When you conceitedly think you are perfect, your pride increases, and, however well-known you become, you end up with increasingly more pointless distractions and more people who are jealous of you, which end up as conditions for mental nonvirtue.

If one loses one's renown, others will no longer be able to harm you and, ultimately, without such distractions, you will be free to achieve enlightenment and happiness. Meditate with joy while thinking that this is the blessing of the Buddha.

Likewise, even if others directly oppress us, we must stop our impatience toward them. If you are harmed by a weapon, of course it hurts your body a bit, but it does not hurt your mind; contemplate how bad words hurt neither one's body or mind.

STOPPING BOTH DISLIKE FOR THE SUCCESS OF ONE'S HARMDOER, AND JOY IN THEIR TROUBLES

Even if through meditating in this way praise and disparagement become equal to you, if you still suddenly experience impatience toward your enemies having good things, it states the following in *Way of the Bodhisattva*:

Why should you be happy,
when your enemy is upset?
Your mental wishes
cannot cause their harm.

Why should you be joyous, though,
If the suffering you wish upon them comes to be?
If you think it brings you satisfaction,
what could be more ruinous than that? [511]

Caught on the unbearably sharp hook,
cast by the fisherman of my afflictions,
held over the cauldrons of hell,
I am sure to be roasted by the guards.

There is no use in getting angry at the happiness found by other sentient beings. Even if you were to get angry, how could it harm them? Thus, even if you are angry at the happiness found by your enemy, as well as it not harming that person, it proliferates the suffering of your unhappy mind, and undermines your mental peace. It does nothing except harm you. **Even if you have already harmed them it is the karma for both yourself and the other to burn in hell. Develop a firm mind of restraint while thinking about this.**

(2′) The patience of accepting suffering

    (a″) The reason we definitely must accept suffering
    (b″) The way to develop acceptance of suffering

        (1″) Stopping absolute dislike toward suffering when it occurs
        (2″) Showing that it is appropriate to accept suffering

(a)) Contemplating the good qualities of suffering

(b)) Contemplating the advantages of patience with suffering's hardships

(c)) How it is not difficult if you start small with your habituation

(c') An extensive explanation from the viewpoint of the bases

All of these are explained as follows: **Thus, you may think that even though you are able to apply the antidote to your hatred of those that harm you, you still cannot bear the suffering that has befallen you. Still, if nothing can be done about that suffering then being upset is pointless, and if something can be done about it then there is no need to be upset.**

The Way to Develop Acceptance of Suffering

The unwanted suffering that has befallen you now is the result of nonvirtue committed in your previous lives. [512] It is because you experience these feelings of suffering in this lifetime that you are able to practice adopting and discarding what you should—otherwise you would just continue to turn the wheel of cyclic existence. Now this suffering has become the root of mentally renouncing cyclic existence and achieving liberation which is nirvana. How kind!

There are many such bad conditions that appear as aids. Take for example the Tibetan refugees: Of course being separated from our country and becoming refugees is an incredibly sad situation. Nevertheless, speaking from a Dharma perspective, we have gained an opportunity to form strong bonds with people from various religious traditions and learn from each other.

Moreover, it has led to Tibetan Buddhism and culture spreading far and wide in the world. Prior to this when Tibet was a free and sovereign country, relations were not built with foreign nations and they withdrew unto themselves. This led to the country lagging behind. To make up in some small way for this disconnection, nowadays most people at least have heard of Tibet and know roughly where it is and so forth.

In this way bad circumstances can become a stimulus for virtue, and through more profound perspectives one's way of life can start to have substance. Having seen why it's worth accepting suffering, which can become like "turning bad omens into good fortune," **it is like the relieving of strong pain from an illness through undergoing harsh treatments such as bleeding, moxibustion, and so forth: instead of the suffering from having to be reborn in the hell of Unrelenting Torment in your life, think that the suffering from illnesses and so forth in this life suffice instead. Contemplate this.**

Moreover, however much suffering arises from tragic circumstances affecting your body, since you have attained a precious human body you are lucky that there is something that can be done about it. We must remember that if it were the body of an animal undergoing such suffering just how much more hardship there would be.

An Extensive Explanation from the Viewpoint of the Bases [513]

There are eight topics in this section.

Accept the Suffering That Is Based on Objects

Having brought about experiences in your actual meditation sessions with respect to the aforementioned topics, in the session breaks accept the suffering based on enhancing Brahmin-like conduct from objects like ragged clothing, and so forth.

Regarding this topic, it is worth understanding how it is covered in the *Great Treatise on the Stages of the Path*. Once there was an Amdo monk from Ganden Jangtsé Monastery who was determined to follow the twelve ascetic practices, thinking that it was unacceptable if he could not practice any one of them. He lived without accommodation or a roof over his head at the foot of a tree in Mundgod, south India, and I praised him at the time. Such persons who are able to put all such teachings into practice are astounding, and thus I have mentioned this here, too, to recollect as an example.

Accept the Suffering Based on the Worldly Concerns of Praise and Depreciation

Accepting the suffering based on the worldly concerns of praise and depreciation, and so forth means to not be concerned with others' praise or depreciation, with getting what you want or not, and stamping down on the eight worldly concerns.

Accept the Suffering from Conduct in Which You Are Not Reclining

Regarding **accepting the suffering from conduct in which you are not reclining**, things that fundamentally harm your health while you are in your sessions or while engaging in virtue are a completely different situation. In general, it is best if you can sit in the seven-point Vairocana posture without leaning back and forth.

After Trehor Kyorpön Rinpoché of Drepung Monastery arrived in India, he bestowed the Guhyasamāja empowerment as requested. At that time he was seated in a peculiar cross-legged posture, which reminded me of the posture Marpa Lotsāwa had referred to as "my sitting posture that other great Tibetan meditators are incapable of." He had spent a long time practicing in isolated places, and since he was so habituated with everything including the sitting postures he did not display the slightest discomfort. [514]

*Accept the Suffering from Upholding the Dharma,
Such as Honoring the Three Jewels*

Accepting the suffering from upholding the Dharma, such as honoring the Three Jewels, is to accept the difficulty associated with singularly engaging in the virtue of veneration and offering service to the aforementioned objects of refuge, upholding the teachings oneself, teaching them to others, reciting daily prayers, and likewise meditating on the meaning of the words of Dharma. However, if you go about this too foolishly, you can end up with increased blood pressure, an increase in wind diseases (*loong*), and so forth, so you should be very careful. Some practitioners use the view that their illnesses are the result of their karma as a pretext to not take medicine and not take care of themselves. This is entirely unacceptable.

Accept the Suffering from Living through Begging

Monastics shave their head and beard, **adopting an unattractive appearance, and wear poor clothing** that is cut and patched due to not being allowed to handle expensive items, **and so forth.** Since they live in pure [Brahmā-like] conduct, they must engage in behavior **desisting from sensory pleasures of singing, dancing, and so forth,** and live off of alms. Once when I went to Thailand, I went with their monks on their morning alms rounds, taking my begging bowl into the streets. It was a source of great happiness and joy to follow the practice of the Vinaya of accepting whatever alms were given. The custom of the monastery I was staying at was to go barefooted, and as I was not accustomed to that I burned my feet due to the strong heat, but aside from that it was also a great spectacle. This **is to accept the suffering from subsisting by begging** for substandard food, and so forth.

Accept the Suffering from Fatigue Due to Persevering in Virtue

Regarding **accepting the suffering from fatigue due to persevering in virtue,** [515] Accomplishing virtuous deeds takes an extended period of time. Therefore, it will not work unless you exert yourself considerably from the outset with study and contemplation. Then, in the middle, giving rise to the meaning of what you have studied in your continuum after you have understood it also requires effort. This is illustrated by the sincere undertaking of hardship by Jetsun Milarepa, for example, and the previous Kadampa masters who relinquished concern for food, clothing, and reputation through their practice of the four entrustments: entrusting your mind to the Dharma, entrusting your practice to a life of poverty, entrusting your life of poverty to death, and entrusting your death to an empty cave. They voluntarily took up spiritual practice by way of great hardship and a firm resolve, striving with joy and enthusiasm. We must act like this.

Accept the Suffering from Helping Sentient Beings through Protecting Their Lives

Accepting the suffering from helping sentient beings through protecting their lives, and so forth, is the patience of taking on the suffering of hardships encountered when engaging in deeds such as the eleven beneficial activities mentioned in the prior context of the ethical conduct of enacting the welfare of sentient beings.

Directly Accept the Suffering from Provisional Acts Such as Giving Up Engaging in Business

Directly accepting the suffering from provisional acts such as giving up engaging in business, and so forth, is to give up activities of a householder, and actions such as business and fieldwork that are not inherently misdeeds, but are for a monastic. **Moreover, through having earnestly familiarized your mind to also accept what you cannot** directly take on right now from among those, [**it is as said in**] *Way of the Bodhisattva*:

There is nothing that does not become easier
through habit.
Thus, if you familiarize yourself with minor harm,
you will be able to have patience even with great harm.

Through gradual habituation you will eventually complete the perfection of patience which does not give thought to anything.

Developing the Patience of Certitude About the Teachings

To have certitude about the teachings one generates the patience of conviction. This has two points:

(a″) The object one has conviction in
(b″) The way to have conviction [516]

The object one has conviction in has eight:

(1″) *The object of faith.* This is the qualities of the Three Jewels.
(2″) *The object to be actualized.* This is the suchness of the two selflessnesses.
(3″) *The object desired.* This is the powers of buddhas and bodhisattvas.
(4″) & (5″). The *objects to be adopted and discarded.* These are the causes and effects of proper and improper engagement [with those].
(6″) *The object of meditation that is to be attained.* This is enlightenment.
(7″) *The object of meditation that is the method.* This is the path trained in by bodhisattvas.

(8″) *The object subsequently practiced through listening and contemplation.* This is the twelve links of excellent speech, and so forth.

THE WAY TO HAVE CONVICTION

Having found certainty as to what those objects are, hold onto them
without discordance and reflect on them again and again. The *Great
Treatise on the Stages of the Path* explains this in accordance with
[Asaṅga's] *Bodhisattva Grounds.*

A SUMMARY

When practicing any kind of patience you must do so by possessing
the six excellences, along with the six completed perfections. Thus,
in order to be able to accomplish well any beneficial activity that is
principally for an altruistic purpose, one must properly conjoin it
with mindfulness and introspection, whether it be during the preparation or actual act. This is the main important point: the six crucial
features—that is, the six perfections—must be complete in each individual deed. In the same way, engaging in loving-kindness toward
others is the foundation upon which one gives advice on increasing
qualities and stopping faults; explains the Dharma; makes offerings
and gives alms such as giving material things; protects others from
frightening situations; and trains in giving rise to the courage to be
able to strive in such things. These are the practices explained in the
four types of generosity.

To correctly enact these one must be unadulterated by faulty behavior of body, speech, and mind, and ensure that one's attitude and
outlook are correct based on the appropriate approach to training in
those virtuous activities for the sake of others—that is, the ethical conduct which is polite and noble behavior. [517] To strive in this way,
one requires patience able to accept hardships without giving them

thought, and to generate perseverance that joyfully engages in virtuous activities. Then, through the adroitness of concentration that is able to remain single-pointedly on the focal object without wavering, one needs to possess intelligent wisdom that can discern right from wrong and what is to be adopted or discarded.

In brief, if the six crucial points of attitude and application that are the six perfections are complete in whatever you undertake from now on, all of your deeds will become excellent paths.

Concluding Verses

The dense forest stream of a collection of virtues accumulated
   throughout lifetimes,
is totally scorched by a single fireball of anger.
This unbearable enemy who has piled up logs of nonvirtue to
   the peak of existence
is the foundation of all my suffering.

From the peak of the steep mountain of karma and afflictions,
   out of control,
an avalanche of bad results falls down
onto those in the gorge of cyclic existence.
Yet who could blame it for its destructive nature?

When you fit yourself well with the impenetrable armor of
   patience,
on the battlefield lined with the army of true origins,
how amazing it is that you can advance toward the abode of
   nirvana,
that cannot be penetrated by striking, smashing, harsh words,
   and weapons.

Training in the Perfection of Joyous Effort

THE TRAINING in the perfection of joyous effort has five parts:

(a') What joyous effort is
(b') How to begin the practice of joyous effort
(c') The divisions of joyous effort
(d') What to do when practicing joyous effort
(e') A summary

What is joyous effort? It states in *Way of the Bodhisattva*:

Any effort that is joyous in virtue.

The perfection of joyous effort is the total culmination of progressively increasing a correct joyful attitude toward accumulating virtue and accomplishing the welfare of sentient beings. [518] Furthermore, it says in the *Ornament of the Mahāyāna Sūtras*:

Joyous effort is supreme among collections of virtue.
By this you subsequently attain the others.
Through joyous effort you immediately achieve the supreme
    state of bliss,
including supramundane and mundane siddhis.

Through joyous effort you attain life's pleasures.
With joyous effort you come to possess total purity.
Through joyous effort you go beyond the perishing collection.
Through joyous effort you awaken into supreme
enlightenment.

The source for all mundane and supramundane happiness and good
is joyous effort.

How to Begin the Practice of Joyous Effort

As it states in *Entering the Middle Way*:

All qualities follow joyous effort.

Anything difficult to accomplish seems easy in the eyes of someone
with joyous effort; they do not perceive it as a struggle. From the
perspective of someone without joyous effort, even small and easy
pursuits seem fundamentally hard. Therefore, with joyous effort you
can easily accomplish all of your desired goals. For this reason it is
extremely important.

The Divisions of Joyous Effort

This has two parts:

(1') Actual divisions
(2') The way to cultivate joyous effort

The actual divisions has three parts:

(a") Armor-like joyous effort
(b") Joyous effort in gathering virtue
(c") Joyous effort in accomplishing the welfare of sentient beings

These outlines are taught thus:

Regarding armor-like joyous effort, it is the thought, "In order to achieve buddhahood to dispel the suffering of one sentient being, if I have to remain in hell for a trillion multiples of three countless eons, in which a thousand great eons are the equivalent of one day, thirty of those making up a month, and twelve of those a year, I would not give up joyous effort. What need is there to mention a shorter amount of time!" [519]

Immeasurable joyous effort is even greater than that. Calculating the period from beginningless samsara to the present time as one day, and thereby calculating months and years, even if [it took] a hundred thousand such years to generate bodhicitta once and see a single buddha, and as many such years as there are grains of sand on the banks of the Ganges River to understand the mind and behavior of a single being, and one would have to do such a thing with every single being, one would not consider it as too long, but would do it joyfully. This is explained as the unsurpassable joyous effort.

Thus, we must start as we did in the context of generosity: by habituating ourselves with generosity through both attitude and deed, beginning with giving a single mouthful, until ultimately being able to give up even one's head or body without hesitation. In the same way, here, one too thinks, "I will engage in just this much virtue this morning," and strive with great joyous effort in the virtue of generosity and so forth as you intended. Eventually you will be able to engage with joyous effort for days, months, years, or until the end of your life, according to your commitment, without feeling that it is difficult or taking a long time. Your joy will keep increasing, resulting in being able to achieve the aforementioned armor-like joyous efforts.

Set a firm motivation that during the actual session you will not let anything else interrupt your analytical or placement meditation, applying the antidotes to the three poisons through recollecting the Three Jewels until the session is complete. It is taught that having stopped your craving for idleness and lesser happiness and applied great joyous effort, even though you may face much hardship in your earlier sessions, eventually upon habituation it will not be difficult and your joy will increase.

The Way to Cultivate Joyous Effort

This has four parts:

   (a″) Eliminating unfavorable conditions that hinder joyous
       effort [520]
   (b″) Amassing a host of favorable conditions
   (c″) Based on those, sincerely devoting yourself to joyous effort as
       you started out
   (d″) How to make the body and mind serviceable through that

Eliminating unfavorable conditions that hinder joyous effort has two parts:

   (1″) Identifying the discordant class
   (2″) How to apply methods to eliminate that

When flashing thoughts of procrastinating laziness persist, thinking, "I have time," consider what *Way of the Bodhisattva* says:

Tasting the bliss of idleness,
and craving for sleep,
one is not saddened by cyclic existence,
which in turn leads to laziness.

It is explained that the causes of the laziness that procrastinates virtue by wasting the day away arise from attachment to lesser pleasures such as sleep and lethargy, and so forth. Therefore, if you end up in a state of mental darkness, for example, where your mind is blank or you cannot think or recollect anything, then do not remain inside your house, but instead **perform your physical conduct where there is a breeze, wear lighter clothing, and also take breaks.** Regarding your focal object, contemplate that just as you see people die regardless of how young or old, you too will also die soon, and finding a nice body such as this after death will be hard. Meditate on this until you develop an understanding of urgency, like there is not even time to drink.

Still, because the antidote has not been perfected, when experiencing craving for inferior pleasures such as idle chatter, contemplate that by being distracted with temporary minor pleasures the door to the holy Dharma is locked and you will be born in lower realms, as it states in *Engaging in Bodhisattva Deeds*:

Why do you give up the cause of infinite joy—
the holy Dharma, supreme among joys—
and take pleasure in the causes of suffering,
distractions, excitement, and so forth?

How to apply methods to eliminate that has three parts:

(a)) Stopping laziness that is procrastination
(b)) Stopping attachment to negative actions
(c)) Stopping discouragement, or self-deprecation

(1)) Stopping discouragement toward the goal

(2)) Stopping discouragement toward the methods for achieving that goal

(3)) Stopping discouragement because any place you are is a place of practice [521]

STOPPING DISCOURAGEMENT TOWARD THE GOAL

Having meditated in this way you may become discouraged by thinking, "It will be hard for me to achieve the goal of the Buddha Bhagavān, since he has eliminated all faults and possesses all qualities." When this occurs, think of these words from *Way of the Bodhisattva*:

> Do not depreciate yourself by thinking,
> "How could I become enlightened?"
> The Tathāgata, proclaimer of truth,
> taught this truth:

> "Flies, biting insects, bees, and
> likewise all insects
> will achieve enlightenment, difficult to attain,
> upon generating the force of perseverance."

> So why should someone like me—
> born a human being, recognizing help from harm—
> not be able to achieve enlightenment,
> as long as I do not give up the conduct of enlightenment?

Encourage yourself by meditating with this thought: "If the Bhagavān, possessed of extraordinary qualities, this buddha who never lied and only spoke truth, **has taught that all sentient beings will achieve buddhahood, I too will certainly achieve buddhahood."**

Not only is it important to have conviction in the Tathāgata's teaching that achieving buddhahood is possible, but it is also crucial to contemplate that the Tathāgata taught this based entirely upon reasoning—that is, in terms of the emptiness of true existence of all phenomena—and based on the mind being in the nature of clear light.

STOPPING DISCOURAGEMENT TOWARD THE METHODS FOR ACHIEVING THAT GOAL

If you find yourself thinking you cannot strive in these methods to achieve buddhahood, in an encouraging manner you must try to ascertain that it is feasible and possible to achieve the resultant state of buddhahood, then also that the ten grounds and five paths that one traverses to achieve buddhahood also have immeasurable qualities individually that can be accomplished. [522]

It can happen that you think, "If this takes so long I doubt someone like myself could achieve it." For example, the mantra path seems difficult to some people because they think it would be hard for them to quickly accomplish an experience or realization despite trying. Some lose hope because the sutra path requires accumulating the collections for three countless eons. When you desire to achieve buddhahood but think that the path is difficult to implement—that is, **when you encourage yourself by thinking, "I will achieve buddhahood," yet believe that you would not be able to give away your body, such as your arms or legs—on this point it states in** Way of the Bodhisattva**:**

> **The Supreme Physician does not utilize**
> **ordinary remedies such as these.**

Through very gentle treatments
he heals innumerable severe illnesses.

The Guide first instructs
One to give vegetables and the like;
familiarizing yourself in this way,
eventually you will give even your flesh.

Once I perceive my body
as I perceive a vegetable and the like,
what difficulty could there be
in giving such things as my flesh?

Contemplate with great joy that you will be able to give your head,
eyes, and so forth when you are able to perceive it as the same as
serving a meal of cooked vegetables; it will not be so hard!

Generally, the degree of difficulty comes from our own capability, and from our perspective on things. Therefore, it is clear that for
someone who has great potential, even a hard task becomes effortless. Moreover, if you have the confidence that things will work out,
the situation seems easy no matter what. Therefore, it is taught that
difficult tasks are only to be attempted once your capacity has been
gradually developed and you have gained confidence. The Bhagavān,
greatly compassionate in his skillfulness, did not teach that beginners
must push themselves to accomplish difficult undertakings of which
they are incapable. [523] Rather, he taught that as the mind gradually
matures, tasks that are initially difficult to accomplish can be undertaken once they appear to be less difficult, due to habituation, and will
not cause fatigue. It is, moreover, as taught with extensive reasoning
in Nāgārjuna's *Precious Garland*.

STOPPING DISCOURAGEMENT BECAUSE ANY PLACE
YOU ARE IS A PLACE OF PRACTICE

You might think, "I cannot bear to take birth in cyclic existence" upon training in the conduct of bodhisattvas. It says this in *Way of the Bodhisattva*:

> Since misdeeds are forsaken there is no suffering.
> Because of knowledge there is no lack of joy.
> Thus it is misconceptions and misdeeds
> that harm the body and mind.
>
> Through merit one has a comfortable body.
> Through knowledge a comfortable mind.
> Why would the compassionate ones be disheartened
> from remaining in samsara for the sake of others?

Meditate while thinking that the cause is not present since bodhisattvas have given up misdeeds, and thus the resultant suffering does not arise.

To gather virtue, strive to honor the Three Jewels, and so forth. To accomplish the welfare of sentient beings, strive in teaching methods for others' riches not to be taken by thieves, and so forth. These were discussed in the section on ethical discipline. Distinguish the differences as per the context and sustain the meditative focal object. Just as in the prior context of the eleven deeds for helping beings, we are instructed to train in engaging the objects based on which we cultivate joyous effort with joy and enthusiasm.

Amassing a Host of Favorable Conditions

This second outline of the four within *the way to cultivate joyous effort* has four parts:

(1") Cultivating the power of aspiration
(2") Cultivating the power of steadfastness
(3") Cultivating the power of joy
(4") Cultivating the power of relinquishment

How does one give rise to joyous effort by eliminating what is discordant to it? **Without being content with giving rise to merely a few of the aforementioned qualities, by recollecting the benefits and disadvantages of training and not training in the bodhisattva conduct, first** cultivate the initial **power of aspiration,** and try to give rise to the intention to engage with joy and enthusiasm in the conduct. [524]

Next, regarding **the "power of steadfastness" that does not abandon the undertaking of joyous effort**: having first analyzed whether you can put into practice right now that which is to be undertaken, if it is something you are unable to undertake right now then do not begin it for the time being, and if you think you can do it, engage in it decisively, and you must bring to completion what you have started.

Even in the case of worldly business, you would not make rash decisions initially, but rather you would analyze whether you should proceed based on your own financial situation and the current state of the market, and come to a decision. Following that, if you diligently pursue business for a few days but then get distracted and involved in other things, you will not see it through until the end.

Thus, in line with having to finish what you start, it is taught that one must train in the three types of pride: pride in action, pride in potential, and pride about afflictions. Pride in action is the courage motivated by the thought, "I will do it myself," in which performing this or that virtue does not depend on others—avoiding the trap of only striving in an activity if others are doing it, and waiting with hesitation if they are not. Pride in potential is the thought, "Others might consider this task difficult to accomplish, but I can do it!" While not performing an action through the conceited affliction of pride and seeing such a motivation as something to forsake, you give rise to pride that venerates sentient beings at the crown of one's head while assuming a lower and humble position. This is the pride about afflictions that has disdain for afflictions. The explanations in the commentaries to *Way of the Bodhisattva* regarding this, and those given by Jé Tsongkhapa when he cites the relevant passages differ slightly. [525]

Next, **the** third **power of joy is to not stop the momentum with great joy** and insatiability. Regarding this, if you are able to skillfully prolong any particular virtuous activity, you will have an insatiability for whatever virtue you practice. Thus, not only can you be joyful even during your daily prayer recitations, some people wake up at two or three in the morning to do their prayers, and continue these sessions for years on end. Some people are exhausted even at the thought of this, but from the side of the practitioners themselves, they experience neither difficulty nor weariness. With great enthusiasm think to yourself everyday that you have gained an opportunity to make your life meaningful, and hold a long session.

If you are not accustomed to joyous effort then however much you sleep you will think, "If only I could sleep a bit more!" and so forth. This is the fault of a lack of habituation. It is hard for so-called "virtuous practice" to shape the mind so quickly, and thus for the sake of confronting an untamed mind a variety of measures must be taken, akin to waging war. Just as different kinds of weapons are used on the battlefield and the power of armies are utilized from earth, sky, and sea, subduing an untamed mind requires striving from many different angles to gradually bring about results.

Moreover, just as when damming water you must continue to block leakages wherever they appear, so too the antidotes appropriate to the stages of growth of an affliction must be employed, and the means for taming this unruly mind must be approached from all angles. Therefore, if you stick to a single practice, no matter how deep you go you will not get far. As such, it is taught that not only is it incredibly important to place imprints for the entirety of the path, but also to take it gradually and sustain it, and through "a hundred methods and a thousand strategies" use great joy to maintain momentum of insatiability. [526]

The fourth, **the power of relinquishment, is understanding the importance of relaxing upon exhaustion.** If you exert yourself with too much joyous effort in virtue you run the risk of your physical strength gradually declining, of facing mental exhaustion, and so forth. Therefore, when your body and mind are fresh, do not lose the enthusiasm from the momentum of the earlier session, and take a break before you become unenthused. If you do this you will want to continue with the later sessions, and thus it is taught you should engage like this. Intense virtuous practice sometimes requires stopping at the right time and resting.

Regarding the actual practice of joyous effort **through these, it states** in *Way of the Bodhisattva*:

> Just as a veteran approaches
> a sword-fight with their enemy,
> so too I will dodge the attacks of afflictions
> and strike hard the afflictions, my enemies.

Just as someone skilled in combat plunges their weapon into the enemy and dodges the incoming blows, in this case, too, one destroys manifest afflictions and defends oneself from the mental wounds of

the dormant afflictions. One develops joyous effort and practices in both of these ways.

Concluding Verses

However much you are wildly preoccupied
in the meaningless bliss of the sleep and lethargy of
    ignorance,
there is no satisfaction,
just like drinking salty water out of thirst.

If, out of anger, you can hold yourself high and try to injure
a powerful enemy you are incapable of vanquishing,
then this despondency regarding attaining buddhahood,
which is entirely achievable, is absurd!

Understanding the apparent urgency of this life,
if you whip yourself along with perseverance, devoid of
    procrastination,
within the holy Dharma that achieves eternal happiness,
you will certainly reach that island of liberation! [527]

Training in the Perfection of Concentration

THIS HAS FIVE PARTS:

(a') What concentration is
(b') How to begin meditation on concentration
(c') The divisions of concentration
(d') How to practice
(e') A summary

Way of the Bodhisattva states:

> Having thus cultivated joyous effort,
> place your mind in meditative stabilization.

Once you have brought to completion the meditation on single-pointedness of mind through the mind abiding without wandering from its focal object, you have perfected concentration. Furthermore, in the teachings of earlier masters, such as in the *Great* and *Middle-Length* lamrim treatises, after the sections on training in the six perfections as the "general training in conduct," they created a separate outline focused on "training in particular in the last two perfections," in which **calm abiding and special insight** are extensively **explained on their own in brief and extensively relating to the topics of concentration and wisdom. However, when condensing the practice of a single topic, the focal object of calm abiding is addressed** in the fifth outline, and the focal object of special insight as the sixth, after which is a summary of the four means of gathering disciples. Accordingly, in this text, the way to meditate on calm abiding is explained in brief in the section on concentration out of the six perfections, and the way to sustain special insight is explained in brief in the context of wisdom.

Therefore, with respect to meditation on calm abiding, which is the practice of concentration or meditative stabilization, it states in *Unravelling the Intention*:

> If beings meditate
> on special insight and calm abiding,
> they are liberated from the bindings of negative tendencies
> and the bindings of signs.

Wisdom entirely eliminates the experience of the bindings of negative tendencies from the root together with its seeds, and concentration suppresses the manifest experience of the bindings of signs. Thus, those two are called calm abiding and special insight, and of all the meditative concentrations of the three vehicles that go by many names, there is not one that is not included within calm abiding and special insight.

In general, all virtuous practices are included within analytical and placement meditations. [528] Thus, both calm abiding and special insight are a great and important summation of the practices that include all meditative concentrations. However profound the practices ranging from generosity to joyous effort may be, they can never directly harm afflictions, and therefore, mainly the practice of wisdom is necessary. Moreover, it is indispensable to give rise to such meditative concentration of conjoined calm abiding and special insight based on concentration, wisdom's assistant. All paths that act as direct antidotes to afflictions are meditative concentrations of conjoined calm abiding and special insight. In order to develop this practice, calm abiding has to be achieved before special insight, and thus the topics of "how to train in calm abiding, the nature of concentration," and "how to train in special insight, the nature of wisdom" are offered.

In general, calm abiding is not unique to Buddhism alone, but something that Buddhists and non-Buddhists have in common. Thus, it appeared in many of the classical Indian philosophical tenets, and there is more or less calm abiding meditation in ancient Christian traditions, too. In particular, there is said to be profound meditative concentration practices in the orthodox sect of Christianity in some countries such as Greece.

Calm abiding is to keep one's mind single-pointedly and firmly on a single, suitable object without wavering. The mind does not scatter to other objects and remains calm, and thus is called calm abiding.

Regarding the further increase in ability of that factor of single-pointedness of mind, it depends upon making the effort to cultivate habituation, since it is a compounded phenomenon. Therefore, through cultivating mindfulness and introspection one sustains meditative concentration. Putting effort into the collection of causes such as staying in conducive places and far from opposing conditions is referred to as "cultivating the collections for calm abiding." With regard to this, Ārya Asaṅga lists a collection of thirteen causes in his *Śrāvaka Grounds*; namely, an appropriate amount of food, exerting effort in yoga instead of sleeping, restraining the doors to the senses, and so forth. Ācārya Kamalaśīla gives a collection of six conducive conditions in his *Stages of Meditation*. Despite a mere difference in extensiveness, the meaning is the same. [529]

The way one knows the object through calm abiding is much more effective, and the potential of mind is heightened based on the crucial point of winds and mind being single engagers.[87] For example, researchers have seen that when a small object is placed in front of someone who tries to move it through focusing single-pointedly on it that they are able to move it. Even though these kinds [of experiments] are not [related to] profound natures of reality, if the mind does not scatter and is totally focused it has great potential. Without that, it is clearly shown the mind cannot affect great potential.

Special insight includes "special insight realizing modes," "special insight realizing varieties," "mundane special insight," and "supramundane special insight." However, special insight principally refers to seeing final reality. Special insight does not settle for an understanding of how things merely appear outwardly when not analyzing or investigating them. Rather, it is a thorough analysis of the final manner of existence through discriminating wisdom that does not mix the many realities of an object, separating them individually. It thus has clear special insight into the nonerroneous mode of existence of things.

Calm abiding continuously employs mindfulness and introspection toward a single object; thus the mind naturally abides on the focal object, and when the joyful bliss of physical and mental pliancy arises through single-pointed meditative stabilization included within the preparations of the first concentration,[88] **it becomes an extraordinary meditative stabilization** of actual calm abiding. **For this reason,** calm abiding is absolutely necessary **for wisdom to cut the bindings of grasping to signs.** [530] This calm abiding that is an extraordinary meditative stabilization conjoined with the bliss of physical and mental pliancy is needed as an assistant for wisdom, **as it states in the *Moon Lamp Sūtra*:**

Through the power of calm abiding one becomes unwavering.
Through special insight one becomes like a mountain.

For example, just as in order to utilize water you need a vessel to contain it, to engage with the object the mind must be unwavering. Thus, in order to see the meaning of reality [like] the unmixed and separate details of a painting, if it is obscured by the darkness of ignorance you must light the lamp of wisdom and look. As the winds of distraction stir it and it becomes unclear, meditative concentration that closes the door to that is indispensable. If you are not able to stop the drifting toward other objects through calm abiding, not only will you have little result with respect to the meaning of reality, but likewise other virtues of karmic causality, love, compassion, recitations, and so forth will bear small fruit. Therefore, if you have single-pointedness within your analysis it enhances even neutral mental activities, let alone virtuous mental activities, since your analysis becomes much more profound. Thus, it is not only within your meditations on emptiness: if you carry out other virtues with a distracted mind such as meditation on love, compassion, recitations, and other practices of methods, they cannot become powerful virtuous activities. As it states in *Way of the Bodhisattva*:

> The person whose mind is distracted
> lives between the fangs of afflictions.

And also:

> All recitations and austerities,
> practiced for however long
> with a distracted mind,
> are taught to be meaningless by the knower of reality.

What is the order that calm abiding and special insight arise? Śāntideva says:

> Having understood that special insight thoroughly possessed
>   of calm abiding
> totally destroys the afflictions,
> seek calm abiding at the outset!

Cutting the root of grasping at a self requires meditating on the wisdom realizing selflessness. [531]

How to Begin Meditation on Concentration

Moreover, without having previously attained the bliss of physical and mental pliancy in dependence upon placement meditation, the bliss of pliancy cannot be induced through the force of analysis. Therefore, special insight cannot be attained without preceding it. Thus, **calm abiding is meditated on prior to it. Regarding this it states in the** *Ornament for the Mahāyāna Sūtras*:

> **The intelligent practice in a place**
> **that is accessible, a nice place,**
> **a healthy environment, with nice acquaintances,**
> **which has supplies for ease in yogic practice.**

This indicates the collections needed for calm abiding, which are the **easy acquisition of conducive conditions for Dharma practice such as food and clothing,** staying in a conducive place, having little desire, feeling contentment, not engaging in many activities, practicing pure ethical discipline, and contemplating the drawbacks of desire. These are taught as the supports to avoid mental distraction.

The line, which "has supplies for ease in yogic practice" indicates that the person practicing calm abiding should be able to easily acquire the necessary requisites of food and drink, and so forth. Moreover, when practicing you should spend the majority of your day meditating single-pointedly, and not meditating for brief periods then spending most of your time on other things. Doing so becomes an obstacle to achieving calm abiding. Likewise, **a place free from the danger of wild animals, robbers and thieves, enemies, and harmful spirits, a nice environment that does not lead to illnesses, the presence** of Dharma friends with compatible views and behavior, and being devoid of all meaningless and distracting commotion are the features of a place in which to practice this Dharma.

However, if one remains in such a conducive place yet still creates causes for distraction of their own accord there is nothing to be done. Therefore, engage in practice based on the six practices and so forth that are the collections needed for calm abiding. First, give up attachment to the joy of having a lot of nice food and clothing. Second, have few desires, as stated in the passage:

> Not content even with what they have,
> and strongly desirous due to not getting it [532]

As stated, fine objects of desire, strong desire toward them, lack of contentment, and so forth, are unsuitable. Third, be content with alms for food and rags for clothes, which is to say, be content with only poor quality food and clothing. However, it is important for us beginners to have a sufficient amount of nutritious food to strengthen our bodies. If you become complacent or negligent with such things it leads to a decline in mental strength, too, and a lack of enthusiasm for virtuous practice. For this reason, it is entirely inappropriate to do with less than you need. Nevertheless, as your experience of meditative concentration gradually becomes more profound and you develop correct wind yoga, you will not be so dependent on outer coarse food anymore.

Moreover, fourth, do not engage in many activities, such as profiting through business, medical treatment, astrology, and so forth. Fifth, no matter what monastic or lay vows you possess, guard them with pure ethical discipline according to your commitment. Sixth, contemplate well the drawbacks of desire and the nature of impermanence.

Having thus prepared the collection of causes, the way to meditate on calm abiding that is the actual practice is a practice of a bodhisattva's path of concentration. Therefore, meditate on bodhicitta for a long time at the outset. In order to give rise to the yoga of calm abiding easily by way of accumulation and purification, it must be preceded by the seven-limb practice and one must supplicate the merit field, and sincerely request blessings.

Regarding the actual practice, **the object you direct your focus upon was taught by the Tathāgata to be the four focal objects of a yogin**: (1) the focal objects for purifying behavior, (2) the focal objects for expertise, (3) the focal object for purifying afflictions, and (4) the pervading focal object. These correspond to the meditator's own dispositions, affinities, imprints, and so forth. [533]

The focal objects for purifying behavior are the following: unpleasantness as an antidote to attachment, love as an antidote to anger, observing the manner of cycling in the forward and reverse orders through the twelve links of **dependent origination as an antidote to ignorance, observing the different parts of the five elements and consciousness individually, and counting the in and out breaths.** As a means to purify the imprints left behind through behavior motivated by strong, manifest afflictions in our previous lifetime and earlier part of this lifetime that are still strong now, meditation on unpleasantness, love, and so forth was taught.

Then, **as for the focal objects for expertise, it is the observation of the five aggregates of form and so forth** that include compounded phenomena, **the eighteen constituents of the eye and so forth** that include all compounded and uncompounded phenomena, and furthermore **the twelve source phenomena, the twelve links of dependent origination, and the virtuous and nonvirtuous causes of karma and effects.** They are called "focal objects for expertise" because they are required for becoming an expert in the future. In terms of the object there is nothing that is not included, and from the perspective of the subject, or observer, it apprehends one of the observed bases just explained that is either an image possessing conceptuality, or an image without conceptuality, and when meditating upon it initially it is one focal object, then gradually one meditates in an elaborate fashion. At this point one is able to include all compounded and uncompounded phenomena within the focal object of special insight. Alternatively, one can make a summary of phenomena like in the following:

> All compounded phenomena are impermanent.
> All contaminated phenomena are suffering.
> All phenomena are empty and selfless.

In brief, all phenomena subsumed within aggregates, constituents, and source phenomena are included within either of the four focal objects.

The focal object for purifying afflictions is, for example, the view having the aspects of peacefulness and coarseness in which that higher relative to the desire realm up to the Sphere of Nothingness[89] is "peaceful," and that below is "coarse." [534] The pervasive focal object is subsumed within all of those. Regarding that, the *Sūtra Requested by Revata* as cited in Asaṅga's *Hearer Grounds* states:

> **Revata, if a monk-meditator, a practitioner of yoga, has behavior uniquely dominated by desire, then he closely focuses the mind on the focal object of unpleasantness; if it is dominated by anger, [he focuses the mind] on love; if dominated by ignorance, then on the dependent-related origination of this condition.** This can refer to both the coarse dependent origination of causes and conditions and the subtle dependent origination of dependent establishment. **If dominated by pride, he focuses his mind on the divisions of the constituents.**

Having been strongly habituated with the afflictions of desire and

so forth in the past, the three poisons are strong even toward minor objects. With respect to the antidotes for those which have been arising for a long time, whichever is the stronger of the afflictions of attachment and so forth must be destroyed, and with respect to those with which we are less habituated over previous lifetimes or the afflictions that we engage in equally within this lifetime, one can choose a focus rather than it be a particular one. It is like, for example, how only a treatment for heat [related illnesses] can be used for a fever that is unrelated to wind illness, but if it is a combination of fever and wind illness, on top of giving fever medicine, minor ingredients from wind medicine must be added.

It is of course possible some people wrongly think that because four focal objects of meditative concentration were taught in sutra that they must meditate on all of them. If you were to do so, it would not assist in mental abidance and furthermore be a cause for distraction.

Therefore, although there are a variety of focal objects in general, a person should take a single suitable object and meditate on it continually for days and months until they achieve calm abiding, even if it takes a year. Otherwise, you will not achieve calm abiding if you switch focal objects, as Āryaśūra states:

Fix your mental thoughts
firmly on a single focal object.
Moving through many focal objects
disturbs the mind with afflictions. [535]

As such, focal objects that get to the crucial point are, as Ācārya Bodhibhadra states,

Meditation on the body as a *khaṭvāṅga* [staff], and focusing on the drops supported by the body, is "calm abiding

focused inwardly" whose foci within the body are taught in connection to tantra. **Observation of enlightened body and speech is "calm abiding focused outwardly."**

Although [Bodhibhadra] of course emphasizes the latter practice, implicit in Ācārya Jñānapāda's refutation of direct-gazing meditation, in which you look at a sacred image placed in front, being unsuitable, is the negation of all "supports of pebbles and sticks" and so on—words of all great meditators as well-known as the wind—and thus in this tradition one must accomplish meditative concentration within one's mental consciousness alone from the outset.

The intention behind statements in some texts that one should first single-pointedly look at focal objects such as the Tathāgata's image and so forth with a sense consciousness is that in order for the aspect of a focal object to clearly appear to mind, one must gain certainty toward the clear aspects of the object through a sense consciousness for the time being. However, the actual meditation is to be done with a mental consciousness, since if one had to stay single-pointedly focused on an object with a sense consciousness there would be no way to maintain that. Therefore, since meditative concentration is achieved in one's mental consciousness, one first clarifies the focal object by looking at an authentically proportionate image of the Tathāgata and thoroughly ascertaining its shapes. Then, one takes the aspects of its meaning generality [mental image] that appear in the mind and meditates on them as one's focal object. This is taught to be "an image with conceptuality."

Furthermore, since all previous masters assert that one achieves calm abiding by way of the eight antidotes that eliminate the five faults, which are taught extensively in the *Great* and *Middle-Length* lamrim treatises, what are the eight mental antidotes to the five faults? It states in Maitreya's *Separation of the Middle from the Extremes*:

Through the serviceability abiding in that,
you will come to attain all goals. [536]

As stated, the way to achieve it is as follows:

This occurs from relying upon the causes
of the eight antidotes that eliminate the five faults.
The five faults are laziness,
forgetting the instructions,
laxity or excitement,
nonapplication and application.

The Five Faults

Laziness is not being joyful toward meditating on the meditative stabilization of calm abiding, and finding pleasure in what is discordant with it. Forgetting, or forgetting the instructions, is to lose the focal object of meditation while the observed object is unclear, or relinquishing the focal object. Although not forgetting the focal object, falling under the sway of laxity or excitement. Even though laxity and excitement were counted together and falling under their sway has been identified, not applying the antidote to abandon them. Instead of emphasizing the focal object when free from laxity and excitement, over-applying the antidote to laxity and excitement.

Having immediately identified these five faults, their antidotes are as stated in *Separation of the Middle from the Extreme*:

The basis and abiding in it,
the cause and the effect,
not forgetting the focal object,
understanding laxity and excitement,

thorough application of abandoning those,
and resting naturally when they have been pacified.

The ability to continuously engage in meditative stabilization with joyous effort is what abides. Which [basis] does it abide in? Since it arises and abides through the aspiration to strive in meditative stabilization, the basis is aspiration—that is, the basis of exertion. That aspiration itself arose from its cause of faith captivated through seeing the qualities of meditative stabilization. Abiding in meditative stabilization under the influence of that faith is to continuously engage in exertion, or joyous effort. Together with the pliancy that is the effect of engagement [in effort], these four destroy laziness that does not want to engage in meditative stabilization.

The antidote to forgetting is stated in [Asaṅga's] *Compendium*:

What is mindfulness? Regarding an object with which you
are familiar, your mind is not forgetful and functions without distraction.

Nonforgetfulness is to not discard whatever focal object you have habituated yourself repeatedly with before and recollect it continuously. [537] The mindfulness possessing three attributes, which does not divert from that focal object to others, destroys forgetfulness.

The antidote to laxity and excitement are as stated in [Bhāvaviveka's] *Heart of the Middle Way*:

Restrain the straying elephant of your mind,
with the ropes of mindfulness,
to the secure pillar of the focal object,
and gradually bring it under control with the iron hook of
wisdom.

If the mind's abidance on the focal object through mindfulness goes under the sway of laxity and excitement, then just like an untamed elephant is tamed with a metal hook, so too introspection acts as the watchman for laxity and excitement and does not let them take control. As it states in *Way of the Bodhisattva*:

> That which constantly checks
> the situation of body and mind—
> that alone, in short,
> is the definition of guarding introspection.

This is the unique cause for the arising of introspection, while cultivating mindfulness is the common cause for the arising of introspection. Through holding the mind and sustaining the continuity of the focal object, laxity and excitement are dispelled. Regarding the elimination of such laxity and excitement, even though the words "laxity and excitement" are as renowned as the wind from the mouths of all great meditators nowadays, most of those people have not identified them beyond the mere names. Among those who have identified them, they do not distinguish laxity and lethargy and take them to be the same. Thus, they identify every laxity as actual meditative concentration and many waste their lives away in the mountains.

It states in Asaṅga's *Compendium*:

> What is excitement? A wholly unpeaceful mind that belongs
> to the category of desire attached to the characteristics of
> pleasant things, and functions to interrupt calm abiding.

Since excitement is explained as a mind not at peace due to attachment to pleasing objects, even though discursive thoughts distracted with one's enemy due to anger are not excitement, since discursive thoughts that interrupt calm abiding and scatter the mind to other things are all obstacles to calm abiding, they must be stopped. [538]

Excitement not only scatters the mind, but since it diverts the meditator toward the object to which they are attached, and it is a significant interruption, it was thus specifically referred to as a fault of meditative concentration. It is not that it is the only one, and it is taught that all scattering through anger and distraction through ethically neutral states of mind must all be stopped.

Likewise, Kamalaśīla's *Second Stages of Meditation* states:

> When the mind does not see the focal object with clarity, like a blind person, or someone entering the dark, or someone with closed eyes, understand that the mind has become lax.

Laxity is identified as a consciousness in which the mere factor of limpidity of mind toward the focal object is present, yet has become unclear and the mode of apprehension has declined due to lacking an acute factor of intensity of the manner of apprehension of the focal object.

Thus, the mind being enveloped in darkness is lethargy, and although laxity is not that, it arises from it. As such, laxity is the mind lacking focus and sharpness, being totally slack and sunken, lacking the ability to hold the focal object along with the factor of fixation, with a touch of boredom.

Lethargy is a factor of ignorance. It is a consciousness having the aspect of bodily and mental heaviness and being unserviceable. It is a nonvirtue or an ethically neutral obscuration, and thus lethargy cannot be virtuous, but laxity can also be virtuous. It is of the type that, within a continuity of mental peace, gradually loses the factor of fixation of the mind on a virtuous focal object and turns into laxity.

When such laxity and excitement occur, the antidotes that abandon them that are the opposite of nonapplication are as stated in Asaṅga's *Compendium*:

> What is intention? It is the mental action of thorough application, functioning to engage the mind in virtue, nonvirtue, and the ethically neutral.

Intention is the mental factor among the fifty-one types of mental factors[90] that induces the mind into either virtue, nonvirtue, or the ethically neutral, and thus if introspection identifies laxity and excitement in this context, it is as [Bhāvaviveka's] *Heart of the Middle Way* states:

> In the case of despondency, make the mind light
> through meditation on vast focal objects. [539]

As this is the fault of withdrawing the mind too much, avert this through slightly expanding the focal object. If it is not dispelled through that, either, and laxity becomes stronger, avert it through temporarily leaving the focal object and contemplating the six— the Three Jewels, giving, ethical discipline, and recollection of the deity—and the advantages of having attained freedoms and opportunities; move around; put your mind on the things you see; wash your face; and sit in a cool place.

However much you expand the focal object is how much a soft and powerless mind is dispelled. Thus, if you put concerted effort into developing strength and contemplating those, it helps to clear away despondency, or lethargy. As such, in order to increasingly uplift the mind, try to stop laxity through a strong factor of firmness. If that does not stop it either, then temporarily set aside the previous focal object and seek out the other methods for uplifting your mind.

Thus, without purposely recollecting the qualities of the Tathāgata's body, speech, and mind as explained previously in the section on refuge, if you take the upright golden body adorned with the noble marks as your focal support and meditate on it, and your frame of mind deteriorates, and you become despondent and are on the verge of falling asleep, for example, then generally, even if the image of the Tathāgata is clear, since there is no factor of firmness from the side of the mind, if you strongly engage in methods to dispel the fault of being too mentally downcast, your mental spirit will lift. And, if you cannot dispel laxity through that either, cultivate joy in the mind by particularly focusing on the qualities of the Tathāgata's body, speech, and mind. Furthermore, if you think of the many ways to develop joy and a relaxed mind, it helps to lift your spirits. If that, too, does not help to dispel laxity, pause your session for the time being and try to refresh yourself by going outside into fresh air, or into the mountains, and so forth, where you have a greater view. Doing so helps to dispel mental despondence from withdrawing the mind inward too much. [540] Regarding that, initially one part of your mind—introspection— must keep watch and be able to identify whether laxity or excitement is interfering with mindfulness's holding [the object].

What, then, is the antidote to excitement? **Bhāvaviveka's *Heart of the Middle Way* states:**

> Excitement must be pacified
> by turning the mind to impermanence and so forth.

Excitement about your desired objects is thwarted through meditation on strong disillusionment such as impermanence and suffering. Excitement is when the mind does not remain on a single focal object as intended due to the fault of being too firm [in its grip] or too elated, and is carried off by any discursive thought. Thus you must try to rein the mind back in. However much effort you put into withdrawing the mind inward, that is how much your mental elevation diminishes, and thus if you contemplate the bad side of things, like the uncertainty of the time of death, how you have wasted your life until now, and that if you continue in this way you risk your human body with freedoms and opportunities becoming meaningless, the suffering of samsara, how you are under the influence of ignorance, and so forth, it helps your mind to deflate and be withdrawn inward, and for your mental elevation to lessen.

Sometimes if you meditate facing a wall your mind is a little less scattered, and if you wear glasses in general it seems to be less distracting if you take them off sometimes. Or, even if your discursiveness and excitement have lessened, if you become mentally unclear, I wonder if putting on your glasses leads to strong mental scattering, which can be of benefit to generate the potential of the factor of clarity.

These workings of laxity and excitement are like, for example, in an educational setting where a teacher is too strict and you become scared and so forth and lose enthusiasm, leading you to be unable to study or to totally mentally withdraw and remain in a dark state where even if you act as if you are trying hard in your studies, your mind is blank. Such states arise from the mind becoming far too despondent and is an approximation of laxity. [541]

If love and encouragement are received from the teacher, then one gains some confidence and those shortcomings clear up. On the other hand, if the teacher is too kind in nurturing the student, when told to study they do not listen, and they remain distracted with games and so forth. These are cases of the mind being lost to excitement and being too distracted with different objects, and thus it is similar in the sense that you must try to overcome it by withdrawing the mind inward through regulating that behavior.

It is a crucial point to meditate on the antidotes to the various distracting discursive thoughts such as anger and so forth that are illustrated by that. In brief, all common causes such as not guarding the doors to the senses, inappropriate amounts of food, sleeping in

the first and last parts of the night, engaging too much with objects of sleep, lethargy, and desire, must all be abandoned.

Then, since applying the antidotes to laxity and excitement when they do not occur is a fault, **regarding the elimination of over-application of the antidotes to laxity and excitement it states in Kamalaśīla's two later** *Stages of Meditation*:

> If you exert yourself when your mind has entered equi-poise, then your mind will become distracted.

The end of the eighth mental abiding is the time when the mind, unaffected by laxity or excitement, is in equilibrium. Therefore, if at that time you exert yourself too much in applying caution regarding laxity and excitement such as uplifting the mind or hooking it inward, since that is a fault of meditative concentration, then neutral application that knows to let go is the antidote to over-implementation of the antidote to laxity and excitement.

There are three types of neutrality, or equanimity: (1) neutral application, (2) neutral feelings, and (3) the neutrality of a mind in equilibrium without attachment or hatred. Thus, from the boundary of the eighth mental abiding, when meditative concentration is without the faults of laxity and excitement, if you exert yourself in application of the antidotes to laxity and excitement, it becomes a condition to impede the mind remaining in a relaxed state. Therefore, you must implement neutral application. [542]

Having merely heard the word "relax" of course some say, "Good relaxation is the best meditation." Yet this a wrong identification of the factor of limpidity of a mind overcome by laxity as the real medi-tation. Here, it is knowing to relax exertion at the right time, and not a relinquishing of the firmness of your manner of apprehension. As for the timing, most great meditators relax [exertion] as soon as they develop a little experience. In our tradition "the destruction of laxity

and excitement" is at the time of the ninth mental abiding, and thus the time for it is different.

There are some differences regarding this. Since mahāmudrā and dzogchen meditation styles are meditations in connection with the yogas of Highest Tantra, the differences in meditation styles that occur must be distinguished as the differences of those. Aside from that, if you let go from the start there is a risk of amassing laxity. Some Chinese acquaintances of mine have told me how some meditators in China have meditation practices, but lack strong feelings of love and compassion, and cannot readily experience feelings in their mind and remain in equanimity.

To take a guess, those persons only wish to engage in placement meditation for extensive periods, and this seems to be the result of a lack of strong habituation from putting effort into method practices of love, compassion, and so forth.

Through this style of meditation, one accumulates laxity and does not comprehend the subtle intensity of the aforementioned factors of the mind's limpidity and clarity. If you do not realize that merely not being distracted by other objects, and remaining vividly on the focal object, does not mean that the meditative concentration is without faults, then you will amass even greater subtle laxity, and it is in dependence on that I believe it is taught that the meditator ends up lacking feelings, for example, or becomes stupid.

Thus, having integrated well into your experience the five faults and the way to practice through the eight applications that are the antidotes to abandon them, you are to practice. [543] Do not think that it is enough to learn the aforementioned words of the explanation as your practice. Not knowing how to integrate the practice on a mental level through listening to the meaning leads to many cases of outwardly directed verbiage resulting in a disconnect between Dharma and the person. Moreover, you may think that since "one essential piece of advice is enough for a fool," the aforementioned

explanations from great treatises are nothing but the wasted fruits of exhausting hardship. If you go to a faraway place, you must be familiar with the entire situation of the paths—either independently or in dependence on others. Setting off bewildered does not achieve the goal. So too, without understanding the crucial points of eliminating the faults of meditation and enhancement, all aspirations to be a lord of siddhas within your determination—back straight and eyes closed—appear to fall in line with the meaning of this passage in *Ascertaining the Three Vows*

> It was taught a fool's meditation on mahāmudrā
> Is likely a cause for an animal [rebirth].

These days this disposition pervades and proliferates in oneself and others like the number of insects in the summer. The omniscient [Butön] said:

> If I speak nonvirtuously I transgress the Dharma.
> If I speak in accordance with the Dharma, Tibetans rise up as
>   my enemies.

So many discussions just to make himself the white crow [outcast]. Having ascertained the points explained previously, the way to accomplish them with respect to a single focal object is as stated in Atiśa's *Lamp for the Path*:

> With respect to any single focal object,
> place the mind in virtue.

The object you focus on at present is generally suitable to be an image [of a buddha], for example, and among those it states in the *King of Concentrations Sūtra*:

The bodhisattva whose mind engages the focal object
of the most beautiful lord of the world
with golden-colored body,
is said to be in equipoise.

As a by-product of observing the Tathāgata's image, one vastly accumulates the merit of recollecting the Buddha. [544] It is similar to the cornerstone of a building filling the role of two walls, or someone settling a business deal, for instance, that automatically relieves them of another concern. Therefore, having first frequently looked at and contemplated paintings, reliefs, and so on of the enlightened body, individually contemplate the shapes of crown protrusion, the face, eyes, arms, legs, and clothes, and even the colors—down to the borders of the whites and blacks of the eyes—without mixing them. Do not pursue the various inverses of those, such as an aspect of standing instead of being seated, or an appearance of white when it is actually blue. Even though the appearance of the actual Buddha and features down to the blacks and whites of the eyes do not appear unmixed from the start, through initially meditating by sustaining a continuity of the mere coarse appearance of the enlightened body's aspects and shapes from seeing the image, in the end it occurs as was explained. However, exhausting yourself with the hopes that it will turn out exactly as it should through merely having practiced becomes an obstacle to meditation. Thus, having set boundaries, even though calm abiding can be achieved through focal objects such as stones and sticks, and the like, in order to accomplish calm abiding and to accumulate merit and purify obscurations in the manner of two needs fulfilled with one deed, since this is a presentation of the way to achieve calm abiding purely from a sutra perspective without being mixed with tantra, it is good if you observe and meditate on an image of the Tathāgata as explained prior.

If you cut through laxity, the enlightened body is vivid and clear, glistening so bright, so to cut through scattered excitement, if you think of the image as weighing down heavily, it is taught that through your imagination influencing the way you direct your thoughts toward the focal object it helps in the elimination of laxity and excitement.

As for us, we have been born in a place where the doctrine of secret mantra has greatly proliferated, and from a young age—without concern for whether the way we are engaging in the path of mantra is correct—we recite secret mantra rituals and meditate on the enlightened body of the meditational deity. Thus if we use as our focal object a clear visualization of our body as the deity's body and meditate on calm abiding, it is excellent because it accords with the way to achieve meditative concentration on the basis of deity yoga. [545]

Although in general it is taught from the perspective of specific intended disciples who have already attained concentration (bsam gtan, dhyāna), in highest mantra specific bodily points are taken as the focus even more so, and since there is a way to accomplish meditative concentration together with the practice of deity yoga, it is good even if such things are taken as focal objects.

What, then, is the way to meditate through visualizing that focal support? Generally, just as it is taught to use an eight-point sitting posture and sit comfortably while practicing in your session, that becomes even more crucial while practicing calm abiding: **(1) on a soft and comfortable seat sit cross-legged or with legs half-crossed, (2) your eyes, slightly open, fall at the tip of the nose, (3) your body is straight, (4) your hands are placed evenly, (5) with the head straight, set it so that nose tip and navel are aligned, (6) your teeth and lips rest naturally, (7) the tip of your tongue touches your palate, (8) your breath moves gently. The activities of counting twenty-one in and out breaths and so forth through possessing this eight-point body posture are taught as methods to stop external distraction.** In more detail, do as explained in the section of the six preparatory practices.

Then, having understood that if you have calm abiding **through**

the strong aspiration induced by faith in the qualities of meditative stabilization any virtuous activity you do becomes powerful and
you see its qualities. **Together with joyous effort that is enthusiastic
toward virtuous activity, visualize the body of the Buddha, which
you have familiarized yourself with prior**—an image of a painting or
relief, around the size of four or five finger widths—**in the aspect of
the actual Buddha in the space in front, in line with your eyebrows,
at a size that suits your mind.** If you do full-length prostrations to that,
visualize it about an arm span away from your fingertips.

Since there is no definitive timespan for calm abiding practice sessions, it is important for beginners to have many short—but good
quality—sessions. [546] As you gradually build familiarity it is good
to extend sessions when they are of good quality.

**With a mind recollecting the focal object without forgetting, by
way of possessing both the intensity of the factor of clarity of abiding uninterruptedly on the focal object, and a firm factor of abiding**
that does not lose the clear focal object and remains serenely **without
scattering to another, hold tightly and meditate just to the point that
tension in the upper body and so forth do not arise.** If holding the
body posture very tightly does not lead to the faults of squeezing or
stretching of the upper body, nor to scattering or excitement, then it is
good to hold it a bit more tightly.

**When you think you have remained on that a bit, without forget-
ting the focal object through mindfulness, check with the guard of
introspection. When you see that the finely tuned factor of clarity
of the object and factor of intensity of the mode of apprehension
have deteriorated, acknowledge that subtle laxity has occurred, and
stop it. If the vivid intensity of the clarity is suddenly lost and there
only remains a mere limpidity, identify it as coarse laxity. When the
aspects of pleasant objects of desire are about to appear, realize that
the aspects of subtle excitement and attachment that have suddenly
arisen are coarse excitement and cut laxity and excitement by way**

of their antidotes—that is, acting unmistakenly in accordance with whether your mood is high or low, and so forth. **Although you must try to stay on the principal focal object with total clear vividness during a one-hour session, if you hold too tightly, strong excitement arises, and if you relax too much strong laxity arises. Therefore, it is very difficult to find the right balance between holding tight and letting go. As such, Master Candragomin states:**

> If I exert myself, excitement ensues.
> If I give that up, I become despondent.
> If it is hard to find the right balance in this,
> what shall I do with my disturbed mind?

A beginner might not be able to perfectly integrate the crucial points exactly to the word of a practice possessed of the eight applications that abandon the five faults. How should they gain practical experience of the "mental placement" from among the nine mental abidings—even though [the mind] does not abide for long on the focal object—and meditate by holding firmly? [547]

[As Tsongkhapa states in his *Foundation of All Good Qualities*:]

> Please bless me to quickly give rise in my continuum
> the path of unified calm abiding and special insight—
> the pacifier of distraction to wrong objects,
> and the proper engager in correct reality.

[Tsongkhapa] labeled a "wrong object" a focal object that is not the currently appropriate focal object, since it is situationally wrong or outside of it. One must thus dispel mental scattering to other focal objects. "Correct reality," in this context refers to the emptiness that is the mode of existence of suchness. Through observing it properly, free from the faults of laxity and excitement, (1) the calm abiding qualified by the bliss of physical and mental pliancy, and (2) with that as its basis, the special insight that is the mind that totally sees suchness and is qualified by the bliss of pliancy induced by the power of repeatedly analyzing the meaning of suchness with individually discriminating wisdom, are achieved sequentially. Then the union of calm abiding and special insight is achieved.

For that sake, initially **during the time of the first mental abiding the factor of abidance of the mind does not remain only on the focal object, and discursive thoughts flow uninterruptedly like a steep mountain stream. Thus, one might wonder whether doing this practice has caused conceptualization to increase. However, this was at a time when one had previously lacked the critical points of practice. For example, even though a traveler may continuously move along a major road, due to having no aspiration to intentionally look, they do not notice other people, but if they intentionally look then they notice many persons, their loads, and so forth. Although the wheels of the undercurrents of conceptual thoughts were turning previously, they went unnoticed. In this context one experiences recognition of the discursive thoughts due to the practice of the mind, and therefore is the context of the first mental abiding called mental placement.**

The protector Maitreya, in his *Ornament for the Mahāyāna Sūtras*, explains how to achieve the nine mental abidings by means of the four attentions and the six forces.

First, you merely direct your mind to the focal object through following instructions to which you have only listened, which is the first force of listening. [548] Then, upon having meditated gradually, you come to have an experience of a relaxation of discursive thoughts wherein they sometimes subside, and sometimes come coursing through, just like a stream in a narrow ravine. At that point, the second mental abiding, called *continuous placement*, which is achieved through the second force of *reflection*, is able to maintain a little continuity on the focal object. Laxity and excitement are strong within these two mental abidings, and only a little meditative concentration is possible; thus this is the occasion of the first of the four attentions called *tight focus*.

Then, upon some slight habituation, you gain an experience of your discursive thoughts becoming weary. You acknowledge that the mind abides when there are no opposing conditions, and does not when met with them, like a reservoir fed by water from three upper parts of a valley. At that point, the third mental abiding called *patched placement* is accomplished through the third force of *mindfulness*, which quickly realizes the mind being distracted and patches it to the focal object again. For example, just as a patch must be added [to torn clothing], after the mind has been able to abide on the focal object for a while it scatters outward and is then withdrawn again and made to abide on the focal object, and, like clothing, it is patched again.

The fourth mental abiding, called *close placement*, withdraws [one's expansive attention] and refines it. The fifth mental abiding, established from the fourth force of *introspection*, called *taming*, is joyful about the qualities of meditative concentration. The sixth mental abiding, called *pacifying*, understands the drawbacks of distraction and stops it. Of the two mental abidings achieved through the fifth force of *joyous effort*—the seventh and eighth— the seventh, called *thoroughly pacifying*, pacifies the affliction of an attached mind through abandoning it with effort. The five mental abidings ranging from the third to the seventh are interfered with by laxity and excitement; thus it is the time of the second of the four attentions—*intermittent focus*. [549]

Then, having meditated sequentially, like an ocean with waves, through slightly applying the antidote of holding mindfulness no matter what discursive thought arises, they go back to their natural place and subside. Thus, you have an experience of an application of remedying discursive thoughts. At that time, you accomplish the eighth mental abiding called *single pointedness* through the fifth force, a *meditative concentration with continuity*. Laxity and excitement do not interfere with the eighth mental abiding, and it is the time of the third of the four attentions called *uninterrupted focus*

Then, having sequentially meditated, no matter what object condition arises, meditative concentration dawns naturally without relying on the effort of the antidote of holding mindfulness, like an ocean without waves. Thus, you gain the equipoise of an experience of not manifestly remedying discursive thoughts. At that time the ninth mental abiding called *balanced placement*, achieved from the sixth force, *total familiarity*, engages the focal object effortlessly. This is therefore the time of the fourth of the four attentions called *spontaneous focus*.

Not understanding that it was in this context that the previous masters considered the effort of stopping laxity and excitement as a fault and considered it the best relaxation, the fault arose of understanding it to mean the relaxing of the factor of intensity of the manner of apprehension. Therefore, one must understand well these crucial points; meditation does not arise just from having a meditation belt, meditation hat, and cord net bag.

Within the explanation of the four attentions in the nine mental abidings, the first two [mental abidings] are labeled *tight focus* and the next five are labeled *interrupted focus*. One might think this is incorrect, because the first two mental abidings must also have interrupted focus, and the next five must also have tight focus. There is no fault in our position, however, because even though the middle five [mental abidings] contain both tight and interrupted manners of focus, the first two [mental abidings] are not labeled "interrupted" since (1) not more than a little abidance arises intermittently between the extremely prevalent laxity and excitement, and (2) during the middle five [mental abidings] the more prevalent meditation on meditative concentration is frequently interrupted by laxity and excitement intermittently. [550]

It is like, for example, if you serve the first of three people meat, the second person meat and cheese, and the third person meat and cheese with melted butter on top, and then label the first person "the one who received meat," and while the second person has meat, instead of labeling them "the one who received meat" you label them "the one who received both things" and even though the third person has both things, it would not be correct to label them "the one who received both things" because they have three things.

Thus you may wonder if the ninth mental abiding is calm abiding, since it is free from subtle laxity and excitement and can be sustained without effort for a long time. Merely this, however, is not posited as calm abiding, as it states in Maitreya's *Ornament for the Mahāyāna Sūtras*:

> Nonapplication comes from familiarity.
> Next, upon great pliancy
> of body and mind being achieved,
> you are said to have attention.

From this context onward it is a similitude of calm abiding explained as *attention* since the achievement of an exceptional joyful bliss of physical and mental pliancy is required to achieve fully qualified calm abiding.

This being the case, you may suspect that there is no pliancy when the meditative concentration of the ninth mental abiding first arises. Even though the subtle pliancy that has arisen is hard to realize because it is minor, the reason that the ninth mental abiding is explained as an attention that is a similitude of calm abiding on these occasions is, for example, like how the filling up of the parts of the full moon of the fifteenth day [of the Tibetan calendar] is a gradual accumulation from the second day onward, yet although the slight part of the moon on the second day is the moon, it is not the moon of the fifteenth day. Likewise, from the subtle factor of pliancy increasing, eventually the negative tendencies belonging to the class of afflictions that were not suitable to employ in virtue as one desired are pacified and mental pliancy arises. Through the power of that, serviceable winds course within the body causing freedom from the negative tendencies of the body, and a pliancy of a body light like cotton arises. In dependence on that a great experience of bliss arises in the body. Through its power the bliss of mental pliancy that is an experience of mental pleasure arises. Furthermore, as soon as physical pliancy has arisen and when expansive mental joy occurs, calm abiding is still not attained by a small margin. Upon that expansive joy diminishing, simultaneous with the attainment of an unwavering pliancy that is a similitude of a meditative concentration remaining [vividly] unstirred on the focal object, calm abiding is achieved. [551]

Therefore, many who believe themselves to be great meditators do not appear to have gotten anywhere according to these great treatises. However, the diminishment of that expansive joy does not cause pliancy to deplete. For example, it is taught to be analogous to how even though the fluttering joy from hearing a nice story subsides after some time, that does not mean it was not a nice story.

Having actualized the calm abiding possessing the exceptional bliss of mental and physical pliancy, the preparation for the first concentration is attained; yet of course these alone cannot suppress manifest afflictions. Well, you might wonder if this does not contradict the earlier explanation that the higher training of meditative concentration and calm abiding can suppress manifest afflictions. That, however, was stated with the intention that the special insight with the aspect of peacefulness and coarseness, and so forth, are also included within calm abiding. Therefore, one still needs to train in the path.

What, then, is the way to train in the path having the aspect of peacefulness and coarseness? **Regarding the way to train, by meditating on special insight having the aspect of peacefulness and coarseness that is a mundane path, (1) the majority of afflictions that are to be abandoned through meditation related to those who dwell in the desire realm subside, (2) an actual first concentration possessing joyful bliss is achieved, and (3) actual clairvoyance and miraculous powers also arise.**

Having meditated sequentially, all manifest afflictions included up to those of the Sphere of Nothingness are abandoned and one achieves the mind of the Peak of Existence. Moreover, having meditated on special insight that analyzes the meaning of the two selflessnesses on the basis of having achieved the preparations for the first concentration, without striving for an actual first concentration and those above that while on a supramundane path, but rather on the basis of having manifested a mere preparation for the first concentration **if one achieves a śrāvaka's path of seeing, for instance, even though one has not directly meditated on an actual first concentration having the aspect of peacefulness and coarseness and those above that, one still implicitly achieves their qualities, and through an uninterrupted path of the path of meditation of any of the three vehicles acting as an antidote to the afflictions they are abandoned from the root.** [552]

Concluding Verses

One's flaws of laziness and so forth are known.
The benefits of the eight applications of faith and so forth
    are seen.

How marvelous is the meditative concentration of calm
    abiding with the bliss of pliancy,
clear and nonconceptual, induced by the nine mental
    abidings!

Having practiced little meditation in the past
the afflictions of the three poisons were undiminished,
    dormant,
and the one pretending to be a blissful, good Dharma
    practitioner
has their pathetic faults revealed by the slightest harm from
    things going wrong.

Though their untamed minds do not remain at all
in the [nine] mental abidings that are common to
    non-Buddhists,
they believe themselves to be enlightened beyond the
    extremes of peace and existence!
They must take a look at themselves.

If it is said in the excellent teachings and the commentaries on
    their intention
that only through difficult points like these does one achieve
    clairvoyance and miraculous powers and so forth,
for the happy-go-lucky, full-bellied sunbathers to have signs
    of achievement
would be like a river spurting forth from a rockface.

Woe! In the past the deceptive distractions
led me to waste my life meaninglessly.
Now I am overjoyed at practicing this way
in a supreme place devoid of commotion.

Having understood the crucial point of the amount of ground
   I can cover,
with bliss pervading my body and mind,
allowing me to set them in the direction of virtue no matter
   the action,
buddhahood, so renowned, is also not far, but close.

The Perfection of Wisdom:
Training in Special Insight

THE GLORIOUS CANDRAKĪRTI states:

> First one clings to self, thinking, "I,"
> and then generates attachment to things, thinking, "Mine."

However strong one's grasping to self, that is how strong one's grasping at mine will be, and therefore in dependence upon the attachment of self-grasping toward all things that are mine growing stronger, all Buddhist tenet systems are in agreement in accepting that grasping at a self forms the root of attachment and hatred.

After achieving calm abiding, no matter what path having the aspect of peacefulness and coarseness you meditate on, leave aside self-grasping being abandoned by it; it will not even be able to lessen its strength. [553] Even if manifest afflictions are temporarily suppressed, since their seeds have not been abandoned, they will arise again when the conditions are met.

Having seen that all phenomena—exemplified by (1) self and the phenomena of the aggregates and so forth that it is designated onto, or (2) the self that experiences, and the phenomena of the aggregates and so forth that are objects of experience, or (3) the self who appropriates, and the phenomena of the aggregates and so forth that are appropriated—do not exist from their own side as they appear to a mistaken awareness. If individually discriminating awareness repeatedly familiarizes and habituates to that, then whatever appears will be understood to be like an illusion, and the grasping to self will be eased.

Since the grasping to self is not fundamental to the nature of mind, it is possible to become free of it. There is no other cause for achieving nirvana other than meditation on selflessness. All other methods, such as love, compassion, and so forth, cannot oppose the grasping at self, thus the state of peaceful nirvana cannot be achieved by them.

Thus, a brief presentation will be given of the differences in the level of subtlety of the assertions of Buddhist tenet systems on the mode of the nonexistence of self, aside from which there is no other door to peace.

The protector Nāgārjuna, in the twenty-fourth chapter of his *Fundamental Wisdom of the Middle Way* refutes the claim by the Proponents of Existence that Madhyamaka is nihilistic, stating that their logic is flawed because they do not understand the necessity of emptiness, its nature, and its meaning. The purpose of reaching certainty regarding emptiness and of meditating on it is to completely uproot wrong views, or rather, wrong awarenesses. However, achieving certainty about the selflessness that is the emptiness of being a self-sufficient, substantial entity, and then meditating on merely that might diminish the coarse view of the perishing aggregates apprehending "I," but it is unable to overcome the solid grasping that apprehends the aggregates and so forth as "mine."

For that reason, the higher tenet systems composed presentations on the selflessness of phenomena. [554] Those who assert a selflessness of phenomena that is an emptiness of duality of apprehended object and apprehending subject, prove that form, sound, and so forth are empty of existing externally. This is because they do not exist as they appear to exist—that is, as established by way of their own characteristics that serve as the referent for the conceptual consciousness that apprehends them.

Thus, through meditating on the path of the emptiness of duality of apprehended and apprehender, one sees that the phenomena of "mine" do not exist from their own side. From this the apprehension, or grasping, at solidity becomes weaker. However, since one still apprehends consciousness as truly existing, one is unable to stop the arising of attachment and hatred based on the feelings of happiness and suffering of inner consciousness. For that reason, the Madhyamaka proponents, without making a distinction between inner and outer, said that all apprehended and apprehenders are empty of true existence.

Within the proponents of the Madhyamaka there are Prāsaṅgika, or Consequentialists, and Svātantrika, or Autonomists. For ease of understanding, you can divide them into those of the Madhyamaka who propound inherent existence, and those of the Madhyamaka who do not propound inherent existence.

Those of the Madhyamaka who propound inherent existence assert that all phenomena—the apprehended and apprehenders—are not established from the side of the object's own unique mode of subsistence without being posited through appearing to a faultless awareness. Still there exists a self-sustaining entity of the object as it appears to a faultless awareness even from the side of the basis of designation. [For them], all reference points of the apprehension of solidity are not stopped and remain.

The Consequentialists, or proponents of the Madhyamaka who do not propound inherent existence, assert that whatever basis of designation, that is, apprehended and apprehender phenomenon, is merely posited through name and term, and is not established at all from the side of the object. Therefore, all reference points of the apprehension of solidity are destroyed, and all objects of grasping of apprehensions of "I" and "mine" are totally eliminated.

Thus, upon thorough analysis, those who assert mere selflessness of persons, those who assert the selflessness of phenomena of nonduality, and those who accept self-characteristics conventionally but not true existence ultimately, are all unable to refute the entirety of the object grasped at by the awareness apprehending a self, which is the root of attachment and hatred. [555] Due to the remainder of the object of negation of the awareness apprehending "I" and "mine" being left over, the nature of the path that achieves liberation is incomplete. Based on that, the protector Nāgārjuna stated:

> Why would the great poisons of the afflictions not arise
> in those whose minds have positions?

As such, if a reference point remains, then attachment and hatred observing that arises, and thus the reference points must be shattered from the root. However, if you accept [them] as [arbitrarily] posited by awareness, or [arbitrarily] created by conception, then you go to the extreme of annihilation. The positing of "merely name, existing only by imputation," and the "infallibility of conventional dependent origination" as noncontradictory is a difficult point of the Madhyamaka view.

If analyzed in this way, the assertions on the view within the lower tenet systems are undermined by logic, and the emptiness of phenomena being inherently established is not undermined by logic, and thus it is the correct path.

In the mother [perfection of wisdom] sutras, the Bhagavān states that all phenomena from form up to space are not established by way of their own nature, not established by way of their own characteristics, and not established inherently, a statement which the protector Nāgārjuna declared is the literal, definitive meaning. One group of followers of his arose comprising Āryadeva, Buddhapālita, Śāntideva, Candrakīrti, and so forth. There was also a group of followers comprising Bhāvaviveka, Jñānagarbha, the great abbot Śāntarakṣita, and Kamalaśīla. The former do not accept self-characteristics conventionally, while the latter do accept self-characteristics conventionally.

Within the group that accept self-characteristics conventionally, two groups arose: (1) those who assert external objects, such as Ācārya Bhāvaviveka, his spiritual sons, and so forth, and (2) those who do not assert external objects such as the great abbot Śāntarakṣita, his spiritual sons, and so forth. Here, the glorious Candrakīrti's position—the system that propounds a lack of inherent existence—is considered supreme, and the view of special insight that will be explained is done so on that basis. [556]

The Tibetan Nyingmapas of the Early Translation period, the glorious Sakyapas, the incomparable Kagyüpas, and the Riwo Gelukpas are all followers of Candrakīrti and proponents of a lack of inherent existence. The manner of explanation of some who accept the great Madhyamaka of other-emptiness is slightly different: they state that the Madhyamaka view as elucidated by Buddhapālita, Candrakīrti, and so forth, is not the exact intent of the protector Nāgārjuna. Moreover, they establish that the protector Nāgārjuna and Asaṅga are of the same intent. They state that since Maitreya's *Sublime Continuum* and the protector Nāgārjuna's *Praise of the Dharmadhātu* are incredibly similar, they interpret the final view from those and declared it as "the great Madhyamaka of other-emptiness."

Regarding the explanations of self-emptiness and other-emptiness: One explanation of self-emptiness is that by the statement "form is empty" [from the *Heart Sūtra*,] form itself is just a mere appearance, and form is empty of its own nature from the side of the object, and thus is "self-empty." Another explanation [of self-emptiness] is that, in the place of one self-empty thing, a pot being empty of "pot" is conventional self-emptiness, and a pot being empty of true existence is ultimate other-emptiness. This is logically unacceptable, because if a pot were empty of "pot," a pot could not be posited. Jé Rinpoché [Tsongkhapa] accepts the first understanding of self-emptiness and does not accept the second. Regarding other-emptiness, he asserts that if you posit a self-characterized form and say it not being established ultimately is [what other-emptiness] applies to, form thus becomes empty of emptiness, and therefore that becomes "other-emptiness."

Although there exist dissimilarities in such explanations and their usage of terminology, it is important to distinguish the teachings of previous Tibetan masters and Indian scholars according to those given to a general audience and those given to a private audience, as explained previously in the *general explanation*. [557]

The Perfection of Wisdom

The way to **train in the perfection of wisdom**, which is special insight, has five parts:

(a') What wisdom is
(b') How to begin cultivating wisdom
(c') The divisions of wisdom
(d') How to practice
(e') A summary

The divisions of wisdom has three parts:

(1') The wisdom realizing the ultimate
(2') The wisdom realizing the conventional
(3') The wisdom realizing the accomplishment of the aims of sentient beings

Wisdom comprises (1) **the wisdom realizing the ultimate—that which sees the meaning of suchness, (2) the wisdom realizing conventionality—that which is wise in the five sciences, and (3) the wisdom understanding how to achieve the aims of sentient beings in this life and the next—freedom from misdeeds, and so forth.**

Upon bringing to completion the habituation of the mind with these three, the perfection of wisdom is totally complete.

As it states in Nāgārjuna's *One Hundred Verses on Wisdom*:

> The root of all qualities, both seen and unseen,
> is wisdom.
> As such, to achieve both,
> thoroughly cultivate wisdom.

The purity of the first five perfections of generosity and so forth— being free from pride and despondency, wherein even offering one's own flesh is like offering a medicinal plant, and, moreover, a bodhisattva wheel-turning monarch not falling under the sway of sensory pleasures, too, depends on wisdom. In brief, since all mundane and supramundane qualities come about in dependence on wisdom, one must cultivate it.

What is important and of concern for us at present is human "intelligent wisdom." We must understand it is advantageous for our goals. For example, even in the case of the stages of the path of the three beings, when it seems that some of their direct ways of thinking are slightly different, or sometimes contradictory, if you correctly understand the purposes and reasons behind that, based on the power of wisdom, you are able to turn it into something lacking contradiction. [558]

Therefore, the need for analysis with wisdom is emphasized in Buddhism, and thus the problems and adversities in our lives can also be eliminated through the intelligence of wisdom. In accordance with the potential and advantages seen from first-hand experience, in short, the protector Nāgārjuna thus stated, "The root of all qualities—seen and unseen—is wisdom." As such, for the sake of easily achieving both seen and unseen qualities one must further enhance wisdom. **Among the many types of such wisdom to be sought out, it is important to meditate on special insight that pacifies coarse and subtle afflictions.**

The methods to completely pacify afflictions together with their imprints are both the mundane and supramundane special insights— illustrated by the special insight realizing modes [of reality]—and must both be meditated on. **Regarding that, you might wonder whether the mundane special insight of peacefulness and coarseness that suppresses manifest afflictions is to be sought out.** It is the special insight realizing selflessness that purifies afflictions together with their imprints that must principally be achieved, **as it states in** *Praise in Honor of One Worthy of Honor*:

> **Those opposed to your teaching**
> **are blinded by delusion.**
> **Even after reaching the peak of existence**
> **suffering arises again, and existence is created.**

Although non-Buddhists and so forth have abandoned the manifest afflictions up to the level of Nothingness and achieved a mind of the Peak of Existence, they are not free from cyclic existence. Therefore, it states in the *King of Samādhi Sūtra*:

> **Although meditating on meditative concentration,**
> **it does not destroy the notion of self.**
> **Through that the afflictions return and thoroughly disturb,**
> **as they did Udraka, who meditated on meditative**
> **concentration here.**[91]

Due to the power of not abandoning self-grasping, as with the non-Buddhist Udraka, the afflictions disturb, and again one falls to the minds of lower states. [559] This being so, how could it be the goal striven for by great-scope disciples? However, if you then think that there was no purpose to the calm abiding previously meditated on with effort, it states in *Praise in Honor of One Worthy of Honor*:

Even if followers of your teachings
do not achieve an actual concentration,
existences can be thwarted,
like the gaze of Māra.

One might doubt that, putting aside the attempt to achieve an actual first concentration and so forth after achieving a preparation for the first concentration, one could attain liberation from cyclic existence through a supramundane special insight meditating on the meaning of selflessness—the view of emptiness. If that were the case, then if omniscience is not attained by this practice of the last perfection, there could be no higher Dharma than that of the middle scope. Such an occurrence of wrong thinking is the mistake of one-sided vision, like the grass seen by a one-eyed yak. Thus, there is a great difference between the two meditations on emptiness of persons of middle scope and this present context of the persons of great scope. Previously, in the section on training in the general conduct, an extensive manner of training in bodhicitta and the bodhisattva conduct was covered. The meditation on emptiness with the assistants of methods such as bodhicitta, generosity, and so on, is "the emptiness endowed with all supreme aspects"—that is, a wisdom realizing emptiness whose potential is much greater. Even though it is similar in being the emptiness meditated on by śrāvaka and pratyekabuddhas to achieve their liberation and the same in being an awareness realizing emptiness, there is a huge difference from the side of method. As such, it can arise as an antidote not only to afflictive obscurations, but also to obscurations to knowledge. Moreover, since the object of meditation of śrāvaka and pratyekabuddhas is neither possessed of all attributes of method, nor has such an assistant of method, it is taught that their solitary wisdom cannot arise as an antidote to obscurations to knowledge.

However, if you wonder whether one can achieve buddhahood through bodhicitta and the method-related conducts among the six perfections alone, one cannot, [560] as Jé Lama Tsongkhapa states [in his *Three Principal Aspects of the Path*]:

> Even though you have become habituated with renunciation
>   and bodhicitta,
> without the wisdom realizing reality,
> you are still unable to cut the root of existence.
> Therefore, strive in means to realize dependent arising.

Not only is bodhicitta necessary, but one must meditate on the path of higher training in wisdom that is conjoined with it—it is not a partial path like that of persons of the middle scope and below.

As such, Jé Rinpoché, in his *Three Principal Aspects of the Path*, could have stated the reason for requiring the view of emptiness with the words, "Therefore strive in means to realize *emptiness*," but he did not; instead, he stated, "Therefore strive in means to realize dependent arising." Rather than using words from the side of emptiness, the fact he used the words "dependent arising" from the side of appearance—the so-called "infallible dependent arising of appearances"—is a highly important point, and thus those words were used in the reason for needing to meditate on the view of emptiness. The protector Nāgārjuna also has many works on the topic of dependent arising, and thus with emptiness appearing as dependent arising and dependent arising appearing as emptiness, in brief, it is a significant point that one must realize emptiness through seeing the meaning of emptiness as dependent arising.

Well then, if you think, "Since calm abiding and special insight are both included within the practice of the trainings of meditative concentration and wisdom in the context of persons of middle scope, why do they need to be conjoined with bodhisattva conduct?"

It states in Nāgārjuna's *Sixty Stanzas on Reasoning*:

By this merit may all beings
complete the collection of merit and pristine wisdom,
and may they attain the two supreme states
that are arisen from merit and pristine wisdom.

To achieve buddhahood, both the rūpakāya and the dharmakāya must be achieved, so in dependence upon what are they accomplished? Candrakīrti states:

Conventional truths are means
and ultimate truths are arisen from means.
Whoever does not know the difference between these two
enters into the bad paths of wrong conceptions. [561]

Implicitly this means:

Whoever correctly knows the difference between these two
enters into good, unmistaken paths.

The foundational view is correctly understanding (1) conventional truths, the appearance aspect, which is that all phenomena are established conventionally and arise interdependently without error between cause and effect, and (2) ultimate truths, the aspect of emptiness, which is that phenomena are not even slightly established by way of their own nature. At the time of the path the collections are accumulated by the powerful conduct of generosity and so forth. Based on this one attains the results which are the rūpakāya and dharmakāya, the ultimate goals of persons of great scope. Therefore, the path of attainment by which one gains those two bodies requires conjoined method and wisdom.

In the context of the practice of wisdom in [Śāntideva's] *Compendium of Trainings*, it first gives the sutra explanation of the presentation of conventional subjects, in which it makes a detailed analysis of each dividing point of the qualities, nature, or potential, of whatever subject it may be, and then after that cites many sutra passages that state they are not established by way of their own nature, are like illusions, are like the city of gandharvas, like a mirage. In accordance with that, having initially brought to mind a subject basis, which has a true and infallible manner of relation of benefit and harm, and ascertained it, in dependence upon the reason of understanding how it is a dependent origination in which it must be established by way of causes, conditions, and mutual dependence, when you thus proclaim that it is empty of inherent existence, there occurs great potential to eliminate the two extremes, and thus one can understand from the previous citation of Candrakīrti stating, "Conventional truths are means, and ultimate truths are arisen from means," that one must proceed with unified method and wisdom.

Thus, **as for the method to achieve those results, I have already given the experiential guide on the way to accumulate the collection of merit. With respect to the stages of practice for accumulating the collection of pristine wisdom, generally, there were four separate tenet systems in the ārya land of India with conflicting views. [562] However, principally it was the Madhyamaka and Yogācāra schools that were renowned. Regarding this, it states in Nāgārjuna's *Precious Garland*:**

> **As this Dharma is profound, the Buddha understood
> that it would be difficult for beings to understand.
> Thus the enlightened sage turned away
> from teaching the Dharma.**

Since it is difficult for others to realize this important point of how to posit the presentations of karmic causality and emptiness as noncontradictory, the Buddha behaved as if it were difficult to accept to turn the wheel of Dharma. The one who would teach that diffi-

THE PERFECTION OF WISDOM

cult point was prophesized by the Victor, in the *Descent into Laṅkā Sūtra*, to be the glorious protector Nāgārjuna.

Not only was he foretold in scripture, if one analyzes with reasoning, too, the way this great being unraveled the intention of the words of the Buddha there is no contradiction to be found. Moreover, that it was said that he is akin to the Buddha with respect to the kind Teacher's general teachings possessing the feature of profundity and in particular the stages of the profound path is due to the fact that however much you investigate the logic of this master the more acceptable it becomes. Therefore, not only are Nāgārjuna's works excellent explanations unrefuted by logic, but based on those the entirety of the words of the Sugata become acceptable and one comes to understand the final intention of the Bhagavān exactly as it is. Therefore, his teachings are like a key, and for that reason he is renowned as the second teacher regarding this teaching. **Although there were many who claimed to be his follower, there is no occasion in which one can achieve liberation through the mere view of accepting that all phenomena are inherently established; thus the glorious Candrakīrti states:**

> Those outside the path of the venerable Ācārya Nāgārjuna,
> have no means for peace.
> They deviate from convention and truth,
> and having deviated will not achieve liberation.

Thus, since one must realize the unmistaken intention of the protector Nāgārjuna, [563] which commentaries on [his intention] should be followed? Jowo Atiśa says:

> Through what is emptiness realized?
> The student of Nāgārjuna—the one prophesized by the
>   Tathāgata—who saw true reality, is Candrakīrti.

Through instructions transmitted by him,
one realizes true reality.

Regarding the following and practice of Candrakīrti's commentaries, Candrakīrti's *Commentary on Āryadeva's "Four Hundred Verses"* states:

> The *self* is any thing's inherent nature of not relying on another, and the nonexistence of that is *selflessness*. This is understood as two, divided by way of phenomena and persons: selflessness of phenomena and selflessness of persons.

What is the order of the two modes of selflessness? Generally, *emptiness*, refers to *empty* of the object of negation, while *-ness* is understood as suchness or that itself. Thus, to understand emptiness one must form an understanding of a manner of being empty of that [object of negation] through understanding the object of negation which it is empty of. Therefore, it states in Āryadeva's *Four Hundred Verses*:

> First overcome the nonmeritorious.
> In the middle, overcome the self.
> Finally, overcome all views.
> The one who understands this is wise indeed.

Wrong views that consider karmic causality as nonexistent, and so forth, were overcome previously in the contexts of the small- and middle-scope beings. It states in Nāgārjuna's *Sixty Stanzas on Reasoning*:

> For the time being, the source of all faults, nihilism,
> has been overcome.

The first stage is refraining from faulty behavior that occurs under the influence of afflictions as indicated by the line, "First overcome the nonmeritorious." **"In the middle"** and so forth indicates **self of persons, and "finally"** and so forth indicates **self of phenomena,** thus indicating **the order that one must overcome them.** This order **was authored from the perspective of practice instructions.**

Alternatively, with regard to the line, "In the middle, overcome the self," aside from a slight difference in difficulty between realizing self-lessness of persons and selflessness of phenomena due to the difference in the subject—the empty basis—there is no difference in subtlety between those two selflessnesses. [564] Moreover, to overcome afflictions one must realize subtle selflessness of persons, and if you realize that, then you possess the potential to refute the grasped object of the apprehension of the aggregates as truly existent. Therefore, achieving the liberation at the point reflected in the line, "In the middle overcome the self" requires realizing selflessness, too. Through splitting that into selflessness of persons and selflessness of phenomena, one can indeed state that "through realizing selflessness of persons liberation is achieved," and that if subtle emptiness is realized one must also realize selflessness of phenomena, it was with the key point in mind that the line, "Finally, overcome all views" is to be applied.

Alternatively, with respect to the line, "In the middle, overcome the self," I wonder if it could be applied to meditation on selflessness for the sake of merely abandoning afflictive obscurations, and with the line, "Finally, overcome all views," one reaches certainty and meditates on emptiness with the attitude of wishing to achieve omniscience for the sake of abandoning the apprehension of true existence not only in one's own continuum but in the continua of all limitless sentient beings. Thus, indirectly, one is meditating for the purpose of abandoning the self-grasping in the continua of all sentient beings. Moreover, one is also meditating on selflessness specifically to accomplish the entirety of the purpose of the wisdom that realizes emptiness through limitless reasonings for the sake of overcoming the stains of mistaken dualistic appearances deposited by self-grasping.

Nāgārjuna states in his *Precious Garland* that, "For as long as you apprehend the aggregates, for that long you will apprehend them as 'I.'" This means that as long as one has an apprehension of the aggregates as truly existing, one will still have an apprehension of a self of persons, and therefore to *completely* realize selflessness of persons one must realize selflessness of phenomena, because it requires that one refute the grasped object of the apprehension of truly existing aggregates.

Although the selflessness of phenomena comes first in the great treatises, it is a crucial point to not confuse their general and specific order in one's practice. [565] Regarding that, **the view of selflessness does not arise in a person who does not believe in karmic causality,** and "the view of selflessness" is not explained on the basis of a merely imputed self. Rather, the main concept is selflessness by reason of being a dependent arising, and thus there is a connection to someone who perfectly understands the manner of dependent arising needing to acquire ascertainment of infallible karmic causality from the depths of their heart. As such, I think it is a case of it being difficult for someone who does not believe in karmic consequences and who does not accept and has no belief in something which is by nature related to dependently arisen karma, to prove noninherent establishment by reason of dependent origination.

Without overcoming the apprehension of a self of persons one cannot overcome the apprehension of a self of phenomena. This statement is referring to a coarse apprehension of a self of persons, and if someone conceives a self-sufficient, substantially existent person through the influence of tenets, they can never overcome the apprehension of a self of phenomena. **The corresponding portion of faults of individual afflictions, such as attachment, were each eliminated previously through their antidotes, but not all faults were elimi-**

nated. This is due to not having eliminated ignorance, their root. Thus, it states in the *Four Hundred Verses*:

> Just as the body sense power pervades the body,
> delusion abides in all [afflictions].
> Therefore, all afflictions, too, are destroyed,
> by destroying delusion.

> If dependent origination is seen,
> ignorance does not occur.
> Thus, with all efforts directed to this
> I will only speak of that.

Just as when a tree is cut from the root all of its branches and flowers dry out, if self-grasping is abandoned all afflictions will be pacified. Therefore, it states in *Entering [the Middle Way]*:

> Having seen that all faults and afflictions
> arise from the view of the transitory collection,
> and having realized that the self is its object,
> the yogin negates the self.

And in *Precious Garland*:

> For as long as you grasp at the aggregates,
> you will apprehend them as "I."
> If there is the apprehension of "I," there is karma,
> And from karma, too, there is birth. [566]

If you have self-grasping, you will accumulate karma, through which you are reborn. Therefore, since the root of cyclic existence is the ignorance of apprehending true existence and apprehending an "I," they

must be overcome. Furthermore, for as long as you have an apprehension of true existence grasping to the aggregates as truly existing
through the influence of tenets, for that long you will apprehend them
as "I." Thus, if you do not refute the grasped object of the apprehension of the aggregates as truly existing, you cannot *completely* realize
selflessness of persons.

With respect to reaching certainty on the two types of selflessness,
the great Dharma king Tsongkhapa supplicated protector Mañjuśrī
who taught the way to give rise to the pure view in his continuum.
Having actualized it accordingly, within the practice for guiding disciples it states to first meditate on selflessness of persons then afterward
selflessness of phenomena, and among the individual transmitted
frameworks there are two: (1) that transmitted via Khedrup Gelek
Palsang that is guidance by way of preliminaries and actual practices,
and (2) that transmitted via Khedrup Sherab Sengé that is guidance by
way of possessing the four types of mindfulness. Whichever of those
two you practice makes no difference. However, this present context
is that of an experiential guide of the perfection of wisdom within the
stages to enlightenment, and therefore the preliminaries are left aside
because they correspond to the aforementioned sequence of practice.

The Practice of the Perfection of Wisdom

The actual practice has two parts: the way to meditate on selflessness
of persons, and the way to meditate on selflessness of phenomena.

Regarding the first, there are many frameworks, such as the logic
of dependent arisings, for instance, having three essential points,
and the logic of the sevenfold reasoning having nine essential
points, and so forth.

The logic of the sevenfold reasoning can be illustrated with a chariot:
a chariot is not suitable to be posited in any of these seven ways: (1)
one with its parts; (2) different from its parts; (3) the support for its

parts; (4) supported by its parts; (5) possessing its parts; (6) the mere collection of its parts existing as individual units; (7) its shape.

Thus, on the basis of this sevenfold reasoning in which if you search for the designated object beyond that which is mere name and merely imputed existence, it is not to be found. One must rely on the nine essential points of (1) ascertaining the object of negation, [567] and (2–8) that if it is inherently established it must definitely exist as one of the seven extremes, together with (9) the essential point of ascertaining the pervasion.

These have been extensively taught in the sublime teachings of Jé Rinpoché, such as in extensive and abbreviated *Special Insight* chapters. Principally, within the analysis based on the four essential points, as given in the experiential guide of the great trailblazer of this tradition—the omniscient Norsang Gyatso—and his spiritual sons, whose experience was passed down from one to another, the first essential point is that of ascertaining the manner that the innate apprehension of "I" apprehends the "I." With respect to this, Buddhapālita states:

> **Regarding the statement, "All phenomena lack a self," if both objects of negation of the self and its absence are not thoroughly identified, it would be like waging a war without knowing the location of the enemy, or like firing an arrow without knowing where the target is.**

It states in *Way of the Bodhisattva*:

> **Without touching upon the imputed thing,**
> **there is no apprehension of its lack of existence.**

There are two manners of explanation regarding this: the first applies the "imputed thing" to the subject that is the basis of imputation, and the second applies it to the object of negation. Regarding the first, if you do not ascertain the phenomena that is directly related to its basis of designation, then you will be unable to realize the negation of its inherent existence using the reason of it being a dependent origination. *Reality* means the negation of true existence on a particular basis—there is no reality without a basis.

When applying "imputed thing" to the object of negation, **it is taught that if the meaning generality of the object of negation** to be negated **does not properly appear to one's mind, one cannot ascertain the meaning of selflessness which is a negation of that. "Persons" refers to the persons who are the six types of migrating beings and the ordinary and ārya beings of the three vehicles. A manner of existence in which they are not designated by awareness and instead are established as self-sustaining from their own side is their "self" or "inherent existence."** The persons who are the basis, or subject, having a manner of subsistence in which they are not merely imputed by awareness and are established as self-sustaining by way of their own nature is "self" or "inherent existence." [568]

Furthermore, among the innate apprehensions of "I" that apprehend an "I" or "self" on the basis of designation **that is the person,** there is not solely the apprehension of a self through the apprehension of true existence, but rather **there are three** manners of arising: **(1) an apprehension of an "I" qualified by being merely imputed by conception onto the basis of designation** which is the general thought of "I," **(2) an apprehension of an "I" qualified by being inherently established, and (3) an apprehension of an "I" not qualified by either of those two**—that is, inherently established or not inherently established.

Regarding the first, it is an awareness apprehending an "I" of persons of someone in whose continuum the Madhyamaka view has been born. For the duration that the compositional factor that is the elimination of the object of negation of inherent existence does not decline, when a person appears to awareness it clearly appears as a person that is merely dependently imputed.

Regarding the second, the apprehension of an "I" qualified by being inherently established, **it is the actual innate apprehension of an "I" in this context that is to be destroyed by the antidote**—that is, the root of all afflictions.

Regarding the third, to those ordinary beings whose minds have not been influenced by tenet systems, there is no differentiation of being imputed through name or inherently established; therefore theirs is a conventional valid cognizer positing "I." Moreover, at all times—whether awake or asleep—we have an acute awareness thinking "I." However, when encountering the conditions of happiness or suffering, as with a mirror and the reflection of a face, it is a very strong manifest awareness, and when those conditions are not encountered, it is slightly unclear. The majority of current instructors on the view have failed to analyze whether it is such a manifest awareness. They profess to practice based on a few empty words regarding the manner the innate apprehension of "I" apprehends the "I," and so forth, and therefore completely miss the point. They are like someone pointing their finger at a vague face and shape of a person and stating, "This is that thief from yesterday!" [567]

Therefore, whether you do or do not have a manifest thought of the direct help or harm others have done to you, visualize again and again something that has already happened prior, like someone accusing you of theft, or the achievement of your goal, for example. While thinking, "I did not even have the thought to steal, yet they accused me of theft!" and getting very angry at the other person, the "I" that is accused of theft appears acutely in the middle of your heart, as if it were visible to the eye or could be touched by the hand. Likewise, the "I" that is the object of benefit in the thought, "They helped me in this way," appears vividly from the middle of your heart.

Thus, from the point of letting the other coarse conceptualizations that are dormant innate apprehensions of "I" develop through a manifest awareness based on either of those two approaches, you must investigate the manner in which that awareness apprehends "I." It is incredibly difficult to investigate both the apprehension of "I" and the manner of its apprehension on the basis of this very mind itself. If the awareness of the manner of apprehension is too strong, the factor of intensity of the mode of apprehension vanishes and becomes unclear. So, how should it be done? Through the power of being accustomed with calm abiding, consolidation occurs on the basis of any focal object of analytical or placement meditation. So, instead of focusing on the body of the Buddha, for example, make manifest the awareness thinking "me" instead, and while the majority of that mind abides with the factor of intensity of clarity, one side of the awareness looks at the manner of apprehension and where it is apprehended. This is taught to be like how two people walking next to each other on a road will look at the road with the main part of their eye and look at their acquaintance from the corner of their eye.

What is the realization of selflessness, or emptiness? It is the elimination of the object of negation that is nonexistent, that something is empty of, without anything remaining to awareness. From the perspective of ascertaining its nonexistence, or emptiness, there is no positive phenomenon that appears, as with the thought, "It is this or that," for example. It is a vacuity which is a mere negation of the object of negation, upon which awareness radiantly abides, or dissolves, or enters. [570]

With respect to the way to identify the object of negation for the sake of reaching a conclusion on suchness, it states in *Four Hundred Verses*:

The seed of existence is consciousness.
Objects are its domain.

If you see that objects lack self,
the seed of existence is halted.

Through apprehending the self of objects, attachment and anger arise,
and due to those one accumulates karma. Therefore, the apprehension of self must be eliminated. Regarding the way to eliminate it, if
you ascertain that its object of the mode of apprehension—that is, the
apprehended self—does not exist even conventionally, the awareness
apprehending self ceases. There is no other method to make it stop.
Therefore, you must come to recognize the manner of apprehension
of the awareness holding to self—that is, if the "self" that is the object
of the mode of apprehension of the awareness apprehending self were
to exist—it must exist in such and such a way. For example, when an
intense awareness thinking "I" arises, the self appears to that awareness as if it were self-sustaining from the side of the object. Of course,
such an awareness also has the mere "I" as its focal object. However,
it does not appear at all as something merely imputed by awareness.
Rather, it appears to exist with the object. Likewise, the modes of
apprehension with respect to any inner or outer phenomena are the
same.

The awareness apprehending it to exist as it appears is the awareness apprehending the object of negation. Its object of the mode of
apprehension does not exist even conventionally. Regarding this, the
great Seventh Dalai Lama stated:

Objects of a dream in the mind of one drunk on sleep, or
the horses and elephants conjured by a magician, and so forth,
are not at all really there—they are merely appearances,
imputed by awareness.

I often quote this passage as it was useful for me to imagine it. It is
clear from this passage that things which appear in dreams—such as

mountain ranges, family homes, and so forth, and the horses and elephants that are a magician's display do not exist on those bases at all, but are instead merely imputed by awareness. The remaining passage states:

> Thus, all phenomena—oneself, others, samsara, nirvana,
> and so forth, are none other than mere imputations
> through awareness and conventional terms.
> They have no existence at all on their bases of designation. [571]

Although these terms have referent meanings—good and bad, samsara and nirvana, self and others, and so forth—their manner of existence is devoid of being a self-sufficient entity, or being nondependent, nor can they be found at all if searched for. Therefore, it is taught that they have absolutely no existence on their bases of designation, either. Furthermore, that text states:

> Even so, from the perspective of the six consciousnesses of
>   ordinary beings
> polluted with the thick sleep of ignorance,
> whatever appears seems actually established on that basis—
> look at our terrible minds!

Since things cannot be found when searched for, ultimately it is a situation of being only suitable to be posited through name without there being other means. Despite that being the case, it does not appear as such to our awareness, and whatever phenomenon appears, it appears as if there is a phenomenon that is the referent of its convention that exists within its basis of designation. Thus, there is a manner of identifying the object of negation where such a concrete appearance that occurs is taught to be the object of negation, and alternatively it was taught:

This manner of subsistence of the "I" and so forth as
    primordially established,
appearing to such a mistaken awareness,
is the subtle object of negation, and thus
it is essential to negate it without remainder in the perspective of
    awareness.

Likewise, Gungthang Rinpoché states:

Because the nature of the view is sought,
it is negated when not found.
Since the unfound basis of designation is not refuted,
a remaining mere name subsequent to that is seen.

That mere name and furthermore all action and agents,
are established through undisputed experience, and thus
all concomitance, faults, and qualities, adoptings and
    discardings—
elaborated conduct—are authenticated.

This teaches that although phenomena appear as existing from the side of the object, they do not exist at all as they appear, and are instead merely posited through name and terminology.

At one point I, myself, was putting effort into searching for the nature of the view as indicated in the lines, "Because the nature of the view is sought, it is negated when not found." [572] Undertaking the search to find the nature of conventional subjects such as a pot and so forth, and not a search for a pot itself, the nonexistence of, or emptiness of, the object of negation was almost appearing to my awareness. However, on later analysis, that turned out to be the self of the Madhyamaka Svātantrika position. When thinking about it from that perspective, in the connecting verses of general Madhyamaka treatises, specifically the special insight chapter in Jé Rinpoché's *Great Treatise on the Stages of the Path*, it says:

> My friends who have trained in the profound Madhyamaka
>   treatises,
> although you find it difficult to posit the dependent origination
>   of causality
> within the absence of inherent existence,
> it would be more gracious if you stated:
> "Such is the system of the Madhyamaka."
> I think it is less difficult to make such a statement.

Similarly, the word "mere" in Jé Rinpoché's usage of "mere name" does not negate the existence of an object that is not name, or that object being established by valid cognition. For example, a pot that is the referent object of the name "pot" exists, but if you search for that object, you cannot find it. It is acceptable to operate on the assumption of the existence of an object that is other than that name, but when searching for it, wondering where it is it, although it is not found, not finding it does not mean the object does not exist. How does one posit existence despite it not being found when searched for? It is taught that aside from "existence through imputation" there is absolutely no other manner of existence.

Well, then, what is the unmistaken subtle object of negation, and what is the vacuity that is the negation of that? Khedrup Norsang Gyatso states:

> Just as there is not the slightest existence of the form in a
>   dream,[92]
> or the illusion of a horse or elephant, other than a mere
>   appearance[93]
> to one's own awareness,

from the Peak of Existence down to the hells
there is only that which is merely imputed by conceptual
   thoughts
of however many sentient beings there are. [573]

This verse teaches that the subtle object of negation is something existing from its own side without being merely imputed by thought. Until that subtle object of negation has been eliminated, one's view remains fabricated and partial. Thus, a Madhyamaka view other than that, that is free from extremes, is also one of the difficult points of the Madhyamaka.

Hereafter, aside from the "I" within the thought of "I" seeming to exist in the middle of the heart, yet not having ascertained it to be established within anything, from now on, through a corner of awareness investigating thoroughly, sometimes it seems to exist with the body. For example, when you state, "Today I am tired," "Today I have to go," or "Today I am staying," the "I" seems to exist with the body, and appears almost as if the place where one points to the "I" is the body itself.

Sometimes it is as if it exists with the mind—that is, occasionally when stating, "Since previous lifetimes, I ..." or, "Yesterday I was sad," or "Today I am happy," one thinks the "I" exists with consciousness. Likewise, no matter what feeling of happiness or sadness arises the "I" seems to exist with that feeling.

Sometimes it is as if it exists with the other aggregates individually, and so forth. What is the manner that the real object of negation appears to an innate awareness **at the end of these various appearances occurring? Together with this body and mind that are inseparable like milk and water,** my body and mind that are controlled, and **an "I"** that is the master of those **will be recognized as something concrete, something that inherently exists from my own side and is primordial. Since this is the first essential point of ascertaining the**

object of negation one should analyze until one's experience reaches the depths of this.

In regard to this it states in the teachings of Khedrup Norsang Gyatso:

> The sun lord Losang [Drakpa] saw
> that the gathering of many disciples who fancied themselves[94]
>   experts
> asserted the great Madhyamaka free from extremes
> to be the logical refutation of the objects of negation[95]
> confined by the terms "own characteristics," "inherent
>   establishment," and "true existence,"
> as posited by awareness. [574]

The fact that Jé Rinpoché emphasized appearances upon suspecting that students of the philosophical texts had fallen into the extreme of annihilation is a very important point. Occasionally, suspecting they had fallen into the extreme of annihilation, he insistently stated the object of negation is "establishment by way of its own characteristics," and "inherent establishment." It states in Changkya Rölpé Dorjé's *Recognizing My Mother: A Song of the View*:

> Now a few of our bright minds,
> through grasping at the terms "self-sustaining," "truly
>   established," and the like,
> leave the wavering appearances as they are
> and search for something with horns to negate.[96]

Tsongkhapa saw that since [they thought] the object of negation that is trapped by the conventional terms "self-characteristics," "truly established," and "inherently established" is an object of negation posited by awareness, the meaning of which is the logical negation of merely that was asserted by them as the great Madhyamaka free of extremes. However, Tsongkhapa taught that this was not so. When thoroughly analyzing this, it is obvious that it is the Madhyamaka Svātantrika manner of negating the object of negation.

Having thus given rise to that in your continuum, if you ascertain the identification of the "I" apprehended by the innate apprehension of "I" and one's five aggregates as self-sustaining in the manner of water poured into water, from merely having performed analysis you will acquire ascertainment, and if not, it becomes something not self-sustaining. Candrakīrti states in *Clear Words*:

> Would the object of the apprehension of self, moreover, be in the nature of the aggregates or different from the aggregates?

Even though the "I" seems to be established in an inseparable manner with the nonindividuated five aggregates, a pot, for instance, would not be called "separate" or "indivisible" with respect to one basis, yet here occurs an aspect of "I" and "aggregates" that are separated as two: a basis of designation and a designated phenomena. Investigate this by thinking, "Is the 'I' that is established as inherently self-sustaining with the aggregates a third alternative that is neither one nor different from the self and the five aggregates?" Since something must be either one or different if it exists, even if it were to truly exist there is nothing beyond being either truly one or truly many. [575] As such, when analyzing which of the two it is, **having compared it with another phenomenon that is a functioning thing and finally realized that there is no third alternative, the conclusion that it is not other than being one or different is the essential point of ascertaining the pervasion.**

Therefore, from having practiced this second essential point, one gains slight experience of one's previous ascertainment doubting that the designated "I" that previously seemed to exist as self-supportingly indivisible with the aggregates that are its basis of designation can not be independent, but either one or different. Following that it is not sufficient to doubt whether it is one or many—one must decide. Therefore, when you investigate whether the "I" apprehended by the innate apprehension of true existence is established as one with both body and mind, generate ascertainment that (1) it is not suitable to be other than one with the body or one with the mind; (2) if it were one with the body it would not be logical to say "my body" which is applied to a basis and an attribute, and one would have to say "my I" and "the body's body," and that it is the same for mind, too. If upon reflecting in this way you can only repeat the words and not fully understand it, consider the following from Nāgārjuna's *Fundamental Wisdom of the Middle Way*:

> When there is no self
> except for the appropriated aggregates,
> the appropriated aggregates are the self.
> In that case, your [proposed] self does not exist.

If the "I" and the aggregates were inherently one, they would be one in terms of all completely inseparable parts. Since they are thus unsuitable to be anything other than partless, with one partless thing an "I" that is the appropriator of the five aggregates, the "five aggregates" that are appropriated by it cannot be posited as two different things. Thus, contemplate by thinking the assertion of "my body" and "my aggregates" becomes meaningless. If by that, too, you do not reach an effective conclusion, then contemplate that by reason of both the "I" and the body being one, after death when the body is cremated, the "I" would also have to be cremated, or just as the "I" reincarnates in a future life, the body would also have to reincarnate. Or, contemplate the fallacy that just as the body does not reincarnate the "I" would also not reincarnate. [576]

Having thus meditated you will understand that it is perhaps not one with the body. Thus, when you think, "So is it one with the mind?" contemplate that since "I" get cold when naked and suffer from hunger and thirst if "I" do not eat or drink, if my mind is born in the formless realm after death, since the mind is also one with the "I" at that time, then there would be a fallacy of needing to utilize the coarse form of food, clothing, and so forth. This line of reasoning is easy to sustain and appropriate for a beginner, yet if you push yourself with wisdom, resolve to elaborate a bit further. As it states in Candrakīrti's *Entering the Middle Way*:

> If the aggregates were the self,
> since there are many, the self would also be many.

Contemplate the fallacies of the consequence of the self becoming many through the following logic: just as there are five aggregates, there would be five selves, or, just as there is only one "I," five aggregates would not be tenable. Likewise, it states in Nāgārjuna's *Fundamental Wisdom of the Middle Way*:

> If the aggregates were the self,
> [the self] would arise and disintegrate.

Since the aggregates naturally arise and disintegrate, one must accept that the self, too, arises and disintegrates. Therefore, both the "I" from one's previous life, and the "I" of this life are not beyond being one or different, and, if they were one, then through the power of being inherently one the stupidity of the animal "I" was in my previous life and its suffering of being exploited would have to be experienced by the human "I" of this life. Moreover, the happinesses of the human of this life would have to be experienced by the animal of one's previous life. Contemplate such absurd consequences. Likewise, it states in Candrakīrti's *Entering the Middle Way*:

> Whatever things are individual by way of their own
>   characteristics,
> are unsuitable to belong to the same continuum.

If the "I" of the previous life and the "I" of the next life were different, then through being different things that are never connected, it would also be unreasonable to recollect that "I was such-and-such in my past life," like Devadatta not recollecting that he was Yajñadatta.

Moreover, the karma I have accumulated to be reborn in a good migration would also be karma performed that goes to waste, because its result that is the ripening of higher status would be enjoyed by another and thus not experienced by me. [577] This is because [according to this wrong view], both the agent of karma and the experiencer of the result are not included within the same basis of the mere "I" and have no relationship. Therefore, if karma so accumulated in a previous life had a positive or negative effect in this life, one would be encountering karma one has not performed. Moreover, if [your own karma] had no positive or negative effect there would be no purpose in adopting virtue and abandoning misdeeds in this life since their results would not ripen upon the "I" of the next life. Having understood this third essential point of the lack of being inherently one through contemplating this, one then thinks that the "I" must be different from the five aggregates. However, *Entering the Middle Way* states:

> There is no self other than the aggregates,
> because there is no apprehension of [the self] without the
>   aggregates.

There is no self that is an object other than the aggregates, because if the aggregates have not been reversed, there is no innate awareness apprehending the self as another object. **Since inherently established different things must be unrelated, just as the five aggregates can be individually distinguished among one another by stating "this is the form aggregate" and so forth, after negating the five aggregates, although needing to make the identification of "this is the I," no matter how finely one analyzes it is not found at all. Moreover, it is not enough that this manner of not finding [the "I"] is a repetition of the empty words "it is not found." It is not, for example, like when a bull becomes lost and one holds to the truth in the words, "It is not in such-and-such valley," but one finally decides that it is unfound only after searching in the top, middle, and lower parts of the valley. Here, too, one finds ascertainment having meditated until reaching a decision, as it states in** *Entering the Middle Way*:

> Since there is no action without an agent,
> it is not that my self does not exist.
> Consequently, a yogi perceives both the self and emptiness of
>   the self
> and thereby becomes liberated.

From then onward it is taught that you have first found the Madhyamaka view when the "I" that is like an inherently established thing that can be seen by the eye or touched by the hand is not found and totally disappears.

If you have identified the self that is the object of negation—that which is self-sufficient and independent—then through seeing whether such an "I" exists as one or different from the aggregates that are its basis of designation gives rise to many errors, eventually you will come to a decision that such an "I" does not exist. [578]

Here, too, the process of that which is ascertained initially by an awareness arisen from study being practiced by an awareness arisen from contemplation and thus achieved by that arisen from meditation is not a fully qualified special insight as in the previous context of calm abiding, but is an ascertainment of a subtle view, like the moon on the second day [of the lunar calendar]. At this time, if one does not have imprints regarding emptiness from previous lifetimes, it would be like one had suddenly lost what was being held in the hand. If one does have imprints, the experience would be as if the jewel lost from one's hand has been regained suddenly.

The manner in which one should sustain the view of selflessness having settled it in that way is, as in the previous context of calm abiding, to rely on the six preparatory practices, adopt the physical posture, use mindfulness and introspection here, too, and meditate on it. Regarding the manner to do so, some people, at the end of performing a preliminary analysis of the view, meditatively sustain suchness in which they do not take anything to mind. This is given as a summary of the first, second, and third refutation of other systems contained in the great chapter on *Special Insight*. Moreover, some practitioners stabilize the previously analyzed view with mindfulness alone. These different styles of meditation lack a unique focus that is different from sustaining calm abiding.

If, during the cultivation of the actual practice, you do not perform analysis, or abide without taking anything to mind, or abide serenely in the context of the view, that means the former does not become a meditation on the view, and the latter abides through using the view as a focal support. However, that is merely the manner of sustaining calm abiding observing suchness; it is not the manner of sustaining special insight. That requires analytical meditation, whereas calm abiding requires placement meditation. This manner of sustaining the practice is very clear in Tsongkhapa's *Middle-Length Exposition on the Stages of the Path* and in treatises on mantra.

THE PERFECTION OF WISDOM

In the Perfection Vehicle, when one strives in the means for inducing ascertainment of an object on the basis of the coarse mind itself, ascertainment can only be induced through analysis. If there is another method for awareness to become more subtle it is clear that in that context, however much awareness becomes subtle with respect to a focal object, it will be that much more able to induce awareness. [579] If your awareness has become subtle through the force of yoga in that way, it will only become that much clearer; it does not become less clear. Therefore, if you perform analysis through having such a practice, it becomes an obstacle to awareness becoming more subtle. When meditating on the view by way of such a practice, only placement meditation is performed, not analytical meditation.

Generally, the fact that only placement meditation is explained in many of the Dzogchen or Mahāmudrā treatises must be understood as a manner of meditation on emptiness in relation to the yoga of Unsurpassable Mantra. From the perspective of the sutras it is as before: special insight requires analytical meditation and is pervasively analytical meditation; however, in relation to the yoga of Unsurpassable Mantra it is taught that special insight can be placement meditation.

Potowa's *Blue Compendium* states:

> Some [wrongly] say that a lack of inherent existence is settled
>   through logic
> during the period of study and contemplation,
> and that during the period of meditation only
>   nonconceptualization is meditated on.
> If this were so, since an unrelated emptiness is meditated
>   upon separately,
> it would not become an antidote.

Therefore, even during meditation,
individually investigate whichever [reasonings] you are
    familiar with—
such as that of lacking one or many, or dependent origination,
    and so forth—
and remain, too, without the slightest conceptualization.

If you meditate like so, it is the antidote to afflictions.
For those who wish to follow the sole deity, [Atiśa,]
and who wish to engage in the system of the perfections,
this is the system of meditation on wisdom.

Many people who consider themselves great meditators state that one settles the view with logical analysis, and during meditation one only meditates without conception, but this is no different than raising your horse well at home and going by foot when heading abroad. Therefore, this is nothing more than one's own fault of slightly misunderstanding the crucial point of how to achieve special insight in dependence upon calm abiding. Thus, in the context of calm abiding, the meaning of the statement that nonconceptualization is required and one should cease conceptualization is that one should not conceptually deviate from the focal object, such as the enlightened body. [580] If, on the other hand, one had to cease all conceptions, since that which takes to mind the aspect of the Tathāgata's body is a conception, if that, too, were stopped, then one would of course lose the focal object. It is an error to think that since all individual analysis on the meaning of selflessness induced by wrong conception, which is the basis of error of nonconceptualization, is conceptual, it therefore should not be done during meditation. This is a misunderstanding of the meaning of calm abiding. The reason is that, in dependence on individual analysis through wisdom affected by the force of calm abiding, the afflicted conceptions such as attachment and so forth do not scatter to other [objects], and the analytical meditation being practiced becomes incredibly clear.

If one analyzes with individually discriminating wisdom before achieving special insight, it harms the factor of abiding, but even if you analyze with discriminating wisdom having already attained special insight, it becomes increasingly more stable on the focal object, as it states in Jé Rinpoché's *Songs of Experience*:

> The meditative concentration achieved by single-pointed
>   meditation
> is not enough; through the correct analysis of individual
>   discrimination
> [generate the meditative concentration]
>   abiding totally firm without wavering on reality.

After accomplishing the union of calm abiding and special insight, no matter how much you analyze the focal object becomes more and more stable through the force of analysis. This is taught as the aftereffect of accomplishing special insight, as **the wisdom of special insight is powerful through merely having firm calm abiding. Furthermore, if you alternate analytical and placement meditation prior to achieving calm abiding it will interfere with calm abiding. However, if after achieving calm abiding you experience the factor of abiding being undermined by forceful analysis, you should do placement meditation, and if you do not feel like analyzing due to too much placement meditation you should perform analytical meditation and alternate in this manner.**

It is not sufficient that analysis be on the meaning of selflessness and placement be on nonconceptualization or any random thing, such as a deity's body. During analytical meditation one contemplates selflessness, and during placement meditation one

is single-pointedly focused on the self's lack of inherent existence, without wavering to other thoughts. Just any sort of nonconceptualization does not suffice, as it states in Kamalaśīla's third *Stages of Meditation*:

> Therefore, within the holy teachings, see that the absence of mindfulness and absence of mental engagement precede correct individual analysis. [581] This is because it is only correct individual analysis that can create the absence of mindfulness and the absence of mental engagement; there is no other way.

As such, the followers of Khedrup Gelek Palsang explain that upon vividly ascertaining the nonexistence of the "I" induced through the four-point analysis, one must practice by prolonging the continuum of that very ascertainment and performing mere recollection of the four-point analysis again and again, and that it is incorrect to meditate by [merely] thinking that the "I" does not exist the way it appears, or that it does not exist as established in that manner of appearance.

There are many traditions that agree that having induced ascertainment, one meditates by thinking that it does not exist as established in that manner of appearance, as do some who uphold the lineage of Khedrup Sherab Sengé.

To summarize, after you have previously settled the four-point analysis through listening and contemplation, you vividly ascertain during your meditation that the "I" as apprehended by the awareness acutely apprehending "I" from the center of the heart does not inherently exist on the basis of designation of the five aggregates. At this point, since that itself is the actual focal object, you must ensure it is not forgotten. Introspection keeps watch on whether the conception apprehending "I" has been eliminated or not, and if it

happens that you need to refresh your memory regarding the manner in which the "I" is not inherently established, through slight
analysis, settle it in equipoise on the thought that it does not exist
in that manner.

At that time, due to your strong habituation with the thought that
apprehends a self, even though you focus tightly and practice, as
with the nine mental abidings in the context of calm abiding, the
apprehension of "I" is too strong and frequent such that the thought
"I am not truly existent" occurs only occasionally. Once you have
habituated yourself gradually, however, the awareness viewing the
self as not truly established will be frequently interrupted by the
apprehension of true existence. Following that, immediately upon
the arising of an awareness apprehending true existence it can be
averted merely through slight mindfulness, and thus it is as if you
are without interruption. Following this, one meditates without
relying on thorough application [of the antidote], as in the case of
the ninth mental abiding, and can relax one's exertion. It is a similitude of the union of calm abiding and special insight, or a slight
factor of it. [582] At that time, just as, for example, "space" is posited
as the mere absence of the object of negation of obstructive contact
on the basis of the transparent whiteness of the sky, the placement
of single-pointed equipoise onto the nonaffirming negation that
is the vacuity of the mere negation of true existence—the object to
be negated—without being interrupted by other phenomena is the
true way of sustaining the space-like meditative equipoise. Without
letting other awarenesses such as the thoughts, "This is emptiness," or,
"It does not exist as it appears" arise, while your awareness engages
the vacuity of the mere negation of the object of negation itself you
must set it in equipoise. While calm abiding is excellently established,
calm abiding being induced by the power of individual analysis and
leading to the *absence of mental engagement* and *absence of mindfulness* is also identified as this.

One might doubt whether various conceptualization and analysis could be causes for nonconceptualization. The *Chapter of Kāśyapa* states:

> Kāśyapa, it is so: Just as, for example, a fire starts from two trees rubbing together in the wind, burning the two trees, in the same way, Kāśyapa, the power of an ārya's wisdom will emerge if correct individual discrimination is present. With its emergence, the correct individual discrimination itself is burned up.

Through analysis, like the rubbing together of a variety of wood-like conceptions, the fire-like view of emptiness emerges, burning up all the wood of conceptualization and annihilating the wood. Through meditation on a conception, clear appearance will dawn with respect to its object, and at that time the conception becomes nonconceptual. Thus the substantial cause of nonconception requires a seed from which nonconception arises without beginning; however, that itself does not need to be nonconception.

Through sustaining and meditating on the continuum of the similitude of special insight attained from the point of absence of thorough application [of the antidote] onward, one attains an exceptional pliancy of body and mind induced by analytical meditation that is even greater than the bliss of physical pliancy induced earlier during calm abiding through the force of equipoise. When that has been attained, one has achieved actual special insight. From then onward it is the "actual path of unified calm abiding and special insight," which I can confidently proclaim as the position of the experts who maintain the pure tradition without confusing fish and turnips. [583]

After attaining special insight, calm abiding and special insight are united through their assisting, or dependence upon, one another.

Therefore, many wise persons and fools of the Sakya and Dakpo Kagyü traditions and so forth state, "If one has conception, it is not the view," meaning that meditation on the view requires the absence of proliferation and reduction of conceptual thoughts. They refute as unreasonable the assertion of the Gelukpas that special insight is the little fish moving to and fro through the still water of calm abiding. Even many of our own followers loudly proclaim that this opponent's position is the ultimate crucial point of the path. However, until one has achieved the fully fledged view of space-like equipoise, if the analysis of a similitude of special insight in which the force of calm abiding has not perished is absent, many who go on the path of calm abiding alone, devoid of special insight, cannot make progress on the path, and after initiating unified calm abiding and special insight that does not rely on exertion, both calm abiding and special insight engage simultaneously with equal force, as taught in the *Great Treatise on the Stages of the Path* through quoting [Ratnā-karaśānti's] *Instructions for the Perfection of Wisdom*, and at that point, since we no longer assert the little fish of special insight darting through the unmoving waters of calm abiding, this is analogous to the sun of refutation and proofs rising while the opponent's position has not yet dawned. The disciples, too, were indeed deceived, like a rabbit calling out danger after hearing a piece of fruit falling in water, by those who did not understand the intention of the *Great* and *Middle-Length* lamrim treatises. Yet, grasping (1) at the way to practice the beginning, middle, and end of the meditation on the path and (2) the manner of arising in one's continuum as the same without making detailed differentiation is similar to proclaiming that there is no difference in the development and decline of the bodies of both a newborn baby and a hundred-year-old person. Think well about this!

What happens during post-meditation after one has practiced space-like equipoise? It states in the *King of Samādhi*:

Just like a mirage, the city of gandharvas,
like an illusion, or a dream,
meditation on characteristics is empty of intrinsic nature.
Know all phenomena to be like this.

During post-meditation, the appearance of the mere name of "I" that remains after refuting the object of negation must appear like an illusion. [584] Thus, even though all phenomena appear, if you are able to see them as untrue, like an illusion, except from what is itself good or bad, you will not develop attachment to something totally and exaggeratedly good, nor will aversion arise toward something that is totally bad due to the superimpositions of incorrect mental attention. Moreover, you must give rise to an awareness seeking omniscience, for example, having discriminated that it is good, and an awareness desiring liberation from afflictions and the ocean of suffering that is cyclic existence which has arisen from them, having discriminated they are bad.

The manner of sustaining the practice of seeing things as illusory can be divided into two: (1) the illusory combination of that to be adopted and discarded, and (2) illusory conventional phenomena appearing yet not being true. Until the object of negation is refuted there is no way the illusoriness of things appearing yet not being true can dawn to awareness, and thus when you have an experience of refuting the subtle object of negation during meditative equipoise, when, through the force of that, conventional appearances dawn vividly during post-meditation, things will appear as established from their own side as before, but you will naturally understand that the appearance does not exist in reality.

The manner of appearance that is a realization of the lack of true existence of the appearance of a dream or [magician's] illusion of horses and elephants is not the manner of appearance of this system. If that were the case, the magician and elders who understand conventions would also have to realize that manner of appearance.

Moreover, through having practiced the previous analysis of the view, appearances that are shimmering and ephemeral, devoid of being identified as this or that, are also not the illusions of this context.

Therefore, merely thinking that the pot that appears to a valid cognition apprehending "pot" exists conventionally, yet is not established from its own side, does not fulfill the meaning of the illusion-like manner of appearance. It requires understanding that whatever appears to exist has a mode of existence in which it is not established as inherently self-substantiating, but rather is dependently arisen, or dependently imputed. Moreover, one must know how to unmistakably posit all presentations of action, and agent, and causality, on the basis of the very mode of existence of being "simply name, existing imputedly," despite noninherent establishment, or not being established from its own side. [585]

It is for this reason that the great master Jé Tsongkhapa states [in his *Three Principal Aspects of the Path*]:

> As long as the two understandings
> of infallible dependent arising of appearances,
> and emptiness free of assertions appear separately,
> one has not realized the intention of the Sage.

This teaches that if you do not gain an understanding of emptiness when inducing ascertainment of dependent origination on the side of appearance, or do not gain an understanding of infallible dependent arising when inducing ascertainment of emptiness—that is, when contemplating either appearances or emptiness the other is left out—you still have not realized the intention of the Sage.

Well, how should the illusory mode of appearance **be? Glorious Dharmakīrti states the reason why realizing the horses and**

elephants conjured by a magician are not horses and elephants does
not harm the inherent establishment of horses and elephants:

> Without refuting its object,
> the [conception of self] cannot be abandoned.
> One abandons desire, anger and so forth
> related to good qualities and faults
> through seeing they do not exist in the object,
> not through removing external appearances.

It is not enough to remove the thorn, for example; it requires refuting
the object of apprehension. Through the power of being deceived by
the immediate cause of error that is the illusionary horses and elephants, they are undeniably seen by the eye consciousness. Yet just
as ordinary adults know there exist no horses and elephants as they
appear, horses and elephants, too, due to deception by a long-term
cause of error, undeniably appear to conventional consciousnesses.
However, they must be understood as like an illusion that is empty
of inherent existence by way of their own nature. Therefore, just as
ascertainment of the lion killing the illusionary elephant and so
forth is induced through seeing it directly, while understanding the
lion conjured by a magician does not exist in reality, so too ascertainment from the bottom of one's heart that the person who does
not exist inherently and appears as illusory accumulates black and
white karma and experiences their ripening. My lama has taught
that this is the feature of this Dharma.

Both real horses and elephants and illusory horses and elephants are
alike in not being inherently established, and also in existing through
mere imputation by names and terms alone. However, it is important
to distinguish that illusory horses and elephants are not established
as horses and elephants conventionally, and that actual horses and
elephants are established as horses and elephants. [586] Just as it is

explained that "emptiness is the meaning of dependent arising and dependent arising is the meaning of emptiness," if you are able to induce a genuine understanding of the presentation in which dependent arising is tenable by reason of emptiness, you will be able to make the above distinction.

The analogy is given through making the following fine distinction: When the inherent establishment of horses and elephants has been refuted through logic, then from the perspective of such a conventional consciousness, the consciousness that apprehends horses and elephants as real—which has an appearance of existence by way of self-characteristics while there is no existence by way of self-characteristics—**is a mistaken consciousness, like the illusory horses and elephants. Yet from the perspective of a worldly consciousness, the consciousness apprehending horses and elephants as real is not mistaken, while the consciousness apprehending the illusory horses and elephants is mistaken. Instead of this, if you contemplate that the horses and elephants are not inherently existent, and then [make the comparison] that the horses and elephants and illusionary horses and elephants are similarly mere convention, it is a great contradiction. This would contradict the meaning of this passage in** *Entering the Middle Way*:

> **That which is apprehended by the flawless six senses**
> **and realized by those of the world,**
> **is verified by the worldly.**

This teaches a mode in which something is not true for ārya beings, but true for the worldly. **Thus, it becomes a deprecation of the conventional. Moreover, Mañjuśrī's instruction to Jé Rinpoché that he must emphasize the side of appearance was also intended with respect to the suspicion that future disciples would fall into the extreme of annihilation through not understanding this crucial** point. Moreover, there are many proofs with respect to the side of appearance in Tsongkhapa's *Great* and *Middle-Length* lamrim treatises and great commentaries on Nāgārjuna's *Fundamental Verses* and Candrakīrti's *Entering the Middle Way*. Thus, the following passage by the lion of speakers, Taktsang Lotsāwa, also appears to be authored based on this basis of confusion:

Having analyzed with many reasonings,
he accepted impure, mistaken appearances as valid.

This is one of the refutations known as "the eighteen great burdens of contradiction directed to Jé Rinpoché" by Taktsang Lotsāwa.

Although the reasoning of dependent arising was not taught in this context, since it is incredibly important it must be supplied from other sources and meditated upon. [587] This is because, although one can induce ascertainment with respect to the side of emptiness in which the imputed object is not found when sought via the reasonings of not being one or many, or the seven-fold reasoning, one is unable to easily induce ascertainment with respect to the way dependent origination is infallible conventionally. It states in the *Fundamental Verses Called "Wisdom"*:

Whatever is a dependent origination
is indeed said to be empty.

Furthermore:

Since there are no phenomena
that are not dependent originations,
there are thus no phenomena
that are not empty.

This has been taught extensively. Based on the logic of dependent relation, dependent origination is the meaning of emptiness, and emptiness is the meaning of dependent origination. Moreover, one must train in this logic of dependent origination that eliminates the two extremes simultaneously, and which has the features of eliminating the extreme of existence through appearance and the extreme of nonexistence through being empty.

Meditation on the Selflessness of Phenomena

Regarding the way to meditate on selflessness of phenomena, the essential point of *identifying the object of negation* is, for example, a body that is not imputed outwardly through the name "body" onto the basis of the complete five limbs—from the crown to the soles of the feet—but instead appears as if is established as self-substantiating from its own side.

Deciding that the body established like that is either one with or different from the body's upper part, lower part, limbs, and so forth, is the essential point of *ascertaining the pervasion*.

If they were one, since "the body's head, legs, arms, flesh, bones, and skin" are ascertained as being separate, individual objects that are the basis of designation and designated object, is the essential point of *lack of being truly one*. If those two were different, since if you mentally eliminate the parts of the body from the crown to the soles of the feet one by one and determine that there is no longer an identification of "body," aside from a mere body imputed outwardly by conception onto the body with five complete limbs, there is no body that is self-substantiating from its own side. This is the essential point of *lack of being truly many*.

It is when ascertainment dawns vividly with respect to those that the view of selflessness of phenomena is initially found.

If the body were inherently established with the form of the complete five limbs without depending on imputation through conception, [588] then one should equally think that a tree with leaves and branches in a forest, and another that has been made into a pillar by a carpenter are both pillars. Likewise, it would be like a baby that still had no name last month but was named Tashi this month, upon seeing the baby at both times one should think, "It is Tashi," but one does not.

Furthermore, this consciousness is imputed onto the basis of designation that is a collection of many parts such as the consciousness of yesterday and the consciousness of today. Moreover, "time" is posited onto a collection of years, months, days, and so forth. If uncompounded space, for instance, is illustrated with respect to a thousand vacant spaces, since each vacant space has a part of uncompounded space, space is posited onto their collection. One can settle the view through analysis of the four essential points with respect to any phenomenon; however, just as [Candrakīrti's] *Clear Words* uses the example that if the chariot burns so too does the parts of the chariot, upon realizing the lack of inherent existence of the self, through the force of stopping the apprehension of the five aggregates, too, that are its basis of designation as inherently existent, one also realizes selflessness of phenomena. The awareness realizing the lack of inherent existence of the person does not think, "The aggregates are not inherently existent." However, without needing to depend again on any other reason, through the force of it previously refuting the subtle object of negation with respect to the person, it possesses the ability to later refute the subtle object of negation with respect to phenomena, such as the aggregates. This is taught from the perspective of coarse convention.

Through the power of having established the view of selflessness of persons and practiced it, it is not difficult to establish one's understanding of selflessness of phenomena. Selflessness of phenomena, furthermore, is as stated in [Āryadeva's] *Four Hundred Stanzas*:

> The viewer of one object
> is said to be the viewer of all.
> The emptiness of one,
> is the emptiness of all.

Moreover, Āryadeva says:

> Whoever sees the suchness of one thing,
> sees the suchness of all things. [589]

If you realize one thing as empty you can realize others [as empty] too. Therefore, due to having practiced with respect to form, for instance, as in the context of selflessness of persons, all phenomena ranging from form to the omniscient mind will appear as not inherently established. Thus the previous masters gave some illustrations within their practice, but if one had to meditate on each phenomena individually, the meditator themselves would first have to accomplish immortality. Since one would not be liberated through a few illustrations, too, made at the time of listening and reflection, one would be set back through the distraction of counting one's hopes and apprehensions, entering into equipoise on the meditative concentration of pretending to be knowledgeable when one is not.

Concluding Verses

> Through the dim-sightedness of the thick darkness of
>   ignorance
> the appearance of the coiled, spotted rope of body and mind

Is apprehended as the scary, poisonous snake of "I."
Through this one experiences all terrors of the three types of
  suffering.

Through the apprehension of "I" that grasps at the true
  existence of the conjured horse,
one endlessly visits all places in cyclic existence without
  control,
not knowing the fault of experiencing it like the happiness
  and suffering of a dream.
How incredibly foolish!

The empty nature of this beloved "I,"
who, although exists, is not found however much it is sought,
leaves no trace, like a flight path in the sky.
Through this one understands the essential point of all
  phenomena being primordially empty.

The suffering of burning in the hells
and the pleasures of enjoying delights of gods and men
while not existing, are experienced, as like an illusion.
This leads to the realization of the essential point of
  appearance: the infallible dependent origination.

When the wheel of the sharp weapon of wisdom—
the infallible middle way of positing
conventional existence and primordial emptiness—starts
  to turn,
the tight bindings of the affliction of self-grasping are cut.

Despite this being the single path traversed
by all āryas of the three vehicles,
Modern day fools who appear to uphold the teachings,
experience it like measuring a fathom in the dark. [590]

Yet, as I recollect the kindness of the supreme, incomparable
    tutor
the sublime voice unmistakenly proclaiming
the profound point, deep like the ocean,
may clouds of offerings of excellent teachings spread.

Training in the Four Ways to Gather Disciples That Ripen Others' Continua

Training in the four ways to gather disciples that ripen others' continua has five parts:

    (i) What the four means of gathering disciples are
    (ii) The reason there are four
    (iii) The function of the four means of gathering disciples
    (iv) The need for those who gather disciples to rely on them
    (v) A slightly elaborate explanation

A slightly elaborate explanation has two parts:

    (a') Pleasant speech that accords with worldly customs
    (b') Pleasant speech that accords with pure Dharma teachings

With respect to how those are taught, **it states in the *Ornament for the Mahāyāna Sūtras*:**

> **Generosity is the same [as before]; teaching [the perfections],**
> **making others accept them, and doing so oneself**
> **are asserted to be pleasant speech, enacting their benefit,**
> **and consistency [in one's behavior].**

In order to ripen the continua of others, in dependence on the four means of gathering disciples for the sake of enacting the welfare of

sentient beings, having trained in the conduct of bodhisattvas—the children of the victors—a retinue is gathered through the generosity of material goods, fearlessness, and Dharma, according to the dispositions and inclinations of disciples. The practice of the perfection of generosity is the first of the four means of gathering disciples— the generosity of what is needed. With a radiant and smiling face directed at the retinue gathered through the power of such generosity, speak pleasantly—the second means of gathering—with good behavior in accordance with worldly norms, such as inquiring about their dispositions and so forth, and talk of the benefits of Dharma to which they are inclined. In particular, give pleasant discourses on the Dharma to those with dull faculties, who engage in various wrong deeds, who are concerned only with this life, the careless monastics, and so forth, in order to lead them onto the correct path.

Since there are many types [of persons] who have thus been made joyful regarding virtue, for those who cannot conceive eternal happiness, forcefully leading them onto the path to liberation, or into the Hīnayāna or Mahāyāna, for instance, is inappropriate for the time being. [591] Thus, it will not benefit the disciple, just as treating a fever with camphor will exacerbate the illness and cause harm unless the fever has first been made to maturate through a decoction. Therefore, for such beginners who cannot conceive of eternal happiness, for their own good temporarily make them train sequentially in small virtues, illustrated by saying, "One must perform such-and-such virtue for the sake of health and longevity," and ultimately guide them in the direction of omniscience. This is the third means for gathering disciples. In order to make others engage in that, too, if you yourself do not participate then others will say, "To tame us you must first tame yourself!" Thus, practicing to a level that is greater, or at least equal, to that of others is consistent behavior, and is the fourth means of gathering disciples.

The Virtuous End: The Concluding Content

Sealing with dedication prayers is indeed included here. Importantly, one might wonder how to continue a practice of the essentials after reaching complete certainty regarding the previous practices. During refuge and bodhicitta, contemplate the sufferings of persons of lesser and middle scope. Following that, for those who integrate lamrim into their practice of secret mantra, exert yourself in confession of misdeeds and accumulation of merit connected to guru yoga, then sustain the focal objects of bodhicitta that increases giving and taking, and of the union of calm abiding and special insight.

Concluding Verses

Having understood and practiced the profound six perfections
through joyous effort that makes the heart courageous,
and wisdom by nature spontaneous,
you will arrive at the peak of unimpeded accomplishment of
    one's own welfare.

Not deviating to the inferior path of peace like śrāvakas and
    pratyekabuddhas,
your endless stream of enlightened activity—
the four means of gathering that matures others—
will resemble a river possessing the eight qualities. [592]

With the adroit wings of unified method and wisdom,
you have soared to the heights of existence and peace,
to finally frolic in the meeting place of the immortal three
   enlightened bodies.
Thus, the incomparable garuḍa has been accomplished here
   and now.

One therefore [first] ripens one's own continuum by accumulating
vast merit and wisdom and actualizes buddhahood in dependence
upon the path of the six perfections. One then ripens the continua
of others and leads them to the ground of omniscience in dependence upon the four means of gathering disciples. These stages of
the path of the three beings, instructions that please the victors, the
quintessence of the holy teachings that bear a lineage, practiced as
naked instructions, are this alone [and nothing else].

Since it is equivalent to a wish-granting jewel that fulfills the
hopes of migrating beings through having practiced it without anything missing, [Tsongkhapa] authored the extensive praise [in *Songs
of Experience*, starting with the lines]:

Since it fulfills the desired aims of all beings without
   exception
it is the wish-fulfilling jewel.

Having thus offered a minor supplement to the contents of the outlines
of *Oral Transmission of Mañjuśrī* in the main section of this virtuous
text, virtue is finally dedicated at the virtuous end through recollecting
the kindness of the Teacher Bhagavān.

Dedication of Virtue through Recollecting
the Kindness of the Teacher

By craving the delights of existence—the fleeting appearances
of this life and the tumultuous barrage of the waves of
desire,
beings are totally immersed in the limitless ocean of cyclic
existence, choked by the terrifying sea monsters that are the
three types of suffering.
If beings defiled by ignorance are without opportunity to
attain even the crystals of personal peace,
then their chances of hearing about—let along actualizing—
the supreme wish-granting jewel of the two aims, are
terribly difficult. [593]

The dense forest of afflictions and knowledge obscurations
has been burned by the fires of the two collections;
the buddhahood of the union of the two bodies free of faults,
the healing paradise of altruistic activity that rejuvenates
upon even hearing or seeing,
is devoid of the wilderness of despair—difficult to bear—
and free from the dangers of the wild animals of the
inferior path.

In order to establish beings into this state, from the center of
the clouds of white teeth within the mouth of the son of
Śuddhodana, guru of migrating beings, who loves not one
but all,
red lightening that is the soft and smooth tongue flashes,
resounding with the thunder of the Dharma of the three
vehicles.

Having thus been impregnated with high status and definite
    goodness,
your disciples thus fan their variegated tail feathers of the ten
    powers
performing the dance of altruism.

The nectar of the incomparable twelve-fold speech of the Sage
swirls as an endless knot at the heart of the two regents,
whose sacred words intoxicated the charioteers Nāgārjuna and
    Asaṅga, who intoned eloquent sayings.
Their famous white dukūla garments beautify the ārya land,
    meeting place of the immortals.

The mirror of emptiness reflects the image of the deeds of the
    six perfections—
radiant with the light of one hundred thousand suns, its
    appearance unceasing,
was drawn into the sky of the snowy land by Atiśa along the
    winds of the special intent,
where his noble tradition was obscured for a long time by
    clouds of ignorance.

[Tsongkhapa], supreme with clear intelligence and renowned
    good fortune,
greatly kind and unable to bear this,
excellently gripped Mañjuśrī's sharp vajra sword of
    intelligence
and cut through the web of deluded misconceptions.

Tsongkhapa, spoken of as the unprecedented "Jahnu"[97] by all,
is expert in differentiating the interpretable and definitive,
    due to having drunk

the rain of the Muni's teachings, the words and commentaries
   on their intention possessing eight branches, fallen from the
   mouths of forefathers.

Even if those desiring to uphold this tradition
totally washed the face of the earth
with a heavy cascading waterfall of their sweat,
wise ones who know the correct way are rare like daytime
   stars. [594]

The assembly of teachers whose loud voices confident in
   explanation, debate, and composition
resound in the ears of the fortunate
like the supreme right-turning Dharma conch.
They are certainly omniscient ones.

The feigned profundity of others
Is an incomplete medicine poisonous for some.
The unrivaled pith of the teachings is complete without
   exception,
thus fulfilling the great purpose of leading the three types of
   beings along the correct path.

The meaning of the words of the two lamrim treatises are
   profound and changeless like the sky.
They do not fit in the hole of feeble intelligence.
Newly composed texts based on good intentions are the waters
   that fall into the two extremes—
either not filling the vessel of intelligence or spilling over
   for some.

The dry branches of words that lack key points
cannot bear the fruit of authentic meaning,
and those covered in the excess leaves of meaningless words
are like painted images of butter lamps, devoid of light.

Therefore, this unprecedented treatise, the new moon,
is replete with all facets of meaning,
yet devoid of the form of the hare of vast words.
So how could it possibly arise within the pond of my
    own mind?

However, when the arrow nocked by the adroit finger of much
    learning
about the essential points of the treatises difficult to realize,
hits the far target of the subtle and fine excellent teachings,
the arrogance of the dexterous archers, boastful of their skill,
    deflates.

Those whose sight is too myopic to peer into the limits
of logical and scriptural analysis,
yet whose tongues dance with nonvirtuous gossip that reaches
    to the Peak of Existence,
should take rest.

If those wearing the cloth hat dyed the color of saffron,
upheld our own teachings it would be marvelous.
But there are many empty-handed ones who have lost the
    exceptional jewels
of scripture and realization of our forefathers to the thief of
    distraction.

The tarnished brass dull-facultied ones habituated with
   ignorance
are referred to as refined gold who uphold the sublime
   teachings.
But having arrived at the great gathering of many experts
they blunder by showing their ugly colors of ignorance.

It is of course difficult that all types of intelligence would be
   complete
from inside a very young egg.
But why is it a bird cannot fly into the sky of explanation and
   accomplishment,
despite spreading their youthful wings? [595]

I will not capture the attention of many untrained persons
who are falsely touted as renowned experts,
yet through this mere partial knowledge of the five sciences,
accomplished through exertion like the poor man's wealth,
   this treatise rises above.

The merit which unravels the complex knot
of the essence of the Buddha's speech, the supreme deed,
is the blazing thousand-spoked wheel of gold.
Through it may I reach the pinnacle of the palace that is the
   four fearlessnesses.

May the great deities protecting the tradition of the
   yellow hat,
Six-armed [Mahākāla] and Karmayama,
burn up the factions of desire-realm gods with fire from
   their eyes,

and raise the banner of scripture and realization at the Peak of
Existence.

Having matured the golden eggs of the guiding treatise with
    the warmth of their mind
may sentient beings produce the good result of the one
    possessing the four bodies—
the creator of the inexhaustible adornment wheel—
and become enlightened.

THE FIFTH DALAI LAMA'S COLOPHON

Some instructional treatises on the stages of the path to enlightenment authored by Chen-ngawa Lodrö Gyaltsen and others are
wordy in the earlier parts and thus do not concentrate on the focal
points, and the latter parts are too condensed to be useful for beginners. Those with mental acumen, who have the eye of intelligence
to view the excellent teachings of the great Tsongkhapa, yet rely on
other words are indeed akin to using a salty well on the banks of a
lake possessing the eight good features.[98] Within this transmitted
lineage of teachings, up until the omniscient Sönam Gyatso, aside
from the two lamrim treatises and the incomparable oral transmissions of the lamas, there was no custom of relying on written notes.
Moreover, up until Chen-ngawa Rinpoché Shönu Chöphel Sangpo,
root verses were composed for the *Essence of Refined Gold*, and supplements were authored for the *Great* and *Middle-Length* lamrim
treatises; aside from that, there were no instruction manuals composed in a systematic style.

    Jampa Rinchen, the master of the Ganden hermitage retreat center
of Palkhor Dewa Chenpo in the upper region of Nyang valley, was
born in the district of É Rigpai Jungné and propounded countless
sutra and tantra. He received extensive practice instructions from

me between two half-moons. [596] He earnestly requested that the instructed focal objects of meditation be committed to writing.

Generally, with regard to practice instructions, it is not beneficial to oneself or others if one has not comprehensively received them from the mouth of a lama who holds the lineage, as they cannot be transmitted through mere reading transmissions or books. Bold individuals who have false authority over Dharma give explanations to others despite not having received the practice instructions themselves. These days, when it is even worse than when the Jowo Kadampas said that those who teach others without having practiced are like pouring from an empty vase into another, I wondered whether writing down the practices clearly as naked instructions was helpful for the continuity of the teachings as a single whole.

Nonetheless, beings of inferior intelligence engaging in this degenerate era incur the faults of wrong explanation through not accurately retaining the spoken words of the lamas. Thus, I thought that there might also be some benefit in dual teachings. Regarding this instruction manual on the stages of the path to enlightenment called *Oral Transmission of Mañjuśrī*, I excellently listened to the stainless oral transmission out of the kindness of guru Mañjuśrī, from the great omniscient Khöntön Paljor Lhundrup (1561–1637), one from the area called Pabongkha, Dharma king of the degenerate age, who does not need to rely on others to understand the entirety of the teachings of the victors. Moreover, I received an in-depth explanation, not missing a single word, of [Tsongkhapa's] *Great Treatise on the Stages of the Path* twice in the presence of the skilled orator, lord of speech, Jetsun Lama Könchok Chöphel. Due to their kindness I am able to raise my chin slightly with the confidence to proclaim this teaching.

I, the fortunate monk from Zahor, Ngawang Losang Gyatso Jikmé Gocha Thupten Langtsö Dé, also known as Jamyang Gewai Shenyen, in the male earth-dog year, or *Vilamba* as it is known in the ārya land, the thirty-second year of the sixty-year cycle, and Wuzu as it is known in the kingdom of the Mañjuśrī emperors;[99] in the month known as *Śrāvaṇa* in Sanskrit, the male-bird month in Tibetan, the Chinese Qiyue, the seventh Hor month; with respect to the *Kāla-cakra Tantra* convention, the *middling joy* that is illumination of the darkness of darkness, the vowel *ā* and consonant *ma*; according to the *Svarodaya Tantra* convention, the second joy of the red direction, vowel *ā* and consonant *cha*; the age of *childhood*; earth element; desirable object of smell; at the planetary junction of the sun and constellation of *Delta Corvi*, at the time junction of the lion, in Palden Drepung, the great seat of Dharma, the great grove of all the Buddha's words and commentaries that have been translated. The scribe, Trinlé Gyatso, from Drongmé, recorded it.

May excellent teachings be realized and virtue flourish!

COMPILER'S COLOPHON

These two volumes consist of (1) a presentation of the basis, path, and result to be known that is illustrated by way of the three: Buddhist tenets, science, and religious doctrine, and the application of those to an approach that is compatible and relative to modern science—that is, related to an introduction on how the short- and long-term welfare of beings can be increased—was given in the *general explanation*, together with (2) a lamrim manual called *The Fourteenth Dalai Lama's Stages of the Path, Volume 2: An Annotated Commentary on the Fifth Dalai Lama's "Oral Transmission of Mañjuśrī"* that is an organization of the intention of the Buddha Bhagavān into the stages of the path of practice on a single seat—a profound method for healing oneself, others, and the environment.

These are the words of the one who is the root of all well-being, freedom, religious and secular matters of the snowy land of Tibet,

THE VIRTUOUS END 703

the supreme guide of all who uphold the Victor's teaching on this earth, the unacquainted friend of persons of various backgrounds with diverse interests in religion, philosophy, and politics, the protector and refuge, the great among great beings, respected as a supreme teacher and guide, a leader for world peace, the fourteenth incarnation of the omniscient victorious lord who holds the white lotus, [598] whose name is Jetsun Jampal Ngawang Losang Yeshé Tenzin Gyatso, the incomparable lord over the three realms of existence, the root guru possessing the three types of great kindness, renowned in the world as "His Holiness the Dalai Lama."

For a long time His Holiness has pledged himself to the three great commitments for healing the world: (1) as a human being himself, the promotion of human values; (2) as a religious practitioner, the promotion of religious harmony; (3) as a Tibetan and someone who carries the name of the Dalai Lama, and in particular as the sole person to whom the lay and ordained Tibetans inside and outside of Tibet place look to with great trust, his third commitment is to the Tibetan cause, and thus he is a spokesperson for the freedom of Tibetans. Therefore, for the sake of accomplishing those goals, the essence of His Holiness's enlightened activity of speech that has been disseminated in all directions and components of his thought are condensed within the first volume *Fourteenth Dalai Lama's Stages of the Path: Guidance for the Modern Practitioner.*

In the year 1040 the great mahātmā, widely renowned as the incomparable Jowo Jé Atiśa, went to the region of Ngari, Tibet, via Nepal, and during his three-year stay authored the *Lamp for the Path to Enlightenment* specifically for the Tibetan disciples of that time appropriate to their inner and outer conditions and what they required. [599] With respect to this original model of all advice renowned as lamrim, among the many literary lamrim works propagated by experts who are not confined to any tradition of Tibetan Buddhism, this second volume of *The Fourteenth Dalai Lama's Stages of the Path* is an annotated commentary that supplements the supreme teaching of the *Oral Transmission of Mañjuśrī: The Instruction Manual for "The Stages of the Path to Enlightenment"* by His Holiness the Great Fifth Dalai Lama.

Up until now His Holiness, the supreme omniscient one, for his whole life, from the common perspective of disciples, too, mastered the vast textual tradition of the experts of glorious Nālandā, such as the ācāryas of the ārya land, Nāgārjuna and his spiritual sons, and through keeping at the heart of his attention mind training in the great treasury that endlessly bestows well-being onto all beings—love, compassion, and precious bodhicitta—the essence of the thought of the Sage, the core interest of the victors and all their spiritual children, gained full ascertainment of emptiness being dependent arising and dependent arising being the meaning of emptiness.

Not only that, but particularly in dependence on His Holiness exchanging experiences with experts from regions that uphold the Buddhist tradition and so forth, these viewpoints regarding Buddhism are vast and profound, and have resulted in an independent text following logic alone. Additionally, in dependence on profound experiences induced through ascertainment this treatise of our Tibetan tradition contains the essence of the victor's sutra and tantra teachings without exception. Moreover, seeing that the Dharma explained herein, and in particular that this presentation of philosophical viewpoints, has the potential to benefit the seven billion people on this earth right now and in the long term, and that the conditions are complete, His Holiness earnestly gave advice to those within the expanse of this great earth of various race, color, aspirations and dispositions on the worthiness of applying short- and long-term virtuous altruistic means. [600]

To encourage people to wholly participate in this, His Holiness has traveled many times to countries within the five continents of this earth for over fifty years. He has propagated the teachings of the philosophical views taught in the Dharma tradition of the Buddha, the incomparable king of the Śākyas, frequently discussed essential advice that issues forth peace and everlasting happiness, has given presentations, counsel, and Dharma teachings to the vast gatherings of persons belonging to diverse races and societies, of differing philosophical views and tenets, and for this has continuously agreed to participate in occasions to grant extensive awards. His Holiness has learned about all the various advancements in new scientific theories from various renowned modern scientists, and through the approach of making exchanges with a multitude of learned people of all levels for more than thirty years, has maintained regular dialogue about the benefits of educating our thinking based on the hopes, outlooks, and so forth of humankind, and on the relationship between Buddhism and science.

Among the many excellent books on unifying traditional and modern knowledge that we continue to be grateful for, through the aspirations of interested persons who requested the publishing of these two volumes of *The Fourteenth Dalai Lama's Stages of the Path*, just like the true principles taught 2500 years ago by the supreme Teacher, this timely masterpiece on subjects applicable to all in this twenty-first century, too, is a clearly composed text approached from the perspective of content that demarcates the definitive and interpretable, in line with what is needed in modern times. [601]

Regarding the practice of Dharma illustrated in the stages of the path to enlightenment and the manner of explanation of the author's interpretation of philosophical views, as continuously directed by His Holiness, the protector and refuge, incomparably kind, since previous lamrim texts and so forth are a tradition of instruction based on the Tibetan society of their respective time, in which the listeners and contemplators were of course not only followers of Buddhism, but also all Tibetans, and moreover, a time when both the teachers and the students were mostly male monastics, whether it be the analogies or meanings, it is obvious the style of writing—even up to the ancillary— is based on the experiences of male monastics within monastic culture.

It is suitable to point out and appraise these as not only being thoroughly compatible with past societies among the snow mountains, but also that they excellently accomplished the needs corresponding to the place, time, and circumstances of those previous eras, different to those of today.

It is now easier to travel to different places on earth and, just as it is said that "the world has become smaller," it is now easier for countless people across the five continents to take interest in, research, appreciate, or be diligent within their faith in the philosophy, religion, and culture of the Tibetan Buddhist traditions, and these endeavors are widely increasing due to the power of intelligence. Therefore, there is a need to take on this opportunity to offer a gift that heals self, others, Buddhists and non-Buddhists in this life and the next, in the short and long term, for the sake of people's understanding of the stages of trainings taught in Buddhism and for the practice of adopting and discarding in accordance with their place, time, and the person's circumstances to be correct. Regarding this need, His Holiness has said it is the legacy of us Dharma teachers, Tibetologists, and so forth on whom the responsibility falls to explain, debate, and author literature. [602] In particular whether giving commentaries, teaching, or propagating, carrying a motivation that merely by reason of us being the same in wanting happiness and not wanting suffering, one assumes that we all have the same situation and background in terms of our way of thinking, life experiences, environment, our societies, and so forth, and taking as authoritative the explanations and analogies given to a small subsect of Tibetan people that is only related to our old society from a thousand years ago and then applying the same model to all persons of broad nationalities in modern times a thousand years later is far too narrow an approach, and becomes inappropriate based on context. This being so, now is not an era in which we "call East wherever we point our finger" under the traditions, pressure, and so forth of dull-facultied followers of faith, but

THE VIRTUOUS END   707

rather of pursuing outcomes that we have analyzed with our own intellect.

Therefore, on top of not being interested in obvious real-life advancements that have come from improvement in modern education, nor in things that have been disproven through logic, if one is still indifferent and stubbornly disregards whether it appeals as an assertion to others, and uses the fact that it is indeed the word of the Buddha as a pretext to cling only to former traditions and be a fundamentalist when engaging in explanation, debate, and composition, having entered into the Buddha's teachings not only are you not fulfilling your prayers and commitments to strive in skillful accomplishment of others' welfare, but this also becomes a cause of difficulty for intelligent persons to accept the teachings. This approach acts as a foundation for wrong views and depreciation of positive Tibetan culture and authentic Buddhist teachings that have a unique, logical style of view, meditation, and conduct. It thus has become an obstacle for the Buddhist teachings and this culture to still spread throughout all times and directions. [603]

Instead of being the steady shoulder that lifts the teachings up once again, this approach could become the boulder that is pushed downhill. Therefore, as it is clear to all, His Holiness continually advises on the importance of a pleasant style of explanation that is factually concordant and appropriate for all. Here now, too, the manner of explanation is not merely in the style of former traditions. [His Holiness] takes into consideration the many situations of foreign and Tibetan persons whether young, adult, or older, monk or nun, layman or woman, who engage in the teachings through being interested in and having faith and respect for religion in general or Buddhism in particular, or those who have aversion or are neutral toward religion, or hold differing political or scientific views, and so forth, and without sectarian bias, follows the waves of the ocean of inclinations and dispositions of beings. Seeing the trend of modern times to seek truth from facts as greatly important, I and others are receiving the benevolence of His

Holiness bestowing the combination of the essence of both the knowledge of valuable philosophical views and the powerful conduct of bodhisattvas as a tradition that is a unification of old and new.

Regarding *The Fourteenth Dalai Lama's Stages of the Path, Volume 2: An Annotated Commentary on the Fifth Dalai Lama's "Oral Transmission of Mañjuśrī"* that is one part among such noble enlightened deeds of speech, it is the result of His Holiness's original intention to kindly author a lamrim of the Fourteenth Dalai Lama, in which the entire draft that followed his instructions, including the title and colophon, which was written and offered to His Holiness, was carefully checked by him at earlier and later times and amendments were made based on his advice.

This excellent explanation takes as its basis the stainless oral advice of His Holiness. With respect to His Holiness's speech, too, the arrangements and connections that were suitable to be made throughout the text of his phrasing—resplendent with blessings and not deficient—were formulated into a clear supplement [to the Fifth Dalai Lama's text] without going beyond His Holiness's intentions, and were not tainted by my own fabrications as I have stated earlier in the author's introduction [in the first volume].

I, Dagyab Loden Sherab, am a lowly disciple who has been delightedly following His Holiness since long ago, who gained firm faith through knowledge of the qualities of the protector's three secrets. I am the one who had the good fortune to endeavor in the service of composing these consolidated volumes utilizing a computer and so forth, these treatises that illuminate the intention of the victor Śākyamuni, the supreme victor the Great Fifth, and the supreme victor the Great Fourteenth, an enlightened deed of speech having inestimable value. By virtue of completing this act of service on the seventh day of the second month of the Tibetan Fire Monkey year of 2143, the good day of the fifteenth day of March of the Western year 2016, may it become a excellent gift that bestows the glory of peace and happi-

ness to all beings regardless of whether they adhere to any particular
religion, political or philosophical view, and may it become the cause
for myself and all other faithful ones to touch the ground of eternal
happiness through the good feast that nourishes through the supreme
guru's mind that is pleased, which we are inseparable from in all lifetimes. Through the compilation of this dedication prayer the ending
has been made firm.

Concluding Prayers [609]

Oṃ svasti.
In the vast sky of limitless knowledge,
from the dense clouds of endless loving care,
may a hundred thousand pleasant rains of the boundless words
    of dependent origination,
fall on the fields of myriad sentient beings and nurture them.

I pay homage to the crowns of Nāgārjuna and Asaṅga,
the great charioteers prophesized to accurately explain
the pith of the subject matter—the vast and profound explicit
    and hidden meanings of
the mother of the victors, the quintessence of all heaps of
    Dharma.

I amass faithful prostrations to all Kadam spiritual friends
who thoroughly illuminated, in the land of snow mountains,
the core meaning of all the countless excellent discourses—
the crux of the stages of the path of the three beings.

How marvelous the warm and gentle *Oral Transmission of
    Mañjuśrī,*
supreme pith instructions on how to practice

the stages of the path endowed with four types of greatness,
having few words, concise meaning, and easy to assimilate.

Through the great treasury of instructions of Losang Gyatso
being completely opened by Tenzin Gyatso,
hordes of invaluable riches of unprecedented explanations
are spread equally as spiritual sustenance for beings in the
     degenerate age.

Through the accomplishment of the power of the excellent, pure
     prayers of victors and their spiritual children,
the stainless Dharma of the Sugata is illuminated
wherever it has not spread or has declined
through courage spurred by powerful love.

Due to this, when the Meru of the Victor's teachings of Tibet
sunk into the ocean of evil times,
the account of Viṣṇu in the form of a turtle
lifting it up through the physical strength of explanation and
     accomplishment was magnificent.

The great Ganges River of the stainless teachings of the Victor,
that has excellently flowed via the tributary of the lords of
     accomplished scholars in the ārya land
into the throat of Jahnu of the land of snows, filling it up,
again spills out as nourishment for beings of this great
     earth. [610]

The renown from gifting to the countless sentient beings of the
     degenerate age not tamed by the victor
an inexhaustible treasury of secret teachings that combine
     into one

all the enlightened deeds of the ocean of victors, numbering as
    many as atoms,
has reached the far shore of existence and peace.

Tibetans of old were covered with a single cloth
of the totally pure tradition
and possessed the Dharma melody of the six-syllable mantra
    without being taught.
The manner they were guided on the path,

would be difficult to make sense of
in the clouds of the twenty-first century
rippling with manifold conceptual thoughts
waving with the winds of desire.

Having seen this, for the sake of beings who are gripped by
the splendor of modern-day civilization
His Holiness disseminated a new and unprecedented manner of
    explanation
in connection with present realities.

Out of the three levels of content of the treatises—
foundational, philosophical, and Dharma of the path—
the first two are trainings for religious persons without
    sectarian bias,
and even the nonreligious.

For that purpose you have given us a good tradition of learning,
    contemplation, and meditation
of a system of diverse knowledge
as appropriate for the vast array of beings

within an excellent explanation through your knowledge of the
    four reliances.

You have composed a timely teaching
for the ears of present-day beings—
a golden explanation totally purified
by the fires of however many types of knowledge exist.

Sarasvatī, toiling,
Plucks a melody on her harp
To express the marvel of this,
yet it remains hidden in the sphere of the unmanifest.

The great master Āryadeva
in his *Four Hundred Verses*
unraveled what was concealed and filled in the incomplete
with respect to Nāgārjuna's root treatises.

Likewise, for the sake of unravelling the profound, difficult-to-
    realize meaning
of *The Oral Transmission of Mañjuśrī*,
His Holiness authored a supplement, applying as appropriate
outlines, explanations, annotations, and so forth.

The Fourteenth Dalai Lama's Stages of the Path is for illuminating
    the intention
of the fourth victor, the son of Śuddhodana,
the lord of victors, Losang Gyatso,
and Tenzin Gyatso, who surpasses the victors. [611]

All excellent explanations based on the place, time, situation,
    and disciples,

that have been lost to forgetfulness
on the many occasions
that the stream of the commentarial guides on lamrim was
    bestowed,

with a pure engagement of devoted exertion and the special
    intent
were collected with effort for a long time, and combined,
edited, and refined into a single treatise;
the one who accepted this responsibility was Loden Sherab.

This general explanation of the Buddha's teachings and
    subsidiary topics,
along with the supplement and annotations to the actual
    treatise,
counted among volumes of scripture that are the guides,
has been published to be of benefit to all fortunate ones.

I dedicate whatever limitless collections of white virtue that
    comes from this
that is like a stainless conch or kumuda flower, supremely white,
not tainted by the defilement of attention to my own aims
for the swift accomplishment of the victorious state of
    omniscience of all mother sentient beings.

I pray that the guide of the world, Tenzin Gyatso's life be long
    and stable,
and his aspirations spontaneously fulfilled,
and that all sentient beings be free from the multitude of
    misfortunes of the degenerate age
and nurtured by the glorious wealth and joy of Dharma.

In particular, may the beings of the Dharma region of Tibet
be free of current inner and outer suffering,
and swiftly and easily attain the good fortune to see
the smiling face of the protector of the land of snows.

*The Fourteenth Dalai Lama's Stages of the Path, Volume 2: An Annotated
Commentary on the Fifth Dalai Lama's "Oral Transmission of Mañjuśrī"* is
a compilation of commentaries on *Oral Transmission of Mañjuśrī* and
many other guides on lamrim treatises given by His Holiness the great
Fourteenth Dalai Lama to Dagyab Kyabgön Chetsang Rinpoché over
the years as a single treatise in the style of a supplement to *Oral Transmission of Mañjuśrī*. During the publication of the two volumes of *The
Fourteenth Dalai Lama's Stages of the Path*, sponsored by both the office
of the Ganden Phodrang and Tibet House Germany, the incomparable
supreme refuge Dagyab Kyabgön Chetsang Rinpoché, with a white
ceremonial scarf and ritual objects, instructed me, the Śākya monk
Samdhong Losang Tenzin, to compose this concluding prayer, that I
offer with faith.

Jaya jagata.

Appendix: Essence of Thought: A Summary of *The Fourteenth Dalai Lama's Stages of the Path, Volume 2*

Compiled by H. E. Dagyab Kyabgön Rinpoché
Translated by Chandra Chiara Ehm
Edited by Ven. Konchog Norbu

What is the philological meaning of the "stages of the path" (Tib. *lam-rim*)? What are the uncommon techniques to subdue the mind that are presented in the stages of the path? What are the origins and primary sources of the stages of the path?

This second volume provides the reader with answers to these foundational questions and concisely illustrates how the stages of the path are divided into three paths, taken up by persons of initial, intermediate, and higher motivation, and what distinguishes them.

From page 104 onward

This section discusses how there is no contradiction between the philosophical teachings and the teachings that lead to realization.

From page 114 onward

In the classical tradition of India's Nalanda University, stages of the path literature outlines a path from the preliminaries to the practice of tantra, integrating practice-oriented approaches from the Theravada, Mahāyāna, and Tantrayāna traditions.

Traditionally, stages of the path texts begin with an introductory chapter on how to rely on a spiritual teacher, even before embarking on the explanations on the practices of the person with an initial motivation. The reasons for this approach are presented here.

From page 115 onward

In order to correctly comprehend and cultivate reliance on a spiritual guide, a perfect human rebirth of leisure and opportunity, and so forth, it is vital to generate faith in and devotion to the Buddhist doctrine. Without such faith and devotion, those concepts are very difficult to transmit, and so this stages of the path commentary, *Oral Transmission of Mañjuśrī*, commences with a short introduction to refuge.

From page 131 onward

Before completely relying on a spiritual teacher, it is crucial to make use of the three methods to investigate a spiritual guide: one should investigate the teacher from a distance, from close by, and over an extended period of time. It does not make any difference if the spiritual guide is a lay person or a monastic. What is important is to rely on a teacher who embodies the distinguishing qualities that characterize a spiritual guide and who has spiritual realization.

This passage further clarifies how many teachers one should rely on, and what permutations there are of spiritual teachers and *tulkus*.[100] There are four options: (1) spiritual guides can be both a spiritual teacher and a tulku, (2) they can be neither one nor the other, (3) they can be a tulku but not a spiritual teacher, or (4) they can be a spiritual guide without being a tulku.

From page 139 onward

From the very beginning, the understanding of regarding the teacher as a buddha has been rooted in the higher paths. In contrast to the tantric approach, however, the Kadampa masters chose to keep this hidden.

[In the tantric context, the unsurpassable Indian scholar Atiśa (982–1054) commented in his *Guhyasamāja Lokeśvara Sādhana* that one should generate identical respect toward the Buddha and a spiritual guide.][101] One of Atiśa's students, Geshé Potowa (1027–1105), emphasized that a teacher can be respectively a buddha, a superior being,[102] or an ordinary being. Gampopa (1079–1153) explained how a teacher can manifest in four possible ways: (1) as an ordinary being, that is, a bodhisattva who is not yet a realized bodhisattva, (2) as a bodhisattva who abides on the higher grounds, (3) as a buddha manifesting in the form of the enjoyment body,[103] or (4) as a buddha manifesting in the form of an emanation body.[104]

According to the *Prajñāpāramitā* sutras the spiritual guide who teaches Mahāyāna Dharma can range from being a person who has not entered a path to a person who has attained complete enlightenment. A practitioner who is still a beginner, though, can only rely on a teacher who is an ordinary being and does not abide on the higher grounds.

From page 144 onward

The stages of the path literature commonly begins with a chapter on relying on a spiritual guide, since this serves as a preliminary condition for the tantric path. However, for someone approaching this literature who is completely new to Buddhism there might be some doubt as to whether the stages of the path should commence with such a chapter on relying on a spiritual teacher.

Therefore, when introducing the graduated path to enlightenment to the modern practitioner, it is essential to focus on foundational topics first. These topics, such as the explanations on dependent arising, refuge, the four noble truths, and the two truths (which exist in a causal relationship), should be explained in a logical and interconnected manner. Only in this way can the modern student comprehend the reasons why the teacher should be relied upon like a buddha. If the students are not introduced to the teachings through such a gradual approach, a danger persists that they might become confused and unsettled, and furthermore might not treat the tantric teachings in a respectful manner.[105]

There are certain traditions in which the practitioner is threatened with the torments of hell if they sever their relationship with their spiritual teacher. Those have strong similarities to theistic intimidations of hell awaiting those who go against the word of God. This kind of approach directly contradicts the Buddhist body of thought, which is to be proven through logical reasoning. Using threats has little benefit and is not harmonious with the attitude and predispositions of a contemporary practitioner.

This discussion is deepened here by shedding light on the reasons why the practice of the graduated paths to enlightenment presented in the traditions of sutra and tantra should be uncoupled and approached individually.

From page 145 onward

It is very rare to find proper devotion displayed by a genuine student, which never wavers despite the faults of the teacher. Devotion should not be based on superstition, but on a firm foundation of logical reasoning. When faith and trust are generated in this way, encountering a teacher's fault can actually strengthen our devotion and be the basis for realization.

From page 156 onward

If one is not supposed to question at all but is expected to regard the teacher solely as a buddha, a doubt may arise as to why scriptures such as Maitreya's *Ornament of the Mahāyāna Sutras* (*Mahāyānasūtrālaṃkāra*) place so much emphasis on the descriptions of the teacher as endowed with the qualities of a peaceful and tamed mind. It is vital to examine whether the teacher possesses the qualities of greater knowledge of the scriptures, ethical personal conduct, great compassion, and control over their attachments.

If the spiritual teacher is truly a buddha or a bodhisattva, those criteria are less relevant, as they are primarily suited for investigating the qualities of ordinary beings.[106] This is why the characteristics described in Maitreya's *Ornament of the Mahāyāna Sutras* and the request to see the teacher as a buddha can appear to be contradictory.

[As Geshé Potowa observes, "It is not about the teacher being a buddha, it is about how we perceive them."[107] Geshé Potowa here refers to the student's perception of the teacher, which depends on their judgment whether to view the teacher as a buddha or not.]

In general, a single teacher can manifest different appearances to different people. He can appear as a friend, as a foe, as an ordinary being, or as a buddha. This being the case, a spiritual guide, dependent on the student's judgement, can be a friend, foe, ordinary being, or buddha. How this concept is not contradictory is described in these pages.

Furthermore, the Dalai Lama has made very clear that there is a palpable need to create boundaries in terms of how vulnerable we allow ourselves to become when putting trust in teachers "displaying" different aspects to different people—teachers who oftentimes label their incorrect ethical behavior as an "inconceivable aspect" for their students.

There are stories in the collected biographies of the Buddhist mahāsiddhas, where the teacher's seemingly unethical behavior was used as a method to strengthen the student's faith and devotion. These were very unconventional methods for non-ordinary students and are surely obsolete today.

For ordinary students, this is an area that causes the greatest distress and confusion. It would be wise indeed to critically analyze the reasons given as to how appearances—the actual behavior of a certain teacher—and the reality of their qualities and characteristics should not be contradictory.

From page 166 onward

In the same way that Dromtönpa passed on the teaching to his student Geshé Potowa by transmitting the lineage of the scriptures, we should rely on our teacher through the scriptural teachings.

If the student trusts a teacher who does not possess substantial knowledge of the scriptures, who is unable to understand the teaching in detail and is therefore unable to compare the scriptures, then there is the danger that the student will develop misunderstandings regarding the study and practice of the Buddhist doctrine.

From page 220 onward

Within the explanations regarding the person with an initial motivation, the concept of reincarnation is discussed. Further discussed is the exploding number of newly recognized reincarnations of former teachers and tulkus, and how they are becoming a nuisance.

This section also addresses what it actually means to "relinquish this life." This does not only refer to abandoning attachment to this very lifetime, but also comprises the understanding that even with this aspiration one need not forfeit one's own happiness or quality of life.

The Buddha distinguished between temporal and ultimate attainments, clearly pointing out that for any kind of attainment, four complete perfections are required: wealth, aspiration, Dharma, and liberation.

At the same time as we concentrate on hearing, contemplating, and meditating, we should also contemplate the present and future well-being of all sentient beings. It is important to take responsibility for society as a whole and to develop a lifestyle that reflects this kind of socially and environmentally responsible attitude. This concerns living a life in which the mind of enlightenment, or *bodhicitta*, is authentically applied.

From page 259 onward

The descriptions of hell realms and the beings that dwell there did not originate in the Buddhist tradition but were already accounted for in the traditions of other ancient world cultures. This section carefully outlines the historical context of hell realms and explains how, due to individual karma, the perception of experiencing them is not necessarily an unchanging predicament.

From page 280 onward

The Buddha, who is supreme among humans; his teaching, the Dharma, which is free from all attachment; and the noble assembly, one's companions on the path—those elements that we commonly associate with Buddhist refuge can, according to the Dalai Lama, also be found in other religious traditions.

From page 308 onward

Citing five different reasons, this section illustrates why we need to keep away from the Dogyal Shugden cult.

From page 393 onward

In Asaṅga's *Compendium of Knowledge* (*Abhidharmasamuccaya*) "affliction" is defined as "a phenomenon that upon arising has the character of thorough disturbance; due to it arising it disturbs the mindstream."

When cultivating compassion, it's quite possible that one might encounter an unbalanced state of mind. However, in comparison to such an afflicted state of mind, the mind of compassion is generated deliberately. For this reason, the Dalai Lama proposes to rephrase the stated definition of "affliction" by adding the aspect of "involuntary," which would render it as "a phenomenon that upon arising has the character of thorough involuntary disturbance; due to it arising it disturbs the mindstream."

From page 420 onward

Today's understanding of pregnancy and birth is in some ways very different from that of the past. The traditional perception of becoming pregnant is one of attachment-based intercourse occurring during the right time of the month. However, in vitro fertilization could make it possible to store genetically flawless semen, ova, and embryos in banks [without relying on attachment-based intercourse]. There would even exist the possibility to choose the individual gender, constitution, body height, and skin and hair color of the future child.[108] Women who are in their sixties could make use of artificial insemination in order to achieve pregnancy [which would imply that pregnancy does not require that one has not reached menopause].

These modern approaches to birth and pregnancy do not at all contradict the law of karma but show us how important it is to cultivate an expansive and profound understanding of the subtle workings of the law of cause and effect.

From page 424 onward

In the phrase "dependent-related arising," "dependent" refers to the understanding that nothing arises without depending on its own causes and conditions; everything exists due to causes and conditions. "Arising," on the other hand, refers to the result that originates from a *similar* cause.

From page 468 onward

The first method to generate bodhicitta, commonly referred to in the Tibetan scriptures as the "seven-fold instructions on cause and effect," should be called the "seven-fold cause-and-effect instructions." The reasons for this are discussed here.

The second method for generating bodhicitta is the meditation of "exchanging self and others." Nagarjuna's *Precious Garland* (*Ratnāvalī*) mentions the term "tradition of vast conduct," the significance of which is shown in the context of the meditation of exchanging oneself with others.

From page 470 onward

Whatever compassion that we generate and cultivate in our daily lives is mainly aimed at those whom we perceive as kind toward us and does not include those who are in a position to harm us. This being the case, it is crucial to contemplate how much our compassion depends on the expression and behavior that others demonstrate toward us. Limitless compassion is not dependent on others being accommodating toward us; it is instead directed toward all sentient beings.

From page 476 onward

The motivation we generate to actualize love and compassion should not be influenced by the self-cherishing of "me" and "mine," but rather by the understanding that all sentient beings have the same aspiration and the same right to be free of suffering and obtain happiness, exactly like ourselves. Only with completely unbiased love and compassion do we have the appropriate conditions to generate a supreme intention and the mind of enlightenment.

When we express our love and compassion only toward those we are close to or those who show us good will, this only creates harm and is of no real benefit. In order to avoid this, emphasizing the meditation on equanimity from the very beginning is extremely important. "Equanimity" here by no means indicates indifference or a stoic passivity, but rather an attitude of immeasurable equanimity free of attachment and aversion.

From page 477 onward

When meditating on equanimity we initially contemplate someone who is close to us and another who we feel aversion toward. Afterward we widen the scope of our meditation to include the citizens of one nation that we feel personally close to, and those of another nation that are unappealing to us.

Upon attaining stability in our meditation, we expand the scope further to include all sentient beings.

From page 490 onward

An understanding of what enlightenment means is not by itself a sufficient cause to generate the authentic mind that strives for enlightenment. Enlightenment is attained through the potential of our own mind. This understanding should be repeatedly scrutinized through logical analysis, and such examination should rely on an in-depth understanding of the four noble truths, the meaning of liberation, and the different approaches to abandoning the mental afflictions.

Another important factor that is taken into account here is the understanding of the relatively gross and subtle levels of our mind; such an understanding is one of the causes to practice in the lineage of highest yoga tantra.

A great deal of attention should be given to the following quotation: "compassion observes sentient beings; wisdom observes enlightenment."

From page 503 onward

While developing and finally realizing the basis, path, and result in our mental continuum, sentient beings, both those who are related to us and those who are not, are of greatest importance. The boundless qualities of the buddhas, and the paths of the noble ones, exist because of sentient beings. For that reason, the magnificence of all the buddhas relies on sentient beings, because the buddhas' excellent qualities rely on the object and the path—which are none other than sentient beings.

From page 510 onward

This section elaborates in great detail the meditation of exchanging oneself with others.

As a first step, we equate ourselves with all sentient beings by recalling that we, like every sentient being, have the same basic disposition of wanting happiness and not wanting suffering.

Until this moment we have always pursued the bad habit of constantly placing ourselves at the center of the universe. This is exactly the pattern that has to be exchanged. We should share our advantages and benefits with others and take upon ourselves the disadvantages and detriment of others.

Even though right now we might not be able to practically be of benefit to others, it is vital that we at least refrain from harming anyone. This is the indispensable groundwork through which we can make use of the essence of our existence.

A truly good person not only cherishes such an attitude toward life but actually adopts it as a lifelong way of life.

From page 518 onward

Tsongkhapa (1357–1419), in both his shorter and his longer stages of the path texts, bases his explanations of the bodhicitta ritual and the bodhisattva vows on the ritual of conferral according to Atiśa.

From page 564 onward

The ethics of refraining from the ten nonvirtues is a central subject of all three of the paths taken up by those of initial, intermediate, and higher motivation, and are described in the stages of the path. This section further explores what differentiates the individual approaches to ethics of the beings of initial, intermediate, and higher capacity.

From page 623 onward

If the focus on placement meditation is too one-sided and disregards meditations concerning the method aspect, such as meditations of love and compassion, we might become apathetic and fall into a subtle state of lethargy.

From page 640 onward

The inability to completely abandon the nonexistent self as the object of grasping is the principal cause of attachment and aversion. Since the mind that apprehends "me" and "mine" is still able to locate such an object of grasping, the path to liberation is necessarily incomplete. While the grasping to a self is still endowed with an object of engagement, attachment and aversion are also still present. This is why this object of engagement has to be abandoned from its root.

In the process of understanding the self of phenomena, which is the object of negation, it is important to always remain vigilant. If each mental concept is apprehended as truly existent, then when trying to abandon those in order to realize selflessness, there would be the danger of falling into the extreme of nihilism.

In reality, all phenomena are merely imputed, and this very imputation itself exists only in dependence on dependent arising. Therefore, the perception of mental creations as truly existent, an actual cause of falling into nihilism, and of phenomena as imputed by way of being dependently arisen, the main cause for the correct understanding of the view of emptiness, stand in contradiction. This is one of the pith instructions of the Madhyamaka school.

From page 643 onward

This section offers an introduction to emptiness of self and the emptiness of other.

From page 648 onward

In short, it is critically important to comprehend the meaning of emptiness as dependent arising.

From page 673 onward

The meditations on the right view in the Mahāmudrā and Dzogchen lineages are mostly practiced in conjunction with stabilizing meditation. This is the same way that a practitioner of highest yoga tantra should meditate on emptiness.

In the sutra vehicle, special insight (only focusing on emptiness in this context) is always an analytical meditation, whereas within the practice of highest yoga tantra, special insight is characterized as a stabilizing meditation.

It is due to our virtue that we have access to such precious teachings.

Glossary

afflictive obscuration (*snyon sgrib, kleśāvaraṇa*). One of the two types of obscurations: afflictive and obscurations to omniscience. Emotional defilements and their seeds that prevent liberation from cyclic existence.

appropriated aggregates (*nyer len gyi phung po*). The five psychophysical aggregates of sentient beings that are acquired due to karma and affliction. They are the five aggregates of: (1) form, (2) feeling, (3) discrimination, (4) compositional factors, and (5) consciousness.

arhat (*dgra bcom pa*). Someone who has achieved the final goal of the śrāvaka and pratyeka vehicles. It is the attainment of nirvāṇa, where all mental afflictions and their causes have been destroyed, never to return.

ārya (*'phags pa*). A being who has achieved the path of seeing—that is, someone who has directly realized emptiness.

calm abiding (*gzhi gnas, śamatha*). A quiescence of mind gained through prolonged focus-based meditation as a way of gaining control over the mind to the point where one is capable of focusing the mind to one's own volition with ease and without distraction.

compositional factors (*saṃskāra*). Formative action concomitant with the production of karmic seeds causing future samsaric existence.

dharmakāya (*chos sku*). Dharma body. The buddha body that perfectly fulfills one's own welfare. It comprises omniscience and its factors of purity—that is, being devoid of natural and adventitious stains.

dharmadhātu (*chos dbyings*). The sphere of reality. Equivalent to ultimate truth, or emptiness.

four concentrations (*bsam gtan, dhyāna*). The four levels of the form realm in Buddhist cosmology.

four reliances (*rton pa bzhi*). (1) Relying on the teachings not the person; (2) relying on the meaning not the words; (3) relying on wisdom not the ordinary mind; (4) relying on the definitive teachings not the interpretable.

grounds and paths (*sa lam*). The path to buddhahood is divided up into five paths and ten grounds. There are specific boundaries for each, determined by one's level of realization.

high status (*mngon mtho, abhyudaya*). A fortunate rebirth in one of the three happy migrations of gods, humans, or demigods.

intended action (*bsam pa'i las*). An action of body or speech motivated by an intention.

karma of intention (*sems pa'i las*). The mental factor that formulates an intended action of body or speech.

mind generation (*cittotpāda*). Equivalent to bodhicitta. A mind that is concomitant with the aspiration to achieve full enlightenment for the sake of others, and is the entrance way to the Mahāyāna.

negative tendencies (*gnas ngan len, duṣṭhula*). Inducing further suffering because of being born into a negative situation.

nirmāṇakāya (*sprul sku*). Emanation body. A buddha's form body that fulfills the welfare of sentient beings.

obscuration (*sgrib pa, avaraṇa*). That which is either an **afflictive obscuration** or an **obscuration to omniscience**. See respective entries.

obscuration to omniscience (*shes sgrib, jñeyāvaraṇa*). That which obscures the knowing of all objects of knowledge. They are the imprints of the apprehension of true existence, together with the dualistic appearances that they cause.

placement meditation (*'jog sgom*). The two general divisions of meditation are (1) placement, and (2) analytical. Placement meditation involves unwavering attention on the focal object.

Prāsaṅgika (*thal 'gyur ba*). Middle Way Consequentialists. Mahāyāna followers of Candrakīrti and so forth, who reject intrinsic existence even on a conventional level.

pratyekabuddha (*rang rgyal, rang sangs rgyas*). Solitary realizers. Hīnayāna practitioners that achieve their respective level of enlightenment in their final lifetimes without relying on the instructions of other masters.

rūpakāya (*gzugs sku*). Form body. The buddha body resulted from the dharmakāya and exists for the welfare of others. It comprises the emanation and enjoyment bodies.

saṃbhogakāya (*long sku*). Enjoyment body. A buddha's form body that fulfills the welfare of ārya bodhisattvas.

spheres and sensory sources (*khams dang skye mched, āyatana*). In the categorizing of phenomena as found in the Abhidharma literature, the eighteen spheres comprise the six types of consciousness, the six sense faculties such as the faculty of the eye, and the six objects of those consciousnesses. This division is based upon each of these eighteen occupying its own "sphere" or entity. The twelve sensory sources are the six faculties paired with the six objects. This division is made on the basis of each pair being a source of a corresponding apprehending consciousness.

śrāvaka (*nyan thos*). Hearers. Hīnayāna practitioners who heard teachings from the Buddha and caused others to hear them.

Svātantrika (*rang rgyud pa*). Middle Way Autonomists. Followers of Bhāvaviveka who refute true existence with [faulty] lines of reasoning in which the members exist by way of their own character.

valid cognition (*tshad ma, pramāṇa*). An incontrovertible awareness.

whispered lineage (*bsnyan brgyud*). Secret tantric teachings that are not committed to writing, but instead passed down orally from master to disciple.

Yogācāra (*sems tsam pa, cittamātra*). A philosophical school of the Great Vehicle, whose core belief is that all existence is undifferentiated from the mind, and thus they do not accept the existence of external phenomena. Hence, they are also known as Mind Only.

Notes

1. This is an indication that not every word in the book was actually spoken by His Holiness. See introduction.
2. There is a discrepancy between *Oral Transmission of Mañjuśrī*, 2012, p. 147, and this text, p. 1. The former reads *zla ba'i* (of the moon) and the latter reads *bdag po'i* (of the lord/owner). After consulting other editions of the root text, the first reading is preferred, especially since it reappears further on in the commentary. The "nurse of the moon" is a metaphor for the ocean.
3. A buddha has thirty-two major and eighty minor marks.
4. An epithet of the Buddha.
5. The Tibetan word used here is *ma ma*, which can be understood as either a caregiver or an ocean.
6. Modes and varieties refer to ultimate truths and conventional truths, respectively.
7. The twenty-seven enlightened deeds are various activities related to placing beings onto the path to enlightenment.
8. The full verse reads: "That which through the knower of all leads hearers seeking pacification to peace, / that which through the knower of paths causes those benefiting migrating beings to achieve the aims of the world, / and through the perfect possession of which the subduers teach these varieties having all aspects; / to the Mothers of the buddhas as well as the host of hearers and bodhisattvas, / I pay homage." English translation by Toh Sze Gee & FPMT Inc., 2008.
9. The Tibetan tradition lists the following: (1) Mahākāśyapa, (2) Ānanda, (3) Śāṇavāsika, (4) Upagupta, (5) Dhītika, (6) Kṛṣṇa, and (7) Sudarśana.
10. *Mchod sbyin bdag po* is a synonym for *zla ba* (moon).
11. Rgyal dbang chos rje, *Rje'i rnam thar chen mo*, 588.
12. Rgyal dbang chos rje, *Rje'i rnam thar chen mo*, 747.
13. Ye shes rtse mo, *'Khrungs rabs*, 309. See also Kunga Gyaltsen.
14. Ye shes rtse mo, *'Khrungs rabs*, 308, 225.
15. Ye shes rtse mo, *'Khrungs rabs*, 304, 221.

16. Ye shes rtse mo, *'Khrungs rabs,* 313.

17. Ye shes rtse mo, *'Khrungs rabs,* 303.

18. Ye shes rtse mo, *'Khrungs rabs,* 216, 303.

19. Ye shes rtse mo, *'Khrungs rabs,* 214.

20. Ye shes rtse mo, *'Khrungs rabs,* 218.

21. Ye shes rtse mo, *'Khrungs rabs,* 221.

22. Ye shes rtse mo, *'Khrungs rabs,* 231.

23. Ye shes rtse mo, *'Khrungs rabs,* 315.

24. Ye shes rtse mo, *'Khrungs rabs,* 252–316.

25. Its lotus base measured 2.88 meters. The Maitreya statue itself was 7.11 meters. In total 9.91 meters in height, including the base.

26. An "arm span" is approximately six feet.

27. Ye shes rtse mo, *'Khrungs rabs,* 285.

28. This would be approximately forty-three hundred kilograms. According to the *Bod rgya tshig mdzod* dictionary, one load (*khal*) of barley is twenty containers, which is clearly [what we would call the equivalent of] twenty-eight half kilos (*rgya ma*) these days. Thus one load of barley is approximately fourteen kilograms.

29. One "bucket" is approximately forty to sixty liters.

30. Ye shes rtse mo, *'Khrungs rabs,* 282.

31. Ye shes rtse mo, *'Khrungs rabs,* 318.

32. Ye shes rtse mo, *'Khrungs rabs,* 220, 335, 256.

33. Rgyal dbang chos rje, *Rnam thar chen mo,* 750.

34. Dung dkar, *Dung dkar tshig mdzod,* 671.

35. Ye shes rtse mo, *'Khrungs rabs,* 311.

36. Ye shes rtse mo, *'Khrungs rabs,* 337.

37. It appears that Jé Gendun Gyatso was individually referred to as the "fifth throneholder of Tashi Lhunpo" and the "fourth Dharma regent." See Dzongtsé Thupten Jampa, *Chos grwa chen po,* page 7, where he writes "the first Dharma regent of the omniscient one, Panchen Sangpo Tashi; the second, Panchen Lungrik Gyatso; the third, Panchen Yeshé Tsemo; the fourth, the omniscient Gendun Gyatso . . ." Moreover, on page 85: "the second throneholder Panchen Sangpo Tashi . . ." Thus there are diverse lists that use the different titles "Dharma regent" and "throneholder."

38. Ye shes rtse mo, *'Khrungs rabs,* 385. Jé Gendun Gyatso's *rnam thar* states: "He came to the seat of Tashi Lhunpo in his thirty-seventh year."

39. Rebkong Jigmé Samdrub, *Gong sa,* 56–81.

40. Although this text reads *khri gsar* ("new throne holder"), his tenure ended several years prior in 1589.

41. Don dor and Bstan 'dzin chos grags, *Grags can mi sna,* 665.

42. *'Khrungs rabs* 2: 524–527.

43. *'Khrungs rabs* 2: 524–527.

44. *'Khrungs rabs* 2: 527.

45. Don dor and Bstan 'dzin chos grags, *Grags can mi sna*, 669.

46. Dung dkar, *Dung dkar tshig mdzod*, 1184.

47. Three authored by Tsongkhapa: (1) the *Great Treatise* (*Lam rim chen mo*); (2) *The Middle-Length Stages of the Path* (*Lam rim 'bring po*); (3) *Songs of Experience* (*Lam rim nyams mgur*); (4) Third Dalai Lama's *Essence of Refined Gold* (*Lam rim gser zhun ma*); (5) Fifth Dalai Lama's *Oral Transmission of Mañjuśrī* (*'jam dpal zhal lung*); (6) Panchen Losang Chökyi Gyaltsen's *Easy Path* (*Bde lam*); (7) Panchen Losang Yeshe's *Swift Path* (*Myur lam*); (8) Dakpo Gomchen Ngawang Drakpa's *Quintessence of Excellent Speech* (*Legs gsung nying khu*).

48. The second and third discernments are ordered as per Tsongkhapa's *Great Treatise on the Stages of the Path*, whereas the Fifth Dalai Lama explains them in reversed order.

49. Note that the order of the three in the root text of the Great Fifth does not match the order in the commentary.

50. These are the four powers of that tantric adept, which the *Dung dkar Dictionary* defines as "pacifying the harm of spirits; increasing lifespan, merit and wealth; gaining control over people and other beings; and defeating enemies."

51. The connotation of a "four-sided path" (*gru bzhi lam*) is probably completeness.

52. The mantra is *Oṃ svabhāvaśuddhāḥ sarvadharmāḥ svabhāvaśuddho 'ham.*

53. The complete verse is "You are the protector of all beings without exception / the deity who destroys the intractable legions of Māra / perfect knower of everything that exists / Bhagavān and retinue, I beseech you to come to this place."

54. His Holiness means that not all lamas are tulkus, and not all tulkus are lamas.

55. When teachers accept services and gifts with the motivation to fulfill students' desires, they themselves accumulate merit.

56. The sequence the Dalai Lama describes here—the two truths, the four truths, refuge, and so forth—corresponds to the ten Mahāyāna key instructions, which are taught in the *Abhisamayālaṃkāra*, a commentary on the *Prajñāpāramitā* sutras. In keeping with the Dalai Lama's intention, Dagyab Rinpoché composed the *Instructions Lamrim in 60 Verses* according to these ten key Instructions. Also, in this lamrim text, the explanations of how to rely on the teacher are explained only at the end of the teachings for persons of middle scope.

57. (1) Nāgārjuna, (2) Āryadeva, (3) Buddhapālita, (4) Bhāvaviveka, (5) Candrakīrti, (6) Śāntideva, (7) Śāntarakṣita, (8) Kamalaśīla, (9) Asaṅga, (10) Ācārya Vasubandhu, (11) Dignāga, (12) Dharmakīrti, (13) Ārya Vimuktisena,

736 THE FOURTEENTH DALAI LAMA'S STAGES OF THE PATH

(14) Haribhadra, (15) Guṇaprabha, (16) Śākyaprabha, (17) Atiśa. See volume 1 for the author's supplication prayer to the seventeen pandits.

58. The full verse is, "May the earth be pure everywhere, / Free of pebbles and so forth, / Even like the palm of the hand / And smooth like lapis lazuli." *Bodhicaryāvatāra*, verse 10.35.

59. "Sun of expounders" is an epithet of Mañjuśrī.

60. The full verse is "With the finest flowers, the finest garlands, / Music, ointments, supreme parasols, / Supreme lamps, and the finest incense, / I make offerings to the victorious ones."

61. The verse is from the *Samantabhadra Prayer*: "All negative deeds that I have done / With my body, speech, and mind / Out of attachment, anger, and ignorance, / I individually confess."

62. "To the Buddhas, those thus gone, / and to the sacred Dharma, spotless and supremely rare, / and to the Buddha's offspring, oceans of good qualities, / that I might gain this precious attitude, I make a perfect offering." (*The Way of the Bodhisattva*, Padmakara Translation Group, Shambhala, 2011.)

63. *Praṇidhānasaptatināmagāthā*, attributed variously to Gzhan la phan pa'i dbyangs Dgon pa pa and Āryaśūra (Beresford, 1979).

64. *The Confession of Downfalls* is otherwise known as the *Sūtra of the Three Heaps*, an excerpt from *Ascertaining the Vinaya*: *Upāli's Questions*. See bibliography.

65. The Tibetan text reads Ahmedabad, but Anandwan is where His Holiness famously went to see Baba Amte and his residence for lepers and the disabled.

66. The outlines "Going for refuge through commitment" and "Going for refuge by refusing to acknowledge other refuges" do not appear in this text.

67. Chang is a type of alcoholic beverage.

68. *Rigs kyis bsrung ba*, literally: protection (*bsrung ba*) by one's own character (*rigs*) in the sense of no willingness. This refers to an unmarried person who is not under the care of a family or another person and does not want to have sexual intercourse. (Dagyab Rinpoché)

69. The Dalai Lama explains this passage according to the customs of ancient India. This does not mean that he considers all the actions listed here to be unethical today. Furthermore, unethical behavior is divided into two categories: (1) unethical behavior by nature, such as rape and sexual abuse, and (2) unethical behavior by cultural custom. Even in former times, actions such as same-sex intercourse were not unethical by nature, but only by cultural habit. (Dagyab Rinpoché)

70. In this passage, the disregard for women in the Indian and Tibetan societies of the older time becomes evident. However, this attitude is still present in many areas even in our highly developed Western society, starting with different

payment for women and men for the same professional activities. (Dagyab Rinpoché)

71. This again reflects the disrespect for women in the ancient context. Yet even today in our highly developed modern society, it is still the case that women are subject to greater danger outside at late hours than men, and women are often still less respected in gatherings than men. (Dagyab Rinpoché)

72. In another edition, three more verses are mentioned that are not included in this text.

73. The five views are (1) view of the transitory collection (*'jig tshogs la lta ba*), (2) wrong views (*log lta*), (3) extreme views (*mthar 'dzin*), (4) holding wrong views as superior (*lta ba mchog 'dzin*), and (5) holding wrong ethics and disciplines as superior (*tshul khrims dang brtul zhugs mchog 'dzin*). The five non-views are (1) attachment (*'dod chags*), (2) anger (*khong khro*), (3) pride (*nga rgyal*), (4) ignorance (*ma rig pa*), and (5) doubt (*the tshom*).

74. The four acts of generosity are (1) material generosity, (2) generosity of Dharma, (3) giving protection from fear, (4) the generosity of love.

75. In Tibetan medical theory a combination illness is an imbalance of two humors. A compounded illness is an imbalance of all three humors (wind, bile, phlegm).

76. The Sera Je edition of the root text reads "not confused regarding karma and effect," whereas this text reads "confused regarding karma and effect."

77. These outlines do not exist in Panchen Losang Yeshe's *Swift Path*. They are also not the exact outlines in Tsongkhapa's *Great Treatise on the Stages of the Path*.

78. To be concomitant with a consciousness entails arising in its retinue and having concomitance by way of five factors: (1) same support, (2) same object, (3) same aspect, (4) same timing, (5) same substantial entity.

79. Neutral application (*'du byed btang snyoms*) refers to the situation in which there is no need to apply antidotes to laxity or distraction during calm abiding meditation.

80. Note from the author: In these verses "child," *bu*, is to be understood as a general term for son or daughter, as is the case in all treatises.

81. From Nāgārjuna's *Fundamental Wisdom of the Middle Way*: "One is liberated through having exhausted karma and affliction. / Karma and affliction derive from conception. / Those derive from elaborations. / Elaborations cease within emptiness."

82. (1) Mañjuśrī, (2) Avalokiteśvara, (3) Vajrapāṇi, (4) Maitreya, (5) Kṣitigarbha, (6) Akaśagarbha, (7) Sarvanivaraṇaviṣkambhin, and (8) Samantabhadra.

83. (1) Kāśyapa, (2) Ānanda, (3) Śāṇavāsika, (4) Upagupta, (5) Dhṛtaka, (6) Kṛṣṇa, and (7) Sudarśana.

84. This refers to King Tri Songdetsen and twenty-four subjects who received teachings from Guru Padmasambhava.

85. The five great forefathers of the Sakya tradition are (1) Sachen Kunga Nyingpo (1092–1158), (2) Sönam Tsemo (1142–1182), (3) Jetsun Drakpa Gyaltsen (1147–1216), (4) Sakya Pandita (1182–1251), and (5) Drogön Chögyal Phakpa (1235–1280).

86. The four great kings are (1) Dhṛtarāṣṭra in the east, (2) Virūḍhaka in the south, (3) Virūpākṣa in the west, and (4) Vaiśravaṇa in the north.

87. This refers to the mind going wherever its wind mount goes, and vice versa.

88. There are four concentrations (*dhyāna*). They constitute the four levels of the Form Realm in Buddhist cosmology.

89. Ci yang med pa'i skye mched, Ākiṃcanyāyatana, the third of the four formless realms.

90. The fifty-one types of mental factors are divided into seven groups in the literature. They are as follows:

> I. *Five omnipresent mental factors*: (1) feeling, (2) discrimination, (3) intention, (4) contact, (5) mental engagement. II. *Five object-ascertaining mental factors*: (6) aspiration, (7) belief, (8) mindfulness, (9) meditative concentration, (10) wisdom. III. *Eleven virtuous mental factors*: (11) faith, (12) shame, (13) embarrassment, (14) nonattachment, (15) nonhatred, (16) nonignorance, (17) effort, (18) pliancy, (19) conscientiousness, (20) equanimity, (21) nonharmfulness. IV. *Six root afflictions*: (22) attachment, (23) anger, (24) pride, (25) ignorance, (26) doubt, (27) afflicted view. V. *Twenty secondary afflictions*: (28) belligerence, (29) resentment, (30) concealment, (31) spite, (32) jealousy, (33) miserliness, (34) deceit, (35) dissimulation (36) haughtiness, (37) harmfulness, (38) nonshame, (39) nonembarrassment, (40) lethargy, (41) excitement, (42) nonfaith, (43) laziness, (44) nonconscientiousness, (45) forgetfulness, (46) nonintrospection, (47) distraction. VI. *Four changeable mental factors*: (48) sleep, (49) regret, (50) investigation, (51) analysis.

List provided by and under copyright of FPMT Education Services.

91. Note from the author: This citation appears to be worded slightly differently than that cited in the *Great Treatise on the Stages of the Path*.

92. Text reads *yod med brtag* but it is taken as a misprint of *yod min lta*.

93. Text reads *sgyu ma'i ltar snang* but is taken as a misprint of *rta glang*.

94. Text reads *mkhas pa 'gyur ba* but another source reads *mkhas rlom*.

95. Text reads *rang ngor shar ba rigs pas brtag pa na* but is taken as a misprint of

rang blos bzhag pa rigs pas bkag pa'i don in accordance with the commentary that follows here.

96. Read instead as published in His Holiness the Dalai Lama's *Lta ba'i dka' gnad gsal sgron* (SJRB-0154): *da lta rang re yi blo gsal 'ga' zhig | tshugs thub bden grub sogs brda la zhen pas | snang ba ling ling de rang sor bzhag nas | dgag rgyu rwa can zhig 'tshol bar snang ste |*

97. In Vedic history, the great sage Jahnu was disturbed by the waters of the Ganges and drank them up. He eventually released them from his ear.

98. The eight good features of water are sweet, cool, soft, light, transparent, clean, not harmful to the throat, and beneficial to the stomach.

99. A reference to the Manchu dynasty in China, the emperors of which were considered emanations of Mañjuśrī.

100. The literal translation of the Tibetan term *tulku* is "emanation body," or "emanation" in shorthand. Today the English designation for *tulku* is "reincarnate lama."

101. The explanation in brackets, that Atiśa does not proscribe viewing the spiritual guide as identical to the Buddha, is a supplement by Dagyab Rinpoché.

102. Skt. *ārya*. A person who has directly realized emptiness on the path of seeing.

103. The enjoyment body (Skt. *saṃbhogakāya*) is one of the four bodies of the Buddha. The enjoyment body is the form in which the enlightened mind appears in order to benefit bodhisattvas who are superior beings.

104. The emanation body (Skt. *nirmāṇakāya*) of a buddha manifests in various forms to ordinary sentient beings.

105. The request to rely upon the teacher like a buddha mainly applies to the tantric context.

106. If the teacher is already a buddha, there is no need to investigate these qualities, as they would be self-evident.

107. The explanation in parentheses is a supplement by Dagyab Rinpoché.

108. However, this kind of use of scientific possibilities is prohibited for ethical reasons.

Bibliography

Sutra and Tantra

Account of Sumāgadhā. Sumagadhāvadāna. Ma ga dha bzang mo'i rtogs pa brjod pa. D346, mdo sde, *am.*

Basis of Discipline. Vinayavastu. 'Dul ba gzhi. D1, 'dul ba, *ta*

Chapter of Kāśyapa. Kāśyapaparivartasūtra. 'Od srung gi le'u. Chapter of the *Basis of Discipline (Vinayavastu).* D87, dkon brtsegs, *cha.*

Chapter of Satyaka. Satyakaparivarta / Ārya-bodhisattvagocaropāyaviṣayavikurvāṇanirdeśa-nāma-mahāyānasūtra, 'Phags pa byang chub sems dpa'i spyod yul gyi thabs kyi yul la rnam par 'phrul ba bstan pa zhes bya ba theg pa chen po'i mdo. D146, mdo sde, *pa.*

Compendium of Sayings. Udānavarga. Ched du brjod pa'i tshoms. D326, mdo sde, *sa.* Translated by W. Woodville Rockhill as *A Collection of Verses from the Buddhist Canon.* London: Routledge, 1982. Revised ed. 2000.

Descent into Laṅkā Sūtra. Laṅkāvatārasūtra. Lang kar gshegs pa'i mdo. D107, mdo sde, *ca.*

Dhāraṇī of the Blaze of the Three Jewels. Āryaratnolkanāmadhāraṇī. Dkon mchog ta la'i gzungs. D847, gzungs, *e.*

Golden Light Sūtra. Āryasuvarṇaprabhāsottamasūtrendrarāja. 'Phags pa gser 'od dam pa mdo sde'i dbang po'i rgyal po. D556, rgyud, *pa.*

King of Samādhi Sūtra. Samādhirājasūtra / Sarvadharmasvabhāvasamatāvipañci-tasamādhirājasūtra. Chos thams cad rang bzhin mnyam pa nyid rnam par sprod pa ting nge 'dzin gyi rgyal po'i mdo. D127, mdo sde, *da.*

Kṣitigharba Sūtra. Daśacakrakṣitigarbha. 'Dus pa chen po las sa'i snying po'i 'khor lo bcu pa'i mdo. D239, mdo sde, *zha.*

Mahāparinirvāṇa Sūtra. 'Phags pa yongs su my a ngan las 'das pa chen po'i mdo. D120 mdo sde, *tha.*

Moon Lamp Sūtra. Candrapradīpasūtra. Zla ba sgron me'i mdo. See: *King of Samādhi Sūtra.*

Perfection of Wisdom in 8000 Verses. Āryāṣṭasāhasrikaprajñāpāramitā. 'Phags pa shes rab kyi phar rol tu phyin pa brgyad stong pa. D10, khri brgyad, *ka.*

Praise by Example. Upamāstava. Dpe la bstod pa. Contained in *Praise in Honor of the One Worthy of Honor.*

Samantabhadra Prayer. Samantabhadracaryāpraṇidhāna. Kun tu bzang po'i smon lam. Final chapter of the *Avataṃsaka Sūtra.* D44, phal chen, *kha.*

Sayings on Impermanence. Mi rtag pa'i tshoms. Contained in the *Compendium of Sayings.*

Sūtra Gathering All Threads. Āryasarvvaidalyasaṃgraha. 'Phags pa rnam pa 'thag pa thams cad bsdus pa. D227, mdo sde, *dza.*

Sūtra of Maitreya's Liberation. Byams pa'i rnam par thar pa'i mdo. Section of *The Stem Array.*

Sūtra of the Meeting of Father and Son. Pitaputrasamagamana. Yab sras mjal ba'i mdo. D60, dkon brtsegs, *nga.*

Sūtra of the Ten Teachings. Daśadharmakasūtra. Chos bcu pa'i mdo. D53, dkon brtsegs, *kha.*

Sūtra of the Three Heaps (The Confession of Downfalls). Āryatriskandhanāmamahāyānasūtra. 'Phags pa phung po gsum pa shes bya ba theg pa chen po'i mdo. D284, mdo sde, *ya.* English translation by Brian Beresford as *Confession of Downfalls.* Dharamsala: Library of Tibetan Works and Archives, 1993.

Sūtra Requested by Brahmā. Brahmāparipṛcchāsūtra. Tshangs pas zhus pa'i mdo. D158, mdo sde, *ba.*

Sūtra Requested by Sāgaramati. Āryasāgaramatiparipṛccha. 'Phags pa blo gros rgya mtshos zhus pa'i mdo. D152, mdo sde, *pha.*

Tantra Bestowing the Initiation of Vajrapāṇi. Vajrapanyabhiṣekamahātantra. Lag na rdo rje dbang bskur ba'i rgyud. D496, rgyud, *da.*

The Jewel Cloud. Āryaratnamegha. Dkon mchog sprin. D231, mdo sde, *wa.*

The Play in Full. Āryalalitavistara. 'Phags pa rgya cher rol pa. D95, mdo sde, *kha.*

The Stem Array. Gaṇḍavyūhasūtra. Sdong pos brgyan pa. Chapter of the *Āvataṃsakanāmamahāvaipulyasūtrā.* D44, phal chen, *ga.*

The Sūtra Requested by Revata. Nam grus zhus pa. Details not found.

The White Lotus of the Good Dharma. Saddharmapuṇḍarīka, Dam pa'i chos pad ma dkar po. D113, mdo sde, *ja.* Translated by Peter Alan Roberts as *The White Lotus of the Good Dharma.* 84000: Translating the Words of the Buddha, 2018.

Unraveling the Intention. Saṃdhinirmocana. 'Phags pa dgongs pa nges par 'grel pa. D106, mdo sde, *ca.* Translated by Buddhavacana Translation Group, Vienna, as *Unraveling the Intent.* 84000: Translating the Words of the Buddha, 2020.

Verses of the Nāga King Drum. No extant Sanskrit. *Klu'i rgyal po rnga sgra'i tshigs su bcad pa.* D325, mdo sde, *sa.*

Śāstra

Āryadeva. *Four Hundred Verses. Catuḥśatakaśāstranāmakārikā. Bstan bcos bzhi brgya pa zhes bya ba'i tshig le'ur byas pa.* D3846, mdo 'grel (dbu ma), *tsha.*

Āryaśūra. *Garland of Birth Stories. Jātakamālā. Skyes pa'i rabs kyi rgyud.* D4150, mdo 'grel (skyes rabs), *hu.* Translated by Jacob. S. Speyer as *Garland of Birth Stories.* New Delhi: Motilal Banarsidass, 1971.

———. *Compendium of the Perfections. Pāramitāsamāsa. Pha rol tu phyin pa bsdus pa zhes bya ba.* D3944, mdo 'grel (dbu ma), *khi.*

Asaṅga. *Bodhisattva Grounds. Yogācārabhūmaubodhisattvabhūmi. Rnal 'byor spyod pa'i sa las byang chub sems dpa'i sa.* D4037, mdo 'grel (sems tsam), *wi.*

———. *Śrāvaka Grounds. Yogācārabhūmauśrāvakabhūmiḥ. Rnal 'byor spyod pa'i sa las nyan thos kyi sa.* D4036, mdo 'grel (sems tsam), *dzi.*

Aśvaghoṣa. *Fifty Verses on Guru Devotion. Gurupañcāśikā. Bla ma lnga bcu pa.* D3721, rgyud 'grel, *tshu.*

———. *Praise in One Hundred and Fifty Verses. Śatapañcāśatkastotra. Brgya lnga bcu pa shes bya ba'i bstod pa.* D1147, bstod tshogs, *ka.*

———. *Eradicating Suffering. Śokavinodana. Mya ngan bsal ba.* D4177, mdo 'grel (spring yig), *nge.*

Atiśa Dīpaṃkara. *Bodhisattva's Garland of Jewels. Bodhisattvamaṇyāvalī. Byang chub sems dpa'i nor bu'i phreng ba.* D3951, mdo 'grel (dbu ma), *khi.*

———. *Lamp for the Path. Bodhipathapradīp. Byang chub lam gyi sgron ma.* D3947, mdo 'grel (dbu ma), *khi.* Translated by Richard Sherbourne, as *A Lamp for the Path and Commentary.* London: George Allen & Unwin, 1983.

———. *Commentary on Lamp for the Path. Bodhimārgapradīpapañjika. Byang chub lam gyi sgron ma'i dka' 'grel.* D3948, mdo 'grel (dbu ma), *khi.* Translated by Richard Sherbourne, as *A Lamp for the Path and Commentary.* London: George Allen & Unwin, 1983.

———. *The Two Truths. Satyadvayāvatāra. Bden pa gnyis la 'jug pa.* D3902, mdo 'grel (dbu ma), *a.*

Bhāvaviveka. *Blaze of Reasoning. Madhyamakahrdayavrttitarkajvālā. Dbu ma'i snying po'i 'grel pa rtog ge 'bar ba.* D3856, mdo 'grel (dbu ma), *dza.*

———. *Heart of the Middle Way. Madhyamakahrdayakārikā. Dbu ma snying po'i tshig le'ur byas pa.* D3855, mdo 'grel (dbu ma), *dza.*

Candragomin. *Letter to a Student. Śiṣyalekha. Slob ma la springs pa'i spring yig.* D4138 mdo 'grel (spring yig), *nge.*

Candrakīrti. *Clear Words. Mūlamadhyamakavrttiprasannapadānāma. Dbu ma rtsa ba'i 'grel pa tshig gsal ba.* D3860, mdo 'grel (dbu ma), *'a.*

———. *Entering the Middle Way. Madhyamakāvatāra. Dbu ma la 'jug pa.* D3861, mdo 'grel (dbu ma), *'a.*

———. *Seventy Verses on Refuge. Triśaraṇagamanasaptati. Gsum la skyabs su 'gro ba bdun cu pa.* D3971, mdo 'grel (dbu ma), *gi,* 251a1–253b2.

———. *Commentary on Āryadeva's "Four Hundred Verses." Bodhisattvayogācāracatuḥśatakaṭīka, Byang chub sems dpa'i rnal 'byor spyod pa bzhi brgya pa'i rgya cher 'grel pa.* D3865, mdo 'grel (dbu ma), *ya.*

Dharmakīrti. *Commentary on the "Compendium of Valid Cognition." Pramāṇavārttikakārikā, Tshad ma rnam 'grel gyi tshig le'ur byas pa.* D4210, mdo 'grel (tshad ma), *ce.*

Dharmamitra. *Vinaya Commentary. Vinayasūtraṭīkā. 'Dul ba'i mdo'i rgya cher 'grel ba.* D4120, mdo 'grel ('dul ba), *'u.*

Dignāga. *Compendium of Valid Cognition. Pramāṇasamuccaya. Tshad ma kun las btus pa.* D4203, mdo 'grel (tshad ma), *ce.*

Guṇaprabha. *Vinaya Sūtra. Vinayasūtra. 'Dul ba'i mdo.* D4117, mdo 'grel ('dul ba), *wu.*

Kamalaśīla. *Three Stages of Meditation. Bhāvanākrama. Sgom pa'i rim pa.* D3915–D3917 mdo 'grel (dbu ma), *ki.*

Maitreya. *Sublime Continuum. Mahāyānottaratantraśāstra. Theg pa chen po rgyud bla ma'i bstan bcos.* D1150, bstod tshogs, *ka.*

———. *Ornament for Clear Realization. Abhisamayālaṃkāranāmaprajñāpāramitopadeśaśāstrakārikā. Shes rab kyi pha rol tu phyin pa'i man ngag gi bstan bcos mngon par rtogs pa'i rgyan.* D3786, mdo 'grel (sher phyin), *ka.*

———. *Ornament for the Sūtras. Mahāyānasūtrālaṃkārakārikā. Theg pa chen po'i mdo sde'i rgyan gyi tshig le'ur byas pa.* D4020, mdo 'grel (sems tsam), *phi.*

———. *King of Prayers of Ārya Maitreya. Āryamaitreyapraṇidhānarāja. 'Phags pa byams pa'i smon lam gyi rgyal po.* D4378, mdo 'grel (bstan bcos sna tshogs), *nyo.*

Mātṛceṭa *Interwoven Praises. Miśrakastotra. Spel mar bstod pa.* D1150, bstod tshogs, *ka.*

———. *Praise in Honor of the One Worthy of Honor. Varṇārhavarṇastotra. Bsngags 'os bsngags bstod.* D1138, bstod tshogs, *ka.*

Nāgābodhi. *Understanding the Explanation. Rnam bshad rig pa.* Details not found.

Nāgārjuna. *Commentary on Bodhicitta. Bodhicittavivaraṇa. Byang chub sems 'grel.* D1801, rgyud 'grel, *ngi.* Translated by Thupten Jinpa as *Commentary on the Awakening Mind.* Montreal: Institute of Tibetan Classics, 2007.

———. *[Exposition on the Essence of] Dependent Origination. Pratītyasamutpādahṛdayavyākhyāna. Rten cing 'brel par 'byung ba'i snying po'i rnam par bshad pa.* D3837, mdo 'grel (dbu ma), *tsa.*

———. *Fundamental Wisdom of the Middle Way. Prajñānāmamūlamadhyamakakārikā. Dbu ma rtsa ba'i tshig le'ur byas pa shes rab.* D3824, mdo 'grel (dbu ma), *tsa.*

———. *One Hundred Verses on Wisdom. Prajñāśatakanāmaprakaraṇa. Shes rab brgya pa zhes bya ba'i rab tu byed pa.* D4328, mdo 'grel (thun mong ba lugs kyi bstan bcos), *ngo.*

——. *Precious Garland of the Middle Way. Rājaparikathāratnavālī. Rgyal po la gtam bya ba rin po che'i phreng ba.* D4158, mdo 'grel (spring yig), *ge.* Translated by Jeffrey Hopkins as *Buddhist Advice for Living and Liberation: Nagarjuna's Precious Garland.* Ithaca: Snow Lion, 1998.

——. *Letter to a Friend. Suhṛllekha. Bshas pa'i spring yig.* D4182, mdo 'grel (spring yig), *nge.* Translated by Lobsang Jamspal as *Nāgārjuna's Letter to King Gautamīputra.* New Delhi: Motilal Banarsidass, 1978.

——. *Sixty Stanzas on Reasoning. Yuktiṣaṣṭikākārikā. Rigs pa drug cu pa.* D3825, mdo 'grel (dbu ma), *tsa.*

——. *Praise of the Dharmadhātu. Dharmadhātustava. Chos kyi dbyings su bstod pa.* D1118, bstod tshogs, *ka.*

Ratnākaraśānti. *Instructions for the Perfection of Wisdom. Prajñāpāramitopadeśa. Shes rab kyi phar rol tu phyin pa'i man ngag.* D4079, mdo 'grel (sems tsam), *hi.*

Śāntideva. *Way of the Bodhisattva. Bodhisattvacaryāvatarā. Byang chub sems dpa'i spyod la 'jug pa.* D3871, mdo 'grel (dbu ma), *la.* Translation by the Padmakara Translation Group as *The Way of the Bodhisattva.* Boulder: Shambhala, 2006.

——. *Śikṣasamuccaya. Bslab pa kun las btus pa.* D3940, mdo 'grel (dbu ma), *khi.* Translated by Cecil Bendall and William Henry Denham Rouse as *Śikṣa Samuccaya.* New Delhi: Motilal Banarsidass, 1971, first published 1922.

Vasubandhu. *Treasury of Knowledge. Abhidharmakośa. Chos mngon pa'i mdzod.* D4089, mdo 'grel (mngon pa), *ku.*

Tibetan Works

Anon. *Clouds of Offerings to Please the Impartial on the Origins of Dogyal (Dol rgyal byung rim gzur gnas dgyes pa'i mchod sprin).* Details not found.

——. *A Jewel Garland of Scattered Texts: A History of the Succession of the Emanations of Ārya Lokeśvara ('Phags pa 'jig rten dbang phyug gi rnam sprul rim byon gyi 'khrungs rab deb ther nor bu'i phreng ba).* Dharamsala: Sku sger yig tshang, 1977.

Changkya Rölpé Dorjé. "Recognizing My Mother: A Song of the View" (*Lta mgur a ma ngos 'dzin*). In *Essential Commentary on Madhyamaka (Dbu ma stong thun chen mo).* Lha mkhar yongs 'dzin bstan pa rgyal mtshan, 1972.

Chekawa. *Seven-Point Mind Training (Blo sbyong don bdun ma).* Translated by Ruth Sonam as *Seven Points for Training the Mind.* Dharamsala: Library of Tibetan Works and Archives, 2014.

Dagyab Loden Sherab. *Instructions Lamrim in 60 Verses (Gdams ngag lam rim),* 2019. Translated by Gavin Kilty. Tibethaus Deutschland, 2021.

Dalai Lama Gendun Drup, First. *Song of the Eastern Snow Mountain* (*Shar gangs ri ma*). Translated by Johan van Manen as *The Song of the Eastern Snow Mountain*. India: Asiatic Society: 1919.

———. *Instruction Manual on the Seven-Point Mahāyāna Mind Training* (*Theg pa chen po'i blo sbyong don bdun ma'i khrid yig*). Details not found.

Dalai Lama Sönam Gyatso, Third. *Essence of Refined Gold* (*Byang chub lam gyi rim pa i khrid yig gser zhun ma*). Translated by Dr. Chok Tenzin Monlam as *The Essence of Superfine Gold: A Guide on the Stages of the Path to Enlightenment*. Dharamsala: Library of Tibetan Works and Archives, 2012.

Dalai Lama Ngawang Losang Gyatso, Fifth. *Oral Transmission of Mañjuśrī* (*Byang chub lam gyi rim pa'i khrid yig 'jam pa'i dbyangs kyi zhal lung*). In *Byang chub lam gyi rim pa'i khrid yig*, vol. 3. Yongzin Lingtsang Labrang, 2012.

Dalai Lama Kelsang Gyatso, Seventh. *Praise to the Noble Avalokiteśvara* (*'Phags bstod*). Translated by Gavin Kilty as *Praise and Prayer to Noble Avalokiteshvara: Bringing Forth the Rains of Happiness and Well-Being*. FPMT Education Department, 2014.

Dalai Lama Tenzin Gyatso, Fourteen. *Stages of the Path, Volume 2: An Annotated Commentary on the Fifth Dalai Lama's "Oral Transmission of Mañjuśrī"* (*Rgyal ba'i dgongs gsal: Byang chub lam gyi rim pa'i 'khrid yig 'jam dpal dbyangs kyi zhal lung zhe bya ba mchan bus bkral ba rgyal ba dgongs gsal mtha' yas skye rgu'i re ba kun skong*). Dharamsala: Dalai Lama Trust, 2016.

———. *Advice Regarding Dogyal: Part One* (*Dol rgyal skor gyi lam ston bka' slob dang po*). Dharamsala: Namgyal Monastery, 2010.

———. *Advice Regarding Dogyal: Part Two* (*Dol rgyal skor gyi lam ston bka' slob gnyis pa*). Dharamsala: Namgyal Monastery, 2010.

Dondor and Tenzin Chödrak. *Sources on the History of Tibet* (*Gangs ljongs lo rgyus thog gi grags can mi sna*). Lhasa: Bod ljongs mi rigs dpe skrun khang, 1993.

Dungkar Lobzang Trinlé. *Dungkar's Tibetological Dictionary* (*Mkhas dbang dung dkar blo bzang 'phrin las mchog gis mdzad pa'i bod rig pa'i tshig mdzod chen mo shes bya rab gsal*). Beijing: China Tibetology Publishing House, 2002.

Dzongtsé Thupten Jampa. *A Marvelous History of Tashi Lhunpo Monastery* (*Chos grwa chen po bkra shis lhun po dpal gyi sde chen phyogs thams cad las rnam par rgyal ba'i gling gi chos 'byung ngo mtshar dad pa'i sgo 'byed*). Dharamsala: Bod kyi dpe mdzod khang, 1991.

Gampopa. *Jewel Ornament of Liberation* (*Dam chos yid bzhin nor bu thar pa rin po che'i rgyan*). Translated by Khenpo Konchog Gyaltsen as *The Jewel Ornament of Liberation: The Wish-Fulfilling Gem of the Noble Teachings*. Ithaca: Snow Lion, 1998.

Gungthang Tenpai Drönmé. *Mirror Illuminating Words of Truth* (*Bden gtam de nyid gsal ba'i me long*). Lhasa: Zhol par khang.

———. *Verses of Advice for Meditating on Impermanence* (*Mi rtag pa sgom tshul gyi bslab bya tshigs su bcad pa*). Translated by Sean Price as *Verses of Advice for Meditating on Impermanence*. Lotsawa House, 2015.

Gyaltsab Darma Rinchen. *Ornament of the Essence* (*Mngon par rtogs pa'i rgyan gyi rtsa ba 'grel ba dang bcas pa'i rnam bshad snying po'i rgyan*). Translated by Toh Sze Gee as *Ornament of the Essence*. FPMT Education Department, 2008.

Gyalwang Chojé Losang Trinlé Namgyal. *Ornament of the Buddha's Teachings: The Biography of the Great Tsongkhapa* (*Rje tsong kha pa chen po'i rnam thar rgyas pa thub bstan mdzes rgyan*). Varanasi: Mtho slob dge ldan spyi las khang, 1967.

Khedrup Gelek Palsang. *Requesting Prayer to the Lamrim Lineage* (*Lam rim gsol 'debs*). Translated as "Requesting Prayer to the Lam-Rim Lineage Gurus," in FPMT Retreat Prayer Book. FPMT Education Department, 2016.

Kunga Gyaltsen. *The Amazing Twelve Deeds: The Biography of the Omniscient Gendun Drup* (*Bla ma thams cad mkhyen pa'i rnam thar ngo mtshar mdzad pa bcu gnyis*). Lhasa: Dga' ldan pho brang.

Langri Tangpa. *Eight Verses of Mind Training* (*Blo sbyong tshigs brgyad ma*). Translated by Ruth Sonam as *Eight Verses for Training the Mind*. Ithaca: Snow Lion Publications, 2006.

Longchenpa. *Resting in the Nature of the Mind* (*Sems nyid ngal gso*). Translated by Herbert Guenther as *Kindly Bent to Ease Us*. San Francisco: Dharma Publishing, 1975.

Pabongkha Rinpoché. *Heart-Spoon: An Exhortation to Remember Impermanence* (*Mi rtag dran bskul snying gi thur ma*). Translated by Lama Zopa Rinpoché and Jampa Gendun as *Heart-Spoon*. FPMT Education Department, 1994.

Panchen Losang Chökyi Gyaltsen. *The Sūtra Ritual of Bhaiṣajyaguru* (*Sman bla'i mdo chog*). Translated as *The Wish-Fulfilling Jewel: Concise Essence Sutra Ritual of Bhagavan Medicine Buddha*. Translator unknown. FPMT Education Department, 2003.

———. *Compassionate Refuge. Skyabs thugs rje ma*. No details found.

———. *The Easy Path: Naked Instructions on the Stages of the Path* (*Lam rim dmar khrid bde lam*). Translated by Rosemary Patton as *The Pearl Garland: An Anthology of Lamrims*. Veneux-Les Sablons: Éd. Guépèle, 2013.

———. *Guru Pūjā*. (*Bla ma mchod pa'i cho ga*). Translated as *Lama Chopa and Tsog Offering*. FPMT Education Department, 2020.

———. *Melody of Laughter of the Intelligent: Answers to Your Questions* (*Dri lan blo bzang bzhad pa'i sgra dbyangs*). Collected Works, vol. 4, 539–60.

Panchen Losang Yeshé. *Swift Path*. (*Lam rim nyur lam*). Translated by Toh Sze Gee as *The Swift Path: A Meditation Manual on the Stages of the Path to Enlightenment*. Boston: Wisdom Publications, 2023.

Panchen Yeshé Tsemo. *The Marvelous Jeweled Necklace: The Biography of Gendun Drup* (*Rje thams cad mkhyen pa dge 'dun grub pa dpal bzang po'i rnam thar ngo mtshar rmad byung nor bu'i phreng ba*). In *Garland of Jewels: The Lives of the Dalai Lamas* (*'Phags pa 'jig rten dbang phyug gi rnam sprul rim byon gyi 'khrungs rabs deb ther nor bu'i 'phreng ba*). Dharmasala: Mdo smad bdus spyi khyab rgyn las khang, 2015.

Patrul Rinpoche. *Words of My Perfect Teacher. Kun bzang bla ma'i zhal lung.* Translated by Padmakara Translation Group as *Words of My Perfect Teacher.* Boulder: Shambhala, 1998.

Potowa. *Blue Compendium* (*Don gyi lam rim beu bum sngon po*). Translated by Ulrike Roesler in *Stages of the Buddha's Teachings: Three Key Texts.* Boston: Wisdom Publications, 2015.

Rebkong Jigmé Samdrub. *Biographies of the Dalai Lamas* (*Sa tā la'i bla ma sku phreng rim byon gyi chos srid mdzad rnam*). Beijing: Krung go'i bod rig pa dpe skrun khang, 2013.

Sakya Pandita. *Clarifying the Sage's Intent* (*Thub pa'i dgongs pa rab tu gsal ba*). In *The Collected Teachings of the Sakya* (*Sa skya pa'i bka' 'bum*), vol. 10, 7–218. Sachen International, 2006.

———. *Treasury of Good Advice* (*Sa skya legs bshad*). Translated by John T. Davenport as *Ordinary Wisdom: Sakya Pandita's Treasury of Good Advice.* Boston: Wisdom Publications, 2000.

Songtsen Gampo (attributed). *Maṇi Kabum* (*Ma ṇi bka' 'bum*). Lhasa: Bod ljongs mi dmangs dpe skrun khang, 2013.

Thokmé Sangpo. *Thirty-Seven Practices of Bodhisattvas* (*Lag len so bdun ma*). Translated by David Tuffley as *The 37 Practices of a Bodhisattva.* Redland Bay: Altiora Publications, 2014.

Tsongkhapa. *The Great Treatise on the Stages of the Path* (*Byang chub lam rim chen mo*). TKSB, volume *pa* (*The Collected Works of Tsongkhapa.* Reproduced from the Tashi Lhunpo edition and reprinted in New Delhi by Ngawang Gelek Demo, 1980). Translated by the Lamrim Chenmo Translation Committee as *The Great Treatise on the Stages of the Path* vols. 1–3. Ithaca: Snow Lion Publications. 2000–2004.

———. *Abbreviated Stages of the Path* (*Lam rim bsdus don / Byang chub lam gyi rim pa'i nyams len gyi rnam gzhag mdor bsdus*). Also known as *Songs of Spiritual Experience* (*Lam rim nyams mgur*). TKSB, volume *kha, Thor bu.* Translated by Geshe Wangyal as "The Concise Meaning of the Stages of the Path." In *The Door of Liberation.* New York: Maurice Girodias Associates, 1973. Revised edition, Boston: Wisdom Publications, 1995.

———. *Abridged Chapter on Special Insight* (*Lhag mthong chung ba*). Found in Tsongkhapa's *Middle-Length Stages of the Path of Enlightenment.*

———. *Applying the Advice of the Three Jewels* (*Bla na med pa'i rin po che gsum gyi gtam gyi sbyor ba*). In *Collected Works,* vol. 2, 139–43. Labrang, 1999. TKSB, volume *kha.*

———. *Clarification of the Intent: An Extensive Explanation of Candrakīrti's "Entering the Middle Way"* (*Dbu ma la 'jug pa'i rgya cher bshad pa dgong pa rab gsal*). Translated by Thupten Jinpa as *Illuminating the Intent: An Exposition of Candrakīrti's "Entering the Middle Way."* TKSB, volume *ma*. Boston: Wisdom Publications, 2021.

———. *Commentary on the Ethics Chapter of Asanga's Bodhisattva Grounds (Byang sa'i tshul khrims le'u'i rnam bshad byang chub gzhung lam)*. TKSB, volume *ka*. Translated by Mark Tatz as *Asanga's Chapter on Ethics, With the Commentary of Tsong-Kha-Pa: The Basic Path to Awakening, The Complete Bodhisattva*. Lewiston: Edwin Mellen Press, 1986.

———. *Essence of Eloquence: Differentiating of the Provisional and Definitive Meanings (Drang ba dang nges pa'i don rnam par 'byed pa'i bstan bcos legs bshad snying po)*. TKSB, volume *pha*. English translation of the Mind Only section can be found in Jeffry Hopkins, *Emptiness in the Mind-Only School of Buddhism*. University of California Press, 1999.

———. *Foundation of All Good Qualities (Yon tan gzhir gyur ma)*. Translated by Geshe Wangyal as "The Foundation of All Excellence." In *The Door of Liberation*. New York: Maurice Girodias Associates, 1973. Revised edition, Boston: Wisdom Publications, 1995.

———. *Golden Rosary of Excellent Explanations (Legs bshad gser gyi phreng ba)*. Translated by Gareth Sparham as *Golden Garland of Eloquence*. Fremont: Jain Pub. Co., 2008.

———. *Great Chapter on Special Insight (Lhag mthong chen mo)*. TKSB volume *pa*. English translation by Lamrim Chenmo Translation Committee in *Great Treatise on the Stages of the Path to Enlightenment, Volume Three*. Ithaca: Snow Lion, 2004.

———. *Middle-Length Stages of the Path (Byang chub lam rim chung ngu)*. TKSB, volume *pha*. Translated by Philip Quarcoo as *The Middle-Length Treatise on the Stages of the Path to Enlightenment*. Boston: Wisdom Publications, 2021.

———. *Ocean of Reasoning: A Thorough Exposition of Mūlamadhyamakakārikā (Dbu ma rtsa ba'i tshig le'ur byas pa shes rab ces bye ba'i rnam bshad rigs pa'i rgya mtsho)*. TKSB, volume *ba*. Translated by Geshe Ngawang Samten and Jay L. Garfield as *Ocean of Reasoning: A Great Commentary on Nāgārjuna's "Mūlamadhyamaka-kārikā."* New York: Oxford University Press, 2006.

———. *Opening the Door to the Supreme Path: A Supplication Prayer for the Lamrim [Lineage] (Lam rim gsol 'debs lam mchog sgo 'byed)*. Found in *Byang chub lam rim gsung chos chen mo'i skabs kyi zhal 'don nyer 'kho phyogs bsgrigs*. India: Jangchup Lamrim Teachings Comittee: 2012. English translation found under the title "Requesting Prayer to the Lam-Rim Lineage Gurus" in *FPMT Retreat Prayer Book: Prayers and Practices for Retreat*. Portland, OR: FPMT, Inc., 2016.

Zhabkar Tsokdruk Randröl. "Repaying My Mother's Kindness" (*Ma yi drin bsab*). *Collected Works*, vol. 12, 549–54. New Delhi: Shechen, 2003.

Works Consulted by the Translator

Shakabpa, W. D. *One Hundred Thousand Moons: An Advanced Political History of Tibet, Volume 1 (Bod kyi srid don rgyal rabs)*. Translated and annotated by Derek F. Maher. Boston: Brill, 2010.

Index

A

Abhidharma, 33, 94, 188, 348
Acala, 11
Account of Sumāgadhā, 180
afflictions, 421, 449, 576, 614, 646
  aggregates and, 380
  arising of, 363
  birth as basis for, 372
  combinations of, 405
  controlling, 399–401, 410–11
  death and, 256
  degree of, 469
  destroying, 97, 436–37, 655
  dormant, 401, 402, 408, 602–3
  drawbacks of, 396–99
  ethical discipline and, 564
  excessive, 443
  five views and five nonviews, 395–96, 737n73
  guru's protection from, 168–69
  identifying, 394–95, 401, 402
  manifest, 602–3
  order of arising, 407
  purifying, focal objects for, 613
  reversing karma from, 356
  root of, 406
  selflessness in overcoming, 653, 674
  separation from, possibility of, 359–60
  six causes, 407–10
  on small- and middle-scope paths, 214

Tibetan and Sanskrit etymologies of, 411
afflictive obscurations, 289, 357, 647, 653
Age of Enlightenment, 263
aggregates, appropriated, 360
  aging and, 374–75
  as *appropriated*, meaning of, 367–86
  and Dharma practice, necessity for, 436
  as focal objects, 612
  grasping, 656
  in higher rebirths, 356
  name and form in, 429
  nirvana without remainder and, 282
  self of persons and, 354–55, 640, 665–66, 667–71
  as support for suffering, 367–68, 372–73, 378, 380
  in view of transitory collection, 403–4
  See also view of transitory collection
aging and death, link of, 430
Ajātaśatru, 349
Akṣobhya statue (Lhasa), 52
Aku Kunsang Tsepa, 48
alms, 109, 585, 588, 611
Altan Khan, 48–49, 50–52, 53, 54, 56
altruism/altruistic intention
  benefits of, 507–9
  of bodhisattvas, 400
  dependability of, 359–60

foundation of, 478–79
generating, 78
infallibility of, 499
in listening to Dharma, 91–92
mindfulness and introspection conjoined with, 588
as root of happiness, 516
See also bodhicitta
Amdo, 61, 72. *See also* Kumbum Monastery
Amitāyus, 237
Amoghasiddhi statue, 31
Amte, Baba, 254–55, 736n65
analogies and examples
bird's flight, 119, 136, 303, 351, 392, 688
butter lamp, 244
caste, 464–65
charcoal made from white sandalwood, 227
chariot, 656, 686
City of Sukhākarā, 516
for compounded phenomena, 89
criminal having hand cut off, 415
fire from two trees rubbing together, 678
hook without ring, 303
ice, 448
for illusion, 680
king and ministers, 359
magician's display, 657, 661, 662, 680–81, 682–84
mango seed measuring ocean, 15
mirror's reflection, 408, 659
nurse of the moon, 2, 3, 733n2, 733n5
pigeon returning to ship, 383
prisoner freed from prison, 358
prisoner in prison, 101
provisions for journey, 250

rope apprehended as snake, 406, 687–88
sky flower, 102
three faults of vessel, 94–95, 108
turtles, 8, 9
turtle's neck in yoke, 207–8
victory banner, 11
water bubble, 244
water poured into water, 667
well-paying job, 92
wish-fulfilling jewel, 10, 694
wish-fulfilling tree, 2, 3, 450
analysis, 738n90
calm abiding and, 609
emphasis on, 645
importance of, 93
and nonconceptual meditation, variant views, 672–76, 678–79
as obstacle, 673
analytical meditation, 606
ethical discipline in, 566, 569
in investigating "I," 660
patience, developing through, 575–76
and placement meditation, relationship between, 198–99, 675
purpose of, 675–76
on relying on spiritual teachers, 153
topics of, 198
See also special insight
Anavatapta Lake, 14
anger, 259, 603, 737n73, 738n90
analytical meditation on, 575–78
antidotes to, 396, 612, 613
in calm abiding, 619
controlling, 399, 400
drawbacks of, 572–73, 589
harm from, 499, 504
identifying, 402
objects of, 408

other afflictions caused by, 564
posture and, 176
self apprehension and, 661
Aṅgulimāla, 349
animals, 257, 258, 277, 583, 625
bardo body for, 419
bodhicitta and, 461
happiness of, 460
karma and, 342, 343
killing, 333–34, 340
liberating, 237
loving instincts of, 481, 483–84
numbers of, 210, 211
suffering of, guided meditations on, 269–71
annihilation, 642–53, 666, 683–84
antidotes, 350, 402
eight applications, 615, 616–23, 629, 635
types of, 395–96
Applying the Advice of the Three Jewels, 103
approach retreats, 37
arhats, 340, 349, 357, 394, 403, 461, 469
Array of Stalks Sūtra, 166, 170
ārya bodhisattvas, 160, 320, 341, 520, 521
Āryadeva, 364, 642. See also *Four Hundred Verses*
āryas, 155, 355, 658, 683, 739n102
Āryaśūra
Compendium of the Perfections, 458–59, 553, 563, 569
on focal objects, 614
Garland of Birth Stories, 78, 90, 267, 547–48
Seventy-Stanza Prayer, 197, 736n63
Asaṅga, 1, 21, 78, 81, 92, 696
on animals, 269

Bodhisattva Grounds, 78
Compendium of Knowledge, 394, 395, 617, 618, 620
homage, 7–9, 709
intent, 643
lineage, 22
Maitreya and, 152
as role model, 507
Śrāvaka Levels, 202–3, 607, 613
Ascertaining the Three Vows, 625
aspiration, 367–86, 600, 617, 628, 738n90
aspirational prayers, 192, 537, 555
aspiring bodhicitta
and engaging bodhicitta, difference in, 525–26, 529–30
possessing the commitment, 519, 522–24, 529
Ascertainment of Valid Cognition (Dharmakīrti), 26
Aśvaghoṣa
Eradicating Suffering, 387
Fifty Verses on Guru Devotion, 142, 143, 163, 164
Praise in One Hundred and Fifty Verses, 287–88, 297, 298
Atiśa Dīpaṃkara Śrījñāna, 1, 19, 46, 163, 230, 519, 674, 696, 739n101
Bodhisattva's Garland of Jewels, 11
on Candrakīrti, 651–52
Commentary on Lamp for the Path to Enlightenment, 130, 563
on gurus, relying on, 124
homage, 9–10, 14, 15
lineages, 22, 78, 79
on refuge, 113
scriptural tradition of, 11
serving, 567–68
in Tibet, 23, 703
visions of, 61, 195

visualizations, 179–81, 518
See also *Lamp for the Path to Enlightenment*
attachment, 230, 359, 737n73, 738n90
  antidotes to, 395–96, 612
  appropriated aggregates and, 367–86
  calm abiding and, 611
  cherishing others and, 499
  in contemplating karma, 345
  dormant, 402
  ethical discipline and, 564
  four types, 428
  helping others and, 576
  to impermanent things, 224–25
  laziness and, 595
  mind and, 259
  objects of, 408
  posture and, 175
  reversing, 370–71
  root of, 363, 639, 641, 642
  and self, dependency on, 360, 661
  in seven-fold cause-and-effect process, 475
  on small-scope path, 215
  at time of death, 419
  visualization for reducing, 401
Augustine, Saint, 262
Avalokiteśvara, 52, 300, 737n82
  Dalai Lamas as emanations of, 56
  in Kadam tradition, 11
  tapestry, 31
  Tibet and, 204
aversion, 176, 225, 230, 259, 345, 359, 363. *See also* anger
awareness
  erroneous and nonerroneous, 427, 447–48
  mistaken, 363, 449, 639–40, 663
  subtle, 673

B
bad conditions as aids, 582–83
bardo
  birth from, 420–21
  days measured in, 419–20
  establishing, 418–19, 429
basis of designation, 403, 641, 658, 662–63, 667–68, 671, 676, 685–86
basket of discipline. *See* Vinaya
basket of manifest knowledge. *See* Abhidharma
basket of sūtras, 93–94
Baso Tulku, 61
bathing ritual, 180–81
Bedi, Freda, 220–21
Bengung Gyal, 174, 402
Bhaiṣajyaguru, 31, 237
Bhāvaviveka, 642, 643
  Blaze of Reason, 21
  Heart of the Middle Way, 333, 617, 620, 621
Bimbisāra, 349
birth
  link of, 430
  suffering of, 367, 370, 371–72, 378, 384, 391
Bodhibhadra, 614–15
bodhicitta, 3, 15, 177, 458, 507, 693
  benefits, ten points on, 461–65
  bodhisattva conduct and, 214
  Buddha's, 502
  in calm abiding, 612
  centrality of, 454–55
  conventional and ultimate, 111
  dark and white practices regarding, 527
  as enlightenment's root, 452–53
  four causes, conditions, strengths, 467–68
  guarding, 524–27

human birth and, 206
increasing, 78
joy of, 500–501
losing, 466
sessions, times and amount, 526
special resolve and, 489–91
two aspirations in, 454
uncontrived, time in generating, 528
visualization, 178
vows, 523, 527, 528, 562–63
wisdom and, 647–48
See also aspiring bodhicitta; engaging bodhicitta; mind generation
bodhicitta ritual
  bodhicitta generation, 518–19, 521–24
  refuge in, 519, 520–21
  sections of, 517
  visualization, 517–18
bodhisattva conduct, 15, 78–79, 84,
  169, 529, 535–36, 541, 600. *See also*
  four ways of gathering disciples;
  six perfections
bodhisattvas
  abandonments of, 357
  afflictions of, 400
  anger of, 572
  anger toward, 572, 573
  bodhicitta of, 460, 461
  causes for, 462
  eight great, 22, 518, 737n82
  ethical discipline of, 565, 566
  lineage, 528
  love of, 463
  Mahāyāna and, 21–22
  merit of, 413
  refuge of, 302–3
  as spiritual teachers, 141
Bodong Panchen Choklé Namgyal, 30
body
  after death, 255

attachment to, 101–2, 419
casting off repeatedly, 387
causally concordant methods for
  acquiring, 346–47
as focal object, 614–15
fragility of, 243–45
generosity of, 558–59
impermanence of, 219, 232
karmic arising of, 258
projected and completed, distinctions, 330
rebirth and, 221
in selflessness meditations, 665, 685,
  686
suffering of, 374, 380
as supreme support, 435
three nonvirtues, 324, 325
at time of death, 248, 253, 254, 418
of wind and mind, 449
See also precious human body
Bökharwa Rinpoché, 49
Bön tradition, 73, 115, 377
Brahmā
  as creator, 405
  rebirth as, 384, 486
  refuge in, 118, 288
  voice of, 183, 296, 518
breath
  as focal object, 612
  in giving and taking meditation,
    511–12
  for meditative stability, 176–77
  and mind, at time of death, 415–16,
    417
buddha bodies, divisions of, 3. *See also*
  four bodies of buddha
Buddha Jewel
  eight qualities of, 283–84
  as excellent friend, 299
  reasonings on, 289–91

recollecting, 291, 294–98, 626, 627
refuge in, 118
as worthy of refuge, four other reasons, 298
Buddha Śākyamuni, 5, 7, 161, 712
buddhahood manifested by, 282–83
epithets, 2, 4, 733n4
images and representations, 31, 173, 312–13, 349, 413, 625–28
infallibility of, 321–22
in Kadam tradition, 11
karmic connection with, 457–58
lineage, 19
Mahāyāna teachings of, 20, 22
past lives, 153, 163
perception of, 152
praises, 1–7, 695
respecting, 443
reverence for, 89–90
as role model, 507
visualizations, 179–81, 517–18, 628
buddhahood, 457
aspiration for, 475–76
bodhicitta and, 462, 465
causes and conditions of, 3–4, 124
as close, 637
despondency regarding, 603
guru's proximity to, 167
method and wisdom required for, 537, 647–48
possibility of, conviction in, 597
time in attaining, 229, 453, 531
as union of two buddha bodies, 649, 695
Buddhajñānapāda, 152–53
Buddhapālita, 642, 643, 657
buddhas, 168, 471
body, speech, mind of, 283
emanations of, 160

karmic causality understood by, 320–21
sentient beings and, 502, 503
Tibetan etymology, 288–89
Buddhism, 308
analysis and investigation of, 293
modern science and, 77–78, 702, 705
and other religions, influences from, 260
refuge and, 113–16, 292–93, 316–17
self-reliance in, 251–52, 292
traditional, 145
See also Tibetan Buddhism
Butön, 12, 73, 625

C
Cakrasaṃvara, 11, 54
calm abiding, 198, 355, 531, 605–6, 660, 672
actualizing, 634–35
beginners in, 629
bodhicitta in, 612
and bodhisattva conduct, conjoined, 648–49
Buddhist and non-Buddhist, 607
causes and conditions of, 607–8
collections needed, 610–11
conceptualization in, variant views on, 674–75
ethics and, 446, 611
focal objects of, 612–15, 625–28
four trainings for, 199
higher training in concentration and, 440
induced by individual analysis, 677
neutral application in, 737n79
nine mental abidings in, 623, 629, 630–33, 636, 677
posture, 627, 628

purpose of, 646–47

relaxation and tightness, balancing, 628–29

self-grasping and, 639

session numbers and length, 628

similitude, 633–34

and special insight, order of, 609–10

and special insight, union of, 465, 606–7, 630, 675, 678–79

without special insight, 679

as wisdom's assistant, 606–7, 608–9

Candragomin, *Letter to a Student*, 205, 373, 459, 629

Candrakīrti, 642, 643, 651

Clear Words, 280, 281, 667, 686

Commentary on "Four Hundred Verses", 652

on "I" and "mine," 639

Seventy Verses on Refuge, 288

on two truths, 649

See also *Entering the Middle Way*

celibacy, 409, 446

Chakyung Drak, 55

Chamdzö Sönam Chöphel, 63, 66, 68, 70

Changkya Rölpé Dorjé, *Recognizing My Mother*, 666

Chapter of Kāśyapa, 678

Chapter of Satyaka, 295–96

Chayulwa Shönu Ö, 25–26

Chekawa Yeshé Dorjé, 25, 512. See also *Seven-Point Mind Training*

Chen-ngawa Lodrö Gyaltsen, 155–56, 700

Chen-ngawa Tsultrim Bar, 14, 15, 25–26, 30, 79

Chenpo Döndrup, 41

Chenpo Yönten Shenyen, 41

cherishing others, 492, 505, 511

advantages of, 469, 497–500, 502–3, 506, 522

bias in, 476–77

as great scope boundary, 84

See also self-cherishing

China

Fifth Dalai Lama in, 68–70

Fourth Dalai Lama in, 63

meditation in, 624

Third Dalai Lama and, 52, 53

Chinese Cultural Revolution, 397

Chödrak Gyatso, Seventh Karmapa, 39

Chöjé Jinpa Dargyé, 66

Chökhor Gyal Monastery, 40, 41, 42, 44, 47, 60

Choklha Öser, Panchen, 38, 39

Chökyab Sangpo, 23

Chökyi Gyaltsen, 185

Chongyé, 47, 66

Chongyé Monastery, 38

Chöphel Sangpo, 184

Christ, 262–63

Christianity

Buddhism and, 301

ghost stories in, 276

hells of, 261–63

meditation in, 607

refuge in, 291–92

in Tibet, 293

clairvoyance, 133, 335, 383, 404, 635, 636

clear appearance, 199, 308, 355, 678

clear light mind, 448–49, 490, 597

clear light of death/dying, 254, 327

cognitive obscurations. *See* knowledge obscurations

Collection of Indicative Verses, 92, 233–34, 240–41

Commentary on "Compendium of Valid Cognition" (Dharmakīrti), 26, 37, 280
  on bodhicitta, 524
  on Buddha's authority, 290
  on compassion, 499–500
  on karma, 394
  on love, 355
  refuge verse in, 304
  on self and afflictions, 406
  on suffering, 385
Communism, 398–99
compassion, 3, 251, 312, 395, 400, 507
  afflicted, 471
  biased, 475
  and bodhicitta, causal order, 467–68
  bodhicitta and, 452, 465
  of bodhisattvas, 102
  Buddha's, 297
  calm abiding and, 609
  dependability of, 359–60
  dependent on others' behavior, 470–71
  as Dharma's root, 311
  in giving and taking, 512
  guided meditation on, 488
  of gurus, 162
  habituation with, 500
  hearing, contemplating, meditating on, 93
  ignorance and, 355
  importance of, 474, 486
  observing sentient beings, 122, 490–91
  for others, suffering from, 488–89, 509–10
  refuge and, 286
  special resolve and, 524, 531, 532
  and wisdom, conjunct arising, 455

Compendium of Determinations, 306–7, 316
compositional action, link of, 427, 429
concentration, 738n90
  completing, 605
  first four perfections in achieving, 544
  gaze and, 176
  higher training of, 440, 634
  of non-Buddhists, 438
  treatises on, 78
  See also four concentrations (*dhyāna*); placement meditation
conception (biological), 420–21
Condensed Mother in Eight-Thousand Verses, 20–21
confession, 191–92, 564
  instructions, 349–50
  in session breaks, 199, 350
  verse, 736n61
Confession of Downfalls, 199, 736n64
consciousness
  of causal period, link of, 429
  concomitant by five factors, 471, 737n78
  as empty of existing by own nature, 283
  erroneous, 282
  as focal object, 612
  karma and, 319
  mistaken, 683
  primary, 259
  six types, 662
  subtle, 221, 223–24
  at time of death, 246, 418
  worldly, 683
contact, link of, 430
conventional truth, 538, 649, 650, 733n6
corpses, 248, 253, 263, 418

covetousness, 325, 337–38, 340

craving, link of, 428, 429, 433

creator gods, 251, 257, 291–92, 405, 447

cremation, 248, 255

crown protrusion, symbolism of, 182

cyclic existence (samsara)
definite rebirth in, 345
nature of, 101, 389
others' suffering in, contemplating, 456
renunciation of, 84, 364–66, 368, 412
stages of entering, 393
suffering of, 216
support for, 435

D

Dagyab Rinpoché, *Instructions Lamrim in Sixty Verses*, 735n56

daily practices
joyous effort in, 601
meditation, 196–97
virtue and nonvirtue, counting, 564

Dakpo Kagyü tradition, 58, 679

Dalai Lama lineage, 24, 51, 61

Damchö Gyaltsen, 185

Dampa, Khenpo, 498

Dampa Sönam Gyaltsen, 73

Dante, 262

Dantik Mountain, 55

Dantik Yangdzong, 72

Dargye-pa Pön Sönam Palsang, 30–31

Darma Rinchen, 185

Dartsedo, 71

death, 51, 286
black and white karma after, 325
causes of, 414
certainty of, 233–40
coarse mind at, 415–16

foundational attitudes toward, 219–25
helpers at time of, 416
joyous effort and, 595
manner of, 246
mindfulness of, 83, 231, 245–52, 263
mindfulness of, not cultivating, 226–30
in selflessness meditations, 668–69
subtle mind at, 416–17
suffering of, 367, 372–73, 377–78, 384, 391
time of, uncertain, 231, 240–45
virtuous mind at, 327
visualizing one's own, 252–55

debate, 33–34

dedication, 193–94, 197, 565, 695–700

definite goodness, 3–4, 7, 111–12, 206, 322, 361, 454, 696

definitive enumeration, meaning of term, 541

definitive meaning, 137, 349, 642

deities
haughty class, 275, 307, 308
meditational, 627
worldly, 307–8

deity yoga, 463, 627

demigods, 205, 206, 371, 381, 383, 396

Demo Tulku, 61

demons, 91, 153, 260, 261–62, 277

dependent establishment, 291, 631

dependent origination, 4–5, 119, 280, 281, 425, 658
and afflictions, loosening basis of, 396
of appearances, 363–64, 681–82
Buddha's unique teaching on, 291
of dependent imputation, 7
emptiness appearing as, 648, 683, 685, 704

ignorance and, 655
infallibility of, 642, 688
karma and, 319–20
reasoning of, 684–85
subtle, 5, 613
Descent into Laṅkā Sūtra, 651
Desi Sangyé Gyatso, 70, 74
desire
    antidote for, 613–14
    excitement as, 618
    posture and, 175
desire realm, 427, 430
    afflictions of, 635
    ethics and, 439
    gods, 382–83, 392, 419, 699–700
    rebirth in, 345
Devadatta, 152
devotion, 147, 152, 160, 161, 162, 165,
    169, 300
Dhāraṇī of the Blaze of the Three Jewels,
    147
Dharma, 96
    abandoning, 106
    accepting suffering from upholding,
    585
    bodhicitta in, 177, 178
    conviction based on reasoning in,
    292
    correct effort in, 122–23
    ethical discipline in teaching, 567
    explanatory and practical, lack of
    difference in, 105
    four greatnesses of, 108
    generosity of, 552, 554–55, 559, 692
    meaning, focusing on, 249
    mindfulness of death and, 226
    as noncontradictory, 100–103, 105
    profundity dependent on inclina-
    tions, 445
    pure origins of, 19, 20

refuge as heart of, 177, 178
reverence for, 89–90
styles of teaching, 115–16
texts, respecting, 313
dharma, meanings of, 289
Dharma Jewel, 306
    contemplating qualities of, 298–300
    eight qualities of, 284
    importance of, 118–19
    as object to be achieved, 82
    reasonings on, 280, 281
Dharma practice
    authentic, rarity of, 190, 211
    conducive conditions for, 610–11
    death and, 237–40, 245–52
    external and internal, 227
    as façade, 286
    for future lives, 323
    hardship in, 228–29
    potential for, 206–7
    self-assessment of, 276–77
    short- and long-term goals of,
    323–24
dharmadhātu, 35, 83, 179, 281, 289,
    305, 538, 539
dharmakāya, 2–3, 160, 182, 283, 456,
    536, 537, 538–39
Dharmakīrti, 26, 681–82. See also
    *Commentary on "Compendium of
    Valid Cognition"*
Dharmakīrtiśrī, 163, 172
Dharmamitra, *Vinaya Commentary*,
    302
Dharmatrāta, 81
Dharmodgata, 163
Dignāga, *Compendium of Valid Cogni-
    tion*, 281, 286–87, 290
disciples. *See* students and disciples
discouragement
    practice places and, 599

toward goal, 595–96
toward methods, 597–98
discriminating wisdom, 292, 412–13,
    608, 639–40, 675
discursive thoughts, 86, 135, 516,
    618–19, 621–23, 630–32
Dogyal Shugden, 71, 308–11
Dol Chumik Karmo, 71
Dönyö Dorjé, Rinpung Sakyong, 39
Dönyö Palden, 41
doubt, 737n73, 738n90
    antidote to, 193
    in bodhicitta, 159
    in gurus, 150–51
    imagined meditation and, 199
    importance of, 137, 148
    in instructions, 166
    in karma, 412
    three kinds, 403
downfalls, four doors to, 442–43
dreams, 657, 661–62, 680, 688
Drepung Loseling Monastery, 38, 52
    Fourth Dalai Lama at, 60, 62
    Great Prayer Festival and, 39, 44
    Second Dalai Lama at, 38, 41, 43
    stupas at, 56, 63
    Third Dalai Lama at, 47
Drogön Chögyal Phakpa, 73
Drokmi Śākya Yeshé, 163
Dromtön Gyalwé Jungné, 27, 135
    Atiśa and, 163, 567–68
    emanations, 34, 38, 46
    on four-sided path, 99–100, 735n51
    on humility, 162
    lineages, 23, 79
    Potowa and, 166
    praise for, 10, 15
    visions of, 61, 195
    visualizations, 180–81, 518
Dromtönpa, King, 314

Drongmepa Sangyé Gyatso, 73
Drophen Ling (aka Ngachö Gön), 71
Drophen Ling medical college, 68
Drupa Sherab, 26
dzogchen meditation, 176, 624, 673
Dzogé Aseng Lama, 48, 52

E
Egyptian religion, 260–61
eight worldly dharmas, 27, 83, 187,
    212, 278, 324–25, 351, 584
eighty mahāsiddhas, 161–62
eleven-fold practice combining mind
    training traditions, 504–5
emanation bodies (nirmāṇakāya), 141,
    160, 739n104
empowerments, 60, 61, 189
emptiness, 280, 413, 660, 696
    bodhicitta and, 464
    certainty in, 640
    clear appearance of, 355
    as dependent arising, 648, 683, 685,
        704
    elaborations ceasing within, 491,
        737n81
    endowed with all supreme aspects,
        647
    as hidden phenomenon, 321
    karmic causality and, 650–51
    meditation of middle and great
        scope persons, difference in, 647,
        648
    of one as emptiness of all, 687
    realized through reasonings, 653–54
    self- and other-, 643–44
    self-cherishing and, 496–97
    stages of, 21
    through hearing, contemplating,
        meditation, 112
    true cessations and, 366–67

enemies
  befriending, 506, 513
  patience toward, 580–81
  reflecting on, 504
  suffering of encountering, 378–79
  suffering of uncertainty and, 386
engaging bodhicitta
  and aspiring bodhicitta, difference
    between, 525–26, 529–30
  vows, when to adopt, 530–32
enjoyment bodies (saṃbhogakāya), 141,
    160, 739n103
enlightenment, 490
  for all sentient beings, 84
  bodhicitta as root of, 452–53
  Tibetan etymologies of, 81, 288–89
  time in accomplishing, 229, 453, 531
Ensapa Sangyé Yeshé, 49
Entering the Middle Way (Candrakīrti),
    26, 38, 670, 684
  on aggregates as self, 669
  on anger, 572
  on bodhisattvas, 462
  on compassion, 474
  on harming, 578
  on "I" and "mine," 406
  on joyous effort, 592
  on patience, 573
  reciting, 195
  on self and its emptiness, 671
  on view of transitory collection, 655
  on worldly consciousness, 683
environment, 222–23, 495, 556, 702
equalizing and exchanging self and
    others, 473, 504–5, 513
  benefits of, 502–3
  cherishing others, contemplating
    benefits, 497–500
  lineage, 469–70
  others prioritized in, 492–94, 510–11

outline, 491
Panchen Yeshe's five divisions, 492
Śāntideva's tradition, 501
self-cherishing contemplation, 495–97
through habituation, 506–7
See also giving and taking
  meditation
equanimity, 624
  in calm abiding, 623
  generating, 225
  guided meditation on, 477–78
  karma and, 329
  order of, 475, 476–77
ethical conduct/discipline, 93, 321,
    449, 588, 599
  calm abiding and, 446, 611
  enacting beings' welfare, 566–69
  as foundation, 354
  of gathering virtue, 565–66
  guarding, benefits of, 444
  identifying, 561, 563
  importance of, 445–46
  in leisure and opportunity, attaining,
    208–9
  of non-Buddhists, 438
  of restraint, 562–65
  six branches, 440
  ten nonvirtues and, 441–42
everyday life
  attitude in, importance of, 509
  cherishing others in, 497–98
  Dharma's influence in, 299
  self-cherishing in, 496
excitement, 738n90
  antidotes, 617–18, 620–22, 627
  beginner's, 122
  identifying, 616, 621, 628–29
  in mental abidings, 630–31
  over-application of antidote, 623
  time of, 624

existence
  craving, antidote to, 394
  link of, 428, 429
  through imputation, 664–65
  See also inherent existence; true
    existence
external objects, 643

F
faith, 738n90
  advantages of, 147–48, 156
  afflicted, 471
  arising naturally, 144, 151
  benefits of, 169
  in calm abiding, 617
  dependability of, 360
  followers of, 292
  generating, 197, 295
  grasping true existence and, 471
  high status and, 4, 7
  in holy beings, 97
  in karma and effect, 326
  in listening, 90, 91
  of others, respecting, 190
  rational and blind, distinguishing,
    147–49
  in refuge, 82–83, 286
  relying on gurus through, 134, 140,
    146–47
  in spiritual teachers, 116
  in Three Jewels, 121, 300
  through reasoning, 196, 279
  treatises for inspiring, 78
  and wisdom, balancing, 293
family and loved ones, 247, 379, 398
fear, 101, 208, 312, 342
  of death, 232, 246, 389
  female rebirth and, 347
  of lower rebirths, 264, 270, 272, 358
  protection from, 160, 737n74

refuge and, 121–22, 279, 286, 287, 300
  of strong compassion, 488–89
  in womb birth, 374
fearlessness, generosity of, 552, 555–56,
    559, 692
feeling, link of, 430
finger-pointing explanations, 91
five degenerations, 444, 452
five elements as focal object, 612
five faults, 616, 629
five great authoritative treatises, 67
focal objects
  four, 612–14
  and mind, relationship of, 620, 621–22
  that get to crucial point, 614–15
  variant views on, 615
  "wrong," 629
forgetfulness, 616, 617, 738n90
form realm, 383, 419, 439. *See also* four
    concentrations (*dhyāna*)
formless realm, 439
  four levels of, 613, 646, 738n89
  gods of, 383
four attentions (in mental abidings),
    630–32
four bodies of buddha, 13, 14, 282,
    283, 458, 490, 739n103
four concentrations (*dhyāna*), 440, 608,
    634, 635, 738n88
four continents, 187–88
four fulfillments, 222
four great kings, 518, 738n86
Four Hundred Verses (Āryadeva), 243,
    712
  on afflictions, destruction of, 655
  on emptiness, 687
  on nonmeritorious actions, 215
  on selflessness, 660–61
  on students, 136
  on suffering, 369

on two selflessness, order of, 652
four immeasurables, 178
Four Medical Tantras, 68
four opponent powers, 191–92, 358,
   443, 564
four powers of tantric adepts, 95,
   735n50
four seals, 224, 284–85, 302
four thought transformations, 115,
   216–17
four truths, 4, 354
   analogy for, 369–70
   analyzing, 322
   definitive enumeration of, 541
   dependent origination and, 363–64
   emptiness in understanding, 281
   liberation through, 459
   order of, 367, 368, 369
   relationship between, 365–66
   sixteen aspects of, 224, 440
   suffering of suffering and, 217
   three trainings and, 439
   twelve links and, 423–24
   See also individual truths
four types of birth, 371, 372, 430. See
   also womb birth
four ways of gathering disciples, 169,
   537, 606, 691–92, 694
four-fold retinue, 203
Fourteenth Dalai Lama's Stages of the
   Path Vol. 2
   compiler's colophon, 702–9
   concluding prayers, 709–14
   modern approach of, 705–8, 711
friends and companions, 312, 351,
   386, 389
Fundamental Wisdom of the Middle Way
   (Nāgārjuna), 26, 38, 684
   on aggregates, 668, 669
   on emptiness, 491, 737n81

on Madhyamaka as nihilistic, refuting, 640

G
Gampopa Sönam Rinchen, 130–31, 518
   Jewel Ornament of Liberation, 80,
      140–41, 142, 143, 156
   Milarepa and, 228–29
Ganden Jangtsé Monastery, 52, 583–84
Ganden Khangsar estate, 58
Ganden Nampar Gyalwé Ling, 58
Ganden Ngamchö festival, 71
Ganden Phodrang, 45, 310, 714
   democracy and, 75
   Fifth Dalai Lama and, 66
   founding, 68
   Fourth Dalai Lama and, 58–59
   power of, 70
   printing house at, 74
Gandenpa Miwang Yülgyal Norbu, 58
Ganga River, 67
Gelek Gyatso, 185
Gelek Palsangpo, Ganden Tripa, 48,
   183, 656, 676
Gelongma Palmo, 135
Geluk tradition, 128, 131–32, 643, 679
Gendun Drup, First Dalai Lama,
   24–25, 238–39
   birth and childhood, 28–29
   Instruction Manual on the Seven-Point
      Mahāyāna Mind Training, 35
   lineage, 88
   monasteries founded, 30–31
   passing, 35
   previous lives, 34
   sacred life examples, 27
   Song of the Eastern Snow Mountain,
      134–35
   supplicating, 183

teachers of and teachings received, 25–27

teachings and spiritual deeds of, 31–34

titles of, 30

visualization, 180–81

vows and ordination, 29

Gendun Gyaltsen, Ganden Tripa, 58, 59, 62

Gendun Gyatso Palsangpo, Second Dalai Lama

  birth and early childhood, 35–36

  as Drepung throneholder, 43

  lineage, 88

  monasteries founded, 40–41

  Palden Lhamo and, 42–43

  passing, 45

  public teachings, 40, 42

  recognition, 36–37

  spiritual deeds, 44

  supplicating, 183

  teachings received, 37–40

  titles, 734n37

  vows and ordination, 37

Gendun Tashi, 47

General Confession, 193

generosity, 3, 208, 209, 321, 588

  attitude possessing three features, 554, 555

  completing, 548, 560

  of Dharma, 552, 554–55, 559, 692

  and ethical discipline, relationship between, 570

  of fearlessness, 552, 555–56, 559, 692

  four acts, 400, 737n74

  in gathering disciples, 692

  habituating with, 593

  identifying, 547

  inappropriate objects and recipients, 558–60

  karma and, 345, 346

  of material things, 552, 556–57

  method and wisdom in, 539

  obstacles, antidotes to, 557–58

  outline of, 549–51

  practicing, 552–53

  ten kinds of recipients, 554

Genghis Khan line, 56

Genju Dutang, 52, 53

giving and taking meditation, 505, 511–12, 556, 693

gods

  birth as, 205, 209

  desire realm, 382–83, 392, 419, 699–700

  non-Buddhist, 117–18, 288, 405

Golden Light Sūtra, 235, 350

golden seal, 69–70

Gomang Khangsar Dorjé Chang, 254

Gomchen Rinchen Tsöndrü Gyaltsen, 54–55

grasping, link of, 428, 429, 433

grasping true existence, 112, 363, 395, 396, 427, 448, 449, 471

Great Fifth. *See* Ngawang Losang Gyatso, Fifth Dalai Lama

Great Prayer Festival (Lhasa), 39, 44, 45, 59–60

Great Treatise on the Stages of the Path (Tsongkhapa), 19, 684

  aspirational prayer in, 195

  on bodhicitta, 465, 466–67, 524–25, 529

  on bodhicitta ritual, 516–17, 519

  on bodhisattva conduct, 535–36

  context of, 143, 144

  on death, 231–32, 378

  on demigods, 383

  on exchanging self and other, 492

  on four greatnesses, 77

  on gurus, 127, 142

on habituation, 506
on heat at time of death, 418
on illness, 377
on karma and effect, 319, 327–28
on leisure and opportunity, 209
on liberation, 360, 361–62
on Madhyamaka, 664
on Mahāyāna, 453, 461
on medium-scope path, 423, 432–33
on merit field, 123
on method and wisdom, 539
on mind training, 472
on occasional and adjoining hells
   in, 268
Oral Transmission of Mañjuśrī and,
   64, 701
perfection treatises and, 79–80
on preparatory practices, 172
on refuge, 285
on relying on gurus, 126, 139–40, 165
representation of, 173
on Śākyamuni, 4
on session length, 122
on shared stages, 114
six perfections in, 544
studying, 198
style of, 16, 85
on suffering, 380–81, 384, 583–84
on three trainings, 440
transmission, 88, 701
on twelve links, 426, 430–31
great-scope-person's path
   arising of, 441
   bodhicitta in, 465
   goal, 458, 496–97, 649
   overview, 84, 455
   preliminaries, 454, 456
Greek tradition, 260
Guhyasamāja, 11
Guhyasamāja Root Tantra, 111, 112

Gunaprabha, *Vinaya Sūtra*, 165
Gungthang Tsang Tenpai Drönmé,
   227, 376
on Dharma, 249
on life, fragility of, 244–45
on mere name, 663
Mirror Illuminating Words of Truth,
   237–38
*Verses of Advice for Meditating on
   Impermanence*, 234–35, 236, 245
Guru Pūjā, 308, 503
guru yoga, 164–65, 179, 693
guru-disciple relationship, 131, 156,
   158, 555
gurus, 123, 194
   in bodhicitta ritual, 518, 519
   as buddhas, viewing, 89, 90,
      142–43, 145–46, 157–59, 739n101,
      739nn105–6
   etymology of, 125
   ordinary aspect of, 155–57
   serving, 164–66, 565, 567–68
   sutric definition, 126–27
   ways of viewing, 140–43
   See also spiritual teachers
Gushrī Khan, 68
Gushrī seal, 53
Gyalkhang Tsepa Paljor Gyatso, Ganden Tripa, 57–58, 734n40
Gyalsé Thokmé Sangpo, 73. *See also
   Thirty-Seven Practices of Bodhisattvas*
Gyaltengpa Chen-nga Rinchen Phel, 26
Gyaltsab Darma Rinchen, 26. *See also
   Ornament of the Essence*
Gyalwa Jampal Gyatso, Eighth Dalai
   Lama, 64–65

H

happiness, 258
   cherishing others and, 499, 502

contaminated, 358
in current life, 222
in equalizing self and others, 493–94
ethics as root, 444
everlasting, skillful means for, 364
in future lives, 218–19, 222, 279
karma and, 326, 329
of others, wishing for, 488, 501–2
through Dharma instructions, 92–93 ·
harm, 145, 508, 569, 599, 659
accepting suffering from, 582–87
from afflictions, 215, 230, 397, 410–11, 499, 504
analyzing, 575–78
attachment and, 230
bodhicitta and, 463–64
from Dogyal Shugden, 308–11
karma and, 341, 414
kindness toward, 513
malice and, 338–39, 340, 402
from meat-eating, 333–34
in past lives, 487–88, 565
patience and, 542–43, 575–81
from suffering of suffering, 217
harsh words, 325, 336–37, 340
Hashang (Chinese monk), 72
hatred, 257, 264, 338, 399, 499, 573, 639, 641, 642. See also anger
hearing, contemplating, meditating, 92–94, 105, 108, 117, 672, 673
Heart Sūtra, 91, 643
hells, 277
bardo body for, 419, 421
Buddhist, divisions of, 263
cold, guided meditations on, 266–67
gods' rebirth in, 383
hot, guided meditations on, 264–66
karmic effects and, 342
in non-Buddhist cosmologies, variant, 260–63

number of beings in, 210, 211
Occasional Hell, 268
proof for, 258–59
Tibetan etymology, 268
See also Reviving Hell; Unrelenting Hell
Helta Mongolians, 52
high status/higher realms, 696
accomplishing agents for, 3–4, 7
bodhicitta and, 454
eight qualities of rebirth, 206
falling from, 388–89
methods for achieving, 111, 115
as object of small-scope persons, 217, 218
six perfections and, 541–42
temporarily striving for, 323–24
See also demigods; gods; human birth
highest yoga tantra, 119–20, 143, 417, 490, 624
Hīnayāna, 6, 9, 10, 21, 489
Hindu tradition, 255
Homer, 260
Hong Taiji, 50–51, 56, 66
Hor Mongolians, 55
Hortön, 25
householders, 32, 445, 446, 552, 564, 586–87
human birth, 178, 252, 515
bardo body for, 419–20
in future lives, 323–24
karma of, projecting and completing, 343
as male, 346, 347
origins of, 257–58
See also leisure and opportunity; precious human body
hungry ghosts, 277–78
bardo body for, 419

beings included in, 273

bodhicitta and, 461

first-hand accounts, 273–76

karmic effects and, 342

number of, 210

suffering of, guided meditations on, 272–73

I

"I"

apprehending, multiple modes of, 407, 688

contemplating, 305–6

dependent imputation of, 360

investigating, 660, 661

See also self

idle chatter, 325, 337, 595

ignorance, 655, 737n73, 738n90

antidotes to, 193, 355, 612, 613

apprehending self, 360

basis of designation and, 662

lethargy and, 619

link of, 385, 426–27

as root of cyclic existence, 354

subtle levels of, 281

two kinds, 289, 403

view of transitory collection and, 406

ignorance grasping true existence, 353, 396, 448, 449, 655–56. See also grasping true existence

impatience, stopping, 579–80

impermanence, 89–90, 286

calm abiding and, 611

contemplating, 83, 225, 232, 263

excitement and, 621

foundational attitudes toward, 219–25

purpose of teaching, 216

subtle and coarse, 224

suffering due to, 385

imprints, 214, 215, 433, 469

of afflictions, 408

for bodhisattva conduct, 531

from emptiness, 672

karma and, 429

purifying, 612, 646

separation from, 449

temporary and perpetual basis of, 428

at time of death, 248–49, 250–51, 418

virtuous, placing, 224, 327

Indra, 388, 450

inexhaustible adornment wheels of three secrets, 283

inference, two types, 321

inherent existence, 413, 673

dependent origination and, 650, 658–59, 664

mistaken awareness of, 360

refutation of, 280

in selflessness meditations, 676, 686

in tenet systems, 354, 363, 395, 641, 643

instructions, 88

experiential, 85, 86, 432

explanatory, 85, 644, 702

generating respect for, 77–78

personal, 104–5

practice, 86, 701

intention, 738n90

in calm abiding, 620

fulfilling, 463

in ten nonvirtues, 332, 334, 335–36, 337, 338, 339

virtuous, 346

introspection

in beneficial activities, 588

in calm abiding, 607, 608, 618, 621, 628

in contemplating karma, 345
ethics and, 443, 444–45
in selflessness meditation, 672,
   676–77
in session breaks, 198, 199
sustaining, 355
Islam, 73, 261, 291–92, 293
Īśvara, 117–18, 288, 405

J
Jahnu, 696, 710, 739n97
Jambudvīpa, 240
Jamchen Chöden, 180–81
Jamchen Chöjé, 41
Jampa Rinchen, 700–701
Jampal Ngawang Losang Yeshé, 184,
   186
Jamyang Dewé Dorjé, 184
Jamyang Drakpa, 74
Jamyang Könchok Chöphel, Ganden
   Trichen, 67
Jamyang Lekpa Chöjor, 38
Jamyang Shepé Dorjé, 184
Jamyang Taklung Drakpa Lodro
   Gyatso, 179
Jamyang Wangyal Dorjé, 67
Jangchup Ö, 23
Jangchup Rinchen, 104, 567–68
jealousy, 192, 383, 508, 564, 738n90
Jenyé Monastery, 39
Jewel Cloud, 165
Jñānagarbha, 642
Jñānapāda, 615
Jowo Jampal Dorjé statue, 66
Jowo Śākyamuni, 52, 59, 66, 67
joyous effort, 599
   actual practice, 602–3
   in calm abiding, 617, 628
   cultivating, four powers in, 600–602
   divisions of, 593–94

hinderances to, eliminating, 594–99
   identifying, 591–92
Judaism, 261

K
Kachen Yongdzin Yeshé Gyaltsen, 64
Kadam tradition, 10–11, 99, 518, 701,
   709
   on dying, 246
   ethics in, 446
   four entrustments in, 586
   sevenfold divinity and teachings
      of, 11
   six treatises of, 78–79
   transmission of, 23–24, 33
   See also New Kadam tradition
Kadampas of Authoritative Treatises,
   78, 79
Kadampas of the Stages of the Path,
   79
Kadam Lineage of Pith Instructions,
   80
Kagyü traditions, 518, 643. *See also*
   Dakpo Kagyü tradition; Karma
   Kagyü tradition; Tshalpa Kagyü
   tradition
Kālacakra teachings, 176, 189
Kalkha Chökhur, 63
Kalön Tripa, 45
Kāmadeva, 486
Kamalaśīla, 642, 735n57. See also
   Three Stages of Meditation
Kamawa Sherab Ö, 25
Kangyur, 31, 56, 81, 105, 166
Kangyurwa, 67
Kantalipa, 153
karma, 96, 360, 421, 441
   aggregates and, 380
   beginning, 114
   body and, 243

certainty and magnification, 328
contemplating, 216, 326, 332
death and, 256
definite and not definite, 344–45,
    348–49
effects, three parts, 341–42
four doors to powerful, 341
fruition, eight qualities of, 346
guru's protection from bad, 168–69
hells' appearance and, 268
ignorance and, 427
of intention, 414
not performed/performed not
    wasted, 329
object, agent, action aspects, 320
potential of, 412–13
projecting, 372, 394
projecting and completing, distinc-
    tions between, 343
reasoning on, 279
rebirth and, 205, 251, 257–59
self-grasping and, 655, 661
in selflessness meditations, 670
on small- and middle-scope paths,
    214, 215
at time of death, 415, 416–17
very subtle, 322
white, black, and variegated dhar-
    mas, 324–25
wrong view of, 405
See also compositional action, link of;
    karmic causality
Karma Kagyü tradition, 39, 42
Karma Phuntsok Namgyal, 60, 61
Karmayama, 699–700
karmic causality
    calm abiding and, 609
    conviction in, 279
    and emptiness, as noncontradictory,
        650–51

foundational attitudes, 319–24
selflessness and, 654
wrong view of, 312
Kātyāyana, 415
Kebak (Chinese monk), 72
Kelsang Gyatso, Seventh Dalai Lama
    on death, 245
    on mere appearances, 661, 662
    Praise to the Noble Avalokiteśvara, 223,
        463–64
    supplication, 184
Kelsang Temple, 31
Khandro Kunsang Dekyong Wangmo,
    135
Kholo Chechin Batur, 53
Khöntön Paljor Lhundrup
    (Pabongkha), 1, 117, 701
    Fifth Dalai Lama and, 67, 74–75
    homage and supplication, 13–15, 184
    on merit field, 307–8
    vows, 48
Khunu Lama Rinpoché Tenzin Gyal-
    tsen, 95, 411
killing
    abandoning, 347
    complete act, 331, 332–34
    karma of, 345–46
    weights of, 340
kindness
    exceptional recollection of, 500, 503,
        504, 513
    importance of, 498
    of mothers, recollecting, 475,
        479–84
    repaying, guided meditation on,
        484–86
    of spiritual teachers, 116, 140, 141,
        152, 154–55, 156, 160–62, 199–200
    temporary benefits of, 508

King of Aspirational Prayers of Ārya Maitreya, 454
King of Samādhi Sūtra, 325–26, 444, 608, 625–26, 646, 679–80
knowledge objects, 297, 320–21, 448–49, 457
knowledge obscurations, 215, 320–21, 357, 497, 647
Könchok Chöphel, 66, 75, 701
Könchok Dalai Khan, 70–71
Kongbu Gyatso Temple, 31
Kṣitigarbha Sūtra, 90
Kumbum Monastery, 54–55
Kunga Delek, 37, 38
Kunsangwa, 26
Kyishö, 44, 53, 63
Kyormo Lung, 46

L
Lachen lineage, 29, 67, 71, 72–73
Lachen Rabsel, 72, 73
laity. *See* householders
Lamp for the Path to Enlightenment (Atiśa), 11, 79, 99, 140
  on focal object, single, 625–28
  on Jangchup Ö, 23
  on middle-scope persons, 356
  as model for stages of path genre, 10, 22, 100, 703
  Oral Transmission of Mañjuśrī and, 64
  on others' suffering, concern for, 455
  on vows, 562
Lang Darma, 10, 23, 72
Langri Tangpa, *Eight Verses of Mind Training*, 162–63, 564
Lantsa script, 29
laxity
  antidotes, 617–18, 620–21, 622, 627
  beginner's, 122
  identifying, 616, 621, 628–29

  and lethargy, distinguishing, 618, 619
  in mental abidings, 630–31
  over-application of antidote, 623
  subtle, 624
  time of, 623–24
laziness, 594–95, 616, 617, 738n90
leisure and opportunity, 101, 102, 116, 206, 212, 422
  contemplating, 83, 205–7
  difficulty, due to nature, 210–11
  difficulty of, analogy, 207–8
  difficulty of, cause, 208–10
  future lives and, 224
  identifying, 202–4
  investigating, 204–5
  purpose of teaching, 216
lethargy, 618, 619, 738n90
Letter to a Friend (Nāgārjuna), 81
  on animal birth, 269
  on confession, 349
  on ethics, 442
  on gods' signs of death, 382
  on hells, 266
  on hungry ghosts, 272
  on leisure, 202
  on life, impermanence of, 244
  on misdeeds done for others, 348
  on suffering, 386, 388
  on three trainings, 437
Lha Chenpo, 25
Lhamo Latso (lake), 40, 42–43
Lhasa, 39, 52, 61, 73–74, 274, 397. *See also* Drepung Loseling Monastery; Ganden Jangtsé Monastery; Great Prayer Festival (Lhasa); Sera Thekchen Ling Monastery
Lhasa Trülnang Temple, 48, 66
  Fifth Dalai Lama at, 67
  Fourth Dalai Lama at, 58, 59, 60

Lhasur Khangwa Sönam Lhundrup,
   25
Lhatsun Losang Tenpa, 43
Lhatsun Sönam Palsang, 183
Lhawang Chökyi Gyaltsen, 54
Lhodrak Namkha Gyaltsen, 24
liberation, 322, 360, 361
   conviction in, 449
   as dependent on oneself, 252
   difficulty of, 229
   identifying, 289–90
   motivations for, 100–101
   possibility of, 258–59
   as quality of mind, 311–12
   as state of peace, 361
   three trainings and, 447–49
   time in accomplishing, 323
   weak attitude toward, 433
life-accomplishing practices, 227, 237
lifespan, 240, 346, 347
   of animals, 270
   of bardo beings, 419, 420
   calculating, 239
   in hells, 266, 267
   of hungry ghosts, 273
   increasing, inability for, 237
   uncertainty of, 241, 244
lineages, 19
   profound view, 22, 78
   vast conduct, 22, 78, 470
Ling Rinpoché, 88, 95, 132, 254
listening, 87–88, 91
   benefits of, 90
   force of, 630
   generating reverence through, 89–90
   importance of, 92–96
   and meditation, integrating, 624–25
   sign of, 276
Lithang, 53. See also Thupten Jamchen
   Ling Monastery

Loden Sherab, 713
Longchenpa, Resting in the Nature of
   Mind, 80
Longdöl Ngawang Losang, 184
Lord of Death, 234, 391
Losang Chödrak, 184
Losang Chökyi Gyaltsen, Panchen,
   41, 62
   Compassionate Refuge, 252–53
   Easy Path, 88, 119, 143, 173, 174
   Fifth Dalai Lama and, 66, 67, 70, 75
   Fourth Dalai Lama and, 59–60
   Guru Pūjā, 119, 161, 308, 503
   Melody of Laughter of the Intelligent, 367
   supplication, 184
Losang Tenzin, 185
Losang Tsultrim Jampa Gyatso, 186
Losang Yeshé, Panchen. See Swift Path
   (Losang Yeshé)
Lotus Sūtra, 56
love, 355, 486, 507
   biased, 475
   in calm abiding, 609, 612
   generosity of, 552
   in giving and taking, 512
   guided meditation on, 487–88
   of mother for only child, 463
loving compassion, 467–68, 568
loving-kindness, 259, 398, 400
   eight qualities of, 486–87
   as foundation, 588
   preference for, 507, 508
lower realms, 370
   causes for rebirth in, 577, 595
   contemplating, guided meditations
      for, 264–73
   karma and, 205, 330, 344
   not falling to, 168
   suffering of, inevitability, 286
   virtue in, difficulty of, 208–9

See also animals; hells; hungry
ghosts
Lumpawa Yeshé Jangchup, 25
Lungrik Gyatso, 36–37
Luther, Martin, 262–63
lying, 325, 335–36, 340

M
Machik Labdrön, 135
Machik Shama, 135
Machu River, 49, 55–56
Madāshasi, Hasujas, 70
Madhyamaka tradition, 650, 663–64
finding view, 671
as free from extremes, 665, 666, 667
influence of, 658–59
Nāgārjuna in, 8–9
as nihilistic, refutation of, 640
of other-emptiness, 643
two subschools of, 641
See also Prāsaṅgika Madhyamaka;
Svātantrika Madhyamaka
Mahākāla, the Six-Armed Protector,
51, 54, 699–700
Mahākāśyapa, 300
mahāmudrā, 624, 673
Mahāparinirvāṇa Sūtra, 419
Mahāyāna, 6, 8, 21
bodhicitta in, 452, 466
entering, 461–65
generating path, 459–60
habituation from prior births, 468
method and wisdom in, 539
preliminaries to, 121–22
six perfections subsumed in, 543
sutra and mantra in, 465
in Tibet, 10
vastness of, 533
weak understanding of, 433
Maitreya, 32, 78, 300, 737n82

Asaṅga's perception of, 152
lineage, 22, 469
representations, 31, 173, 734n25
*Separation of the Middle from the
Extremes*, 615–17
visualization, 179–81
See also *Ornament for Clear Realization*; *Ornament for the Mahāyāna
Sūtras*; *Sublime Continuum*
malice, 325, 338–39, 340
Manchu Qing dynasty, 68, 739n99
Manchu River, 49
mandala offerings, 91, 187–88, 193
Mañjuśrī, 21, 78, 106, 300, 737n82
epithet of, 736n59
guru visualized as, 179
Khöntön Paljor Lhundrup and, 13,
14, 701
lineage, 22, 469
representations of, 173
Tsongkhapa and, 656, 683, 696
visualization, 179–81
Mañjuśrī emperors, 70, 702, 739n99
Mañjuśrīmitra, 153
mantras
carved by First Dalai Lama, 28
before Dharma teachings, 91
maṇi, 28
svabhāva-śuddhāḥ, 120, 179, 735n52
Mar Śākyamuni, 72
Māra, 158, 298, 647
Marpa Lotsāwa, 163, 518, 584
Mātṛceṭa
Interwoven Praises, 425
*Praise in Honor of One Worthy of
Honor*, 117, 297, 646–47
Maudgalyāyana, 300
meat-eating, 270–71
meditation
direct-gazing, 615

gaze in, 176
glance, 195
and reasoning, relationship of, 152
relaxation and, 623–24
sign of, 276
stabilizing, 94
sustaining, general, 196–97
meditation seat, 174–75
meditative equipoise, 538, 540, 677, 679
Melungpa Lochok Dorjé, 67
mental factors, fifty-one, 620, 738n90
mere imputation, 662, 682–83
mere name, 618, 657, 663, 664, 680
merely name, existing only by impu-
    tation, 642, 681
merit
  depleting, 253
  of five beings, rejoicing in, 192
  of gurus, 134, 735n55
  lifespan and, 237
  in material offerings, 164
  mind training and, 479
  recipients of, power and, 341
merit field
  beings included in, 307–8
  bodhicitta and, 462
  in bodhicitta ritual, 518, 519
  generating, 119
  guru as, 167
  in highest yoga tantra, 120
  inviting, 180
  recitation, 179, 736n58
  relying on, 123–24, 413
  serving, 565
  visualization, 179–81
Meru, Mount, 187–88, 269
Meru Dratsang, 65
method, 647
  six perfections and, 543

and wisdom, inseparability of, 452,
    537, 539–40, 649–50
Middle-Length Mother in Twenty-
    Thousand Verses, 20–21
Middle-Length Stages of the Path (aka
    Condensed Exposition on the Stages of
    the Path, Tsongkhapa), 80, 684, 700
  on bodhicitta, 529
  on bodhicitta ritual, 519
  occasional and adjoining hells in,
    268
  representation of, 173
  on special insight, 16
  studying, 198
  style, 85
middle/medium-scope-person's path,
    423, 478
  arising of, 441
  attitude in, 101
  bodhicitta in, 454
  goals of, 356–58, 455–56
  measure of, 432–33
  overviews, 83, 353–55
  shared paths, 440
  support for, 437
Milarepa Shepé Dorjé, 146, 163, 173,
    230
  on confession, 191
  on corpses, 248
  hardships of, 586
  on perseverance, 228–29
  visualization, 518
mind
  afflictions and, 400–401
  changing manifestations of, 259
  coarse and subtle, importance of
    distinguishing, 490
  controlling, 444–45
  experiencer as, 263
  levels of subtlety, 78

in selflessness of persons meditation, 665
taming, 196–97
three nonvirtues of, 325
at time of death, 248, 253
untamed, confronting, 601–2
mind generation, 305–6, 454–55, 491
power of, 282
practicing, 223
recitation verse, 124
recollecting benefits of, 526
without ritual, 517
of three persons, 113–14
mind training, 25, 32
benefits of, 515–16
and stages of the path treatises,
combined, 80
techniques, 78
two traditions, 472–73
mindfulness, 738n90
in beneficial activities, 588
in calm abiding, 607, 608, 617, 628,
631
ethics and, 443, 444–45
in selflessness meditation, 672, 677
sustaining, 355
Ming Wanli emperor, 62–63
miraculous powers, 569, 635, 636
miserliness, 187, 188, 557, 738n90
monasticism, 705–6
accepting suffering in, 585
ease in life and death in, 247
ethical discipline in, 563
misbehavior in, 315
repairing downfalls, 350
suffering in, 379
in Thailand, 313–14, 585
three changes of, 314
Möndröl Pandita Tsewang Döndrup, 67
Mongolia

and China, disputes between, 70
Dharma in, 50–51
Fourth Dalai Lama's birth in, 56
ritual sacrifices in, 50
Third Dalai Lama in, 48, 56
Tibetan presence in, 53
Mönlam Pelwa, 38
Moon Lamp Sūtra. See *King of Samādhi
Sūtra*
*Mother in One Hundred Thousand Verses
(Extensive Mother)*, 20–21
mother sentient beings, 457, 474, 475
guided meditation on, 478–79
repaying kindness of, 484–86
motivation, 178
ignorance as, 427
in karmic weight, 320, 340
in listening to Dharma, 95–96,
97–98, 137
in offerings, 173–74
in refuge, 303
by three poisons, 331, 333, 334, 335,
336, 337–38, 339
two types, 499
Mūlasarvāstivādin lineage, 72–73, 572
mundane path, 635

N
Nāgabodhi, *Understanding the Explanation*, 206
Nāgārjuna, 1, 21, 78, 92, 696, 704, 712
on Buddha, 5
Commentary on Bodhicitta, 81, 111,
112, 470
on gurus, qualities of, 129
on hells, 264
homage, 7–9, 709
intent of, 643
Jewel Rosary, 290
on liberation, 360–61

lineage, 22
on lower rebirths, 273
method of, 293
One Hundred Verses on Wisdom, 645
on positions, 642
Praise of the Dharmadhātu, 643
renown of, 651
as role model, 507
Sixty Stanzas on Reasoning, 282, 536,
    648–49, 652
on twelve links, 424
See also *Fundamental Wisdom of the
    Middle Way; Letter to a Friend; Pre-
    cious Garland of the Middle Way*
nāgas, 269, 273
Nālandā Monastery, 114, 161–62, 704,
    735n57
name and form, link of, 429
Namgyal Monastery, 273–74
Namkha Gyaltsen, 185
Nanda, 349
Nangdzé Dorjé, 184
Nāropa, 153, 163, 166
Narthang, 25, 26, 29
Nechung Dharmapāla, 275, 308
Nedong, 44, 45, 47, 48
Nelpa Sakyong Ngawang Lhunpo, 39
Nenying Gyalpo, 38
Nenyön grove, 68–69
Nesur, 14
neutral application, 477, 619, 623,
    737n79
New Kadam tradition, 11–12, 13, 26,
    518. See also Geluk tradition
Ngawang Chokden, 184
Ngawang Chözin, 185
Ngawang Jampa, 185
Ngawang Losang Gyatso, Fifth Dalai
    Lama, 75, 309, 310–11, 710, 712
    Autobiography, 73

in Beijing, 68–70
birth and recognition, 66
criticism of, sectarian, 71
Ganden Phodrang, 45, 70
Khöntön Paljor Lhundrup and,
    13–15, 67, 74–75
legacy, 75
names of, 701–2
passing, 74
regents, 70, 73
supplication, 184
teachings received, 67, 74–75
visualization, 180–81
vows and ordinations, 66–67, 71–73
written works, 75–76
See also *Oral Transmission of
    Mañjuśrī*
Ngawang Losang Thupten, 186
Ngawang Nyendrak, 185
Ngawang Tashi Drakpa, 44, 45
Ngok Lekpé Sherab, 38, 135, 180–81,
    195, 518
Ngorchen Kunga Sangpo, 73
Niguma, 135
nihilism. *See* annihilation
nirmāṇakāya. *See* emanation bodies
    (*nirmāṇakāya*)
nirvana
    cause for, 640
    of holy beings, 234–35
    of medium-scope persons, 357
    nonabiding/without remainder,
        282, 302, 391, 458
    partial, 456, 496
nonaffirming negation, 677
nonattachment, 544–45, 547, 738n90
nonconceptualization, 673–76, 678–79
nonhuman beings, existence of,
    275–76
nonsectarianism, 67, 73–74, 76

nonviolence, 4, 508
nonvirtue, 96, 177
  accumulating, 209
  of animals, 271
  confessing, 191, 192
  projecting, 330
  truth causing, 336
  See also ten nonvirtues
Norbu Sang, 183
Norbulingka, 238, 498
Norsang Gyatso, 40, 657, 664–65, 666
Nothingness level, 646
Nyang valley, 43, 700
Nyathri Tsanpo, 518
Nyingma tradition, 48, 74, 75–76, 518,
  643
Nyugrumpa, 462

O
object of negation
  identifying, 657–58, 660–62, 665–67,
    671, 685
  importance of understanding, 652
  as mere negation, 677
  in post-meditation, 680
  remainders, 642
  subtle, 663, 664–65, 686
obscurations to omniscience. See
  knowledge obscurations
Odé Gungyal, 38
offerings
  arranging, 173–74
  attitude during, 188–90
  to gurus, 164, 181
  merit from, 124
  recitations, 189, 191, 736n60
  tea, 189
  teaching Dharma for, 555
  water, 191
  See also mandala offerings

old age, 367, 370, 372, 374–76, 384, 391
Old and New Testaments, 261
Ölkha Dzingchi, 60
Ölkhawa, 39
omniscience, 3, 7
  causes and conditions for, 536
  conviction in, 449
  human birth and, 206
  knowing all modes and varieties of
    phenomena, 170–71
  possibility of, 259
  time in accomplishing, 323
Ön Tashi Dokha, 25
Önyer Kundun Rinpoché Chösang
  Trinlé, 58
Opening the Gate to the Supreme Path,
  195
Oral Transmission of Mañjuśrī, 704,
  712, 714
  all teachings subsumed in, 106
  Atiśa's homage, 9–10
  Buddha's homage, 1–7
  colophon, 700–702
  concluding verses, 693–94
  cultural context of, 705–7
  dedication, 695–700
  Kadam tradition in, 10–11
  Khöntön Paljor Lhundrup's homage,
    13–15
  Nāgārjuna's and Asaṅga's homage,
    7–9
  pledge to compose, 15–16, 451
  praise for, 694, 709–10
  preparatory practice, reciting, 196
  style of, 16–17
  sufferings in, order of, 381
  transmission of, 64–66, 88
  Tsongkhapa's homage, 11–12
  visualization in, suitability for, 120
Ordos, 52–53

organ donation, 556
Ornament for Clear Realization (Maitreya), 21, 735n56
homage, 7, 108, 733n8
on mind generation, 468
reciting, 195
on victors, attachment to, 471
Ornament for the Mahāyāna Sūtras (Maitreya), 36, 78, 541
on attention, 633
on bodhicitta, 468
on four ways of gathering disciples, 691
on joyous effort, 591–92
on knowledge, 171
on mental attention and wisdom, 198
on nine mental abidings, 630
on practice places, 610
on refuge, 305
on six perfections, levels of, 545
on spiritual teachers, qualities, 126, 157
Yogācāra tenets in, 129
Ornament of the Essence (Gyaltsab Darma Rinchen), 79, 529
Orö Mongolians, 52–53
other-emptiness, 643–44
other-powered, 360, 378
Outlines of the Stages of the Path to Enlightenment, 113

P
Pabongkha, *Heart-Spoon*, 253
Padmasambhava, 738n84
Palden Lhamo, 42–43, 55, 296
Palden Yeshé, 185
Pāli Dharma lineage, 114
Palkhor Dewa Chenpo, 43, 700
palms, joining, 182–83

Panchen, title of, 33
past life recollection, 220–21
path of accumulation, 141, 143, 299, 530, 531–32
path of meditation, 118, 635
path of preparation, 299, 344
path of seeing, 118, 635
patience, 588, 589
accepting suffering, 582–87
anger and, 504
benefits of, 573
of certitude in teachings, 587–88
completing, 572, 587
identifying, 571–72
impatience, stopping, 579–80
outlines, 573–75, 581–82
Patrul Rinpoché, *Words of My Perfect Teacher*, 80
Peak of Existence, 392, 451, 635, 646
Pehar, 308
perfection of wisdom, 452
divisions of, 536, 644–45
practice of, 649–50
preliminaries, 656
See also special insight
perfection of wisdom sutras, 89, 366–67
categories of, 20–21
commentaries on, 651–52
definitive meaning of, 642
on gurus, boundaries for, 141–42
intended audience, 21–22
lamrim and, 80, 81
on the Tathāgata, 290
Perfection Vehicle, 673
Period of Miracles, 31
perseverance, 589, 603
pervasive suffering of conditionality. *See under* three types of suffering

Pabongkha. *See* Khöntön Paljor Lhundrup (Pabongkha)
Phakdé Lotsāwa Ngakrampa, 47
Phakdru Desi, 44
phenomena
basis of designation, 658
compounded, nine analogies for, 89
dependent origination of, 364
self of, 354
summary, in calm abiding, 613
See also selflessness of phenomena
Phuchungwa Shönu Gyaltsen, 14, 15,
30, 31, 424–25, 432
Phuntsok Shenphen Monastery, 52
pith instructions, 79, 104, 105, 106
placement meditation, 198, 606, 673
and analytical meditation, relationship between, 198–99, 675
ethical discipline in, 566, 569
in investigating "I," 660
purpose of, 675–76
See also calm abiding
places of practice
any place as, 599
for calm abiding, 610–11
cleaning and arranging, 172–73
locations for, 88–89
Play in Full Sūtra, 239, 374–75, 376,
377
pledge beings, 119, 179, 295
pliancy, physical and mental, 738n90
analysis and, 610
as antidote, 617
in calm abiding, 608, 633–34, 636
in special insight, 630, 678
post-meditation, 679–81
posture
eight-point, 174, 627
for Mahāyāna refuge, 520
seven-point Vairocana, 175–77, 584

Potala palace, 68, 74
Potowa Rinchen Sal, 23, 30
Blue Compendium, 673–74
on gurus, 124–25, 156
Kadam Treasury of Gems, 140
on karma, 321
lineage, 78
on mandala offerings, 188
passing of, 166
praise for, 14, 15
on suffering, 389
Praise by Example, 294–95
Prajñāpāramitā in 8000 Verses, 173
Prāsaṅgika Madhyamaka, 319, 354,
395, 427, 641
pratyekabuddha path, 98, 302–3, 459
enlightenment in, 520
love on, 298
meditation objects of, 647
realization of, 465
surpassing, 461–62
Prayer of Samantabhadra, 187, 197,
736n61
preceptor-patron relationships, 50,
53, 60
Precious Garland of the Middle Way
(Nāgārjuna), 3–4, 22, 81, 503, 598
audience for, 112
on bodhicitta, 451–52
on buddhas, marks of, 453
on death, causes for, 242
on Dharma, difficulty of, 650
on equalizing and exchanging self
and others, 470
on faith and wisdom, 7
on giving and taking, 511
on higher rebirths, 111
on love, 486
on self-grasping, 655
on virtue and nonvirtue, 325

precious human body, 271, 460,
　500, 583. *See also* leisure and
　opportunity
preliminaries and preparatory
　practices
　and actual practices, distinguishing,
　　107–8
　concluding, 197
　reciting, 196
　relying on spiritual teachers as, 144
　small and middle-scope paths as,
　　113–14, 214, 218
　See also seven-limb practice
pride, 151, 580, 737n73, 738n90
　antidotes to, 182, 613
　controlling, 399
　in Dharma practice, 276
　divine, 308
　thrones and, 90
　types, 402–3, 600–601
Proponents of Existence, 640
prostrations, 89, 628
　in confession, 349
　instructions, 182–83
　in session breaks, 199
　supplication during, 183–87
Purchok Ngawang Jampa, 182
pure appearance, 28, 135, 142, 157,
　200, 310
pure perception, 151, 159

R
Rabjampa Sönam Drakpa, 61
Rabjampa Tsultrim Öser, 41
Rachen Lotsāwa, 62
reasoning
　in equalizing and exchanging self
　　and others, 470
　liberation and, 447–48
　one or many, 665–71, 684, 685

in relying on gurus, 148–49, 152
scripture and, 77
sevenfold, 656–57, 684
rebirth, 102, 263, 389
　certainty in, 203
　doubts about, eliminating, 220–22
　imprints and, 248–49
　karma and, 205, 251, 257–59
　karma at time of death and, 416–18
　repeated, suffering of, 388
　in selflessness meditation, 668–70
　small scope persons and, 83
recitations, advice for, 195–96
refuge, 280, 693
　in abandoning nonvirtue, 279
　actual, basis for, 319
　based on emptiness, 281, 289
　based on faith gained through wis-
　　dom, 292
　based on superior distinctions,
　　300–302
　causal, 303
　causes of, 285–87
　common and uncommon, 121–22,
　　284–85
　in defining Buddhists, 113–16, 292–93,
　　316–17
　higher rebirths and, 219
　and karma, relationship of, 322
　losing, 317
　Mahāyāna, 304, 305, 519, 520–21
　purpose, 123–24, 520
　suitability for, 196
refuge objects, 117–19, 286–87
　distinct Mahāyāna, 520
　identifying, 287–91
　qualities, recollection of, 303
　for small and middle scope persons,
　　82–83
　visualizing, 119

worldly gods, 307–11

refuge prayers
  accumulating, 120–21, 122
  verses, 122, 123, 303–4, 520–21

refuge precepts, 306–7
  amount and time of taking, 315
  benefits of, 315–18
  in *Compendium of Determinations*,
    306–7, 316
  prescriptive, 312–15
  proscriptive, 307–12

regret, 191–92, 230, 553, 564

rejoicing, 192, 565

relics, 63, 235

religious communities, 399

relying on spiritual teachers, 112, 467
  analytical and placement meditation
    on, 198
  benefits of, 167–69
  contemplations, 149–50, 153–54
  disadvantages of not, 170
  order of teaching, 113–16
  in prayers, 171
  as preliminary practice, 144
  as root of path, 124–26
  suitable number, 134–35
  sustaining meditation on, 197
  in sutra and tantra, intentions of,
    157–59
  through faith, 134, 146–47
  through practice, 163–67
  through requisites, 134
  through wisdom, 134

renunciation, 358, 361, 451
  in confession, 349
  of cyclic existence, 84, 364–66, 368,
    412
  fleeting, 579
  through four thought transforma-
    tions, 216–17

result not corresponding to cause, 282

Reting Monastery, 23, 38, 49, 58, 66,
  195

Reviving Hell, 264–65, 266

Rigzin Tenpa Rinpoché, 195

Rikzin Terdak Lingpa, 67

Rinchen Ling, 60

Rinchen Sangpo, 72

Rinpung family, 39, 44, 48

Riwo Dechen, 39

roots of virtue, 305, 536, 572, 579

rūpakāya, 2–3, 182, 283, 536, 537,
  538–39

S

Sadāprarudita, 163, 171

Sakya Pandita Kunga Gyaltsen, 72–73
  Clarifying the Sage's Intent, 80
  Treasury of Good Advice, 293

Sakya tradition, 643, 679
  Fifth Dalai Lama and, 67, 75
  five great forefathers, 518, 738n85
  "four explanations" of, 86–87
  patron relationships, 50
  Second Dalai Lama and, 42

Śākyaśrībhadra lineage, 72, 73

Samantabhadra Prayer, 518, 521

samaya beings. *See* pledge beings

saṃbhogakāya. *See* enjoyment bodies
  (*saṃbhogakāya*)

Samding Dorjé Phakmo, 135

Samdhong Losang Tenzin, 714

Sāmkhya tradition, 243

samsara. *See* cyclic existence (samsara)

Samyé Monastery, 38

Sangha Jewel, 284, 300, 306, 313–15

Sangphu Monastery, 32, 34, 38, 44

Sangyé Rinchen, Genden Tripa, 58,
  59, 62

Śāntarakṣita, 72, 642, 643

Śāntideva, 642
  Compendium of Trainings, 32, 78–79,
    81, 530
  tulku, 61
  See also *Way of the Bodhisattva*
Śāntipa, 113
Sarasvatī, 37, 712
Śāriputra, 300
Sayings on Impermanence, 233
science, modern
  body in, 243–44
  Buddhism and, 77–78, 702, 705
  on compassion, 489
  on life on earth, 258
  on mental well-being, 508
  on mothers' love, 481
  on world, 494
Sechil Buwa, 25
secret mantra vehicle
  bodhicitta in, 463
  discouragement in, 597
  of early translation period, 13
  First Dalai Lama's practice, 29
  gurus in, 158–59
  lamrim in, 102–3, 693
  meditation in, 627
  motivation in, 95, 227
  in New Kadam, 11–12
  ninefold breath in, 177
  preliminaries, 107
  special insight in, 673
  and sūtrayāna, union of, 143–45
  symbolism in, 225
  in Tibet, 10
  winds and mind in, 283
  wrathful motivation in, 499
self, 354–55
  afflictions and, 406–7
  basis of designation, 658
  emptiness of, 671

in exchanging self and other, 510
  rebirth and, 250–51
  three ways of arising, 658–60
  See also selflessness; view of transi-
    tory collection
self-characteristics, 641–43, 666–67,
  683
self-cherishing
  in exchanging self and others, 506,
    510, 511
  faults of, identifying, 495–97, 502
  forsaking, 513
self-grasping
  abandoning, 215
  afflictions and, 655
  cutting root, 610, 688
  easing, 639–40, 641
  levels of, 7
  of others, meditating for abandon-
    ment, 653
selflessness
  analyzing, 412–13
  as Buddha's unique teaching, 291
  certainty in, 656
  meditation on, 640
  realization of, 660
  by reason of dependent arising,
    654–55
  symbols of, 225
  two modes, order of, 652–56
  two modes, relationship of, 654,
    686–87
  view of, 111–12
selflessness of persons, 281, 688
  aggregates in, 354–55, 640, 665–66,
    667–71
  body in, 665, 668–69
  coarse, 6–7, 654–55
  frameworks for, 656–57
  higher training in wisdom and, 129

limits in realizing, 641–42
mind in, 665, 668, 669
object of negation in, 657–58, 660–65
self in, three ways of arising, 658–60
subtle, 653
summary, 676–78
view, sustaining, 672–74
selflessness of phenomena, 281
coarse, 6–7
in higher tenet systems, 640–42
higher training in wisdom and, 129
meditation on, 685–87, 688
self-sufficient substantial entities, 640,
641, 654, 662, 671
sense consciousness, 150–51, 176, 615
sense pleasures, 191, 386–87, 645
sentient beings, 177
accepting suffering of helping, 586
anger toward happiness of, 581
dispositions of, 457
kindness of, 500, 503, 504
limitless, 479
love for, 463
not abandoning, 526–27
pride that venerates, 601
Sera Thekchen Ling Monastery, 52
Fourth Dalai Lama at, 60
Great Prayer Festival and, 39, 44
Second Dalai Lama at, 41, 45
Third Dalai Lama at, 47
Serlingpa, 22
session breaks
accepting suffering in, 583
confession during, 199, 350
ethical discipline in, 565–66
generosity during, 558
relaxation in, importance of, 602
sustaining meditation during,
198–99
Setön Künrik, 163

Seven Limb Prayer, 518, 521
seven patriarchs, 518, 737n83
seven precious royal emblems, 191
seven successors to the teachings, 8,
161–62, 733n9, 737n83
seven-fold cause-and-effect instructions, 470, 492, 503, 504–5
altruistic intention as foundation,
478–79
approximations of experience in,
530–31
compassion, meditation on, 488
equanimity as basis, 475–78
lineage of, 469–70
love, meditation on, 487–88
loving-kindness meditation, 486–87
on mother sentient beings, 474, 475,
479–86
order of, 473–74
outline, 472–73
seven-limb practice, 172, 181–82
confession, 191–92
dedication, 193–94
mandala offering, 187–91
order of, 194
prostrations, 182–87
rejoicing, 192
teachers, requesting to remain, 193
wheel of Dharma, requesting to
turn, 193
Seven-Point Mind Training (Chekawa),
107, 511
sexual misconduct, 334–35, 340,
736nn68–69
Shabkar Tsokdruk Rangdröl, Repaying My Mother's Kindness, 481–83,
737n80
Shakya Gyaltsen, 185
Shamar Garwang Chökyi Wangchuk,
59

Sharawa, 25, 78, 433, 446, 551–52
Sharayugur family line, 55
Shartsé Lopön Dradül, 60
Sherab Sengé, 25, 26, 88, 180–81, 183, 656, 676
Shingkyong Nangso, 54
Shuksep Jetsunma, 135
Shunzhi emperor, 68–70
sickness
  bearing suffering from, 583
  compounded, 405, 737n75
  death and, 242, 253
  karma and, 585
  suffering of, 367, 372, 376–77, 384
Śikhandin, 415
Sikkim, 189
Simrak Shaki Semo, 135
six classes of beings, 276, 384, 484, 658
six discernments, 87–88, 96–97, 735n48
six forces (in mental abidings), 630–32
six perfections, 169, 536, 694, 696
  aspiring and engaging bodhicitta in, order of, 529–31
  attitude possessing three features, 554
  coarse and subtle, 545
  completing, 588–89
  definitive enumeration, 541–44
  inferior and superior, 545
  order, 544–45
  outlines, 540, 545–46
  wisdom in, role of, 645
  See also individual perfections
six sense sources, link of, 429–30
skillful means, 364, 400, 536–37
sky burial, 254
small-scope-person's path, 218, 432
  attitude in, 101

bodhicitta in, 454
common stages, 324
completion of, 357–58
fear and faith united in, 300
goals of, 356
overview, 82–83
as preliminaries, 113–14
support for, 436
society
  exploitation in, 271
  responsibility toward, 222–23
  self-cherishing in, 495
Son Dharma collections, 46
Sönam Chokden Tenpé Gyaltsen, 67
Sönam Chokdrup, 67
Sönam Drakpa, Panchen, 309
Sönam Drakpa Gyatso, Third Dalai Lama, 309
  birth and recognition, 46–47
  death anniversary, 57
  Essence of Refined Gold, 117, 172, 179, 180, 304, 529, 700
  journey to Mongolia, 49–50
  lineage, 88
  monasteries founded, 53–55
  in Mongolia, 51–52
  passing, 56
  supplication, 184
  teachings received, 47–48
  vows and ordinations, 47, 48
Sönam Gelek Palsang, 62, 309
Songtsen Gampo, 10, 54
  Maṇi Kabum, 133–34, 138–39
  visualization, 518
special insight, 16, 355, 465, 531, 605–6
  analytical meditation in, 672, 673
  and bodhisattva conduct, conjoined, 648–49
  and calm abiding, order of, 609–10

and calm abiding, union of, 465,
606–7, 630, 675, 678–79
four trainings for, 199
misunderstanding, 674–75
with peacefulness and coarseness,
635
pliancy in, 630, 678
purpose, 608
similitude and actual, 678
training in wisdom and, 440
types, 608, 645–46
special resolve, 477, 513
aspirational bodhicitta and, 524
bodhicitta and, 486
generating, 531, 532
love and compassion generated in,
489–91
and repaying kindness, difference
between, 491
speech, divisive, 325, 336
Sphere of Nothingness, 613, 635,
738n89
spiritual teachers, 19, 91, 160
attributes of, 130–31
Buddha and, 154–55
discipline of, 127–28
enemies as, 504
finding fault in, 149–51
four categories of, 140–41
gender of, 135
humility of, 162–63
investigating, 132–34, 148
in Mahāyāna, qualities, 126–29
nonvirtuous, 165–66, 170, 408
pleasing, 163, 166
See also gurus; kindness; relying on
spiritual teachers
śrāvaka path, 302–3, 459
anger on, 578
enlightenment in, 520

knowledge of, 103
love on, 298
meditation objects of, 647
realization of, 465
surpassing, 461–62
Śrī Bhūti, 184
stages of the path (lamrim)
eight great manuals of, 80, 735n47
84000 heaps of Dharma in, 106
four greatnesses, 98, 103, 104, 106,
107
as guide for dying, 249
guru as buddha in, 144
as prerequisite to secret mantra,
102–3
sutric and tantric perspectives in,
145
three special attributes, 98
transmission of, 22–24, 25–26, 79
treatises of, 6, 80–81, 697–98, 700
stages of the path of three persons,
81–82, 694, 697
abandonments on, 214
boundaries of, 84
equality of, 458
ethical discipline, distinctions in, 565
lack of contradiction in, 645
Lamp for the Path and, 10
preliminary paths in, 214, 218
progression on, 214–16
purpose of, 442
purpose of teachings for, 6
refuge and, 287, 302
relationship between, 107, 115
shared paths, 219, 423
transmission of, 23–24, 99
by way of twelve links (Phuchungwa), 424–25, 431–32
See also great-scope-person's path;

middle/medium-scope-person's
path; small-scope-person's path
stealing, 334, 340
Stem Array Sūtra, 161
stream entry, 349
students and disciples, 136–37, 138–39,
166
study, 93, 104, 293
stupas, 55, 56, 63
Sublime Continuum (Maitreya), 643
on bodhisattvas, 464
on buddhahood, 283
on Dharma and sangha, 284
on four truths, 369
suffering, 96, 112, 646
accepting, eight bases for, 582–87
of body, 258
of certain becoming, 384
compositional, 367
contemplating, 370–71, 621
of dissatisfaction, 386–87
eight types, 370, 371, 380–81
in equalizing self and others, 493–94
of hot hells, 264–66
karma and, 326, 329, 330
of not getting what you want,
379–80
of others, concern for, 84, 455,
456–57
of pleasantness, parting from, 379
root of, 390
six types, 380–81, 386–89
three types of beings and, 468
of unpleasant, encountering, 378–79
See also three types of suffering; true
sufferings
suicide, 397, 576
Sukhāvatī, 206
Sunakṣatra, 152

Sunggyal Draklha, spirit mediums
of, 55
Sungrabpa, 47
supplication prayers
Opening the Door to the Supreme Path,
79
to stages of the path lineage gurus,
91, 183–87
and tantra, blending, 194–96
supramundane path, 635
sutra basket, 93–94
Sūtra Gathering All Threads, 106
Sūtra of Maitreya's Liberation, 524
Sūtra of the Meeting of Father and Son,
153
Sūtra of the Ten Teachings, 147
Sūtra of the Three Heaps, 191, 349. See
also *Confession of Downfalls*
Sūtra on the Basis of Discipline, 326
Sūtra Requested by Brahmā, 440, 443–44
Sūtra Requested by Revata, 613
Sūtra Requested by Sāgaramati, 81, 91,
193
Sūtra Ritual of Bhaiṣajyaguru, 179
Svātantrika Madhyamaka, 641, 663–64,
667
Swift Path (Losang Yeshé), 88
on bodhicitta, 461
on exchanging self and other, 492,
495
giving and taking in, 511
on gurus, viewing as buddhas, 143

T

Taikha Palace, 69
Taklung Monastery, 58
Taklungpa, 39
Taktsang Lotsāwa, 684
*Tantra Bestowing the Initiation
Vajrapāṇi*, 142, 170

Tantrayāna. *See* secret mantra vehicle
Tārā, 11, 31, 46
Tashi Lhunpo
 conflicts at, 34
 Fifth Dalai Lama at, 70
 First Dalai Lama at, 29, 238–39
 founding, 30–31
 Fourth Dalai Lama at, 60
 Panchen lamas at, 33, 59
 Second Dalai Lama at, 36–37, 38,
  40–42, 43, 732n38
Tashi Tabten, Sakyong, 49
tathāgata essence, 493, 508–9
television, afflictions from, 409
Ten Mahāyāna Key Instructions,
 735n56
ten nonvirtues, 206, 331
 abandoning, 217, 219, 279, 332,
  440–42, 497, 563
 common to all religions, 311
 four factors and, 332
 higher rebirth and, 111
 investigating, 345
 karma and, 324, 342
 of others, 223
 self-cherishing and, 495
 small scope persons and, 82–83
 on three paths, 214–15
 weights of, 339–40
 wrong view as heaviest, 339
ten perfections, 536
ten virtues, 50–51, 343, 345, 347, 348,
 358
tenet systems, 222, 293
 afflictions in, 395
 collection of wisdom in, 650
 emergence of, 6
 inherent existence in, 354, 363, 395,
  641–42, 643
 on self, modes of, 640–44

 self-grasping in, 639
 two truths in, 363
Tengyur, 81, 105, 166
Tenzin Dorjé Dayan Khan, 70
Tenzin Gyatso, Fourteenth Dalai
 Lama, 710
 activities of, 704–5
 personal recollections of, 238–39,
  247–48, 498, 663–64
 political power of, 45
 praise to, 702–3, 712
 prayer for, 713
 in Thailand, 585
Terdak Lingpa, 75
Thailand, 313–14, 585
Thekchen Chökhor Ling, 51, 54
Theravada tradition, 183, 204
thirty-seven limbs of enlightenment,
 282, 354
Thirty-Seven Practices of Bodhisattvas
 (Thokmé Sangpo), 307
thirty-two major and eighty minor
 marks, 2, 733n3
Thönyön Gyalwa, 44
Thothori Nyantsan, 10, 518
Three Jewels, 177, 279, 281–82
 accepting suffering from honoring,
  585
 differences in Buddhist traditions,
  282
 faith in, 121, 300
 as final refuge, 288
 in gathering virtue, 565
 protection of, 119, 123
 relationship between, 299–300
 See also Buddha Jewel; Dharma
  Jewel; Sangha Jewel
three poisons, 96, 371
 control by, 449
 definite karma and, 344

influence of, 150–51
investigating, 345
rebirth and, 257
strength of, 614
three principal aspects of path, 413,
    522
Three Stages of Meditation (Kamalaśīla),
    607, 619, 623, 676
three trainings, 197, 355, 422, 437, 565
    human birth and, 206
    identifying, 438
    liberation and, 447–49
    for middle-scope persons, 83
    objects of abandonment, 438–39
    order of, 354–56, 439
    purposes of, 102
    relationship between, 444
    result of, 439
    six perfections and, 543
    spiritual teachers' mastery of, 127–29
    as wish-fulfilling tree, 450
three types of suffering, 121, 383–84,
    421, 688
    suffering of change, 358, 367, 384–85,
        468
    suffering of conditioning, 356, 367,
        385, 468, 469
    suffering of suffering, 217, 358, 367,
        384, 468
thrones, 89–90
Thupten Gyatso, Thirteenth Dalai
    Lama, 310
Thupten Jamchen Ling Monastery,
    53–54
Thupten Lungtok Namgyal Trinlé, 186
Thupten Sönam, possession of,
    274–75
Tibet, 204, 703
    autonomy of, 323–24, 364
    bad conditions as aids in, 582–83

as central land, 203
Chinese authorities in, 526–27
Chinese torture in, 498
democracy in, 75
Dharma practice in, 209, 711
elderly in, respecting, 376
exile from, 246–47
generosity in, 557
government of, 45
gurus in, 131, 135
political authority in, 68
prayer for, 713
religion in, 115
well-being of, 310
Tibet House Germany, 714
Tibetan Buddhism, 143–45, 706
    Christian interest in, 301
    early dissemination period, 9, 10, 13,
        72, 80
    fundamentalism in, 707
    god and spirit worship in, 310
    later dissemination, 72–73
    major lineages of, 310
    monasticism in, respecting, 314
    spreading, 582–83
Tilopa, 153, 163, 166
Tokden Jampal Gyatso, 24–25
Tölung Gelpo Nakha, 48
Tongkhor Yönten Gyatso, 53
trainees, two types, 292
transference of consciousness, 419
transmission, importance of, 19–20, 701
Treasury of Knowledge (Vasubandhu),
    5, 417
    on bardo beings, lifespan, 419
    cosmology of, 188
    on definite karmas, 344
    on hells, lifespan in, 266
    on Jambudvīpa, lifespan in, 240
    on karma at time of death, 415

on virtuous and nonvirtuous acts, 331

on worlds arisen from karma, 268

treatises, four interrelated aspects, 137

Trehor Geshé Palden Drakpa, 141–42

Trehor Kyorpön Rinpoché, 141–42, 584

Trerabpa, 74

Tri Songdetsen, 10, 52, 64, 738n84

Trijang Rinpoché, 132, 274–75, 308, 310, 397

Trinlé Gyatso (scribe), 702

triple basket, 21, 93–94

Trophu Ganden Temple, 31

Trophu Lotsāwa Jampa Pal, 72

true cessations, 118, 258, 280, 366–67

true existence, 301, 360, 597, 643

analyzing, 360, 405, 668

apprehension of, abandoning for others, 653–54

apprehension of, antidote to, 4, 7, 354–55

faith and, 471

as object of negation, 658, 666

in selflessness meditations, 677

in tenet systems, 641–42

See also grasping true existence; ignorance grasping true existence

true origins, 281, 353–54, 369, 394

true paths, 118, 258, 280, 281, 289, 538

true sufferings, 281, 367, 369, 423–24

Trungpa Taphu, 276

Tsandrapala of Gyatön, 29

Tsang Rabsel, 72

Tsang region, 28, 35, 39, 66

Tsangpa Gyaré, 390

Tsangpa Önshang, 60–61

Tsangpa Panchen Rigpa Sengé, 49

Tsangpa tradition, 60–61

Tsangpo River, 397

Tselé Natsok Rangdröl, 555

Tsethang, 39

Tshalpa Kagyü tradition, 42

Tsöndrü Gyaltsen, 185

Tsongkhapa, 1, 58, 74, 79–80, 99, 166, 195, 230, 309, 656

Abbreviated Stages of the Path, 364–65

appearances emphasized by, 666, 683–85

birthplace, 54

as buddha, 146

on Buddha's speech, 5

Commentary on Nāgārjuna's Fundamental Verses, 26

Commentary on the "Ethics" Chapter of "Asaṅga's Bodhisattva Grounds," 528–29, 566

Confession through the Four Powers, 349

on death, 227

Differentiating the Definitive and Interpretable, 26

Foundation of All Good Qualities, 390, 629

Gendun Drup and, 25–26

Gendun Gyatso's recollection of, 36

Golden Rosary, 79

Great Fifth's study of, 13

Lamp for the Five Stages, 39

lineages, 20, 23–24, 79

miraculous powers of, 62

Praise of Dependent Origination, 290

praises, 11–12, 451, 696–97

Requesting Prayer to the Lamrim Lineage, 20

secret biography of, 38–39

on self- and other-emptiness, 643–44

Songs of Experience, 98, 99, 441, 694

Three Principal Aspects of the Path, 216, 648, 681

on transmission, 19–20

visualizations, 180–81, 518
vow lineage of, 73
See also *Great Treatise on the Stages of the Path*; *Middle-Length Stages of the Path* (aka *Condensed Exposition on the Stages of the Path*)
tukdam meditation, 254
Tulku Drakpa Gyaltsen, 309
tulkus, 739n100
  false, 309
  and lamas, four possibilities between, 131–32
  past life recollection of, 220–21
Tumtön Lodrö Drakpa, 25
Turing Khan, 55–56
Tuṣita, 53
twelve links of dependent origination, 354
  as focal object, 612
  lifetimes to complete, number of, 430–31
  projecting and actual causes and results, 427–30
  three types of beings and, 431–32
  two sequences of, 425–26, 434
  ways of presenting, 424–25
twenty-seven enlightened deeds, 3, 733n7
two collections, 694, 695
  bodhicitta and, 462–63, 464
  completing, 169, 541
  discouragement toward, 597
  method and wisdom in, 539–40
  preliminary accumulations of, 172
  refuge and, 306
  two buddha bodies and, 3, 536
two great trailblazers/charioteers, 8–9, 20, 99. *See also* Asaṅga; Nāgārjuna
two obscurations, 106, 118, 169, 357.

See also afflictive obscurations; knowledge obscurations
two truths, 3, 4, 362–63, 539, 649, 650, 733n6
two welfares, 169, 453, 542–43, 569, 694, 695

U
Ü, 29–30
Udayana, 349
Udraka, 646
ultimate truth, 539, 649, 650, 733n6
unethical behavior, by nature and by custom, distinguishing, 736n69
universal monarchs, 384, 388, 486, 645
Unpleasant Sound continent (*Uttarakuru*), 240
Unravelling the Intention, 606
Unrelenting Hell, 263, 264, 266, 351, 396, 503, 583
Ü-Tsang, 53, 63

V
Vaibhāṣika tradition, 319
Vairocana, 54
Vajra-Bell-Holder tradition, 47
Vajrabhairava, 11
Vajradhara, 143, 179
Vajrapāṇi, 237, 737n82
Vajravārāhī, 153
Vajrayāna (Vajra Vehicle). *See* secret mantra vehicle
valid cognition, 321, 448, 515, 659, 664, 681
Vasubandhu. See *Treasury of Knowledge*
verses of auspiciousness, 49
Verses of the Nāga King Drum, 485
Vidyākokila, 22
view of transitory collection, 354–55, 403–4, 406, 655, 737n73

views
  holding as supreme, 404, 552,
    737n73
  holding discipline and asceticism as
    supreme, 404, 737n73
  holding to extremes, 404, 737n73
  partial, 665
  related to objects, 6–7
  searching for nature of, 663–64
  See also wrong views
Vinaya, 72, 93, 182, 446
virtue, 96, 322
  completing, 330
  facade of, 228
  gathering, 599
  increasing, 193
  insatiability for, 601
  training of, 578–79
  See also ten virtues
Viṣṇu, 9, 118, 288, 405, 710
vows
  bodhisattva, 523, 527, 528, 529,
    562–63
  cherishing, 354
  eight-limbed, 61
  facade of, 228
  guarding, 611
  of householders, 445, 446
  individual liberation, 72, 441, 442–43,
    562, 563
  monastic, 445–46
  refuge as support for, 317
Vulture's Peak, 21–22

W
Wangchuk Rabten, 67
water, eight features of, 700, 739n98
Way of the Bodhisattva (Śāntideva), 32,
    78–79, 81, 487, 489, 556
  on afflictions, 396, 410–11
  on anger, 572, 573
  on animals, 270
  on bad migrations, 358
  on bodhicitta, 453–54, 460, 463
  on bodhicitta, aspiring and engag-
    ing, 525
  on bodhisattvas, 413
  on body, giving away, 558
  on calm abiding and special insight,
    609–10
  on cherishing enemies, 504
  on death, 245–46
  on discouragement, 596
  on enemies, 581
  on equalizing and exchanging self
    and others, 470, 493, 501, 502
  on ethical discipline, 561
  on familiarization, 506
  on generosity, 548
  on harming, 575–76, 577
  on hells, 268–69
  on human birth, turtle analogy,
    207–8
  on introspection, 618
  on joyous effort, 591, 597–98, 602
  on karmic results, 414–15
  on laziness, 594–95
  on lifespan, human, 239–40
  on misdeeds, harm from, 599
  on object of negation, 657
  on others' suffering, 509–10
  on patience, 571, 586–87
  on praise and renown, 580
  on sentient beings, kindness of, 500
  on sentient beings and Victor, 177
  seven-limb practice in, 194, 736n62
  on spiritual teachers, 129–30
  on suffering, 389
  on virtue, 285

wealth, material, 117, 129, 222, 351,
    497
  afflictions increased by, 398
  covetousness toward, 338
  death and, 237, 239, 246–47, 378
  Dharma used for, 227
  generosity with, 542, 552, 556–57
  offering, 164
  pride in, 403
  suffering from, 390, 398, 486, 495,
    567
welfare of others
  aspiration for, 458
  contemplating, 178
  discouragement about, 599
  mind generation for, 468
  mind-training approach to, 476
  partial enactment of, 457
  special resolve for, 490–91, 513
  as their own nirvana, 469
wheel of Dharma, 21, 365, 366
White Lotus of the Good Dharma, 413
White Mañjuśrī sādhana, 37
winds
  mind and, 283, 607–8, 738n87
  pliancy and, 634
  posture and, 175–76
  yoga of, 611
wisdom, 738n90
  definite goodness and, 4
  intelligent, 589, 645
  observing enlightenment, 490–91
  perspective of, 6–7
  realizing emptiness, 3, 452, 466,
    539–40, 647
  realizing selflessness, 94, 128, 129,
    289, 355, 465, 610
  relying on gurus through, 134
  training in, 355
  visible appearance of, 22

See also perfection of wisdom
wisdom beings, 119
wisdom truth body. See dharmakāya
womb birth, 206, 371–72, 373–74, 391,
    419, 420–21, 479, 484
women, 135, 347, 736n70, 737n71
wrong livelihoods, 111, 174
wrong views, 9, 10, 204, 325, 707,
    737n73
  antidote to, 194
  complete path of, 339
  degrees of, 311
  overcoming, 652
  rebirth and, 203
  two types, 404–5
  weights of, 340

Y

Yargyab, 60–61
Yarlung, 47, 60
Yeshé Gyaltsen, 185
Yeshé Gyatso, 185
Yeshé Tsemo, Panchen, 37, 38, 40–41
Yo Gejung, 72
Yogācāra tradition, 9, 129, 650
Yönten Gyatso, Fourth Dalai Lama
  birth and recognition, 56–58
  Ganden Phodrang installation,
    58–59
  passing, 63
  travels and teachings of, 60–61
  vows and ordinations, 62
Yönten Gyatso Tenpé Nyima Gyaltsen
    Palsangpo, 44

Z

Zahor, 66, 701
Zina Lugya clan, 55
Zurchen Chöying Randröl, 67, 75

A Short Biography of His Holiness the Fourteenth Dalai Lama

HIS HOLINESS THE DALAI LAMA is the spiritual leader of the Tibetan people and is a beacon of inspiration for Buddhists and non-Buddhists alike. He has persistently reached out across religious and political lines in his mission to advance peace and understanding in the world. In doing so, he embodies his motto "My religion is kindness."

He was born in 1935 in the northwestern Tibetan province of Amdo and enthroned as the Fourteenth Dalai Lama in 1940 in Lhasa, the capital of Tibet. He was educated in a traditional manner in the Potala Palace, the official residence of the Dalai Lamas. In 1950, at the time of the Communist annexation of Tibet, he assumed his responsibilities as head of state. He traveled to Beijing in 1954 to negotiate Tibetan autonomy with Mao Zedong and other Communist leaders.

In 1959, in the wake of the failed Tibetan uprising, shortly after completing his traditional *geshé* degree, he sought exile in India and set up his exile government. The next year he initiated the exile government's transition to democracy.

For his efforts to ensure the survival of the Tibetan people and their culture, and for his advocacy of peaceful resistance to Communist rule in Tibet, in 1989 he was awarded with the Nobel Peace Prize.

He has traveled globally to minister to Tibetan exile communities, advocate for peace, teach kindness and compassion, meet with religious and political leaders, and explore with scientists the many ways in which Buddhism and science can learn from each other.

His Holiness stepped down from his role as head of state in 2011, following the inauguration of the first democratically elected Tibetan president. Since then he has dedicated himself to his four commitments:

1. As a human being, he is committed to developing the intrinsic and fundamental qualities of goodness that exist in all of us.
2. As a Buddhist monk, he is committed to encouraging harmony among the world's regions.
3. As a Tibetan he is committed to working for the welfare of the Tibetan people.
4. As a follower of the Indian Nalanda tradition of Buddhism he is committed to preserving this ancient Indian knowledge tradition.

Readers are encouraged to learn more about His Holiness's life through his autobiographies and biographies.

Dalai Lama. *Freedom in Exile*. San Francisco: Harper Collins, 1991.

Dalai Lama. *My Land and My People*. New York: McGraw-Hill, 1962.

Dalai Lama and Sofia Stril-Rever. *My Spiritual Journey*. New York: HarperOne, 2011.

Norman, Alexander. *The Dalai Lama: An Extraordinary Life*. Boston: Mariner Books, 2020.

Tenzin Geyche Tethong and Jane Moore. *His Holiness the Fourteenth Dalai Lama: An Illustrated Biography*. Northampton, MA: Interlink Books, 2020.

A detailed biography of His Holiness the Dalai Lama is being published by the Norbulingka Institute in Dharamsala, India, under the title of *Rgya chen snying rje'i rol mtsho*. The publication began in 2009. Twenty-four of a planned fifty volumes have been released, covering through to the year 1995.

A Short Biography of His Eminence Dagyab Kyabgön Rinpoché

His Eminence Loden Sherab Dagyab Kyabgön Rinpoché was born in 1940 in Minyak, eastern Tibet, into a peasant family. At the age of four he was recognized as the Ninth Kyabgön (patron) of the Dagyab region. He belongs to the third ranking of tulkus in Tibet and holds the honorary title of Hothokthu Nomanhan.

Rinpoché studied the major and minor subjects, such as the Buddhist psycho-ethical philosophy and grammar, poetry, and astronomy, at the monastic university of Drepung, earning a geshé degree and the reputation as an exceptional scholar.

In 1959 Rinpoché fled to India with His Holiness the Fourteenth Dalai Lama. Since that time, the two have established a tight and personal bond. His Holiness has full confidence in Rinpoché, as is shown by his asking Rinpoché to compile the present work based on His Holiness's teachings given over the past several decades.

In 1964 His Holiness appointed Rinpoché as first director of Tibet House New Delhi. This developed into an internationally recognized institute for the preservation and promotion of Tibetan culture.

In 1966 he accepted a position at the University of Bonn, Germany, as a Tibetologist at the Institute of Central Asian Studies. He served as an international research fellow and lecturer for thirty-eight years, until his retirement in 2004. His main field of research was Buddhist art, symbolism, and iconography. He is the author of several books. A list of publications can be viewed at www.dagyab-rinpoche.com.

In the 1980s he was asked by a group of Germans interested in Buddhism to become a spiritual teacher, and in response he founded a Buddhist community, Chödzong, in southern Germany. Since then he has also taught in other European countries, North and South American, and Asia.

Rinpoché is the founder of Tibet House Germany (Tibethaus Deutschland), which is under the patronage of His Holiness the Dalai Lama. As the successor organization of Chödzong, it was established in Frankfurt in 2005 as the Tibetan Buddhist Cultural and Educational Institute Tibet House Germany. Rinpoché still serves as its spiritual director together with H. E. Zong Rinpoché. The institute has five departments: Buddhism, Personality and Society, Art and Culture, Medicine, and Science.

Rinpoché mainly teaches at Tibet House Germany and its rural retreat center, Berghof, where he gives sutra and tantra teachings as well as talks on Tibetan culture, in both the German and English languages. Since 2000 he has visited Singapore yearly to teach at Gaden Shartse Dro-Phen Ling. He has also taught in Tibetan monasteries in Tibet and India. Since 2020 he has been giving online teachings to participants from many Eastern and Western countries, including China.

H. E. Dagyab Kyabgön Rinpoché is known to hold a large number of transmissions of the Geluk lineage, as well as many Sakya and Kagyü lineage transmissions, and he teaches the full range of Tibetan Buddhism, beginning with the cultivation of the basic human values— which His Holiness has emphasized for many years as the foundation of all religions—up to the two stages of Highest Tantra. His ability to transmit the rich tradition in all its diversity and depth, and at the same time teach according to the human needs and realities of today's time and culture, is greatly appreciated by his students. With encouragement, without pressure or coercion, he always emphasizes the benefits of changing one's mind, the taking of daily life as the main field of spiritual practice, and the strengthening of one's capacity to be a good human being.

He and his wife, Norden, moved from Bonn to Berlin after his retirement to be close to their two children and five grandchildren. Rinpoché continues to focus on writing biographies and books about Buddhism and Tibetan history and language, as well as on teaching in different countries. His dedication to pass on as much of his inexhaustible knowledge as possible, and otherwise to be of service, still guides his activities.

Also Available from the Dalai Lama and Wisdom Publications

Buddhism
One Teacher, Many Traditions

The Compassionate Life

Ecology, Ethics, and Interdependence
The Dalai Lama in Conversation with Leading Thinkers on Climate Change

Essence of the Heart Sutra
The Dalai Lama's Heart of Wisdom Teachings

The Essence of Tsongkhapa's Teachings
The Dalai Lama on the Three Principal Aspects of the Path

The Fourteenth Dalai Lama's Stages of the Path, vol 1
Guidance for the Modern Practitioner

The Good Heart
A Buddhist Perspective on the Teachings of Jesus

Imagine All the People
A Conversation with the Dalai Lama on Money, Politics, and Life as It Could Be

Kalachakra Tantra
Rite of Initiation

The *Library of Wisdom and Compassion* series:
Volume 1. Approaching the Buddhist Path
Volume 2. The Foundation of Buddhist Practice
Volume 3. Saṃsāra, Nirvāṇa, and Buddha Nature
Volume 4. Following in the Buddha's Footsteps
Volume 5. In Praise of Great Compassion
Volume 6. Courageous Compassion
Volume 7. Searching for the Self
Volume 8. Realizing the Profound View
Volume 9. Appearing and Empty

The Life of My Teacher
A Biography of Kyabjé Ling Rinpoché

Meditation on the Nature of Mind

The Middle Way
Faith Grounded in Reason

Mind in Comfort and Ease
The Vision of Enlightenment in the Great Perfection

MindScience
An East-West Dialogue

Opening the Eye of New Awareness

Practicing Wisdom
The Perfection of Shantideva's Bodhisattva Way

Science and Philosophy in the Indian Buddhist Classics, vol. 1
The Physical World

Science and Philosophy in the Indian Buddhist Classics, vol. 2
The Mind

Science and Philosophy in the Indian Buddhist Classics, vol. 3
Philosophical Schools

Science and Philosophy in the Indian Buddhist Classics, vol. 4
Philosophical Topics

Sleeping, Dreaming, and Dying
An Exploration of Consciousness

The Wheel of Life
Buddhist Perspectives on Cause and Effect

The World of Tibetan Buddhism
An Overview of Its Philosophy and Practice

About Wisdom Publications

Wisdom Publications is the leading publisher of classic and contemporary Buddhist books and practical works on mindfulness. To learn more about us or to explore our other books, please visit our website at wisdomexperience.org or contact us at the address below.

Wisdom Publications
132 Perry Street
New York, NY 10014 USA

We are a 501(c)(3) organization, and donations in support of our mission are tax deductible.

Wisdom Publications is affiliated with the Foundation for the Preservation of the Mahayana Tradition (FPMT).